KENNETH O. MORGAN is f[...]
versity of Wales, honorary [...] Oriel
Colleges, Oxford, and Labour peer. He has been for over
thirty years one of Britain's leading modern historians. His
many books include *Wales in British Politics, 1868–1922* (1963),
Lloyd George (1974), *Keir Hardie* (1975), *Consensus and Disunity*
(1979), *Rebirth of a Nation: Wales 1880–1980* (1981), *Labour in
Power 1945–1951* (1984), *Labour People* (1987), *The People's Peace*
(1989) and *Callaghan: A Life* (1997). He was elected a Fellow
of the British Academy in 1983, and was married to the historian and criminologist, the late Jane Morgan.

From the reviews of *Michael Foot*:

'This magnificent biography . . . is everything an authorised
biography should be. It's compendious, meticulously re-
searched with the collaboration of its subject, and contains
every fact you are ever likely to want to know about him . . .
it's also clear, lucid and readable'   *Guardian*

'Morgan's judgements of Foot are elegantly balanced . . . Foot
was, and still is, a great man who deservedly inspires affection
as well as admiration'   ROY HATTERSLEY, *Observer*

'I was engrossed. Kenneth Morgan's superb portrait . . . is
much more than another Labour biography. It is a portrait in
bright oils of a master parliamentary literary-political agitator,
in a society congenitally hard to rouse'   *Prospect*

Wales in British Politics, 1868–1922
David Lloyd George: Welsh Radical as World Statesman
Freedom or Sacrilege?
The Age of Lloyd George
Lloyd George Family Letters (ed.)
Lloyd George
Keir Hardie: Radical and Socialist
Consensus and Disunity
(with Jane Morgan) Portrait of a Progressive
Rebirth of a Nation: Wales 1880–1980
Labour in Power 1945–1951
The Oxford Illustrated History of Britain (ed.)
Labour People
The People's Peace: Britain Since 1945
Modern Wales: Politics, Places and People
The Young Oxford History of Britain and Ireland (ed.)
Callaghan: A Life
Crime, Protest and Police in Modern British Society (ed.)
The Twentieth Century

For Joseph

CONTENTS

ILLUSTRATIONS

The infant Michael.

Michael's father and grandfather at Lady Well House, Regent Street, Plymouth, 1902. (*Isaac Foot papers*)

The seven Foot children, *c.*1920. (*Isaac Foot papers*)

Pencrebar, near Callington, Cornwall, the Foot family home from 1927.

The Leighton Park school first eleven, 1930. (*The Leightonian, 1930*)

Michael as an undergraduate at Wadham, *c.*1932.

Michael and John Cripps during their Oxford Union American debating tour, October 1934.

Labour candidate for Monmouth, November 1935.

Sir Stafford Cripps. (*Popperfoto*)

The Foot family in the late 1930s. (*Tribune*)

Michael as assistant editor of the *Evening Standard*, with Dingle, 1941. (*Isaac Foot papers*)

Michael in his flat, Park Street, Mayfair, 1943. (*Pictorial Press*)

Jill Craigie making the film *The Way we Live*, 1944.

Jill around the time Michael met her.

Michael photographed by Jill in his Park Street flat, 1946. (*Pictorial Press*)

Dingle, Hugh, Isaac, John, Michael and Christopher at Pencrebar in the late 1940s. (*Isaac Foot papers*)

Aneurin Bevan speaking in Ebbw Vale, Michael listening, 1947. (*R. L. Jenkins*)

Michael Foot MP speaking at a local carnival, 1950. (*Charles H. Morgan*)

In the News, BBC Television, 10 February 1951. (*Haywood Magee/ Getty Images*)

Free Speech, ITV, 1954.

Michael and Jill at Paddock Cottage, on Beaverbrook's Cherkley estate, c.1955. (*Michael Ward*)

Joan Vickers defeats Michael at Devonport in the general election, May 1955. (*PA/Empics*)

Michael dismissed in the annual *Tribune* vs *New Statesman* cricket match, late 1950s.

Michael, Isaac, Hugh and Christopher watching Plymouth Argyle play at Home Park, 1958.

Michael, Vanessa and Jill, Ebbw Vale by-election, November 1960. (*Daily Herald/Science and Society Picture Library*)

Vicky cartoon of himself and Michael in full spate (early 1960s).

CND en route to Aldermaston: Michael, James Cameron and Michael's step-grandson Jason Lehel, Trafalgar Square, 30 March 1964. (*Alpha/S. & G.*)

Michael and Lord Beaverbrook, Italy, 1964.

Cartoon by Glan Williams, *Sunday Citizen*, 17 July 1966. (*Centre for the Study of Cartoons and Caricature, University of Kent*)

Michael at the Aneurin Bevan memorial stones, Waun-y-Pound, near Tredegar. (*Terry Kirk/Financial Times*)

Co-Op beauty contest, early 1970s.

At a Yorkshire miners' demonstration, Doncaster, June 1971. (*NCB Yorkshire Regional Photographic Department*)

Marching for the miners, Doncaster, June 1971. (*NCB Yorkshire Regional Photographic Department*)

Party conference, Blackpool, October 1973. (*Colin Davey/Camera Press*)

Leaving number 10 after a crucial Cabinet meeting on whether to join the Common Market, 18 March 1975. (*Alpha/S. & G.*)

With Indira Gandhi in New Delhi, December 1976.

Labour Party/TUC Rally against Racialism, Trafalgar Square, 21 November 1976. (*Jan Overbury*)

Cartoon by Garland, *Daily Telegraph*, 1977. (*Nicholas Garland/Daily Telegraph Syndication*)

On the platform with Jim Callaghan, party conference, 5 October 1977. (*PA/Empics*)

With Jack Jones of the Transport Workers at Jones's leaving party, Royal Festival Hall, 20 February 1978. (*Peter Cade/Getty Images*)

Arriving at St Patrick's cathedral, Dublin, to lecture on Jonathan Swift, 18 October 1980. (*Irish Times*)

Haranguing the faithful, 1981. (*Roger Hutchings/Camera Press*)

Michael and Jill with their dogs on Hampstead Heath. (*Harry Dempster/Daily Express*)

Michael and Denis Healey at Heathrow, on their way to meet Leonid Brezhnev in Moscow, 15 September 1981. (*PA/Empics*)

Garland cartoon, *Daily Telegraph*, 13 November 1981. (*Centre for the Study of Cartoons and Caricature, University of Kent*)

Michael with Tony Blair, Westminster, 1982. (*PA/Empics*)

On the number 24 bus, 23 May 1983. (*Rex Features*)

With Neil Kinnock in Tredegar, 1988. (*R. L. Jenkins*)

Michael and Dizzy on Hampstead Heath.

At the Open University with with Lord Callaghan, Tony Blair and Dr John Daniel, *c.*1990. (*The Open University*)

Eightieth birthday party, 23 July 1993.

Portrait of Michael by Graham Jones, 1998. (*Palace of Westminster and courtesy of Sir Patrick Cormack MP*)

PREFACE

Michael Foot has had a very long and colourful life. He was chronicler and participant in central aspects of British twentieth-century history. His first general election found him crusading for Lloyd George's Liberal Party in 1929. His twentieth and last saw him campaigning for Labour in his old seat, Ebbw Vale/Blaenau Gwent, seventy-six years later. He spans the worlds of Stafford Cripps and Tony Blair. He was a doughty opponent of appeasement in the later 1930s: his book *Guilty Men* made him famous at the age of twenty-seven. He was vocal in condemning the invasion of Iraq in 2003. He stands, and feels himself to stand, in the great and honourable tradition of dissenting 'trouble-makers', the heir to Fox and Paine, Hazlitt and Cobbett. He played in his life many parts. As icon of the socialist left, he was custodian and communicator of British socialism. He was the greatest pamphleteer perhaps since John Wilkes, a formidable editor, and author of a glittering biography of his idol, Nye Bevan. He was a scintillating parliamentarian, an inveterate critic and peacemonger as Bevanite, Tribunite and founder member of CND, yet also a belligerent patriot and internationalist from Dunkirk to Dubrovnik. He was a central figure and champion of the unions in the Labour governments of the 1970s, a key player in Old Labour's last phase. Less happily, he was for almost three tormented years Labour's leader. Perhaps most important of all, he was a deeply cultured and literate man whose learning was absolutely central to his politics. He was heir to the Edwardian men of letters, the Liberals Morley or Birrell, and politically more innovative than either. Over sixty years he was an inspirational and civilizing force, if a deeply controversial one. His passing will symbolize a world we have lost.

When Michael Foot asked me if I would write a new authorized biography, I was, of course, both excited and honoured. At the same time, I had some doubts. After writing a large biography of one veteran

Labour leader, Jim Callaghan, I wondered whether it would be wise to write another, especially on someone so removed from Callaghan's own wing of the party. Although Callaghan and Foot worked with immense loyalty as colleagues in the Labour government of 1976–79, they were very different as men and as democratic socialists. Someone who worked for them both told me that they were not 'best buddies', while Jim Callaghan himself, just before he died in March 2005, showed himself to be a bit wary of my new project. Another point was that, while I had never really been on the right in Labour terms since I first joined the party in 1955, I was not really Old Labour either, despite the stereotypes of amiable journalists who have vainly tried to depict me as its 'laureate'. On the contrary, I have always been a liberal devolutionist rather than a state centralist (being Welsh may have something to do with that), while on several major issues my views were not those of Michael Foot, notably on CND and on Europe. Although an admirer of Bevan (whose features adorn the sticker on my car window), I was not a Bevanite. And finally, at the start of 2003 I was doing something else, namely writing an academic book on the public memory in twentieth-century Britain. I have always been a historian rather than a biographer; only six of my books have been biographies. I was also an active member of the Lords (dissident Labour), an institution of whose abolition Michael Foot has always been an ardent supporter.

But as soon I began work and began talking to Michael Foot about his career, my doubts immediately dissolved. Having written on Jim Callaghan's equally fascinating career proved to be a huge stimulus, both in seeing somewhat similar episodes from another perspective, and in finding contrasts and comparisons between two totally different men, each capable of the greatness of spirit to work with someone to whom he was not naturally attuned. The fact that I started from a somewhat different political (and perhaps literary) standpoint from Michael Foot was in itself exciting in trying to examine his principles and his crusades from the outside. Michael himself was typically honourable and honest in recognizing that I came from somewhere else on the Labour continuum, and that in any case I was writing as a detached scholar and lifelong academic. It is characteristic that he has made no effort to read, let alone censor, anything I have written. His view of freedom of expression and interpretation, and the need to pursue them uninhibitedly and audaciously, has been most admirably exemplified in his approach to his own biographer, and I greatly respect that. Even membership of a non-elected House has not, perhaps, been a barrier. And finally, to someone working on the public memory, there is no finer custodian or exemplar of it than Michael Foot, deeply aware, as hardly any contemporary politicians are, of the vital importance of the past – history, legend, memory and myth intertwined – in shaping the present and pointing the way ahead. So writing on Michael Foot has enormously stimulated my earlier interests. As I have moved into my eighth decade, it has given me several new ones: I know far more about Montaigne, Swift or Hazlitt, for example, than I ever did before, and my mind is much the richer for it. In all ways, I have found writing about Michael deeply stimulating. This book has been great fun to write, and it would be nice to think that some readers might find it fun to read. No doubt I shall find out.

There is another personal aspect too. Back in 1981 I received a letter from Jill Craigie, Michael's wife, in effect suggesting that I might write his life. She invited my wife Jane and me to their house in Pilgrims Lane for a delightful dinner and talk. In fact, for whatever reason, the offer was never actually made – to my relief at that time, as I was then heavily involved with two long books, two small children and a beautiful and dynamic young wife, as well as being a busy Oxford tutor. I was not exactly looking out for ways of filling up my empty hours. I met Jill for the last time in the autumn of 1997 at an event at Congress House, near the British Museum, to celebrate the centenary of Nye Bevan's birth. She had not been well, and she looked ill and rather sad as she came up to me and (without needing to explain) said quietly that we both knew she should have taken a different decision years earlier. I felt deeply moved, but mumbled something to the effect that I was still very much alive, and that there was still time. Jill died two years later. I would like to think that in writing this book I have been fulfilling a kind of secret bond of trust between us. I well know she would not have agreed with all its contents, but it would have been fun to have been appropriately chastised by this tough, determined but warm, loyal and lovable woman.

My main debt of gratitude is, of course, to Michael Foot himself.

Apart from honouring me by asking me to write the book, he was always freely available for formal interviews or offhand chats, always open in making his papers (when they could be unearthed!) available to me, and quite astonishingly kind in giving me some of his own or his father's books, several of them rare. He is an extraordinarily warm and generous person, a man of unforced, spontaneous learning. Simply to work through his personal edition of Montaigne's writings, read in Hereford hospital after a serious car crash in late 1963 and covered with his own scholarly pencilled annotations, is in itself an education. Whether at home in his Pilgrims Lane basement rooms or cheerfully installed in an upstairs dining room over the goulash, raspberries and white wine at the Gay Hussar in Greek Street, talking to this ever-young nonagenarian has been nothing less than a joy, and I count myself fortunate indeed. I am also greatly indebted to the quite selfless kindness of Jenny Stringer, who has not only looked after Michael but in many ways looked after me as well during the writing of this book. I am also very grateful to Sheila Noble, who allowed me to look through Michael's papers in her own possession in Clapham. Kay, Baroness Andrews, was kind in making the initial connections, her interest in the book no doubt shaped by her background as a citizen of Tredegar. I am also grateful to Michael's many nice housekeepers who gave me so many splendid lunches. I particularly recall lunchtime conversations in Welsh with two of them, observed by Michael with amused tolerance. I have never met the authors of two earlier biographies, Mervyn Jones, and Simon Hoggart and David Leigh, but I would also wish to thank them for valuable information in their books which has helped me, especially on the personal aspects.

I am also hugely indebted, of course, to the kindness of Michael's friends and colleagues. I have greatly benefited from formal interviews with Ian Aitken, Lord Barnett, Francis Beckett, Tony Benn, Albert Booth, the late Lord Bruce, the late Lord Callaghan, the late Baroness Castle, the late Dick Clements, Roger Dawe, Lord Evans of Parkside, Alan Fox, Vesna Gamulin, Geoffrey Goodman, Brian Gosschalk, Baroness Gould, Lord Hattersley, Lord Healey, Lord Hunt of Tanworth, Jack Jones, Dr Hrvoje Kacic, Sir Gerald Kaufman MP, Lord Kinnock, Jacqui Lait MP, Sir Thomas McCaffrey, Keith McDowall, Lord McNally, Baroness Mallalieu, Nada Maric, the late Lord Merlyn-Rees,

Lord Morris of Aberavon, the late Lord Murray of Epping Forest, Sue Nye, the late Lord Orme, Lord Owen, Lord Paul, Sir Michael Quinlan, Caerwyn Roderick, Clive Saville, Lord Steel, Sir Kenneth Stowe, Elizabeth Thomas, Hugh Thomas, Lord Varley, Lord Wedderburn, Baroness Williams of Crosby, Vivian Williams and Sir Robert Worcester.

I am also grateful for valuable information gained from, amongst others, Dr Christopher Allsopp, Lord Anderson of Swansea, Sir Kenneth Barnes, Lord Biffen, Lord Brookman, Dr Alan Budd, Lord Burlison, Lord Carter, Lord Corbett, Sir Patrick Cormack MP, Lord Dubs, Lord Eatwell, Robert Edwards, Dr Hywel Francis MP, John Fraser, Baroness Gale, Jadran Gamulin, Lord Gilmour, Baroness Golding, Dr Andrew Graham, Lord Graham of Edmonton, Peter Hain MP, Lord Hogg, Lord Howe of Aberavon, Lord Irvine, Baroness Jay of Paddington, the late Lord Jay of Battersea, Lord Jones of Deeside, William Keegan, Paul Levy, Lord Lipsey, Lord Mason, Mrs John Powell, Professor Siegbert Prawer, Lord Prior, Lord Rodgers, Lord Sheldon, Dr Elizabeth Shore, Robert Taylor, Baroness Turner of Camden, Dennis Turner and Alan Watkins. I am also indebted to Francis Beckett for audio-visual material. Sheila Noble and Alan Fox were particularly helpful in giving me illustrations.

All academic writers are massively indebted to the philanthropic race of librarians. The staff of the House of Lords Library have been extraordinarily helpful, not least their former chief, David Lewis Jones from Aberaeron – *diolch yn fawr iawn i ti am dy caredigrwydd*. The librarian of the Reform Club, Simon Blundell, has been eternally helpful. I am also much indebted to the staff of the People's History Museum, Manchester, where Michael Foot's formal papers are so admirably housed, especially my old friend Stephen Bird. The helpful staff of the New Bodleian Library in charge of the newspaper stacks; my old friend John Graham Jones of the Political Archive, the National Library of Wales, Aberystwyth; Drs Allen Packwood and Andrew Riley at Churchill College, Cambridge; Ms Mari Takayanagi of the House of Lords Record Office; Ms Sally Pagan of Edinburgh University Library; and Ms Rachel Hertz at the Harry Ransom Humanities Center, the University of Texas at Austin, have all been kindness itself, while the library staff of The Queen's College, Oxford, have served me cheerfully as they have done since 1966. I am truly fortunate in my college, its Provost and Fellows, and all its staff.

I am delighted that the Right Honourable Tony Blair allowed me to publish one of his private letters. I am also very grateful for permission to publish material where trustees own the copyright, notably the Beaverbrook Papers in the House of Lords Record Office; to Baroness Jay for material from the private papers of Lord Callaghan in her possession; and to Sir Patrick Cormack MP for showing me the portrait of Michael Foot in 1 Parliament Street as well as to the artist, Graham Jones, for allowing me to use it in illustrating this book.

For the second time, a manuscript of mine has been read by my old friend Professor David Howell of the University of York. His extraordinary learning and attention to detail have both saved me from many errors and much enriched my knowledge on matters ranging from trade union elections to the goal-scoring exploits of Plymouth Argyle. The *Dictionary of Labour Biography* is in the best of hands. My MS was also read by my daughter Katherine, and she too was immensely helpful for her insights both as a civil servant and as a young person.

I am also much indebted to Alison and Owain Morgan for generously giving me material on and insights into the career of Isaac Foot, whose life they have published with Michael; Chris Ballinger of Brasenose College, Oxford, for great help with the more recent National Archive records; to my colleague at Queen's, Nick Owen, for giving me material on Indian politics in the thirties; to Clive Saville for sending me fascinating information on his time with Michael Foot in Whitehall; to my old friend Professor Dai Smith for material on Raymond Williams, whose biography he is writing; to another old friend, Professor Roger Morgan, and to John Allinson for sending much helpful information on Leighton Park School; to an almost lifelong colleague, Professor Wm Roger Louis, for help at the Harry Ransom Center, Austin, Texas; and to Dr Peter Gaunt, Professor John Morrill and Dr Stephen Davies for informing me about the Cromwell Association. I have also benefited from the learning of Dr James Ward and my Lords colleague Ted Rowlands for guidance on Dean Swift. Indeed the companionship of many gifted and humane colleagues in the Lords has been a boon beyond measure, since I have had expert

advice from Bhikhu, Lord Parekh, on Indian affairs, from Bill, Lord
Wedderburn, on the complexities of labour law, and from Trevor,
Lord Smith of Clifton, with shrewd thoughts on many matters from
the benches of the Liberal Democrats. Anne-Marie Motard of the
University of Montpellier has always been a reassuring force. My
literary agent, Bruce Hunter, has been friend and wise adviser as for
decades past, and my editor at HarperCollins, Richard Johnson, has
made my first experience with that great publishing house quite
delightful, as has my wonderful copy-editor, Robert Lacey. Since one
of my unfortunate common experiences with Michael Foot is to have
been the victim in a serious car crash, in my case in 2004, I would also
like to thank Professor David Murray of the Nuffield Orthopaedic
Centre, Oxford, for restoring me physically (twice).

Most authors owe much to their families. Partly through adversity,
ours is closer than most. I am hugely grateful to my two amazing
children, David and Katherine, for their love, moral support, knowledge of word processors and unfailing enthusiasm for their obsessive
bookish father; to my lovely daughter-in-law Liz, another writer in the
making; and to my little grandson Joseph, a free-thinking, free-walking
radical to whom this book is dedicated. This is my first big book since
1973 in which my beloved late wife, Jane, played no part. Yet maybe
she was present after all. In 1987, at the parliamentary launch party of
my book *Labour People*, one of the politicians dealt with there (very
favourably) ignored the publishers' invitation. He also ignored us in the
Commons corridor as we approached the terrace room. By contrast,
Michael Foot had replied at once, and made a very warm and witty
speech at the event. 'No surprise there,' said Jane with finality. 'Michael
Foot is a gentleman.' As always, she was right.

KENNETH O. MORGAN
Long Hanborough,
May Day 2006

1

NONCONFORMIST PATRICIAN
(1913–1934)

On a fine sunny evening on 14 July 2003, the Prime Minister, Tony Blair, hosted a reception in Downing Street. But this was a New Labour event with a difference. It was attended not only by the predictable great and good of the British Labour movement and the associated media, but also by a rich variety of rebels and dissenters, veterans of CND, *Tribune* and Troops Out, a representative sample of those people that the historian A. J. P. Taylor had christened, in a famous book in 1957, Britain's 'troublemakers'. They were there to honour a frail old man of almost ninety, compelled to be seated but full of life and nodding his head in synchronized animation. This was Michael Foot, an almost legendary icon on the Old Left, one-time leader of the Labour Party, long-term oppositionist parliamentarian, editor and essayist, pamphleteer and man of letters, a scourge of Guilty Men in high places ever since he first made his name in that famous wartime tract published just after Dunkirk, sixty-three years earlier. This reception was merely the most spectacular of many events designed to make July 2003 a month of celebration of Michael's latest landmark. That same week there was to be a massed gathering of his friends at his favourite Gay Hussar restaurant in Greek Street, Soho, at which the eminent journalist Geoffrey Goodman presided and Michael was awarded a shirt of his beloved Plymouth Argyle football team bearing the number 90 on its back. He had, he was told, been formally registered as part of the Argyle squad with the Football League, perhaps to reinforce his team's left-wing attack. The following week there was another reception in the very epicentre of the establishment, this time the Foreign Office in Carlton Gardens, genially presided over by the Foreign Secretary Jack Straw, Member for Blackburn and successor and protégé of Michael's old comrade and love, Barbara Castle. He described how Michael had made in the House of Commons in 1981 the finest speech that he, Straw, had ever heard.

But the evening in the Downing Street garden on 14 July, Bastille Day appropriately, was the highlight. It was set, as Foot would have particularly appreciated, in a place steeped in history, where the newly elected Labour Prime Minister Clement Attlee had convened his excited ministers in 1945 and Lloyd George's 'garden suburb' of private advisers had once conducted intrigues and manoeuvres from temporary huts set amongst the flowerbeds. People wondered what Tony Blair himself might say about so traditional and committed an Old Labour stalwart. In fact his speech was charming, generous and relaxed. He recalled Michael's dedication to human rights (though not to social-ism), and paid especial tribute to his strong backing of the young Blair's effort to become candidate for the Sedgefield constituency in 1983 – a reflection no doubt of Foot's positive response to Blair's early cam-paign in the Beaconsfield by-election in 1982, and also perhaps of his determination to ward off the selection of a hard-left Bennite, Les Huckfield. Michael, in response, spoke at much greater length and with less precision, although, to the joy of some present, he did manage an amiable throwaway reference to George Galloway, a far-left socialist shortly to be expelled from the Labour Party for his support for Saddam Hussein. The whole occasion was entirely relaxed and enjoyable, Old and New Labour as one, poachers and gamekeepers drinking in com-mon celebratory cause. Vocal protests from demonstrators outside in Whitehall directed against Downing Street's later visitor that evening, Israel's Prime Minister Ariel Sharon (with which many in the garden sympathized), were satisfactorily inaudible. As they left, people com-mented on how relaxed Tony Blair looked even at a time of pressure during an inquiry by the Commons Foreign Affairs Committee into the origins of the invasion of Iraq four months earlier. This was made especially difficult by the embarrassed evidence from the government scientist, arms expert and apparent whistle-blower, Dr David Kelly. Honouring Michael Foot, himself a vocal critic of the Iraq war, meant for the moment the burying of hatchets all round.

Four days later, the birthday bonhomie disappeared. The body of the tormented David Kelly was discovered in woodland at Southmoor, near his home in southern Oxfordshire. Suicide was suspected. Angry friends accused Tony Blair of indirect complicity. Foot's birthday party was to prove almost the last happy evening that the Prime Minister would know for many months to come. The shadow of Kelly and the other consequences of the Iraq venture would haunt him right down to the general election of May 2005, which saw Labour's majority fall by almost a hundred. But whatever these events meant for Tony Blair, they were perhaps not a bad symbol for the career of Michael Foot – loyal acclaim from the party, genial genuflection from the establishment, but an underlying background of conflict, tension and tragedy throughout the near century of which he was chronicler and survivor.

This unique combination of elitism and dissent went right back to Michael Foot's ancestral roots. His family and forebears shaped his outlook and style more than they do for many public figures. More important, he himself believed that their influence was decisive, and often paid testimony to their historic importance, by word and by pen. It was a background of West Country dissent that dated from the historic conflict between Crown and Parliament under Charles I. Cromwell was very much the people's Oliver for the tenant farmers and craftsmen of Somerset, Devon and Cornwall. But it was also a tradition of patriotic dissent, of dissent militant. Francis Drake was an earlier hero for the community from which the Foots had sprung, his freebooting illegalities discounted amidst the beguiling beat of Drake's Drum. In August 1940 Isaac Foot, Michael's father, was to give a famous broadcast, 'Drake's Drum Beats Again', comparing the little boats at Dunkirk with Drake's men o'war. Similarly it was Cromwell the warrior whom Michael and all the Foots celebrated – the victor of the battles of Marston Moor, Naseby and Dunbar, the man who supported the execution of his king and conducted a forceful, navy-based foreign and commercial policy – quite as much as the champion of civil and religious liberties. It is not at all surprising that Michael, 'inveterate peacemonger', unilateralist and moral disarmer, should also brandish the terrible swift sword of retribution in the Falklands and in Croatia and Bosnia later on. Like the legend of John Brown's body, his prophetic truth would go marching on.

The Foot dynasty of Devon were robust specimens of West Country self-sufficient artisans. In the main they were village carpenters and wheelwrights, working on the Devon side of the river Tamar which separates that county from Cornwall. On balance, the Foot dynasty were Devonian English, indeed very English, not Brythonic or Cornish Celts. The earliest traced of them is John Foot, who is known to have married Grace Glanvill in the Devon village of Whitchurch, near Tavistock, on 21 October 1703. Then came successively Thomas Foot (born 1716), another Thomas Foot (1744–1823), John Foot (1775–1841) and James Foot (1803–58), all resident in the hinterland of Plymouth, all Methodists subscribing in their quiet way to that city's tradition of vibrant nonconformity, and with folk memories of Plymouth's role as a bastion of parliamentarianism, almost republicanism, during the civil wars of the 1640s. Men recalled the siege of Plymouth during those wars, and the citizens' proud resolve not to be starved by the royalist armies into surrender. There was a permanent monument to it in Freedom Fields, close to the later home of Isaac Foot and his family. The man who really established the Foot tradition and mystique was Michael's grandfather, the elder Isaac (1843–1927).[1] A carpenter and part-time undertaker by profession, he moved to Plymouth from Horrabridge in north Devon, reportedly with just £5 in his pocket. He built his own house, branched out as a small entrepreneur and as such took a more public role in the civic life of Plymouth. A passionate Methodist and teetotaller, he was anxious to civilize the somewhat turbulent seaport in which he lived, and left as his legacy a Mission Hall in Notte Street, near the city centre, which he himself had financed and built, along with Congress Hall for the Salvation Army. His son, the younger Isaac (1880–1960), began life with clear expectations of a professional career. He qualified as a solicitor, and after a brief period in London was articled to a solicitor back in Plymouth, married a Scots fellow Methodist, Eva Mackintosh, in 1904, set up his own firm of solicitors, Foot and Bowden, in the same year, and moved to live in Lipson Terrace, a comfortable upmarket road in the northern part of the town. It was in this secure bourgeois enclave that the seven children of the Foot dynasty were born.

Isaac Foot, Michael's father, was the sixth of eight children, of whom five were to live to a considerable age.[2] He was a memorable personality of dominating influence. As its patriarch, he was passionate in his defence of the Foot family. When he wrote to congratulate Michael on a fine maiden speech in Parliament in August 1945, at the same time he condemned Churchill for not appointing his other son Dingle to the Privy Council after his service at the Ministry of Economic Warfare: 'I shall never forgive him for that. Now the Foot family move to the attack. When folk attack the Foot family, they are biting granite.'³ His outlook and lifestyle were challenging and highly individual. Of all the seven children of this Liberal patriarch it was Michael who was said most to resemble him. Until his nineties Michael would readily turn to his father's views on politics and literature, on Cromwell or Napoleon, on Swift or Hazlitt or Burke, to bolster his own line of argument. Isaac Foot had been a radical youth, and at the age of eighteen was attracted to H. M. Hyndman's Marxist party the Social Democratic Federation (SDF),⁴ but not for long. He was one of many young professional men stirred by the Liberal landslide victory in the general election of January 1906, when both the two Plymouth seats were captured by Liberals from the Conservatives. In 1907 he was elected a Liberal councillor and rose to become Deputy Mayor in 1920, at hand to take an enthusiastic part in the celebrations of the tercentenary of the sailing from the city of the *Mayflower*. He was basically an old Liberal, committed to the traditional battles with the bishop, the squire and especially the brewer. He shared to the full the nonconformist crusade for civic equality which made Devon, Cornwall and (to a lesser degree) Somerset more similar to the political outlook of rural Wales than to the rest of southern England. But Isaac responded very positively also to Lloyd George's social radicalism, his 'People's Budget' of 1909 with its new taxes to pay for social reform, which the Lords rejected, and the successful battle with the Upper House in 1909–11, resulting in the passage of the Parliament Act. Despite the huge Liberal schism created later by the 'coupon election' in December 1918, when Lloyd George and his followers continued in coalition with the Unionists (Conservatives), the Welshman remained something of a Foot family talisman from then on. Isaac Foot actually stood for Parliament in January 1910 as Liberal candidate for Totnes, but was heavily defeated by the Conservative. He stood again in December 1910, this time for Bodmin, a seat held by another Liberal the previous January by the slender margin of fifty votes, and was defeated there by an even narrower margin, just forty-one votes. The turnout was 86.6 per cent in this traditionally hard-fought seat, and Foot stayed on as candidate.

During the war he was among those numerous West Country Liberals who took the side of the fallen Asquith after Lloyd George had ousted the Prime Minister in a *putsch* involving leading Conservatives and press men like Max Aitken (soon to become Lord Beaverbrook) in December 1916. Isaac Foot had in any case been a strong critic on libertarian grounds of the conscription measure passed by the Asquith coalition that May, and defended many conscientious objectors in tribunals during the war. This was not popular, and ensured his heavy defeat in a second contest for Bodmin in the general election of December 1918; he also failed in a by-election in Plymouth in 1919, after which the successful Conservative candidate Nancy, Lady Astor became the first woman MP to take her seat in Parliament. But Isaac hung on, and eventually won Bodmin in a by-election in February 1922 with a strong majority of over three thousand. He held on to the seat in the general elections of 1922 and 1923, lost in 1924 and was returned again to represent the same constituency in 1929 and then in 1931 when (from 3 September) he served in Ramsay MacDonald's National Government as Minister for the Mines.

Isaac Foot was in every sense a prominent figure in the political and civic life of Plymouth and the West Country. In all he fought Bodmin seven times, and established himself as a powerful politician of charisma and pugnacity. As an orator (and later a broadcaster) he was remarkable, drawing from his lay preaching in Cornish chapels a revivalist style and a vivid vocabulary with which righteously to smite the opposing Philistines. In the 1930s he was to become Vice-President of the Methodist Conference. But for all his devout Methodism and moralism, he showed little compunction in using fair means or foul to make his political points. 'He fought with the gloves off,' was his son's later reflection. He threw himself into electioneering with gusto, taunting the Tories such as the Astor family interest in Plymouth with popular refrains such as 'Who's that knocking at my door?'. He was a fund of political and other jokes, and was liable to break into comic songs, sung in a rich Devonian accent.

He showed himself to be equally forceful in following one of his

main private interests, the Cromwell Association, of which he was a
founder member and which he served as secretary from 1938 and
chairman until 1951. Here he would staunchly defend Oliver's reputation and integrity against all comers. There is reference to Isaac on
the monument unveiled in 1939 to mark Cromwell's great victory at
Marston Moor in 1644. Here indeed, as Michael Foot was to describe
him, was 'a Rupert for the Roundheads'.[5] Episcopal opponents were
particularly relished. On 20 February 1949, in his seventieth year, Isaac
had a ferocious duel in the *Observer* with the Bishop of London, who
had dared to impugn Cromwell's reputation as a champion of liberty
and toleration. Isaac swept the charges contemptuously back in his
face. The Bishop's accusation that Cromwell had condemned prelacy
was, however, joyfully endorsed.[6] Isaac flung at him one of Cromwell's
contemporaries, who scorned

> You reverend prelates, clothed in sleeve of lawn
> Too meek to murmur, and too proud to fawn
> Who, still submissive in their Maker's nod
> Adore their Sovereign and respect their God.

In Isaac's mind, old flames of controversy over tithe, church rate,
university tests or Welsh disestablishment still burned fiercely. Cromwell's reputation went through many vicissitudes over the centuries,
from Whigs hailing the champion of parliamentary liberties, to Vic-
torians who saw his Major-Generals as the last refuge of military rule
in Britain, on to working-class radicals who revered 'the People's
Oliver'. For Isaac, Cromwell was simply the great liberator, Milton's
'chief of men', in peace and in war. In 1941 he published with Oxford
University Press *Cromwell Speaks!*, a compendium of militant and patriotic quotations from the great man's letters and speeches, to help in
sustaining the national morale at a time of supreme crisis. His Cromwell
Association made a point of honouring their hero's statue on Cromwell
Green in front of the Palace of Westminster, a memorial which had
been bitterly attacked by Irish MPs in the 1890s. Isaac Foot was a true
believer. He celebrated Cromwell and Milton in the same passionate
vein as another Liberal politician, the late-Victorian man of letters
Augustine Birrell, did in his 1905 biography of Andrew Marvell. John
Gross has written that, for thousands of old Liberals, 'the seventeenth

century was alive with an intensity that now seems hard to credit'.[7] It might have been Isaac – indeed all the Foots down the generations – that he had in mind.

Michael fully inherited this Cromwellian creed, without the roundhead puritanism. Like his elder brother John, he later became a Vice-President of the Cromwell Association, and he gave an eloquent address to it on 2 September 1995, in part a tribute to his father. He had assured the Chairman beforehand (surely quite unnecessarily), 'My remarks will not be critical in any sense and would not offend members of the Cromwell Association.' At the age of eighty-two, the ardour of the old believer was quite undimmed. A wreath was laid at Cromwell's statue (the main theme of Foot's speech), there were readings from the psalms and the singing of Bunyan's imperishable hymn, so evocative to a Plymouth pilgrim, 'He who would true valour see'. As late as September 2005 Michael attended the Cromwell Day service in the chapel of Central Hall, Westminster, and wrote warmly to the Association to convey his pleasure at the event: 'I trust that several members of our family will be joining the Association soon.'[8] On the other hand, he was sufficiently the disciple of his friend H. N. Brailsford to recognize fully the force behind the progressive egalitarian doctrines of the Levellers as well. Michael drew from his father not simply a cult of Cromwell, the popular tribune who brought blessings like the abolition of the House of Lords or tolerance towards the Jews, but also the need to defend his heroes with the maximum of pugnacity. When he himself entered Parliament, his father encouraged a creed of *fortiter in re*, not to confine his blows upon opponents to the regions above the belt, but to fight either dirty or clean as circumstances dictated, and Michael duly responded. Isaac Foot remained a keen observer of all his sons' political progress, but Michael, who advanced from Cromwellian republicanism into a Labour Party of self-proclaimed levellers, was perhaps the most cherished of them all. Isaac would surely have endorsed Michael's warm commendation in November 2005 of a book by his own former legal adviser, the civil rights lawyer Geoffrey Robertson QC. This commemorated John Cooke, who successfully prosecuted the trial of Charles I for treason which led to the King's execution in 1649. It was an event of which Michael Foot, humanist and opponent of capital punishment, strongly approved.

This bond between father and son was illustrated by Isaac's splendid lecture comparing Oliver Cromwell and Abraham Lincoln given to the Royal Society of Literature in April 1944. Michael Foot's copy of the published version was inscribed 'To Michael with love and Cromwellian Salutations from Dad, 23 February 1945'. It seems almost as if Cromwell was a member of the family, a particularly cherished great-uncle. Dingle Foot was to recall that there were twenty to thirty busts or portraits of Oliver in their home. The Cromwellian aspect was obviously well absorbed by Michael. Lincoln, however, he found less appealing, perhaps too conservatively inclined, especially on race questions, and indeed American inspiration generally was less influential on a politician so robustly English. By far the most attractive American for the young Michael was Thomas Jefferson, not so much in his role as an American revolutionary as that of a transatlantic voice for western European enlightenment.

For all his partisanship, Isaac's cheerful, generous personality won him good friends across a wide spectrum, and indeed these came to include the much-abused Astors themselves. He was always active in the municipal life of Plymouth, and became its Lord Mayor after the end of the war in 1945. He patronized the city's religious and musical life, and also sporting events in football and cricket: Isaac began a unanimous Foot tradition of supporting Plymouth Argyle FC, based at Home Park and elected to the Football League in 1920. It was a family link that continued from Isaac's vocal terrace support in the 1920s to Michael's becoming a club director in the 1980s.

But Isaac's main influence on his sons and daughters, and especially on Michael, lay not in politics but in books. From his early years he was, as Michael was frequently to describe him, a 'bibliophilial drunkard' whose appetite was 'gargantuan and insatiable'.[9] He had an obsession for rare and other books of all kinds, especially historical, literary and religious. His collecting began when, as a young clerk in London, he spent as much as he could of his fourteen shillings weekly pay in the second-hand bookshops of Charing Cross Road. In his later years every room in his large home at Pencrebar, even (improbably) the laundry room, was crammed full of carefully arranged and notated volumes. He would read for four or five hours every day; he would read as he walked to work, he read in his bath, he would have read in his sleep were it possible. Much of his library was sold off to the University of California, Santa Barbara, for a surprisingly low figure of £50,000 after his death in 1960,[10] less than £1 per book. Other materials went to Berkeley and UC Los Angeles, so sadly the library was dispersed: it had expanded to perhaps sixty thousand books, including no fewer than 240 Bibles, among them priceless octavo and quarto editions of Tyndale's New Testament of 1536, and many medieval illuminated manuscripts, along with an immense range of antiquarian works by or about Shakespeare, Montaigne (130 volumes), Milton, Swift, Pope, Johnson, Burke, Hazlitt, Wordsworth, Carlyle, Hardy, Conrad and some unexpected intruders onto the old puritan's shelves, such as the sonnets of Oscar Wilde's lover, Lord Alfred Douglas. The inventory of UC Santa Barbara library listed three thousand English Civil War tracts, over two thousand volumes on the French Revolutionary period, and over a thousand on the American Civil War, amongst his historical collection. A colossal holding on literature included over three hundred volumes on and by Milton, including first and second editions of *Paradise Lost* and a first edition of *Areopagitica*. The religious holdings were equally immense, including titles on and by Luther and Calvin, a hundred contemporary Erasmus imprints, vast collections on Richard Baxter's Congregationalism, and a Quaker collection of more than two hundred volumes. Isaac Foot also ranged around the classics: one especially priceless book was the 1488 edition of Homer printed in Florence.

Somehow all these volumes were crammed into Pencrebar, though only just. Isaac designated a Bible room and a French Revolution room; when he developed an interest in Abraham Lincoln later in life there was an American Congress room. Many books were extremely rare, yet there was apparently the minimum of security against fire or theft. His home was a shrine to what George Gissing had called 'the shadow of the valley of books'. So extreme was his mania for collection that A. L. Rowse, a historian at All Souls, Oxford, and no inconsiderable bibliophile himself, claimed that Isaac Foot's second wife was in tears as one room after another was annexed for his literary stockpiling, supplemented by bookcases to occupy what little room remained. 'He has the obstinacy of a senile fixation,' was Rowse's harsh verdict.[11] But clearly for the young (and middle-aged) Michael his father's passion for the printed word was breathtakingly exciting, the key to a civilized life. In return, Isaac delighted in Michael's own emerging skills as a powerful writer of serious literary books. The publication of *The Pen and the Sword* in 1957, written after Michael had lost his Devonport seat in the 1955 general election, perhaps gave Isaac more pleasure than any other feature of his son's career. 'Let the boy be known for his books,' he lovingly observed.

Isaac's influence was profound on all his children, but on Michael most of all. Michael's journey into the Labour Party, a unique adventure for the Foot family, did not threaten their relationship; if anything, it made it stronger. Isaac responded by offering Michael the example of Hazlitt as the supreme inspiration any real radical could ever want. He gave him a passion for language, written and spoken; Michael's politics were politics of the book. He spelled out for the readers of the *Evening Standard* (1 June 1964) his philosophy of life, drawn from the critic Logan Pearsall Smith: 'To read and to act is not achieved by many. And yet to act and not to read is barbarism.' It was books, as much as the sufferings of his fellow men, that made Michael a socialist and nurtured his unique brilliance as a communicator. More specifically, it was Isaac who directed him to the unique qualities of Swift and Hazlitt, Michael Foot's prime allies in his assaults on twentieth-century political opponents, his friends in good times and bad. The more measured influence of Montaigne, the cool, sceptical essayist of sixteenth-century France, but also the mentor of Foot's hero Swift, was another legacy from Isaac when Michael turned to Montaigne's essays in hospital after a serious car crash in 1963. Another hero was John Milton, not only a matchless poet but in *Areopagitica* a timeless champion of a free press.

On the other hand, Michael's growing love of literature was self-nurtured also. Isaac's literary enthusiasms were mainly pre-Romantic and shaped by a puritan heritage. Michael's own passionate temperament gave him heroes of a different kind, in particular his beloved Byron, for whose poetry Isaac had no particular regard and which had been fiercely criticized by one of Michael's own heroes, Hazlitt. Without Isaac's affection and inspiration, Michael Foot's career would have been far less distinctive. But it might also have been less dogmatic and he might have been more open to argument from others. Isaac's literary giants, it seemed, were almost gods, to be treated with near-sanctity. None of them could be lightly impugned. There was also a curious formality, almost a distance, between father and son. When Isaac ran into debt as a result of his solicitor's business being disrupted during the war when his offices in Plymouth were bombed out, quite apart from his manic book purchasing, Michael, now with a good income from the *Evening Standard*, loaned him successive sums of money to help him out, ranging from £110 in May 1940 to £875 in March 1941. Each was accompanied by a highly detailed formal IOU drawn up in legalistic terms by Isaac. An IOU of £2,095 up to September 1942 set out both the capital sum and the interest upon it at £4 per annum as a first charge on Isaac's estate, a strangely formal arrangement perhaps between a father and a son.[12] Having Isaac as a father was both an inspiration and a challenge, but without doubt he contributed most of the components of his son's passionate but unquestionably bookish socialism.

Michael Foot's mother, Eva Mackintosh, was also a powerful personality in her way, even if tending to be swamped at home and in spirit by Isaac's intemperate bibliophilia. Born in 1878 and a year and a half older than Isaac, she was of Scottish and Cornish background, and a strong Methodist like her husband. Indeed, it was on a Wesleyan Guild Methodist outing that Isaac first set eyes on her. With a characteristic Foot blend of impulsiveness and caution, he proposed to her almost immediately and was accepted, but then remained engaged for three years while he built up his solicitor's practice. They married in 1904, in Callington, a village a few miles north of Plymouth where Eva had latterly lived. It was a long and immensely happy marriage, ended only when Eva unexpectedly died in May 1946, after which Isaac somewhat disconcertingly for the family married a second time. Eva had traditional non-feminist views, which clearly extended to her two daughters, Jennifer and Sally, both of whom had somewhat restricted lives. Her son John's egalitarian-minded American fiancée evidently found this disturbing when she first visited the Foot household.

Five of Eva's seven children, including Michael, were given the second name Mackintosh (an allegedly useful asset when brother Dingle stood as Liberal candidate in Dundee). She wrote occasional letters to the local *Western Morning News* under the thinly-concealed *nom de plume* of 'Mother of Seven'. Hugh Foot wrote in his memoirs of how his mother made them all laugh 'at ourselves and at each other'.[13] Eva was not only happy being a warm and spirited mother, but also gave every encouragement to the professional careers of her talented sons. She was thoroughly at home in a political setting, being herself a robust Liberal, and perhaps more instinctively attracted to radicalism of the Lloyd George type than other members of the family. Michael's defection to Labour in 1934 was a shock for them all, but Eva appears to have taken the news better than some. When Michael campaigned for Devonport as a Labour candidate in 1945, a meeting was interrupted by the delivery of a large Cornish pasty from his mother, a Methodist's material peace offering and also a signal that her socialist son was no less favoured than husband Isaac and sons Dingle and John, all Liberal candidates in 1945 (and, unlike Michael, all defeated).

The family background of the Foots is of quite exceptional importance: the historian John Vincent once called their home, referring to the Hertfordshire seat of the Cecils, 'a West Country Hatfield'. There were five sons: the eldest Dingle (1905–78), the second Hugh (1907–90), the third John (1909–99), the fourth son and fifth child, Michael (born in 1913), and the youngest son and sixth child, Christopher (1918–84). All went on to have, to varying degrees, fulfilling professional careers. By contrast the daughters, Margaret Elizabeth, known as Sally (1911–65), and Jennifer (1916–2002), had lives that were domestically confined. Jennifer married, but Sally never did. It was a large and lively household, with much family fun and frivolity and a high degree of competitiveness in the playing of games, especially cricket and football, in which Isaac enthusiastically joined. They lived in Lipson Terrace from 1904 until in 1927 they moved to a large white Victorian manor house, Pencrebar, near Callington, some eight miles north of Plymouth, overlooking the Cornish moorland. With its 'wide sashed windows, large rooms and wide sweeping lawns and shrubberies', it became a focal point for West Country nonconformist Liberalism and a much-loved family home, as well as a depository for Isaac's vast library.[14]

It was in every sense a close-knit family which made demands of all the children, but enriched them too. They all recalled a cheerful and secure childhood. Hugh noted that 'we had and needed few outside friends'. The eldest boy, Dingle, with whom Michael had little to do at first because of the eight-year gap between them, immediately showed himself to be talented. He was thought to be the ablest Foot at the time, and Michael later considered him the funniest orator amongst them.[15] As all the Foot boys did, he went to a private second-ary school, in his case Bembridge School on the Isle of Wight, where he was taught by a former Liberal MP, J. H. Whitehouse, who was now the school's headmaster. Dingle went on to Balliol College, Oxford, where he became President of the Liberal Club in 1927 and rose to be President of the Union in 1928, also gaining a second-class honours degree in law. He entered chambers in 1930, becoming a barrister of international distinction, and in 1931 he was elected as Liberal (though pro-government) MP for Dundee, which he rep-resented until 1945. One problem was the physical disability of a tubercular arm. The second son, Hugh, went to Leighton Park, the famous Quaker school near Reading which Michael later attended, and then on to St John's College, Cambridge, where he showed a notably un-Foot-like enthusiasm for the college rowing club but also became President of the Liberal Club and of the Cambridge Union. There was some fraternal joshing about his alleged relative lack of intellectual sharpness – Michael described him caustically and unfairly in the *Evening Standard* in 1961 as 'never considered the brightest of the brood'. But Hugh, like his brothers, ended up with a second-class degree. In fact Michael always had a strong relationship with 'Mac', as Hugh came to be known, including a cheerful period as the lodger of Hugh and his wife in the later 1930s. His assessment of his brother concluded: 'All in all a credit to the family and I can't say fairer than that, can I?' With Hugh's son Paul, the friendship was to be stronger still.

John, the third son and another charming and eloquent Liberal, seemed as talented as any of them. He too went to Bembridge School and Balliol College like Dingle, took a degree in law and also became President of the Liberal Club and the Union, a remarkable dynastic achievement which Michael was soon to extend. He became a solicitor and in due time took over from Isaac as senior partner in the family firm Foot & Bowden. But his political antennae seemed no less acute than those of his two brothers, and he was four times a Liberal candidate, for Basingstoke in 1934 and 1935, and for his father's old stamping ground of Bodmin in 1945 and 1950. Unexpectedly he failed to win the latter, and ended up as Baron Foot of Buckland Monachorum, though with a radical outlook on social and defence issues very similar to those of his firebrand brother Michael. The two were both Cromwellian enthusiasts, and were very close. Michael would say of John, 'He was the best speaker of the lot of us.'[16] The two daughters, Jennifer and Sally, as mentioned, were not encouraged to develop their talents, while the youngest son, Christopher, settled down, none too happily, as a local solicitor.

This was the background into which Michael Mackintosh Foot was born on 23 July 1913. It was cradle, crucible and cauldron for him. The tone was set by Isaac. It was distinguished by a passion for both literature and music (the latter less pronounced in Michael's case until he met Jill Craigie, who introduced him to Mozart), especially Bach's choral music, and a passionate devotion to the grand old causes of nineteenth-century Liberalism. It was an intimate family whose members kept up warm relations throughout their lives. Michael and his brothers addressed each other in letters or telephone conversations with the words 'pit and rock'. This private code recalled a famous phrase from the Book of Isaiah: 'Look unto the rock whence ye are hewn and to the hole of the pit whence ye are digged.' Hugh thus communicated with Michael while serving at a tense period as Governor of Cyprus in the late 1950s. Life in the Foot family seems to have been inspiring and somewhat pressurizing at the same time, being conducted at a high level of intensity, both political and religious. One newspaper described the household as characterized by 'bacon for breakfast, Liberalism for lunch and Deuteronomy for dinner'.[17]

One strict rule was abstinence from alcohol until the age of twenty-one, after which the sons would qualify for a small legacy from their grandfather: Michael and John celebrated their release from this thraldom by getting drunk together on a trip to Paris, in pursuit of culture and self-liberation, in 1934. The child Michael, dominated by his three older brothers, Dingle, Hugh and John, was to find a particular kinship with his slightly older sister Sally. A major factor here was that both suffered from severe eczema – a hereditary condition, apparently – and in Michael's case from growing asthma as well. Outdoor games were to some extent denied him, and he turned naturally to indoor bookish pursuits, where Sally was a natural mentor and guide, with her own unfulfilled artistic and literary talents which later brought friendship, for instance, with Louis MacNeice. Sally introduced Michael to novels and poems which were to stay with him for ever. He would say that she taught him how to read. His lifelong attachment to female relationships, many of a bookish kind, undoubtedly stemmed from his loyal Sally, and his posthumous essay on her, 'Sally's Broomstick', is deeply felt.[18] Her cruel death in the 1960s was a particular blow to him.

It may be that Sally's presence was a calm refuge in an otherwise hyperactive family. One of the adverse consequences for some of the Foot family was a kind of depressive alcoholism, perhaps a reaction against the dynastic prescription of total abstinence in youth. Dingle ended his career in this sad condition, as did his youngest brother Christopher, whose life ended young, and so too did his sister Sally. Indeed, Sally's death through apparent drowning may have been more tragic still. Christopher had to give up his solicitor's work early through some kind of psychological illness. It was Michael, for all his mixed health, who was usually seen as the most stable and normal. So family life was not always as relaxed as when Isaac was telling his stories or Michael was organizing children's games at parties. Keeping up with the Foots could bring its own pressures.

Every Foot from Isaac onwards showed the influence of family. All shared the unyielding attachment to books, to Cromwell and the West Country, to Plymouth Hoe and Plymouth Argyle. All in important senses remained liberal, or at least libertarian, at heart. Most were political, but with a politics fired in the crucible of Foot family argument, rhetoric and dissent. Nothing showed this continuing tradition more clearly than the sadly posthumous book *The Vote* by Hugh Foot's journalist son Paul, long a pillar of the *Socialist Worker* and a writer of a caustic brilliance equalled only by his cherished uncle Michael.[19] Paul was named after the favourite saint; his brother Oliver derived his name from another cult hero. Paul Foot's book is on many fronts a debate within the family. It conducts a sporadic, if affectionate, argument with Michael in denouncing his adhesion to a right-wing, disappointingly parliamentary Labour Party. The debate would be continued towards the end of Paul's life, blighted as it was by illness, on the pavement outside bookshops in the Charing Cross Road, with both bibliophile disputants, uncle and nephew, waving their sticks about to the occasional alarm of passers-by. Paul's book also engages in a covert dispute with his Aunt Jill, a devotee of the suffragettes, but mainly of the Tory Christabel Pankhurst and her mother Emmeline, whereas Paul Foot (like most socialists) found the social radicalism of Sylvia Pankhurst, the lover of the Labour Party's founder Keir Hardie, by far the most appealing.

But the most startling family argument of all for Paul was with his deceased grandfather Isaac, pillar of the Cromwell Association over so many years. Where Cromwell to Isaac (and to Michael too) was the people's Oliver, champion of liberty, to Paul he was the establishment enemy of the Levellers, who rebutted the dangerous democracy voiced by Rainboro, Lilburne and their friends at Putney in 1647. Paul was indirectly announcing that he was the first Foot to break away from the family shibboleths, that Cromwell was no real hero for the popular, let alone the socialist, cause, and that in the earliest campaign for the vote the puritan establishment was essentially an obstacle. Those political continuities, traced by Liberals over the centuries from Putney to the Parliament Act, were in reality an illusion. Paul Foot's was an iconoclastic book, but it was notable that it was the family's boat that had first to be rocked, if not sunk without trace.

His uncle Michael's early years were comfortable and elitist. The First World War made little direct impact upon him, unlike say the youthful Jim Callaghan down the coast at Portsmouth, whose father served in the navy and fought at Jutland. None of the Foots had any experience of this or any other war. Basically they had disliked every one since 1651. The dominant feature of Michael's upbringing is the abiding stamp of loyalty to Plymouth itself. It symbolized for him Britain's worldwide mercantile glories, as well of course as embodying an eternal legend of defence against foreign conquest in the great days of Drake. Plymouth, English to its core, was not therefore the natural base for a devotee of European integration. In 1972 Michael spoke strongly in support of his Conservative successor as MP for Devonport, Joan Vickers, in resisting proposals in Peter Walker's Local Government

Bill to merge Plymouth with the surrounding area. There was, declared
Foot, a 'deep lack of affinity between Plymouth and the County of
Devon'. In family vein, he went on:

> Charles I tried to subdue Plymouth and failed, and Freedom
> Fields is a monument which bears that out. Charles II tried to
> subdue the people of Plymouth by establishing a citadel with
> the guns facing not seawards towards Plymouth sound but
> inwards, but he, too, failed.

Foot had the joy of representing Devonport in that city for ten years
in Parliament, from 1945 to 1955, and hung on as a predictably unsuccessful candidate in 1959, a decision that Aneurin Bevan declared was
'quixotic'.[20] Well into his nineties, journeys with his friend Peter Jones
to see Plymouth Argyle do battle at Home Park were a staple of life.
Contact with his private secretary, Roger Dawe, at the Department of
Employment in 1974 was greatly eased by the latter's Devonian and
Methodist origins, and his being a fellow Argyle supporter.

   During the First World War the Foots moved to Ramsland House
in St Cleers, on the edge of the Cornish moors. But Michael always
identified intensely with Plymouth, the city which was his boyhood
home, where his father was Lord Mayor and where he fell in love
with Jill. And to a degree Plymouth identified with him, indeed with
all the Foots. David Owen, a future Cabinet colleague and Member
for Devonport, grew up there in the fifties under the shadow of the
Foots as a dominating dynasty. In the 1970s Michael and Jill, somewhat
remarkably, managed to persuade the local authority in Hampstead to
rename their road Pilgrims Lane, in tribute to his native city's most
famous exports, and the nickname also of its football team. In later life
he would recall happy episodes from his childhood, such as visits to
the Palace Theatre. One such recollection became memorable, when
in a Commons debate in October 1980 during Labour's leadership
election he spoke of a conjuror who smashed with a hammer a gold
watch belonging to a member of the audience, but then forgot the
rest of the trick. But it remains open to conjecture how far this was a
real Plymouth, or rather an affectionate amalgam of fact, legend and
folk memory, specific and selective associations from the Armada to
the Blitz, ready for instant political mobilization in argument. Michael

Foot's historical reading and personal background formed a highly usable background. This was true of all his interpretations of past scions of the liberty tree, from the Levellers to the suffragettes, and it applied equally to his vision of a post-modernist Plymouth.

That does not mean, of course, that his childhood memories were necessarily entirely benign. Michael's schooling was delayed by his severe asthma in 1919, which led him to go to London at the age of six to obtain medical advice. Indeed, his awareness of ill-health and fear of being thought unattractive were important threads in his early years: a robust life into his nineties was not what the doctors might have predicted. His first school in 1919 was a local preparatory school, Plymouth College for Girls, perhaps not a total success for a six-year-old boy. In Recitation, his school report commented, 'His expression is very good; he should speak out more' – seldom an injunction needed in later life. Another subject was Needlework – 'Good, but he works too slowly.'[21] In 1921 he went on to Plymouth College and Manna-mead School. Going there was not without its hazards, especially being harassed by local bullies as he made his way across Freedom Fields. In 1923, at the age of ten, he went away to a private boarding school, Forres, in Swanage on the Dorset coast. His brother John was already a pupil there. Michael's progress was often interrupted by bronchial complaints; nor did the school's occasional penchant for caning its pupils (including Michael himself for one alleged misdemeanour) appeal to him. But he seems to have developed well, and his head-master, R. M. Chadwick, wrote enthusiastically when he left Forres in 1927 of the immense contribution he had made, and how his name should be inscribed on the school Honours Board. He was first in his form in every subject from Latin to Scripture, while he had also done well in sport as captain of games – 'a very good example of all-round keenness'. An earlier report at Christmas 1926 had commended his football skills – 'Fast and a very good shot at goal. Much more deter-mined than he was last season.' The headmaster added in his final remarks, 'We have all grown very fond of him during his time with us and he will leave a big gap. We look forward to making Christopher's acquaintance next term.'[22]

The fourteen-year-old Michael's next destination was another pri-vate school, Leighton Park, the Quaker boarding school near Reading which his older brother Hugh had already attended (as a scholar, unlike Michael). Founded in 1890, Leighton Park was an elitist school in its way, and was sometimes referred to as 'the Quaker Eton'. Years later A. J. P. Taylor told Lord Beaverbrook, 'Michael had been educated at Leighton Park, the snob Quaker school, and I at Bootham [York], the non-snob one.' Beaverbrook gleefully responded (ignoring Taylor's extremely wealthy cotton-merchant father), 'You and I are sons of the people. Michael is an aristocrat.'[23] But Leighton Park had much cachet amongst nonconformists in both England and Wales. Its liberal Quaker ethos meant that there was no fagging, no corporal punishment and certainly no cadet corps. Its historian, Kenneth Wright, wrote that it was 'an unconventional school producing unconventional people who did not fit into predetermined moulds'. It attracted droves of liberal Cadburys from Bourneville and liberal Rowntrees from York, putative pacifists one and all. Michael seems to have found both the teaching and the atmosphere of the school generally congenial. Later on in life he was fiercely to denounce the public schools in the *Daily Herald* for their atmosphere of snobbery, but clearly Leighton Park escaped this particular contagion. Its school magazine, *The Leightonian*, gives at that time a cheerful sense of irreverent informality.

At first Michael's schooling was much interrupted by ill-health. His return for his second term in 1928 was delayed by impetigo and bronchial problems, while his weight was relatively slight. But he soon got into his school subjects with gusto – or at least into those parts of the work which interested him. These clearly did not include a great deal of science. By the spring term of 1928 his science teacher lamented that 'he has not much aptitude for this subject' (chemistry). Physics was adjudged to be no better. A year later, science of any kind has disappeared from his schooling, a not untypical instance of the second-ary education of the time. By contrast, his mathematics was highly praised for arithmetic, algebra and geometry, with marks in the high eighties in each. But by the end of 1929 that also has vanished from his ken. Michael Foot was never a particularly numerate politician. By contrast, the humanities were going well, especially all kinds of litera-ture, and history, for which he had a fine Welsh teacher. His parents were also pleased to see that he scored 92 per cent in scripture in the summer term of 1928. In the spring term of 1930 his report praised the 'mastery' he demonstrated in a paper on the Italian Risorgimento (surely a particularly congenial theme for a romantic young radical), while in European history generally he was thought to be working with 'considerable intelligence and interest'. The one weakness in his work on humanities subjects appeared to be modern languages. Neither in French nor in German did he distinguish himself. French lessons in the spring of 1930 showed that 'his vocabulary is weak', and he scored a mere 37 per cent.[24] Surprisingly for a man with such a quick and adaptable mind, this remained a weak point throughout his life. He was never a confident linguist; he gloried in the novels of Stendhal and the poems of Heine, but he read them in translation. But in that he was typical of the political generation of his time. He got his School Certificate with honours in 1930, and his Higher School Certificate a year later.

Leighton Park in general seems to have been very good for the teenage Michael Foot academically, and he also flourished in other ways. He was an active member of School House, and in 1930 he became a school prefect. *The Leightonian* records several of his other activities. He played a role in Gilbert and Sullivan's *The Pirates of Penzance* as Sergeant of Police. An old boy of the school wrote that 'Foot's performance will go down in the school's history': the audience got him to sing one of his songs three times, and 'in each encore he was even funnier than before'. Despite his asthma and eczema he took his full part in school games, and was commended on his performances as a wing forward in the first rugby XV ('his dribbling is his best feature', though his tackling was also sound) and especially at cricket – 'a good forceful batsman, an excellent cover point fielder and a good bowler who keeps a steady line'. He took six wickets for twenty runs against Bedales, and topped the school bowling averages in 1931, with fifteen wickets at an average of 10.73 apiece.[25] Years later he was to demonstrate his cricketing skills when playing for *Tribune* against the *New Statesman*: the latter's captain and political correspondent, Alan Watkins, came to realize that asking his fast bowlers to be charitable to an amiable old gent was a big mistake. Tennis and rugby fives were other games at which he represented the school. He also began to display talent in the school debating society, which he restarted, and took part as the Liberal candidate in the school mock election on 30 May 1929. He won with fifty-six votes, against thirty-eight for the

Conservatives and eleven for Labour – a more substantial majority than he ever gained at Devonport, and one of relatively few Liberal victories that year.

This was a time of much political energy in the Foot household. Their new home in Pencrebar became a significant salon for West Country Liberalism, with Lloyd George himself a visitor. The young Michael Foot was heard to deliver impromptu speeches to garden parties even at the tender age of twelve. Past divisions between Coalition and Asquithian Liberals set aside, the Foot household campaigned *en bloc* on behalf of Lloyd George's last crusade in the 1929 election with its famous Orange Book to promote economic recovery, *We Can Conquer Unemployment*. The Liberals' eventual tally of seats was a mere fifty-nine, and Ramsay MacDonald became Prime Minister for the second time, Labour ending up with 289 seats, the largest number in the House. But there was much joy with the return of Isaac again for Bodmin, though with a majority of less than a thousand over Gerald Joseph Harrison, the Conservative who had defeated him in 1924. Isaac took a prominent front-bench role in the new House, and was appointed as a Liberal member of the Round Table conference on India in 1930. Michael's elder brother Dingle had also made his first attempt on Parliament, but was defeated by a Conservative in Tiverton, despite polling over 42 per cent of the vote. Hugh was now entering the diplomatic service, and would soon embark on a long connection with the Middle East by serving in Palestine. The schoolboy Michael, a vigorous campaigner for Lloyd Georgian Liberalism in 1929 with its multi-coloured cures for economic stagnation, the Green, Yellow and Orange Books, yielded to none of them in the passion of his political commitment. Lloyd George's battle hymn, 'God gave the Land to the People', was a very popular song at Pencrebar. It was always one of Michael's favourites, next to 'The Marseillaise' and 'The Red Flag'. In *The Leightonian* (March 1931) he set out his Liberal creed in idealistic terms: 'The Liberal Party alone had the courage to think out new schemes and the men of vision to put them into effect . . . It wages a war for liberty, justice and the abolition of poverty.' The party was no meek middle way, but 'possesses ideals, unshared alike by Tories who are a little sentimental and Socialists who are a little timid'.

The most distinctive feature of Michael's political involvement at this time was in the peace movement. This was hardly surprising for a pupil of Liberal background attending a distinctively Quaker school. Leighton Park's headmaster, Edgar Castle, was a *Manchester Guardian* reader and a strong supporter of world disarmament. A League of Nations branch flourished at the school, in which Foot was active. He wrote in *The Leightonian* (March 1931) a sharp critique of scouting as an activity for young people. Its specious militarism and patriotism, and the unquestioned authority of the scoutmaster, were appropriate targets for the seventeen-year-old boy: 'Scouting must not, hermit-like, shut itself off from the modern world.' He added one phrase intriguing for the student of his career: 'We are not meant to play at backwoodsmen all our lives.'

At the age of eighteen, between 7 August and 4 September 1931, in the summer vacation after his last term at Leighton Park, Michael made his most decisive, emphatic gesture yet by taking part in a young people's peace crusade that took him abroad for the second time (he had had a trip to Holland in May 1931). He went with another boy, L. H. Doncaster, on a John Sherborne bursary which covered all the costs save for £10. They travelled as far as Colmar in Alsace, sleeping rough on 'a bed of straw in the village schoolroom or a haystack in the cowshed', though making only limited contact with the other marchers, who were entirely French- and German-speaking. They sang collectively a French song, 'Nous faisons serment d'alliance', the words of which were fresh in Michael's mind seventy-five years later. He paid tribute to their one mobile assistance, a donkey who discharged his duties 'in a manner which would have put Balaam's ass to shame'. Michael pressed on to Strasbourg and then to Germany, to the Black Forest. Here, for the first time, he heard the name of Adolf Hitler. It was virtually a holiday, but he enjoyed 'a pervading sense of self-righteousness', for all this was done in the cause of peace. The child was father of the Aldermaston marcher. He had enjoyed his schooldays, and his school seemed pleased with its association with him. In the late 1940s the brass plate from his time at Leighton Park was still on display on the door of his old study in School House. In 1990 he spoke at length, wallowing in happy nostalgia, at a school centenary dinner in a private dining room in the Commons. He remained a faithful Old Leightonian to the end.[26]

The decisive change of life for the young radical was to come in 1931, when he followed Dingle and John in becoming an undergraduate at Oxford. This had long been a cherished ambition for Isaac, despite the considerable sums he was obliged to pay for Dingle, Hugh and John at the older universities. Michael at school showed a quick intelligence and literary flair, especially in his history essays. But his teachers' assessment of his abilities was sufficiently cautious that he was sent forward for entrance examination not to Balliol, the destination of Dingle and John before him, but to the less prestigious Wadham in the same college group, where the competition for places might be less demanding. He took papers in his favoured subjects of Modern History and English, but his greatest good fortune came in his general paper, in which a question asked candidates what proposals should be made by the current Round Table conference in London considering the future governance of India. As noted, Isaac Foot was himself a Liberal member of that conference, with first-hand knowledge of the views of Gandhi and others on India's future. The night before he sat the paper Michael had had dinner with his father at the National Liberal Club in London, and Isaac had given him a lengthy briefing on future proposals for an Indian federation, along with discourses on the social and economic problems of Indian Untouchables and others. Michael's examination answer in Oxford the following day was therefore unusually authoritative. His interview with Wadham's tutors went equally well, especially a discussion with Lord David Cecil, then at the college. Asked by Cecil which historians he particularly admired, Foot naturally shone. His enthusiastic defence of Macaulay's *History of England*, reinforced by some additional warm comments on Macaulay's kinsman George Otto Trevelyan, saw him comfortably home, a college award-holder as an exhibitioner.[27]

So it was to Wadham that he went for the Michaelmas term in October 1931. He stayed for the next three years, the first two years in college, the third in lodgings in the city with his close friend John Cripps. It was a dampish house quite near the river, which did not improve his asthma. Foot's devotion to his remarkably beautiful college henceforth was unshakeable. Half a century later, in his volume of essays *Loyalists and Loners*, he hailed it as 'of all places the greenest and most gracious, the peerless and the most perfect in the whole green glory of Oxford'. Wadham's virtues were innumerable: it was founded early in the seventeenth century by a woman, Dorothy Wadham, it nurtured the philosophical learning of John Wilkins, the seamanship of Robert Blake, the church-building of Christopher Wren, it spanned almost every aspect of Michael Foot's intellectual universe. He later became friendly with its formidable future Warden Maurice Bowra, famous for epigrams such as 'Buggers can't be choosers.' Bowra was no socialist, but he shared Foot's eclectic antiquarianism. On one bizarre occasion in August 1962 he tried to act as a kind of peacemaker between Foot and the Labour leader Hugh Gaitskell when they found themselves, perhaps to their mutual horror, in the same bar in the small Italian town of Portofino, but Gaitskell's enmity was implacable.[28] No honour pleased Foot more than to be elected an Honorary Fellow of the college in later years. Michael Foot was a supreme Oxford man, but also passionate for the collegiate atmosphere of his college. Dorothy Wadham was so admirable a woman that, in his whimsical view, had she lived centuries later she would have applied for membership of the Labour Party.

Foot's years at Wadham down to June 1934 were enriching in every way. After eighteen years in the evangelical intensity of Plymouth, Pencrebar and Leighton Park, he moved into a different atmosphere and he blossomed in it. Previously somewhat withdrawn and bookish, worried about his health and his complexion, he emerged as an attractive, gregarious young man. He had interesting and intelligent friends (almost all male, as befitted the ethos of the time) of various backgrounds and nationalities, and enjoyed a full social life, quite apart from his ventures into student politics. There were lectures by eminent scholars in the examination schools – G. D. H. Cole's lectures on William Cobbett he particularly enjoyed – and visiting celebrities of all kinds. One such he got to know personally, and with whom he was destined to have a complex relationship, was the philosopher Bertrand Russell, who lectured to the Oxford Liberal Club during Foot's term as chairman. His book *The Conquest of Happiness* (1933) had a powerful effect on the young Michael Foot, not only in his views on political matters but also on personal morality.[29] Foot, a natural romantic much influenced by his reading of Rousseau, was fast moving on from the Methodist ethic. To apply his own memorable description of Aneurin Bevan, the puritan was an increasingly sensual puritan.

His prime objective, of course, was to gain a reasonable degree. Here the results were adequate, but perhaps no more. Michael had chosen not to read History, the natural choice for him, his passion and hobby for many years past, but the newer school of Politics, Philosophy and Economics, also known as Modern Greats. This was not perhaps the best choice. The Politics papers were fine, not least because they were heavily historical in slant, and were to remain so until the 1960s. He did, however, regret that his passion for late-eighteenth-century history, through liberal authors such as George Otto Trevelyan and J. L. Hammond's study of Charles James Fox, was diverted to having to focus on Lewis Namier's structural studies of Georgian politics and his 'formidable lists of figures'.[30] Economics he found less appealing, in part because of his relative lack of interest in maths or statistics. His tutor, Russell Bretherton, a brilliant twenty-five-year-old who taught both economics and modern history, was congenial enough as a staunch supporter of the expansionist economic theories of J. M. Keynes (as understood before the latter's *General Theory* of 1936). He was also friendly with the Christ Church economics don Roy Harrod, Keynes's later biographer. Bretherton was certainly a man of parts. His later publications included *Country Inns and Alehouses*, while he also developed much expertise as an entomologist specializing in butterflies. After the war he was to become an important civil servant, working under Harold Wilson at the Board of Trade and under Peter Thorneycroft at the Treasury (where he proved to be a strong European). At any rate, Bretherton's Keynesian doctrines got Foot through his economics papers in the schools. But Philosophy, even in the days before Oxford plunged into the arid realms of logical positivism, he found less than riveting, too abstract and detached from real life. In the end last-minute swotting of a textbook survey by Bertrand Russell, one of his political heroes, saw him stagger through. He told *The Leightonian* that 'after two years' hard work at Philosophy, I know less about it than when I began'.[31] But his eventual honourable but unremarkable second-class honours suggested that perhaps PPE was not the ideal school for him. Then as always Michael Foot was never a man for socio-economic detail. He was a sounding board for historical mood and movement, and literary interpretation of it, rather than an analyst, still less a desiccated calculating machine.

In every other respect, Michael found life at Oxford great fun. He operated on a broad university basis and soon became a celebrated figure in journals and political clubs. Photographs of the time show a smart young man with neatly trimmed hair, a broad forehead and spectacles, invariably with a serious expression on his face, but evidently with a sense of humour. He played a little gentle soccer for Wadham. His old school magazine was told that 'in the intervals of debating, politics and work . . . on occasions he announces pontifically from the depths of an armchair that one should constantly aim at acquiring not knowledge, but the Larger Vision. He also tells us that he has fully recovered from the effects of a recent holiday involving "cricket and all that" in Denmark.'[32]

The most interesting of the various social bodies he joined was the Lotus Club, an Anglo-Indian dining club of around fifty members at a time, twenty-five British and twenty-five Indian. It had been formed by an Indian, G. A. Chettur, in the mid-twenties to counter charges that Indians at Oxford were inbred and cliquey, basing their social life on the Majlis. Michael was always attracted to Indians, and at Oxford he made friends with several of them, notably D. F. Karaka, who was to succeed him as President of the Union, the first Indian so to serve, and whose early autobiographical work *The Pulse of Oxford*, published in 1933, conveys much of the gaiety of university life at that time. The Lotus Club invited guest speakers, and to Michael's joy one of them was his father Isaac. The club, Michael wrote to him, 'is a society existing for the promotion of friendship between Englishmen and Indians. Presumably you are supposed to make a speech about India.' He stoked up his father's enthusiasm for a visit to Oxford by mentioning a recent successful visit by Lloyd George, with whom Michael had breakfast.[33]

But activities like the Lotus Club were really indications that by far Michael's strongest interests during his three years at Oxford were political. Even measured against the university careers of his brothers Dingle and John, with whom he was constantly compared, his progress was remarkable. He became President of the Liberal Club in 1932, at the start of his second year, and was triumphantly elected President of the Oxford Union in June 1933, at the end of it. In October 1933 the undergraduate magazine *Isis* made him an 'Isis Idol', a supreme accolade amongst the student body. Quite apart from his powerful background in Liberal politics, Michael went up to Oxford at a critical moment which would have stirred any politically sensitive young man. In August 1931, just before he started at Wadham, a huge political and financial crisis in Britain saw the collapse of the second Labour government, and Ramsay MacDonald become, totally unexpectedly, Prime Minister of an all-party National Government. The Labour Party was divided and crushed at the general election that October, while the economy plunged into mass depression and heavy unemployment. For all subsequent Labour leaders, from Lansbury to Foot, MacDonald went down in the party's annals as a legendary traitor who blackened the very name of leadership in the people's party. Foot would mention his name darkly when he was a Cabinet minister during the financial crisis of the IMF loan in 1976. Meanwhile, the Liberal Party divided into three after the election: the National Liberals led by Sir John Simon (allied to the Tories), the mainstream followers of Sir Herbert Samuel, and Lloyd George's family group of just four. Isaac Foot was returned unopposed at the election at Bodmin as a supporter of the mainstream group which followed Sir Herbert Samuel as wary members of the new government, rather than of Lloyd George, who led his family group into permanent opposition. Dingle Foot, returned for Dundee, took the same line as his father, though he later veered somewhat to the right.

Michael, a devoted Lloyd Georgian, did not approve at all of his family's near apostasy. He chided his father amiably enough in early 1932:

> Well, I hope you are feeling thoroughly uncomfortable in your present position. I hope that the responsibility for a niggardly disarmament policy and blustering (?) dealing with Ireland rests heavily on your shoulders. I hope that you squirm in your pronouncement of each tariff order. I suppose you will vote with patriotic resignation for the further cuts and a raising of the school leaving age. I suppose you shout with the best of them when Sir Samuel Hoare exclaims 'that the dogs bark but the caravan still goes on'. Nevertheless, this is the greatest

economic crisis in the history of mankind and national unity must be preserved.

Much love. Michael.[34]

In fact the Samuel Liberals left the government *en bloc* in October 1932, when the government introduced tariffs and imperial preference to protect British industry and thus end a century of free trade, so father and son were for a time politically reunited. Dingle, however, remained alarmingly acceptable to the National Government, so much so that he was comfortably returned again for the two-Member Dundee constituency in 1935 without Conservative opposition, in harness with Florence Horsburgh.

Beyond the local vagaries of British politics it was an alarming world, in which democracy and international peace themselves were increasingly threatened. The menace posed itself most sharply when Hitler came to power in Germany in January 1933. With totalitarian regimes installed in Germany, Italy and the Soviet Union, and the economies of major industrial nations in ruins as a result of the Depression, the relative tranquillity of Foot's childhood in the twenties had disappeared. However, these were developments about which he read, rather than experiencing them at first hand as did the young Hugh Gaitskell or Denis Healey, say. Certainly they reaffirmed his commitment to liberal values. Unlike some famous Cambridge contemporaries, the siren call of Communism never seduced him.

Michael Foot was at this time still unshakeably a Liberal, albeit a left-wing one. The Liberal Club was then a powerful force in Oxford, with Lloyd George especially, according to Foot's friend D. F. Karaka, evoking 'little short of hero-worship'.[35] This was no mere youthful staging post: Foot's Liberalism went to the core of his being. He was a devout free trader and civil libertarian. Although he had effectively lost his religious faith, the popular ethic of West Country nonconformity was still a guiding star. The *Oxford Magazine* recorded a speech of his at the Union in October 1932 in which 'he destroyed the case for tariffs, condemned the Tariff Boards and laughed at Peter Pan industries which never grew up'. The writer added wryly, 'This is the first speech, I think, in which Mr Foot has not mentioned the name of Mr Lloyd George. It was perhaps the best speech of the evening.'[36] Foot's

Liberalism remained unflinching throughout his undergraduate years, and he affirmed it in an article, 'Why I am a Liberal', published in the *News Chronicle* in 4 April 1934, commissioned by that Liberal newspaper's editor, Aylmer Vallance. Liberalism, he claimed, had largely created the 'social and democratic institutions which this country already enjoys'. Above all, it was committed to the League of Nations and international peace: 'I am a Liberal, first of all, because of the unfaltering resistance which liberalism is pledged to offer to those twin dangers of fascism and war.'[37] There and elsewhere, his undergraduate speeches and articles show the centrality of international issues in underlining his liberalism, but it went to the core of his being. In later years, Barbara Castle would note that referring to his 'Why I am a Liberal' article could annoy Michael Foot and move him on to other subjects.[38]

However, it can scarcely be doubted that essential aspects of his early student beliefs stayed with him thereafter, even after his transformation to left-wing socialism. He always remained a strong champion of human rights, active in the National Council for Civil Liberties or in campaigns against censorship; even more strongly was he the Whiggish champion of parliamentary liberties. His jousting with Tony Benn in the early 1980s testified to his unshakeable commitment to the parliamentary route to socialism. Shirley Williams, a Cabinet colleague in the later 1970s, always saw Foot as a man who was never a statist nor a natural centralizer, a natural champion of devolution and popular participation, in some sense always a Liberal.[39] It was a view shared, more improbably, by Barbara Castle, who confided in her diaries her irritation with the basic rationalist Liberalism of 'the collective Foot type'.[40] To her he was a kind of conformist amongst the nonconformists.

The centrality of international issues in underpinning Michael's Liberalism emerged even more strongly in his activities in the Oxford Union. From his first performances in debates in the autumn of 1931 he showed himself to have star quality, and to be a quite outstanding debater even in a House of remarkably talented young men. His speeches were lively and well spiced with humour. In a debate in May 1933 on a motion 'That this House would prefer Fascism to Socialism', the President, the future Labour minister Anthony Greenwood, recorded that Foot 'made a delightful speech which had nothing at all to do with the motion'. He cheerfully moved a frivolous end-of-term motion in December 1932 that 'This House would hang up its Christmas stocking'. The following summer he ridiculed a government of which its Prime Minister 'would never rest until German measles was called the pox Britannica'.[41]

But his ultimate purposes were always deadly serious, and he could stir heart, mind and soul as very few speakers could. Foot indeed, Liberal as he was, is a central exhibit in the left-wing pacifism widely prevalent in the Oxford of the time. Frank Hardie, a famous President of the Union, wrote later of the sea-change in the attitudes of speakers in debates after the crisis of 1931. A serious tone replaced the flippancy of the recent past. The significance of the famous motion of 9 February 1933 'That this House would not fight for King and Country' (in which Foot, perhaps surprisingly, did not speak, though he certainly voted for it) may have been exaggerated by Churchill and others as a symbol of the feebleness of the public mood at the time, but it certainly reflected important currents amongst the undergraduate population. Foot himself wrote in the *Cherwell* in October 1933 of how 'Oxford politics in the past few years have taken a decidedly radical turn'.[42] The new mood of undergraduates was shown by an anti-war demonstration alongside the Martyrs' Memorial on Armistice Day in November 1932, which caused much controversy. There were important new left-wing clubs formed, notably the far-left October Club and the Anti-War Committee, whose members came into conflict with the university proctors for its verbal attacks on the Oxford University Officers' Training Corps.[43] Attempts at censorship like Randolph Churchill's ill-judged motion at the Union later on, which tried to expunge the 'King and Country' vote from the record, provoked violent reaction. Many of the movers and shakers amongst undergraduates were associated with radical, anti-war positions.

Several of them became close friends of Michael Foot. Among them were men of high talent (women were marginalized in a highly chauvinist university at that time). Frank Hardie, President of the Union in Hilary term 1933 during the King and Country debate, was a charismatic President of the University Labour Club. Anthony Greenwood, President of the Union in Trinity term 1933 and a handsome man popular with women undergraduates, saw the pro-Communist October Club founded in his rooms in Balliol – and later suppressed by the proctors. Paul Reilly of Hertford College, the son of a famous architect, was another young man of the far left, and a long-term friend of Michael Foot. He was later to be an important figure in industrial design and director of the Design Council. Foot's most important close friendship was with John Cripps of Balliol College. He was a patrician socialist with whom Foot shared a house in his final year at Oxford and with whom he was to visit America on a debating tour in 1934, and who was to become a major figure in countryside matters. Unlike his friends Reilly and Foot, he gained a first in the Schools. It was through John's father, Sir Stafford Cripps, an outspoken MP and voice of far-left views after the collapse of the Labour government (in which he had served as Solicitor-General) in 1931, that Michael Foot was to secure his first important *entrée* into the Labour Party.

For Michael the Union, as the focus of Oxford social and political life, was the institution to conquer, and he made astonishingly swift progress. Dingle and John had both been Presidents in the twenties, and as it happened both spoke in Union debates in the Trinity term of 1932. A speech of John's was described as 'stupendous' in the *Oxford Magazine*.[44] As for Michael, his brand of revivalist Liberal oratory swept opponents aside. Elected early on to the Library Committee, he was elected Treasurer for Hilary term 1932, then became Librarian, and in June 1933 defeated David Graham, ex-Librarian, in winning the presidency by a large majority. Anthony Greenwood graciously wrote a balanced and delicate appraisal of his election: 'He would do well to pay a little more attention to the serious parts of his speeches. At present he seldom really deals with the subject. But it was a great oratorical effort and fully justified the result of the polling. I hope that Mr Foot will have a very happy term in the chair which has become almost a monopoly of his family.' Foot's election brought much joy. Greenwood wrote privately to congratulate him: 'I thought your speech last Thursday was first rate, as it was in the Eights Week debate.'[45] His mother Eva wrote with almost a sense of inevitability: 'Do you think Graham really thought of getting it?' Isaac combined paternal warmth with practicality:

> The Foot colours have been kept flying high. I send you a
> cheque for ten pounds and made a further pull in the overdraft.
> If invested in the Abbey Road it will be worth about eighty
> pounds at the age of ninety. No swollen head, my lad.[46]

In the event, Michael's term as President passed by satisfactorily,
though inevitably silently on his part. He returned to debating the
following term in loud support of a motion that 'the presence of four
hundred and seventy Conservatives in the House is a national disaster'.
Towards Tories, Foot observed, he had 'an inflexible loathing'.

His experiences in the Oxford Union profoundly shaped Foot's
political image. The Union nurtured his particular style of oratory,
heavily sarcastic towards opponents, the swift marshalling of key points
of an argument, the deliberate focus on the opposition's strongest point
before destroying it, the inexorable advance towards an unanswerable
conclusion. Reinforced by ample quotations from historical and literary
eminences, Foot's speeches were hard to rebut. From this time on he
was to become celebrated as an incomparable revivalist stump speaker.
Equally, the sometimes more measured approach necessary in House
of Commons debates, or in television interviews, was much harder to
capture. But his unique debating style, with a distinctive rhythm and
cadences, and unorthodox changes of emphasis that made him hard to
interrupt, was central to his political fame.

The dominant theme of his speeches at the time was always resistance to war. Foot is a good example of the rebellion of the young in
the later twenties and earlier thirties, responding eagerly to anti-war
works like *All Quiet on the Western Front* or *Goodbye to All That*, using
images that exposed 'merchants of death', denouncing the 'system of
Versailles' and calling for a new international order with open coven-
ants openly arrived at. One book on the wartime experience that made
a particularly deep impression on him was the poet Edmund Blunden's
Undertones of War (1928). Foot's credo came out very clearly in a
compilation of four essays by recent Oxford undergraduates, *Young
Oxford and War*, published by Selwyn Blount in 1934, under the
unexpected editorship of a rising Indian politician, V. K. Krishna
Menon, and with a brief foreword by Harold Laski.[47] The authors
were a varied group. R. G. Freeman was a Communist and President
of the short-lived October Club. Frank Hardie, the former Union

President, wrote 'as a pacifist and a socialist'. Keith Steel-Maitland, whose chapter was easily the most practical and down-to-earth, was a moderate Conservative.

Finally there was Michael Foot, writing passionately as a near-pacifist Liberal. He condemned the rise of militarism in schools and universities in recent years: 'There can be no real distinction between defence and offence in the modern world.' He quoted freely from anti-war Union of Democratic Control authors like G. Lowes Dickinson and Norman Angell, author of *International Anarchy*, a phrase which appeared with much frequency in Foot's early writings. He applauded the pacifist arguments advanced by Quakers and others, and pointed to the success of German Protestants in, so he claimed, resisting Hitler. Pacifism implied 'unilateral disarmament' and argued that evil should not be resisted with evil. The broad pacifist movement was plagued by internal divisions but could focus on ending international anarchy and 'the elimination of force from the conduct of international affairs'. His was by no means a complete or unqualified pacifist argument. A properly constituted collective peace force to provide a backing of law 'does not contain the elements objected to by the pacifist'. But instances in which resort to arms could ever be accepted by one of Foot's outlook seemed hard to spell out in practical terms. It was a young man's tract, rich in idealism, uncertain in logic, lacking in any kind of practical detail. But it embodied themes that were constantly to recur in Foot's later career.

Foot emerged from Oxford with a glowing reputation as a potential young politician, even perhaps a future minister, Cripps and others thought. As noted, he announced his release from Oxford life with a trip to Paris with his brother John, spent in part breaking their vow of abstinence from alcohol, in part pursuing in vain a pretty young French girl Michael had met at Pencrebar the previous year. His student days had officially come to an end, but there was an interesting coda that autumn. With his close friend John Cripps he went to the United States for the first time in a debating tour on behalf of the Oxford Union. America was neither a country nor a culture that had impinged greatly on Michael's early years, although he enjoyed aspects of its artistic life such as the films of Walt Disney and the voluptuous Mae West, and had some emerging interest in writers such as Emerson and Thoreau. Politically, like many young Englishmen, he had much enthusiasm for Franklin Roosevelt's New Deal programme, which he regarded as an attempt to shore up social welfare and progressive economics against backwoods Republican reactionaries during the Great Depression, and indeed as an inspiration to the world. But it belonged 'over there', and had little directly to offer the young Foot (though this was equally true of young Labour economists like Hugh Gaitskell, Douglas Jay or Evan Durbin at the same period).

It was a gruelling visit, with twenty-two debates between 26 October and 4 December 1934.[48] They went mostly to universities on the eastern seaboard, ranging from Yale and Penn State to Bates College, Maine. The last two debates took them almost seven hundred miles west, as far as Michigan. Michael Foot and John Cripps, 'two quiet young chaps wearing glasses', as they were described in the *Atlanta Journal*,[49] were usually given left-wing motions to defend, which they both did with much success, defending trade unions, condemning military training in schools, attacking isolationism in American foreign policy. The old Liberal in Foot emerged in a robust attack on American trade policy at New Rochelle, New York, on 26 November: 'If you uphold an isolationist policy, you can no longer remain a great creditor nation, you can no longer remain a great exporting nation.' The result would be the same economic collapse and mass unemployment that were then so visible in Britain. He and Cripps were invariably triumphant in these debating jousts, and a succession of student newspapers wrote in praise of their wit and eloquence. Foot's 'brilliant rebuttal' in a motion on the need for trade unions was praised in *Yale News*,[50] although there were some murmurs that the Oxford Union seemed a bit facetious by American standards. There were also random interviews in which Michael told the Americans of the importance of Mickey Mouse to the British view of transatlantic culture.[51] The tour was, in its way, an important episode for Foot. America was never so appealing that it shaped his political or other views: despite his enthusiasm for most aspects of Roosevelt's New Deal, he was too intensely English for that. But the visit enlarged his vision in many respects. For instance, one aspect he noticed was the apparently much greater prominence of women in higher education in the US, notably in some distinguished women's colleges at which he and Cripps spoke. The trip took him out of his familiar English radical world for a while, and helped him to grow up.

Michael Foot's early years made him a distinctive, perhaps unique, kind of politician. He somehow bridged new and old, the brave new world radicalism of the post-war generation alongside the cultural depth of a Victorian man of letters. He was in many ways an old young man; equally he remained an eternally youthful spirit well into extreme old age. He drew from his origins a passionate attachment to the traditions of his family, and of Plymouth and the West Country more generally. He acquired an immense stock of vivid, easily mobilized political and literary influences and allusions. An apt quotation from Foot could spear opponents at will. His political connections were strong, first with Lloyd Georgian Liberalism, though perhaps Stafford Cripps might direct him towards new horizons. As a young debater at Oxford he acquired a fluency and poise in debate, buttressed by a kind of cultural confidence that pushed him towards a public career. He discovered that he could speak and he could write, with passion, conviction and often brilliance. He had all the idealistic fervour of a young anti-war radical at that time. Yet perhaps the abiding legacy from his younger days was an ability to place himself in historical context. When he reflected on current political and social issues, Drake and Cromwell, Tom Paine and Hazlitt, even aberrant turncoats like Edmund Burke, were at his shoulder. He felt himself to be somehow their heir, a past and future king of libertarian dissent, but searching still for a coherent movement to lead or even to join. But, whatever his future, he would share with the inspirational Isaac a demonic energy to pursue great causes. For 'He trespasses upon his duty who sleeps upon his watch.' No Foot ever dared do that.

2

CRIPPS TO BEAVERBROOK
(1934–1940)

When Michael Foot's hero, David Lloyd George, came to London as a young man at the age of seventeen in November 1880, he set eyes on the House of Commons for the first time. In his diary he admitted to having 'eyed the assembly in a spirit similar to that in which William the Conqueror eyed England on his visit to Edward the Confessor, the region of his future domain. Oh, vanity!'[1] Five years later he unveiled to his future wife, Maggie Owen, the force of his terrifying ambition: 'My supreme idea is to get on . . . I am prepared to thrust even love itself under the wheels of my juggernaut if it obstructs the way,'[2] and he was as good as his word. Michael Foot, by contrast, felt no such overpowering urge. Although the son and brother of Liberal MPs (and possessed of a good deal more historical knowledge of the Norman Conquest than Lloyd George), he had no driving political ambition. To none of his friends did he suggest that he might consider becoming a parliamentary candidate. Indeed, when he came down from Oxford in June 1934, even when he returned from the United States six months later, he had no idea of what he might do in life. His brothers were finding their feet professionally, Dingle in chambers as a barrister as well as being an MP, Hugh in the Colonial Service, John in the solicitors' firm Foot & Bowden back in Plymouth. But none of these routine occupations appealed to Michael's imagination even though he too, in his way, sought 'to get on'.

In fact he spent his first six months after graduating very much on the move. There was the jolly visit to Paris with John mentioned earlier, on which he spent a small legacy of £50 from his grandfather, a reward for earlier abstemiousness, successfully chasing culture, less successfully chasing girls, gleefully downing his windfall with glasses of

Pernod. There followed a far more significant trip for the longer term
when he went on across Europe, taking a train to Venice – very much
his cherished city in later years – and then a boat from Trieste to Haifa
to join his elder brother Hugh ('Mac'), now serving in the Colonial
Service amongst the continuing tensions of Palestine. Hitherto Michael
had had no particular interest in the tensions between Jews and Arabs,
although most British Liberals, from Lloyd George downwards, had a
broad sympathy for the Jews and for the Zionist movement. Churchill's
philo-Semitism when a pre-war Liberal MP was well known. But
Michael Foot's trip in 1934 had a major impact upon him. It was to
stimulate the first of many controversial crusades. He first became
aware of the qualities of the Jews on the slow boat to Haifa, since
virtually all the other passengers on it were Jewish. One of them was
an ardent chess player with whom Foot first played serious chess. On
this voyage his Jewish friend won every time, but Foot was to become
'one of the strongest players in the House of Commons' in later years.[3]

    When he reached Palestine Michael stayed with his brother Hugh
at Nablus, in the famous biblical region of Samaria. For one hellfire
Welsh nonconformist preacher the very name had been a symbol of
communal turbulence: 'What was Samaria? Samaria was the Merthyr
Tydfil of the land of Canaan.'[4] In 1934 it was no more tranquil, with
a small number of Jewish settlers in a prolonged stand-off with a large
Arab community scattered throughout desert villages. Michael quickly
realized the complexities of the situation in Palestine, a region left
in conflict and possible chaos after the ambiguous pledges to both
communities made by Lloyd George's government after the disastrously imprecise Balfour Declaration of 1917. But whereas brother
Hugh, like most in the Colonial Service, was a warm sympathizer with
the Arabs, it was the plight of the beleaguered Jewish minority that
haunted Michael all his life. After a few tense weeks in Nablus he
returned home by a circuitous route, including a cheap ship from
Beirut, his first flight, from Athens to Salonika, and a stopping train
through Yugoslavia and back to England. There followed his debating
tour in America with John Cripps. He returned home just in time for
Christmas, after which the more practical problems of getting and
spending had to be resolved.

    The way that things worked out for him had a critical effect on his entire life. In the absence of any attractive alternative his thoughts turned to writing a work of history, in which the present-day moral would emerge. His chosen area was the life of Charles James Fox, to whom he had been pointed by his reading of George Otto Trevelyan and others, and who had interested him when working for prizes at Leighton Park school. Fox had much appeal as a subject. He was a critic of the overmighty authority of George III and his King's Friends. He was a colourful personality, sexually liberated – usually a feature of Foot's chosen heroes, including Hazlitt, Byron and H. G. Wells. He was a literate apostle of the Enlightenment. Above all, he championed the ideals of the French Revolution and of civil liberty through dark times in peace and in war. Foot was always a passionate supporter of the revolutionaries of 1789: they drew him to Tom Paine and to Hazlitt in his reading. A fellow chess enthusiast, Charles James Fox inspired Foot as an essential link in a native English radical tradition that bound the Levellers in Putney church to Cobden and Bright and Lloyd George and Bertrand Russell and the anti-war apostles of the Union of Democratic Control in 1914: the relationship of all this to the separate complexities of the socialist tradition was something he had yet to work out. Fox was naturally opposition-minded; he was seen by A. J. P. Taylor as the founder of the dynasty of 'trouble-makers' which his 1957 Ford's Lectures at Oxford celebrated, and whose steps the Campaign for Nuclear Disarmament consciously followed. Fox had kept alive the red flame of radical courage during the bleak Pittite years. He was the most natural of subjects for the post-Oxford idealist Michael Foot.

But the book never happened. Foot had no money, no publisher, not even a synopsis to wave around. Instead he found himself trapped in a humdrum office job, which was to change his life. It was to become a central point of self-reference and self-definition in his own later interpretation of his career. This arose from his friendship with John Cripps, which led him to spend much time in vacations at 'Goodfellows' in the west Oxfordshire village of Filkins, the squire's home of John's father, the famous advocate and by now socialist firebrand Sir Stafford Cripps. He also went on holiday with the Cripps family to the Scilly Isles. Foot's relationship with Stafford Cripps soon became a decisive one. He needed a hero and a patron: in Cripps, as later in Beaverbrook, he found both. 'Goodfellows' fascinated him with its array of visiting Labour, trade union and socialist celebrities. He met George Lansbury, Labour's current evangelistic pacifist leader, whose pacifism appeared even to Foot surreal, but with whom he became friendly in Lansbury's last years. He was impressed by Ernest Bevin, the Transport and General Workers Union's General Secretary, as an authentic working-class leader of much strength of personality; much less so by the taciturn Clem Attlee. A far more potent influence than either was one occasional visitor, the young Welsh MP Aneurin Bevan, who was to shape his destiny for ever. There were also young people like Geoffrey Wilson, an idealistic Quaker who was to become Stafford Cripps's private secretary on his ambassadorial visit to Moscow in 1940. Clearly, amidst such company Foot's traditional Liberalism would be facing a severe challenge. But Cripps was attracted by his son's interesting and knowledgeable young friend, anxious to help him forward and to enlist his literary and oratorical talents for his own versions of the socialist cause. Cripps's brother Leonard, a ship-owner and a director of the Holt shipping firm's Blue Funnel Line which traded with southern Africa and the Far East, needed a personal assistant. His nephew John had been pencilled in for this post, but John (a caustic critic of his uncle's right-wing views) suggested his friend Michael instead. Thus it was that on 1 January 1935 the impressionable young Foot began work amidst the cranes and bunkers of the alien shipyards of Liverpool's docks.

Michael Foot's time in industrial Liverpool was not a relaxed one, and he left after barely nine months. But for ever afterwards he would give this period a legendary Damascus-like status as the time when he first witnessed social hardship and became a left-wing socialist. It is important to try to establish how far the poverty of working-class Liverpool was pivotal in this conversion, and indeed what kind of socialism it was to which he was drawn. Certainly he found his job in the Blue Funnel Line boring and undemanding. He used as much time as he could in making notes on the back of business correspondence on the career and ideas of Charles James Fox. He had hoped that his new job might entail some overseas travel, for which he had now acquired a taste, but none was forthcoming and he was office-bound. Foot told his mother how heartily he disliked all the people he worked with and for. Leonard Cripps was boring, Sir Richard Holt 'the last word in malignant density'. Others had 'stunted intelligences', while the routine duties were 'dull as ditchwater'.[5]

But Liverpool, the first industrial working-class city of which he had any experience, was far more compelling. He found lodgings in a Yiddish-speaking Jewish home which his recent visit to Palestine made congenial. He spent time exploring the shabby backstreets of the dockside areas. He also transferred his footballing interests, at least for a time, to supporting Everton at Goodison Park. He treasured in later life an 'Ode to Everton' that he composed in 1935, which was printed in the *Liverpool Daily Post*. It laid particular emphasis on 'Dixie's priceless head', a reference to the prolific goal-scoring centre-forward 'Dixie' Dean.[6] But crucially, within a month of arriving on Merseyside the old West Country Liberal had joined the Labour Party as an active, ardent crusader and canvasser. (Oddly, in accounts of his career he tends to give 1934, not 1935, as the date of his conversion.) Michael had got religion, and wanted the world to know. Soon he was an energetic participant in the committee meetings and street-corner campaigning of the Liverpool Labour Party. He met congenial comrades here, including two future parliamentary colleagues, Sydney Silverman, an eloquent Jewish lawyer, and the formidable and pugnacious Bessie Braddock and her husband Jack, both ex-Communists. To what extent Michael's conversion was the consequence of empirical observation might, however, be examined. After all, commentators have wondered how far George Orwell's famous book of the same period was actually the product of first-hand observation of Wigan Pier. John Vincent once commented in an *Observer* book review that 'a man who describes as flabby Lancashire cheese which is crumbly gives himself away at once'.

Without doubt, Michael Foot's compassionate heart and soul were deeply stirred by the poverty he saw in the dockside community and in Liverpool's backstreets. It was a maritime city with a weak manufacturing base, and thus very high unemployment, painfully evident on street corners amidst its shabby terraces. Equally clearly, his speeches and articles while at Oxford show a young man moving rapidly leftwards in his revulsion for militarism and dictatorship. His criticisms of socialism in 'Why I am a Liberal' are half-hearted questionings of the merits of centralization. Most of his close friends at Oxford – John

Cripps, Paul Reilly, Tony Greenwood – were emphatically Labour. And without doubt his acquaintance with Stafford Cripps and the bracing radical atmosphere of 'Goodfellows' were a powerful influence too. But, most characteristically, Michael's conversion came through the medium of books – and indeed not sober works of socio-economic analysis, but imaginative works of fiction. While crawling to his office on Liverpool's trams, his mind was focused not only on the slums through which he passed but on the books he read on his journey. Arnold Bennett was a particularly powerful stimulant: his *How to Live on Twenty-Four Hours a Day* (1910) made a lasting impact on the young socialist. It is actually a short book, not at all one of Bennett's masterpieces, but Foot no doubt appreciated the chapter on 'Serious Reading', which lavished great praise on Hazlitt's essay 'Poetry in General' – 'the best thing of its kind in English'.[7] Foot also read extensively the novels of H. G. Wells, destined to loom alongside Cripps and Bevan as supreme inspirations. *Tono-Bungay*'s relatively brief account of socialist ideas was exciting to him, more perhaps for its subtle exposé of the immoralities of free-market competitive capitalism. Bernard Shaw was another important influence, though he was less favoured because of his criticisms of Wells's *Short History of the World*.[8] Foot's was an undoctrinaire ethical socialism, a gospel of words and ideas, similar to that which had impelled young men like Attlee or Dalton into the Independent Labour Party. On more immediate matters, Foot was excited by Bertrand Russell's *Proposed Roads to Freedom*. Economic theory does not seem to have interested him. At first he was innocent of connections with Marxism, although by 1937 he was instructing the equally young Barbara Betts (the future Barbara Castle) in the intellectual delights of *Das Kapital*. His ideology, such as it was, kept its distance from the formal programmes of the Labour Party, still in 1935 trying to redefine its policies after the catastrophe of 1931 had laid bare the emptiness of its economic notions, and perhaps also the wider problem of attempting to modify and humanize a capitalist order which it ultimately wished to abolish.

Nor was Michael Foot a Fabian. He had met Beatrice Webb at Stafford Cripps's home, and did not take to her admonitory style. He did not become a socialist in order to promote orderly administration by a bureaucratic elite; nor, without a background in local government at any level, was he inspired by the heady vision of 'gas and water socialism'. The first book by the Webbs that he read, and indeed responded to positively, was their *Industrial Democracy*, which he read together with Barbara Betts at her Bloomsbury flat. Years later, in 1959, he took sharp issue with the Fabian historian Margaret Cole on the Webbs' vision of socialism: 'I think there is running through a great deal of what they wrote . . . a strong bureaucratic, anti-libertarian attitude which often reveals what I think is a real contempt for those who are engaged in Socialist agitation, protest and activities of that nature.' He pointed out Beatrice's patrician absence of interest in the great propaganda work of Robert Blatchford, editor of the early socialist newspaper the *Clarion* (he might have added her contempt for Keir Hardie and George Lansbury as well). For much of their career the Webbs were unconvinced that the Labour movement was the instrument of change, rather than a generally-defined 'permeation' and gradualism. Revealingly, Foot added as a criticism the Webbs' uncritical adulation of the Soviet Union and Communist doctrine, in contrast to the far more critical approach of his old journalist friend and mentor H. N. Brailsford, historian and intellectual guru of the socialist left.[9] Foot's conclusions appear to endorse many of H. G. Wells's assaults on the Fabian high command in the Edwardian period, and the general line of criticism indicated in one of his favourite books, *The New Machiavelli*. It was a battle of the books which Margaret Cole was most unlikely ever to win. For Foot, then, socialism was a greater liberalism, a doctrine of social and aesthetic liberation. It implied new values and a new society. It made Michael in time the natural disciple of the imaginative crusader Aneurin Bevan and the natural husband of the cultural socialist, Jill.

In this quest, Stafford Cripps seemed at this period the natural messiah. Since the 1931 schism, with the defection of MacDonald and his Chancellor Philip Snowden to become allies of the Tories, Cripps had led a sharp advance to the left. He preached a style of socialism that went far beyond the cautious parliamentary parameters within which Labour had grown up. He joined the far-left Socialist League, a movement of middle-class intellectuals, formed in 1932, in large part from the ILP when it disaffiliated from the Labour Party. It was a movement in which Michael Foot was shortly to enlist. Cripps campaigned to promote a new foreign policy in alliance with the Soviet Union: the League of Nations was dismissed as 'the International Burglars' Union'. He also pressed for the social ownership of all major industries and utilities, based not on state nationalization but on workers' control. At the 1933 party conference Cripps proclaimed in Marxist terms that a socialist government would never receive fair treatment under capitalism, with the City, the Civil Service and the establishment all ranged against it. He called for some form of emergency government to entrench socialism in our time. In January 1934 he caused even greater alarm and shock by suggesting that Buckingham Palace would be foremost amongst the institutions seeking to defeat an incoming Labour government. This doctrine horrified leaders such as Dalton, Attlee and Morrison: Beatrice Webb thought him an extremist and his ideas revolutionary. By the 1935 general election Cripps's erratic behaviour meant that his star was soon to wane. He himself recognized the fact by giving private financial help to Clem Attlee as assistant party leader in Lansbury's last phase. But to the young Michael Foot, a books-driven evangelist yearning for a cause, Cripps was the most obvious instrument of creating a new socialist society.

Foot's conversion to socialism was, naturally, a huge shock to his traditionally Liberal family. Nothing like it had ever happened at Pencrebar. What made things worse was that they discovered his conversion to Labour indirectly, when the *Daily Herald* picked up a short comment in the Oxford undergraduate magazine *Isis*. But the shock was far from terminal: it was nowhere near as bad as a Foot becoming a Tory (the family's response to Dingle's effective electoral pact with the Tories in Dundee is not recorded). Isaac was shaken at first by his son's transformation. However, he cheerfully told Michael that if he was to move from liberalism to socialism, he ought to absorb the thoughts of a real radical. An even more intense perusal was needed of the thoughts of William Hazlitt (who, among other things, was a republican who voiced public grief on hearing of Napoleon's deeply regrettable defeat at Waterloo).[10] Even the Labour Party could be better understood by recourse to the bookshelves of Pencrebar. Michael's mother Eva seems to have been more immediately upset by the news, and he had to write to her explaining his belief that only socialism, rather than any form of liberalism, had the answer to problems of poverty and peace. But in time his mother came to a more complete appreciation than Isaac ever did of the reasons for Michael's becoming a socialist. Certainly her Labour son's political advance was as important to her as that of any of her Liberal brood.

Michael Foot's earliest activities as a left socialist in the streets of Liverpool had, of course, immediate social evils to condemn. But what is striking about his socialism, then and always, is how far this very English rebel, who travelled relatively little until his old age and was dedicated to worshipping the liberty tree of his country's past, framed his socialism in an international context. This, of course, was common to many idealistic young people in the thirties, with the rise of totalitarian dictatorship and the threat of a global confrontation with the democratic peoples. Foot played his full part in campaigning against fascism, for the Popular Front in Spain, and in denouncing Chamberlainite appeasement. But he had perspectives of his own in relation to two important countries further afield – India and Palestine.

Since his undergraduate days, Foot had had a special affinity with India and the Indians. He liked their food, he admired their culture; perhaps, as Philip Snowden said of Keir Hardie, India 'appealed to the seer and the mystic in him'. He had listened avidly to his father's accounts of the views of Mahatma Gandhi during the Round Table conference which explored the future government of India in 1930–31. He had been active in the Anglo-Indian Lotus Club. In the Oxford Union he was friendly with progressive Indians like the sharp young Parsee D. F. Karaka, whose memoirs testified to Foot's generosity of spirit and enthusiasm for multiculturalism.[11] Foot carried on this involvement right through the thirties. Long after Indian independence in 1947, devotion to India was a golden thread in his career. India embodied key political and cultural values that he cherished. A major influence from 1934 onwards was his contact with Krishna Menon, a member of St Pancras borough council until 1947. Menon's energetic work as chairman of the St Pancras Education and Library Committee, especially on library and arts provision for children, was greatly admired. He first met Michael when he edited the book *Young Oxford and War*, to which Michael contributed, and Michael was to be much associated with him in campaigning for the Socialist League in London. Krishna Menon was an exciting guru: Foot's visits to his legal office at 169 The Strand always remained memorable for him. He joined the strongly pro-Congress Commonwealth of India League (previously the Home Rule for India League), of which Krishna Menon had been General Secretary since 1930, and read Indian newspapers avidly. At this period Foot's instinct was to call for gradualism in the demands of the Congress, and he wrote urging Indian nationalists to cooperate with the authorities as the new Indian constitution was being drafted at Westminster in 1934–35. Krishna Menon's tendency to build links between Congress and the British Communist Party was something that disturbed Foot later in that decade.

But Indian self-government was a glowing ideal for him throughout the thirties, merged into the Labour Party's campaigns for social justice and world peace. This was widely true of younger socialists in Britain, contrasting with a relative lack of interest in Africa. Several of Foot's most admired fellow-socialists were zealous in the Commonwealth of India League. Thus he discussed the subcontinent on long walks with H. N. Brailsford, who had first-hand knowledge of India, was a personal friend of Gandhi and was to write *Subject India* for the Left Book Club during the war.[12] Harold Laski was another key socialist intellectual much concerned with Indian independence: he had after all served on the special jury in the O'Dwyer v. Nair libel case that followed the dismissal of General Dyer, the perpetrator of the massacre at Amritsar in 1919, and was shocked by the sheer racialism that it revealed, especially from the judge. Aneurin Bevan, shortly to be Foot's closest political ally and mentor, always gave India a high priority, as did Bevan's wife Jennie Lee, while amongst Foot's literary heroes H. G. Wells was another ally on Indian matters: *The New Machiavelli* was an important text for opponents of the Raj. Amongst Indian leaders, in addition to Krishna Menon, Foot also met Pandit Nehru and heard him speak in 1938 at a meeting on Spain. Foot's continuing links with the Nehru family – Nehru's daughter Indira and her sons Sanjay and Rajiv Gandhi especially – remained important for the next half-century and more.

Foot was always amongst those who encouraged Indian nationalists when war broke out in 1939 to try to work with the British government, certainly not to join the radical nationalist movement associated with Subhas Chandra Bose, who sought aid from the invading Japanese to overthrow the Raj. On the other hand, the authoritarian policies of the Viceroy, the Marquess of Linlithgow, which saw the arrest of Gandhi, Nehru, Patel and other Congress leaders following the 'Quit India' campaign in 1942, aroused Foot's shock and fury. They made the downfall of empire all the more inevitable. His involvement with Indian nationalism was such that, not for the last time in his career, he aroused the interest of MI5. It sponsored Indian Political Intelligence, a secret espionage body which infiltrated the India Office to keep watch on 'subversives' such as Communists, nationalists and 'terrorists' (undefined) operating outside India. It reported direct to the Secretary of State for India through the Public and Judicial Department of the India Office, and to the government of India through the intelligence bureau of the Home Department. Thus it reported on a meeting organized by Mrs Rebecca Sieff, of the Marks & Spencer family, in the Savoy Hotel on 28 October 1941 to consider asking the British government to include India within the scope of the Atlantic Charter. The thirty-four people present included intellectuals of great distinction such as H. G. Wells and Professor J. B. S. Haldane, along with Kingsley Martin and the Labour MPs Sydney Silverman, W. G. Cove and Reg Sorensen. There were two Indians present, Dr P. C. Bhandari and Krishna Menon. Michael Foot, still only twenty-nine, chaired this august meeting. After a diversionary protest from a sole Fabian present it was decided to send a deputation to Churchill, to include Julian Huxley, the writer Storm Jameson, Mrs Sieff, Krishna Menon and Michael Foot, though to no effect.[13]

. Foot's passion for India provided an important context for his socialism. He remained on good terms with the notoriously prickly Krishna Menon after Nehru appointed him High Commissioner in London in 1947. There were also continuing links with people like Karaka, editor of a famous weekly, *Current*, a great admirer of Gandhi in his last period but a critic of Nehru.[14] Foot continued to enjoy fame in India as a man sympathetic to the country even at the time of difficulties with Pakistan in the 1960s, and with close access to Mrs Gandhi during some important visits to the subcontinent in the 1970s. On the long-running dispute with Pakistan over Kashmir, and the 1975 State of Emergency, Foot always resolutely took the Indian side, even at the cost of much flak from close friends like the journalist

James Cameron and his Indian wife Moni. He encouraged Sheikh Abdullah, the Muslim nationalist leader in Kashmir, to promote the cause of integration into India.

Foot retained close relations with leading Indians. An early one was the author Mulk Raj Anand, 'India's Dickens', a well-known habitué of Bloomsbury in the 1930s and a friend of Virginia Woolf and T. S. Eliot. Foot was especially moved by Anand's sensitive chronicle of the world of the Untouchables, as indeed was Foot's friend Indira Gandhi.[15] Another Indian friend and admirer, years later, was the industrialist Swraj Paul, who established a steel mill (opened there by Indira Gandhi) in Foot's Ebbw Vale constituency after the closure of much of its old steelworks. Yet another was the celebrated *Observer* cartoonist 'Abu' (Abu Abraham), a kind of Indian version of Foot's friend 'Vicky'.[16] Foot's later visits to India between 1973 and 1997 were of central importance for him, not only for Indian matters but also in pursuing the cause of world disarmament. He rejoiced in the Congress's return to power in 2004, since the new Prime Minister, the Sikh Manmohan Singh, was an old personal friend.

India thus provided an important early dimension of Foot's socialism, even if he was always inclined to exaggerate the degree to which the post-Menon Congress really had a socialist philosophy. It made him close to socialist authors like Brailsford, Wells and Laski, all much engaged in the affairs of the subcontinent. At the same time Cripps, himself highly knowledgeable about India, became more distant from the Congress as time went on, and the controversial episode of his disastrously ambiguous 'offer' of dominion status in 1942 led to a serious breach with Nehru. India, then, intensified Foot's socialism. But it also proved to be a major factor for him in questioning Cripps's political judgement, and they quarrelled again, as they had done over the Unity campaign with the Communists in the late thirties. India thus partly led Foot to measure his distance from the man who had been his major inspiration in making him a socialist in the first place. It should also be added that Foot's deep political interest in India never extended to a serious concern with problems of trade, aid or development in Third World countries. In this, as in other respects, his lack of interest in economic questions limited his curiosity about matters that stimulated his socialist conscience on other grounds.

Palestine was the other country to attract his attention as a new-born socialist. Ever since his visit to see Hugh there in 1934, he had been deeply absorbed by the country. He had by now met Jewish friends like Sydney Silverman in the Labour movement, while the Labour Party considered itself to have important bonds with Jewish Labour figures in Palestine like David Ben-Gurion and Golda Meir. Indeed, there was a small Jewish movement in Britain, Poale Zion, that was affiliated to the Labour Party. Michael's visit to see Hugh 'Mac' in 1934 inspired his intuitive concern, but also a sense of the complexities of the region. An instinctive attachment to Zionism was challenged by a sense of the Arab desperation which broke into open rebellion in the later 1930s. Hugh Foot himself took the strongly pro-Arab line dominant in the Foreign and Colonial Service. In the 1960s, at the UN and in Harold Wilson's government, he was passion-ately pro-Palestinian. In 1967 he largely drafted UN Resolution 242, which for the first time attempted to check perceived Israeli aggressive incursions and settlements over the West Bank of the Jordan. Most of the other Foots tended to gravitate to this line also. When Hugh died in 1990, remarkably enough, Palestinian Arab flags were draped over his coffin, at the request of his son Paul.[17] But in this, as in other ways, Michael was a dissenter within his dissenting family.

By the time war was under way, his support for the Jews was a pivot of his political outlook. It became even more pronounced after the war when he, Richard Crossman, Ian Mikardo and others on the left became passionate critics of Foreign Secretary Ernest Bevin's strongly pro-Arab policy. There were important personal factors in shaping Michael's views: friends in the party like Teddy Kollek, later Mayor of Jerusalem and both friend and foe of Arthur Koestler; and certainly his fondness for Lily Ernst, the Jewish Yugoslav girlfriend/ mistress of Lord Beaverbrook. In the war years he met Arthur Koestler, the most ardent of Zionists, who went as far as endorsing the attacks of the terrorist Stern gang on British troops. Foot's newspaper *Tribune* was to employ influential Jewish, and strongly pro-Israel, contributors like Jon Kimche, Evelyn Anderson and its literary editor, Tosco Fyvel. But obviously the dominant element was the torment of the Jewish people under the Nazi regime, even if the dimensions of the Holocaust were not yet widely known. It made Michael Foot a strong champion of a partitioned Palestine with recognition of a Jewish state of Israel. Only much later, in the 1970s, following, among other things, fierce debate on the Palestine issue amongst the Tribune group of MPs, did he come to modify an old entrenched position, and to join others on the left to call for an Israeli withdrawal from settlements on the West Bank. The Jews, he felt, 'had wrecked their own case'.[18] In any case, a sternly nationalist Likud-led administration seemed far removed from the old comradeship in the era of Ben-Gurion and the socialism of the kibbutz.

Otherwise the new-born socialist followed the standard position of the Liberal-Labour left, endorsing European regimes such as the Popular Front governments of France and Spain in 1936, condemning terrorist dictatorship in Germany and Italy (especially the latter, in the case of one who had many Italian friends and who revered the works of the socialist novelist Ignazio Silone). Towards the League of Nations Foot's view was a characteristic confusion of pacifism with pacificism, collective security being bracketed with the ending of all wars. After all, the Soviet Union itself was now a member of Cripps's 'burglars' union' (as he had once called the League of Nations). Only some on the Labour left began to recognize the emptiness of their diagnosis, individual MPs like Hugh Dalton and especially the TUC, concerned for the fate of trade union comrades under Hitler and Mussolini.

One country, however, was never close to Michael Foot's world view – the Soviet Union. His growing interest in the Marxist interpretation of history never translated into sympathy for Russia under Stalin. He did not share the simple-minded certainties of contemporary young Cambridge intellectuals like Blunt, Burgess and Maclean. It is utterly ironic that in the 1990s disaffected and unreliable informants of MI5 such as Oleg Gordievsky began to spread rumours that Foot (or 'Agent Boot') had been a Soviet 'agent of influence'. Right-wingers in the security service who had let genuine spies such as Kim Philby slip through the net actually gave them some credence. On the contrary, Foot rejected with scorn the totally uncritical enthusiasm for Russia shown by the Webbs or Bernard Shaw. He praised H. G. Wells for having a famous dialogue with Stalin in 1934 but in no way being taken in by him. It was a cause of a breach with Cripps that his old icon proved so undiscriminating in his allies in the Unity Front, seeking common cause with the Communists in the later thirties. Foot was quick to respond to news of Stalin's purges in 1937–38; least of all those on the democratic socialist left could he be accused of fellow-travelling. The simple-minded journalistic claims at the time of *l'affaire* Blunt that all intelligent young people inevitably migrated towards Communism as the strongest resistance to fascism in the thirties have little substance. A broad-church Labour Party was the invariable desti-nation of almost all of them, even in the pro-Russia climate of the later stages of the war. Like most of his fellow Bevanites and Tribunites, Michael Foot was a redoubtable voice of anti-Communism. Nor did he ever accord to the Russian Revolution of 1917 the special place in his historical affections that was claimed by the events in France in 1789.

By the late summer of 1935, for all the seductive appeal of Liverpool socialism, Michael Foot was restless. He was thoroughly bored in his job with the Blue Funnel Line. His thoughts turned again to writing a biography of Charles James Fox, and publishers were approached about this for a 'Brief Lives' series. Another historical subject that appealed to him was English radicals during the time of the French Revolution, a special place being accorded to Tom Paine. He did discuss the possibility of a book on this theme with Harold Laski, whom he heard lecture at the LSE and who was an inspirational force for so many young socialists in Britain and throughout the Common-wealth. But nothing came of it, and it was politics which seemed to beckon more powerfully. The Labour Party had been making some headway since the dark days of 1931, winning famous by-elections such as that in East Fulham in 1933. Foot himself was active in a by-election in the Wavertree division of Liverpool in February 1935. Here J.J. Cleary won the seat for Labour for the first time, after the Conservative vote had been badly split by an independent candidature from Randolph Churchill, standing on behalf of his father's distinctly illiberal views on India. Pacifist-inclined though he was, Foot recog-nized the departure of George Lansbury as Labour leader after the 1935 party conference as inevitable. Who precisely he would have favoured as Lansbury's successor is unclear. He had no trust in Herbert Morrison, and regarded Attlee as taciturn and colourless. On balance, perhaps, he tended to favour that patriotic (if drunken) Freemason Arthur Greenwood, father of his student friend Tony.

Suddenly in October, right on cue after successful Royal Jubilee celebrations which the Prime Minister, Stanley Baldwin, orchestrated with characteristic deftness, a general election was called. Michael Foot suddenly decided that he wished to be part of it. He travelled down to Labour's headquarters in Transport House to see the party's General Secretary, Jim Middleton (whose wife Lucy was to be a fellow Plymouth MP in 1945), and asked if there were any vacancies for Labour candidates. Given a list of long-shot constituencies with no record of Labour strength at all, Michael Foot, for no clear reason, selected Monmouth in south Wales. It had never been a seat that Labour expected to capture, although in a by-election in 1934 their candidate had won 35 per cent of the vote. That evening he took a train down to Monmouthshire, and was seen by the local agent Tom Powell and a handful of local officials. On the last day of October he was formally adopted as Labour candidate at a meeting chaired by Ivor Harries, President of the Monmouth division Labour Party. Polling day was barely a fortnight away. It was a disgracefully short period of campaigning and a forlorn hope for Labour, in a constituency the new candidate had never previously visited or even seen. Still, Michael Foot, at the age of twenty-two, was into serious politics for the first time.[19]

Monmouth was the most Tory seat in Wales. Indeed, English in speech, squirearchical in tradition, it was hardly a Welsh seat at all. It lay in what the literary theorist Raymond Williams, a native, was to call 'border country'. It was mostly an anglicized enclave along the Welsh marches, far more similar to rural Herefordshire or Worcestershire than to the radical or socialist traditions of Wales. Its outlook bore little resemblance to the nonconformist values of West Country England either. It was marked by the remaining influences of great houses – Lord Tredegar or the Dukes of Beaufort. It was strong hunting country, and the Beaufort Hunt was an ancient local institution: here was a pastime that Foot particularly disliked, for social as much as for humane reasons. Monmouth was also an area of immense natural beauty, hailed by early enthusiasts for the 'picturesque', along the river Wye and around Tintern Abbey, immortalized by Michael Foot's much-admired Wordsworth. The *South Wales Argus*, published in Newport, detailed the placid panorama of rural Gwent 'from Grosmont to Magor, and from Llanfihangel-Crossenny to Chepstow'.[20] There were pockets of Labour strength in the western parts of the constituency close to the mining valleys further west, while there was a strong railway interest around Abergavenny in the north-east, including the family of Raymond Williams. The fifteen-year-old Williams and his railwayman father, an activist in the Labour Party, campaigned for Foot. In fact the youthful Labour candidate did not impress the schoolboy Williams: 'He was a new phenomenon, straight out of the Oxford Union, who did sound a bit odd in Pandy village hall. I said to my father: "What has this to do with the Labour Party?" '[21]

Monmouth had remained stolidly Conservative/Unionist during the Liberal ascendancy in Wales in the later nineteenth century, until the famous Liberal upsurge of 1906 when Major-General Sir Ivor Philipps captured the seat and held it until the end of the First World War. Since then it had been solidly Tory. In 1931 the Conservative candidate, Sir Leolin Forestier-Walker, held it easily in a straight fight with Labour, with a fourteen-thousand majority and 70 per cent of the vote. Michael Foot's slender hopes were given an early buffeting at a meeting in Usk when his agent greeted the electors with the immortal words, 'Here we are again in bloody old Tory Usk.' The Conservative member since a by-election in 1934 was Major J. A. Herbert, a Tory of imperialist persuasion, later to be Governor of Bengal.

Nevertheless, the fledgling Labour candidate fought a spirited, even sparkling, campaign. Foot's address and his speeches focused on the twin themes of peace and poverty. 'The armaments race must be stopped now,' and the League of Nations must be supported, including in the current crisis caused by the Italian invasion of Abyssinia. At home there should be public ownership of all major industries and banks ('exchange' had been added to 'production' and 'distribution' in Clause 4 of the Labour Party's constitution at the 1934 party conference) together with social reforms, some of which were targeted on farm labourers, including a minimum wage and the abolition of tied cottages.[22] His early speeches at Caerleon and Chepstow defied the ethos of the constituency by being uncompromisingly socialist: 'The community should take into its own hands the factories and land in order that the masses should share in the abundance.' 'One small section' should not be allowed to 'exploit the masses' (applause).[23] In an article in the local newspaper he wrote that 'Labour advocates as the main feature of its programme the national ownership of the factories and other wealth.' The private owners of the means of production were 'enemies of society at large'. There were vague echoes of Wells in imprecise calls to adopt scientific methods of production and to promote new inventions.[24] At Caldecot he urged that unemployment (rife in many parts of the constituency) should be made a national charge. Always there were assaults on the National Government's record on international peace and its failure to promote disarmament. He attributed the recent increase in stock exchange prices to the rise in armament shares. He shrugged off criticisms that, at twenty-two, he was too young to be a Member of Parliament. After an evening meeting at Rolls Hall, Monmouth, the press recorded that 'never before has a Labour candidate received such applause at the close of an address'.[25]

There were, inevitably, few outside speakers in Labour's forlorn Monmouth campaign. Foot was assisted by Stafford Cripps's youthful protégé, the Quaker Geoffrey Wilson, and indeed Cripps came down to pay the young candidate a remarkable tribute, saying that he hoped to see him in an incoming Labour administration after the polls. Cripps was as robust as Foot: the Labour Party 'sought to get rid of private ownership of production . . . in order to give the workers a decent life'.[26] There was also a resounding eve-of-poll meeting, addressed by two coming stars, Aneurin Bevan and James Griffiths. It rained heavily on polling day. The outcome was a reduced Conservative majority of 9,848. Major Herbert polled 23,262 votes and Foot 13,454. Labour was to remain a relatively weak force in the constituency thereafter, until a passing victory in 1966 and a more sustained period of power in 1997–2005 under the banner of New Labour. But old or new, the Labour Party was never going to find it easy in so traditional an area.

Nevertheless, Foot had fought a spirited and creditable campaign. He told the post-election crowd in Agincourt Square, Monmouth, 'We shall go on fighting until we are victorious.'[27] The Labour poll had increased by three thousand, and was the highest ever in the constituency. The Tory *Western Mail*, which had left Foot's campaign virtually unreported, quoted him as saying: 'I have enjoyed myself in the Monmouth division more than I can say.'[28] He never thought of fighting Monmouth again, and in 1938 was to be adopted in his native Plymouth for the Devonport division, not obviously a more hopeful prospect. But he had caught the bug for electioneering. This general election, incidentally, was mostly unfortunate for the Foots. While Dingle, bolstered by an electoral pact with the Tories, romped home in two-Member Dundee, John Foot came eight thousand behind the Conservative in Basingstoke. More calamitous, father Isaac was unseated by the Tories at Bodmin after a ferocious personalized campaign directed against 'Pussyfoot'. He particularly resented the campaign against him by two neighbouring 'National Liberal' ministers, Walter Runciman (Member for St Ives) and Leslie Hore-Belisha (Member for Plymouth, Devonport). Isaac bitterly quoted against them Lord Alfred Douglas's poem of betrayal, 'The Broken Covenant':

> And when all men shall sing his praise to me
> I'll not gainsay. But I shall know his soul
> Lies in the bosom of Iscariot.

Hore-Belisha, representing part of Isaac's own Plymouth, was one who would lodge in the collective Foot memory, leaving the entire family eager for revenge. Another sharp critic of Isaac, as it happened, was the author of the 'Crossbencher' column of Beaverbrook's *Sunday Express*. This was a young journalist called Peter Howard – with whom Michael was later to co-author *Guilty Men*. Isaac was to try to return to Westminster when he fought a by-election in 1937 after the egregious Runciman went to the Lords. Narrowly, by 210 votes only, he lost again.

After the election, Foot had no job and no immediate objective. He lived in lodgings in London, at 33 Cambridge Terrace, near Paddington station, which he rented for thirty shillings a week, and often seemed lonely. Nearly seventy years later, he recalled how on Christmas Day 1935, at the age of twenty-two, he found himself all alone in London with nowhere to go, nothing to do, and no girlfriend for comfort. Then he discovered that Plymouth Argyle were playing Tottenham Hotspur at White Hart Lane on Christmas morning. He took the bus to Tottenham and saw Argyle triumph by 2–1, one of their goals being scored by their record goal-scorer Sammy Black, perhaps the finest player ever to don the black-and-green shirt of the 'Pilgrims'. To celebrate, Foot went to the Criterion restaurant in Piccadilly to enjoy his Christmas turkey: 'Never in the realms of human conflict had two away points been so spectacularly or insouciantly garnered by one man.'[29] To add to the joy, the next day Plymouth defeated Spurs again, this time at Home Park. But it still sounds like a bleak and lonely time in an unfriendly metropolis.

In fact, he found a role and companionship for the next year or more through the Socialist League and the patronage of Sir Stafford Cripps. The Socialist League was still a lively force amongst urban intellectuals after the 1935 election campaign, though in retrospect it may have passed such a peak as it attained following defeats at the 1934 Labour Party conference at Southport.[30] Certainly it had no mass appeal, and membership was at best a couple of thousand. Its programme consisted of the immediate abolition of capitalism at home, with mass nationalization and the extinction of the rich. It opposed rearmament, called for a general strike against war, and declared socialism to be the remedy for imperialistic rivalries between the great powers. Even at the time, it seemed a programme of remarkable emptiness. The dream of a general strike by workers of all countries had been shown to be a total chimera in August 1914. Nevertheless it was, characteristically, to this fringe movement of intellectuals rather than to the mainstream party that the young Foot now devoted his energies, basing himself on the militant London Area Committee of the League. In 1936 much of his time was taken up with propaganda work, making tub-thumping speeches on socialism in our time on street corners in places like Mornington Crescent and Camden Town in north London, and sometimes on Hampstead Heath. His close friend Barbara Castle has left a striking picture of him at this period – witty, learned and articulate, his spectacles giving him a diffident and myopic air which young women might find attractive, a general air of casualness, perhaps outright scruffiness in his dress, whirling his arms around theatrically in high passion.[31] More courageously, he often attended Mosleyite fascist meetings, engaging in loud heckling with an almost foolhardy recklessness, but getting away unscathed – unlike Frank Pakenham, the future Lord Longford, who was severely beaten up and hospitalized after a blackshirt meeting in Oxford town hall.

The Socialist League had some hopes of progress in 1936. Like the Bennites decades later, its adherents felt that Labour's ability to win no more than 154 seats at the previous year's general election showed the need for a far more radical, even revolutionary, approach. It based itself on a variety of fragments – former members of the ILP, which had disaffiliated from the Labour Party in 1932, intellectuals like William Mellor, linked with G. D. H. Cole in his SSIP (Society for Socialist Inquiry and Propaganda), some like D. N. Pritt who were effectively Communists under another name. It was a melange of the English (or Anglo-Scottish) far left. The election of Popular Front governments in France and Spain, with Communist backing, in the summer of 1936, gave the movement some encouragement. But it remained a fringe movement always: Ben Pimlott has cited evidence to show that eight 'mass demonstrations' attracted only twelve thousand supporters in total, and that the League's almost one hundred local committees were extremely small, save perhaps for Foot's London Area Committee.[32] A fatal weakness was the total absence of any trade union base: it was seen as a fringe body of middle-class suburban intellectuals. In 1937 it embarked on a new initiative, the Unity Campaign, which aimed to forge an alliance with the Communists: Stafford Cripps and Harry Pollitt spoke from the same platform. Pollitt indeed, uniquely amongst British Communists, was to become someone Foot particularly admired from that time onwards. A new newspaper was created on 1 January 1937, under the powerful editorship of William Mellor – this was *Tribune*, of which very much more anon, to which Foot was a founding contributor.

But the League's campaign soon plunged into fatal difficulties. Internally there was endless ideological and tactical bickering between myriad socialist splinter groups. More seriously, externally the Labour Party's NEC inevitably reacted strongly to any kind of formal link with the Communists, whose approaches it had always firmly rebuffed. Leading figures like Morrison and Bevin spoke out aggressively against the League. On 24 March Labour's NEC declared that all members of the League would be expelled. Less than two months later, on 17 May, the League held a conference at Leicester in which anguished debate occurred: H. N. Brailsford, a veteran socialist intellectual and one of Foot's heroes, wrote that he wished to resign from the League.

The decision was taken to disband the Socialist League, and it never re-emerged. Stafford Cripps pursued his crusade for a Unity Front of all on the left on his own, drawing on his own immense funds acquired as a celebrated lawyer, and became a fringe figure, destined in 1939 to be expelled from the Labour Party himself.

Foot's involvement in the Socialist League was therefore quixotic and fruitless. But it left an important personal legacy in the important friends the lonely young bachelor now acquired. It was in the League that he became close to Krishna Menon, unwell for much of the time but soon to become a local councillor in St Pancras. Another colleague was the *Daily Mirror* journalist and future MP Garry Allighan, later defended by Foot in 1947 when he was harshly expelled by the House of Commons for breach of parliamentary privilege. But much his most important new friend, who filled personal as well as political needs, was the fiery and distinctly attractive red-haired Bradford girl Barbara Betts, with whom he campaigned for the League throughout London. She had been engaged in left-wing politics since graduating from St Hilda's in Oxford, and was now deeply involved in a passionate affair with William Mellor, a leading League intellectual and also a married man.[33] But she and Michael Foot took to each other at once. She found his air of intellectual diffidence combined with political passion deeply attractive. Foot was manifestly in love with her, while understanding and respecting her relationship with Mellor. They spent much time in each other's company, and when Barbara in the course of 1936 rented a new flat in Coram Street, Bloomsbury, Michael was a frequent visitor for whom she cooked many meals. Sometimes they found the money to have dinner together at Chez Victor in Soho. They also paid joint visits to see Cripps in Filkins.

At this time the relationship seems to have been a fairly equal one, with perhaps Foot the more important intellectual force, but Barbara far from docile. Foot, not normally an enthusiast for political philosophy, had recently discovered Marx's socialist writings. He spent many evenings in Barbara's attic flat, sometimes on the roof outside, reading passages from *Das Kapital* to her and discussing their importance, thereby deflecting her from perhaps the more congenial task of reading Dickens's *Martin Chuzzlewit*. More alarmingly, he gave her driving lessons in his new car. Eventually, as he gaily commented at Barbara's memorial service in 2002, his car became a write-off, while Barbara went on to become Minister of Transport. Despite hints from Foot to the contrary in later life and her own lifelong flirtatious style, Barbara insisted that there was never any sexual dimension to their friendship at all.[34] When they went on holiday together to Brittany in 1938, at the time of the Munich conference, despite the encouragement of a cheerful landlady they slept in separate rooms, though with a connecting door: the only excitement came when Michael had a severe bronchial attack in the middle of the night and took refuge in his inhaler. For all that, Barbara Castle (as she became when she married the journalist Ted Castle in 1944) and Michael Foot were basic points of socialist reference for each other, yardsticks for each other's socialist purity. They became less close when Foot came under the spell of Beaverbrook, but the relationship remained strong. Colleagues felt they shared a kind of instinctive closeness that was sublime but asexual. It survived various conflicts – the row over *In Place of Strife* in 1969, Barbara's sacking from his government by Jim Callaghan in 1976, even a sharp book review of the *Castle Diaries* by Michael Foot. Throughout their long lives, she was one of the few who always called him 'Mike'.

Perhaps, despite the wishes of his mother (who had never met her), Michael could never have married Barbara anyway. He soon became far more confident with young women, and Barbara speculated that he did not find her beautiful enough. He might also have found her relentless ideological nagging tiresome. On their Brittany holiday she 'lectured Michael relentlessly about world politics'. Michael himself commented that a week with Barbara gave a whole new meaning to the phrase 'Peace in our Time'.[35] Two other personal points may be made. They were both deeply involved with the career of Nye Bevan, a red-blooded Celt who made frequent passes at Barbara which she did not obviously discourage. Also Barbara, who tended not to get on with other attractive young women, never had a friendly relationship with Michael's later wife, Jill. Indeed, like Jennie Lee, whom Bevan had married in 1934, she positively rejected the central tenet of Jill Craigie's value system, her unyielding feminism.

Overshadowing Foot's world in 1936–37 was the erratic but charismatic presence of Stafford Cripps, his point of entry into socialist politics. It was Cripps who directed one somewhat strange venture in

1936, in effect Foot's first book, though one he chose not to mention in his *Who's Who* entry. This was a volume of nearly three hundred pages, published by the left-wing publisher newly set up by Victor Gollancz. It was entitled *The Struggle for Peace*. Just over 150 pages consisted of a text on international affairs by Cripps; the remaining 127 pages consisted of 'References' written by Foot, in effect around forty thousand words of extended notes on Cripps's text.[36] These show Foot in the most intensely Marxist vein he was ever to demonstrate throughout his life. They do not provide a tribute to the young man's critical faculties, and it is not surprising that he should try to expunge the memory of them thereafter. They focus on armaments expenditure by the great powers, on economic imperialism, on the cruelties and exploitation by Britain of its colonies, in a seemingly mechanical fashion.

In this book, while Foot often quotes from left-wing authors at home, notably Brailsford and Leonard Barnes, most of his sources come from the far left or from Communists, especially the famous Indian theoretician of the Leninist view of empire, R. Palme Dutt, who is repeatedly praised. He is commended for his 'graphic description' of world rearmament; his account of the prospects for increasing productive capacity in *Fascism and Social Revolution* is 'a brilliant analysis'. As it happened, when Foot met the doctrinaire Palme Dutt later on, he never got on with him.[37] Other works cited are even more remarkable. The source for a stated link between military strategy and the profit motive is Bukharin's article on 'Imperial Communism'. Most remarkable of all is the work on which a treatment of the economic exploitation of the colonies is based – Stalin's *Marxism and the National Question*. Stalin's conclusion that colonial rebellions must inevitably be socialist is endorsed (and a letter from a young African nationalist resident in London, Joshua Nkomo, is thrown in for confirmation). Foot adds: 'The methods by which the Soviet government has dealt with the colonial peoples reveal a real basis for cooperation with so-called backward peoples as soon as the power of capitalism within the imperialist nation has been effectively broken. This subject is dealt with in the Webbs' *Soviet Communism* and Joshua Kunitz's book *Dawn Over Samarkand*.'[38] At least Foot's notes are more fun to read than Cripps's leaden text on such themes as 'working-class unity is the only true foundation for world peace'. But they too are eminently forgettable. Equally, it is clear that they are quite untypical of Foot's libertarian and pluralist approach to socialism, and reflect contemporary pressure from Stafford Cripps on his young co-author. Unlike young men such as Denis Healey who joined the Communist Party in the thirties, Foot's thinking never advanced any formal structural analysis based on the dialectic. He seldom made important reference to Marx in his later writings, other than to say how thrilling his (remarkably vague) vision of a post-capitalist utopia really was. Nor did he find the one contemporary example of Communism in practice at all appealing. He visited Stalin's Russia for just two days – a stay in Leningrad at the end of a holiday in Helsinki with brother Dingle in 1937 – and disliked it. He was not to go again until an official visit as Labour leader in 1981.

Foot now did show signs of having a clearer idea of his career. For a young man obsessed with words and politics, journalism beckoned as an inevitably appealing career. But it was a slow start. He persuaded Kingsley Martin, editor of the establishment organ of the left the *New Statesman*, to give him a temporary job on his magazine. He spent almost a year there in 1936–37 to little effect, on a meagre annual stipend of £250. His abiding memory was of sessions every Thursday night with Allen Hutt of the *Daily Worker*, who taught him about the intricacies of typography as well as stimulating his ideas on socialism and his resistance to fascism. But Kingsley Martin was not over-impressed with his young recruit. Foot, he thought, was 'not a bad journalist but not A plus'. It seems in retrospect an amazing misjudge-ment by an often dangerously opinionated and dogmatic man. Michael himself looked back without affection on 'semi-freelance penury' in Martin's offices.[39] Martin later realized his mistake. In November 1943 he wrote to Beaverbrook saying that he had heard that Foot was ceasing to be editor of the *Evening Standard* and asking permission for him to write occasional articles for the *New Statesman*, but Beaverbrook courteously refused.[40] Despite much subsequent collaboration, from the Second Front campaign in 1943 to CND in 1958, Foot and Martin, like the *New Statesman* and *Tribune*, were never close. In the late thirties, and for much of his career, Martin, like Victor Gollancz, was a sentimental fellow-traveller, liable to suppress material by Wells, Orwell and others which criticized Stalin and the Soviet Union. Contrary to what was sometimes implied by right-wing commentators, that could never be said of the libertarian democrat Michael Foot.

Stafford Cripps ensured that his distinctly hard-up protégé found a more enjoyable job almost immediately. In January 1937, as noted above, the weekly *Tribune* came into being as the voice of the far left. Its editor was William Mellor, the paramour of Barbara Betts. Michael Foot received a staff post on it, while Barbara also contributed as a freelance. They wrote a column together on trade union matters under the name of 'Judex'. Foot wrote later of his own role as 'cook's assistant and chief bottle-washer in the backroom'.[41] So, in fairly humble fashion, began Foot's association with this famous organ of the Labour left, which continued for the rest of his life, as editor, director, board member and patron. It was to *Tribune* rather than Victor Gollancz's more conventional Left Book Club, let alone the official Labour Party, that he hitched his star.

For a time working on *Tribune* seemed rather fun. It kept Foot in close touch with Cripps, whose massive private funding enabled the paper, with its few thousand readers, to keep going. Writing twenty-one years later, Foot cheerfully recalled that working with Mellor was 'like living in the foothills of Vesuvius. Yet, between the eruptions, the exhilaration was tremendous.' For Mellor, 'socialist principles were as hard as granite'.[42] The newspaper had a distinguished editorial board of Cripps (the chairman), Laski, Brailsford, George Strauss, Ellen Wilkinson and an up-and-coming and highly charismatic Welsh backbench MP, Aneurin Bevan, who wrote a weekly parliamentary column. Foot saw him only occasionally at this time, but the ideological and personal spell that Bevan cast was largely to determine the rest of his career. *Tribune* also brought Foot into contact with influential foreign émigrés, notably Julius Braunthal of the Austrian Socialists, who wrote for *Tribune* regularly. Foot much admired his later multi-volume history of the Socialist International, and in 1948 wrote a powerful preface to his *Tragedy of Austria*, a plea for closer cooperation between German and Austrian socialists. Foot was to observe here: 'No one with any kindred feeling can read the story of Red Vienna without being a better socialist for it.'[43] Despite all its writing talent, much of 1937 was occupied for *Tribune* with sorting out the mess after the dissolution of the Socialist League. There were more promising avenues to pursue as well. One of them was championing the right of constituency parties to be directly represented through election to Labour's National Executive, which happened at party conference in 1937. But throughout 1938 there were endless strains, to which Cripps was a major contributing factor. They were occasioned, as so often on the left, by difficult relations with other leftish bodies, such as the Left Book Club, whose publisher Victor Gollancz was a distinctly combustible character, and at this time of sentimentally pro-Soviet fellow-travelling outlook. In the background were the show trials and purges in the Soviet Union, of which Barbara Betts wrote quite uncritically under guidance from Intourist, and which D. N. Pritt QC hailed as showing how the rule of law was entrenched under Stalin, but which Michael Foot, ex-Liberal, condemned from the start. He particularly objected to *Tribune*'s refusal even to mention the show trials of Nikolai Bukharin and other victims.

Tribune reached a crisis point in July 1938. Cripps sought an agreement with Gollancz to merge the journal with the Left Book Club, so that it could pursue an uninhibited Unity Front, pro-Soviet policy. This meant the resignation of *Tribune*'s editor William Mellor, a tetchy and difficult man for all his personal charm. Cripps offered the post of replacement editor to the unknown twenty-five-year-old assistant editor Michael Foot. It was a deeply attractive offer, and it speaks much for the strength of character of the young man that he promptly refused. In part he resented what he saw as the disloyal, even treacherous way in which Mellor had been presented with a *fait accompli*. Beyond that, he would be expected as editor to endorse the Unity Front approach, and defend the Soviet Union against its critics.[44] Both were unthinkable. In a letter which he has not kept, Foot wrote to Cripps resigning from *Tribune*. Cripps, en route to Jamaica to try to remedy his gastric problems, replied on 25 July kindly but firmly urging him to change his mind. He could not be expected to pay thousands of pounds towards a paper in whose policies he did not believe. Nor could he be ignored as chairman of the board. 'I only elaborate these points, Mike dear, to try and show you that I am not such a completely negligible political factor in the *Tribune* as you seem from your letter to think.'

H. N. Brailsford was a man for whom Foot had a high regard,

dating from the time when as a young man just out of school he read the left-wing newspaper *New Leader*, which Brailsford edited. His classic book *Shelley, Godwin and Their Circle* (1913) celebrated the 'democratical' radicalism of the French Revolutionary period which Foot most venerated, while his *War of Steel and Gold* (published in May 1914) was a famous analysis of the economic roots of international conflict. Brailsford now strongly disagreed with the pro-Soviet line that Cripps wished *Tribune* to take, and had been appalled by the trial of Bukharin. Under Stalin, he felt, the Soviet Union had become 'a bloody tyranny ruled by terror and lies'. Yet he too wrote to Foot on 6 August, trying to persuade him to change his mind.[45] He wrote sympathetically as someone who had himself three times resigned during his journalistic career. But he argued now that Foot and Mellor were not standing against the proprietors on a matter of policy (a debatable point), and also that Foot should not capitulate in advance against Gollancz, though he added, 'Like you, I distrust him and am highly critical of the Left Book Club.' In worldly fashion he noted that 'to run a good paper matters more than to perform prodigies of conscience'. He offered to speak to Cripps when he returned, and invited Foot to his Buckinghamshire home for a weekend to talk matters through.

But Foot would not be moved by these senior figures. After hanging on for a few weeks until a new editor, the obscure near-Communist H. J. Hartshorn, was appointed, Foot cut his links with *Tribune*. Brailsford was to conclude that the young man was right. He wrote again to Foot a few days later, largely agreeing with him: 'I agree in thinking that Gollancz is a sinister influence. But I have a feeling that the Socialist Left is allowing itself to be driven from all its strategical positions by the C. P. With great subtlety it drove the Socialist League to suicide, & now it is capturing the Tribune. Much as I respect Cripps as a man, I fear he's a disastrous strategist.'[46] In this instructive episode, Foot's judgement and instincts were fundamentally sound. Quite apart from his genuine outrage at the treatment of Mellor, to become editor of *Tribune* would have compromised him morally at that time, and marginalized him within the Labour movement. Persistent rebel though he was, Foot would never leave the mainstream when a crisis beckoned. Thus it was when he veered away from CND after 1961, when he joined the Shadow Cabinet in 1970, when he stuck to Jim Callaghan's ailing government through thick and thin after 1976, and when he struck back at Bennites and Militants in 1982. Although he continued to respect Cripps, Foot now saw him as a naïve and highly fallible messiah. At the start of the war Cripps was to be expelled from the Labour Party for pursuing his Unity Campaign again. During the war years he was to come full circle, and now called for an alliance with progressive Tories. Nor did he show up well on India in the end. Foot's life of Aneurin Bevan (in two volumes, published in 1962 and 1973) is distinctly qualified in its praise: 'Cripps was a political innocent. He knew little of the Labour movement, less of its history . . . His Marxist slogans were undigested; he declared the class war without ever having studied the contours of the battlefield.'[47] Nye Bevan was a different and altogether more convincing prophet.

It was a troubled summer of 1938 for Foot. He had no job and no immediate likelihood of one, though still brooding about possible books on modern history. In December he did acquire a practical commitment since, undeterred by his Monmouth experience, he had been nominated Labour candidate for the Devonport division in his native Plymouth. Presumably this would be contested in a 1940 general election. But since that seat had been held in 1935 with a majority of over eleven thousand and 68 per cent of the vote by a notable National Liberal Cabinet minister, Leslie Hore-Belisha, his prospects there looked extremely remote. The European scene that summer was becoming increasingly alarming, with the Sudetenland crisis in Czechoslovakia following Hitler's Anschluss with Austria. Foot was in Brittany on holiday with Barbara when the Munich crisis took place; he returned to find Prime Minister Neville Chamberlain's diplomatic 'peace in our time' coup with Hitler trumpeted to the skies by publications ranging from Kingsley Martin's *New Statesman* to the *Express* newspapers of the right-wing press magnate and perennial political controversialist Lord Beaverbrook. Foot was unable to share in this euphoria, and sensed a great surrender. Since the civil war in Spain he was a pacifist no longer. Franco's assault on the Spanish Popular Front, along with Hitler's military assistance for him, convinced Foot that the democratic powers had to mobilize force in return. But then came a wholly unanticipated opportunity. Aneurin Bevan had privately mentioned Foot's resignation from *Tribune* to his friend Beaverbrook. 'I've got a young bloody knight-errant here,' Bevan was said to have observed. Foot was invited down to Cherkley, Beaverbrook's Surrey retreat near Leatherhead, to summarize and interpret the latest news. Beaverbrook was immediately struck by him. After lunch that day Foot was made a feature writer on the *Evening Standard*, Beaverbrook's London daily, at a stipend of £450 a year, soon to rise higher.[48] He had exchanged one patron for another, the erratic Cripps for the mercurial Beaverbrook. He had a platform and first-hand access to critical political events. After so many miserable episodes while campaigning on the left, he had made a fresh start. It was to make him famous.

Foot's close, almost filial, relationship with Beaverbrook has always been deeply contested and highly controversial. Probably its most enduring legacy for him was his close attachment not to Beaverbrook but to his left-wing younger friend Aneurin Bevan, whom Foot now got to know well for the first time. But in the months that led to war, and many of the years that followed, it was the unpredictable Canadian press lord, now aged sixty and seemingly close to retirement, who carved out Foot's destiny. It seemed at the time – and in many ways still does – a most improbable friendship. Clearly, the real basis was simply personal. In a very few months Foot had become, in his own words, 'a favoured son', one of the family. Foot's essay on Beaverbrook in his book *Debts of Honour* (1980) breathes the deepest affection in every line: 'I loved him, not merely as a friend, but a second father even though I had . . . the most excellent of fathers of my own.' He pours scorn on the view, widely held on the left, that Beaverbrook was 'a kind of Dracula, Svengali, Iago and Mephistopheles rolled into one'.[49] Foot fell for Beaverbrook's charm, vivacity and mental agility, his rare ability to attract to his circle an extraordinary range of fascinating personalities – Churchill, Brendan Bracken and Aneurin Bevan; H. G. Wells and his Russian mistress Moura Budberg; the Russian ambassador Ivan Maisky; the American ambassador Joseph Kennedy. All in all, the 'old man' was simply fun.

It should be added that Foot fell not only for Beaverbrook's own charms but for those of his glamorous young mistress, the former ballet dancer Lily Ernst. Known to them as 'Esther', she encouraged Foot's interest in Jewish matters. But she interested him physically as well. She was 'a lively Jugoslav-born Jewish girl',[50] and the ever-susceptible romantic Michael Foot, with a penchant for middle Europeans, fell passionately in love with her. It was more than her beauty: she also introduced Foot to one of his cherished poets, Heinrich Heine, a man much influenced by an even greater hero, Byron. Lily Ernst brought him a volume (in English translation) of Heine's romantic poems, which she and Michael discussed avidly. As was the case with Barbara Betts, she was the partner of another man, and Beaverbrook had actually smuggled her out of Vienna just before the Anschluss. Thus Foot remained caught up, devoted but distant, in another non-sexual relationship. But in 1939–40 Lily Ernst became another major reason for his wanting to keep close to Beaverbrook and his court.

For his part, Beaverbrook evidently delighted in Foot's personality, his stories, his radical irreverence, and especially his feel for history and literature, with which he used deliberately to beguile the older man. Foot's admiration could turn into open flattery, historical analogies at the ready. He laid praise on with a trowel when his master became Minister of Aircraft Production in May 1940, telling Beaverbrook, 'Gibbon wrote of the Emperor Theodosius that "the public safety seemed to depend on the life and abilities of a single man". As we read the news of the air battle it seems the same today.'[51] Beaverbrook, whose knowledge of the Emperor Theodosius was probably somewhat sketchy, lapped this kind of thing up. He came to have the highest regard for Foot's writing for the *Evening Standard*, as assistant editor and then, from April 1942, as editor. He admired 'the splendid work that you do in the early mornings in the Evening Standard . . . It is in the early mornings that I admire you most. When a man is admired most in the early morning he is a great fellow.'[52] But even more he adored Foot's warm and witty companionship, which filled a gap in his life. Foot responded with a distinctly sycophantic piece in the *Daily Express* about the *Evening Standard*: 'Cobdenites and anarchists, True blues and pale pinks, radicals and roaring diehards may all make their contribution to this ultra-Conservative journal.'[53] The leader column was sternly independent in viewpoint: 'It doesn't care a fig for anyone.'

What is one to make of the Foot–Beaverbrook relationship? A man may make friends with anyone he wishes, male or female, and there is no scientific law governing these things. The immediate mutual attraction is understandable, but so too is the sharp political and personal breach after 1945. Perhaps what really needs explanation is why they got together again in 1948 and their continued close friendship thereafter, even as Foot pressed on towards the further reaches of the socialist left. Foot always felt at ease with Beaverbrook, and accepted his many kindnesses without feeling that he was being patronized. He describes with simple, perhaps naïve, gratitude being very soon taken by Beaverbrook on the Blue Train to Cannes and Monte Carlo, the trip being wound up with a stay in the Paris Ritz. It was, Foot explains, all part of learning how to write a good newspaper column. He was to accept Beaverbrook's frequent comments on the contents of his columns or leading articles – Beaverbrook was notorious as the most interfering of newspaper owners, with his own personal agenda ranging from Empire Free Trade to appeasement of Germany – cheerfully and modestly enough.

Beaverbrook also put a room in his London flat at Foot's disposal, and Foot sought – and gained – permission to bring a few books, including 'the heavily-marked works of Jonathan Swift' along with works by Marat, Bakunin, Cromwell, Stalin 'and other successful terrorists'. In 1950 Beaverbrook's kindnesses included a large donation to *Tribune* when Foot was sued for libel after his attack on Tory press barons, 'Lower than Kemsley'. It saved the paper from liquidation. It also helped that the *Daily Express* took out full-page advertisements in *Tribune*, which cannot have boosted the circulation of Beaverbrook's newspaper empire. The 'old man' also took to Jill, and for some time in the early fifties the Foots lived in a grace-and-favour cottage on the Cherkley estate. Foot always felt confident that his freedom of expression or thought was not compromised in any way by his association with Beaverbrook, certainly not that he was being bought. It should be added that he was only the first of many left-wing journalists to work for Beaverbrook newspapers and to relish the experience. Robert Edwards came from *Tribune* to become a distinguished editor of the *Daily Express*. The historian A. J. P. Taylor, who first met Beaverbrook in 1956 after giving a glowing review of one of his books, *Men and Power*, was another from the left who came to love Beaverbrook; he became the custodian of his collections of private papers, and wrote a highly favourable biography of the old man after his death. Beaverbrook, wrote Taylor of his beloved 'Max', was a man 'who stirred things up'.

But there is still something to be explained. Beaverbrook may well have been a delightful dinner companion and stimulating friend. What he clearly was not was someone at all in tune with Michael Foot's passionate socialism. Foot has frequently called him 'a genuine radical', of which his being a Canadian Presbyterian was a major aspect. He admired a fellow nonconformist outsider like Lloyd George, the centre of a kind of alternative, anti-establishment circle of devotees drawn from all parties and none. Beaverbrook was certainly a mischievous iconoclast. He thought it enormous fun when a dinner-party would end with Michael Foot and Alan Taylor standing to sing 'The Red Flag'. But he was not in any meaningful political sense a radical. Where Foot was a passionate anti-capitalist of Liberal free-trade background, Beaverbrook was a buccaneering champion of the free market, along with tariffs within a protective imperial system. His *Express*'s crusader bore the chains of a shackled capitalism throughout the years of the Attlee government after 1945. In international affairs he was foremost amongst the appeasers, a warm supporter of Lloyd George's lamentable visit to Hitler in 1936, an advocate of Britain leaving the League of Nations, a warm supporter of Munich, an associate of the defeatist Irish-American ambassador to Britain Joe Kennedy, a man who felt that war in September 1939 was a huge error. As Michael Foot became the fierce champion of resistance to fascism in 1938–39, he acknowledged that his employer and patron took a totally different view. Foot rightly claimed that Beaverbrook was an excellent listener to alternative views, and that all viewpoints on the international scene were represented, and powerfully expressed, at his private gatherings at Cherkley.

But listening and tolerating are passive virtues, and not the same as giving positive support. In Beaverbrook's case they appeared to be an alternative to it, and Foot skirted the point with some delicacy. Readers of Foot's 1940 book *Guilty Men* would search in vain for any hint that the wealthy Canadian press baron was ever amongst the appeasers. This does not imply that Foot was a hypocrite, since his advocacy of his own radical views became ever bolder. He did not sacrifice his integrity as a commentator and critic. But it does suggest that the relationship with Beaverbrook was not at all an extension of his own ideas, but something that existed on a totally different plane. For Foot, as to a degree for Bevan, Beaverbrook acted as someone who could transmute revolutionary thoughts and passionate oratory into a private dialogue, detached from key aspects of real life and ultimately harmless. Those who came close to him were always in danger of becoming licensed rebels.

What Foot did gain from his work on the *Standard*, in addition to a much higher standard of life, was a genuinely stimulating atmosphere in which to work. He progressed rapidly, acting as assistant on the Diary and writing signed historical feature articles on personalities like the Turkish leader Kemal Ataturk. He impressed his employer, and in 1940 became assistant editor. His closest friend from day one was the relatively youthful editor of the *Standard*, Frank Owen, a highly gifted former Liberal MP with alleged Trotskyite tendencies (he was later to write a biography of Lloyd George) and an ardent anti-appeaser.[54] He combined enterprising journalism with a distinctly raffish lifestyle, marked by vast consumption of spirits and a bewildering array of attractive girlfriends. He hurled himself into a hectic private life as frenetic as his editing of the *Standard*. In the end it all proved to be too much, and Owen ended up a pathetic alcoholic. He drew Foot, now rapidly shedding the inhibitions of Pencrebar and West Country Methodism, into this way of life, the more so when they shared a flat in wartime London. Owen contrived a series of sartorial signals on a coat-stand if he was seducing or otherwise entertaining a young woman. He was also a man of much fascinating information, specializing in military matters. He had good contacts with Basil Liddell Hart, Orde Wingate and even Lord Louis Mountbatten. On the eve of war he boldly led a staff deputation to Beaverbrook urging him to change his personal stance on appeasement, or at least to allow his editors to endorse war against Hitler. Beaverbrook, a caustic critic of the Foreign Secretary Lord Halifax's diplomacy, agreed half-heartedly to do so, although Foot describes him as 'sulking in his appeasers' tent' for some time to come.[55] It was not Lloyd George's war, and it was not yet Beaverbrook's either.

The outbreak of war in September 1939 was, of course, an immense trauma for Beaverbrook's journalists as for everyone else. From the start, Michael Foot was a passionate advocate of total resistance to Hitler. On 9 September his impassioned leader in the *Standard*, headed 'No!', urged that any peace proposals should be totally rejected.[56] But he could only promote this militant stance through the printed word, since his asthma meant that he was turned down for military service, as was Dingle with his tubercular arm. Unfriendly questions were asked about this by Plymouth Tories in 1945. In the end, John and Christopher were the only Foot boys to see active service. Foot had now joined Owen in writing highly patriotic leading articles for the *Standard* from a strongly pro-war stance. The paper's leader as early as 9 September 1939 declared: 'There will be no quitting here. Britain is pledged to see the finish of Hitlerism.' Another on 11 November announced: 'The world knows that we are fighting to prevent this Continent from being transformed into a second Dachau prison camp.' On 6 July 1940, after Churchill's elevation to the premiership, another leader addressed its readers in epic terms: 'You are a member of the nation which stood erect, when all others had fallen or been battered to their knees, against the most black-hearted despotism which ever declared war on the human race.' A few days earlier, Hitler was warned: 'He has challenged the toughest people in the world and does not know it. He may even reckon on a breed of Pétainism. He does not know that, if such there are, we shall finish them before he has a chance to finish us.' However, in the period of 'phoney war' that lasted until May 1940, it was difficult to see what the outcome of such stirring rhetoric might be.

Foot's most characteristic writing came in signed feature articles filling in the historical background to current crises, with themes ranging from Drake's Drum to the strategic entanglements in the Middle East. Readers of the *Standard* were treated to learned discourses on the Treaty of Brest-Litovsk in 1918, or even the battles between Carnot's French Revolutionary army and the Austrians in 1793. He also wrote caustically on the collapse of the Norway campaign in April 1940, comparing it with Gallipoli in the First World War, though taking care not to emphasize the role of Churchill, permanently identi-fied with the Gallipoli disaster, but also widely seen as the only hope of victory now.[57]

Foot also found time to produce his first solely-authored book,

Armistice 1918–39, a volume of 274 pages on post-1918 European history published by Harrap, and appearing in March 1940. It came out of a series of sketches of leading political personalities in the press, and the main strength of the book lies in its vignettes of people as varied as the German Communist Rosa Luxemburg, Hitler, Mussolini, Mustafa Kemal, Aristide Briand, Stanley Baldwin, Anthony Eden and Jan Masaryk. The approach is historical, with brief leftish commentary on contemporary issues. The style is brisk and sardonic. The preface gives the reader due warning: 'No attempt is made at impartiality. Unbiased historians are as insufferable as the people who profess no politics.' There is comment on the 'Young England' MPs like Bob Boothby, Duff Cooper, Oliver Stanley and Victor Cazalet who flocked to back Eden after his resignation as Foreign Secretary in 1938. Baldwin, 'standing in lonely eminence like a hillock in the Fen country', is condemned on Churchillian grounds for promoting party over country.[58] Churchill himself is criticized over the Russian Revolution and the General Strike, but is relatively lightly handled. Lloyd George gets off more or less scot free. There is a sketchy conclusion. In general the book is not memorable, though fun to read. Its most striking feature is that, despite his enthusiasm for Rosa Luxemburg, the dogmatic Marxism Foot displayed in the notes to Cripps's book in 1936 has by now totally disappeared. Stalin's purges do not escape mention. However ephemeral, the book did confirm that the *Standard*'s leader-writer had the capacity to write sustained work on his own.

In May 1940 there was a national crisis. In the Commons there came the famous Norway debate of 7–8 May, after which Chamberlain's discredited regime gave way to Churchill's all-party coalition. Beaverbrook, as mentioned, became Minister of Aircraft Production a few days later, despite his own decidedly equivocal attitude to the fall of Chamberlain. Foot was present at the Norway debate; indeed he and Frank Owen were, remarkably, put in touch by Beaverbrook with the veteran Lloyd George at this time, to encourage him to help in overthrowing Chamberlain and then to offer his services for the new Churchill administration.[59] But Foot felt the need for a far more direct role than simply being a comfortable journalistic commentator on a war for which others were sacrificing their lives. The architects of appeasement, from Chamberlain and Halifax downwards, were still around, and in key positions in the Cabinet. They must be indicted and removed from power. Since 10 May Foot had been working closely with Frank Owen, a sharp critic of recent military disasters, in penning a series of inspirational leading articles in the *Standard* to strike a note of defiance. But something much more was needed to shock the national conscience.

There was also another possible colleague, someone that Foot knew less well. This was Peter Howard, previously author of the 'Crossbencher' column in the *Sunday Express* (with both Isaac and Dingle Foot amongst his previous targets, incidentally).[60] Howard, a handsome former English rugby captain, specialized in the caustic personal portrait. Foot and Owen were quite unaware that he was about to become a leading evangelist for Dr Frank Buchman's Moral Rearmament. This movement was deeply suspect to all democrats, since Buchman's pronouncements on current events showed an alarming sympathy for Hitler and indulged in a crude anti-Communism. The author Rose Macaulay observed that 'the Gestapo was riddled with Buchmanites'. But Howard's religious inclinations, to which he largely devoted the remaining twenty-five years of his life, were not yet known. The three men met in the *Standard* offices on the night of 31 May. Foot had heard first-hand evidence of mismanagement by the high command from survivors of the mass evacuation of British servicemen from Dunkirk. Something decisive was urgently needed to galvanize public opinion into realizing how incompetent and morally indefensible the conduct of affairs had been for years past, how essential it was to give mass support to the new Churchill government, above all to spell out the atrocious record of the politicians responsible for past errors, and send them packing. Following some convivial sessions in the Café Royal, the three Express group journalists thus hit on the idea of writing an instant book.[61] The precise contents and shape would be left to serendipity and spontaneous combustion. Michael Foot was the main inspiration.

It was he who won the agreement of his old *bête noire* Victor Gollancz to take it on for immediate publication, he who enlisted Ralph Pinker as literary agent (a disastrous choice, as events proved). Most important, it was Foot who provided a title, in a meeting with his friends in the Two Brewers in the Gray's Inn Road. Still deep in

his reading on the French Revolution, he recalled a popular demonstration at the Convention Assembly in 1793. Those present demanded,
they told the convention, 'a dozen guilty men'. That, Foot believed,
was what the British people demanded now, and *Guilty Men* is the
title the book was given.

Since leaving Oxford, Foot's career had been as haphazard as that
of many intelligent young men unclear about their future. The relationship with Cripps, the abortive crusading for the Socialist League
and writing for *Tribune* had been bruising affairs. He had a record of
association with some flamboyant failures. His writings were not yet
significant. His flight from Liberalism had as yet little positive to show.
The most important by-product was a series of strong personal relationships, important as he grew to maturity, with Cripps, Barbara Betts,
Aneurin Bevan, Frank Owen, and of course Beaverbrook. At each
stage of his life, starting with his father and Lloyd George, Foot seemed
to find comfort in worshipping a messiah, a hero-figure, as a supreme
point of reference, just as he did in his reading of literature. His
psychology appeared to require one. He had unexpectedly lurched
into a significant post at the *Standard* and was for the first time well
paid. He had enjoyed an extrovert lifestyle and had lively friends of
both sexes which allowed an intense, almost donnish, personality to
blossom. But there had been no clear direction or design hitherto to
harness his undoubted talents, no big idea to impress a nation enduring
a crisis of survival. Now, with Owen and Howard to help, Foot sensed
the prospects of a personal statement of a new kind. It would be deeply
controversial to denounce government ministers at a time of total war.
It might be disastrously counter-productive. But in 1711 such a venture
had been a triumph for his and Isaac's literary icon Jonathan Swift.
True, Swift was trying to stop a war and drive a Churchill (Marlborough) out of power, whereas for his admirer in 1940 the purpose
was the exact opposite. Still, for him too it could be his finest hour.

3

PURSUING GUILTY MEN
(1940—1945)

The three young men wrote their book in four days, from 1 to 4 June 1940.[1] The first two days were spent in Howard's country home in Suffolk. The last two were spent in the *Standard* offices in Fleet Street – or rather *on* the *Standard* offices, since much of the writing was done on the roof whenever Foot and Owen were not engaged in producing their newspaper. The book was almost literally written in white heat, since the background was air raid preparations around St Paul's anticipating attacks from the Luftwaffe. *Guilty Men* was not a long work. It eventually ran to 125 pages, divided up into twenty-four short chapters. These were split up on a rough and ready basis between the three authors, eight chapters each. Foot himself wrote the first chapter, 'The Beaches of Dunkirk', based largely on accounts given at the time by survivors. When an author had finished a chapter he read it aloud to the other two, and incorporated their comments and corrections on the spot. On 5 June Foot handed the manuscript to Gollancz, who matched the high tempo of the authors by reading it and accepting it for publication the same day. Proofs were rushed through, and a month later on 5 July *Guilty Men* was on sale. Foot was uncharacteristically nervous about it, and wondered whether it would achieve the desired effect. But it was from the very outset a sensational success. It was the most influential wartime tract Britain had known for over two hundred years, and the best-selling ever.

The tone of the book is caustic and satirical. It makes no attempt to be even-handed. The purpose was to pillory and to condemn the National Government. Left-wing sympathy for ideas of appeasement was simply ignored. *Guilty Men* assailed leading political figures, many of them still in the Cabinet, including the previous Prime Minister, Neville Chamberlain, for a catastrophic failure to defend the country or prepare it for war. It did so with a relish that went far beyond that of media interrogators like Jeremy Paxman or John Humphrys in a later age. There had been nothing like its uninhibited venom since the Regency period. *Guilty Men* was Gillray and Rowlandson in breathless prose. It is a remarkable tribute to the survival of traditional liberties in wartime Britain that it appeared at all.

The book consists of a series of brief vignettes of key episodes or personalities, the latter invariably foolish or dishonest. Of Foot's eight chapters the first was the most powerful, and it set the style for what was to follow. He condemned Dunkirk as 'a shambles', and drew powerfully on oral testimony from survivors. It was 'flesh against steel'; 'they never had a fair chance'. 'It is the story of an Army doomed *before* they took the field.' The soldiers were heroes all – and so too were the sailors and civilian seamen who braved the perils of German bombing to bring them safely home. The son of Plymouth was the last to neglect the naval glories of the 'miracle of Dunkirk'. The second chapter, apparently written by Frank Owen, went back to the origins of appeasement as the authors saw them – the miserable conspiracy that saw the National Government formed in 1931. Ramsay MacDonald is reported as telling Baldwin on Crewe station as early as the 1929 election, 'Well, whatever happens, we shall keep the Welshman out.'[2] Lloyd George is indeed a hero in the wings throughout, and Churchill enjoys similar status during this 'regime of little men'. In asides that the book made famous, MacDonald emerges to express his joy at the delight of aristocratic wives like Lady Londonderry at his success; Baldwin is lazy and inept as he pronounces that the bombers would always get through.

Each subsequent chapter has a named cast list, each member of which is a contributor to tragedy and dishonour. Chamberlain is obviously the chief villain, and the account of his surrender at Munich, probably written by Foot, is drenched with sarcasm at the expense of the 'umbrella man', as is the treatment of the 'Golden Age' of the subsequent six months before Hitler occupied Prague in March 1939 and the state of Czechoslovakia ceased to exist. The later chapters consist of a series of satirical studies of government ministers, and the book winds up dramatically with Hitler's blitzkrieg in France, Dunkirk and the downfall of Chamberlain. The final three paragraphs are printed in capital letters, as suggested to Gollancz by Rose Macaulay. They end with a plea that 'the men who are now repairing the breaches in our walls should not carry along with them those who let the walls fall into ruin . . . Let the guilty men retire.'

Despite the joint authorship and the breathless haste with which it was composed, the book does hang together remarkably well as a chronicle of passion and patriotism. Foot contributed some of the key chapters. Frank Owen wrote much of the military and naval detail, including the final chapter, where his particular expertise lay. Peter Howard, the sharpshooter of the 'Crossbencher' column, wrote many of the individual character studies on ministers like Leslie Burgin, Sir Horace Wilson, the Tory Chief Whip David Margesson, Lord Stamp, W. S. Morrison, Reginald Dorman-Smith, Lord Stanhope at the Admiralty and above all Samuel Hoare, 'the new titan', appointed to the Air Ministry for the third catastrophic time. Howard's most famous target is the pre-war Defence Minister Sir Thomas Inskip, speared for all time as 'Caligula's horse', depicted as a complacent, stupid, 'bum-faced evangelical'. One of Howard's known chapters is that which includes Bevin's demolition of the pacifist Lansbury at the 1935 Labour Party conference. Foot, an admirer of Lansbury's socialist crusading at Poplar and elsewhere, nevertheless felt that 'in that Howard was justi-fied'. Foot himself supplied one of the briefer character sketches, of Ernest Brown, the minister dealing with unemployment, which he attributed in large measure to wet weather: 'He was still lamenting the weather when he was removed from his office – to another post.'[3] The fact that Brown was one of the Simonite National Liberals who were anathema to Isaac Foot gave Michael's ironic dismissal a special relish. Another incidental target was Walter Runciman, whose visit to Prague in August 1938 as Chamberlain's emissary was an especially shoddy prelude to surrender: he too was a National Liberal who had helped to undermine Isaac Foot in Bodmin. The book sped along, but its overall theme had a kind of Platonic unity which justified the use of a single pseudonym for its authors. This was 'Cato', the populist Censor of ancient Rome who to Michael Foot was an appropriate model as 'a good republican'. Along with 'Cassius', his pen name when writing *The Trial of Mussolini*, and 'John Marullus', his later *nom de plume* in *Tribune*, Cato was a memorial to Foot's classical interests. Of course, writing a book in Beaverbrook's offices in work time made anonymity essential.

The book is an obvious patchwork, but a pungent and powerful one. Foot himself later felt that *Guilty Men* had been overrated, and that it had less merit than his next book, *The Trial of Mussolini* (1943) – which, of course, was his work alone. There is a moving introduction, a brisk, highly personalized scene-setting, then a series of mostly effective personality studies, and an upbeat finale. Government ministers are skewered in turn; a digression is the treatment of the Civil Service head Sir Horace Wilson, chief appeaser and responsible for the fact that 'the dead hand of bureaucracy grips us by the throat'. There is a catchphrase or anecdote on almost every page. Many of them have had eternal life in popular memory ever since. It was *Guilty Men* that first drilled permanently into the public consciousness Chamberlain's umbrella, Baldwin's 'appalling frankness', 'peace in our time', faraway countries of which we know nothing, Hitler 'missing the bus'. They are as much part of the essential cultural equipment of British people now as are nursery rhymes or pop songs. Appeasement is guaranteed always to be a dirty word.

The broader public interpretation of the thirties, of course, is owed to Churchill, maker of history during the war, writer of it subsequently. But Churchill's majestic, if often misleading, volumes were offered to a public whose images were already set in stone. The leftish journalists had blazed the trail. Everyone knew who the villains of the thirties were, and why they could never be forgiven. Since the heroes of *Guilty Men*, apart from Churchill, were really the ordinary British people, seen as citizens no less than as subjects, the book fostered a natural sense of a people's war which should be followed by a people's peace. Successive polls of historians designed to assess the rating of twentieth-century British Prime Ministers always saw Neville Chamberlain close to bottom of the poll, his considerable achievements in promoting economic recovery in the thirties set aside even by scholars. If the purpose of popular tracts is to create a demonology, *Guilty Men* was an outstanding success.

Like any popularized version of historical fact, its simplistic analysis has since been seriously undermined. As the pre-1939 public records became available, revisionist scholars such as David Edgerton showed that the rearmament record of Baldwin and his colleagues over warships and aircraft production was far more commendable than the Express Newspapers journalists allowed. They have even been given credit for encouraging a mood of national defiance after Munich. Chamberlain, of course, has had many defenders. So have Hoare, the Chancellor of the Exchequer Kingsley Wood and his predecessor John Simon. Even Thomas Inskip's entry in the new version of the *Dictionary of National Biography* in 2004 concluded that he was far from hopeless; in coordinating defence he showed the, perhaps unheroic, qualities of 'weighing evidence and drawing unemotional conclusions'. Halifax has been the subject of a sympathetic biography (1991) by Andrew Roberts – though oddly the Foreign Secretary makes no appearance at all in the pages of Foot and his colleagues. But of course *Guilty Men* was concerned not with timeless verities but with transforming the public mood. This it did with great brilliance and brio. It would not have done so if its arguments were historically worthless. The combined learning of subsequent scholars like Donald Cameron Watt, Alastair Parker, Richard Overy and Martin Gilbert suggests that the verdict on Britain's political leadership in the thirties still strongly favours the journalistic critics rather than the academic dissenters. Parker's brilliant *Chamberlain and Appeasement* (1997) fatally undermines the counter-revisionists and lists all Chamberlain's calamitous miscalculations. Watt's definitive *How the War Came* (1989) is a shattering indictment of Chamberlain and his ministers. *Guilty Men*, a rough-and-tumble polemic of no scholarly quality at all, has been proved right in its instincts, and the British public knew it to be so.

From the start the book sold by the tens of thousands – over 200,000 by the end of the year, and 220,000 in all. It went through no fewer than seven reprints during July 1940 alone. Gollancz and Foot's nervousness about gambling on so daring a book at such a tense time was shown to be baseless.[4] Many technical obstacles in marketing were successfully overcome, notably the wilful refusal of W. H. Smith's and Wyman's bookshops to have it on their shelves (a far more serious problem then than it would later have been). Other shops showed great caution in confessing that the dread work was actually in stock.

Most unusually for him, Gollancz had to distribute it on a 'sale or return' basis. Thousands of copies were sold not in shops at all but on street kerbs. Foot and friends pushed barrowloads of the book for a quick sale in London's West End. Their sales pitches in Soho and Leicester Square caused some excitement among prostitutes and their clients, who thought it was an instruction manual on sex. Sales swept on and on; *Guilty Men* went through more than thirty impressions in six months, and received plenty of reviews. In an excellent diversion, the anonymous book was actually reviewed by Michael Foot himself in the *Standard*, where he inevitably found points for disagreement. No one had any idea who the author might be: journalistic licence seems to have been more restrained in those days, though of course the book had been produced in unusually secretive circumstances, and without secretarial help. Some wondered whether the former First Lord of the Admiralty Duff Cooper, who had famously resigned from the government after Munich, might be responsible, but the prose style would surely quash such an idea. Only slightly more plausible was the suggested authorship of Randolph Churchill. Not until a good deal later, via sources still unclear, did the truth sneak out.

Guilty Men was the work of a trio, but it has always been Michael Foot with whom it has been identified. As Frank Owen and particularly Peter Howard retreated from the public eye, Foot's continued prominence, and continued identification with its message, meant that man and book were inextricably linked for ever. Crises in the Falklands, Croatia or Bosnia, involving alleged surrender in foreign affairs, made the connection all the firmer. The book did not make him rich; unfortunately the authors lost serious money because Pinker, their agent, appears to have run away with some of the proceeds. But Foot gained something more precious – what Gibbon called 'everlasting fame'. It was a mixed blessing in some ways, as it was hard to have a satisfactory career after peaking so young. It also meant that Foot was typecast as a partisan polemicist, a caustic critic rather than a constructive politician. This diminished his public image. It could also make him seem a dated figure, stuck in a time-warp. Analogies with the bad old days of the thirties would continue to come all too easily to him, to the point of self-parody. Even during the 1983 general election campaign he was still returning to the themes and personalities of *Guilty Men*.

As a publicist and commentator Foot would henceforth stand on a pedestal all his own. His work chimed in with a sense of 1940 as a climactic moment for the national identity. He was a socialist, but also manifestly a patriotic one, admired across the spectrum. At the age of twenty-seven, or at least when his identity was known, he became at a stroke almost the most celebrated journalist of his day, quite as famous as Brailsford, Lowes Dickinson or others of the anti-war writers he had so admired in his youth. In a wider sense, his identification with the thesis of *Guilty Men* moved him on to a new level of authority. Popular contempt for appeasing dictators became a theme endlessly fanned in the media over the next sixty years through the obsessive interest of the British in the Second World War – on stage, screen and television. Heroic young men fighting the Battle of Britain, escaping from Colditz, blowing up the Mohne and Eder dams, would follow the Queen's Christmas broadcast. 'The Dambusters March' rivalled 'Land of Hope and Glory' as an alternative national anthem. There were endless uncritical historical sagas on Churchill, as well as several magisterial biographies. Popular polls found Churchill to be the greatest Briton of all time, leaving Shakespeare, Newton and Darwin trailing in his wake.

But in a way Foot had already pointed the way for him, like a socialists' John the Baptist. His timeless journalism had become an essential part of the triumph over Nazism. The message stuck, and in unlikely places. During the invasion of Iraq in 2003, President George W. Bush, on whose study desk a bust of Churchill reportedly stood, repeatedly cited the perils of appeasement of dictators, as shown by British policy in the thirties (when, incidentally, the United States was made almost inert by its policy of isolation). Bush urged that Saddam Hussein be resisted as uncompromisingly as Hitler had been. Tony Blair, whose own rhetoric became increasingly Churchillian as he neared a pre-planned war (presented as a response to an alleged threat to national security from non-existent weapons), took the same line. Yet one of their mentors in their subconscious (or those of their speechwriters or spinners) was none other than the aged socialist peacemonger and Hampstead sage, himself a fierce opponent of the Iraq war, who addressed the massive anti-war march in London on 15 February 2003 to that effect. Since Saddam Hussein was manifestly

no Hitler, and he had no *Mein Kampf* on display, perhaps Foot's grasp
of logic and of the historical facts was more robust than theirs. At any
rate, as his old friend A. J. P. Taylor would have said, here was one of
history's 'curious twists'.

After the publication of *Guilty Men*, Foot's work for Beaverbrook
on the *Standard* continued to flourish. In May 1941 he took over the
influential 'Londoner's Diary' column. Then, in April 1942, still well
short of his thirtieth birthday, he actually became the newspaper's
editor when Frank Owen was called up to serve in the RAF. Beaverbrook himself had not known at all about the authorship of *Guilty
Men*: it was technically in breach of contract for Foot and the others
to write their book while employed by him. But when he did discover
the truth, he showed no particular concern. Indeed, he was cheerfully
to tell Halifax, who had asked about his personal finances, that he lived
comfortably enough from the royalties from *Guilty Men*.[5] In any case,
far from being attacked in the book as the appeaser he was, he had
received honourable mention at the end, along with Churchill, Bevin
and Morrison, as one of the four strong men in the new government
who could rescue the nation.

Foot had no crises of conscience about writing leading articles or
otherwise producing copy for a newspaper owned by a right-wing
capitalist he was to denounce in 1944 as an 'ante-deluvian monster'.
In fact Beaverbrook himself agreed entirely with *Standard* campaigns
such as that to promote a second front in western Europe, and became
strongly supportive of the Soviet Union long before it was invaded by
Hitler. His own wartime career also fitted in comfortably with his
newspaper's challenging line. His appointments, first as Minister of
Aircraft Production and then Minister of Supply, fulfilling a role somewhat similar to the one Lloyd George had played so brilliantly at
Munitions in 1915–16, were exactly in line with the strong executive
leadership for which the *Standard* called.

Relations between editor and proprietor, then, continued to
flourish. Foot's letters, which had begun with 'Dear Lord Beaverbrook', now started with 'Dear Max'. Beaverbrook himself seemed
generally pleased with the way his young protégé was handling matters.
Later on, addressing the Royal Commission on the Press, he did appear
to make some slightly dismissive remarks about Foot: 'He is a very

clever fellow, a most excellent boy. And then suddenly he was projected into the editorship of the paper before he was ready for it . . .
Michael Foot believed that I made him a journalist.'[6] But Beaverbrook
offered these views in March 1948, when he and Foot were estranged
politically. There is no evidence that he felt any major concern in the
two wartime years when Foot sat behind the editor's desk. There were
those who surmised that Foot was getting too comfortable in his
editorial role. Beaverbrook's right-hand man E. J. Robertson, the long-
term general manager of Express Newspapers, wrote in August 1942
that 'On a number of occasions I have noted that Frank [Owen] is
jealous of Michael Foot.' Owen feared losing his editorship for good
as a result of being called up by the RAF, but put up a façade to cover
his anxieties. Whether these fears were justified is impossible to say
although the prospect of Owen's possibly standing as an independent
candidate in the Maldon by-election two months earlier had ruffled
some of Beaverbrook's feathers. In the event Maldon was captured
by another Beaverbrook journalist standing as an independent, Tom
Driberg, who appeared in the pages of the *Express* as 'William Hickey'.
Foot and Owen actually remained very good friends. Owen went on
to serve as Press Editor in South East Asia Command later in the war,
and apparently turned somewhat against Beaverbrook in 1945, as did
Foot. His later decline into penury and alcoholism elicited a good deal
of sympathy from Foot, who took up his case to receive benefits with
the social services while serving as a Cabinet minister in 1977–78.
Owen's death in 1979 was marked by a particularly warm tribute from
his old comrade, appropriately in the columns of the *Evening Standard*
they had both once edited. In addition, Foot wrote a vivid celebration
of him in the *Dictionary of National Biography*.[7]

Beaverbrook, as was his wont, continued to take a keen interest in
the contents of his newspapers, and Foot received occasional queries,
which had to be handled carefully. In September 1942 he vigorously
rebutted complaints from George Malcolm Thomson, Beaverbrook's
ghost writer on foreign affairs and general sidekick, about the *Standard*'s campaign for a second front in 1943. Thomson's remarks on
Germany's 1914 Schlieffen Plan to invade France through Belgium
betrayed 'a gross historical ignorance and give me much pain'. Thomson
would have to 'find other grounds for his sinister campaign against the

second front'.[8] In November 1942 Foot dealt no less vigorously with Beaverbrook's own murmurings that *Standard* leaders were damaging relations with Franco's Spain. Foot responded that almost any honest report on Spain, detailing the well-known German influence there, would be used as a pretext for saying the British press was stirring up trouble, and trying to censor it.[9] This Beaverbrook steadfastly refused to do. Foot also defended comments about the Finns. While expressing sympathy with them for being invaded by the Soviet Union, he insisted that the *Standard* had always resisted 'giving them assistance which would land us in difficulties with the Russians'.

More serious were Beaverbrook's reservations about three articles in May 1942 signed by 'Thomas Rainboro', the name of the famous Leveller of 1647. These appeared not in the *Standard* but in a very different paper, *Tribune*, with which Foot retained an unofficial personal connection. They consisted of stinging attacks on Churchill, called 'the modern War Lord', for major strategic errors including the failure to protect Greece and resistance to a second front. Remarkably, these were written from an RAF camp in Andover by Frank Owen, recently called up, and drew on his military expertise acquired from Liddell Hart, Wingate and others. Beaverbrook, as Mervyn Jones has shown, evidently knew the secret of their authorship, and indeed agreed with their main thrust, but then became alarmed at possible consequences; he demanded that any future articles be suppressed, and Foot drove to Andover to ensure that they were.[10] His only direct connection with the articles had been to write an erudite explanation in *Tribune* as to who the original Rainboro was. As regards the *Standard*, one area where Foot was willing to concede error was when Beaverbrook turned to matters of literary style amongst his columnists, and to phrases that 'will not do'. He instanced 'generations yet unborn' and 'bore his burdens bravely' as infelicities; we might simply see them as journalistic clichés.[11]

But on wider matters, until well into 1943 Foot's Beaverbrook connection remained brisk and effective. His employer warmly approved of his consistent support for the Soviet Union before and after Hitler's invasion: on 22 June 1941 Foot, who was staying at a house party at Cherkley at the time, went downstairs in the morning and played 'The Internationale' on the gramophone at high volume.

He warmly applauded his old patron Sir Stafford Cripps for his work in fostering Anglo–Soviet friendship in his time as ambassador in Moscow up to the start of 1942. Beaverbrook gave moral support to this. Indeed, his tolerance for his young editor was remarkable. He learnt without apparent dismay of Foot's presence at meetings shared with Communists like Harry Pollitt on behalf of the 'Russia Today' movement in 1941, urging a firm Anglo–Soviet alliance in full Popular Front mode. Russia's involvement in the war greatly excited Foot. He and Frank Owen had frequent sessions in Owen's Lincoln's Inn flat in 1941 with Harry Pollitt, the British Communist Party leader, for whom Foot had especial admiration. Jon Kimche was another important link with Communist activists like Wilfred McCartney. Bevan and Jennie Lee, however, also in contact with the Communists in 'Russia Today', were far less 'forgiving' than Foot was inclined to be.[12] By contrast, the entry of the United States into the war after Pearl Harbor did not excite anything like the same obsessive enthusiasm from Foot and his friends. Roosevelt the war leader seemed less captivating than Roosevelt the New Dealer, while in any case America was never a country that captured Foot's sustained attention.

Under Foot the *Standard* became a more radical newspaper. It also became a more high-quality one. He drew to its columns a wide range of eminent contributors. A highly influential one was H. G. Wells, whom Foot saw as a prophetic figure and who had enormously influenced his conversion to socialism in his Liverpool days. Foot became personally friendly with Wells, and equally so with his Russian partner Moura Budberg, 'the magnificent Moura', whose colourful life had included being the long-term mistress of both the British agent Robert Bruce Lockhart and the great Russian writer Maxim Gorki. A learned Polish follower of Trotsky, Isaac Deutscher, wrote for the *Standard* on contemporary themes. So did Jon Kimche of the ILP, an ardent Zionist and another émigré, later to edit *Tribune*. He owned a socialist bookshop near Ludgate Circus and shared to the full Foot's literary enthusiasm for Hazlitt and others, but he also supplied essential military expertise for Foot's paper, which had been somewhat lost when Frank Owen left the editorship. Kimche's role illustrates the close links between Beaverbrook's *Evening Standard* and *Tribune* at this time, for which Foot and indeed Owen were in large measure responsible. The two publications worked closely in covert ways, notably over the campaign for a second front or affairs in Greece. The *Standard*'s coverage of international affairs greatly gained from expertise gleaned through people writing for *Tribune*. In addition to Kimche on military matters and Deutscher on eastern Europe, there was also excellent analysis of Franco's Spain by the Spanish socialist historian A. Ramon Olivera.

A more exciting journalistic recruit still was Arthur Koestler, a Hungarian Jew and ex-Communist. Foot first met him when Koestler was wearing the uniform of the Pioneer Corps, albeit in the comfortable ambience of the Savoy Grill. A previous place of residence for him, as an ex-Communist immigrant, had been Pentonville prison. His breathtaking book *Darkness at Noon* (1940) had exposed the Stalin show trials in unforgettable language, and explained his earlier conversion to Communism in terms of a psychoanalytical theory of political neurosis. In *Loyalists and Loners* (1986), Foot later described the book's indelible impact upon him: 'I can recall reading it right through one night, horror-struck, over-powered, enthralled.'[13] Koestler on his side was much attracted by Foot as a highly intelligent, literate socialist 'whose projection about the future was untrammelled by a sense of guilt about the past'.[14] Despite Koestler's notoriously combustible, even violent, temperament, he and Foot struck up a strong political affinity. They also shared an enthusiasm for chess and for Foot's girlfriend from 1942, Connie Ernst (no relation to Lily). Koestler's biographer has commented that Koestler was important for Foot, and later for Richard Crossman, for 'unshackling their socialism from the Soviet incubus', but he was very much pushing at an open door on that front. Foot helped him in introducing him to a rich range of socialist writers, intellectuals and activists, and their relationship was often very close. However, Koestler's relations with the *Standard* came to a shuddering end when he revealed a darker side of his personality. A series of articles in the *Standard* in June and July 1942, 'The Idle Thoughts of Sidney Sound', supposedly conveying the reveries of 'typical' figures on the London underground, caused alarm for their erotic quality, and they were wound up.[15] Foot remained on warm terms with Koestler for several years, and worked closely with him in promoting the cause of the Jews after the war. But this other Koestler, with an almost sadistic approach to young women, was eventually to reveal himself to Foot, to his personal anguish. He was startled later on to hear that Koestler had been involved with British espionage work, and lamented his sympathies with ideological anti-Communism, what Crossman was to call Koestler's 'entry ticket into McCarthyite America'.

Koestler was one of three remarkable writers who imposed themselves on Foot's sensibilities at this time, and was the one with whom Foot was most intimate. The other two were George Orwell and Ignazio Silone.[16] As it happened, two of this trio, Koestler and Silone, heartily disliked one another. After the war, at the international Congress of Writers in 1949, Silone advocated 'spiritual resistance' towards Communism, whereas Koestler urged an aggressive head-on confrontation and sneered at Silone as a pacifist. Koestler and Silone were two of the six famous ex-Communist, though still left-wing, writers who contributed to the famous volume *The God that Failed* after the war, while of course Orwell's anti-Communism became legendary from his account of the Spanish Civil War *Homage to Catalonia* (1938) onwards. Their influence is essential to the understanding of Michael Foot as a public figure; they also demonstrate the foolishness of attempts by shadowy agents in later years to depict Foot as any kind of Communist dupe. Foot got to know Orwell through *Tribune*, where he wrote a famous column, 'As I Please', which was often attacked by the *Tribune* management for being over-critical of the Soviet Union, but was always defended by Aneurin Bevan and Michael Foot. These wartime years saw Orwell at his greatest, in Foot's view. He was thrilled by *The Lion and the Unicorn* in 1941, and the way it uniquely captured 'a patriotic English socialist moment', in the words of their joint friend Tosco Fyvel. But Orwell had left *Tribune* by the time Foot became editor after the war, and disappeared to a remote Scottish island. Michael and Jill were closer to Orwell's controversial widow Sonia in the decades after his death. Later revelations that Orwell, like Koestler, had been providing information about his friends to MI5 did not increase Foot's affection for him, though he remained an admirer of his writings, including *Animal Farm* and (to a degree) *Nineteen Eighty-Four*. The latter, however, he claimed had been taken by American cold warriors (and the *Daily Mail*) to be more of an anti-Soviet document than was in fact the case. In *Loyalists and Loners* Foot wrote of

Nineteen Eighty-Four leaving a 'taste of sourness, even defeatism'. He applauded Bernard Crick's fine biography (1980) for showing that Orwell, to his dying day, was a democratic socialist.

Perhaps the biggest impact on Foot's literary and political sensibilities, however, came from the third of the trio, the Italian ex-Communist Ignazio Silone, at the time in long-term exile from Mussolini's Italy in Switzerland. He had joined the Communist Party when very young in the 1920s, but soon found its intellectual tyranny unbearable and was expelled in 1931 when he refused to denounce the ideas of Trotsky. Foot first became aware of Silone's work when he read a translation of the social novel *Fontemara*, originally published in Zürich in German in 1933. It remained an iconic work for Foot all his life, and in 1984 he wrote a foreword to a new English-language edition which explained how Silone's taut but passionate prose enshrined the idea of democratic socialism for him. At this time Silone was little known in the English-speaking world, and Foot played a major role in familiarizing the British public with him after 1945. Most of Silone's books, including perhaps the most famous, *Bread and Wine*, were novels, but the one that made the most intense impression on Foot was a work of non-fiction, *School for Dictators* (1939), a vivid account of the horrors of Mussolini's fascism and the persecution of the Italian left during his period of power. Foot's introduction to *Fontemara* even compares *School for Dictators* with Machiavelli's *The Prince*. After the war Foot found Silone's affirmation of socialist values inspirational, and quotations from him appeared frequently in Foot's writings thereafter, including the famous story about Saint-Simon, 'Get up M. le Comte, you have work to do.' By the time of his death in 1978, Silone had become an honoured figure in the literary canon of the socialist left. He was a central figure in Foot's political odyssey. The first of Foot's three meetings with him in Rome in 1949, when Foot was on a Labour National Executive delegation, was among the most memorable encounters of his life. Most movingly, he quoted Stendhal in relation to Silone as a thinker: 'Only a great mind dares to express itself simply.'

One way and another, the *Standard* years meant that Foot was having a thoroughly good, comfortable war. Jill Craigie was later to twit him as a 'Mayfair socialist'. He had built up an impressive social reputation as a man worth knowing. He moved in attractive intellectual and literary circles, friendly with a rich array of writers like Koestler, Orwell, H. G. Wells and Moura Budberg and others. Koestler's friend Dylan Thomas, then living in Chelsea and hanging around its pubs, was also a visitor to Foot's top-floor flat at 62 Park Street, Mayfair, keeping pace with Koestler in drinking the drinks cabinet dry. As a younger man Foot kept up an extraordinarily unhealthy lifestyle – no exercise, little fresh air, a good deal of drink, mainly of spirits, and smoking sixty to seventy Woodbines a day, which did not help his asthma. But he remained remarkably energetic nevertheless. He also acquired a new, much closer girlfriend, Connie Ernst, a dark-haired Jewish New Yorker working in London for the US Office of War Information. With her he had a serious relationship from 1943 onwards, and he was to propose marriage on a visit to New York in 1945. They became for two years a consistent partnership, and would invite friends to dine with them at the White Tower, a Greek restaurant in Soho. Through Connie he got to know other American intellectuals, notably Ernest Hemingway, whom he greatly liked, and his second wife Mary Welsh. It was Mary who helped him in renting the flat in Park Street (drawn to his attention by Connie Ernst). Here he could live in some style, pore over Swift and Hazlitt, listen to music, play chess with Koestler and others. Nor was the rent crippling – just thirty shillings a week. There he stored some of his precious wartime literary purchases, many bought from Kimche, including a first edition of Gibbon's *Decline and Fall of the Roman Empire*. To the joy of Isaac, Michael's rising salary enabled him to pursue his literary enthusiasms further, and to buy S. S. Howe's famous library of volumes of Hazlitt. The master essayist's thoughts gripped him with ever greater intensity (and as a result often featured in the columns of the *Evening Standard*). Foot was later to tell Edmund Blunden how being a 'worshipper' of Hazlitt led to a strong interest in Leigh Hunt and his *Examiner*, subjects of two of Blunden's own books which Foot enormously enjoyed: 'My criticism of your book on Leigh Hunt was that Hazlitt did not come out as well as his blindest admirers insist he must. But that is a mere trifle compared with so much on the other side.'[17]

In many respects there was a remarkable ferment of intellectual life during the war. It was one of the great formative periods in modern

British history, when creative writers, commentators, planners, economists and artists came together with new blueprints for reconstruction
and new dreams of renewal. Michael Foot, man of words and putative
man of action, was a pivotal figure in it.

But by late 1943 it was clear that his somewhat unnatural base in
the Tory *Evening Standard*, and his filial relationship with Beaverbrook,
were undergoing a change. After all, Foot was Labour candidate for
Plymouth, Devonport, and a post-war election was perhaps on the
horizon. In addition, he was increasingly restless for a wider crusading
role, far beyond the editorial desk. His book published by Gollancz in
late 1943, *The Trial of Mussolini*, written once again in breach of his
editorial contract with the *Standard*, was a sign of this and caused
Beaverbrook some anxiety. He remained keen to retain Foot's services,
and offered him a new role instead, as feature writer and book reviewer.
Foot's generous, even affectionate, response on 1 November 1943
suggested that a parting of the ways might not be too far off. He
suggested two possible courses of action to Beaverbrook. The first was
continuing to act as editor of the *Standard* for just one more year, since
he intended to fight Devonport for Labour at the next general election:
'I certainly intend to become a politician and to devote what energies
I possess to the annihilation of the Conservative influence in politics.'
The second was that he continue to write for Beaverbrook newspapers
on such terms as their owner proposed, so long as 'I am not required
to do anything in defiance of my views and that I have freedom to
engage in such nefarious activities as I choose in writing books or on
the platform'.[18] They chose the first course, amicably enough, but
things were getting progressively more difficult, especially after D-Day
the following June, which made the ending of the war a far more
proximate possibility.

So Foot wrote a letter of transparent honesty and integrity to
Beaverbrook a few days later:

> The main idea I have is that your ideas and mine are bound to
> become more and more irreconcilable . . . There does not seem
> to be much sense in my continuing to write leaders for a news-
> paper group whose opinions I do not share and some of whose
> opinions I strongly dissent from . . . The leaders which I now
> write are hardly worth writing since they are non-commital and

> from my point of view I am associated with a newspaper group
> against whose policies (but not against the proprietor) I am
> resolved to wage perpetual war. Somehow things were different
> before. The compromise worked and certainly greatly to my
> advantage. But I do not see how it could work very much
> longer.

Foot felt, 'as an ambitious and intransigent socialist', that he could find
another newspaper in which to express himself. He did not see how
Beaverbrook could reasonably run a column by him: 'At the present
I am engaged in writing stuff in which I have no particular interest,
and I would like to do something different.' He therefore asked
Beaverbrook to release him from his obligations to newspaper and
owner.[19] Beaverbrook did release him, in tones of sadness and regret.
It was a deeply civilized break-up on both sides. But it was a peculiarly
sharp one. In a few months Foot was denouncing his old patron's
right-wing views with fire and fury in newspaper columns and
speeches. Much more completely than before, he was his own man.

He now threw himself into an even more frenetic range of activities
than before. Chief amongst them, given his now perceived talent as
part-author of *Guilty Men*, was inevitably the writing of books. He
produced two short but effective tracts in the later wartime period, both
highly partisan in a way that the earlier book never was. Each was written
at Pencrebar. *The Trial of Mussolini*, as noted, appeared without Beaverbrook's knowledge and caused him concern. It was written, Foot told
him, to protest against the hypocrisy of those who denounced Mussolini
at his fall but had upheld his views for twenty years previously. The
idea came to him at the time of the removal of Mussolini and the
appointment of Marshal Badoglio as potential peace-making head of
the Italian government in July 1943. Foot visualized the forthcoming
post-war trial of the dictator and, using the same theatrical method as
in *Guilty Men*, cast the various pre-war British ministers who had
appeased him as witnesses at the tribunal. He had been given much
information on circumstances in Italy by the son of Vittorio Orlando,
the Italian Prime Minister during the 1919 Paris peace conference.[20] A
more profound underlying influence was Ignazio Silone. But the book
would really be about British foreign policy, not Italy. He offered the
idea once again to Victor Gollancz, who seized it avidly for another

of his 'yellow perils', as the volumes of the yellow-jacketed Left Book Club were known. He received the manuscript on 20 August, and it was published in October, with a confident print run of 100,000 copies. Foot wrote the book in three weeks. His *nom de plume*, again, was drawn from classical antiquity – not 'Cato' this time but 'Cassius', the assassin of an earlier not-so-sawdust Caesar.

The Trial of Mussolini is a short polemic, only eighty-two pages and perhaps forty thousand words long, but it is most cleverly written, with much subtle argument. Its style of dramatic personal confrontation between judge and witnesses meant that it lent itself to being turned into dramatic form by political and dramatic societies. George Orwell praised it as such in his review in *Tribune*. Foot himself considered it a better and more complete book than *Guilty Men*.[21] The conceit of a public trial with eminent witnesses is skilfully sustained throughout. Although the action concerns the trial of Mussolini, the dictator in many ways comes out strongly, giving a vigorous defence of his policies and making short work of any British claims to moral superiority in the area of 'wars of aggression'. Really it is the witnesses who are in the dock. Successively, Austen Chamberlain describes an amiable meeting with Mussolini in 1924, when Chamberlain was Foreign Secretary. Lord Rothermere, owner of the *Daily Mail*, relates how in 1928 he stated that 'Mussolini will probably dominate the history of the twentieth century as Napoleon dominated that of the early nineteenth century.' Neville Chamberlain confirms the long-held support of British Tories for the Italian dictator. Lord Simon testifies to British double-dealing over Abyssinia. Sir Samuel Hoare is condemned by counsel as 'disingenuous' over his notorious pact with Pierre Laval, the future Prime Minister of the Vichy government, about the Italian invasion of Abyssinia in 1935. Halifax and Leo Amery offer similar testimony. Special attention is paid to Hore-Belisha, Foot's target in Devonport, who had visited Rome in 1938 and received a bronze medallion from Mussolini. Even Churchill receives a momentary glance of disapproval. The judge concludes in emotional tones to draw a distinction between the English people and 'the England of the Chamberlains, the Simons, the Hoares' and the rest of the Tory Party which consorted with Fascism and connived at imperialist war.[22]

The Guilty Men are thus given another pasting, though perhaps in an over-complex way. *The Trial of Mussolini* sold slightly less well than 'Cato's' work of 1940, but sales still rose to 150,000. It aroused some criticism as being anti-patriotic. Gollancz sturdily defended the author: 'Michael Foot . . . would be interested to find himself described as seditious. So would his father, old Isaac . . . So would the electors of Devonport, who, if they have the wit to understand the true meaning of British honour and British interests, will in a few weeks' time [*sic*] be returning Michael to Parliament.' The reviews, however, were very favourable, especially one from the Conservative Catholic Christopher Hollis. Another, more predictable admirer was Isaac Foot: 'He is a fine boy and . . . he has a fire in his belly.' [23] But Foot this time made less of an impact. At least the book made him more money than its predecessor, with no absconding agent this time. It also confirmed his unique skill as a patriotic pamphleteer.

There had been announced another project of Foot's, to appear in the 'Searchlight Books' series published by Secker & Warburg under the editorship of George Orwell and Tosco Fyvel, both active in the world of *Tribune/New Statesman* left journalism. Ten books appeared in the series in 1941–42, covering various projections for post-war reconstruction, by such notable authors as Sebastian Haffner, T. C. Worsley, Ritchie Calder and Joyce Cary. The series was launched in 1941 by Orwell's own famous study of the British national character *The Lion and the Unicorn*, which, rather modestly, sold over ten thousand copies. Michael Foot was announced as the author of a forthcoming work entitled *Above All Things – Liberty*. But the publishers' printers at Portsmouth, along with their stock and paper, were destroyed by the Luftwaffe in 1942, so nothing came of it.

In November 1944 Foot published another squib with Gollancz, this time of overtly party political slant, with an election now on the horizon. This was *Brendan and Beverley*, a book of just seventy-eight pages. Foot's name appeared as the author, and he was now formally identified as the writer and co-writer of the two earlier works. This one was a parody of an imagined conversation between two Conservatives, Brendan Bracken, who was close to Churchill and was now Minister of Information, and Sir Beverley Baxter, a right-wing Canadian MP, a strongly imperialist Chamberlainite throughout, and Member for Wood Green and Southgate. In the same month Foot wrote savagely to *The Times* denouncing Baxter as a pro-Chamberlain appeaser, and dismissing a book of his as 'a satire on political sycophancy'.[24] *Brendan and Beverley* takes the form of a dialogue between the two Conservatives named in Disraeli's *Coningsby*, 'Taper' (Bracken) and 'Tadpole' (Baxter). They give their different versions of Conservative philosophy, but neither is convincing. Baxter was a particular *bête noire* of Foot's, and he is the more obvious target, but 'Taper' also gives a poor performance. He defends the Churchill coalition, of which Foot was now a strong critic, 'since it can do down ideas of reform'. There is a patriotic peroration on Churchillian lines, but it is given to an unnamed Labour politician.[25]

This book did not sell well: its message was too oblique for the general public, and it anticipated an election which was not yet called. What it did do was confirm the sharp breach with Beaverbrook, who was close to both Taper and Tadpole. Brendan Bracken was a frequent house-guest at Cherkley, and was actively involved with Beaverbrook in preparing the Conservatives' propaganda campaign in the coming election. Baxter had actually been editor of the *Daily Express* up to 1933, and was later to serve as theatre critic of the *Evening Standard*. Attacking them both, as a way of pronouncing anathema on all Tories and their works, was Foot's clearest possible declaration of divorce.

Foot was now very much a doer as much as a commentator. From 1943 to 1945 he engaged in a bewildering miscellany of protest movements, all characteristic of the rich crucible of the war years. He remained active in the India League and friendly with Krishna Menon. He was now campaigning actively for the Zionist cause, and was prominent on the Anglo-Palestine Committee, chaired by Israel Sieff, managing director of Marks & Spencer, and also including Frank Owen, Kingsley Martin, David Astor and Lord Pakenham. Foot himself addressed it on the plight of Hungarian Jewry in 1944.[26] There was the League for the Rights of Man, with which Gollancz was identified and which became more vigorous after the United Nations came into being after the war. He was also a member of the National Council for Civil Liberties, founded in 1934, which had kept watch on the preservation of civil liberties during wartime. There were various bodies to affirm solidarity with the Soviet Union. Foot also kept very close to the intense milieu of political and literary protest, the natural

habitat of writers like Orwell, Koestler and Fyvel, the world of the
Penguin Special, the Left Book Club, Searchlight Books, Cyril Con-
nolly's literary periodical *Horizon*, and such transatlantic equivalents as
Partisan Review and *Dissent* in New York. All this protest literature was
fundamental to the wartime cultural hegemony of the British dissenting
left. Michael Foot, barely into his thirties, was an increasingly influential part of it.

Finally, in this potpourri of leftish idealism, Foot was a member of
the so-called '1941 Committee' formed by J. B. Priestley and well
described by the historian Paul Addison as 'a perfect photosnap of the
new progressive Establishment rising from the waves'.[27] It included
not only Priestley himself and his wife Jacquetta Hawkes (both of
whom Foot now got to know for the first time) but also Richard
Acland, Thomas Balogh, Ritchie Calder, Kingsley Martin, Tom Win-
tringham and the Rev. Mervyn Stockwood, all of whom were later
colleagues of Foot in CND, which it partly anticipated. However,
the 1941 Committee was more broadly based, since it also included
mainstream Labour figures like Douglas Jay and Christopher Mayhew,
and even a one-nation Conservative, Peter Thorneycroft, leader of the
Tory Reform Group. It faded away when several of its key figures
(though not Foot) joined Acland's new Common Wealth Party the
following year.

Despite all this manifold activity, which began long before his
resignation as editor of the *Standard* in August 1944, the bedrock of
Foot's world was now the Labour Party, albeit via left-wing movements, non-Communist though pro-Russian, kicking hard against the
restraints of being yoked in Churchill's coalition. Foot was never an
admirer of Attlee's leadership, and the wartime years underlined the
fact. One protest in which he was involved was the Bristol Central
by-election of February 1943, one of many awkward by-elections for
the government at this time. Here there was an Independent Labour
candidate in the person of Jennie Lee, Aneurin Bevan's wife, who had
recently left the ILP but who declined Acland's invitation to join the
Common Wealth Party and ran on an Independent Labour platform
to campaign for socialist policies and a break with the coalition. The
ILP ran a candidate against her out of revenge. The entire affair was
distinctly embarrassing for the Labour Party. However, Foot (despite

being editor of the *Standard*) went to Bristol to campaign hard on
behalf of Jennie Lee and against the idea of an electoral truce. Unfortunately Bristol Central, which included the city's central business area,
was the least promising of the five Bristol seats, and there was a very
low poll since so many voters were away during wartime. Jennie Lee
lost by 1,500 votes to the widow of the former Conservative Member,
Lady Apsley, and there was actually a swing to the government, in
contrast to almost all other contests at the time.[28] This was a solitary
venture by Foot, who of course was free to electioneer without
inhibition after he left employment with Beaverbrook.

Bristol Central tended to confirm that Foot, having broken with
Cripps, was finding another inspirational guru in Jennie Lee's husband.
Going out of his way to campaign for her showed how he was swinging
from Beaverbrook to Bevan. He had known Nye for some years,
dating from a meeting during the Monmouth election in 1935, and
had got much closer to him during his time on *Tribune*. Bevan, as we
have seen, was one of Beaverbrook's many left-wing associates, and it
was he who recommended Foot for a job with Express Newspapers
in 1938. He was at this time editor of *Tribune* himself, though his
talents did not really lie in the field of journalism. But in the wartime
period, with Bevan emerging as a towering critic of Churchill and the
coalition on many issues, Foot became his most intimate ally. In 1944
they collaborated in campaigns on the future of Poland, and especially
in attacking Churchill for British military intervention in the civil war
in Greece. Foot would be more than his comrade. He would be his
Boswell, his Engels, his John the Baptist, and of course his parliamentary heir.

Long after his death in 1960 Bevan remained the most important
person in Foot's life, not excluding Jill. He was central to Foot's every
crisis of conscience, the permanent sounding board for his socialist
values. Their difference of view over nuclear weapons was more sear-
ing for Foot's psychology than any divorce could have been. Foot's
passionate admiration for this brilliant, articulate tribune, who came
not from the literate suburban bourgeoisie but from Tredegar in the
working-class cauldron of the Welsh mining valleys, was unshakeable.
Bevan stood with Foot on every possible issue. He was a citizen of the
world. He strongly endorsed Indian independence, a free state for the

Jews, friendship with the Soviet Union and an early second front, public ownership as the basis of a socialist transformation, a welfare state, and a free and open society. Foot was excited by the nature of Bevan's socialism, with its background in south Wales syndicalism and ideas of industrial democracy as opposed to bureaucratic statism. He admired his libertarian Marxism, his natural use of language, his open-mindedness towards other cultures, his brilliance as an orator both on the stump and increasingly in the Commons.

Most of all, he admired his style. Bevan was a vivid, colourful man, with a love of painting and literature; he was captivated by a book like Stendhal's *Le Rouge et le noir*. He shared with Foot a liking for the more exotic versions of liberal philosophy, notably the works of the Uruguayan author José Rodo. He had a genuine love of complex ideological debate, attacking the enemy's argument at its strongest point. Also, in Foot's brilliant phrase, he was 'a sensual puritan', with a shared love of Venice and an attraction to women that went far beyond his own beguiling but wayward wife. He dressed well, he liked to dine well at the Café Royal, he enjoyed wine, especially Italian. He far transcended the other, more staid Welsh MPs dining on the 'Welsh table' in the Commons: Jim Callaghan would say Nye would only join them for a meal when he was in political trouble.[29] Bevan straddled the worlds of politics, the arts and journalism. His associates ranged from Koestler to Brendan Bracken, who provoked him by calling him a 'lounge lizard, a Bollinger Bolshevik'. Bevan was a captivating figure. If often difficult and egotistic, he was also perhaps the most original and visionary politician ever produced by the British working-class movement. In addition he had a range of skills that left his people the National Health Service, Britain's greatest contribution to civilization in the twentieth century. He proved himself an artist in the uses of power. He loved Michael for his literacy, his integrity and his courage, his love of the romantics. Bevan liked to declaim aloud the poetry of Keats and Wordsworth, and was another enthusiast for Wells, though he could never quite fathom Foot's regard for Swift. Bevan's *Why Not Trust the Tories?*, a brilliant philippic published in 1944, showed a heavy influence from Foot, not least the famous peroration citing Rainboro of the Levellers in the Putney debates. To Foot, nothing more confirmed his low opinion of Attlee and his near-hatred of Gaitskell than what he felt was their conspiracy to remove Nye in 1951. For Bevan represented everything he felt was most worthwhile in this world: 'More than any other in his age he kept alive the idea of democratic socialism,' and gave it a vibrant and audacious quality.[30] Foot's own equally audacious biography was to provide him with the most glittering of memorials after he was gone.

After leaving Express Newspapers, Foot needed employment. In fact it had already been guaranteed. In the summer of 1944 he became a regular columnist for the *Daily Herald*, a post which he retained until 1963. He had not had much regard for the paper in recent years, after its brilliant beginning in the Lansbury years after 1913. It was taken over in 1929 by Lord Southwood, owner of Odhams Press, 'a small-minded man interested only in profits', in Foot's view, and 'an absurd figure to be in charge of a Labour paper'.[31] However, Foot did have an immense regard for the *Herald*'s editor, Percy Cudlipp, a native of Cardiff. Like Foot he had been a very youthful editor of the *Evening Standard*; indeed, he was appointed by Beaverbrook at the even younger age of twenty-seven. Along with his brother Hugh of the *Daily Mirror*, Percy transformed the popular left-wing press: 'He could do anything on a newspaper. He could take anybody's copy and make it better.' In later life Foot declared that Cudlipp was 'the greatest of all the popular editors'.[32] He was also an autodidact, a man of considerable culture, with a love of music, a flair for light verse and a close friendship with John Betjeman. Cudlipp had long been angling for Foot's services, and he moved to the *Herald* immediately on leaving the *Standard*. He would write two columns a week, on Tuesdays and Fridays, for less remuneration than on the *Standard*, but with more scope to do other things, including write for *Tribune*. Cudlipp would prove to be a stout defender of him when he later got into trouble with Transport House.

The newspaper introduced Foot as 'the brilliant young left-wing author and journalist', and his first column appeared on 15 August 1944. After an initial appeal to idealism, it dealt with the congenial theme of the need to avoid any secret treaties that might pervert a post-war settlement. His columns gave Foot ample scope to cover a vast swathe of topics, mostly international, succinctly and even violently, with ample use of historical analogy and literary quotation. On 25 August he hailed the liberation of Paris, with much citation of Fox,

Tom Paine, Hazlitt, Wordsworth, Shelley, Byron and others from his Valhalla of heroes. He took time out on 15 September to rebut Bernard Shaw's characteristically perverse clarion call against all political parties, and advised him to look at the reconstruction needs in Plymouth which the Tory caucus was trying to wreck. Two weeks later came the cry that 'only the international faith of Socialism can win the final triumph – Shout it from the housetops!' There followed a lengthy series of familiar assaults on individual Tories, 'guilty men' one and all – Leslie Burgin, W. S. Morrison, Lord Woolton, Lord Linlithgow (the Viceroy who had imprisoned Nehru), Lord Croft. There is on 5 December a good Labour kick at the Liberal William Beveridge for wanting industry to remain in private hands and opposing redistributive taxation: 'He travels on the *Queen Mary* yet believes he is Columbus!' Over the new year he is denouncing the 'tragedy' of Britain's intervention in Greece, though also challenging far-left critics by condemning Russian involvement through the Lublin government in Poland: 'Will the Poles have liberty?' On 20 March 1945 he is drenching with ridicule the hapless National Liberals like Ernest Brown. The opportunity is predictably seized to stick more darts into the Member for Devonport, Leslie Hore-Belisha, 'a lonely giant' who not only received a medal from Mussolini but also voted to remove Churchill from office in 1942, while Rommel was close to Alexandria. On 5 April there is a moving tribute to a genuine Liberal, David Lloyd George, whose great life had come to an end, but whose career was marked by tragedy because he had been compelled to govern with the Tories (this, of course, at a time when Labour ministers were still entrenched in Churchill's coalition). It is lively, knockabout stuff, but fierce, even vicious, with skilful one-sided argument and a populist approach for the voting public.

But his most serious enterprise was becoming an MP, and Plymouth therefore called him more and more. A seat Labour had never looked like winning, Devonport was located in a part of Britain in which, as Andrew Thorpe has shown, Labour was traditionally very weak. It was clearly going to be a tough contest. Isaac had anticipated this with some relish: 'You didn't commit yourself to a clean fight, I hope?'[33] Early on, Foot was challenged at meetings there in 1944 about his not doing military service, and had to explain his medical circumstances, the asthma which led to his being given Grade IV. He insisted he had not been a conscientious objector. He was also interrogated about having worked for the right-wing Beaverbrook press. The *Standard* was a very good paper under his editorship, he said: 'He had left of his own free will because someone was trying to interfere with his rights as to what he wanted to write in that newspaper.'[34] Needlessly, he threw back provocations of his own, including much personal insult (never anti-Semitic) of Hore-Belisha.

The Labour Party had made progress in Plymouth since the early 1930s. The council had a Labour majority, and Foot was later to pay tribute to some of the key local personalities, Harry Mason (the council leader), Harry Wright (its finance officer) and Bert Medland, one of the MPs elected in 1945, and later to serve as Foot's election adviser in 1950.[35] But it was still going to be a very tough contest in a city that had undergone tough experiences. Plymouth, a place with much ancient slum housing, had also been a significant victim of the blitz, as was the fate of all seaports and naval centres. On 20–21 March 1941 there was heavy bombing by Heinkels, as it happened while George VI and Queen Elizabeth were visiting the naval barracks and dockyards. The centre of the city was set ablaze, leaving 292 civilians dead. Worse was to follow on 21–23 and 28–29 April, when many tragedies occurred. Seventy-two people were killed when an air-raid shelter in Portland Square was hit, and so were ninety-six sailors in the naval barracks. In the final assault on 29 April, the Devonport High School for Girls was hit, forty-three sailors were killed on HMS *Raleigh*, and 100,000 books destroyed by fire in the Central Library. The rebuilding of Plymouth after the war inevitably became a theme of bitter political contention. Foot wrote an article in *Reynolds News* in October 1944, 'Plymouth is Betrayed', condemning the government for refusing to grant national funding to assist the local council's Plymouth Plan. Lord Astor, the outgoing Conservative Mayor of Plymouth, supported the plan, as did his wife.[36] So too did the incoming Mayor, none other than Isaac Foot. But Hore-Belisha insisted that local reconstruction could only be a local responsibility. The entire issue occasioned intense debate. The clerk of a local district council warned Isaac Foot that his son's support of the 'extravagant' city plan, 'creating unnecessary overspill', might lose him half his supporters.[37] Foot also gave his

backing to the plan of the celebrated town planner Patrick Abercrombie for Plymouth in 1943, which would have created a large,
multi-purpose Tamarside local authority.

By the early spring of 1945, the end of the war was clearly in sight.
Twelve days after VE-Day on 8 May, the Labour Party decided to leave
the Churchill coalition. A purely Conservative 'caretaker' government
took over, to prepare the way for a general election, eventually
announced as to be held on 5 July – or rather, it was a government
which also included some of the ghostly National Liberals, known
briskly to Michael's brother Dingle as the 'Vichy Liberals'.[38] To Foot's
immense derision, the man appointed as the new Minister of National
Insurance in Churchill's 'caretaker' government was none other
than Mussolini's erstwhile acquaintance Leslie Hore-Belisha, perhaps
another Caligula's horse; though not of Cabinet rank.

Michael Foot's journalism reached a climax now. In mid-April he
was sent by the *Herald* to San Francisco to cover the conference to
launch the new United Nations; it was his first visit to America since
his debating tour with John Cripps in 1934. He wrote eight somewhat
atmospheric articles describing the conference, which were published
in the *Herald* between 17 April and 29 May. He focused mainly on
trying to convey the mood of the conference, discussed some of the
issues, notably Poland and the Lublin government, and assessed some
key personalities including the Soviet Foreign Minister Molotov,
whom he found 'mysterious' and who of course he knew as a key
figure in the pre-war show trials. He had a number of interesting encounters, notably with the future Australian Foreign Minister Dr H. V.
Evatt. In a relaxed aside he noted that at one meeting he sat next to
the romantic French film actor Charles Boyer.[39]

But Foot was anxious to return home. There was a vital election
to fight, and time was getting short. He also had an even more pressing
reason to get back, something to change his life even more fundamentally than his election to Parliament. He had met Jill Craigie.[40] Previously his affections had focused strongly on Connie Ernst, who had
returned to New York at the end of 1944 and whom he had asked to
marry him. He travelled to San Francisco via New York, and was with
Connie on 12 April 1945, the day President Roosevelt died. But, to
the disappointment of Koestler amongst others, Connie regretfully but

decisively declined the offer: she did not wish to live in post-war London. She went on to marry Simon Michael Bessie, a publisher who in the 1960s actually became Foot's publisher and remained friendly with him, even though his marriage to Connie ended in divorce. Bessie was also to publish in America the works of Jill's later great friend and heroine Rebecca West.

Jill Craigie was quite a different proposition from Connie. Part Scots, part Russian, she was two years older than Michael. Although only thirty-four, she had already been married twice, and had a young daughter. Her first marriage had ended before the war, and she was now in an unsatisfactory marriage with a playwright and screenwriter, Jeffrey Dell. Jill was a notable example of how London's cultural life was galvanized by the experience of war. She went into films, and wrote an ambitious documentary, *Out of Chaos*, in 1943, inspired by the socialist philosophy of William Morris. She focused on the war artists, and got to know eminent figures like Paul Nash, Graham Sutherland, Stanley Spencer and especially Henry Moore. She also met the writer on urban theory Lewis Mumford during the war, and the influence of his book *The City in History* inspired her to make a documentary on the rebuilding of a war-damaged city. A title that suggested itself was 'The Way we Live Now', and one possible city for the location of the film was Plymouth, where Patrick Abercrombie was to be part-architect of a post-war city plan.

In the autumn of 1944 she met Michael Foot at a party given at his home in Montpellier Row, Twickenham, by the eminent architect Sir Charles Reilly, the father of Foot's Oxford friend Paul. Foot invited her to dinner at 'a very posh restaurant', the Ivy in Covent Garden. Evidently they instantly attracted each other. Foot was captivated by her charm and beauty. She was 'a raging beauty thrust on susceptible wartime London . . . She had the colouring of an English rose but everything else was a romantic, mysterious addition.'[41] He told his mother, who worried about his bachelor status, 'That's the girl for me.' Her attraction for him is very understandable. Apart from her beauty, throughout her life Jill had a sensitive, rapt way of being deeply appealing to men of all ages. No woman listened with more intense attention to the conversation of men, not least Welsh men. But she also had close women friends, including Jenny Stringer in later life.

She had in her few years in London attracted the interest, personal as well as intellectual, of an extraordinary group of celebrities: Paul Nash, Henry Moore, Charles Reilly and even the aged Ralph Vaughan-Williams all flirted with her. Another strong admirer was the former Cabinet minister and son of the former Prime Minister, Malcolm MacDonald, who proposed marriage. She looked after his Hampstead house for a time, her neighbour, improbably enough, being General de Gaulle.[42]

Jill also attracted Michael with her quick intelligence, her artistic flair, her social poise and (possibly) her vigorous feminism. She herself was immediately smitten by Michael, his honesty, his air of myopic charm. It was love at first sight, even if in Michael's case it was short sight. The severe eczema which had worried him in his relationships with women was of no consequence to her. She and Michael both had unfinished relationships to unscramble. Jill ended matters with Jeffrey Dell and briefly moved into the Hampstead house of a fellow film-maker, William Macquitty: she was a Hampstead personality years before Michael. Meanwhile Michael had to sort matters out with Connie Ernst.

The relationship between Jill and Michael developed rapidly. His still somewhat undeveloped sexual experience flourished under her confident tutelage. She visited her 'Mayfair socialist' several times in 62 Park Street, bought him a new gramophone and encouraged his interests in Mozart and in opera generally.[43] Most important, she told him of her plan to make a documentary on Plymouth, and came down there to work with him on it. Foot himself appeared in the film, looking unusually well-tailored in a smart dark suit. She promised to help in his election campaign. When he went off to America the prospect of her moving into 62 Park Street, cramped though it would be, was a real one.

The partnership of Michael and Jill is a *leitmotiv* through the rest of this book. It was a marriage of two strong-minded people, each of whom had powerful relationships with the opposite sex, while remaining faithful and trusting. Each gave the other a kind of radiant confidence that lasted for the next fifty-five years. Jill admired Michael's socialist passion, his literacy, his lack of affectation, his generosity in personal relationships, his humanity. Without changing his personality or his style, she wanted him to succeed. He admired her dedication to work on the feminist movement, while her artistic interests and many friends in the cultural world greatly developed his own somewhat eclectic interests. They did almost everything together: the constituency visits, the trips to Venice or later Dubrovnik, the joint reading of lyric poetry or the prose of Wells or Conrad. Just Plymouth Argyle remained for men only. For Michael, a romantic, passionate man, Jill was the perfect partner.

To what extent her tastes fitted in with his kind of politics is another question. She was not a person with naturally strong political understanding, even though she would respond to great campaigns and was as committed a supporter of nuclear disarmament as Foot himself. In old age they crusaded passionately together about the plight of Croatia and Bosnia after the collapse of Yugoslavia, when her expertise in film direction was invaluable. Her advice on political matters, beyond the purely personal, could be unhelpful, and her strong views encouraged Foot's own fierce and unyielding dogmatism. This trait could be offputting for powerful women of similar outlook, notably Barbara Castle and sometimes Jennie Lee. Barbara Castle's letters would address Jill, in not altogether friendly fashion, as 'my feminist friend'. She observed of Jill in her memoirs, 'Michael used to be as brutal with her as he was with me.'[44] There were other close political women friends of Michael who found Jill difficult to warm to. She was better liked in Ebbw Vale/Blaenau Gwent, Michael's constituency from 1960 to 1992, than she ever was in Devonport. Many criticized her after they married for not looking after Michael properly and for allowing him to go to work, even as a minister, scruffily dressed, with shabby suits or cardigans worn out at the elbows. But even in politics Jill could be an invaluable ally, smoothing Beaverbrook's feathers, rebuilding ties with Bevan after the clash of 1957, nurturing links with the labour movement across the spectrum in the troubles of the early eighties. The Labour Party cherishes its great partnerships – Sidney and Beatrice Webb, Douglas and Margaret Cole, the Callaghans, the Kinnocks, the Blairs. In this pantheon the touchingly loyal team of Michael and Jill may confidently be placed.

Foot came back post-haste to Plymouth at the end of 1944, urged to do so by Jill Craigie, who was waiting in the city for him. He was formally endorsed as candidate at Victory Hall, Keysham, on 8 June 1945. He warmed up with yet more abuse of Hore-Belisha, enquiring as to which party he thought he belonged. In the *Herald* he derided the term 'National' which was being appropriated by the Conservatives, and referred to 'the sheer native density of the Tory mind'. He ridiculed 'the antics of the Beaverbrooks and the Baxters, the Brackens and the Belishas – yes, and the Churchills', lumping together friends and foes new and old.[45] His *Herald* articles rammed his message home with the aid of old friends from the past – Hazlitt on Peterloo, Paine, Cobbett, the Chartists, the Tolpuddle Martyrs, Keir Hardie, Ben Tillett and Tom Mann, a legendary roll-call of all the saints who for their labours rest. Like other Labour candidates, he raged at the extraordinary campaign being conducted for the Tories by Beaverbrook and Bracken. The first radio election broadcast by Churchill, in which he compared Attlee and his colleagues to some kind of Gestapo, 'no doubt humanely administered in the first instance', seemed totally repulsive so soon after newsreels had appeared of the German concentration camps. Attlee won applause in saying that the voice was that of Churchill but the mind was that of Foot's former patron, Beaverbrook.

On the stump in Plymouth, Foot fought a fiercely socialist campaign. Inevitably he confined himself to his constituency, with the occasional foray to help Lucy Middleton, the Labour candidate in the neighbouring constituency of Plymouth Sutton. Housing and employment were perhaps the major issues. Foot pressed again the need for help for the Plymouth plan, and for financial aid from the Admiralty for an extension of the Devonport dockyard. He had powerful support from Aneurin Bevan at the Guildhall in Devonport. The Tories, Bevan declared, were only puppets of big business: 'I have seen their limbs twitch as the puppet-masters pull the string.' He called for the nationalization of coal, steel and the Bank of England. With reference to the Conservatives in the Lords, Bevan demanded, with rhetoric and reason, 'Why should we have to put up with this antediluvian chamber of pampered parasites?'[46] Foot himself, for all his neo-pacifist past, strongly upheld the need to refurbish the dockyard and strengthen the Royal Navy (cue for more references to the Spanish Armada and Drake's Drum).

The hapless Hore-Belisha was battered to the end. He was accused of failing to give the British Army proper equipment in Belgium in 1940, of having contemplated war with Russia, and of genuflection before Mussolini and also Franco. 'Where, oh where, is our wandering boy tonight?' speculated Foot.[47] Hore-Belisha's brief record as Minister for National Insurance was said to have included refusing full compensation for servicemen and their families, and the idea of family allowances. Credit for the invention of Belisha beacons was omitted. Michael was not the only Foot engaged in these polemics against an old adversary compared by Isaac Foot back in 1935 with Judas Iscariot. Not far away in Liskeard, Cornwall, brother John ('Major') Foot repeated, with even greater passion, Michael's points about the Mussolini medal and the vote against Churchill in 1942 that disfigured Hore-Belisha's past. He shouted at Hore-Belisha from the balcony of the Liskeard Liberal Club as he passed through the town centre a few yards away: 'Has such a reckless adventurer ever come into politics and public life who has had [sic] so much folly in such a short time? I hope my brother is going to do a very good job of clearing up and putting this man out of public life for ever.'[48] The family solidarity of the Foots took precedence over any thought of narrow partisanship.

The influence of Michael Foot and his works was also apparent in Labour's national campaign. Ernest Bevin and scores of other Labour candidates used 'guilty men' themes and vocabulary in attacking the Tories' pre-war record on foreign and defence policy, and drawing a distinction between Winston Churchill, the war leader, and the party which he was now leading in the election. Labour published a pamphlet on these lines entitled *The Guilty Party*, while the Conservatives' riposte, perhaps unwisely entitled *Guilty Men?*, which focused on such themes as Labour's pre-war opposition to conscription, tended to have its concluding question mark forgotten.[49]

On polling day, 5 July, the local Plymouth newspaper, the Conservative-inclined *Western Morning News*, forecast a five thousand majority for Hore-Belisha. It also prophesied that Isaac Foot would 'sweep' Tavistock and John Foot would carry Bodmin.[50] In the Foot household it was agreed that the three Liberals, including Dingle in Dundee, would all get home. The one member of the family who stood no chance at all, despite his plucky campaign, was Michael in his straight fight in Devonport. There followed an uneasy wait of three weeks while service votes were collected. On 26 July the dramatic news came through. The dams had broken. Labour had made over two hundred gains and won 393 seats, a landslide majority of more than 180 over the Tories. The great war leader, Churchill, had been cataclysmically overthrown by the almost anonymous Attlee, on whom Hore-Belisha had poured derision as Harold Laski's 'office-boy'. And Devonport had shared in this triumph, as had indeed the other two Plymouth constituencies. A brief tenure of Plymouth Drake in 1929–31 had been Labour's sole victory in the city before. Now Bert Medland, a retired civil servant who had been Labour's Mayor of Plymouth in 1935, won the Drake constituency, while Lucy Middleton, the wife of the long-term former party General Secretary whom Michael had met before the 1935 election, captured Sutton as well.

In Devonport Michael Foot had won on a 14 per cent swing, gained on a poll of 71.1 per cent, with 13,395 votes to Hore-Belisha's 11,382, a majority of 2,013, or 8.2 per cent. The election expenses showed how frugal the Labour campaign had been. Foot had just £30 of charged personal expenses, plus £23.18s.3d. for his agent. By contrast, the defeated Hore-Belisha ran up £148.7s. personal expenses and no less than £106.10s.10d. for his agent.[51] Contrary to forecasts, Michael was in fact the only Foot to be returned amidst a general Liberal collapse everywhere in the country. Isaac, now Lord Mayor of Plymouth, lost to the Tories in Tavistock by nearly six thousand. John trailed by over two thousand in Bodmin. Most stunning of all, Dingle came fifteen thousand votes behind the two Labour candidates (one being John Strachey) in the two-Member constituency of Dundee. In the *News Chronicle* Ian Mackay noted that Michael Foot was one of several Labour journalists elected, including J. P. W. Mallalieu, Maurice Webb, Haydn Davies, Garry Allighan, Hector McNeill, Tom Driberg, Vernon Bartlett and Konni Zilliacus, a new sociological trend.[52] After the Devonport result was declared there was mass public rejoicing around the Guildhall in Plymouth. Then Michael and his new love Jill more privately celebrated victory and the new dawn, political and personal, that it would surely bring.

His election to Parliament marked the climax of an extraordinary war for Michael Foot. It had made him a prominent editor, an instantly known countrywide campaigner and a nationally celebrated author.

Guilty Men had made him a celebrity of a kind while still in his late twenties. It attached the sheen of patriotism to his socialism. Some critics later surmised that he remained stuck in that war, eternally berating Chamberlain and his acolytes, celebrating El Alamein, Stalingrad and the invasion of Normandy, still holding fast to the values and ideas of that increasingly distant conflict. Memories of the Second World War, nourished more avidly in Britain than in any other combatant country, right down to the sixtieth anniversary of VE-Day in 2005, remained an essential framework for the sense of historic identity. They encouraged a vision of a dauntless island race standing alone while other, feebler Continental nations plunged into collaboration or collapse. The memory worked against the sense that Britain was part of Europe. It fostered a long-term anti-Germanism. But it was legitimate, too, to declare that the war had brought not only a great triumph for courage and perseverance, but also a great opportunity to avoid the betrayals of post-1918 which older men like Attlee, Bevin, Morrison and Cripps recalled all too well. After all, it was their victory, just as much as Churchill's. One government minister, the seventy-six-year-old Lord Addison, had actually been part of that earlier post-war government as Minister of Health, and was well aware of the broken pledges then which had led to his own eventual resignation from the Liberals to join the Labour Party.

For Michael Foot, for all his bewildering changes of outlook and occupation since his Oxford days, it was a thrilling moment, another 1789. As his old friend A. J. P. Taylor was memorably to write in the final sentence of *English History 1914–1945*, 'England had risen, just the same.'[53] In the columns of the press the new Michael Foot MP recalled the French socialist thinker Saint-Simon asking his servant to tell him every morning: 'Get up, M. le Comte, because you have great things to do.' It was a story he had picked up from one of his cherished books, Ignazio Silone's *School for Dictators*. Foot did not believe in servants, but the mood and the message were no less resonant, just the same.

4

LOYAL OPPOSITIONIST
(1945—1951)

Like the legendary shot fired at the bridge at Concord, Massachusetts, that heralded the American War of Independence, 'the Election rings around the World!', Foot excitedly told the readers of the *Daily Herald*.[1] Labour's socialist programme, as announced in the King's Speech, was 'the Boldest Adventure, the Greatest Crusade'. Labour had become the nation. Historical analogies with past revolutionaries from Cromwell to Garibaldi poured from his pen. In Westminster the new *soi-disant* revolutionaries, the 393 (shortly 394) Labour MPs, were sworn in immediately. Will Griffiths led a chorus of 'The Red Flag' in the Commons in which Foot joined enthusiastically. From the very start, dramatic events unfolded: the next four weeks saw the Potsdam conference, the dropping of atomic bombs on Hiroshima and Nagasaki, VJ-Day marking the end of the war in Japan on 15 August, the abrupt ending of Lend-Lease by the Americans on 21 August, the new committee on the use of atomic energy, all of them to colour Foot's views fundamentally for the remainder of his career. He felt thoroughly at home in his new surroundings. He enjoyed the buzz in the lobbies as a great progressive programme was launched – a National Health Service, nationalization of the mines, independence for India, all part of what the new Chancellor Hugh Dalton called 'the flowing tide' of socialism. Foot also liked the parliamentary atmosphere, the chatter and conspiracy in smoking room and tea room, the ready access to Fleet Street friends. He enjoyed too some of the extra-mural activities, especially the group of MPs who played chess. Leslie Hale was his favoured opponent. Foot was recognized as being amongst the best parliamentary players, though it was agreed that the strongest was Julius Silverman. Others of note were Douglas Jay, Reginald Paget, Maurice

Edelman and Maurice Orbach, with Jim Callaghan another, less talented, enthusiast. The world's dominant players were Russian, and Foot met several grandmasters when an international tournament was held in London in 1946.

Best of all, Foot made attractive new friends amongst the Labour backbenchers. All of them, predictably, were on the left, paid-up members of the awkward squad. Four were particularly important for him. Richard Crossman was a didactic former Oxford philosophy don who had written on Plato and Socrates. Foot first met him when Crossman arranged a social event at the Savoy Grill after Parliament assembled. It was Palestine that first drew them together, but they remained intellectual comrades from then on, even posthumously, when Foot was involved in the publication of Crossman's diaries. Another long-term ally was Ian Mikardo, a bright but prickly left-winger who, unusually for Labour, was a business consultant. He was of rabbinical Jewish background and had strong views on Palestine. It was he who had moved the famous Reading resolution committing the party firmly to wholesale nationalization at party conference in December 1944, when Foot first met him. Mikardo later described his friendship with Foot as 'one of the most precious things in my life'. Tom Driberg was an old colleague on Beaverbrook newspapers, writer of the 'William Hickey' column. Foot remained tolerant of his ex-Communism and particularly conspicuous homosexual exploits, which almost led to his prosecution, and reacted loyally when journalists asserted that Driberg had been a double agent, both for the KGB and MI5. There is no doubt that many of his contemporaries placed less trust in Driberg's character and reliability than Foot did.[2]

Perhaps Foot's most congenial friend was J. P. W. Mallalieu, commonly known as 'Curly', a man of many talents. He had been a fine sportsman at Cheltenham College and Oxford, and won a rugby blue as a stand-off half. He had an exciting war in the navy, and published a best-selling book about it, *Very Ordinary Seaman*. He wrote a financial column in the *New Statesman*, 'Other People's Money', and a weekly parliamentary sketch in *Tribune*. He became a great admirer of Nye Bevan, while his friendship with Foot was such that for a few months in 1953 Michael and Jill lived with him and his family. However, Mallalieu never supported CND, and actually became a navy minister under Harold Wilson in 1964, which put him beyond the pale for many on the left. Foot's memories of him, however, were always affectionate. As a sign of it he gave his daughter Ann (later Baroness) Mallalieu a present of a book on fox-hunting, a strong enthusiasm of hers even though Foot detested the pastime.[3]

These men found other left-wing comrades early on in the new Parliament. Others with whom Foot had close relations were Harold Davies, Leslie Hale, Stephen Swingler, Will Griffiths, Hugh Delargy and the playwright Benn Levy (along with his beautiful American actress wife, Constance Cummings). Along with them was a friend of far longer standing, Barbara Castle, in the House as MP for Blackburn and the only one of them who had a government job, as PPS for Cripps at the Board of Trade. In his memoirs Mikardo lists some others in their circle: the Australian lawyer and keen European federalist R. W. G. ('Kim') Mackay, George Wigg, Donald Bruce and Wing-Commander Ernest Millington, who had been returned as a Common Wealth candidate at the election but then joined Labour. Occasionally they were joined by mavericks like Woodrow Wyatt, or even figures on the party right like the independent-minded barrister R. T. Paget, who simply enjoyed their company on social grounds. In addition, there were one or two incorrigible rebels who flitted in and out but really pursued their own path, like Sydney Silverman, a disputatious Jewish lawyer, and S. O. Davies, ex-miner and Marxist Welsh national-ist who sat for Keir Hardie's old seat of Merthyr Tydfil and like him supported Welsh home rule. In 1946 came another maverick, Emrys Hughes, Keir Hardie's Welsh son-in-law who sat for South Ayrshire. He too was almost impossible to tie down.

This distinctly miscellaneous group of around twenty or so formed an identifiable collection of dissenters. Michael Foot was one of its most eminent members, and the most highly esteemed as a communicator. It is difficult to discern any wider influence on the labour movement. Only Crossman attempted to write a statement of political philosophy. Their socialism came across most clearly in their view of foreign policy. Most of them were middle-class journalists: trade unionists (other than members of the NUJ) were very rare. Until the growth of unrest over the anti-Soviet drift of Bevin's foreign policy the following spring, they were little more than just kindred souls, closet critics in the tea room and the bar. They all favoured strongly socialist policies at home, which meant planning, controls and an uncompromising programme of public ownership of the means of production and the redistribution of wealth. But in its first two years, the government itself seemed to pursue this policy with such zest that there was little to complain about. It was really in the more difficult period of Morrisonian 'consolidation' in 1948–50, when the nationalizations effectively came to an end, that complaints arose. Nor did Commonwealth or colonial policy generate any great dissent. The left could justify everything, from the transfer of power in India to an unsuccessful attempt to grow groundnuts in Tanganyika. The major areas of criticism almost entirely involved foreign relations, and were largely offshoots of the early stages of the Cold War. To this should be added concern over Palestine, since almost all of them were passionately pro-Jewish and totally opposed to Bevin's policy.

The members of the group were all instinctively oppositionists. Not one was seriously considered for government office, nor did they expect (or perhaps want) to be. Men like Mikardo or Driberg had backbench mindsets then and always. Until Bevan's resignation as Minister of Health in April 1951, their influence upon either government or party policy was minimal, and in inverse proportion to their prominence as journalists. To call them 'Labour's Conscience', as one text has done, seems remarkably inflated.[4] Foot himself, a highly individual journalist with a past record of campaigns for the Socialist League and employment by Lord Beaverbrook, was considered unreliable, a gadfly, a meteor, the ultimate symbol of a party of protest, not a party of power. His activity was largely focused outside Parliament. The prospect of front-bench status seemed at this stage quite bizarre.

These Labour MPs were soft left, but no more than that. With the possible exception of Geoffrey Bing, a barrister later to be Kwame Nkrumah's Attorney-General in Ghana, they all felt themselves to be located within the capacious reaches of the party's broad church – only just, in some cases. They were quite distinct from a much smaller, more extreme group – D. N. Pritt, John Platts-Mills, Konni Zilliacus, Leslie Solley and Lester Hutchinson (all later to be expelled from the party), along with William Warbey, Tom Braddock and Ronald Chamberlain. The French political commentator Bertrand de Jouvenel distinguished

in 1949 between what he curiously called 'the pacifist head' of Crossman and 'the Russophil head' of Zilliacus.[5] These hard-left dissentients,
consistently pro-Soviet and anti-American, were scarcely within the
Labour tabernacle at all. They tended to keep their own counsel. Their
role in the party was minute, though they could sometimes ally with
Foot's friends, as in the famous 'stab in the back' motion on foreign
affairs in November 1946 (see page 121). They might be joined also
by virtual pacifists like Rhys Davies or Reg Sorensen. But Foot's friends
were more in the mainstream. Foot himself, like Crossman, had always
been anti-Stalinist. He never took the sentimental view that 'left could
speak to left'. From 1948 his attitude towards the Soviet Union hard-
ened, as did that of Bevan. Foot and Crossman were foremost among
those inspired by the anti-Communist thrust of Arthur Koestler's *Darkness at Noon*, not to mention those famous tracts against totalitarianism,
especially *Nineteen Eighty-Four* and *Animal Farm*, written by the eminent recent *Tribune* columnist George Orwell. However blurred the
boundaries might be on the more sectarian left of the parliamentary
Labour Party, a fundamental divide between the future Bevanites and
Tribunites, and the fellow-travelling fringe, was always apparent. With
the two Communist MPs, William Gallacher and Philip Piratin, Foot
had almost nothing to do, although he retained his admiration for
Harry Pollitt, whom he considered a more considerable politician. He
always felt that Pollitt's return to Parliament for Rhondda West in 1945
(the Labour candidate, Mainwaring, beat him by just 972 votes) would
have been politically valuable.

Foot's contacts and manoeuvres in the new House were always
with other backbenchers. His links with government ministers were
mostly tenuous. He had scant enthusiasm for either Attlee or the Lord
President Herbert Morrison, and clearly underestimated them both.
The former he regarded as colourless and uninspired, and a wartime
advocate of coalitionism; Morrison he saw as just a machine man,
who wanted to curb backbenchers' independence – unfairly so, since
Morrison had shown much interest in ideas and policy-making before
the war. For Ernest Bevin, the new Foreign Secretary, Foot began
with a higher regard. Relations were sufficiently good for Bevin to ask
him to go on a fact-finding mission to Persia (Iran) in February 1946.
The purpose was to assess Russian infiltration in that country, from

which Russian and British troops were due to withdraw on 2 March (in fact the British had already left).There was also anxiety that the Russians were taking root in Persian Azerbaijan, through the Tudeh party. Foot's colleague was a Conservative ex-brigadier, Anthony Head, which led to predictable jokes about 'Head and Foot', and they had extensive talks with Tudeh leaders. Foot was convinced after this visit that there was abundant evidence for Soviet Russia's intended domination of Iran. He also wrote in the *Daily Herald* in somewhat prophetic terms about the dangers to Anglo-American oil, including the refinery at Abadan, and made many sensible suggestions about changing the relationship between the British heirs of imperialism and the Persian authorities. But Bevin took little interest, and nothing tangible resulted from what was Foot's one and only official activity on behalf of a British government until 1974.[6] But by the end of 1946, Bevin's robust confrontational stance with the Soviet Union, and even more his blatantly anti-Jewish policy in Palestine, had earned him Foot's anathema.

Nor was Foot in any sense a protégé of Hugh Dalton, the Chancellor of the Exchequer and patron of youth, as were centre-right figures like Gaitskell and Callaghan, along with Anthony Crosland and Denis Healey (neither yet an MP), to whom was added for a time Barbara Castle. In one rare exchange, Dalton wrote to rebuke Foot over factual inaccuracies in *Tribune* over the convertibility of sterling, with particular reference to the precise roles as advisers of Otto Niemeyer, Lord Catto and Wilfred Eady. Foot replied courteously, although he pressed the need for the Treasury to employ 'more socialist economists' to assist in 'carrying out a Socialist policy'.[7] The only one of the government's big five with whom he had ever been close was, of course, Sir Stafford Cripps, now President of the Board of Trade and eventually Chancellor of the Exchequer, but he had shed his links with *Tribune* and they seldom saw each other now. Cripps replied to a query from Foot about the Organization for European Economic Cooperation in 1948 in purely formal terms.[8]

Foot was close to no other minister, with the obvious and seminal exception of Aneurin Bevan. With Foot working closely with Jennie Lee on the editorial board of *Tribune*, he served as a permanent socialist sounding-board for Labour's Minister of Health as he pushed through the National Health Service. Their relationship became closer still after 1949, as Bevan found himself increasingly at odds with the drift of foreign and defence policy. Indeed, Foot, while increasingly critical of Attlee's government, found his special relationship with Bevan made this one aspect of his parliamentary role rewarding, as he pressed Bevan to challenge government policy. Jennie Lee by contrast found the entire experience between 1945 and 1951 frustrating and depressing.[9]

Foot later felt his speeches in the 1945–51 Parliament fell short of the highest standard. They were too complicated in structure, and perhaps too rhetorical. Sometimes the Oxford Union debates did not seem far away. He sounded more like a journalist in Parliament than a parliamentarian; his father was later to express concern on this point. But he began splendidly. His maiden speech, focusing on foreign policy, on 20 August 1945, was a clear success.[10] He complimented the King's Speech in characteristic terms: 'Oliver Cromwell could have hardly done a better job himself in the realm of foreign affairs.' He proceeded with Guilty Men-type attacks on Churchill and other leading Conservatives for their pre-war sympathies with Mussolini and Franco, along with right-wing monarchs like King George of the Hellenes. He declared that Britain enjoyed both a conception of political liberty denied to the Russians and a conception of economic liberty not shared by the Americans. This 'unique combination of treasures' gave it 'the commanding position of leadership if we choose to exercise it'. He wound up with a passionate affirmation of the socialist patriotism common at the time:

> At the end of this great war and after this great election, the British people can play as conspicuous a part before the gaze of all mankind as they played in 1940. Hitler has left behind his terrible legacies – racial hatred, love of violence, hunger, homelessness, famine and death. Surely it is the duty of our great country not to be content with some secondary role, but rather to seek the abatement of those evils by the assertion and example of a much more positive democracy. As we look out across this stricken Continent and as we see a new hope in the struggle to be born across this wilderness of shattered faiths, may it not be our destiny as the freest and most democratic and a socialist power to stand between the living and the dead and stay the flames?

The following speaker, the Conservative Ian Orr-Ewing, congratulated Foot in the customary fashion as 'the sole survivor of a family
which has been for many years represented in this House'. Back home,
Father Isaac wrote with paternal pride: 'Congratulations! I knew you
could do it. When people have said you had not the [parliamentary]
style I said to myself "Just you wait, my lads!" And now you've shown
the beggars.'[11] Journalists also gave Foot a good press. Even *The Times*
gave him some prominence.[12] The *New Statesman* commented that the
speech and its reception showed that 'the House still likes a first rate
verbal pamphleteer'. Hannen Swaffer observed that Foot spoke 'with
the vehemence of a Hyde Park orator', presumably meant as a compliment, while his colleague Tom Driberg, himself no great orator, wrote
in the *Sunday Express* that Foot was 'a little too platform but fiery and
fluent'.[13]

He made another major speech that autumn, on one of his special
themes, Germany – the destruction of its economy, the diminution of
its boundaries, the impoverishment of its people. The *leitmotiv* was
obviously the need not to repeat the errors of 1919. But what stamped
him as one of the awkward squad of the parliamentary left was the
famous vote against the terms of the American loan negotiated by
John Maynard Keynes with much difficulty.[14] There was criticism in
Cabinet both of the reduced amount of the loan, $4 billion, and the
commercial rate of interest attached to it. But most criticisms focused
on two other aspects. They were both part of what Keynes's biographer
Robert Skidelsky has shown was a calculated American attempt to
undermine Britain's financial predominance, with a dogmatic US
insistence on free-market arrangements and scant regard for Britain's
post-war difficulties which Keynes called 'an economic Dunkirk'. The
first of these two provisions was an insistence on an immediate multilateral liberalization of trade; the second was that sterling should become freely convertible into dollars, this to take effect in July 1947.
Emanuel Shinwell and Bevan had both fiercely attacked these proposals
in Cabinet on 5 December, but had been rebuffed.[15]

In the Commons, over seventy Conservatives voted against the
terms on 13 December: their most effective voice was Robert Boothby,
later Michael Foot's weekly sparring partner on television's *In the News*,
who called the loan 'an economic Munich'. They were joined by

twenty-three Labour rebels, nearly all on the soft left – Foot, Hugh Delargy, Barbara Castle, Benn Levy, Raymond Blackburn, W. G. Cove – along with some less likely rebels like Maurice Edelman and James Callaghan. Those on the furthest left like Konni Zilliacus, along with the two Communist MPs, Willie Gallacher and Phil Piratin, supported the government. Foot did not speak in the debate, but his general view emerged in *Tribune*.[16] He saw the terms of the loan as reflecting the advice of defeatist economists about a huge balance of payments deficit looming in 1946, and a victory for 'money power' which would prevent the payment of sterling debts to India, Egypt, Palestine and other colonized powers. Foot had no expertise in international finance (and he was hostile to the Bretton Woods agreement for international currency stabilization concluded with the US in 1944), but he felt instinctively that the loan was part of a long-term American strategy to destroy British independence in foreign as well as economic policy. He told Dalton of his total opposition to convertibility. Hard-headed economic historians have in the main endorsed the general line of his instinctive criticisms. The catastrophic convertibility of sterling in July–August 1947 lasted barely a month.

The vote against the US loan (which the government won easily) confirmed Foot's role as a critic. He spoke thereafter on domestic matters many times. On his home base, he dutifully paid due attention to the needs of Devonport and other dockyards, for all his frequent calls for cuts in arms spending. But he made most impact in the House on foreign policy issues. A central one throughout 1946–47 was the condition of Germany, made the more desperate by the forced immigration of hundreds of thousands of German refugees from eastern Europe. Here his closest associate was his old publisher, Victor Gollancz, whose compassion was moved by the starvation amongst the German population. He and Foot spoke at a mass meeting in the Albert Hall on 26 November 1945 to raise awareness of the plight of German children. Other speakers were Labour's Richard Stokes, Air Vice-Marshal Hugh Champion de Crespigny (who had almost won Newark for Labour in 1945), and Eleanor Rathbone and Sir Arthur Salter, both independents.[17] Foot also came together with Gollancz and Stokes to form the Save Europe Now (SEN) campaign; Bertrand Russell and Canon John Collins were amongst the other committee members, and Peggy Duff was secretary, so there was some overlap with CND later. Others prominent were Lord Lindsay, former Master of Balliol, and the Bishop of Chichester. The campaign went on for two years, attempting to persuade the government to encourage British citizens to either surrender some of their food coupons for the Germans or else send food parcels. SEN saw Foot at his most idealistic and far-sighted.[18]

In the House, he described how 'something like famine' prevailed in Germany, where food rations had fallen from the starvation level of 1,500 calories per day to as low as seven hundred. His solution for finding the relevant resources was to cease to pay for large occupying forces in Germany, and to make further arms reductions in the Middle and Far East. He pleaded for a discussion of the principles underlying British foreign policy. One ray of light was the compassionate, if short-lived, policy for social reconstruction of Lord Pakenham as Minister for Germany after 1945, which Foot saw as a kind of anticipation of the Marshall Plan. Foot's view of the German problem was a comprehensive one. He urged the need for a political reconstruction with decentralized institutions, but also warned of the long-term dangers of Germany's being divided into eastern and western zones. He warned against 'an anti-German mania' like the lunatic plan devised during the war by Sir Robert Vansittart of the Foreign Office for Germany to be reduced to a purely pastoral economy. On the other hand, like other British socialists he found it hard to make common cause with his comrades in the German Social Democratic Party, since their leader, Kurt Schumacher, demanded early German reunification and spoke in alarmingly nationalist terms, with frequent use of the word *Reich*. Not until 1949, with the impact of the Marshall Plan on its economy and a stable constitution, did West Germany progress, albeit under the long-term rule of Konrad Adenauer's right-wing Christian Democrats, and not under the still notionally Marxist SDP.

An even stronger concern in Foot's Commons speeches was the growing violence and political disintegration in Palestine. By 1946 the region was in near chaos. There was unending tension between Jews and Arabs; a mounting exodus of Jews to Palestine after the Holocaust, with US support, despite determined efforts by Bevin and the British government to prevent it; and open guerrilla warfare by Jewish paramilitary or terrorist groups, the Haganah and Irgun Zvei Leumi, against the British forces stationed in Palestine. They were reinforced by the violent Stern Gang. The destruction of the King David Hotel in Jerusalem by the Irgun on 22 July 1946, with the loss of ninety-one lives, caused an especial shock to a populace not inured to long-term terrorism.

As a pillar of the Palestine Committee, Michael Foot was among those who hoped that a potentially pro-Jewish Labour government would begin a new departure after the long saga of bitterness following the Balfour Declaration in 1917. But he was to be horrified by Bevin's policy. Britain's refusal to grant more than a minimum number of immigration visas (a mere 1,500 a month at first), the inhumane efforts to prevent the sailing of the *Exodus* in 1946 with its refugees from the prison camps, the refusal to contemplate a Jewish state, worst of all what seemed to be the blatant anti-Semitism of the British Foreign Office, caused immense shock. Foot's zeal for a state of Israel was reinforced by his renewal of contact with Arthur Koestler, who wrote that Foot was now 'very anti-Bolshie'; Foot helped Koestler by pressing the Home Office to speed up a visa for his aged Hungarian mother. He wrote frequently on Palestine in *Tribune*, and denounced Bevin for not admitting 100,000 Jewish displaced persons into Palestine immediately. Another strong influence was his new friend Richard Crossman. Previously pro-Arab and, by his own confession, anti-Semitic, Crossman's membership of an Anglo-American committee of inquiry into Palestine turned him into a fervent Zionist. It urged an immediate agreement to certificates for 100,000 Jewish immigrants: Bevin treated this with contempt, and in effect sought to continue the pre-war policy towards the Jews.

The names of Crossman and Foot were attached to a particularly effective thirty-two-page pamphlet for Gollancz in the autumn of 1946, *A Palestine Munich?*. In fact much of it, including the entire first section, was written by Arthur Koestler.[19] It detailed the restrictive immigration policy up to 1939 and the rise of Jewish and Arab resistance. The 1939 White Paper, calling for a future Arab Federation in Palestine with highly restricted Jewish immigration, was dismissed as a bribe to the Arabs to prevent their sympathizing with Germany. The pamphlet called for the government to allow full immigration of Jews up to the limit of Palestine's capacity to absorb them, and not to use force of arms to endorse what Labour ministers themselves had called a Palestine Munich. A promise of early independence to the Palestinian Arabs would mean 'an Anglo–Jewish war'. The booklet's political solution, in the absence of one being suggested from the Foreign Office, was a partitioned Palestine free of American military involvement, consisting of a 'Judean state' based on large-scale immigration, and an Arab state, with the central mountain region transferred to the Kingdom of Transjordan. At this point Britain would withdraw its forces, and self-interest would compel both the new Jewish and Arab states to collaborate and to come to terms with each other. It was the most cogent statement by pro-Jewish Labour representatives yet written, and it was predictably dismissed out of hand by all Arab representatives. Basically, it reflected Koestler's totally one-sided Jewish sympathies (he wrote in support of the Stern Gang's operations), and got nowhere. As it happened, Koestler greatly disliked Israel when he moved there, quarrelled with Prime Minister David Ben-Gurion and old friends like Teddy Kollek, and rapidly returned to Britain amidst acrimony all round.[20]

Through *Tribune*, and to a far lesser extent through his *Daily Herald* column (which usually was safely loyalist), Foot kept up his campaign on behalf of the Jews in 1947–48. The British government, in which the Colonial Secretary Arthur Creech-Jones was given the poisoned chalice of Palestine, offered no way forward. Creech-Jones's partition proposals collapsed; Bevin's proposal for five more years of British trusteeship offered nothing new; the United Nations came out with a scheme for immediate partition which Bevin promptly rejected. In the end the British government, harassed by the huge support costs of maintaining troops in Palestine, decided simply to pull its forces out, and withdrew them by 15 May 1948. Attlee quoted the precedent of the withdrawal from India. But there the British government had produced an agreed scheme for a political settlement that would follow. In Palestine there was none. The Foreign Office imagined that the various Arab armies would simply drive the Jews into the sea. The successful creation of the state of Israel in 1949 astonished everybody. Foot, of course, was delighted that a Jewish state had come into being against the odds. In an adjournment debate on 12 August 1947 he had called for the early withdrawal of British forces. The British people themselves were delighted to see their troops withdrawn from a violent land, but it was impossible to see the Palestine settlement as anything other than a shambles and a catastrophe. Foot might hope that the Jewish people would enter a more settled phase after August 1948. In fact, their tragedy was to haunt him and the world for the remainder of his life.

His main concern in *Tribune* columns and Commons speeches, though, was the deepening crisis in relations with Russia. Throughout 1946, especially in Germany, the eastern Mediterranean and the Middle East, the atmosphere seemed ever darker. Of all the commentators on the left, Michael Foot was one of the most outspoken in denouncing Russian policy in eastern Europe after the war. In the press he condemned Russia's intimidation of the socialists in Poland, its pressure upon Yugoslavia, its totalitarian control of eastern Germany.[21] Beyond Europe, his visit to Iran had convinced him of Russian dreams of domination in the Middle East as well. On the other hand, he shared the anxiety common on the left at the drift towards a full-scale military alliance with the United States. Churchill's 'iron curtain' speech at Fulton, Missouri, in March terrified him. Dissatisfaction with Bevin's policy built up amongst Labour MPs in 1946, and finally spilled over, with a critical letter sent to Attlee on 29 October by a group of twenty-one Labour backbenchers urging that a democratic socialist Britain ought to pursue a genuine 'middle way' between American 'free enterprise' and Russian totalitarianism. They were far from being a far-left caucus; they included Crossman, Foot, Levy and Silverman, but also Callaghan and Woodrow Wyatt. A few days later Crossman circulated an amendment to the Address which urged 'full Socialist planning and control' of the world's resources, and 'a democratic and constructive Socialist alternative to the otherwise inevitable conflict between American capitalism and Soviet Communism'. In the end, forty-three Labour MPs put their names to it; among them, in addition to Crossman, were Levy, Silverman and Michael Foot. The name of Jennie Lee, Bevan's wife, indicated that at least one Cabinet minister was unhappy too.[22]

Crossman moved his amendment on 18 November 1946, though he lessened its impact from the start by saying he would not call a division.[23] In sharp terms, he asked the government to reject proposals for an Anglo–American military alliance, and asked whether precise arrangements in terms of arms sharing and staff discussions were already under way. Since Bevin was away in New York, Attlee himself replied, mildly criticizing Crossman's speech as totally one-sided. Two Scottish ILP members mischievously moved Crossman's amendment to a vote, and the government won by 353 to 0, with several Labour abstentions, including Foot. But left-wing anxiety about British foreign policy moved onto a new stage two months later when the 'Truman doctrine' for US military aid to potential victims of Soviet aggression resulted in new American military involvement in Greece and Turkey. Talks at the Council of Foreign Ministers in New York had effectively broken down. Talk of a Cold War, an iron curtain and even a possible third world war became commonplace.

Michael Foot had taken little part in the Crossman amendment debate, and indeed had been under fire himself from the left for being too anti-Soviet in *Tribune*. He remained so in the *Daily Herald*, and satirized Molotov's plans for 'European confusion'.[24] But he also now became a leader of the most significant protest against government policy since the general election. Some left-wing MPs now began to meet regularly to prepare plans: led by Crossman, Foot and Mikardo, they also included Stephen Swingler, Harold Davies, Mallalieu, Benn Levy, Kim Mackay and Woodrow Wyatt. They met against a background of a serious fuel crisis in the severe winter of early 1947, and amidst fears that Labour's socialist advance was slowing down. The economic crisis of the summer of 1947 was another major factor. The outcome was *Keep Left*, a pamphlet which appeared in May 1947, in time for the party conference at Margate.[25] It was the product of a draft 'red paper' worked out with Foot and Mikardo at Richard Crossman's home at Radnage in Buckinghamshire. It included calls for more socialist planning in domestic policies, but what caught the imagination were the criticisms of foreign and defence policy, its call for Britain to stand aloof from confrontations between America and Russia, to withdraw its troops worldwide, and to demobilize rather than embark on conscription. Some of this was the work of Crossman, especially a chapter on 'The Job Abroad' and passages on international affairs more generally. But another key author was Michael Foot, whose contribution focused on the domestic economic scene, notably 'socialist planning'

Clockwise from top left Rebel in the making: the infant Michael.

The two Isaacs: Michael's father and grandfather at Lady Well House, Regent Street, Plymouth, 1902.

Pencrebar, near Callington, Cornwall, the Foot family home from 1927.

The seven Foot children: left to right, John, Michael, Christopher, Dingle, Sally, Hugh ('Mac') and Jennifer, c.1920.

The Leighton Park school first eleven, 1930, Michael standing, second from left.

Left Michael by the Thames as an undergraduate at Wadham, c.1932.

Above Michael and John Cripps, with two Smith College students, during their Oxford Union American debating tour, October 1934.

Michael as Labour candidate for Monmouth, November 1935.

Left Sir Stafford Cripps in Popular Front mode, 1935.

Below The Foot family in the late 1930s: *standing*, Christopher, Michael, Hugh, Dingle and John; *seated*, Sylvia (Hugh's wife), Anne (John's wife), Isaac, Eva, Sally and Dorothy (Dingle's wife).

Left Michael as assistant editor of the *Evening Standard*, with Dingle, Parliamentary Secretary to the Minister for Economic Warfare, 1941.

Relaxing with Bernard Shaw: Michael in his flat on Park Street, Mayfair, 1943.

Above Jill Craigie making the film *The Way we Live*, with Peter Watson, City Engineer and joint designer of the post-war plan for Plymouth, 1944.

Right 'A raging beauty thrust on susceptible wartime London': Jill around the time Michael met her.

Michael photographed by Jill in his Park Street flat, 1946.

Father and sons: *left to right*, Dingle, Hugh, Isaac, John, Michael and Christopher, at Pencrebar in the late 1940s.

and tighter controls on capital and labour. With his other outlets in the press, he was typecast as a symbol of Keep Left from then on.

Foot's viewpoint was an amalgam of socialism, patriotism and anti-militarism. Britain's international role would be the product of the success of its socialist achievement at home. It would offer moral leadership. Foot's answer to the problems of the world was a third force in which democratic socialist Britain would join with comrades in western Europe. Bevan had called for one during the war. It would stand apart equally from the military adventures of both the United States and the Soviet Union: 'The cause of British socialism and the cause of British independence and the cause of world sanity are indissolubly bound together.'[26] The extent to which Foot was identified with a version of a federal united Europe at this time is worth underlining. The later defender of British parliamentary sovereignty against the encroachments of Brussels was in 1946–48 advocating 'a United States of Europe'. It would build a customs union, and plan the coordination of heavy industries. Most of all, it would conduct its own foreign policy and support the Third World with development programmes, bulk commodity purchase and fair trade.

Foot was never a European federalist to the same degree as Kim Mackay, who was influenced by the constitutional arrangements of his native Australia. He cherished Parliament too much. His vision of western Europe was as a socialist-led Europe: the voice he usually quoted as representative of Continental Europe was the veteran French socialist leader Léon Blum. Along with Crossman, Mikardo and others on the left, Foot continued to champion European unity in this form – even though a major difficulty now was that the left in both France and Italy was preponderantly Communist. In May 1948 he was amongst those disciplined by Transport House for attending the founding conference for the Council of Europe at The Hague, where the main event was a visionary speech by Winston Churchill. A 'Europe Group' was formed amongst Labour MPs on 2 December 1946, with Kim Mackay as its chairman. Foot was amongst those, including Crossman, Mikardo, George Wigg and Barbara Castle, who joined in a second wave a few weeks later.[27] It conducted discussions on policy with the French and other socialist parties, and remained active until late 1949.

And yet, the impact of Keep Left was short-lived. At the Margate conference the government produced its own counter-pamphlet, *Cards on the Table* (actually written by Denis Healey of Transport House's international department). Ernest Bevin crushed his miscellaneous critics with an overwhelming conference speech in which he famously condemned the 'stab in the back' and the disloyalty of the Crossman amendment. Its author became widely known as 'double Crossman' from then on. In *Tribune* Foot was sceptical about Bevin's easy rhetorical triumph, and critical of the 'listlessness, almost indifference' of the debates on international affairs.[28] He listed key unanswered questions, notably 'What role are we to play as the foremost European power?'

But in fact it was events which finally undermined the socialist federal argument of Keep Left. Soon after party conference, the US Secretary of State George Marshall announced his famous plan for European economic recovery, his proposals initially covering the Soviet Union as well. Soon the Organization for European Economic Cooperation (OEEC) was working out schemes for the mobilization and distribution of aid in western Europe, to the huge advantage of the ailing British economy. The foreign policy of the Soviet Union became more and indefensible for a democratic socialist like Foot. He became a champion of anti-Communist dissidents in eastern Europe. He particularly admired Milovan Djilas's work of political theory *The New Class* (1957), and the Montenegrin intellectual was to be a guest in the Foots' Hampstead home on several occasions later. In April 1948 Foot argued strongly against the telegram sent to Pietro Nenni, signed initially by thirty-seven Labour MPs (fifteen of whom subsequently disavowed supporting it), backing his left-wing Italian Socialist Party, rather than the right-wing Saragat socialist grouping. Foot, never considered as a possible signatory on any of the lists of possible supporters, wrote in *Tribune* that the Nenni telegram was 'an act of sabotage against the declared policy of the party', and gave the impression that a large section of the Labour Party would welcome a Communist victory at the polls in Italy. Both as a libertarian and an admirer of Silone, Foot could never endorse such a policy. A hysterical letter of protest from the near-Communist Tom Braddock was ignored.[29] Other key events in 1948 which reinforced Foot's anti-Communism were successively the 'coup' in February which put Czechoslovakia under Soviet control, the schism with Tito in Yugoslavia (whom Foot solidly defended until his imprisonment of Djilas alienated him from the government of Belgrade) and, most decisively, the Soviet blockade of west Berlin in 1948–49: this last led even Aneurin Bevan to propose that Britain should send in tanks through the Soviet zone to bring in essential supplies. Foot in *Tribune* and in Parliament symbolized the new mood. He was particularly moved by events in Czechoslovakia; he had Czech socialist friends, and went with Crossman and Wigg on a mission to the country just after the Communist coup. In November 1948 Foot warmly applauded the election of Harry Truman as US President: he had no sympathy for the fellow-travelling left-wing challenge of Henry Wallace.[30] The creation of NATO, largely under Bevin's aegis, in the spring of 1949 was as warmly applauded by Foot in *Tribune* as by the party mainstream, and he publicly rebuked Mikardo for opposing it.[31] 'The Futility of Mr Priestley' ridiculed a future comrade in CND for regarding the USA and the Soviet Union as equally anti-democratic.

Many of the criticisms of Bevin's foreign policy from Foot and others were cogent and well-informed. But they are mainly important as anticipations of the later Bevanites. In the 1940s they struck many of the right notes at the wrong time. It was difficult to suggest an alternative foreign policy at a time when Stalin seemed so threatening and so obdurate. The era of post-Stalin 'peaceful existence' lay many years off. A socialist-led federal Europe was never more than a pipe-dream; the 'western union' which Britain did lead into being in the Brussels Treaty of March 1948 was limited and functional, geared heavily to defence issues, and in no sense a 'third force'.

These events left Michael Foot with a sense of frustration. Bevin's foreign policy showed 'a clean sheet of failure', yet there seemed no viable alternative. In practice, like his friends and colleagues Koestler and Orwell he trod the path of a regretful but firm anti-Communism. The Keep Left group re-formed (without Foot) in July 1949, and drew on the expertise of Oxford economists such as Thomas Balogh and David Worswick in producing the pamphlet *Keeping Left*, which twelve Labour MPs signed. But Keep Left had lost impetus, and tended to fragment. It was a highly miscellaneous group at the best of times. The effect of all this on the career of Michael Foot was mixed: because of his greater prominence and articulacy, involvement with the left tended to heighten suspicion of him in the party as irresponsible or disloyal. Some comrades did not like him anyway. Hugh Gaitskell, his later nemesis, writing after the Durham miners' gala in August 1948, found Foot 'rather strange. He never seems to talk except when making speeches, and was most silent and reserved all the time.' Jennie Lee, he added, was 'a very stupid woman'.[32]

And yet there is much to Foot's credit. On both Germany and Palestine he voiced an unpopular cause with a blend of idealism and hard fact. On the origins of the Cold War, without lapsing into what Marx called 'infantile leftism', he raised perfectly proper questions about the robotic confrontation into which Bevin was dragged at the Council of Foreign Ministers meetings in 1946–47. In questioning Soviet foreign policy, the extent to which it posed a military threat to the West and the viability of Britain's huge overseas commitments, his judgements became the conventional wisdom years later. Even at the time, they crystallized some of the discontent amongst the left-wing middle-class intelligentsia of which Tosco Fyvel wrote in *Tribune*.[33] At the very least, Foot was surely right in urging a debate on fundamental geopolitical principles. On Europe, his enthusiasm for closer union was part of a wider critique of British foreign policy, and his vision of a united Europe was distinctly vague. Even so, the European opportunity was an immense gap in Britain's world view after 1945. Some of the Labour left picked it up more rapidly than many on the right, such as Gaitskell with his uncritical Atlanticism.

The most tentative area of Foot's analysis of international relations, then and always, was his view of the United States. Unlike his father Isaac, who had been on an extensive morale-boosting lecture tour in 1943, Michael was no 'special relationship' man. He had relatively few close American contacts (though he had almost married one of them), and many of them were critics, like the venerable journalist Walter Lippman, the trade unionist Walter Reuther, or the left-wing humorous columnist Dorothy Parker. He was excited by New York City, but rarely visited America, and had limited appreciation of its history or geopolitics. He seldom reviewed books on American history after the time of Tom Paine. His view of America hovered somewhere midway between Henry Wallace and Harry Truman, as he veered between ideological suspicion of American capitalism and endorsement of the visionary Marshall Plan and the military necessity for NATO. Nye Bevan was much the same. But at least in 1945–51 Foot could explore a range of options for relations with the US, compared with the confrontational atmosphere of the fifties between East and West, over China and the bomb above all.

On domestic issues, Foot's Commons speeches followed a fairly unremarkable course in their calls for more socialism. He did not seem to specialize in any particular topic. However, there was one domestic theme on which he took the lead – the influence and political imbalance of the press. Here he was following the lead of his own union, the National Union of Journalists. He launched fierce attacks on the monopolistic right-wing proprietors who controlled at least 80 per cent of British newspapers. Lords Kemsley and Rothermere were his main targets, but Beaverbrook also, his once revered patron, did not escape his barbs. In July 1946 he joined over a hundred Labour MPs, several of them journalists, in asking for an inquiry into the 'monopolistic tendencies' in the British press. On 29 October he seconded a motion in the House by Haydn Davies calling for a Royal Commission on the concentration of ownership of newspapers. Almost ritualistically, he threw in personal abuse of key proprietors: he could not understand why the Attorney-General, Sir Hartley Shawcross, had apologized to them for using the term 'gutter press'.[34] As it happened, Foot was pushing an open door, since ministers as powerful as Dalton and Morrison lent their support, and a Royal Commission duly went about its work in 1947–49 under the erudite chairmanship of an Oxford classics don, Sir David Ross.

When Foot gave evidence before it on 12 November 1947 he attacked newspaper chains which were taking over local journals (including in Plymouth) and the interference of proprietors with editorial freedom.[35] His examples were drawn from his own experience under Beaverbrook. His most startling allegations concerned the 'blacklists' which Beaverbrook maintained, including the refusal to review plays by Noël Coward, concerts conducted by Sir Thomas Beecham or the film *Proud Valley*, which featured the left-wing black American baritone Paul Robeson. Kemsley, he said, also ran a blacklist – for a time none other than Beaverbrook himself was on it! In a second appearance before the inquiry on 18 December, he urged something like American anti-trust legislation to prevent multiple ownership, though this was opposed later by another witness, the American lawyer Morris L. Ernst (the father of Foot's former love Connie).[36] Foot gave a confident performance on both occasions, and dealt firmly with a somewhat patronizing enquiry from Lady Violet Bonham Carter. But, predictably, the Royal Commission's findings were mundane. They saw no danger in the concentration of press ownership, and proposed merely the weak option of a Press Council, run by the newspapers themselves, to consider complaints.[37] *Tribune* denounced the report as 'tepid and unimaginative', and the Press Council proved a frail reed over the decades. Aneurin Bevan, who had drifted away from his pre-war connection with Beaverbrook, was to denounce Britain's capitalist press as 'the most prostituted in the world'.

Foot's grievances against the Tory-run daily press continued to fester, not least with Express Newspapers, which pilloried the Labour government mercilessly. But if the Royal Commission had no major impact, his relations with Beaverbrook were certainly affected. The old press proprietor was evidently upset by Foot's attacks after their close relationship, even though his own evidence to the Royal Commission made almost no direct reference to it. Friends proposed a reconciliation, and Beaverbrook himself wrote to Foot expressing his sadness at their estrangement: 'The separation that has lasted too long has distressed me. The reunion will give me joy.' Foot accepted an invitation to a dinner in honour of the old man's seventieth birthday at the Savoy in early 1949. Invited to speak impromptu, he delighted Beaverbrook with a quotation about a venerable sage from Milton's *Paradise Lost*, which he then revealed referred to Beelzebub. This comparison seems to have been in Foot's mind for some time: in *Tribune* on 26 November 1948, 'Beelzebub Wants the Job' had compared Churchill to his infernal majesty.[38] At the Savoy, though, the magic of friendship was restored, the presence of Jill, whom the old man much liked, being a major contributory factor. Express Newspapers did not change its anti-socialist politics, and neither did Beaverbrook. But his affectionate relationship with Foot was henceforth unshakeable. In all the political crises of the fifties, Foot remained in the closest touch with his former employer, an almost filial and purely personal connection at a time when he was in the bitterest conflict with right-wing comrades in the Labour Party. Each materially helped the other. Beaverbrook helped *Tribune* with money, and would provide Michael and Jill with a temporary home. Foot was the vital link in introducing Beaverbrook to one of his closest friends, the Oxford historian A. J. P. Taylor.[39] And he virtually never attacked the Beaverbrook press again.

With his parliamentary career stuck on the backbenches, and many of his left-wing crusades running into the sand, Michael Foot's dominant interest in these post-war years lay in journalism. The distinguished labour correspondent Geoffrey Goodman, who first met him around 1950, felt that Foot was generally seen then as a pamphleteer and journalist rather than as an MP.[40] His natural milieu was having a drink and a gossip in a pub opposite the law courts with the Socialist Journalists group, including Ted and Barbara Castle, Ritchie Calder and Margaret Stewart of the *News Chronicle*. Younger journalists like Goodman, Mervyn Jones, Ian Aitken and Dick Clements were soon to join them. Foot still wrote for the *Herald* twice a week. One speciality here, as always, was fierce personal satire. In 1948, on lines similar to *Guilty Men*, he wrote a series of character sketches of 'People in Politics'. These turned out to be all Tories, and were nearly all unflattering – Lord Salisbury, Lord Woolton, Anthony Eden, Rab Butler, Oliver Stanley, Sir Waldron Smithers, Alan Lennox-Boyd, Oliver Lyttelton, Ralph Assheton, Harold Macmillan, Richard Law, W. S. Morrison, Lord Hinchingbrooke, Sir David Maxwell-Fyfe and Walter Elliot successively received unsparing attention. Woolton was ridiculed for the huge profits made by the Lewis's department store over which he presided. Of Eden, it was said that his 'polite' resignation from the Chamberlain government in 1938 'left not a ripple on the political waters'. Macmillan retained an Edwardian flourish, 'but the ardours of Young England have gone'. Lennox-Boyd was an imperialist supporter of Franco's fascist regime who was 'as unchanging as Stonehenge'. Most exotic of all was the far-right member for Orpington, Sir Waldron Smithers, 'our best preserved specimen of Neolithic man . . . No one would really be surprised if he turned up one day in goatskin and sandals.' The only one of Foot's victims to be accorded significant praise was Robert Boothby, who sailed piratically 'under the skull and crossbones'. Foot wondered why he remained a Tory at all.[41]

Invariably Foot's columns for Percy Cudlipp in the *Herald* were Labour orthodox in tone, and seldom rocked the boat. When in 1949 his column turned to a kind of 'Any Questions' format, his responses were mild enough. Some were of later interest. Thus on 21 January 1949 he committed himself to the view that 'The Labour Party does not believe in unilateral disarmament. It wants the other countries to agree to disarm but until that agreement is reached . . . it believes in maintaining adequate defence forces.'[42] Of course he was talking here of conventional forces, not the prospect of nuclear weapons. Still, later on a very different note was struck.

But it was in the columns of *Tribune* that Foot's talents expressed themselves most fully. He had been linked with the paper anew, through Bevan, when he left the *Standard* and joined the *Tribune* editorial board in 1945. He also became a director. The following year he shared the editorial role with Jon Kimche, but Kimche, after several rows with the board, was eventually dismissed following an unauthorized visit to Palestine. Foot then worked with Evelyn Anderson, a German Social Democrat, as co-editor. She was a woman of ability, but seemed obsessed with Russian perfidy in eastern Europe. With her limited understanding of the British Labour movement, she departed in 1948. Foot then became the senior editor himself, in partnership with Jennie Lee.[43] *Tribune* now became a more important component of the British weekly political press, and Foot's editorial role added to the mystique that had surrounded him since *Guilty Men*. *Tribune* had always been a struggling publication. It had no money, and sales, at perhaps ten thousand copies (so far as the facts could be uncovered), were disappointing under both Kimche and Anderson. What it did have was Michael, charismatic and irreplaceable. From his paper-strewn office at 222 The Strand, he did everything on the newspaper. Keir Hardie had been similarly omnicompetent when he founded and edited the old ILP newspaper, the *Labour Leader*, in 1894. He not only wrote major articles on long, stuffy train journeys, but also the women's column under the name of 'Lily Bell' and even children's stories – 'Donald the Pit Pony', for instance.[44] Foot, also an MP, was more active still. His business manager, Peggy Duff, called him, affectionately enough, 'the great panjandrum, the Beaverbrook of *Tribune*'.[45] With his Express Newspapers background, he took a close interest in the technicalities of typesetting. He was also much involved in the strategy of marketing and distribution, an important matter, because large bookshop chains like W. H. Smith refused to sell so left-wing a publication. Robert Edwards gives a memorable portrait of Foot at that time, suffering from insomnia and asthma, scratching his blistered wrists, yawning and smoking almost simultaneously. Enveloped in the debris and the stench of up to seventy daily Woodbines, he seemed almost tormented, older than his thirty-odd years.[46] Yet he was also inspirational to all who worked with him.

Most crucial of all, he was indefatigable in raising money, including from his own somewhat limited resources. He could not now turn to senior colleagues like Cripps, Bevan or George Strauss, because they were all Cabinet ministers. He got help from sympathetic capitalists, from Jack Hilton, from the Sieffs of Marks & Spencer (for his staunch support for Israel), from the accountant and Labour MP John Diamond, and increasingly from Howard Samuel, property developer and head of the publishing firm MacGibbon & Kee.

He spread his net more widely still. In the 'Lower than Kemsley' libel case resulting from a fierce attack on the press baron Lord Kemsley in 1950, not only *Tribune* but its directors personally, including Foot and Jennie Lee, were threatened with bankruptcy. This followed the issue of *Tribune* published on 2 March 1950, which fiercely attacked the *Evening Standard*'s editor Herbert Gunn for scandalously suggesting a link between Klaus Emil Fuchs, the atomic bomb spy, and the Minister of Food John Strachey, a former Communist. Foot headed the article 'Lower than Kemsley', an echo of Bevan's 'lower than vermin' attack on the Tories in 1948 and directed against the owner of the *Daily Mail*, a particular *bête noire* of Foot's. *Tribune*, among other insults, spoke of journalists 'watching without shame or protest the prostitution of their trade'. But he would find essential help of £3,000 in fighting the case from Lord Beaverbrook (the owner of the *Standard*, of course), due in large measure to the personal influence of Jill with his old boss. Even so, it was a financial mercy that in 1952 Foot and *Tribune* eventually won the day in the House of Lords.[47]

Foot took his responsibility for what was a small, struggling newspaper very seriously. He venerated the craft of political journalism: Dean Swift, the nemesis of the Duke of Marlborough in 1711, was a model from the past here. In the more recent tradition of Labour journalism he had two particular inspirations. One was Robert Blatchford of the *Clarion* (and the Clarion vans which sold it), always a hero despite his fiercely pro-war nationalism both during the Boer War and in August 1914. Foot not only revered him as an editor and writer, but also honoured him in his lesser-known role as a literary critic. The other was George Lansbury's brilliant *Daily Herald* in its first incarnation before 1914, which featured some of the most celebrated of writers, including Shaw, Wells and Hilaire Belloc, along with the matchless cartoons of the Australian Will Dyson. Foot had a special admiration for Lansbury's achievements at the *Herald*, where he acted at one time both as chairman of the board of directors and as editor, given that he had no training as a journalist at all. At the present time, Kingsley Martin's *New Statesman* was a yardstick – but also a competitor. Like Blatchford at the *Clarion*, Foot wanted *Tribune* to be well-written, punchy in style, and to a degree fun to read. He hoped to emulate the back half of the *New Statesman*, directed by its brilliant literary editor V. S. Pritchett. So he had on his staff some highly literate and intellectual colleagues. A star associate was George Orwell, who served as literary editor for a while and wrote a famously anarchic column, 'As I Please', for some time after the war, along with many other miscellaneous columns and reviews. There were also Tosco Fyvel, Orwell's successor as literary editor, and the drama critic Kenneth Bruce Bain, who wrote under the name of Richard Findlater. Soon talented young political journalists were to come in, Robert Edwards and later an industrial relations specialist, Ian Aitken. Another young recruit, who joined the newspaper as a secretary after the 1950 election, was a Cambridge graduate, Elizabeth Thomas. At first she found it difficult to establish a settled relationship with Foot, who seemed shy and nervy, while his incessant smoking was off-putting. But she persevered, worked closely with him on all issues, rose to become literary editor of *Tribune* some years later, and began a close friendship that lasted well over half a century.[48] This unusual, gifted man, often distant in manner, with an awkward tendency to call women, even Jill, 'my dear child', had also a charm and a cultural dynamism which Elizabeth found magnetic. Women frequently did.

In 1948 and 1949 *Tribune* under Foot's editorship kept up its robust commentary on domestic issues. But in general, with an election approaching, it was supportive of the government in its editorial comment. This aroused some anger among MPs of the further left. Tom Braddock accused the journal of currying favour with those in high places (unspecified), while Konni Zilliacus attacked it, only to be denounced for his 'host of delusions' in return.[49] *Tribune*'s columns featured several articles by Roy Jenkins, a young MP elected in a by-election for Southwark in 1948, praising the government's economic performance, especially the buoyancy of exports to dollar areas (a yearly rate of £234 million for 1948 was quoted, as against £164 million in 1947). When Cripps was forced to devalue the pound in September 1949, Foot in *Tribune* staunchly defended the decision as a progressive alternative to Tory policies of wage-cutting, although he acknowledged that its success depended on 'the understanding and self-discipline' of the workers. Evidently there were divided counsels on the paper's editorial board here, since Ian Mikardo expressed doubts on devaluing the pound unless it was accompanied by other policies, notably severe cuts in military expenditure.[50] But *Tribune* felt that things were going so well at home – with the buoyant effect of devaluing the pound, and iron and steel nationalization carrying on the tide of public ownership – that a general election could have been called in 1949. Attlee's decision to soldier on was, however, accepted amiably enough.

In its views of foreign policy, *Tribune* at this time was even more loyalist. It was fiercely critical of Soviet policy throughout, especially the blockade of west Berlin, and scornful of fellow-travellers. The views once linked with 'Keep Left' disappeared from its pages. Crossman was moved to declare that Ernest Bevin's policies, Palestine excepted, were indistinguishable from those of the parliamentary left. There were good reasons for *Tribune* being especially loyalist at this time, apart from the turn of current events. With the paper in constant financial difficulties, Foot persuaded the Labour Party General Secretary, Morgan Phillips, to buy space for official party propaganda: this helped with the accounts.[51] The 'Labour Party Pages' were uncommonly boring, but they did seem to locate *Tribune* in or near the party mainstream. In December 1949 Foot asked Phillips for a larger grant, since *Tribune* needed to raise its circulation by four to five thousand, but without success.[52]

Foot was to a degree part of the party establishment himself now, since he sat on the National Executive Committee. After being runner-up in the constituency section elections previously, he was comfortably elected in 1948, displacing a minister, Philip Noel-Baker. In 1949 he came second of the seven elected. Many awkward issues came up on the NEC, especially the party decision to expel a handful of far-left MPs. Foot was never one of life's witch-hunters, and he supported Bevan on the NEC in April 1949 in urging that Konni Zilliacus's expulsion be rescinded to give him a chance to state that he would support party policy. But Bevan's arguments were basically concerned with procedure, and he made no complaint when Sam Watson's motion to reaffirm the expulsion of both Zilliacus and Leslie Solley was comfortably carried. In fact Bevan later wrote to the Welsh transport workers' leader Huw T. Edwards that he fully backed the removal of Zilliacus 'because of his close associations abroad with the enemies of Labour and Social Democracy'. He had 'passed beyond the bounds of all reasonable toleration'.[53] There is no evidence that his good friend Michael Foot dissented from this tough view. There was one great joy for him while on the NEC. In 1949 he went on a party deputation to Rome, and met for the first time one of his great literary heroes, the socialist novelist Ignazio Silone, who delighted him by criticizing the Labour government for being 'too nervous'.[54] But otherwise Foot's short period on the NEC was, on balance, not a happy one. There was a cantankerous atmosphere, with trade union representatives hostile to middle-class socialist ideologues. Some in the women's section of the NEC were notably aggressive, especially Edith Summerskill and Bessie Braddock. Foot himself largely stood alone as a symbol of left opinion in the constituency parties, although Tom Driberg did join him in 1949. He left the NEC in 1950 with some relief, and stayed away for over twenty years; it was only when several leading Bevanites came on in the fifties that it seemed to him a worthwhile body.

The latter stages of this Parliament found Foot dissatisfied with his public life on various fronts. He was well-known as a nationwide campaigner and stump orator at miners' galas and the like. But his speeches in the Commons were making limited impact, and the front bench paid them little attention. The NEC was mostly a chore and a bore. His *Tribune*, with barely ten thousand people buying it, always seemed to be struggling: the next spring the 'Lower than Kemsley' libel case produced a crisis which could have been terminal.

But, more positively, his private life was now settled and happy. He looked older and his health was far from perfect. But the asthma was under control, while a medical treatment recommended by Bevan, the Minister of Health after all, would in time remove the eczema that plagued him. He and Jill were now in a strong, enduring relationship, though the puritanical standards of the day meant that they could not really live together. Jill lived in Hollyberry House in Hampstead, Michael in his 'chaste' top-floor flat in 62 Park Street, Mayfair.[55] They had to threaten with reprisals in the press about the private life of his employer a journalist who saw them together in 1948 in a hotel in Nice where they had spent a 'honeymoon' in July 1946. They got married on Trafalgar Day, 21 October 1949, in Hampstead registry office. Isaac Foot and Paul Reilly (now with the Council for Industrial Design) were the witnesses. Isaac was someone for whom Jill had real affection, and she handled him with much sensitivity. After their marriage she reassured him about Michael's appearance: 'He has had his hair cut you will be pleased to hear and he looks very neat and tidy so that everyone at the House is now teasing him about it.' This metamorphosis was not to last long. The West Country press reported that Foot's bride was 'a talented film producer'. Foot added that she was 'a keen Socialist'.[56] Jill had continued to be professionally very active, making a documentary film for UNESCO and working for radio. Her documentary on the rebuilding of Plymouth, *The Way we Live*, was shown at the Cannes film festival in 1946. Perhaps her main achievement was *Blue Scar*, a film about the nationalization of the mines set in Abergwynfi in south Wales, and shown in 1949. It was not successful commercially, and was too sentimental and perhaps too uncritical about a community for which she had intense admiration. A historian of Welsh film saw it as blighted by class stereotypes and some ambivalence about the mining community after nationalization.[57] But, he added, 'there is no doubt that Craigie was happiest when working on location in South Wales'. It began her love affair with the valleys, which helped with the transition to Ebbw Vale later on.

Jill fitted in happily enough with Michael's parliamentary activities;

she hugely admired Nye Bevan, but had a predictably awkward relationship with Barbara Castle. She was marvellous with Beaverbrook. She was also devotedly supportive of her husband, and kept up his spirits in the course of the 'Lower than Kemsley' libel case when there was a real prospect of their facing financial catastrophe. She was a sparkling hostess at her dinner parties, to which artists, actors and film-makers would be invited. She also enjoyed going to politicians' social gatherings. Whether others always enjoyed her presence is questionable. One who must have had reservations was Harold Wilson, President of the Board of Trade, whom Jill always made a point of nagging mercilessly at parties about the government's failure to do more for the British film industry.[58] The Foots' now had a home together for the first time, 33 Rosslyn Hill, Hampstead, a terrace house leased from the Ecclesiastical Commissioners, a mile or so from the Heath. It was a small household, just Michael, Jill and her teenage daughter Julie, who viewed Michael for some time with a certain coolness. One decisive personal decision was taken when Jill became pregnant. They decided on a private abortion, since neither of them felt able to make the commitment of time and energy necessary to a small child. Like many of their friends on the left – the Bevans, the Castles, Driberg and others – the Foot blood family thus remained childless.

The other vital aspect of Foot's private life was his ties with his family. A major blow came in May 1946 when his mother Eva, at sixty-eight years of age, suddenly died of a heart attack in East Grinstead hospital. Isaac learnt of the news while on a train which stopped specially for him at Reading station. At a simple funeral service on 17 May the assembled Foot family sang her favourite hymn, 'For all the saints who from their labours rest'. Michael, more than most of the family, felt the loss of his mother keenly. He had always found her warm, tolerant and understanding, not least for the famous Cornish pasty she sent to Devonport during the 1945 election. But Isaac himself continued a robust and active life, to Michael's joy. In February 1949 Michael sent him a cheerful telegram after his vigorous defence of Cromwell in the press to rebut sharp criticisms of the Protector by the Bishop of London: 'Hazlitt applauds, Swift rejoices, even the martyred Marat finds comfort for his wounds. Michael and Jill.' More practically, in 1948 Michael had to have Isaac to provide financial security when, not for the first time, he had to dip into his own reserves to cover debts incurred by *Tribune*.[59]

At the end of 1949 Michael found himself travelling down to Devon for the unexpected second marriage of his father to his house-keeper, Kitty Dawe, a widow from Liskeard. She did not share either Isaac's literary or political interests, and found his bibliomania hard to reconcile with her view of house and home. But they lived together harmoniously enough. Inevitably, the various Foot brothers and sisters were going their separate ways, yet the family was still an instinctively close one, with its familiar watchwords like 'pit and rock'. Michael's strongest relationships appear to have been with his brother John, still a Liberal and a parliamentary candidate, and his sister Sally with her love of poetry, horses and the countryside. But all the Foots kept in touch with one another. Newspaper photographs showed Isaac, Dingle, Hugh, John and Michael (and sometimes Christopher) watching the ancestral team, Plymouth Argyle, at Home Park. Their expressions suggest that home defeats were not unknown.

In 1950 Michael faced a major political challenge in defending his Devonport seat, won against the odds from the Tories in 1945. The prospects were still unpredictable. One factor was that the 1949 redistribution had cut down the Plymouth seats from three to two, Devonport and Sutton. On balance, perhaps Labour's position in Devonport had been marginally improved. The Drake constituency had been abolished, and its former Labour Member, H. M. Medland, was to serve as Foot's election strategist.[60] Michael Foot had been a good, conscientious constituency member; he had worked hard on conditions in the dockyards, especially the working of the 1947 Dock Labour Scheme, which ended the casualization of labour, and felt optimistic.

He had been preparing for the general election in a more general context. In *Tribune* he had pressed for an election long before Attlee finally called one for February 1950. Also, with Donald Bruce, a left-wing accountant who served as Bevan's PPS at the Department of Health, he had written what was in effect a pre-election tract, published again by Gollancz in the usual 'yellow peril' jacket. It was entitled *Who are the Patriots?*: in reply it provoked a counter tract, *Patriots? My Foot!* by a far-right Scottish Catholic journalist, Colm Brogan, the brother of a famous Liberal professor and radio personality. One of Brogan's specialities was anti-Semitism: he almost suggested that Labour, with all its Jewish MPs, was not a British party at all.[61]

The Foot–Bruce booklet's 115 pages were unremittingly partisan, but also highly effective. While Donald Bruce supplied much of the hard data on economic and social policy, the entire work bears the imprint of Michael Foot on every page. The Foreword emphasized that 'the Guilty Men are Still at Large'. *Who are the Patriots?* then followed what Foot later called the Bevan maxim for debate – 'Seize the enemy's stronghold; capture that and all other outposts will fall in the same assault.'[62] The facts were marshalled economically, stylishly and with a sense of history, and the pamphlet ended with a visionary conclusion ('The Revolution must go on'). There are touches even closer to Foot's enthusiasms. The dedication is to Benjamin Disraeli, a confirmed hero of his, 'who wouldn't have stood for this Tory gang at any price'; quotations from *Coningsby* and others of his novels are sprinkled throughout. Special attention is also paid to the Tory press, not excluding Beaverbrook, who is pilloried for seeing R. A. Butler's Industrial Charter as 'another variation of the old planned economy of the Socialists'.[63] This was written just before Foot's reconciliation with his old master at the Savoy in early 1949. Churchill, an earlier hero in wartime days, is repeatedly condemned for reactionary attitudes. Often at this period Foot was busy cutting Winston down to size. In *Tribune* on 8 October 1948 he dealt fiercely with *Gathering Storm*, the first volume of Churchill's history of the Second World War, in a book review. Sharp and accurate comments were made on Churchill's distortions of fact, including his own role as an appeaser towards Mussolini and Franco. Remarkably, Foot compared Churchill's 'personal conceit and arrogance' to Hitler's in *Mein Kampf*.[64] *Who are the Patriots?* is a powerful document to appeal to the converted, but was inevitably of short-term impact. Since there was in fact no election in 1949 it sold poorly. Gollancz had had a print run of only five thousand at first, and paid a meagre royalty. Foot did not mention it later in his *Who's Who* entry.

Attlee called a general election unexpectedly for 23 February 1950; the reason, apparently, was the moral repugnance of the Chancellor, Sir Stafford Cripps, towards having a pre-election budget to bribe the voters. The campaign was tranquil, even dull; no particular scares or 'stunts' materialized. The Conservatives made what they could of unsuccessful development plans like those for groundnuts in Tanganyika and Gambia eggs as instances of Labour's socialist extravagance with public money; Labour linked the Tories with responsibility for pre-war mass unemployment and reminded the electorate that they had voted against the National Health Service. But it was also a tense, grand confrontation between Attlee and Churchill. Almost the last pre-television election, it marked the climax of two-party politics, with high political consciousness and the public well aware of their class polarization. Men and women readily identified themselves as working- or middle-class; almost three-quarters of the electors placed themselves in the former category. The election was evolutionary Britain's version of a class war. Despite years of rationing and austerity, enthusiasm was still high amongst natural Labour supporters, and no by-election had been lost by the government in the entire 1945–50 Parliament, an astonishing record. Full employment, a welfare state, 'fair shares' were all hugely appreciated. On the other hand, the collectivist mood (with attendant high personal taxation) had waned since 1945. A growing consumerist ethic gave impetus to Churchill's appeal to 'set the people free', contrasting the Tory ladder with the Labour queue. Opinion polls had shown voters swinging against the government in the wake of rationing, austerity and scarcity of basic commodities, including food. In addition, the redistribution of constituencies seemed likely, in effect, to give the Conservatives many extra seats, while huge Labour majorities piled up mountains of 'wasted votes' in mining and other industrial areas. Devonport was, after redistribution, the largest seat in the west of England, with almost seventy thousand voters.

Media attention was riveted by Devonport, largely because of the candidates. Foot was a Labour star throughout the media, and shortly on television too. His opponent was even more of a celebrity, none other than Randolph Churchill, erratic and often alcoholic son of the Conservative leader. As it happened, he and Foot knew each other well from weekends with Beaverbrook at Cherkley, and enjoyed a good relationship. In the election campaign Foot and Churchill hurled invective and personal abuse at each other. Notes for one of Foot's speeches show him describing Randolph Churchill as 'a throwback to the nineteenth century. He thinks that politics is a matter of stunts, scares, handshakes and synthetic smiles for the ladies.' But they remained remarkably friendly – far more so than were Churchill and the local Conservative Party, who found their candidate difficult and tetchy. A remarkable sight at the end of some days was Churchill being dumped on his own by his party workers, perhaps in some rural backwater, and then being taken up by the Labour candidate and Jill for a fraternal evening drink. Sometimes the Labour candidate and his wife would see the Conservative candidate safely on his train.[65] There was also a Liberal candidate, A. C. Cann, who was distinctly embarrassed when evidence was produced of a former association with the British Union of Fascists. Like his party, he was no threat.

The campaign attracted many celebrities. Winston Churchill spoke on behalf of his son early on at the Forum cinema in Devonport. Bevan spoke for Foot to an immense audience the same evening. It was an extraordinary performance, an eighty-minute display of rhetoric and logic without notes: Foot's life of Bevan later recaptured its inspirational quality.[66] A more unexpected supporting speaker for Foot was Herbert Morrison, one of his *bêtes noires*. He amiably observed that 'Michael Foot has been a good and lively member of the House, particularly happy when he was knocking the Tories about,' and hailed him as a 'great journalist and pamphleteer'.[67] Foot's speeches focused almost entirely on domestic issues – health, education, employment and housing – where Labour felt it was on firm ground. He strongly endorsed Lewis Silkin's Town and Country Planning Bill of 1947, which gave local authorities enhanced powers over the environment and future development. He had hailed it in the *Daily Herald* at the time as 'the Plymouth Resurrection Bill' which had brought new hope to the blitzed cities of England. A tricky point was that on education he had to declare his friendliness towards Catholic schools in working-class communities. One of his supporting speakers, unusually for those days, was his wife Jill: this produced a sharp exchange with the *Daily Express* about 'an eve of the poll stunt'.[68] As before, John Foot, again fighting Bodmin as a Liberal candidate, weighed in with support for his socialist brother. The result showed that Randolph Churchill had been a less effective opponent than Hore-Belisha in 1945. Foot polled 30,812 to Churchill's 27,329, a majority of 3,483, compared with

2,013 in 1945. There was a 2.5 per cent swing from Labour to the Conservatives nationally. Foot in Plymouth, on a poll of around 80 per cent, thus did better than his party, though he may have benefited from Cann, the ex-Tory Liberal candidate who polled 2,766 votes, probably mainly from the Conservatives. But, with some losses in middle-class constituencies in the south-east among voters fed up with austerity and controls, Labour nationally only scraped home with a majority of six, with 315 MPs against 298 Conservatives and allies, nine Liberals and two Irish nationalists. Labour had polled significantly more votes than the Tories – 13,266,176 (46.1 per cent) against 12,492,404 (43.5). But the voting system was balanced against them, while redistribution may have cost Labour sixty seats. What it meant for someone like Foot was that, with so tiny a majority and the prospect of another election very soon, there was a premium on loyalty, and the need at all costs to avoid splits in the party.

This was broadly reflected in Foot's writings in the months after the election. In the face of ferocious Tory 'harrying' in the Commons and a sustained campaign by the Tory press, including Express Newspapers, Labour put on a strong show of unity, even fraternity. This was shown at a conference of Cabinet, NEC and trade union leaders at Beatrice Webb House, Dorking, on 20–21 May.[69] Here virtually every speaker, even Aneurin Bevan, endorsed a version of Morrisonian 'consolidation' on domestic policy. The existing nationalizations should be made to work better before the principle was extended. Foot, present as a member of the NEC, introduced a little ginger of his own in criticizing the inadequacy of Morrison's definition of socialism, but he did not seriously diverge from the consensus. His later view was that 'Dorking ended in deadlock and Morrison turned, as was his custom, to renew the contest elsewhere.'[70] But most of the others felt more positive. Foot himself kept up a campaign to capture new ideological ground. His advice in *Tribune* on 'How to win the next election' consisted of the reassertion of socialist principle over nationalization and a free health service.[71] Morrison was chided for wanting to stand pat on past achievements rather than pressing on with nationalizing steel, ship-building or chemicals, and for soft-pedalling the egalitarian ideals that underlay the case for socialism. But these were contributions to party debate, not threats of revolt.

Tribune, in constant financial trouble, changed its strategy as the voice of socialism in September 1950, when it was forced to go fortnightly instead of weekly, alongside publishing a series of five pamphlets. Foot wrote two of these. *Still at Large* was a series of satirical portraits on 'Guilty Men' lines, prefaced by a two-page summary of the history of England from the 1381 Peasants' Revolt onwards. *Full Speed Ahead* appeared under the name of Saint-Just, a French revolutionary. Yet these tracts were perfectly compatible with mainstream policy, and need not have alarmed the apparatchiks. One particularly might have been acceptable in Transport House, *Fair Shares for the Rich*, written by none other than Roy Jenkins. When Morgan Phillips, the party's General Secretary, judged that Methodism should be placed far above Marx in the making of British socialism, *Tribune* mildly demurred. Yet Michael Foot, reared in Wesleyanism in the chapels of south Devon, could hardly complain at due honour being granted to Methodism. There was more criticism of the TUC for rejecting a wages policy. It was illogical to plan everything else and leave wages untouched.[72] Barbara Castle would echo this view in 1969, but without Foot's support.

In foreign policy too, Foot remained publicly well within the fold. The greatest challenge of all came with the North Korean invasion of South Korea in late June 1950. Here was a dangerous international crisis. Yet *Tribune* came down strongly in favour of defending South Korea against attack and supporting the United Nations in sending troops to do so, largely American forces under General Douglas MacArthur.[73] The sending of British troops to Korea was also endorsed since they had UN backing. Constantly Foot is urging comrades about the folly of appeasing aggressors, or the sentimental errors into which they fell in the 1930s.[74] Most of the other members of the Keep Left group took the same view, though Ian Mikardo strongly dissented and resigned as a director of *Tribune*. A small minority of far-left MPs such as Sydney Silverman and S. O. Davies, who criticized UN action, were fiercely attacked. 'The aggression of the North Koreans was and remains an international crime of the first order,' wrote Foot; for them to equate the American government with the Kremlin was absurd.[75] At home, Labour's policy of planning, public ownership and redistribution would ensure that Britain could cope with the economic strain of further rearmament. Collective security and democratic socialism could proceed side by side. Labour's party conference in October used the union block vote to defeat a left-wing motion criticizing Bevin's foreign policy by 4,861,000 to 881,000. The star of the show was Nye Bevan, with a passionate plea for party unity.

Labour Party apparatchiks felt they could still live with, and cope with, Michael Foot. He embarked on a new venture from August 1950, when he first appeared on television in the BBC weekly political debates series *In the News*, with the Conservative Bob Boothby, the former independent MP W. J. Brown and soon the Oxford historian A. J. P. Taylor as the most regular fellow members of the team, and Edgar Lustgarten in the chair. They were convivial occasions, with lavish hospitality from the BBC, an initial gathering at the Albany off Piccadilly and a lavish meal at the Écu de France restaurant, followed by a drink at the Prince of Wales pub near the Lime Grove studios, before transmission actually began at 10 o'clock on Friday evenings. Not surprisingly after all this, the programmes were vigorous and lively, a blend of wit and passion which entertained the viewers. All four team members were chosen because they were unorthodox, even heretics, in party terms. But at first Morgan Phillips and the Labour whips took Foot's forthright, aggressive appearances with equanimity. It was the later birth of 'Bevanism' that caused all the protests.[76]

Then it all fell apart. A massive crisis pole-axed the Labour Party, from which it took a decade to recover. The post-war solidarity ('Pulling through together') disintegrated. The legacy of the new crisis scarred Michael Foot, along with allies like Barbara Castle and Ian Mikardo, for the next thirty years; there were reverberations during Foot's leadership of the party in 1980–83 (Tony Benn was never any kind of Bevanite). The crisis began in Cabinet on 1 August 1950, when Bevan openly voiced concern about the new £3,400-million rearmament programme for 1951–54 and the principles underlying Labour's international policy. The unemotional tones of the formal Cabinet record do not entirely obliterate the flavour of his complaints: 'Our foreign policy had hitherto been based on the view that the best method of defence against Russian Imperialism was to improve the social and economic conditions of the countries now threatened by Communist encroachment. The United States government seemed now to be abandoning this social and political defence in favour of a military defence. He believed that this change of policy was mis-judged . . .'[77] This intervention, ignored by Gaitskell's and Morrison's biographers and memoirs from the Labour right, suggested a major rift, without precedent in the course of Attlee's government.

It was common knowledge that Bevan had been unhappy with aspects of government policy since the Cabinet arguments over whether to press on with nationalizing iron and steel in the summer of 1947. He did not like Morrisonian 'consolidation'. He had had furious debates with his old *Tribune* comrade Stafford Cripps when the Treasury proposed levying charges on medical prescriptions. In the end a fudge was produced for the 1950 election under which prescrip-tion charges were accepted, but in principle only. A Cabinet commit-tee was set up to monitor soaring expenditure on the NHS, but no charges were imposed. The argument rumbled on throughout the summer of 1950.[78] But the Korean War gave it a new cogency. A soaring rearmament programme imposed new strains on the economy and threatened a regime of spending cuts, along with retrenchment and charges at the point of use which might undermine the welfare state. The NHS, Bevan's prized creation, could not escape.

Bevan's anxiety about the drift of policy was reinforced by personal grievance. Attlee, often insensitive in these matters, had not seen fit to promote Bevan after five years of extraordinary achievement at Health. In January 1951 he did move, but only sideways to the Ministry of Labour. When in October 1950 Cripps, a dying man, had to be replaced as Chancellor, the man appointed was the relative political newcomer Hugh Gaitskell, a socialist like Bevan but firmly on the party right. Bevan's anger knew no bounds. He and Gaitskell had met at Cripps's private dinner parties. They had not liked each other, quite apart from the social gulf between a product of Winchester and New College, Oxford, and a native of the mining community of Tredegar. Bevan once tried, amiably enough, to spell it out as a temperamental difference between an eighteenth-century rationalist like Gaitskell and a nineteenth-century romantic like himself. But he also felt there was an ideological emptiness about Gaitskell: 'He's nothing, nothing, nothing.'[79] A clash was inescapable.

The outcome is one of the best-known and most decisive episodes of British post-war history.[80] The clash between Gaitskell, defending the American alliance, justifying the revised rearmament programme of £4,700 million and insisting on imposing charges on the NHS whatever the political fallout, and Bevan, pointing to the damage to the economy from so excessive an arms burden, and defending to the death 'my health service' as a beacon of socialist promise throughout the world, has a titanic quality. The battle between the politicians, Hugh and Nye, became a battle between the biographers, with Philip Williams and Michael Foot locked in dispute over matters great and small in their works on Gaitskell and Bevan. Both have suffered for it. Only Attlee, whose own leadership in the final crisis was supine, even allowing for a temporary stay in hospital in April, has largely escaped scot free, although the opening up of the Cabinet records of the time from 1982 onwards (which Philip Williams did not use) raised new questions about his lack of leadership. Michael Foot's supporting role is still a matter of controversy. But beyond dispute, as player and as historian he had an influence on what resulted.

Bevan had used him as a sounding board for his discontent before and after the general election. By the autumn of 1950 Foot was in daily contact. He urged his friend to take a decisive stand; if Foot's eloquence was ineffective, in the Bevan household the other *Tribune* editor, Jennie Lee, would be even more forceful. Foot reacted to Gaitskell's promotion to Chancellor with as much fury as Bevan. It was followed by a series of increasingly alarming developments at home and abroad. The Americans appeared to be moving into a newly aggressive phase of policy. General MacArthur, threatening an advance towards the Chinese frontier across the Yalu river, seemed almost out of control. There were rumours that the US might use the atomic bomb in Korea. In alarm, Attlee went to Washington for talks with Truman and his Secretary of State Dean Acheson. He claimed to have been given adequate reassurances from the American government about nuclear weapons, but there were serious conditions he had to accept in return. One was the prospect of German rearmament, disturbing to many on the left. Another was Britain's agreement to take on a huge new rearmament programme of £3,400 million, soon to rise to £4,700 million. American defence chiefs were even talking of it growing to £6,000 million. Despite all its economic problems,

Britain's per capita burden of defence spending would be higher than that of the United States. In addition, Britain was concerned at the aggressive approach shown towards China, which Britain had formally recognized in 1949, while the Americans were committed to the Chiang Kai-shek regime in Formosa (now Taiwan), which they insisted was the legitimate Chinese government.

These issues came out in a critical meeting of the Cabinet on 25 January 1951.[81] Gaitskell spelled out the case for financing the new defence budget. He itemized with appalling frankness the various economic difficulties that the defence budget would cause – the damage to exports and investment, the bottlenecks in supplies, a shortage of machine tools, labour difficulties, a net reduction in consumer living standards – almost as if he were arguing the other way. But he justified the programme on political grounds, as a sign of solidarity with Britain's American allies. Bevan spoke strongly against the new armaments programme. He reinforced the economic arguments against it, and emphasized the damage to the social and economic fabric. It was noticeable that Gaitskell, the supposed hard-headed economist, spoke as a politician, defending the arms budget almost out of instinct. By contrast Bevan, the supposed emotional Welsh firebrand, based his arguments on solid, almost incontrovertible, economic fact. However, many of the big guns in the Cabinet – Morrison, Dalton, Attlee himself – spoke in support of Gaitskell, and the programme went through. Since Bevan had spoken convincingly on behalf of an increase in the arms budget in a major debate as recently as 15 January, it was hoped that perhaps the crisis was over.

In fact it was only just beginning, and Foot was to be a crucial part of it. For it was clear that Gaitskell, a long-standing advocate of the need for prescription charges as part of a general programme of cost-cutting at home, had health service charges in his sights. On 15 March he proposed charges on spectacles and dentures, and prescription charges as well. On 22 March he put these proposals to full Cabinet. Bevan, furiously angry at an attack on his cherished National Health Service, launched a violent assault, backed up unexpectedly by Harold Wilson. 'He thought it deplorable that, for the sake of £23 million in a very large budget, the principle of a free health service should be abandoned . . . The government were now proposing to depart from

Labour principle for the sake of a paltry increase in revenue.'[82] Privately, Bevan suspected that Morrison, Gaitskell and others were engaged in a conspiracy to evict him from the Cabinet. In conversation with Dalton he attacked 'rootless men like Gaitskell and Gordon Walker', the latter being the right-wing Commonwealth Relations Secretary. Personalities and policies were intertwined.

Gaitskell stood firm on his proposals, and offered to resign if his budget plans were turned down; Attlee, temporarily in St Mary's hospital for an examination of his duodenum, gave little guidance, other than offering Bevan a somewhat fatuous historical comparison with the resignation of Lord Randolph Churchill after a dispute over the defence estimates during the second Salisbury governmemnt in December 1886. Attempts at mediation, first by Ernest Bevin just before his death, then by the aged Lord Addison, then by some junior ministers led by Callaghan and Arthur Blenkinsop, all failed. Gaitskell duly introduced his budget, with charges on spectacles and dentures, on 10 April, and the entire political world waited to see what Aneurin Bevan would do. There was one significant clue to be heard already. Gaitskell's announcement of the NHS charges was met with a solitary cry of 'Shame' from the Labour benches. It came from Jennie Lee.

It was at this point that Michael Foot became a major player in the drama. Throughout March he and Jennie Lee were urging Bevan to stick to his guns and, if necessary, to resign if NHS charges were imposed. In an under-reported aside during a speech at Bermondsey on 3 April, Bevan said he would do so. Foot himself was as furious about Gaitskell's budget as was Bevan. Philip Williams, Gaitskell's biographer, depicts Foot elsewhere as inserting into his narratives a more hostile view of Attlee and his colleagues than Bevan held, but that hardly applies in this case. On 6 April Foot had warned in *Tribune* of the perils of sacrificing socialist principles, as had happened when MacDonald cut unemployment benefit in 1931. On 19 April Bevan announced that he could not vote for the NHS charges proposed in Gaitskell's budget. The following day *Tribune* led off with a truly ferocious unsigned personal attack on Gaitskell written by Michael Foot, under the title 'A Dangerous Budget'. He focused attention on Gaitskell's health service charges: 'It was the first major attempt to dismantle the social service structure which Labour has built up in the

last five years.' He added, 'It is hard to avoid the conclusion that Mr
Gaitskell shares the detestation of Treasury officials for the principle of
a free health service.'[83]

This was bad enough, but Foot's final passage aroused near apo-
plexy: 'The only way to defeat the Tories is by a united Labour
movement which does not, like Philip Snowden, desert Socialism at
the moment of crisis.' Present policies should be reversed 'before we
are led back to another 1931'. The very comparison with Philip
Snowden, remembered in Labour folk tradition as one of the arch-
traitors of the past, second only to Ramsay MacDonald himself, roused
enormous anger. On 22 April it was announced that Bevan had indeed
resigned, along with Harold Wilson, President of the Board of Trade,
and John Freeman, a junior minister. Bevan's somewhat incoherent
resignation speech on 25 April, with Foot sitting next to him, raised
the temperature still further, as did an angry meeting of the parliamentary party. Dalton commented, during a furious statement about 'my
health service' by Bevan, 'This is Mosley speaking.'[84] Oswald Mosley
might be seen as located in an even lower circle of Labour's legendary
Inferno than his Prime Minister, Ramsay MacDonald.

This editorial in *Tribune* ensured that Foot would be identified as
a leader of the anti-Gaitskell movement. He had already been preparing
for the crisis, rejoining the somewhat shadowy Keep Left group,
chaired by Crossman, on 17 October 1950 after leaving the National
Executive: 'Michael Foot's return to the group was warmly welcomed.'[85] On 12 December he had signed a resolution urging, among
other things, that China should be admitted to the Security Council
of the UN; that Formosa, presently controlled by Chiang Kai-shek,
should be returned to it; and that the rearmament programme (at that
time only £3,600 million) should not be proceeded with. Bevan's
resignation from the government was announced on 22 April. This
gave the rump of Keep Left a huge injection of new vitality. In
February they had numbered no more than ten: members like George
Wigg had resigned. But on 26 April Foot and Ian Mikardo convened
a meeting attended by fifteen Labour MPs; they included Bevan,
Wilson and John Freeman. The others were Richard Acland, Barbara
Castle, Harold Davies, Leslie Hale and Richard Crossman of the Keep
Left group, along with Hugh Delargy, Will Griffiths, Kim Mackay,

Tom Driberg and Jennie Lee. The minutes were kept by Jo Richardson, the personal assistant of Ian Mikardo, in many ways the organizing genius of the group.[86] A series of brains trusts were to be held in different towns. People now began to speak of 'the Bevanites'. The *Statist*, a right-wing journal, added that 'the true mind behind the fat façade of Mr Bevan is the Robespierre mind of that sea-green incorruptible, febrile class-conscious agitator, Mr Michael Foot'.[87] No doubt Michael was happy to be compared with a Jacobin, if not that particular one.

He was also feared for his links with Fleet Street: for instance, he was thought to be constantly leaking private party matters to Hugh Massingham, the political correspondent of the *Observer*. Foot's angry, finger-jabbing debating style was already known to television viewers of *In the News*. Polls showed that many of them saw him as a latter-day Robespierre, 'intolerant, humourless and fanatical', quite different from the diffident personal charm he could show in day-to-day personal relationships. His black-rimmed spectacles, over-long and untidy black hair brushed back from his temples, and vaguely Bohemian mode of dress caused citizens of middle England much alarm, while giving to many a sixth-former the secret delights of forbidden fruit. By July, from Morgan Phillips downwards, party officials were writing to the BBC governors complaining that Foot was not a suitable Labour representative on the programme, since he was a doctrinaire schismatic, with an agenda of his own.[88]

The outcome, inevitably, was a pamphlet, *One Way Only*, published in July. It bore a foreword signed by Bevan, Wilson and Freeman, but most of it appears to have been written by Foot. He has since described it as 'an essay in qualified judgements'. It was not as tentative as that. But much of it was quite moderate, even unexceptionable, with sections on the world crisis in raw materials, keeping down prices at home, and especially on world poverty being addressed by development programmes under the UN's Point Four programme, such as the 1950 Colombo Plan, to aid economic and social development in South-East Asia and the Pacific. There was, however, a separate passage, probably written by Bevan but perhaps by Foot, which attacked the cost of the rearmament programme and urged that restraint be imposed on American foreign policy. Hugh Dalton, no mean conspirator himself, felt that pages written by Foot were 'both very anti-American and very anti-Russian'.[89] It was not, however, an inflammatory document. *Tribune* pointed out, for instance, that it did not advocate unilateral disarmament.[90] But what observers noted was that it looked like a separate manifesto from a party within a party. Michael Foot appeared to be its presiding (some thought its evil) genius.

It was a tetchy summer and early autumn for both government and party. Trade union leaders, while unhappy themselves with aspects of Gaitskell's budget and voting down wage restraint, condemned the Bevanite group in fierce terms. They especially objected to attacks on union leaders like Arthur Deakin that appeared in a second Bevanite pamphlet, *Going our Way*. The Bevanites countered by preparing an all-out assault on the elected constituency section places on the NEC at the October party conference. After all, Driberg, Barbara Castle and Mikardo were already there. The government generally was weary, after six very hard years (and almost eleven years consecutively in office for men like Attlee, Morrison and Dalton). There were new problems in abundance. In Persia there had been a summer crisis over the nationalization of Anglo-Persian Oil by the Persian government. Morrison and Shinwell talked in jingoistic terms about sending British troops to Abadan, but a majority of ministers, including Gaitskell, voted them down.[91] Difficulties also mounted in Egypt, until in October the Egyptian Prime Minister Nahas Pasha announced that the 1936 treaty with Britain would be abrogated. He demanded that the British military presence in the Suez Canal base be removed. Another confrontation threatened.

Most serious of all, the economy now lurched into new difficulties, imperilling the financing of the ambitious rearmament programme. A massive balance of payments crisis, largely caused by a rise in the cost of raw materials, resulted in a gold and dollar deficit of $638 million for the period July–September. Gaitskell responded, among other things, by imposing a three-year dividend limitation, which won him some rare praise from Foot and his friends.[92] He also went to Washington and Ottawa in September for talks with Louis Snyder, the US Secretary of the Treasury, and his Canadian counterpart. These did not go well: Gaitskell thought Snyder 'a pretty small-minded, small town semi-isolationist', though a 'burden-sharing' scheme was cobbled together.[93] However, Gaitskell was compelled to say at Ottawa that the pace of rearmament must slow down, and warned of the dangers of a worldwide inflation in the prices of raw materials. *Tribune* was exultant: 'A gleam of sanity is at last breaking through.' Foot's article was cheerfully headed 'Has Gaitskell Joined the Bevanites?'

At this remarkably unpromising moment, Attlee decided to call a general election for October. It was the second time that he had called one apparently on his own whim, and again for unusual reasons. In February 1950 the reason had been Cripps's unwillingness to introduce a pre-election budget, with the hint of electoral bribery. This time it was a proposed visit of the King to Commonwealth countries in the near future – in the event George VI fell fatally ill and never went. However, at a thinly-attended Cabinet of seven on 19 September, Attlee announced, without warning, his decision to call an election. Morrison and Gaitskell, both abroad, were thunderstruck. The Labour Party seemed ill-prepared, with quarrels among its leading figures. The preparation of the manifesto produced much argument on the NEC between trade union and Bevanite figures, both on defence issues and on the case for more socialism. At party conference, without apparent irony, Bevan made a powerful speech about not underestimating Labour's natural instinct for unity. In the newspapers, opinion polls showed a 7 per cent Tory lead precisely because the reverse appeared true.

Yet the campaign went remarkably well. Despite all the rows between supporters and opponents of Bevan, the morale of party workers in the constituencies was high. There was still huge enthusiasm for 'our' government amongst the British working class, Devonport dockyard workers included. In the end there was a high turnout of 82.6 per cent (compared with 83.9 in 1950). Labour was to poll 13,948,883 votes, the highest ever until it was surpassed by the Conservatives in 1992 (when, obviously, the electorate was much larger). Labour polled 230,000 more than the Conservatives, who obtained 48 per cent of the vote as against Labour's 48.8 per cent. Labour lost just twenty-three seats, most of them in suburban areas of London and the south-east. And they lost the election, winning 295 seats to the Conservatives' 321. By comparison, Tony Blair's New Labour in 1997 polled just 44.4 per cent of the votes, and obtained an overall majority of 179. In October 1951 it was a tense and highly partisan election. Conservative onslaughts on 'socialism' were countered with Labour claims that Tories were warmongers who would send British troops to the Suez Canal and the Persian Gulf. 'Whose finger on the trigger?' asked the pro-Labour *Daily Mirror*. In Wales, Churchill was taunted for sending in troops to deal with striking miners at Tonypandy back in 1910, a cherished (and historically accurate) component of Labour's usable past.

This angry mood showed itself in Devonport, where the Conservative candidate was once again Randolph Churchill. There was little of the previous geniality this time. Churchill attacked Foot as 'Bevan's principal hatchet-man', and offended Jill by referring to Michael's not having done military service.[94] In return, Foot denounced 'British MacArthurs' in the Tory Party who would send troops to Persia. His main supporting speaker again was Aneurin Bevan, whose hour-long speech at the Guildhall was 'untroubled by hecklers', according to the local journalist. Bevan did not forget to give due praise to a former Plymouth Mayor, Isaac Foot, 'a human dynamo of ideas'.[95] Jill, who had recently been unwell, also spoke in the campaign, helping out Michael as he lost his voice. Randolph Churchill's main supporting speaker was again his father, who addressed ten thousand excited people on Plymouth Hoe. He also brought in the old MP, Leslie Hore-Belisha, perhaps not the most appetizing of electoral assets. In a straight fight, Michael Foot triumphed again, with a 2,390 majority, a good result in the circumstances. Randolph Churchill heard the results in the Embassy ballroom, with tears in his eyes. He and Foot were to remain good friends. Later in the fifties Foot read the manuscript of his biography of Lord Derby. Foot also took the witness stand on Churchill's behalf in a difficult libel case in October 1956, despite fears that he might lose his job on the *Herald* for political reasons: 'Rather than see his friend go down he volunteered to go into the box. He undoubtedly made a considerable impression on the jury.' Charles Wintour, later to edit the *Evening Standard*, told Beaverbrook, 'The hero of the day is Michael Foot.'[96] But despite, or because of, these pleasant associations with Foot, Randolph Churchill never fought an election again. It would, however, be his father back in 10 Downing

Street. Foot returned to Westminster to fight new battles, this time perhaps mainly against his own comrades.

The Attlee years ended tumultuously for Michael Foot. In retirement, he wrote warmly of that government as 'this most gifted, intelligent and idealistic Cabinet'.[97] Its programme of nationalization, a planned economy, a welfare state, full employment and 'fair shares' based on redistributive taxation was the most complete achievement of democratic socialism that Britain had ever seen, with the NHS and Indian independence as its glorious highlights. Much of the time until the outbreak of the Korean War in June 1950 Foot's criticisms of Attlee's government were muted. Even on foreign affairs, the 'Keep Left' critique of 1947 turned into a more orthodox view of accepting the need for collective defence against a perceived Soviet threat. Foot had supported the Marshall Plan, the creation of NATO, and sending troops to South Korea. He did not protest against the manufacture of a British nuclear deterrent because it was never announced, and the relevant Cabinet committee authorizing it, GEN 163, was kept totally secret. Foot later said that he never knew of its existence until Britain's first atomic bomb testing took place in the Pacific in October 1952.[98] Aneurin Bevan surely did. But for most of the time it was a government he was happy, even proud, to support – not really in the Commons, where his influence was limited, but in nationwide speech-making and of course with his ever-fluent pen. *Tribune*, for all its financial weakness and the legal threat from Lord Kemsley, kept a strong socialist critique alive, while Foot's own reputation as author and pamphleteer was enhanced.

But the ending of the government was so utterly miserable that memory of the Attlee years was inevitably soured. Foot's recollection of them in his biography of Nye Bevan twenty years on was one-sided and often bitter, especially towards Attlee himself. Hugh Gaitskell he was to demonize mercilessly for the rest of his days. In fact, despite the criticisms rightly made by Philip Williams of Foot's account – its sprinkling of factual inaccuracies and distorting use of selective quotation – most of what he says in his life of Bevan is perfectly sound.[99] On balance it is a better account than that of Williams, who ignored the public records altogether. Bevan's economic critique of Gaitskell's 1951 budget was confirmed by the response of the Churchill government in 1951–54, when the arms programme was greatly scaled down on broadly Bevanite lines. We were all Bevanites now, even if a little late. Gaitskell's one and only budget was a fairly calamitous one, which harmed domestic investment and raised taxes excessively, quite apart from the defence issue. The need to restrain American policy in the Far East, that of Secretary of State John Foster Dulles especially, with its commitment to propping up puppet regimes in Formosa (and later in South Vietnam), also became clearer. But fundamentally it was the image of party civil war that impressed observers, and depressed Foot himself. Thereafter, until Tony Blair's huge victory in 1997, Labour was felt to be inherently disunited, and for that reason usually unelectable.

The schism in his party in the spring and summer of 1951 was to shape Foot's career for years to come. He had acquired celebrity status as an icon of the left, a star of pamphlet, platform and now television. Only Bevan had a stronger reputation on the left. But memories of the Attlee years ensured that Foot, unlike Nye, would invariably be seen in the mould of Hardie or Lansbury, as an agitator of protest, not a politician of power.

5

BEVANITE AND TRIBUNITE
(1951–1960)

For the next ten years, Michael Foot's world was to be shaped by the life and death of one man, the lost leader, Aneurin Bevan. To its relief, Labour had lost the October 1951 general election by only a narrow margin, while it was reinvigorated by gifted young MPs like Roy Jenkins (elected 1948), Tony Crosland (elected 1950) and Denis Healey (elected in a by-election in 1952). The book *New Fabian Essays* (1952), to which all three contributed along with Ian Mikardo, John Strachey and others, showed that there was plenty of intellectual energy in the ranks. The South African émigrée Rita Hinden restarted *Socialist Commentary* as a highly intelligent organ of the centre-right. Labour could also draw comfort from its Conservative opponents. Soon Churchill's government was plunged into as serious financial difficulties as Attlee's had been, with the Chancellor of the Exchequer R. A. Butler in major disagreement with colleagues over the 'Robot' plan to float the pound, allowing it to find its own level and letting 'the reserves take the strain'. Nevertheless, almost from the start of the new Parliament, Labour was obsessed with its own internecine conflicts, the battle between right and left personified in the titanic struggle between Hugh Gaitskell and Aneurin Bevan. Since both of them were socialists, it was a less clear-cut divide than that between *soi-disant* Old and New Labour in the 1990s. But it dominated the party's history for years. It also determined the work and priorities of Michael Foot from then on.

Trouble began early in the new Parliament. As always, it concerned foreign and defence policy, more particularly relations with the Americans. On 26 November 1951, thirty-five Labour MPs defied the whips to protest against the Japanese peace treaty, since it was opposed by the Russians and included China and India, while a further hundred abstained. There was a graver crisis on 5 March 1952, when Bevan and his supporters again ignored the whips and put forward an amendment which condemned the rearmament programme. This produced no fewer than fifty-seven rebels, about double the familiar core group of 'Bevanites'. In each case Foot was amongst them. He had already in *Tribune* highlighted Churchill's decision to roll on the rearmament programme for a further year.[1] This further underlined the foolishness of Gaitskell for insisting on his paltry £23 million of NHS charges. Foot and Bevan both felt they might now be expelled from the parliamentary party, and had anxious discussions as to how to respond. In fact, the parliamentary party a few days later broadly accepted a moderate motion from Strachey and George Strauss (both to be identified later with the 'Keep Calm' group, along with James Callaghan) which merely confirmed party standing orders and left the personal aspects untouched. Attlee's authority seemed to be buckling under the challenge. Relations in the party at Westminster remained tense during the summer. At a calamitous party conference at the end of September, animosity and bad temper were everywhere. The conference was held in Morecambe, a distinctly downmarket Lancashire resort. Crossman described it as 'a minor Blackpool, dumped down on mud flats with a four-mile promenade'.[2] The weather was dreadful, rain with biting winds, and everybody caught colds trudging along that bleak, exposed promenade. No political party ever went there again for its conference. Foot described the conference as 'rowdy, convulsive, vulgar, splenetic'; the episode for which Morecambe is best remembered came when Will Lawther of the National Union of Miners shouted at a left-wing heckler, 'Shut yer gob.' One important landmark was that Bevanites captured six of the seven constituency section places on the NEC: Foot chose not to stand because it would undermine his role as a detached journalist. Immediately after the conference a bitter speech by Gaitskell at Stalybridge made things worse still: Foot saw it as a British version of McCarthyism. Gaitskell denounced the conference for 'mob rule' and attacked the Bevanites elected to the NEC as 'frustrated journalists'. As it happened, Foot was not amongst them, but his name cannot have been far from Gaitskell's thoughts. Relations between the two comrades verged on hatred.[3]

Attlee now asserted his leadership. In an unusually blunt speech at the Royal Festival Hall in London he told the Bevanites: 'Stop this sectionalism. Work with the team. Turn your guns on the enemy not your friends.' A meeting of the parliamentary party on 24 October called for the disbandment of all 'group organizations' in the party other than those officially affiliated. After that, the Bevan group formally disbanded, but it continued to hold meetings all over the country, variously condemning American policy in the Far East, the threat of German rearmament and the costs of the rearmament programme. The audiences were invariably large and appreciative.

For Foot, the decisive question was what Nye would do. In fact his hero was distinctly uncertain and ill-tempered. On occasions he and Foot had discussed the theoretical possibility of leaving the party altogether. But neither seriously contemplated that. Bevan was very alarmed by the Morecambe conference, which looked as if it could produce a permanent split in the party. He told Crossman that what the Bevanites should do was not operate as a private group but act as a socialist ginger group which all members of the party could potentially join. Crossman dissented from this. Foot, who was also present, remained silent: it may be assumed that his instinct was to agree with Bevan.[4] After that, Bevan stood for the Shadow Cabinet in November, and was elected twelfth and last (Harold Wilson, who was also showing signs of backing away from any split, came thirteenth, a point of significance later on). For the next seventeen months Bevan acted in orthodox fashion as a front-bench spokesman on health and housing issues, even though the atmosphere in the party remained cool. Overseas issues were still divisive. Like Foot, Bevan strongly opposed any proposals for German rearmament, but that issue did not have quite the same capacity to damage party unity as the problems of the Far East or nuclear weapons. After all, centre-right figures like Dalton and Callaghan opposed rearming the Germans too. The Bevanites decided not to challenge the whips on that. Bevan stood for the deputy leadership against Morrison in November 1952 and was predictably heavily defeated, by 194 to eighty-two. But then the atmosphere suddenly improved. Crossman noted that 'the Bevanite and anti-Bevanite feuding has melted away . . . everybody is rather shamefacedly aware that both sides are on the same side after all'.[5] Whether Foot shared this complacency is very doubtful, but relations did seem to improve throughout 1953.

Then, quite unexpectedly, there was a major eruption on 13 April 1954. Bevan objected to proposals made by Anthony Eden, the Foreign Secretary, that the winding-up of the war in Indo-China should be followed by the creation of a new security alliance in south-east Asia, the future South-East Asia Treaty Organization (SEATO). It was a bombshell to everyone that he challenged the party leadership on so marginal an issue. This time Attlee had to respond, and it was announced the following day that Bevan had resigned from the Shadow Cabinet. To the dismay – but hardly the surprise – of Foot, Crossman and other colleagues, Harold Wilson, the runner-up in the Shadow Cabinet elections, then decided to take Bevan's place rather than appear as Nye's poodle. Although Mikardo reconvened the old Bevanite group, it was now visibly weakening. Bevan's bad-tempered performance at the 1954 party conference, coloured by his first defeat for the party treasurership, did not increase his stature. He complained angrily (at a *Tribune* rally) of the influence of 'desiccated calculating machines', a reference either to Attlee or Gaitskell (or conceivably both) which caused much offence.

In March 1955 came yet another crisis when it was announced that Britain was going to manufacture the hydrogen bomb. Bevan was not opposed to this decision in principle, any more than he had ever resisted manufacture (as opposed to testing) of the A-bomb earlier on. Michael Foot, by contrast, like Barbara Castle and Jennie Lee, was always an instinctive unilateralist who wanted Britain to renounce such weapons completely on moral grounds. Before the Commons debate Bevan accepted the view of Foot and Jennie Lee and came out strongly against party policy on the grounds of opposing 'first use'. He also called for four-power talks between the USA, the USSR, Britain and France to discuss the future of nuclear weapons, a view which the party leadership accepted. The debate was made memorable for Foot because, in his final Commons speech, Churchill delivered a powerful warning about the spread of nuclear weapons, which Bevan's speech echoed.[6] But at the end of the debate Bevan almost contemptuously challenged his party's views, and interrupted Attlee's winding-up speech in peremptory fashion. He asked whether Labour would support the British use of thermonuclear weapons in the face of a conventional armed attack. It was a crucial issue which Attlee had failed to address; nor did he now. But Bevan's ferocity towards his own party leadership alienated many sympathizers. Foot joined Bevan and several former Bevanites among the sixty-two Labour Members who disobeyed the whips and abstained. The whip was withdrawn from Bevan as a result. Gaitskell tried hard to use this as a reason for drumming Bevan out of the party entirely. Bevan in reply called on the six 'Bevanite' members of the NEC (now including Wilson) to resign if he were. Foot, like Jennie Lee, as always urged Bevan to fight on and not to 'grovel' before the party leadership. But Crossman and Wilson, neither of whom Bevan fully trusted, took a different view. It was noted that several Bevanites – Wilson, Crossman, John Freeman, Leslie Hale, Stephen Swingler and Hugh Delargy – had voted for the official opposition line. Wilson indeed had effectively ceased to be any kind of Bevanite at all.

In the event, Bevan was persuaded (not by Foot) to reverse gear, and apologized to Attlee before the NEC subcommittee. There was a general election coming up soon; to Gaitskell's huge disappointment, Bevan's expulsion was rejected on the full NEC by just one vote, fourteen to thirteen; the whip was restored. In Barbara Castle's reflective verdict, 'Nye was saved by Attlee's distaste for Hugh Gaitskell's bigoted destructiveness.'[7] But the Bevanite group now quietly disbanded for good, and never re-emerged. Later, in December 1955, after Labour's general election defeat, Attlee resigned the leadership and Gaitskell comfortably defeated Bevan and Morrison to take his place. Harold Wilson and other former Bevanites voted for Gaitskell. Even Crossman, who had severely criticized Bevan's tactics on the H-bomb, came close to doing so too.

The Bevanite period thus ended ingloriously. Yet it is an important phase in the career of Michael Foot. He was Bevan's main champion through the power of the printed word. At every stage he urged Bevan to fight back. Through his columns in *Tribune* he became the voice of dissent at every stage, while he roused intense dislike in the party centre-right, who felt Bevan to be out of control. Nye's Commons speeches seemed to take flight oratorically so as to leave any thoughts of compromise behind. There was immense bad blood as the Gaitskellites denounced the Bevanites as a crypto-Communist conspiracy. The extent of this animosity was invariably minimized thirty years later, when the Bevanites were deemed to have been 'the legitimate left', committed to the parliamentary approach, in contrast to the Bennites of the 1980s, who were anti-parliamentary and by definition illegitimate. The normality of the Bevanites was not a view the Gaitskellites endorsed in 1951–54. They also offered derisive comment at the comfortable bourgeois lifestyle of these supposed socialist firebrands, especially when Lord Faringdon of Buscot Park had them driven to Bevanite-run campaign meetings in his Rolls-Royce. Patronage (perhaps on mischievous grounds) from the capitalist enemy, notably Beaverbrook newspapers, was also noted. The comrades were growing apart, and solidarity evaporating. Dalton found it an 'awkward coincidence' when he had to travel on the same train as Foot to a meeting. Foot insisted that no MP could obey the dictates of 'a majority vote at a private meeting'. It unnerved the party hierarchy that he remained one of Labour's supposed spokesmen on the television programme *In the News*, where he could make Bevanite propaganda. He was actually much the least popular of the four regular team members with the viewers. A. J. P. Taylor refused to appear on the programme in April 1953, when Foot was excluded and more orthodox Labour people like Callaghan and J. B. Hynd took his place. In the end, in late 1954 *In the News*, with Foot now back and in full flow, moved to the new ITV under the title *Free Speech*.[8] The ill-will rumbled on.

The Bevanites were a short-lived group. After a period of thriving growth from April 1951 to December 1952, they formally disbanded. Then, after resurrection in April 1954 they simply petered out as Bevan himself got into one row after another. Yet their political importance is considerable. As an articulate body, comprising mainly lawyers and journalists, they had a powerful impact on opinion in the constituencies. Mainly for this reason, Labour Party membership reached unprecedented heights after the electoral defeat in 1951. The circulation of *Tribune*, a major factor in the surge of Bevanism in the constituencies, increased considerably, to perhaps eighteen thousand.[9] The Bevanite MPs – at most thirty-one according to current calculations – kept a strong socialist message alive in the grassroots, even if their main themes always concerned foreign and defence policy. Over 150 invariably successful public forums or 'brains trusts' had been held by late 1954, often in improbable nerve-centres of socialism, such as amongst the disgusted citizenry of Tunbridge Wells. Foot, marooned in his *Tribune* offices, was one of the more occasional performers. A note by Rose Cohen and Jo Richardson showed that of the thirty-one sympathetic MPs, Ian Mikardo attended forty-six brains trusts, Harold Davies forty-three and Leslie Hale twenty-two, but Foot only three.[10] But in any case, the Bevanites operated largely as individuals. Foot and Barbara Castle always maintained that other people greatly exaggerated the element of planned organization.[11] There was a core of MPs who met regularly in the smoking room of the Commons or the pubs of Fleet Street – Crossman, Mikardo, Castle and certainly Foot. More signs of there being an organized group perhaps came from rather jolly buffet lunches every Tuesday in Crossman's elegant residence in Vincent Square for the six NEC Bevanites together with Foot, Jennie Lee, Mallalieu and the Oxford economist Thomas Balogh. These were all paying guests. Others flitted in and out of Bevanite gatherings according to chance or whim. Individualists like Fenner Brockway, Sydney Silverman or Emrys Hughes were almost impossible to tie down in any group, even a splinter group. In Foot parlance they represented 'the dissidence of dissent', like the Fifth Monarchy men of the English Civil War. Possible recruits to the Bevanite ranks like Woodrow Wyatt, Desmond Donnelly, George Thomas and Cledwyn Hughes soon retreated to the centre ground.

What united the members of the group was personal loyalty to Nye Bevan. But it was a much looser tie than that of Blairites to Tony Blair after 1997. Whether Bevan himself actually was, or ever wanted to be, a Bevanite is debatable. He gave his supporters only intermittent encouragement, and he distrusted both Crossman and Wilson. Barbara Castle recalls that 'he hated teamwork and would sit brooding in his Cliveden Place flat with a few close allies from Tribune, notably his wife Jennie and Michael Foot'.[12] Basically, he disliked the whole idea of conspiratorial private groups so beloved of Ian Mikardo. Anyway, Bevan was increasingly abroad, with long visits to India, China and even the USA, and unable to keep closely in touch with his followers. And yet his galvanizing presence in the House lent a constant touch of inspiration which kept the Bevanite movement alive.

The main weakness of Bevanism, however, lay not in the way-wardness of its individuals or the uncertainties of its titular leader, but in the meagreness of its doctrine. On practical issues the Bevanites had many central questions to ask and much to contribute. Internationally, Foot and others perceptively anticipated the world of co-existence and disengagement, the world of the Rapacki plan for a nuclear-free zone in central Europe, including a united Germany, and possible non-alignment after 1956. Foot himself brilliantly deployed his knowledge of historical evidence to show that the case for an atomic deterrent power for the West was quite misconceived. The Russians had not often launched an aggressive war, with Poland in 1919, Finland in 1940, Poland again in 1940 and Japan in 1945 the only instances. Many key tenets of the West's defence strategy were thus fundamentally flawed.

But it is difficult to uncover many documents to illustrate Bevanite political theory as a body of ideas. The nearest equivalent is Crossman's independent-minded chapter 'Towards a Philosophy of Socialism' in the *New Fabian Essays*. His main argument there was the need for socialism to break away from linkage with corporatist ideas: 'the planned economy and the centralization of power are no longer socialist objectives'.[13] Crossman could hardly be said to be offering a Bevanite analysis. Indeed, he was explicitly calling for Labour to reject the residual Marxism with which many Bevanites, including Foot, felt comfortable. Another very important document was Aneurin Bevan's own *In Place of Fear*, a brilliantly written series of fragments, some recycled from the past, published in 1952. On some it had a profound influence: Barbara Castle wrote of it that 'Nye's analysis made a permanent impact on my political thinking.'[14] But the book was really a series of personal statements on behalf of a libertarian form of democratic socialism and tackling global poverty. Full of beguiling phrases, they hardly offered any ideological structure firm enough for his disciples to embrace. Otherwise, Bevanite writings in newspaper columns tended to repeat the achievements of 1945–51, so far as they went, and to call for more public ownership and public spending. They said little that was new.

Surprisingly, the Bevanites, so committed were they to public ownership and 'socialist planning' of the economy, did not respond to contemporary suggestions that the essence of socialism lay elsewhere – that 'socialism was about equality'. They always preferred economic to sociological emphasis. They did not take the opportunity to reshape the ideological debate in the party. It was left to Anthony Crosland of the party right to do so with his *Future of Socialism* in 1956, which provided a fundamental new analysis for a generation to come. With Douglas Jay's *Socialism in the New Society* appearing in 1962, the Gaitskellites manifestly had all the best tunes. As was argued by the 'Keep Calm' group which included Callaghan and Strachey, the Bevanites were too consumed by animosity towards Gaitskell (and he towards them) to examine whether his vision of socialism (which certainly included room for more public ownership and control of the 'commanding heights of the economy') was really so different from their own. Harold Wilson was a manager, not a theorist. He never wrote anything on political ideas. Effectively he ceased to be a real Bevanite when he took his leader's place on the Shadow Cabinet in 1954. Ironically, it was Wilson's election as party leader in February 1963 which the Bevanites later regarded as their supreme achievement. Before a portrait of Bevan, they drank a toast to the lost leader.[15] He had won at last. But their opportunity to recast the ideas of the Labour movement or to redefine the meaning of post-Marxist socialism in Britain had long since passed.

Foot's contributions to Bevanism naturally came most effectively in his writing. He still wrote a column in the *Daily Herald*, alternating with Douglas Jay, whose austere contributions, indicating a professional knowledge of economics, were very different in style and content. But Foot was relatively restrained here. The *Herald* was not a platform for radicalism. Its editor, Percy Cudlipp, became a critic of Bevan himself, which caused some strain with his columnist. Foot, however, did come out with a ringing endorsement when Bevan lost the whip for a second time after the H-bomb debate in March 1955. 'I Stand by Bevan' on 18 March argued that Bevan's points were entirely reasonable, and criticized Attlee for being afraid of healthy debate.[16]

But Foot's main journalistic activities, of course, came through his manifold activities in the Strand office of *Tribune*. The years of the Bevanite revolt were that newspaper's most glorious period. When it resumed weekly publication in late 1952 it became news as never before. It had moved away from the arguments of the early Cold War years after 1945, when Jon Kimche and Evelyn Anderson were focusing on eastern Europe. It now ranged over a myriad of issues at home and around the world. Foot's influence on the newspaper was still central, but he operated now mainly as a manager. He had given up the editor's chair to a remarkably young successor, the twenty-six-year-old Robert Edwards. At Ian Mikardo's suggestion Edwards had joined the staff from a provincial newspaper in 1948, and supplemented his meagre payment of £12 a week with investigative journalism. He got on well with Foot himself: when Edwards's leaders on the bomb were criticized by Jennie Lee as too right-wing, Foot defended him on the grounds of editorial freedom.[17] As has been seen, circulation in Edwards's time at *Tribune*, the climax of Bevanism, rose impressively. Foot, always generous to colleagues, believed that the paper became livelier under Edwards, with a more clearly defined point of view.

Otherwise, the paper had problems. *Tribune* editorial meetings were sometimes discordant, with clashes between Edwards and Peggy Duff, the business manager. Foot, as chairman of the editorial board, took the side of Edwards. The other directors had given Foot a hundred shares so that he could outvote the others, in effect a block vote. Duff later recalled ruefully that, as with the removal of Jon Kimche earlier, Foot had a ruthless side to him which was not always detected. She was sacked on the spot for dissent.[18] However, relations were sufficiently repaired for Foot and Duff later to collaborate on CND. Eventually, after three successful years, Edwards became another link between *Tribune* and Beaverbrook Newspapers, moving to the *Evening Standard* in December 1954 and becoming in time editor of the *Daily Express*. Foot took up the editorial baton again after the 1955 general election, and remained there until his election to Parliament for Ebbw Vale five years later.

In the Bevanite period in the early fifties, Foot's work for *Tribune* was endlessly demanding. He remained its chief fund-raiser. Prospects of any help from the Labour Party, of course, were now zero, so he turned to the capitalists. The most successful link was with Howard Samuel, a millionaire property developer and publisher who pumped much money in to support the causes endorsed by Bevan, of whom he was a great admirer. Beaverbrook continued to send the occasional cheque, for his own whimsical reasons. His largesse, as will be seen, extended to the editor's personal needs as well as to those of his paper.

But, as noted earlier, by far the most important event to affect the finances of *Tribune* was the eventual removal of the black cloud of the 'Lower than Kemsley' libel case. Lord Kemsley, owner of the *Daily Mail*, was a political enemy, a former champion of Chamberlain and appeasement, and bitterly anti-socialist. Kemsley Newspapers had sued, with the apparent intention of driving both *Tribune* and perhaps its editors into bankruptcy. Kemsley won the case, but the verdict was overturned by the Court of Appeal. A key judgement was that delivered by Lord Birkett, a champion of free speech and, as it happened, an old Liberal friend of Isaac Foot. Eventually in the House of Lords in May 1952 *Tribune* had its appeal verdict confirmed, on the basis of its attack on Kemsley being fair comment. One helpful intermediary was the Tory Minister of Labour Sir Walter Monckton, who appeared for Kemsley in the Court of Appeal but then advised his client not to take the case any further, but to drop it. A colossal worry for Foot, not only as editor but also as the husband of a deeply anxious Jill, was finally eliminated, and *Tribune* entered a flourishing period.[19] Ironically, later on Foot was to become friendly (Jill thought perhaps too friendly) with the wife of Kemsley's nephew, the right-wing *saloniste* Lady Pamela Berry.

Foot was also still active as a journalist as well as fund-raiser. He wrote extensively during Robert Edwards's editorship under the pen name of 'John Marullus', a tribune under Julius Caesar and a more recondite classical reference than 'Cato' and 'Cassius'. In similar vein, *Tribune*'s future editor Dick Clements was to write as 'Flavius'. 'John Marullus' was a caustic commentator on the world, and certainly widely read, not least by Herbert Morrison. It was Foot who landed the newspaper in another huge row in October 1954 when he launched a fierce attack on trade union leaders in general, and Arthur Deakin of the transport workers' union the TGWU in particular. Foot had long resented the one-sided way in which Transport House and its allies on the NEC interpreted personal attacks on party colleagues. Morrison had delivered a sharp condemnation of Aneurin Bevan in Rita Hinden's *Socialist Commentary* early in 1954, but escaped any censure. Foot, however, reacted aggressively after Arthur Deakin, their General Secretary, disciplined members of his union when they took sympathetic action on behalf of dockers who were members of another, smaller union, the National Amalgamated Stevedores Union. Foot directed a fierce, highly personalized attack on Deakin entitled 'A Slander on the Dockers' in *Tribune* on 22 October. He had in any case long resented Deakin's role as chief bear-baiter in promoting the leadership's vendetta (as Foot saw it) against Bevan. In a speech in Birmingham on 17 October, Deakin had accused Communists of being behind recent London dock and bus strikes. There was 'a conspiracy to create chaos and confusion'. Foot now accused the union leader of intolerance and worse: the dockers' strike was not caused by Communist elements, said Foot, but by a major issue of principle – that of compulsory overtime. Deakin himself had seriously traduced the stevedores as being led by 'a moronic crowd of irresponsible adventurers'.[20]

The Labour Party's National Executive met on the twenty-seventh and then wrote to *Tribune* in stern terms, asking the three editorial board members, Foot, Jennie Lee and Mallalieu, how they could reconcile such a personal attack with loyalty to the party. Foot reacted in memorable terms. In a six-thousand-word article in *Tribune*, entirely his own work, he strongly upheld Labour's traditions of free speech, and pointed out how left-wing figures like Keir Hardie, Tom Mann, Ben Tillett and more recently Aneurin Bevan had been attacked far more viciously by right-wing elements in the past: 'We shall continue to print the truth as we see it. We trust that others will do the same.' If Arthur Deakin attacked the Stevedores Union, he must expect to be attacked in return. Union leaders, Foot added, were not 'a special breed of humanity, always to be shielded from the rough breezes of democracy, rare birds to be protected by special game laws'. It was a brilliant, really unanswerable philippic. It was published as a pamphlet entitled *The Case for Freedom – an Answer to Morgan Phillips and the NEC*, which sold well in dockland.[21]

In fact, nothing happened: Morgan Phillips told Crossman that he had been surprised at the ferocity of the NEC's reaction, and that no expulsions were contemplated.[22] What this episode did, other than confirm Foot's reputation as a polemicist, was to show the huge gulf between him and the trade unions, or at least their leaders. He was aware of this himself, and in 1953–54 brought a talented young journalist, Ian Aitken, a labour correspondent on Beaverbrook's newspapers, onto the staff of *Tribune* to give a trade union perspective.[23] But at this stage Foot had no close associates among any of the unions. This was, incidentally, also true of Barbara Castle, which had a bearing on her attitude in *In Place of Strife* in 1968. Foot's general attitude was to see the unions as undemocratic reactionary monoliths, using their block vote to shore up the leadership against left-wing critics, and to keep at bay the advance of socialism. Like all the Bevanites, Foot was at home essentially with the middle-class world of suburban socialism. So it continued until Frank Cousins, and more especially Jack Jones, entered his life and opened his eyes.

Tribune in the Bevanite years was the nerve-centre of a lively intellectual world. The presence of a highly intelligent woman, Elizabeth Thomas, on its staff, moving steadily up the ranks to become literary editor, was a signal.[24] Foot himself had a growing and attractive range of friends. He was on warm terms with three young journalist colleagues, Ian Aitken and Geoffrey Goodman, on the *Express* and *News Chronicle* respectively by 1954, and Tom Baistow, also on the *News Chronicle*; he would enjoy meeting them for a drink or perhaps a meal at the George, a pub near the Tribune offices on The Strand. Foot was always unembarrassed at his bourgeois and comfortable lifestyle, and happy to make a political point of it. When he dined at Leoni's, an Italian restaurant in Soho, he would point out that it was 'where Karl Marx had once found sanctuary'. A new venue for meeting friends was the Gay Hussar, just off Soho Square in Greek Street, founded in 1953 by a recent Hungarian immigrant, Victor Sassie. It became famous for its goulash and the powerful red wine 'Bull's Blood'. For the remainder of his days it would be an important landmark, almost a shrine, for Michael Foot, the social venue where he felt most at home. It was reassuringly close to the bookshops of Charing Cross Road and to the burial place of his greatest literary hero, William Hazlitt, in St Ann's Soho. Foot donated copies of all his own books to the restaurant's growing shelves of left-wing volumes, and his portrait was prominent on its walls. It was natural that the main celebration of his ninetieth birthday in 2003 should take place in an upstairs dining room in what had for decades been his second home.[25]

At the Gay Hussar he lunched with other important new friends too. One was James Cameron, a crusading left-wing journalist on the

Lib–Lab *News Chronicle* who had made his name with thrilling dispatches during the Korean War. He shared with Foot a deep love of India, and indeed added to his appeal for Foot when he married an Indian woman, Moneesha Sarka ('Moni'), another close friend. Cameron stood shoulder to shoulder with Foot in many a subsequent campaign, especially on marches to Aldermaston. Perhaps closer still was 'Vicky', Victor Weisz, a compassionate, tormented man who was to commit suicide during the atrocities of the Vietnam War. He became the greatest British cartoonist since the heyday of David Low, chiefly in the *News Chronicle* but later, less successfully, in the *Express*. Viennese Jewish and passionately socialist, Vicky became a master draughtsman: his famous depiction of Harold Macmillan as 'Supermac' perhaps did Labour little good at general elections. Often attracted to cartoonists, like Abu and Austin later on, Foot admired Vicky's radicalism, his quixotic outlook, his *mitteleuropa* romanticism. They shared a common passion for the German romantic poet Heinrich Heine. To Foot, Vicky's presence showed the best of the British liberal tradition, welcoming an immigrant to our shores to enrich our culture. With him, as with few others of his friends, Foot found friendship turning into communion and love.[26]

Michael Foot, for all his public image of prickly, aggressive dogmatism which upset the right-wing papers and television viewers, was indeed a warm and generous man. He did not forget his friends. He lived for their intimacy and steeped himself in their ideas. But with one friend the ties were abruptly snapped. This was Arthur Koestler, a frequent visitor and drinking companion. In May 1952 Koestler was with Jill in the Foots' Hampstead home, after visiting local pubs, and insisted that she make him some lunch. As she was doing so, he attacked her physically and raped her. Screaming and shaken, she felt herself being hit again and again. In the end she staggered outside, bruised and with her clothes torn, trying to regain some kind of composure but deeply distressed. She told Michael afterwards that Koestler had attacked her, but apparently did not tell him that she had been raped. They took no legal action, in the presumed anti-feminist climate of the time which would have assumed that Jill had invited Koestler's sexual attentions. No mention was made of the incident for forty-three years, until, in the unlikely setting of a review of David

Cesarani's biography of Koestler in the *Financial Times*, Foot observed almost casually that 'Koestler had tried to rape my wife'. There was an unedifying attempt by one of Koestler's biographers to dispute the facts, but the news surprised no one who had known the writer personally. His unfeeling attitude towards women was well-known. Tony Crosland had called him a 'serial rapist'; Richard Crossman, whose wife Zita had suffered a similar attempt, said that Koestler was 'a hell of a raper'. Extraordinarily enough, the Foots resumed some kind of contact with Koestler after this episode, and Foot made no reference to it in an essay on Koestler in *Debts of Honour* (1980). But the magic for Foot of close intimacy with his fellow Zionist, brilliant author of *Darkness at Noon*, evaporated for ever.[27]

The rape episode was only one of many that made these years less than comfortable for Jill Craigie. Her relationship with Michael was content if childless by mutual agreement. She found professional opportunities, if more sporadically, including as screenwriter for the successful film *The Million Pound Note* (1954), an adaptation of a story by Mark Twain, which led to a close friendship with its main actor, Gregory Peck. But there were rows with Michael about the Bevanite campaign, and money worries. The financial disaster threatened by the Kemsley libel case caused her anxiety. Money seemed short, not least with the costs of her daughter Julie's education. Charles Wintour told Beaverbrook, 'I get the impression that the Foots could use a little more too. They like to live reasonably well, and furnishing their house, small though it is, must have been quite an item, paid for by Jill.'[28]

Just before this, on 10–11 December 1954, Michael and Jill had moved into a new home. They had had to leave their house in Rosslyn Hill in 1953, when the Ecclesiastical Commissioners refused to renew their lease, which confirmed Foot's hostile view of all Churches. They spent a few months in another Hampstead house, 4 Hampstead Hill Gardens. There it was very much a hand-to-mouth existence, including reportedly for a time sleeping in their car. They were then given shelter by Foot's friend J. P. W. Mallalieu and his wife, and lived with them in Hampton Court for six months before some domestic disagreement between Jill and Mrs Mallalieu put an end to the arrangement.[29] Again they were homeless. But again the old patron, Beaverbrook, helped out with rare generosity. He gave them the use, rent-free, of Paddock Cottage on the Cherkley estate. The Foots, or rather Jill, decorated and maintained it at their own expense. The Beaverbrook home was attractively located. Jill said that it meant living in the countryside; this was questioned by Michael's country-loving sister Sally, who retorted that they were really living in a private park.[30] It was nevertheless remarkably generous of Beaverbrook to give them use of the cottage, effectively as a second home, for years to come. It was, in turn, remarkably insouciant of Foot to accept the gift of a right-wing millionaire capitalist, even if he did not advertise the fact to the *Tribune* staff. Here was perhaps a more intimate donation than the free summer holidays provided for Tony and Cherie Blair by various rich Continental friends after 1997, which led to sceptical press comment. There were suggestions that Foot used his contacts with Beaverbrook to encourage Express Newspapers to push his own views, including stirring up criticism of Bevan during the rift between him and Foot during 1958.[31] This may not have been so, but there certainly was a highly personal, almost naïve, quasi-paternal relationship between the press magnate and the editor of *Tribune*. In the meantime, in December 1954, as noted, the Foots moved into a new house in St John's Wood, 32A Abbey Road, where they were to live for the next ten years. It was a modern house in an expensive area of London, and apparently entailed Jill selling a minor painting by Renoir once given her by an admirer, Malcolm MacDonald. The £2,000 this sale realized provided one-third of the cost of their new house.

In May 1955 the new Prime Minister, Anthony Eden, called a general election shortly after he had succeeded the octogenarian Churchill in Downing Street. This was bound to be a difficult campaign for Labour. Prosperity and consumer affluence had been growing since the end of the Korean War in 1953, and the falling cost of raw materials worldwide gave a gratuitous boost to the balance of payments. In addition, the Conservatives had not met the left's bleak expectations about a Tory government: Walter Monckton as Minister of Labour had been notably amiable towards the unions, as indeed had Winston Churchill himself. Labour's own seemingly endless wranglings, mostly involving Foot's intimate friend Bevan, gave the Conservatives a moral advantage and, save for occasional intervals such as from August to November 1954, they usually led in the opinion polls.

It was clear that it would also be a difficult contest for Foot. His Devonport seat might be considered marginal, even though local journalists felt that he would scrape home. Randolph Churchill had left the political scene, but Foot's Conservative opponent was the most formidable he had yet experienced. This was Miss Joan Vickers, who had served nine years on the London County Council, and who had worked in the Colonial Service and with war prisoners, along with the Red Cross. Her strong experience of social work, and her appeal to women voters, whom she talked to in shops or cinema queues, gave her many advantages. The constituency had perhaps changed in her favour since 1951, with new private housing on its fringes, plus some help from redistribution.[32] On the other hand, there was a Liberal candidate, A. Russell Mayne, a Plymouth-born estate agent, who might siphon off a few crucial Conservative votes.

It was a quiet campaign, with television eating into the enthusiasm for public meetings: 'Devonport has never heard such a muted Michael Foot,' wrote the *Western Morning News*'s lobby correspondent.[33] Foot's was not only a quiet campaign, but possibly not a very sensible one. He made no attempt to moderate his views on defence spending and especially on the bomb, which was not perhaps the best line to take before service voters and their families. He spoke strongly on such traditional socialist issues as the steel and road haulage industries, which the Tories had denationalized, along with nationalizing ICI and the rest of the chemical industry, also not vote-winners. His supporting speakers were what a local journalist called 'the Bevanite circus', Bevan himself, Jennie Lee and the pacifist Methodist Dr Donald Soper.[34] Votes seemed to be slipping away, though Foot's agent Ron Lemin still felt his man would get home. But on polling day there was heavy rain in the evening, when most Labour voters went out to vote. The turnout fell from 82 per cent in 1951 to 77 per cent. So, in the closest of finishes, Joan Vickers polled 24,821 votes against Foot's 24,721, and the Liberal's 3,100. Foot was out by just one hundred after a recount. Nationally, Labour's poll fell by a million and a half, and there was a 2.5 per cent swing to the Conservatives. With a majority of sixty-eight over Labour, four or five more years of Tory rule were guaranteed. Isaac Foot wrote sensitively to his son, telling him that his own six electoral defeats were more honourable than his five victories, and sending him a valuable first edition of Swift.[35] But it was still an immense blow for Michael. His life would have to start all over again.

After the election he had time on his hands and a living to earn. He still had *Tribune*, of course, and became its editor again in December. He was still writing weekly columns for the *Daily Herald*, though they give the impression of being in the way of throwaway ephemera. His bank account benefited from the *Herald*, but his heart was always in *Tribune*. With his new freedom he changed the direction of his life, as will be seen in the next chapter, and spent the next twelve months fulfilling an old ambition by writing a serious book about Dean Swift. In *Tribune* he wrote about matters great and small. There were several opportunities for light relief, including Princess Margaret's affair with the divorced Group Captain Peter Townsend and other aspects of the life of the royal family. When it was reported that Grace Kelly and her husband Prince Rainier were looking for someone to run the finances of Monaco, Foot suggested that Macmillan should move there from the British Treasury.[36] More seriously, he kept up solid support for Bevan, and encouraged his bid to become leader when Attlee retired in November 1955. But Gaitskell was easily elected, with 157 MPs' votes to Bevan's seventy and Herbert Morrison's forty. It was known that Gaitskell's supporters included Harold Wilson, who soon became Shadow Chancellor. More striking was Bevan's return to the fold. He became shadow spokesman for colonial policy, then defeated George Brown to become Party Treasurer at the 1956 party conference at Blackpool. Shortly afterwards Gaitskell made him shadow foreign affairs spokesman, and they collaborated together henceforth, with perhaps less difficulty than is implied by Foot's account in his biography of Bevan.

By far the greatest political event of this period was the Suez crisis, when British troops were sent into Egypt in October–November 1956. Soon after it was over, and Eden had resigned as Prime Minister, it emerged that it had resulted from secret collusion between Britain, France and Israel to invade Egypt, following President Nasser's decision to nationalize the Suez Canal. Here was a natural opportunity for Foot's exposé journalism, and with a *Tribune* colleague, Mervyn Jones, he produced in rapid time a 264-page book which was published on 1 April 1957 by Gollancz with the familiar yellow jacket, under the title *Guilty Men, 1957: Macmillan etc.*[37] The subtitle perhaps caused most comment, since Harold Macmillan was now Prime Minister, and the extent of his bizarre manoeuvrings, first to promote the Suez adventure, then to stop it following severe US pressure on the reserves and on sterling, was not yet known. Foot was again identified as 'part-author of *Guilty Men*', and there were excellent cartoons from his friend Vicky. Much the liveliest part of the book is the first few pages, 'At the Palace', with the usual satirical sketches of Conservative leaders at the time of Macmillan's out-manoeuvring of Butler to become Prime Minister in January. After that there is a fairly dense narrative account of the events from their origins, from Gladstone's sending troops to the region in 1882, to Eden's ignominious withdrawal. While Gaitskell does receive incidental praise for opposing the Suez venture in the end, the book's finale inevitably comes from a broadside by Bevan in the Commons on 19 December. In fact Bevan himself, with his deep sympathies for Israel, had been somewhat more equivocal than Gaitskell in pronouncing on the crisis: Tory newspapers considered him almost a patriot compared with his traitorous leader.[38] Foot, however, seems to have had no difficulty in condemning the Suez invasion; it gave him even more grist for his mill when he attacked Tony Blair's involvement in the Iraq invasion in 2003. His criticisms, however, focused almost entirely on the illegalities committed by Eden and the French premier, Guy Mollet. Israel's response he saw as the result of Arab provocation. On balance the new *Guilty Men* lacked the sparkle, originality and element of surprise of its 1940 predecessor. Reviewers felt it was too partisan to be wholly effective. Other books on Suez followed, with fuller and fresher revelations that left it behind.

The aftermath of Suez was relatively short-lived, so immediate and complete was the Anglo–French climbdown. By the time Foot's Suez book appeared, public debate was being increasingly dominated by an even more momentous issue, namely Britain's development and testing of nuclear weapons. This had always been an uneasy problem between Aneurin Bevan and Michael Foot, and often caused tensions on Tribune's editorial board, which Bevan sometimes attended. There was much anxiety among Labour MPs when repeated British tests took place on Christmas Island in the Pacific. On 24 May *Tribune* published an article by Bevan, 'Destroy the Bombs Before They Destroy Us'.[39]

Everyone could agree with this; the question was how to do so. In August there came a very different clarion call from the octogenarian philosopher Bertrand Russell which called passionately for a unilateral renunciation of nuclear weapons, whose development, let alone use, he called 'a vast atrocity'. Michael Foot strongly committed *Tribune* to this standpoint, arguing that using nuclear weapons would simply mean worldwide mass suicide.

He was not closely in touch with Bevan in the run-up to the party conference in Brighton at the start of October 1957. In the *Tribune* of 4 October, Foot's focus was on the debate on the policy document 'Industry and Society', a modest statement of Labour attitudes to further nationalization, including regulation of private industry and the purchase of shares by the government. Gaitskell's defence of it, wrote Foot, was 'evasive and unconvincing', though Bevan found it quite adequate as a transitional view.[40] But the crucial debate, which took place on 2 October, was on a unilateralist amendment to the official party motion on nuclear weapons. Aneurin Bevan's view was a matter of intense speculation on the left, and it was known that he was wrestling with his conscience in painful fashion. In fact, Foot had already guessed beforehand that Bevan would not endorse unilateralism.[41] He knew that Bevan was impressed by talks he had had with Nikita Khrushchev in Moscow during the summer. The Russian leader had insisted that it was essential for meaningful great-power diplomacy for Britain to retain its own nuclear weaponry and thus make its own contribution to any settlement. Barbara Castle and others had also given indications to Foot of Bevan's likely attitude, while a Tribune meeting the day before saw Bevan confirming this view. It was clinched at a long meeting that evening, involving several bottles of whisky, with the Durham miners' leader Sam Watson.

Even so, Bevan's speech at conference the next day was a huge shock to Michael Foot and to almost all the old Bevanite and Tribunite supporters. It was a confused speech, revealing the torment and intellectual self-torture that Bevan had undergone over months past. Crossman thought it 'a ghastly performance', though 'immensely impressive' when heckling began and the old bull was enraged by his tormentors.[42] Bevan conceded the need to stop nuclear tests, and the urgency of getting rid of all nuclear weapons in rapid time. But his essential point was that if it renounced its own weapons unilaterally, Britain would lose any influence on future negotiations, it would be ignored by the Americans, whom we had to influence, and it would become a laughing-stock throughout the world. In effect, it would cease to be a great power. But, as John Campbell has rightly observed, it was not what Bevan said, but the way he said it.[43] Goaded by waves of heckling from his former supporters on the left, he talked of their wishing to send a British Foreign Secretary 'naked into the conference chamber'. In the most wounding phrase of all, he almost screamed, 'You call that statesmanship? I call it an emotional spasm.' That evening, with James Cameron, Geoffrey Goodman and other friends, Foot sat miserably in a Brighton bar. His god had failed. Nye, his idol, his hero, his supreme fount of inspiration and hope, had betrayed the principles in which they all believed. It was easily the most wounding experience of Foot's life.

But, passionate as he was about Britain's renouncing the use of nuclear weapons, he recovered from his immediate gloom to deliver a measured response in *Tribune*. In 'Bevan and the H-Bomb' on 11 October, Foot deployed a range of strong arguments. Countries like India, West Germany and China exercised great influence on world events without having an H-bomb. Britain's stance meant a total dependence on the United States, and a permanent confrontation between massed alliances and pacts all over the world. Worst of all, Britain was committing itself to a horrific and utterly immoral weapon whose use would mean collective suicide.[44]

Foot's position gained massive endorsement from individuals in the party and beyond. One of them was Frank Cousins, the new General Secretary of the Transport and General Workers' Union, who had delivered an emotional speech condemning nuclear weapons, and using his daughter as a symbol of the new generation he wished to protect. Although never close to Bevan, Cousins was to become an important figure in Foot's life, his first significant friend amongst the union leaders. He and his wife Nance were to be frequent dinner guests of the Foots.[45] In the pages, especially the correspondence columns, of *Tribune*, the debate about Bevan continued to rage. Mervyn Jones has told us that Foot, anxious to preserve some kind of balance, actually wrote letters himself to support Bevan's position. On 18 October *Tribune* published a counter-article from Jennie Lee which in effect repeated her husband's line at conference. The Russians, she wrote, would be contemptuous of a country that dismantled its own weaponry without any regard to others. Foot speculated that these were not perhaps Jennie Lee's own feelings, but the evidence from Patricia Hollis's biography is that she too had been converted to Nye's point of view.[46] Bevan himself wrote in *Tribune* too, on the continuing importance of the nation state and the need to retain the ability to act independently in world affairs. The entire *Tribune* staff were much divided, and board meetings were angry. Bob Millar, the business manager, was strongly pro-Bevan, and reportedly leaked news of divisions among the board to the *Daily Mail*.[47] There was no meeting of minds on so fundamental an issue, especially after the Campaign for Nuclear Disarmament was formed early in 1958. As will be seen, its first Easter march to Aldermaston heralded a new stage in the mass protest and debate over Britain's possession of nuclear weapons. So far as Michael Foot was concerned, he and his hero were hopelessly at odds. They met less and less frequently; they were driven far apart by a fundamental difference of principle. Thrown out of Parliament, his party self-destructing, his idol disappointing his old friends, Michael Foot had never felt more depressed.

The rift with Bevan continued for a considerable time, perhaps well over a year, certainly longer than Foot indicates in his biography of Bevan, where the whole affair is dealt with, understandably, briefly and in a general way. Throughout 1958, as Labour's foreign affairs spokesman, Bevan showed no sign of relenting in his views on Britain retaining its nuclear weapons. He even moved towards the proposition that Britain should endorse the possible first use of tactical atomic weapons, a view put forward by the Labour right, notably by the defence spokesman George Brown. Gaitskell and Bevan, if never personally close, were now proving a strong team in foreign policy debates. They agreed about the cessation of nuclear tests, and the need to convene four-power talks to stop them. Together they also took the initiative in pressing for a scheme for disengagement in central Europe, with the eventual reunification of Germany: they both endorsed the Rapacki plan for central Europe put forward by the Polish government. Foot seemed more and more a fringe figure, sad and forlorn. His meetings with Bevan were infrequent.

At one of these meetings some time in 1958, a legendary clash occurred. After a somewhat alcoholic reception at the Polish embassy, Bevan and Jennie Lee went back to the Foots' home in St John's Wood, where a passionate argument broke out between Bevan and Foot over the H-bomb. Voices were raised, and it even seemed possible that the two men might come to blows, a unique event for Michael Foot. Instead Bevan vented his fury on one of Jill's antique Sheraton chairs, which he smashed to the floor before leaving, violently angry. The next morning Jill rang up Jennie Lee to try to mend fences (though not, unfortunately, the Sheraton chair), and a kind of personal reconciliation was managed.[48] But the episode showed the potential for a permanent rift or worse. Jennie Lee herself was furious at what she took to be *Tribune*'s personal attacks on Bevan. She also had her own strong grievances about *Tribune* policy, especially what she took to be Foot's surprisingly sympathetic remarks towards Tito and his ruthless treatment of dissidents like Milovan Djilas and the Yugoslav Vladimir Dedijer.[49] Certainly the newspaper laid major emphasis on the nuclear weapons issue, and became in effect the organ of the Campaign for Nuclear Disarmament. Its new deputy editor, Dick Clements, whom Foot had met on the *Daily Herald* and who had previously edited *Socialist Advance* for Transport House, ran a weekly banner headline on the front page: 'The Paper which Wants to Abolish the Bomb'.[50]

The impasse went on. In June 1958 Gaitskell reported to Hugh Dalton that Bevan's relations with Foot 'were now very bad and that Foot was trying to stir up Beaverbrook to attack Bevan'. Dalton responded that he had noticed references to Bevan in the *Sunday* and *Daily Express* 'which suggested that Bevan was no longer on the White List'.[51] Geoffrey Goodman, who saw Foot a great deal at this time, believed that he was in a state of 'emotional disrepair' after his quarrel with Bevan, and has questioned whether their relationship was ever properly repaired. Bevan is quoted as saying, 'Deep down, Michael is still a Liberal,' and a compliment was not intended.[52] Even as late as June 1959 Richard Crossman's diary records Foot as being deeply depressed: 'When I suggested we might recreate an informal group with Nye to discuss nuclear weapons, Michael told me he had no kind of relations with Nye. Only once this year had he seen him. He had

been over to the farm just after Aldermaston. He had a pleasant afternoon but only because each side had carefully avoided discussing
anything serious at all. In fact, Michael and Nye have had no political
contact for over a year.' Foot is reported as saying gloomily that
Crossman, Tony Greenwood and Barbara Castle would be better off
talking to Bevan: 'I'm no good these days.'[53] Foot's whole career
seemed to be on hold. He was no longer the most famous Foot. Dingle
had finally joined the Labour Party at the time of the 1955 election,
and was elected Labour Member for Ipswich in 1957 (the decisive
agent seems to have been not Michael, but Dingle's close friend and
fellow ex-left-wing Liberal Megan Lloyd George, daughter of the
former Prime Minister). Hugh was now winning golden opinions for
his statesmanlike role as Governor of Cyprus in handling the alarming
threat from Greek Cypriot EOKA terrorists waging a relentless guerrilla campaign against British rule. Michael appeared more a querulous
gadfly, buzzing about in the wings.

He worked off some of his frustration with attacks on the Labour
Party leadership, and especially the whips, for trying to suppress free
debate within the parliamentary party. *Tribune* at this time is full of
complaints about the repressive use of standing orders to this end. In
1959 Foot published, in a series of small pamphlets for Pall Mall Press,
Parliament in Danger!. It had previously appeared in article form in the
Observer, with whose political correspondent, Hugh Massingham, he
was friendly. Foot here made several strong points about the stifling
effect on political life of an over-disciplinary party system, drawing on
impressive historical examples, notably Edmund Burke, that famous
champion of the independence of MPs. He proposed a number of
procedural reforms, including more free votes in the Commons and
the opening up of closed meetings of parliamentary parties. He was
himself to exemplify some of the merits (and also some of the draw-
backs) of this approach when he returned to the Commons. But it was
noticeable that the pamphlet had the air of settling old scores. The
champions of rigid party discipline seemed to be mainly on the Labour
side, notably Attlee, Morrison and Gaitskell. The last-named was
sharply taken to task for drawing a distinction between an MP's vote
and his 'judgement, thought and speech'.[54] At least Foot could sometimes extract humour from a bleak situation. On 28 November 1958

the sage 'John Marullus' can be found ironically complimenting Transport House for publishing *The Future Labour Offers You* in the green and black colours of Plymouth Argyle. Perhaps this offered 'an unconscious act of appeasement towards *Tribune*'.[55]

One unexpected diversion came in France. In May 1958 the *Daily Herald* dispatched Foot to Paris to report on the political turmoil surrounding the fall of the Fourth Republic and the emergence of de Gaulle as leader. He took this very seriously, writing to his agent Peter Jackson, 'events which have been happening in France may be extremely important for all of us, just as what happened in Germany twenty years ago eventually resulted in the bombing of Plymouth. The *Daily Herald* has in my view been by far the best paper in Britain reporting events in France, just as it has improved greatly in other respects in recent months.'[56] Predictably, Foot was fiercely critical of de Gaulle's role in the crisis. This 'self-appointed national saviour' was the beneficiary of a conspiracy between the military and the politicians, together with the craven Vichy-like appeasement offered by the Pflimlin government, the last administration of the Fourth Republic, which effectively sacrificed the old republic by yielding to pressure from military leaders in Algeria.

Finally Foot launched an attack on President René Coty, formerly a leading figure under Vichy and famous for the manufacture of perfume, who, he declared, had surrendered supinely to illegality like Pétain before him. This was too much for the French authorities, and for the first and only time in his life Foot faced physical danger, and was imprisoned without explanation in the Paris prefecture with another British journalist. An alarmed Jill did not know where he was. The *Herald*'s Paris correspondent, David Ross, a regular contributor to *Tribune*, later blamed himself for not making clearer to Foot the risks he was running. Eventually Foot was flown back home, where he denounced Coty in Cobbett-like terms, with some help from the Bard: 'Coty . . . is the Great Nothing of the Fourth Republic . . . All the perfumes of Arabia will not sweeten the name of Coty.'[57] It should be added that as de Gaulle's presidency unfolded in the sixties, Foot's views became a good deal more cordial, particularly after the withdrawal of French troops from Algeria and the diplomatic stance of resistance towards the United States shown by de Gaulle on numerous issues.

Foot desperately needed a more prominent platform and a stronger voice. CND and *Tribune* were essentially locations on the fringe, even in the Labour Party. Above all, he wanted to return to the Commons. In the summer of 1959 he and Bevan at last had a proper reconciliation, and much of the old warmth returned. For Foot it was a kiss of life. There had been prospects of a safe seat before. The MP for Aberavon, W. G. Cove, sympathetic to the Bevanites, had approached Foot suggesting that he inherit his twenty-thousand-odd majority. Trade unions in the constituency had written in numbers asking Foot to put his name forward. He had also been approached about by-elections in Wednesbury, Ipswich (where Dingle was elected Labour Member in 1957), Gloucester, Gateshead and St Helens, and also about nomination for Bishop Auckland, all of them seats with strong Labour majorities. But he felt committed to Devonport, 'quixotic' though Nye Bevan thought this to be.[58]

His home town, however, was now anything but a hopeful prospect. The Conservative Member for his old constituency, Joan Vickers, had been a good MP since 1955, and had built up a strong personal vote, especially amongst women. She had pushed issues like the treatment of wives deserted by their husbands, and had been prominent in debates on the many African questions that loomed large at this time. There was also a likelihood that population movements would help the Conservatives, with many old Labour areas affected by the drift of people into neighbouring Sutton and to dormitory areas outside the city.[59] On the other hand, there were still eighteen thousand rock-solid Labour voters amongst the dockyard workers of Devonport. But a poll in the *Daily Express* on 14 March 1959 showed a huge lead of 18.5 per cent for Joan Vickers over Michael Foot. Its reporter, Francis Cassavetti, concluded that Foot had no hope of winning the seat back.[60]

The Labour Party in Devonport had been energetic, and conducted 100 per cent canvasses in many areas. Foot, however, had a problem with his agent Peter Jackson, an anxious man of somewhat unstable personality. He wrote to Foot in June 1958 expressing concern about his absences from the constituency, notably his eventful visit to Paris for the *Herald*. He also voiced alarm at Foot's heavy involvement in the Campaign for Nuclear Disarmament. Foot, needless to say, rejected the latter point: 'I believe that the policy of the British government on the subject is utterly disastrous.' He added, 'If we are going . . . to have a strong Labour Government (and any other kind of Government is worse than useless) we must be prepared to make a much more aggressive attack on the Tories, [and] explain Labour policy more persistently.' In November Jackson was expressing further anxiety about the state of organization in Devonport, and wrote a somewhat panicky letter direct to Labour's General Secretary Morgan Phillips. He talked of a 'showdown' in the local party.[61] Foot's response was measured and firm. There should be no showdown: 'There were feuds and quarrels inside the Party when you took over and there has certainly been much too much inertia among many people in the Party about getting on with the job of propaganda,' but things had improved. He particularly resisted Jackson's suggestion of the member of the National Executive coming down to Plymouth to sort things out. He also defended his own proposal for a special *Tribune* publicity project to be launched in the constituency – 'This I am sure could be one of the finest pieces of propaganda attempted by any constituency party in the country.'[62] Reluctantly, the agent climbed down.

Harold Macmillan called a general election for 8 October 1959, and Labour began the campaign in good heart, with the polls mostly putting them in the lead nationwide. In Devonport, with the constant support of Jill and his terrier Vanessa (a present from his stepdaughter Julie), Foot campaigned with more punch than in 1955. He emphasized the rise in unemployment in Plymouth to three thousand (double the national average), along with new initiatives on pensions and education.[63] There were various 'soak the rich' recommendations to deal with speculators much in the news, like the property developer Charles Clore, through a capital gains tax. But he also made no effort to soft-pedal on the nuclear issue: 'Most people know I go further than many of my colleagues in the Labour Party. Nuclear weapons are no use to us. To use them would mean national suicide. They are futile as well as evil.'[64] He had few supporting speakers. As in 1955 the constituency was visited by the Methodist pacifist Donald Soper, a passionate member of CND. More seriously, Aneurin Bevan, due to attend a large Labour rally in Plymouth after an appearance in Swansea, was unable to come, since he was suffering from what the press called 'influenza and a severe sinus infection'.[65] Foot always knew that Joan

Vickers would win. There was an increased turnout of 78.62 per cent, compared with 77.15 per cent in 1955, which was thought to favour Labour. But the Conservatives ended up with a large 6,454 majority. Labour's vote fell by 2,700 to 22,027. Nationally, the Conservatives took 49.3 per cent of the vote to Labour's 43.9 per cent, a nationwide swing of 1 per cent; Devonport's swing was far greater than this. Foot was gallant in defeat: he told his agent Peter Jackson that he lost because of the 'general swing', not because of his own views. In many wards the Labour vote had held up strongly.[66] But he was out again. Jill was near tears. Poor Jackson was to take the defeat very badly, and subsequently his life collapsed, with breakdowns, divorce and suspected suicide. For Michael Foot the result meant that he remained a figure on the fringe.[67]

Things got even worse. Aneurin Bevan produced a riveting final performance at the post-election party conference, with a breathtaking speech that rescued Gaitskell over the party's policy on the economy and private ownership. He made brilliant use of Lenin's views on the commanding heights of the economy to reconcile Gaitskell's speech with that of Barbara Castle, who struck a far more socialist note. But he also used his considerable influence to suppress Gaitskell's maladroit suggestion that the party jettison Clause Four of its constitution, the commitment to nationalization, and even more Douglas Jay's weird proposal in *Forward* after the election that Labour change its name, because it seemed old-fashioned. Foot believed that a right-wing conspiracy had been foiled by his old hero. In *Tribune* he noted the very different terms in which Gaitskell and Bevan had spoken of socialism. All Bevan's old charisma and power were on display. The magic was back.

But Foot knew that in reality Nye was a very sick man. That was why he had failed to speak at Devonport. At a meeting of the *Tribune* board, according to Foot, Bevan 'saw Gaitskell and Gaitskellism as more of a threat than ever to the kind of socialism he had dreamed of and fought for all his life'.[68] The leader's 'mixed economy' programme did not appear to Bevan to be socialism at all. Shortly after Christmas Foot saw him, and Bevan was at his sparkling best in a rumbustious conversation. Two days later he had an operation for malignant cancer in Hampstead's Royal Free hospital. He was declining fast, with Jennie

Lee, and old comrades like Michael Foot, his closest friend from Tredegar Archie Lush and his doctor Dai Davies, in constant attendance. In late March 1960 he gave a non-political interview to journalists, with some cautionary words for future authors (and their reviewers): 'I understand that Mr Macmillan reads political biographies. I have never been able to achieve that degree of credulity.' He quoted (in English translation) from Eifion Wyn's famous Welsh *awdl* (poem) 'Cwm Pennant' – 'O Lord why did you make the world so beautiful and the life of the old shepherd so short?'[69] On 6 July he died in his sleep. Foot was distraught. On 8 July there appeared in *Tribune* his beautifully crafted appreciation of Bevan, 'the most *principled* great political leader of the century'. Foot's biography conveyed the pathos of the moment even more poignantly: 'he was like a great tree hacked down wantonly in full leaf'.[70]

In their final conversations Bevan and Foot had discussed an important political matter. Bevan had urgently pressed his friend to succeed him as Member of Parliament for Ebbw Vale. With much support from Bill Harry and other Bevan intimates in the constituency, Foot now actively sought the nomination.[71] But this proved to be very difficult. Foot, as a unilateralist, and perhaps even more as an Englishman, was not necessarily the most appropriate candidate for a south Wales constituency. Even Bevan himself had not met with universal popularity in his home territory: he was regarded as a London-based politician. Foot's passionate support for CND was suspect in many quarters, not least the steel union with its right-wing, Gaitskellite leadership. The Ebbw Vale steelworks was central to the industrial future of the constituency. When the shortlist for the Labour candidacy was announced after a very disorderly process, to general astonishment Michael Foot's name was not even on it. Nor was the miners' nominee, Frank Whatley. The five people on the list, all male as was customary in south Wales, were a modest group – Ron Evans (Bevan's old agent), Fred Evans (a teacher and later MP for Caerphilly), Gordon Parry from Pembrokeshire, Dr K. G. Pendse and Tom Williams, a barrister and former MP.[72] None approached Foot's reputation or charisma. Much pressure was now applied to the constituency party to change its mind. In particular Frank Cousins, staying in London with Geoffrey Goodman at the time, picked up the phone and demanded of his

TGWU members in Ebbw Vale that they ensure that Foot was a candidate.[73] Archie Lush, Bevan's old colleague, also put pressure on local party officials. On 19 September the general management committee added both Foot and Whatley's names to the shortlist. At the selection meeting on 24 September, Foot made a powerful speech which laid the fullest emphasis on his unilateralism and opposition to Britain's possession of nuclear weapons. In the first ballot he received sixty-seven votes, the runner-up being Ron Evans. Foot was selected on the third ballot.[74] Evans, a generous man, took his defeat in the best of spirits. Indeed, he would serve as Foot's agent, and remained a close personal friend until his death in 1991.[75]

The by-election came in mid-November, following on from an exceptionally bitter and divisive party conference at Scarborough in which Foot took a leading part. There was no question of Foot's not winning easily – Bevan's majority had been over twenty thousand in 1959. In his campaign Foot laid particular emphasis on the steel industry: nationalization was a major issue, since the Richard Thomas & Baldwin works in Ebbw Vale was shortly to be denationalized.[76] His election address declared that the sell-off of RTB was 'nothing short of an outrage'. He also supported a substantial pay increase for the miners. At meetings in Ebbw Vale, Tredegar and Glyncoed, nearly all his supporting speakers came from the left. They included Judith Hart, Harold Wilson, Ian Mikardo, Will Griffiths, Richard Crossman, Sydney Silverman and even Konni Zilliacus, now back once again on the Labour benches, though scarcely diluted in his ideas.[77] The only representatives of the centre-right were John Morris, the new MP for Aberavon, and Jim Callaghan. The latter took sharp issue with Foot's views on defence policy, for which he was both heckled and applauded. After the poll, Callaghan wrote to Ron Evans that it had been agreed he would say something on defence 'as unprovocatively as possible'.[78] Easily the most embarrassing document was a formal letter of support from the party leader. Gaitskell noted that he and Foot 'disagreed strongly' on foreign and defence policy: 'But I understand that much of your campaign has been fought on home affairs.' He wished Foot luck in the campaign for Democratic Socialism (Gaitskell's capitals), but it was hardly a cordial endorsement.[79]

Foot's speeches were, as always, aggressive. He had fierce exchanges with the right-wing Conservative candidate, Sir Brandon Rhys-Williams, over the way the Tories had savaged Nye Bevan. Williams was informed that he possessed 'pin-headed intellectual capacity'.[80] Seven by-election results were announced on 18 November. Labour lost six of them in Tory-held seats in different parts of the country. But in Ebbw Vale it was totally different. Foot swept home with a majority of 16,729: he polled 20,528 votes against Williams's 3,799. Williams, like the Liberal and Plaid Cymru candidates, lost his deposit. Foot's share of the vote was 68.7 per cent, compared with 81 per cent for Bevan in 1959. But there had been only two candidates in the general election; in November 1960 there were four. It was a victory, Foot told the Ebbw Vale electors, using the same formulation as he had before the Monmouth voters in 1935, for socialism and peace. The electors had demanded 'a new foreign policy which repudiates nuclear strategy altogether'.[81] Foot's great friend Vicky produced an appropriate cartoon of Gaitskell reading the Ebbw Vale result in a newspaper. He is shown lamenting, 'Oh, dear, we've won.' Foot was particularly excited by a congratulatory letter from the author Compton Mackenzie, a supporter of CND: 'I can't tell you how delighted I was to receive it – from one of my heroes!'[82]

Foot's return to Parliament, symbolically as Member for Aneurin Bevan's constituency and ancestral home, rounded off a troubled and frustrating decade. Politically, he had little to show for his endeavours. He had spent more than five years out of Parliament. Both in and out of the House, he had been in constant quarrels with parliamentary and party colleagues. Some he relished, notably his long vendetta against Gaitskell. Easily the most wounding and stressful was his breach with Bevan. Like Hazlitt's famous disputes, it was 'the quarrel of the age'. Even at Nye's death, scars in their relationship remained. In November 1960 Foot's Labour Party also seemed at a low ebb, Gaitskell and the left wing, which now had many large unions in support, being passionately at odds with each other over policy towards the bomb. Gaitskell had said at Scarborough that he intended to 'fight, fight and fight again'. His opponents were equally combative. Ever since Bevan's resignation in April 1951 the party had seemed to be engaged in a long civil war, with years of Conservative rule as a result. As he resumed his role on the backbenches, Foot was still haunted by the legacy of

Bevan. Indeed, it would dominate his thoughts as totally as Bevan himself had when was alive, since he had agreed to Jennie Lee's proposal that he should be her husband's official biographer. Crossman prophesied that it would be his 'one and only' masterpiece.[83]

Foot, many felt, would now take over 'the mantle of Nye'. But the nature, or even the existence, of that elusive garment was much contested. Would Foot be still the incorrigible Bevanite freelance, crusading for a purer form of socialism, whatever the destructive outcome for Labour ever returning to power? Or, as he moved towards his fifties, would he turn into the more accommodating Nye of post-1956, still doctrinally on the left but working constructively for the Labour coalition to recapture power? Or would he avoid both choices and focus largely on being a polemical man of letters, a kind of political dilettante, seeking inspiration mainly from a selective view of the past and the wisdom of ancient texts, as he appeared to do after electoral defeat in 1955? On Foot's choice and his still half-developed idea of leadership much would depend as he contemplated a political rebirth.

6

CLASSIC AND ROMANTIC

'You will be glad to see Michael back in the House again. You are a rich man to have so many wonderful children.' So wrote Jennie Lee to Isaac Foot in late October 1960.[1] But two weeks after his son's election for Ebbw Vale, Isaac died, at the age of eighty. For Michael, probably the son Isaac felt closest to, it was deeply upsetting. He received the news on the day of his first speech in the Commons as Member for Ebbw Vale; not surprisingly, his speech, inevitably on the bomb, was not one of his best. Isaac had always declared that while being a politician was a defensible proposition, being a writer was a supreme vocation. Although he wrote little himself, he always encouraged Michael to become a writer of books, serious and scholarly works of literature that would stand the test of time, not ephemeral journalistic squibs. It was Isaac who directly inspired the most original and exciting new departure in Michael's career in the fifties, his volume on Dean Swift, *The Pen and the Sword*. In encouraging his son to turn his attention away from the political duel between Gaitskell and Bevan to that between the Duke of Marlborough and Robert Harley in the reign of Queen Anne, Isaac helped to show the world a new, and deeply rewarding, dimension of Michael's many talents.

Jonathan Swift, an ambiguous political figure at various times held to be Old Whig or neo-Jacobite Tory, had long been a hero of the Liberal Foot family. Isaac had handed this gospel on to Michael early in his life. The suggestion, after his defeat in Devonport in the 1955 election, that Michael should turn his energies to a book on Swift came directly from Isaac, as he fully acknowledged. It was a book he had been meditating for many years.[2] He wrote it not by way of orthodox research into manuscript materials in university or other libraries but through work done in Paddock Cottage on Beaverbrook's Cherkley estate, interspersed with visits to Pencrebar.[3] His essential sources were from his father's remarkable two-hundred-book collection of Swift's published correspondence and writings. It was in that sense a work of filio-piety and inherited scholarship.

Another person close to Foot who held Swift in the highest esteem was George Orwell. He had been brought up on *Gulliver's Travels* since he was a small child, and had remained obsessed by its author ever since. *Animal Farm* was commonly taken as a Swiftian satire on the modern hegemonic state. While being repelled by some aspects of Swift, Orwell hugely admired his incisive prose and his uninhibited style in challenging authority. In the essay 'Politics vs. Literature' (1948) he celebrated Swift for his rejection of the totalitarian police state that Orwell himself so memorably condemned in *Nineteen Eighty-Four*. Foot himself wrote of Swift's 'horror of state tyranny' as one of his most appealing features.[4] His interpretations of Swift, however, differed from those of Orwell in major respects. Orwell saw *Gulliver's Travels* as radical conservative propaganda (as commentators such as Ian Higgins have seen it as coded Jacobitism). Foot rather regarded Swift as a visionary social critic, a view which many scholars have found a refreshing corrective.[5]

Foot's literary heroes from the past also felt particularly inspired by Swift's work. Hazlitt, who perhaps held equal place to Swift in Foot's affections, was a great admirer of Swift's originality and boldness. So were Byron and, later on, H. G. Wells. When Foot discovered another of his father's heroes, Montaigne, whose *Essais* (1580) he read while recovering in hospital after his car accident in 1963, he found yet another precious link, since Montaigne's writings had been a great inspiration to Swift himself in the development of the essay form. The high regard in which Swift held Montaigne, as Foot showed, was confirmed by his giving a copy of his works to Stella, one of his two close women friends.[6] There was thus a kind of celestial literary descent, ranging from Montaigne, the sceptical *politique* of sixteenth-century Bordeaux, down to H. G. Wells, the suburban London socialist, three hundred years later. To Foot, Swift was the essential link in this inspired genealogy. Swift was no sort of socialist, but without understanding or appreciating him and his values, Michael Foot could not have been one either.

Other aspects of Swift also appealed to a man like Foot. One was his personality. It was marked by alternating extremes of humanity and misanthropy. Orwell saw Swift as 'a diseased writer'. He was 'permanently in a depressed mood rather as though someone suffering from jaundice or the after-effects of influenza should have the energy to write books . . . In the queerest way, pleasure and disgust are linked together.'[7] Foot's brother John, who enormously admired *The Pen and the Sword*, also wrote, 'Mind you, Swift is a disgusting fellow.'[8] Swift's was certainly an unstable personality, as the various shifts of mood in the four books of *Gulliver's Travels* suggest. It was a strange man who devoted poems to ageing whores, or whose satirical solution for Irish poverty in his *Modest Proposal* was to introduce cannibalism: the Irish should breed their children only for eating them. There were many suggestions that he may even have gone mad, and he certainly had a dismal death. But Foot cited medical and literary evidence, originally amassed by the doctor father of Oscar Wilde in the mid-nineteenth century, which showed that Swift's decline was physical rather than psychological. To him, Swift was the more fascinating precisely because of his angular, tormented personality. It made his comic writing the more spontaneous, his satire the more uninhibited, his visionary consciousness, as in his treatment of the Houyhnhnms and Yahoos in *Gulliver's Travels* as embodiments of Stoic reason and Epicurean passion respectively, the more searching and intriguing. Swift's frequent lapses into lugubrious misanthropy gave his writing a keener edge.

Foot also warmed to Swift as an outsider, both literary and political. The obscure backwoods Irish clergyman who stormed into English political debate in 1709–11 had yet to make much of a mark in the world. Even *A Tale of a Tub* (1704) had not impressed the public, partly because it was anonymous. Swift was a frustrated genius with huge ambitions unfulfilled. It was a type that always appealed to Foot. So did a very different personality, the outsider Jewish adventurer Benjamin Disraeli, another of his unlikely heroes. Perhaps Beaverbrook, the Canadian outsider who also invaded the English establishment, could be bracketed with them too. There was a kind of instinctive minority-mindedness in Foot which made the individual rebel like Swift, locked into a kind of permanent self-made exile, attractive to him. He liked a man who could shock and destabilize the

establishment single-handed, as Swift did to the Whig Junto in England
or the Protestant Ascendancy in Ireland. Similarly, Foot warmed to
H. G. Wells's undeniably destructive attacks on the old guard of the
Fabian Society, especially the Webbs. The fact that Swift, like Hazlitt,
was also an Irishman, who championed a kind of Irish nationalism and
attacked the class pretensions of the Ascendancy, reinforced his claim
to Foot's sympathies. After returning to Ireland in 1714 Swift pleaded
for his native land to be freed from its economic and political servitude
under English rule. Even if it was accompanied by a marked lack of
confidence in the Irish themselves, this still gave the latter stages of
Swift's controversial career a kind of nobility.[9] This aspect was also a
factor in Foot's intense admiration for yet another Irishman, Edmund
Burke, even in his most reactionary phase of opposition to the French
Revolution. The fact that Swift was a clergyman might have caused
problems for an agnostic like Michael Foot. But he argued that, far
from Swift being a sound churchman, it was debatable whether he was
even a Christian at all. Certainly, a writer who saw 'religious cant as
flatulence and charity as suppressed lust' was not overwhelmed by
piety.[10]

Swift's attitude towards women also made him congenial to Foot,
who insisted that he was a great defender of women's rights. He took
a particular delight years later, in October 1993, when in the presence
of Mary Robinson, the President of the Irish Republic, at the fourth
annual Swift seminar at Celbridge, County Kildare (Swift's friend
'Vanessa's' home), he hailed this aspect of Swift's public outlook. But
the implications for Swift's private life also fascinated Foot. Swift's
experiences with women both harmonized and humanized his life and
work. At times he could pour contempt on the entire female species;
some of his later poems, notably in 1730–31, were distinctly scatologi-
cal. But there was a frequent idealization of women as well. His
relations with his two famous close friends, 'Stella' (Esther Johnson)
and 'Vanessa' (Esther Van Homrigh), helped to make his personality
more complex and humane. Foot felt quite certain that Swift genuinely
loved both women. Almost all Foot's chosen literary heroes had distinctly powerful libidos. Talent was always reinforced by testosterone.
There was Hazlitt's inordinate passion for his landlady's daughter Sarah
Walker, and the scandal caused by his sexually-charged *Liber Amoris*,

which haunted his reputation after his death. Byron's serial infidelities, from Augusta Leigh to Lady Caroline Lamb, are too well-known to need rehearsal here: Foot objected to Fiona MacCarthy's life of Byron (2002), which suggested homosexual tendencies. H. G. Wells's irregular liaisons left a trail of human turmoil, from poor Amber Reeves during his Fabian days, on to Rebecca West and then Moura Budberg. Bertrand Russell was another much-married contemporary whose sex life entailed casual cruelty, but his gospel of liberated relationships was an important part of Foot's philosophical outlook from the time he joined the Labour Party. One of his early formative literary influences was Rousseau, in the posthumously published *Confessions* as well as in the earlier *Émile*. It may be instructive that Charles James Fox, the prospective subject of his projected historical work back in the 1930s, combined 'Jacobin' radicalism with a libertine lifestyle. He was not only radical but raffish. Daniel Defoe Foot admired not so much for *Robinson Crusoe* as for the racy chronicles of *Moll Flanders* and *Roxana*. Even William Blake's gentle mysticism was demythologized. 'Jerusalem', Foot liked to argue, was really a poem in defence of free love, 'arrows of desire' indeed, enlivening England's green and distinctly pleasant land.[11]

Swift was another in this category. Foot relished the fact that Vanessa's home was now a monastery and that the monks kept her portrait in the neighbouring abbey, with positive benefits for the tourist trade. He was never an author to cherish the orthodox or the morally conventional. The puritanism of the Pilgrim Fathers he left behind on Plymouth Hoe. And in each case he insisted that, whatever the sexual pain, the women in his heroes' lives always enjoyed the experience too – though it was a view from which his wife Jill, among others, often dissented, especially in relation to H. G. Wells and Rebecca West.

But ultimately the compelling feature of Jonathan Swift for Foot was his satirical brilliance as commentator and critic. To use a favourite Foot word, he admired Swift's *audacity*. He was versatile enough both to run the marathon and to sprint the hundred metres. He could not only conduct a prolonged examination of the human condition in *Gulliver's Travels*, but could also operate with brutal intensity as a journalist of exposure in his pamphlet *The Conduct of the Allies*. It was this quality of passion, expressed in bewitching language of apparent simplicity, which made Michael Foot his most devoted of disciples, and a sort of heir in an honoured line of literary descent. It was particularly for that reason that Foot turned so fiercely against Dr Johnson, who had written with such scorn of Swift's greatest achievement, even claiming that it was his recondite facts, not his literary style, that made *The Conduct of the Allies* at all interesting. Johnson had also spread the legend of Swift's madness. Foot's savagery towards Johnson was equalled only by his venom towards Hugh Gaitskell. Dr Johnson was wrong in his judgements on Swift. There was a more fundamental reason for smiting him hip and thigh – he was 'a bloody old Tory'. But then, many thought then and later, so was Jonathan Swift. It mattered little to Michael Foot. Decades later, his brother John observed, 'I note in passing that your absurd prejudice against the great Dr Johnson is as virulent as ever.'[12]

It is instructive that the phase of Swift's life which Foot chose as the subject for a book was his venture into politics, soon after he moved to London from Ireland. He focuses on a totally political tract by Swift in which his usual self-satire or irony are absent. The years 1710–11, which *The Pen and the Sword* covers, were a dramatic period of violent party controversy. The state seemed in great danger, with the royal succession precarious and the return of the Jacobites a constant threat: indeed, in 1715 the Old Pretender launched his bid for power. Queen Anne's later years saw crisis after crisis, from the impeachment of Dr Sacheverell to the downfall of the Duke of Marlborough. Rumours of treason were in the air. The period saw Godolphin and the Whig Junto, who since 1702 had kept the country at war with France in the so-called War of Spanish Succession, manoeuvred out of office by the resurgent Tories headed by Harley and St John, and the indirect help of Queen Anne herself. Secret negotiations began with the French. But peace was still some way off.

Then came the intervention of the virtually unknown pamphleteer Jonathan Swift. He had secured the patronage of Harley, and used the venom of his pen to dish the Whigs and sell a Tory peace to a sceptical public. He did so initially in his newspaper the *Examiner*, and then most brilliantly in *The Conduct of the Allies*, published in November 1711. It flayed the Whigs for perpetuating the war for their own personal ambitions and corrupt financial ends, and argued for the acceptance of the peace terms concluded secretly with the French by the Tory ministers. Most audaciously, it claimed that the war, instead of being a struggle for national survival against the overwhelming power of Louis XIV's France, had been wholly unjustified in the first place, and totally against Britain's interests. It had been a prolonged conspiracy by the 'monied men', who made huge profits through trading in stocks and 'lending upon great interest and premiums', but also placed enormous tax burdens on the country gentleman at home.

Most dramatically of all, the book turned opinion against the Duke of Marlborough, the greatest man of the age. Swift dismissed him as a land-based commander with no understanding of sea power or of maritime trade (an argument that appealed to the Plymouth-bred Foot). He also alleged (on the basis of virtually no evidence) that Marlborough had waged war for his own financial benefit, and that he was consumed by avarice and ambition. For years he had received secret payments from Britain's allies which were 'unwarrantable and illegal'.[13] This was why the country had been at war for so long and with no apparent benefit. Swift pressed the insular arguments, popular with Tory Jacobites, that the Houses of Orange and Hanover had ensured that Dutch and German interests were pursued at the expense of those of Britain. He proclaimed the venality of the mercenary Dutch and the ingratitude of the duplicitous Austrians. 'We are thus become the *Dupes and Bubbles of Europe*,' wrote Swift. On the personal side, Marlborough was also said to have put pressure on the Queen to make him General for life. Some even believed that the Duke, whose Blenheim palace, built by Vanbrugh at Woodstock near Oxford, was almost to rival Versailles in its baroque magnificence, himself sought to become King. But then along came the little vicar of Laracor to barge him off his pedestal and cut him down to size.

Swift's pamphlet was a sensational publishing triumph. The thousand copies of the first edition sold out in two days; the second within five hours. By the sixth edition, eleven thousand copies had been sold in two months. Daniel Defoe also wrote tracts against the war at this period, but with nothing like Swift's panache or success.[14] Opinion turned against Marlborough. The war was wound up with the aid of the Queen, who created twelve Tory peers in late December to get the peace terms through the House of Lords. Marlborough, who had terrified Europe on its battlefields for ten years, was cast into the dust. Ormonde took his place as Captain-General. It was a victory, if not a particularly honourable one, for the peacemongers, and amongst the great journalistic coups of all time.

Foot portrays these complex episodes with bold colours; he gives them an immediacy that makes his book intensely exciting throughout. He begins with an incisive gallery of the *dramatis personae*: Swift himself, the Whig aristocrat Thomas Wharton ('the epitome of a loose-living, arrogant, Church-hating Whig'), Harley, St John, the Queen and Marlborough. His overall treatment of them, while vigorous, is more balanced and subtle than his pamphleteering or his weekly journalism were inclined to be. The contrasts between the two great Tories, St John and Harley, are brought out – St John brilliant and self-indulgent, Harley sinuous and secretive. Swift, the former Whig, went privately to see Harley the Tory and left 'with mischief in my heart'. Marlborough is something of an off-stage presence, but his greatness as a general is fully acknowledged. There is pathos as well as a sense of justice in his downfall. This was indeed a highly controversial part of the entire story, and Swift has been widely condemned for inaccuracy and unfairness. Foot later professed himself uncertain whether his father Isaac's sympathies lay with Swift or with Marlborough on the matter. At least Michael Foot does not attempt to exact any kind of revenge from Marlborough's great living descendant, who was also his biographer. On the contrary, Foot's bibliography generously acclaims the great qualities of Winston Churchill's life of the Duke.

The core of his book is the relationship between the press and Parliament. Both are described with great skill. Foot provides a vigorous account of the rise of Grub Street, and its growing influence in the world of the coffee-house intelligentsia. His treatment of the birth of the popular press is a central theme of the book, and a contribution to our knowledge of the subject. The great virtue of the press, in his view, was its sense of independence and its championing of free comment. Writers like Swift and Defoe are thus praised for promoting the cause of journalistic freedom and bringing about the decline of journalistic sycophancy. Thereby, Foot argues, the entire quality of our literature was elevated: 'Never again did the craft of writing suffer quite the same debasement as Dryden had endured.' Events in Parliament are also deftly handled: the qualities of the Tory Robert Harley as parliamentarian and political manoeuvrer are amply praised. One of Foot's specialities comes out in his discussion of parliamentary procedure. He is also excellent on relations between the two houses, the Tory government of Harley and St John matched against the Whig majority in the Lords. Foot explains the initial defeat of the Whig 'No Peace without Spain' lobby in February 1711, and the final crisis which led to Queen Anne's creation of twelve new Tory peers to ensure a government majority and the eventual safe arrival of peace with France. As with Roy Jenkins's biographies of Asquith, Gladstone and Winston Churchill, there is an added fascination because the author is a practitioner of politics in the real world, not merely a detached scholar immured in his ivory tower.

Foot's book is concerned with men in action. But it also has an implied heroine – not the dull but dutiful Queen, but the imperious but magnificent Sarah, Duchess of Marlborough, 'a tremendous figure'.[15] Although she plays a marginal part in the final crisis of 1711–12, Foot wrote in Debts of Honour in praise of the sharpness of Sarah's political intelligence and the magic of her personality. This he bracketed in the title of his chapter on her with 'Praise for women in general'; Jill Craigie evidently agreed with this assessment. The patronizing misogyny of Professor J. H. Plumb of Cambridge University, who had criticized Sarah's 'viragoish temperament', is splendidly dismissed as 'a caricature'.[16] (Plumb had also given a somewhat mixed review of The Pen and the Sword in 1957 – Foot's literary arsenal never neglected the small arms of the tu quoque.) Elsewhere in the same book, A. L. Rowse of All Souls in Oxford is duly chastised for his treatment of Stella and Vanessa: 'Nothing . . . could be more pitiful than Dr Rowse's attempt to foist upon Swift his own contempt for women.'[17] One major quality in Sarah was her generosity of spirit. Nothing better illustrated this for Foot than her warm praise of Gulliver's Travels later on.

Swift himself is criticized by Foot for being unfair to the Duchess. Yet clearly he is the hero, or perhaps the anti-hero, of Foot's book. Foot later described how, initially somewhat sceptical about the tone of The Conduct of the Allies, he 'became more and more converted by what Swift was writing'. Foot sees him as 'the prince of journalists', a ferocious, fearless critic of independent judgement.[18] A later scholar,

Irving Ehrenpreis, condemned the fact that in writing about the Whigs, Swift 'abandons plain fact and rational inference, relying instead upon innuendo'.[19] But Foot treats Swift's clinical attacks as being all of a piece. His sharpness, his immediate recognition of the killer fact (usually derived from secret government documents to which his Whig opponents had no access and no opportunity to refute), contributed to what Ehrenpreis calls his 'dramatic immediacy'.[20] He overthrew an overmighty subject, he ended a war, and he reversed the course of history. Not even *Guilty Men* had quite managed that.

For all its colourful style, Foot's is a work of history, not of historical journalism. All his other books, on Bevan, Byron and Wells (and, one might guess, his unwritten life of Fox as well), were highly partisan accounts of heroic figures. Swift here is not depicted as a giant: he operates on the human scale. *The Pen and the Sword* is detached, at times almost pedantic in its scholarship. Scholars in 2005 regarded it as still the most exhaustive work on the subject, and important for an understanding of the politics of Queen Anne's reign. Foot's book is a remarkable work for a non-professional writer. It was read through prior to publication, not by a historian but by *Tribune*'s drama critic Richard Findlater, and also by Foot's father Isaac.[21] The book is set in its own time, and deserves to be considered separately from its author's career in contemporary politics and journalism, socialism, Bevanism, the campaign against the bomb. Attempts have been made, for example, to relate Foot's treatment of Swift's relationship with Harley to his own patronage by Beaverbrook, but that does not really add to our understanding. The contemporary connections lie at a deeper level.

One reviewer of the book, the strongly Conservative Kenneth Young, later author of a biography of Stanley Baldwin, writing in the *Daily Telegraph* under the heading 'Swift's "Guilty" Men', was baffled why Michael Foot, the left-wing Labour partisan, should turn his talents to the study of the politics of Queen Anne's reign. After some dithering, Young offered the lame view that Foot might be taking tips from 'the most vicious and successful political pamphleteer in our history'. But the connections are not so great a mystery. After all, Foot, a famous journalist, was celebrating a remarkable predecessor who effectively created the press as the Fourth Estate of the realm. More-

over, the great theme celebrated in *The Pen and the Sword* is the cause
of peace. Swift's achievement in 1711–12 was to convert the country
to winding up a war. He disaggregated real patriotism from the pursuit
of military glory as conducted (so he claimed) by Marlborough and
the Whigs. He did this not only in *The Conduct of the Allies* but in all
his most influential writings. *Gulliver's Travels*, Foot controversially
claimed, was 'still the most powerful of pacifist pamphlets'.[22] Linked
with this was a principled rejection of foreign entanglements, a subtle
kind of xenophobia. This came out even more clearly in Swift's
Remarks on the Barrier Treaty (1712), with its scathing attacks on the
Dutch for their deceit and avarice. Michael Foot was a very English
patriot who was for long a reluctant European. He warmed to the
spectacle of a freelance Irishman who identified himself with the patriotic prejudices of parochial English country gentlemen whose world
he knew only at second or third hand. Foot also responded to Swift's
hostility to a moneyed Establishment, the power that used to follow
Land now having gone over to Money. He celebrated especially Swift's
insistence on a nation's constitution being based on traditional principles, underpinned by the rule of law as a function of citizenship:
'Freedom consists of a People being governed by Laws made with
their own Consent, and Slavery on the contrary.'[23] George Orwell
wrote of Swift as having the outlook of a 'Tory anarchist'. This may
be a self-description, or even a self-parody. Michael Foot was neither
a Tory nor an anarchist, but as a self-liberated critic he could respond
to both. Perhaps it was what Aneurin Bevan had in mind when he
said to Geoffrey Goodman in 1959 that 'Deep down, Michael is still a
Liberal.'[24]

The Pen and the Sword appeared in the early autumn of 1957, a
little later than Foot and Mervyn Jones's book on Suez. Published by
MacGibbon & Kee, it was widely reviewed and well received. The
famous man of letters and one-time diplomat Harold Nicolson, no
admirer of Swift himself, and the recipient of a sharpish review by
Foot of his own *Congress of Vienna* in the *New Statesman* years earlier,
gave it lavish praise in the *Observer*. So did other reviewers as diverse as
Lord Samuel, Hannen Swaffer and Foot's good friend James Cameron
('tremendously full and stimulating account'). Isaac Foot was delighted
with the book. He wrote to his son Hugh, appointed Governor of

Cyprus in succession to the fiercely military Sir John Harding at the very time of *The Pen and the Sword* being published: 'Anyone can be an MP or Governor of Cyprus. But this is the summit of the Foot family's achievement – an historic work that will be read in many a year's time.'[25] How Hugh Foot responded to this paternal blessing is not recorded, but he was always a good-natured, uncompetitive son.

Although it was not widely noticed in historical journals, the book was reviewed in the *Sunday Times* by J. H. Plumb, the leading historian of early-eighteenth-century England. He dismissed it as a work of journalism – 'not a satisfactory book' – that failed to explain the violence of the political press. Yet he too felt that 'a great deal of sense' was scattered throughout its pages. Patronizingly, he concluded that 'it will do less harm than many a scholarly monograph'. By contrast, Harold Nicolson praised it both as a guide to the political complexities of the time and especially as a study of earlier political journalism, even if Foot gave Swift 'a political stature he did not in fact possess'.[26] The book also attracted the kind of learned discourse with other scholars in the field which can extend the impact of individual monographs by academic osmosis. In particular, Foot conducted from 1959 a fruitful correspondence with a distinguished Swift scholar, Kathleen Williams, which he acknowledged with typical generosity. It was she who surprised and delighted him by showing him the full importance of Swift's indebtedness to Montaigne. It was also she who directed his reading towards the *Drapier's Letters* and the other rich evidence of his radicalism from Swift's brilliant last Irish phase. Not the least aspect of Dr Williams's appeal was that her home town was one first encountered by Foot at the 1935 general election – 'bloody old Tory Usk'.

At this distance of time Michael Foot's book has passed into the penumbra of largely forgotten works on the Whig Supremacy. Since it was written scholars have transformed our understanding of the complexities of politics between the Glorious Revolution and the ascendancy of Walpole.[27] Yet Michael Foot, an amateur historian but one of many insights, played his part in that transformation. One of the most important passages in *The Pen and the Sword* comes in an appendix. Here he demolishes the argument of an American scholar, Robert Walcott, who had tried, in a book published the previous year, to transfer Lewis Namier's analysis of the politics of interests, located usually in the mid- and later eighteenth century, to the reign of Queen Anne.[28] Foot showed convincingly that this was totally mistaken. In Queen Anne's reign it was transcendently clear that the terms 'Whig' and 'Tory' had profound ideological meaning, and that it was a time of intense party contention. This is now the conventional wisdom amongst scholars. The whole Namierite methodology was condemned by A. J. P. Taylor, Foot's close friend and Namier's former university colleague at Manchester, as 'taking the mind out of history'. Foot, in his modest way, was amongst those putting it back in. He and others rebuffed the teachings of value-free Namierite historians and linguistic Oxford philosophers. For him they were but scholastic ghost writers for an unfeeling, unbending Toryism.

An amateur historian, Foot had the imagination to see the past – all of it – not as a static nexus of structures and economic interests, but as a dynamic universe with its own inherent dialectic. His book shows how he had moved on from Macaulay, Trevelyan and the Whig interpretation of linear progress safeguarded by Parliament in which he was brought up in his West Country youth. Historical change was the product of secular clashes of ideas and social forces, with the popular press acting as both its engine and its arena, leaving great personalities, even a Marlborough, helpless in its wake. The total inability of Marlborough to come to terms with the rising power of Grub Street is a dominant theme of both Dean Swift and Michael Foot. Thereafter, Swift was a constant visitor to Foot's columns, book reviews and parliamentary speeches. He did not return to write about Swift again until his retirement in the 1980s; he was busy doing other things. But the conceptual approach of his book in 1957 crystallized much of his outlook in the intervening years, when he became one of the major political figures in Britain.

Both in what it says and in what it implied about Foot's world view, *The Pen and the Sword* is an important document in understanding him, more so than hundreds of his journalistic throw-offs and show-offs. It is his most scholarly book and probably his best, one still well worth reading. His judgements were certainly daring, and the radical peace-mongering Swift whom Foot depicts was not one recognized by all other scholars. J. A. Downie saw Swift as fundamentally a 'true, loyal Whig', even though *The Conduct of the Allies* was aimed at sympathetic Tory readers. Ian Higgins, in sharp contrast, saw in almost all of Swift's writings 'a disaffected High Church extremist with Jacobite inclinations'. Even *Gulliver's Travels*, on this interpretation, exemplified 'the Church Tory doctrine of non-resistance and passive obedience'.[29] Foot takes a bolder stance in seeing Swift as an iconoclastic radical from *The Tale of a Tub* in 1708 to the Irish writings of the 1720s, and his case deserves to be taken seriously. His later biography of Aneurin Bevan rightly became famous for its political passion and personal commitment; it is also most brilliantly written, with breathtaking panache. But it is, in the best sense, a polemic. In this earlier study of a remote crisis in the age of Queen Anne, far removed from contemporary controversies, Michael Foot showed the talent to write historical literature of high quality, and to handle the English language sensitively in doing so. These abilities were to give him a unique place in the culture of his people in the later twentieth century.

By the time critics and commentators were calmly reviewing Michael Foot's contribution to the understanding of Queen Anne's reign, in the contemporary political world he was being plunged into passionate controversy. As in Swift's day, it centred on the sacred cause of peace. But now it was the overwhelming menace of the bomb, and of nuclear weapons in general, that tormented the British left and gave central impulsion to Foot's career. It had already led to his devastating breach with Aneurin Bevan after Bevan's 1957 conference speech. But, far beyond personalities, it led Foot into a mass movement of popular protest that took him well outside the orthodox confines of the Labour Party, almost beyond party politics altogether. This was the Campaign for Nuclear Disarmament, a central preoccupation for the rest of his life.

The Campaign came into being in the early months of 1958, in the wake of nationwide alarm at Britain's development of her own H-bomb programme. Its message, characteristically, was first proclaimed to the world not by a politician but by a man of letters, in J. B. Priestley's article 'Britain and the Nuclear Bomb' in the *New Statesman* on 2 November 1957. Priestley's passionate outcry against weapons whose use was suicidal and whose purpose was morally obscene struck a powerful chord. A private meeting of professional and intellectual eminences was held on 21 January 1958 in the house of Canon John Collins of St Paul's at 2 Amen Court, next to the cathedral. Among those present were the scientist author Ritchie Calder, Kingsley Martin, Peggy Duff and Professor Joseph Rothblat. The last-named was a particularly notable recruit since he was a Nobel Prize-winning nuclear physicist who had worked on the Manhattan Project at Los Alamos which had developed the first nuclear weapons, but had resigned from his work and rebelled against the entire nuclear strategy. Michael Foot, whose *Tribune* had long advocated the abolition of Britain's nuclear deterrent, was also amongst the pioneers. Bertrand Russell was nominated as President of the new body, with among others Richard Acland, James Cameron, the Bishop of Chichester and Sir Julian Huxley invited to join.[30] In many ways it was a reprise of the associates with whom Foot had worked on the 1941 Committee and the 'Save Europe Now' movement after the war, an identifiable group of progressive intellectuals and campaigners. Foot was a leading figure from the start. On 28 January it was he who proposed that Canon Collins be made Chairman, Ritchie Calder Vice-Chairman and Peggy Duff (of mixed recollection from *Tribune* days) Organizing Secretary.[31] A twelve-person committee headed by Russell and Collins was appointed; Foot was one of them, and with Collins and Rothblat was empowered to sign the cheques. Along with Priestley, Calder and Cameron he would serve on a separate public relations committee.

In the next few weeks and months, CND became the new sensation of British public life. Meetings were held on 13 and 27 February, 18 March and 14 April, all of which Foot attended. A large public meeting was held to launch it at Central Hall, Westminster, on 17 February. Five thousand people attended, while overflow meetings were arranged in Church House, Caxton Hall and elsewhere to cater for thousands of others unable to get in. Foot spoke powerfully there, but the most memorable speech came from his old friend and *In the News* colleague A. J. P. Taylor, who now became a nationwide CND crusader. He raised huge applause when he proposed to his audience that pro-nuclear MPs should be called 'murderers'.[32] Young people, properly dressed in the regulation protest uniform of the day of dufflecoats and blue jeans, flocked to its meetings. There were innumerable extramural activities by students, notably the Oxford University contingents who demonstrated outside the US air base at Brize Norton.

The very youth of much of the membership aroused doubts among some senior CND figures about the likely longevity of their movement. However, dissenters and idealists of all ages were thrilled by its direct, single-issue moral imperative.

Foot, a nationally known face from 'Free Speech' appearances and *In the News*, was much the most prominent of the politicians enlisted. But what was most striking about CND – and in the end one of its major weaknesses – was its ability to enlist people like Canon Collins, Priestley, Russell and Stephen King-Hall, who were independent-minded progressive intellectuals of no formal party affiliation at all. It was unpolitical, perhaps even anti-political, in its appeal. Religious leaders from all Churches joined in. They took their stand like latter-day Luthers: Aldermaston weapons establishment was their equivalent of the church door at Wittenberg. One outstanding feature of CND was its ability to attract major figures from the arts. Benjamin Britten, Barbara Hepworth, Henry Moore, John Osborne, Arnold Wesker, Peggy Ashcroft, Michael and Vanessa Redgrave and Iris Murdoch were among its distinguished supporters.

A symbolic gesture was needed to give the movement a lift-off. What was decided upon had the stamp of genius. A vast inaugural meeting, attended by perhaps fifty thousand people, was held in Trafalgar Square, symbolically at Easter, the season of universal redemption. A mass protest march then took place to Aldermaston, the nuclear weapons research establishment in Berkshire, forty miles away. The annual Eastertime Aldermaston march, a deeply serious event but also an entertaining folk festival, complete with the 'skiffle groups' of the day, became the badge of honour of CND. It made it lodge in the public awareness for years to come.

From the first, Michael Foot was one of CND's iconic figures, the most famous of the politicians swept along by the unpolitical. His identification with the movement contributed to his electoral defeat at Devonport in 1959, and was perhaps a reason for his victory in Ebbw Vale the following year. He was an omnipresent figure, denouncing the infamy of the bomb-makers and their political voices like Gaitskell from the plinth of Nelson's Column in Trafalgar Square, and in mass rallies all over Britain. His 'shaggy white bitch', Vanessa, was a familiar participant in the Aldermaston marches, despite the distance involved, accompanied by her equally shaggy master. Jill Craigie was as passionate a CND demonstrator as was Foot himself, while his brother John, a Liberal, was also strong in support.

CND had some overlap with the old Bevanite group. Ian Mikardo, for instance, threw himself into the movement and became a key organization man as he had been with the Bevanites, while his secretary Jo Richardson assisted Peggy Duff on the administrative side.[33] On the other hand, Barbara Castle, while a member of CND, never joined the Aldermaston marches, since she distrusted the simplifications of single-issue campaigns.[34] Richard Crossman had nothing at all to do with it, while Harold Wilson, as a champion of NATO, was actually opposed. Cleverly, he placed the emphasis not on the existence of the bomb as such, but rather on Britain's so-called independent nuclear deterrent, which the cancellation of the Blue Streak project was, in any case, soon likely to make a logistical and economic contradiction.

Close friends of Foot's outside Parliament like Geoffrey Goodman were doubtful about unilateralism. Aneurin Bevan, of course, had given CND no support: it was the physical embodiment of the 'emotional spasm' of the 1957 party conference. The party leadership, from Gaitskell down, was totally hostile to a movement which they regarded as permeated by the far left, and more hostile to themselves than to the Tory government. Yet some prominent MPs not active in Bevanism did play an active part in the CND movement, notably Anthony Greenwood, who was even persuaded in 1961 to run against Gaitskell for the Labour Party leadership. There was also an influx of young members later to be prominent in the party, such as Stan Orme of the Manchester District Committee of the Amalgamated Engineering Union (AEU) and Joyce Gould, in time to become National Party Organizer.[35] Two decades later CND membership was claimed by a young trainee barrister, apolitical at university, Tony Blair.

Michael Foot's own passionate endorsement of the anti-nuclear campaign, of course, rang out loud and clear week by week from the pages of *Tribune*. The front page advertised prominently the fact that it was the newspaper that wanted to abolish the bomb. When Foot gave up the editorship in 1960 after being elected for Ebbw Vale, his successor Richard Clements, although a CND supporter himself, felt that the nuclear issue was being overdone to an extent that harmed sales.[36] *Tribune* was a difficult paper to manage anyway. There were rows about relations with Bevan after 1957, and about the unlawful campaigns of Russell's Committee of 100 after 1960. Clements felt that *Tribune* should have 'a policy for everything', and that this was compromised by an obsession with the bomb to the exclusion of much else.[37]

Foot, however, refused to retreat in any way on what he regarded as the supreme issue of the time and the key to the survival of humanity itself. Like Swift, but with more consistent idealism, he was giving himself to the cause of peace. Ever since news of the first atomic bomb tests by Britain had come through in 1953, he had been adamant that such weapons were abhorrent and immoral in every way. As he wrote to his agent in Devonport, Peter Jackson, in June 1958: 'There can be no subject more important than this one of what we are going to do about these weapons which can blow us all to pieces. I believe that the policy of the British government on the subject is utterly disastrous.'[38]

Foot regarded the medical and biological evidence of the catastrophic effect of using nuclear weapons as beyond dispute. First use of them in a war was unthinkable: apart from other considerations, it would be an act of collective suicide, since everyone would be obliterated. Even testing them would be harmful to future generations: CND campaigners quoted facts about the health of babies and pregnant women in New Mexico around the Los Alamos testing area. It followed also that dependence on someone else to drop bombs on our behalf or to save our skins was immoral. Hence an alliance system which imposed on Britain a humiliating reliance on the United States, with its notoriously erratic foreign policy in the Far East and elsewhere, was equally objectionable.

Britain should therefore, in the view of CND activists (though Foot himself was significantly unclear on this), leave NATO with its strategy of nuclear deterrence. All global alliances should be broken up, and the policy of non-alignment promoted. Britain should instead use her unique moral example to promote the cause of unilateral disarmament throughout the world, starting perhaps with Commonwealth countries like India (a cherished nation for CND). They hoped, even assumed, that other countries would rush to follow Britain's lead, but this was not a condition of Britain renouncing its own nuclear weapons, which would follow whatever the rest of the world did or thought. Foot tended to argue that countries which had no nuclear weapons had all the greater influence in international affairs – he would cite India, Indonesia, Yugoslavia, Egypt and, curiously, Ghana, seen as an early African instance of a post-colonial state. The resources wasted on potential world suicide should be devoted to world poverty and the regeneration of the planet. Foot never deviated from this policy.

Meanwhile CND seemed to be carrying all before it. The Aldermaston march of 1959 attracted even larger crowds than 1958. CND has been accused of being almost entirely a middle-class movement, a sop to the guilt-complex of the comfortably-off and the high-minded. But its membership was starting to include working-class people, especially trade unionists, too. Frank Cousins, Secretary of the Transport and General Workers' Union, was merely the best-known of many key union officials, while union members like the young Stan Orme were recruited in large numbers. It was all very dramatic. As in the marches against the invasion of Iraq in 2003, it was noted that at a time of alleged political apathy or cynicism during a dull period of single-party rule, hundreds of thousands, even millions, could be mobilized to crusade for a mighty cause. In John Osborne's *Look Back in Anger*, first performed at London's Royal Court theatre in May 1956, Jimmy Porter had claimed that there were 'no great causes left': 'I want to hear a warm, thrilling voice cry out Hallelujah.' Arnold Wesker's trilogy of plays *Chicken Soup with Barley* (1958), *Roots* (1958) and *I'm Talking About Jerusalem* (1960) contrasted the high community ideals of old Jewish socialists in the East End with the mindless lack of commitment of the present generation. CND appeared to change all that, especially among young people. Through its power over the public mind gospel, man and society would be born again. In the spring of 1960, despite Macmillan's large Tory election victory the previous year, a new level of support was recorded when 100,000 people attended the final stages of the march to Aldermaston. Opinion polls showed that a record proportion of 33 per cent of the British population wanted to ban the bomb, and everything connected with Britain's and the world's nuclear arsenal.

While CND was passionate and unambiguous about the end, the

means were less certain. So many of the movement's members were young or apolitical that it was hard to formulate a strategy. Kingsley Martin asked Mervyn Jones at one large rally, 'What on earth are we going to do with all these people?' Nor was it clear who or what would decide policy, since CND had almost a mania for democracy. It claimed to be an undifferentiated mass movement of the people at large, with no effective internal organizational structure to discuss policy or strategic options at all. Mostly, the Campaign just wanted to change society, by mass protest or moral persuasion. The walls of Jericho would come tumbling down soon enough. But harder-headed politicians felt that it would come to nothing without a political platform. That could only mean the Labour Party. This was emphatically the view of Michael Foot, who could not imagine a political existence outside his party, and who felt that, with a change of leadership and policy, it could become the great cleansing agent of reform and a nuclear-free country. There had been intense argument within CND on this point. The *Bulletin* of the movement in January 1959 contained an article by Foot calling for the election of a Labour government at the next election, and one by Michael Croft arguing the exact opposite. After the 1959 general election, Labour CND activists within the constituencies and the trade unions launched a mighty campaign to capture their party. They obtained the natural adherence of many who had no close interest in the nuclear threat, which they saw as abstract and remote from everyday experience, but who simply wanted to be rid of the party leader Hugh Gaitskell after all the revisionism, the attempt to scrap Clause Four and the feud with the Bevanites.

The TUC voted for unilateralism at its 1960 conference, with large unions like the TGWU casting their block votes in favour (and the Engineers voting both ways). At the Labour Party conference in Scarborough there was a mighty debate, led off by an extraordinarily muddled but emotionally powerful speech by Frank Cousins. He was backed up by Foot and others. In the pro-Gaitskell pages of the *Daily Herald* Foot had argued that a Britain 'absolutely tied to NATO whatever follies NATO commits (like rearming Germany)' would have little influence, whereas if it denounced the insanity of the nuclear strategy it would have a major impact in the UN and the world.[39] Beforehand it was clear, after switches in their votes by key unions like the AEU, that the Labour Party, the architect of NATO in Ernie Bevin's days, was going to endorse a policy of unilateralism. Gaitskell's final speech at Scarborough was an astonishing oratorical achievement, fired with an emotion once thought improbable from him. His cry that those who opposed the resolution would 'fight, fight and fight again to save the party we love' was thought to be unforgivably divisive by his opponents, an inspiring clarion call for renewal by his multilateralist supporters. The official policy was defeated by just under 297,000 votes in a total of six million, with individuals like Wilson and Crossman striving in vain for some kind of compromise proposition. The unilateralist victory is often attributed to left-wingers in the constituency parties, as were the triumphs of the Bennites in the early 1980s. But in fact it was the unions, especially the TGWU block vote of over a million, that settled the outcome.

Michael Foot was exultant, yet deeply apprehensive, after the Scarborough vote. He told Margaret Cole of his personal efforts to try to negotiate a compromise with Crossman, Walter Padley of the Union of Shop, Distributive and Allied Workers (USDAW) and others.[40] Foot did not want to break up the Labour Party, especially in alliance with inexperienced supporters strong in idealism but weak in political common sense. The opinion polls after Scarborough showed that it was Gaitskell's arguments, not the miscellaneous ranks of CND, which commanded the support of the great majority of the British people. It was known, too, that the Gaitskellites were being all too true to their word in fighting back. They had most of the party's major figures behind them, men like George Brown, Jim Callaghan and Patrick Gordon Walker, while it was known that a strong centre-right group, the Campaign for Democratic Socialism (CDS), was being mobilized in the constituency parties to capture control from the left. Its organizers included younger people like William Rodgers, Brian Walden and Gaitskell's future biographer Philip Williams. Crossman noted in his diary on 14 December 1960, two months after the party conference, that Foot's 'commitment to CND is a bit of an embarrassment, since he really knows in his heart of hearts that the Party can't be completely unilateralist'.[41] Nor did Foot really support Britain's leaving NATO, which he had himself so strongly backed at the time of its foundation in 1949.

As 1961 wore on, the strength of CDS rapidly grew, as that of CND waned. Much of its finance came not from the grassroots but from wealthy businessmen such as Charles Forte, and there was also evidence of some linkage with the American CIA. However, Crossman's judgement fairly noted that the left 'is taking a terrible beating . . . up and down the country in the conferences I address . . . [because of] the passion to stop wrangling, combined with a really savage disillusionment against unilateralism. People are seeing more and more that what we need is not merely a protest but a will to power.'[42] The tide was turning. Three of the six major unions changed sides compared with their positions in 1960, even if the extent to which they forsook unilateralism as a policy is debatable. To a degree some of them just wanted to support the party's leader. The TUC supported Labour's official defence policy, critical of an independent British deterrent but clearly multilateralist, by almost three to one. At the party conference at Blackpool a unilateralist defence motion sponsored by the TGWU was defeated by 4,309,000 to 1,891,000. The unilateralist crusade was fast losing momentum. Michael Foot was witnessing a repeat of the erosion and demoralization he had experienced with Bevanism six years earlier. He continued to campaign for CND. When a mass demonstration was held at Holy Loch in 1962 to protest against the manufacture of Polaris submarines with their nuclear warheads, Foot was the main speaker.

The decline of unilateralism was reinforced by a great schism within CND itself. This had always seemed probable with so unpolitical and unworldly a leadership. With prima donnas like Canon Collins, J. B. Priestley and Bertrand Russell, rows about strategy or priorities were always likely. Despite great marches, passionate speeches and massive media attention, nothing seemed to have changed. Both government and opposition were committed to retaining Britain's nuclear strike force, however dependent it was on US patronage. The great majority of the British people seemed to feel that a threat of nuclear obliteration was theoretical at most. They had no inclination for Britain, still a great power, to throw away its influence and go it alone.

Much more was needed if CND was to make any effective point at all. Pressure now grew within the organization for a campaign of direct action. There had already been demonstrations against the siting in Britain of US Thor missile bases by a Direct Action Committee, contrary to orders from the CND executive. Now a new surge developed, led by the near-nonagenarian philosopher Bertrand Russell, a veteran of high-minded moral protest since long before the First World War. On 18 February 1961 he led hundreds in a sit-down protest outside the Ministry of Defence in Whitehall. Unfortunately the prospect of martyrdom was extinguished, since the police took no action, and officials even handed the protesters materials with which to attach their protest documents to the ministry door. CND now went into swift decline. Russell formed a militant body, the Committee of 100, to engage in direct action on the lines of the suffragettes in the past. Many identified as the evil genius of the Committee Russell's young American friend Ralph Schoenman. The Committee seemed to be expounding not pacifism, certainly not socialism, but something akin to nihilism. A fundamental split in the movement followed. Leading figures like Collins, Priestley and A. J. P. Taylor resigned from CND. The Committee of 100's sit-downs in Trafalgar Square and elsewhere aroused not public support but public exasperation. The success of Bertrand Russell in being arrested and put in prison for seven days did not inspire many erstwhile followers.

Michael Foot was not enthused either. He was still passionate about abandoning nuclear weapons, and made an effective protest in the Commons on civil liberties grounds when Ralph Schoenman was imprisoned. He cited Gandhi, the Tolpuddle Martyrs and other past dissidents to justify acts of civil disobedience. But he was fundamentally a rationalist and positivist who was not in favour of breaking the law. A poorly attended demonstration at the US Air Force base in Wethersfield, Essex, at the end of 1961 showed that the momentum had gone. Major events in 1962–63 confirmed the decline and fall of the first great anti-nuclear movement. By March 1963 the momentum even seemed to have left the Aldermaston march.[43] Thus the Cuban missile crisis of October 1962 seemed to show the irrelevance of whether Britain had the bomb or not in the face of a great confrontation between the superpowers. In the summer of 1963 multilateralists could argue that there was actually some achievement to show, when the international test-ban treaty was signed in Moscow, Lord Hailsham being the almost nominal signatory for Britain. Now under Harold

Wilson's leadership following the sudden death of Gaitskell in January, the Labour Party concentrated on unity. It abandoned 'theology' and focused on industrial, not nuclear, science. *Tribune* got back to writing on other topics. Students found other issues, closer to their campuses, about which to demonstrate. As in Bob Dylan's sad songs of anti-military protest, it was all over now.

The Campaign for Nuclear Disarmament was a major episode in Michael Foot's career as a politician of protest. It touched him deeply, and he never gave up his faith in the rightness of unilateralism. Councillor Olive Gibbs in Oxford, a prominent CND campaigner, wrote in 1964 of the need for Labour Party members who were also in CND 'to show, quite uncompromisingly, that Nuclear Disarmament and peace take precedence over all other policies'. She told Foot, 'You, thank God, have never done anything else . . .'[44] When CND revived in the later 1970s, this time largely from within the left rather than across the spectrum, in response to a new escalation of nuclear weaponry, Foot was again an eager supporter. He rallied the female faithful at Greenham Common. The Labour Party adopted unilateralism in its manifesto, and under Foot's leadership fought the 1983 general election on that basis. Under his successor as party leader Neil Kinnock the policy was reversed, but Foot's commitment did not change. He continued to participate in international peace conferences to promote the cause, notably a famous one in India in 1997, at which he discovered that he now had an unlikely ally in Robert McNamara, the former US Secretary of Defense. Foot's late book *Dr Strangelove, I Presume* (1997) struck many of his familiar notes, especially over the dangers of nuclear proliferation in the Middle and Far East.

In retrospect, the failure of CND seems almost preordained. It was a large, miscellaneous rallying call for enthusiastic political amateurs. Although dedicated to one single issue, it brought in supporters for a variety of reasons. There were environmental activists concerned about the dangers of nuclear testing and the hazards of nuclear waste. There were nationalists in Scotland and Wales who had their distinct agendas. And there were thousands and thousands of highly intelligent young people, many of them on university campuses, who responded to CND as a form of generational revolt. Some joined the movement because it was a protest against current American foreign and defence policy, others simply because they opposed Gaitskell. Olive Gibbs wrote to Foot about 'this element in C. N. D. which seems to hate the Labour Party more than it does the Bomb, and certainly more than it hates the Tories'. The Campaign's leaders were miscellaneous and highly individualist, with scant reputation as team players. The tactics were always sketchy. Well before the emergence of the Committee of 100, there was always a fundamental division between those dedicated to moral protest for its own sake, and those like Foot and Ian Mikardo who saw little point in CND unless it intended to convert and capture the Labour Party. Foot vehemently opposed a proposal from Stuart Hall of the quasi-Marxist New Left that CND should run its own parliamentary candidates, certainly that they should oppose Labour candidates. At the 1962 CND conference he condemned attempts to run independent unilateralists at by-elections. There was also a clear gulf between those who were simply pacifists and those who championed alternatively the case for conventional weapons.

Perhaps, though, CND's major weakness lay in its purposes. As A. J. P. Taylor was to observe, the movement was the heir of British imperialism.[45] It assumed that if a great nation like Britain took a decisive moral stand, then the rest of the world would be sufficiently stirred to do likewise. There was a kind of nationalist pride in the vision of Britain as the moral leader of mankind. In fact, most British people felt that unilateralism would reduce their country to near impotence in world affairs. Critics cited the pacifism of the 1930s to argue the dangers of futile moral gestures. Like George Lansbury then, CND seemed to be hawking its conscience around from demo to demo, rather than confronting the realities of power politics. Michael Foot, for all his sympathies with the anti-nuclear movement, had been there before. Much of his political career since 1945 had been devoted to ensuring that the British left did not lapse into the illusions of the appeasement years. CND collapsed in 1962–63, but emotionally Foot had left them long since. Certainly he was too much of a Labour loyalist to tear his party apart. When he served in the Wilson and Callaghan governments of 1974–79 he never once raised the issue of nuclear weapons, not even when proposals for Trident and Cruise missiles emerged from talks between Callaghan and US President Jimmy Carter in 1978–79. In the end he was reconciled to the view that disarmament was a matter not for instant protest, but rather for the diplomatic long haul.

And yet the unilateralist movement was a great and noble cause. It focused the public's mind on a potential holocaust being planned in their name. It was defeated not because the British public had a different view of defence policy, but because of its indifference. CND was the first significant body to confront and spell out the colossal dangers arising from the nuclear arms race of the superpowers. If some of its arguments seemed tenuous and its tactics naïve, it was its opponents who seemed content to avoid the major questions and to repeat traditional Cold War shibboleths. There was always an absurdity in arguing that the supreme usefulness of nuclear weapons lay in the fact that they would never be used. And even after the test-ban treaty in 1963, the nuclear arms race continued. In the 1980s both the Americans and the Russians pressed on with alarming new technical developments, such as the US 'Star Wars' programme. The Russian SS20 missiles, targeting central Europe, raised the spectre of new terrors, not least for the Germans. The dangers of nuclear proliferation became all the starker in the 1990s when India and Pakistan, locked in constant disputes over Kashmir, both developed nuclear weapons. Nuclear-powered warheads provided a backdrop, too, to the ever dangerous conflict between Israel and the Arab states. In the new century, new nuclear programmes by both North Korea and Iran, purportedly for domestic energy purposes but with a clear possible military implication, aroused much alarm and led to pressure from the UN. The Cold War had gone but the menace was unchanged.

Foot and CND argued in the late 1950s that somewhere, somehow, a stand had to be taken. If they greatly exaggerated Britain's potential influence in the world, so too, even more, did the supporters of the bomb. Like Nye Bevan, CND's opponents argued that Britain would be naked in any conference chamber if it renounced nuclear weapons. But the extent of Britain's influence was never measured. Like the supposed 'special relationship' with the United States, it was an untested shibboleth. The case for a separate British deterrent was all the harder to make when the cancellation of the US Skybolt missile programme in 1962 showed how Britain's independent weaponry was totally reliant on American charity. Conservatives and Gaitskellites took it for granted that the possession of nuclear weapons, even in that indirect form, gave Britain influence with the Americans, but little in world history for the remainder of the century gave any support for that view. Britain remained subordinate, and increasingly ignored, whatever the state of its nuclear programme. The key decisions in British defence policy would be dictated by American assessments and priorities. This totally unbalanced 'Anglo-Saxon' relationship was a factor causing difficulties between Britain and other European countries long after Britain joined the European Union. In 2003, claims that President George W. Bush's policy in invading Iraq was seriously influenced by Britain's independent viewpoint, resulting from its military status, seemed questionable. Perhaps the decision to take the Iraq question to the UN was a formal response to Tony Blair's pleas, based on pressure from domestic British opinion. But the decision to avoid a decisive UN resolution and invade Iraq anyway, as previously decided in Texas a year earlier, a policy in flagrant breach of international law, made Britain's role appear marginal at best.[46]

By that time, several old Gaitskellites who had voiced the conventional arguments in the 1960s accepted that events had confirmed their futility. Denis Healey was one notable figure who changed his stance, as did many former Gaitskellites who migrated to the Social Democratic Party in the 1980s. Even Roy Jenkins was heard to murmur doubts. On the Tory side, Enoch Powell's total opposition to the British deterrent, which he thought implied an inflated and totally wrong view of Britain's role, was one strong bond in his unlikely but close friendship with Michael Foot.[47] Foot could claim, therefore, that the passage of time had brought its own vindication, and that his labours on behalf of CND had not been wholly in vain.

The thrust of Michael Foot's varied activities in the 1950s, both as writer and politician, suggests important themes for estimating his career. In his book on Swift he was writing serious history on the Augustan age. In CND he was throwing himself heart and soul into an emotional popular crusade. At first sight it might seem that the author and the activist had little contact with one another. Perhaps they were even at odds. Anthony Powell has written of the tension within George Orwell between politics and literature: 'The former both attracted and repelled him, the latter, closer to his heart, was at the same time tainted with the odour of escape.'[48] With Michael Foot there was no such tension. Writing on Swift or Hazlitt was not a form of escapism. It was neither a casual part-time hobby before he resumed his day job, nor simply lodged in a cultural hinterland, as Denis Healey's profound knowledge of art and philosophy was for him. Literature was always centre stage in Foot's life, inseparably intertwined with all his humane values and central to his politics. In more modest form, it compared with the importance of Gladstone's ideas on Homer for his work as a politician.

Foot's devotion to Swift's social critique and his participation in CND were joint components of a lifelong devotion to a humanist ideal. As he put it to the present author, 'it all fitted in'.[49] The writer and the movement shared the same recklessness. They both embodied his favoured *audacity*. Swift, for all his cynicism, was an agent of liberation and renewal, challenging the stale stereotypes of Anne's England in the causes of freedom and peace. He also savaged 'the crimes committed in the name of a strutting, shouting patriotism'. *Gulliver's Travels* was in part a mordant, subversive reflection on the cult of war. In the 1980s Foot published a lecture on 'Byron and the Bomb'. One feels that 'Swift and the Bomb' would have been an equally natural theme. Swift attracted Foot precisely because he was an outsider, the enemy of the Establishment, untypical of the classical orthodoxies of the Augustan age. None of the luminaries of that age obsessed Foot in the same way as Swift. He would not have wanted to write about the equally political Addison or Steele, not even Alexander Pope, who in any case interested him much less than Swift, his lifelong inspiration. Long before Foot's death, it was proposed that his memorial meeting at Conway Hall would feature centrally a reading from Swift's dramatic poem 'The Day of Judgement', the event being rounded off by the singing of 'The Marseillaise', 'Yr Hen Wlad fy Nhadau' and 'The Red Flag'. CND was a rough-and-ready offshoot of a democratic age, almost a shambles at times. But it embodied the values of Hazlitt, the young Wordsworth and the still younger Keats, Byron and Wells – and, in Foot's controversial opinion, those of his great mentor Jonathan Swift.

Almost a quarter of a century later, in November 1980, Jim Callaghan announced his retirement as leader of the Labour Party. To

much surprise, Michael Foot announced his intention of standing in
the election to appoint his successor. He had just been away on a
lecturing visit. The venue was the pulpit of St Patrick's cathedral in
Dublin; his topic was the life and death of Dean Swift. During this
visit the Dublin telephone lines hummed with lengthy calls from union
leaders, Neil Kinnock and others. No one knew for certain what Foot
would do. But he came back to Hampstead to tell the world that he
would stand. Back in 1967, when he was in Dublin for a conference
marking the tercentenary of Swift's birth, he had had to abandon a
visit to Vanessa's home in Celbridge to return to Westminster for a
three-line whip.[50] But now in 1980 it was Swift first, the Labour Party
afterwards. For once in his life Michael Foot felt absolutely certain that
he had got things in the right order.

TOWARDS THE MAINSTREAM
(1960—1968)

Michael Foot began his second life in Ebbw Vale following his election as the constituency's MP in November 1960. After Swift and CND, he needed his heroes and great causes. But he would have to discover them again within the Labour Party, so often a disappointment to him and yet still 'the last, best hope' of progressives everywhere. Ebbw Vale, Nye Bevan's home and an apparently authentic and uncorrupted working-class community, was a good place in which to start the process of discovery. It was an important part of the Welsh coalfield, with a vivid industrial and political history all its own.

The constituency straddled three valleys at the north-west end of the Gwent coalfield, those of the Ebbw, Sirhowy and Rhymney rivers. It contained four towns, Tredegar, Ebbw Vale, Rhymney and the smaller community of Abertysswg. To a degree, so Foot recalled, Rhymney town acted as something of a buffer between the occasional rivalry of Tredegar and Ebbw Vale. Tredegar, at the head of the Sirhowy valley, was the metropolis of the area and its administrative centre. Its centrepiece was Bedwellty House, a comfortable Georgian building, formerly the home of Lord Tredegar. It now contained the chamber of the local urban district council, where the youthful Aneurin Bevan had first proclaimed his message to the world. Later it housed a local museum with prints and photographs of the area's industrial history, and fine portraits of its eminent MPs, Bevan, Michael Foot and Neil Kinnock. Nye Bevan postcards and car stickers were for sale. The house is surrounded by a pleasant little park, once the private preserve of the Morgan family, successive Lord Tredegars, now a public amenity for the enjoyment of the citizens of Tredegar and their families.

As the historian John Elliott has admirably demonstrated, the long industrial history of the Ebbw valleys from the 1780s was in many ways highly distinctive, even unique.[1] They were unusual, for example, in the existence of a major engineering works there in the 1850s. Of course coal, both house coal and steam and coking coal, had been crucial to the region's economic life for a century and a half. At their peak in 1913, there were twenty-eight pits in the Ebbw valleys alone, employing 26,000 men, but there had been a decline during the stagnation of the inter-war years. It was followed by some recovery during the war, and a good deal more under the post-1945 Labour government.

But, unusually for south Wales, iron- and steel-making had been even more dominant there. Rhymney, where Thomas Jones, Deputy Secretary to the Cabinet under Lloyd George, was born, was in Jones's childhood a virtual company town, dominated by the Rhymney ironworks, but that was long gone. In 1960, by far the most important steel plant was the old Ebbw Vale works. After years of difficulty and the threat of closure, it had been given a new lease of life in the later 1930s when a long campaign, greatly assisted by the steel-owner Sir William Firth, a good friend of Aneurin Bevan, secured massive government support to build a totally new plant at Ebbw Vale. The first continuous steel strip mill in Europe, it began operations in 1938. After a century and more of crises, beginning with the threat from the invention of hot blast in 1829, Ebbw Vale found itself 'at the vanguard of the most radical transformation of British industry since the inventions of Bessemer and Gilchrist Thomas in the 1850s and the 1870s'.[2] Owned by Richard Thomas & Co., and then by British Steel after nationalization, it flourished in the immediate post-war years, finding huge markets in the car industry for sheet steel production, as indeed south Wales as a whole benefited from the Attlee government's regional policy. It was a 'depressed area' no longer.

By the time Foot went to Ebbw Vale, however, the bulk of the steel manufacture in south Wales had moved down to the coast, to the mighty works at Margam, Port Talbot, in 1947, and in 1962 to the even newer Spencer works on the mud-flats at Llanwern, near Newport. These were new, totally modernized technologically, and readily accessible for land and maritime transport. The Ebbw Vale works, marooned at the top end of narrow, winding valleys (where Nye Bevan claimed space was so cramped that the rivers had to flow sideways), was inevitably vulnerable. From the time he became Ebbw Vale's MP, Michael Foot was constantly dogged by fears for its future. Debates about steel renationalization in the sixties, and whether it could mean industrial regeneration, had a particular relevance here. Ebbw Vale's steelworks, with its eight thousand employees, was pivotal to the economic future of the area, including coal as well as small tinplate and engineering enterprises. It was equally important for Michael Foot's relationship with his new constituents. A cloud hovered over their valley communities from then on.

Nevertheless, his time at Ebbw Vale was from the first deeply satisfying for Michael Foot, and for Jill also. Even though he kept in touch with good Plymouth comrades like his former agent Ron Lemin, he felt happier in Ebbw Vale: he also thought he made better speeches as its MP.[3] He felt totally at ease with his working-class constituents, whom he naturally tended to romanticize as an impregnable citadel of the purest socialist values. He wrote passionately about them in the *Daily Herald*, contrasting Ebbw Vale as a proud, class-conscious 'real community' with the meretricious values of Tory consumerism, what Harold Wilson was to call 'the candy-floss society'.[4] Foot liked everything about Ebbw Vale. There were its compact mining terraces, originally built by the coal-owners and owned by their occupants from their early stages; the neat little workers' houses with the piano in the 'front room'; the passion for education supposedly financed by 'the pence of the poor'; sturdy chapels, mainly Baptist or *Annibynol* (Welsh Independent), with evocative names like Sardis, Saron, Siloh and Siloam, recalling Foot's Methodist youth; the cheerful community life in working-class clubs and pubs like the Castle in Cwm, the Co-ops, the packed adult education classes and the equally popular bingo halls; the physical strength of Ebbw Vale rugby club, perhaps the strongest Welsh club side in the fifties, still producing international players like Denzil Williams, who would become the then most capped Welsh forward of all time with over thirty caps and who was an electrician in the steelworks. Foot dedicated more than one book to the people of Tredegar, Ebbw Vale, Rhymney and Abertysswg. He loved the bleak, bare hills above Tredegar where he had so often walked and talked with Nye Bevan, like the historic site at Waun-y-Pound where in 1972 Bevan's massive memorial stones would be set in place to commemorate for all time how Nye 'spoke to the people of his constituency and the World'.

Foot particularly admired Ebbw Vale's pride in its working-class past. He liked to quote Nye Bevan on how, when he was lost in the swirling mists up on the Waun, he would look back to see where he had come from before striding confidently on. You needed to know where you had been to understand where you were at present, and to plan the way ahead. No one on earth would have responded more wholeheartedly to this than Michael Foot, himself the self-professed heir of radical authors and activists over the centuries. He understood the importance for Ebbw Vale of its turbulent, protesting past. Indeed, while historians had focused on the rich experiences of Merthyr Tydfil and the Rhondda as crucibles of change, the Gwent valleys to the east were no less significant. There had been successively the great Tredegar miners' strike of 1816; the 'Scotch Cattle' attacks by workers in the 1820s against the company shop; the Chartist ironworkers and colliers who marched down the Gwent valleys in 1839 to free the fiery orator Henry Vincent from Newport gaol, only to be shot down by troops of the 45th Regiment outside the Westgate Hotel; the syndicalists who published their revolutionary tracts on industrial democracy in 1912; the miners (and their wives) who maintained solidarity and class pride during 'Black Friday' in 1921 when the leaders of transport and rail unions declined to strike in support of the miners; the general strike of 1926; and the stay-down stoppages in the Six Bells colliery directed against non-union labour in nearby Abertillery nine years later; the common people of the valleys who sustained Aneurin Bevan in his crusades for socialism and social justice.

This was a rich and inspiring inheritance, still visible in miners' libraries and pithead banners in the 1960s. It was commemorated not just in marches and museums but in literature, oral culture and folk memory. The rightly detested private coal-owners, with their record of industrial exploitation and cruelty, responsible for wage cuts, lock-outs and murderous criminal negligence over pit safety, were as omni-present as thirty years earlier. The great commemorative poet of the area was Idris Davies, Gwent's bard of industrial protest, author of 'Gwalia Deserta' and such iconic verse as 'Do You Remember 1926?'. Michael Foot believed passionately in all this, to his innermost soul.

Idris Davies was Gwent's Byron as far as he was concerned. It was natural that one organization in which he took a keen interest was *Llafur* (Labour), the Welsh Labour history society, founded by both academics (including the present writer) and trade unionists to promote serious historical enquiry. It delighted Michael that when he addressed *Llafur* in Swansea in 1973 on the theme of Aneurin Bevan he was introduced by a famous proletarian chronicler, the diminutive Professor Gwyn A. Williams of Dowlais, who referred to him in French Revolutionary terms as 'Citizen Foot'.[5]

In Ebbw Vale he soon made friends aplenty. He became particularly friendly with his agent, and erstwhile challenger for the Labour nomination in the constituency, Ron Evans. A former steelworker, Ron seemed to Foot to embody almost all the south Wales virtues – his dedication to socialism and peace, his love of choral music, his rugby skills when he had played for the Ebbw Vale works in his younger days. Only in his unusual lack of eloquence (which might have cost him the Labour nomination) did the admirable Evans seem in any way deficient. He acted as a kind of minder for Foot at party conferences when Labour right-wingers (like Wilfred Fienburgh earlier) adopted a threatening tone towards him, but were deterred by Evans' burly frame.[6] Another stalwart was Bill Harry, a strong supporter of Bevan, though opposed to him on the bomb. Two other close friends were Alan and Megan Fox, whom Foot first met in 1963 when Alan was a ward secretary in Tredegar.[7] They remained warm comrades from then on, down to the dispute over the Labour nomination on an all-women shortlist in 2005. Jill also loved Ebbw Vale, her fascination with south Wales dating from her time making the film *Blue Scar*. She spent much time in the constituency, and was greatly liked there, taking part in various local activities. However, women in the constituency, steeped in working-class respectability, with shiny shoes and short haircuts, had admired Aneurin Bevan's smart blue suits and silk ties. By contrast, Michael Foot's shabby clothing, with shapeless suits and pullovers with holes in the elbows, was not always appreciated, and his wife was sometimes blamed for it.

But there were never any political problems in Ebbw Vale. Foot proceeded to win eight successive general election contests there between 1964 and 1987. His majorities were always upwards of sixteen thousand, and he usually polled between 70 and 75 per cent of the vote. Generally, his opponents, Conservative, Liberal and Plaid Cymru, all lost their deposits. Election campaigns in so totally Labour a working-class stronghold were purely nominal. The most successful of his electoral opponents, so far as it went, was a popular local publican, Angus Donaldson, who ran as a Liberal in 1970, and in February and October 1974. In February 1974, when the Liberal vote nationally rose sharply, Donaldson achieved his best result, with nearly five thousand votes and 16.8 per cent of the poll. But he was obviously no threat at all. In the early 1970s Plaid Cymru showed some strength in the constituency, and won seats on the local council in Rhymney, where the Welsh language was still to be heard. But they never troubled Labour at general election times, and invariably ended up last. The Conservatives would put up a promising young man like Jonathan Evans (later an MP and MEP elsewhere) to give him a chance to cut his teeth in an obviously hopeless cause. Throughout, Foot's impregnable strength in his constituency, like that of all the other Labour valleys MPs, was taken for granted. Ebbw Vale was beyond challenge – at least until the 2005 election, when Peter Law, a strong Labour councillor and Welsh Assembly Member from the locality, defeated the official female Labour candidate on a 48 per cent swing. This was a freak result, in protest against the imposition of an all-woman shortlist for the Labour candidacy. Nothing remotely like that happened while Michael Foot was its Member between 1960 and 1992.

Michael and Jill made a home in Ebbw Vale. In 1961 they bought a house at 10 Morgan Street, one of a row of old ironworkers' houses built by the owners in the 1820s in the centre of Tredegar, near the town clock, and quite near Bevan's family home in Charles Street. It was in a very dilapidated state, with the roof falling in, when the Foots bought it, but Jill made sure that some of the original features were kept, including a spiral stone staircase. When the Foots were away it was looked after by their neighbours Mr and Mrs Tagg, who ran a sweet shop. They were great enthusiasts for opera, and Michael and Jill sometimes took them to see the Welsh National Opera in Cardiff; on one memorable occasion they went to La Scala in Milan.[8] For many years Foot went down to the constituency every weekend, and held his surgeries in his Morgan Street home. Much of his work there concerned the employment and medical problems typical of older industrial communities in the coalfields.

It was generally agreed that he was a highly conscientious and hard-working constituency Member. He worked particularly hard when the steelworks got into serious difficulty in 1974 when he was a Cabinet minister. He became popular locally, even though a few scars remained after the nominating process, and his constant rebelliousness as an MP in his early years as Member for Ebbw Vale was not always acceptable in a constituency which was basically Labour loyalist. This emerged with some ferocity during the arguments over the Ebbw Vale steel closures in 1975, when steelworkers hurled abuse at this Englishman who had succeeded the great Aneurin, and accused him of being a traitor. In fact Foot worked desperately hard to keep steelmaking alive in the Ebbw valleys. To this end he found a good friend in John Powell, the head of the Ebbw Vale steelworks and politically a Conservative (somewhat to the concern of Ron Evans and others). Foot was much entertained by the discovery of a Tory in Ebbw Vale, a species he claimed was as rare as a particularly obscure kind of seabird. He and Powell made common cause through the 1970s, to the extent that Foot wrote to Sir Keith Joseph as Secretary of State for Industry after Margaret Thatcher took office in 1979, proposing that Powell be appointed head of the British Steel Corporation. But the Thatcher government was unlikely to appoint a steel-owner so perverse as to be a friend of the famous left-wing firebrand Michael Foot.[9]

In Ebbw Vale Foot naturally inherited that famous mythical garment, the Mantle of Nye. He was Bevan's successor not just as MP but as the leading voice of the socialist left. He gave up the editorship of *Tribune*, which went to Dick Clements, but remained constantly active in Parliament, in the *Daily Herald* and on the platform throughout the country. In fact the spirit of Bevan was constantly at his shoulder from the start, because after intense discussion with Jennie Lee and also Dick Crossman, he began work on a massive two-volume authorized biography of his late, great comrade. The first volume of his life of Aneurin Bevan was published in 1962 by MacGibbon & Kee after some difficulty with Harrap, who argued, curiously, that they still had a moral if not a legal claim to his work after they had published *Armistice 1918–1939* twenty-two years earlier.

Foot had plenty of time to devote to his writing of Bevan's life. He re-entered the House of Commons at the high noon of conflict within the Labour Party over unilateralism, following Gaitskell's defeat at party conference in October 1960 and his pledge to 'fight and fight again'. From his return to Parliament Foot turned his energies to denouncing the party leadership. He lashed out at Gaitskell with bitter and belligerent words. At his first parliamentary party meeting there was uproar over whether unilateralists could be put on a committee to consider Labour defence policy. Gaitskell terminated the meeting after a few minutes; figures on the right called for the dissidents to be expelled. Foot followed this up with attacks on Gaitskell over both peace and public ownership in *Tribune*, for which he still wrote as he wished. Ironically, he followed them on 25 November with an article entitled 'How We Can Unite the Labour Movement'.[10] Unity and loyalty did not seem to be concepts widely identified with the Member for Ebbw Vale. In the new year, even as CND showed signs of going into recession, he was condemning Gaitskell on all fronts in a highly personal way. He denounced him for nominating Labour life peers through his own patronage after the passage of the 1958 Peerages Act. Gaitskell's argument was that if there was a House of Lords still in existence, Labour should be represented within it. In fact this would also be Foot's argument when he nominated Labour life peers as leader in 1983, but in 1961 it seemed to him to be class betrayal. In March 1961 the inevitable happened. Foot was among five Labour MPs who, after previously disobeying the party whip on the Army estimates, did so again on the Air estimates. Instead of abstaining as agreed in the PLP meeting, they voted against the government on a unilateralist amendment. Foot's colleagues included none of the old Bevanites, but three incorrigible individualists, Sydney Silverman, S. O. Davies and Emrys Hughes, along with, more surprisingly, a Scottish unilateralist MP of otherwise unimpeachable orthodoxy, William Baxter.[11]

For Herbert Bowden, the Chief Whip, this disobedience by the five was the last straw. At a parliamentary party meeting a proposal that the whip be withdrawn from them was carried by ninety to sixty-three. Foot's passionate self-defence, which referred to the part the bomb had played in his own campaign at Ebbw Vale, was swept aside, and a long period of isolation followed, longer than Bevan had

ever known. Foot's parliamentary life continued much the same, and
he received the endorsement of his constituency. But he was obviously
even more of a marginal figure than before, unable to take part in PLP
discussions on defence or other policy. Even worse, he was unable to
play any part after Gaitskell's unexpected death in January 1963, and
could neither vote nor campaign for Harold Wilson when he was elected
leader in Gaitskell's place. His exclusion lasted well over two years. Wilson, after becoming leader, then put pressure on Herbert Bowden, a
reluctant Chief Whip, but progress remained slow. When Foot wrote
to Bowden in February 1963 saying that they would like to 'resume
our places' in the parliamentary party, the Chief Whip argued that they
had not given assurances that they would not make 'personal attacks' on
fellow MPs. Foot wrote a conciliatory second letter, and finally on
29 May 1963, after over three months of dithering and renewed pressure
from Wilson, Bowden told him that the whip had been restored at last.[12]

In the interim, Foot had kept active. He told Ron Evans that the
National Executive had declined to 'take note' of his expulsion, and
joked that of the five expelled, Baxter was so reluctant a rebel that
Emrys Hughes threatened to withdraw their whip from him and send
him back to the clutches of the Labour Party. But it did mean that his
parliamentary role for over two years was symbolic and little more.
One somewhat melancholy task at that time was to arrange with his
brothers, including his younger brother Christopher, a solicitor, for
the sale of their late father's immense library of sixty thousand books
with all its literary and historical treasures. The books went to the
University of California for £50,000; the university had originally
offered £45,000, but still they got an absolute bargain. It was John
Foot who handled the final legal details of the transaction, although,
contrary to what has been suggested, Michael did approve of the sale
in general terms.[13] As regards the Labour Party, he was excited by
Harold Wilson's election as leader and anxious to have the whip
restored, but the party hierarchy moved with all deliberate speed.
Michael Foot's activities and speeches in the Commons from the spring
of 1961 to the summer of 1963, variously attacking the bomb, Europe
and Gaitskell, were of little importance. Nor was CND any conso-
lation, being racked by division. It was, politically, a totally unprofitable
time for Foot.

What was of more importance was his life of Aneurin Bevan. He worked and wrote with astonishing speed, writing the first volume of 512 pages in less than a year and a half. Some of his material came from Donald Bruce, his co-author of *Who are the Patriots?* in 1949, who had been Bevan's PPS and had now left front-line politics. Foot had rather mixed feelings about Bruce, left-wing though he was. He felt that, like his later Cabinet colleague Peter Shore, his animus towards the European Common Market was excessive.[14] The first volume of Foot's book covers Bevan's life from his birth in 1897 to his entry into Attlee's Cabinet in 1945. It was published by MacGibbon & Kee in September 1962, shortly before party conference, and in America by Atheneum, run by Foot's friend Michael Bessie, the husband of Foot's former great love Connie Ernst, and who proved to be a firm ally of left-wing British authors in the United States, including Rebecca West.[15] The book was serialized in the *Sunday Times* and was a clear publishing success, selling fifteen thousand copies in hardback and a similar number in paperback. It has remained in print ever since as a powerful and vivid work of literature, of first-rate importance in studying the Labour left in the earlier part of the twentieth century. It will always remain one of the great achievements for which Michael Foot is remembered.

It is, however, not a straightforward book to assess. It is the most personal work that Foot ever wrote. This is even truer of the second volume, published in 1973, covering the years from 1945 to Bevan's death in 1960, in which his disputes with Attlee and Gaitskell are dealt with unsparingly and at length. Foot's book is not so much a history as a saga like *The Mabinogion*, a heroic chronicle of the life of a Welsh giant. It is written firmly in the light of the famous injunction in Ecclesiastes, 'Let us now praise famous men.' As such it is easy to criticize. It is a polemic, and hopelessly one-sided. The author Anthony Hern, whom Charles Wintour asked to judge it for possible serialization in the *Evening Standard*, commented that it was 'biography by way of idolatry. Everybody, including (indeed, almost especially) Churchill is out of step but Nye.' Two months later Hern called Foot's first volume (most surprisingly, it must be said) 'disappointingly dull. It is a work of piety not critical biography.' He added (revealing his own ignorance of the source materials) that it had no access to private papers or diaries. Foot 'admits he worshipped Bevan'.[16] Nobody could seriously argue that the book is other than totally partisan. It is a tribute to a man regarded by Foot as Britain's greatest socialist and an inspiration for men and women of the left throughout the world. There is no criticism of Bevan at all. Passages of it, especially the chapters dealing with the Second World War, exaggerate Bevan's importance. The negative consequences of his frequent rebellions against his own party are never considered – no doubt because Foot in 1960–61 was equally difficult himself. John Campbell, who wrote a very different kind of biography of Bevan twenty-five years later, argued that Foot concealed the fact that Bevan's career was essentially a failure, as was his great cause, the ideal of democratic socialism.[17] He also felt that through extreme partisanship and identification with his subject, Foot misrepresented his hero and underplayed his urge for power and his success in using it when in government. There is much in these arguments.

At the same time, Foot's is undoubtedly an important book, and of the greatest interest for all students of the Labour Party. Naturally it has been made out of date by the availability of other records, especially the Cabinet and other government documents in the National Archive which illuminate Bevan's record as Minister of Health, and then of Labour, after 1945. But Foot's, like every other work of history, is an interim statement, rooted in its own period and much influenced by his own political location at the time. In any case, it might be noted that the use of new public records has in key respects vindicated, rather than reversed, Foot's conclusions, notably over the arguments about Gaitskell's 1951 budget and the reasons for Bevan's resignation.[18]

In passing, it might be noted in relation to Campbell's criticism that he himself is hardly less partisan. His own book of 1987 implicitly celebrates the breakaway Social Democratic Party, which he himself had promoted in a campaign biography of Roy Jenkins, and which in 1989 was itself to collapse in chaos and confusion. It ends with sharp comments on Neil Kinnock. The assumption in 1987 was that the Labour Party was in a state of irretrievable collapse, and that Bevan was part of the wreckage. The young MP for Sedgefield had not emerged on the horizon; three successive Labour electoral triumphs were impossible to imagine. The great achievement of Michael Foot's biography is that, more than anything else written on Bevan, it marvellously illuminates the quality of the man and his socialism. It is a testimony not only to the politics of Nye but the poetry of Nye. Dai Smith's writings on Bevan have most acutely latched on to that vital aspect. Foot's fifth chapter, 'The Man', is a uniquely vivid and penetrating, if romanticized, study of Bevan's personality and domestic life. It embodies the viewpoint of that other great biographer, Ben Pimlott, that a political biography should be 'the egotistical creation of its author'.[19] The writer should make a personal statement, as a novelist does, certainly like a great portrait painter striving to convey the essence of his subject as he sees him or her at any given time, not merely reproduce a likeness. In the deepest sense, a biography should convey *understanding*.

Foot is shrewd on Bevan's relationships – not perhaps with Jennie Lee (who was very much alive, and who influenced the interpretation at key points, including the deletion of references to Bevan's love affairs),[20] but certainly with figures like Cripps and Beaverbrook, both of them central to Foot's own career as well. Foot was a Welsh Member now, of course, and he also gives a full and illuminating account in his first four chapters of the important strands of Bevan's Welsh inheritance, the influence of the syndicalist industrial unionism of 1911–12, his time in the working-men's neo-Marxist Central Labour College after the First World War, and his role in the South Wales Miners' Federation, the beloved 'Fed', during the Depression years. He also covers faithfully Bevan's critique of the limitations of Wales, especially the 'cramped atmosphere' of the nonconformist chapels which is perceptively described. By contrast, John Campbell's book, much more comprehensive on later developments, gets him from birth in 1897 to election to Parliament in 1929 in just twenty-eight brisk pages. It is a bit like the old *Encyclopaedia Britannica* entry, 'For Wales, see England'.

Some of the least satisfactory passages in Foot's book cover internal party wrangles (thus the partisan treatment of Bevan's expulsion from the party in 1939 neutralizes some of its value), and some of the research is indeed slapdash, as Philip Williams complained. But there is also excellent discussion of more objective matters, such as the rescue of Ebbw Vale steelworks in 1938, or the military intervention in Greece in 1944. The account of party politics during the Second World War is still one of the most valuable there is. The reasons why so many in the Labour Party rebelled against a continuation of Churchill's coalition in 1944–45 emerge with particular clarity from Foot's account. Finally, the book is brilliantly written, full of colour, commitment and (yet again) Foot's cherished audacity. It brings home the emotional appeal of democratic socialism for an entire generation as hardly any other book manages quite to do. Attlee reviewed the book in the *Observer*. He is himself much chastised in Foot's pages. But he was a generous man, and he recognized in the book an element of greatness which gave it a universality common to all the best authors. People would not read Foot to get a complete or reliable understanding of the Labour Party up to 1945. But they would not get one without reading it either. As Dylan Thomas observed of the old shepherd who made ritual observations to the moon, 'You'd be a damn fool if you didn't.'

The first volume of Foot's Bevan book came out to much applause, not only from the left, of which he was the new darling, his socialism as unquestioning and unsullied as ever. He told the *Spectator* that the socialist case remained unanswerable. Who, after all, would win the economic race, 'the Communist states, who are turning out trained technicians at an unexampled pace, or the Western powers who contentedly spend more on advertising than education'?[21] It was an article of faith with him for years to come.

But in his personal career he was still a rebel if not without a cause, at least without a parliamentary party, without a strategy or an obvious role. He probably found Parliament less fun than did his brother Dingle, now a centre-right Labour Member for Ipswich. However, Harold Wilson's election as leader to succeed Gaitskell in February 1963 gave him immense encouragement. Crossman's diary recorded Foot as being 'genuinely and enormously excited'. When the party whip was restored in May, he could look forward to a far more constructive role in supporting an ex-Bevanite leader who appeared really to be a kind of socialist. Macmillan's government was running into disarray on various fronts, including balance of payments crises, the pressure from black Africans to wind up the Central African Federation, failure to enter the European Common Market, and, most directly important for the Prime Minister, the evident failure of his leadership as shown in a variety of alleged scandals, of which the most famous was the Profumo affair. Humiliated in the media, a target for the new satire of *Private Eye* and *Beyond the Fringe*, Macmillan resigned as Prime Minister in October 1963. To the delight of Labour, his successor looked like a distinctly passé refugee from the Scottish grouse moors, Lord Home, shortly to be rechristened Sir Alec Douglas-Home. Harold Wilson poured scorn on the 'Fourteenth Earl'. In fact Douglas-Home proved to be a far shrewder Prime Minister than had been expected, and led a strong Conservative fightback. He turned the tables on the Labour leader, pointing out that he was himself 'the fourteenth Mr Wilson'.

Nevertheless, the prospect was clearly there for Michael Foot to charge into the attack, with pen, voice, heart and soul, against a failing Tory government and to help bring to an end the long phase of Tory rule, known in Labour circles as 'thirteen wasted years'. There were already promising parliamentary opportunities, including speaking early on in support of Anthony Wedgwood Benn (as he was then known) as he campaigned to renounce his hereditary peerage on the death of his father, Viscount Stansgate, and stay in the Commons. Foot urged 'cutting the throat' of the House of Lords once and for all. But he also had the unusual experience of a rebuke from Sydney Silverman for being insufficiently radical, since Foot was at least prepared to accept the status quo to enable Wedgwood Benn to keep his seat.[22] This did not happen very often.

Then, on 21 October 1963, it all came to an end, almost for ever. Jill, not perhaps the safest of drivers, was driving on a B road between Abergavenny and Ross-on-Wye when she failed to stop at a red light and was driven into by a large lorry carrying supplies of Lucozade (not Michael's favourite tipple from then on). There was a horrendous crash. Michael sustained a broken left leg, the fracture of all his ribs and, most alarming of all, a punctured lung. Jill's hand was crushed when it was run over by the lorry. Also in the car was Jill's baby grandson Jason, who was unhurt, and their dog Vanessa, who was retrieved later. Michael and Jill were taken to Hereford general hospital, where he had the wit and the strength to insist that he be put in an ordinary NHS ward. But his injuries were desperately serious, and at first it was feared he would die. Friends and admirers, from

Beaverbrook to Councillor Olive Gibbs, were horrified, and obituaries were prepared. In fact he showed extraordinary resilience, and made a remarkably swift recovery. The hospital's bulletins became more hopeful by the day, and on 29 October, just eight days after the accident, it was stated that no more bulletins need be issued. Elizabeth Thomas from *Tribune* was almost the first to see him in hospital. On 31 October she wrote to Ron Evans, Foot's agent:

> The hospital are quite staggered by his powers of recovery. He still gets terribly tired and finds talking difficult and tiring, so won't be allowed any visitors awhile. It will be a long uphill job for both Michael and Jill but I am sure the worst is over. What a terrible week it has been![23]

Foot finally left hospital on 19 November, just under a month after the accident. He wrote to Ron Evans on 7 January 1964 that it would be another three or four weeks before he was able to walk, but doctors assured him that he would make a complete recovery.[24] He was certainly now back in the real world. He added: 'I think the Labour Party is on the eve of the greatest opportunity it has had since 1945.' In his statements to the press he took every opportunity to emphasize the marvels of the National Health Service, even in a country town like Hereford, and how he had opted for an ordinary ward instead of being transferred to a large hospital in London. It was another vindication of Nye's great vision. He and Jill went on a recuperative trip to Morocco, where Michael improved rapidly in the sunshine but poor Jill was in constant pain from her shattered hand. They caught up with Randolph Churchill in Marrakesh, where he was staying at his father's favourite haunt, the Mamounia Hotel. In its elegant gardens, amidst the terraced flowerbeds and the fountains, the two former contestants in Devonport had their usual jolly and somewhat alcoholic encounters. By the spring Foot was well enough to take a modest part in Cardiff's May Day march: the present writer was in a packed audience in the Cory Hall to hear him flay the Tory government with all his old panache. He commented on the recently ennobled Lord Blakenham, previously known to the world as the Conservative Minister for Labour John Hare, a man 'who wouldn't say boo to a goose', that 'it is marvellous what a little ermine will do for a man's ego'.

Foot's accident left its mark on him. He walked with a limp from then on, and needed a stick for his walks with his dog on Hampstead Heath. This gave a savage right-wing press ample scope when he was party leader in 1980–83 to pour derision on him for physical infirmity, if not senility. On the other hand, there were health benefits as well. For whatever medical reason, he left hospital free of asthma for the first time, and after smoking up to seventy Woodbines a day for the past thirty years, he now became a permanent non-smoker. He had already got rid of his long-lasting eczema, thanks in large measure to Nye's Vitamin C prescriptions and gift of an infra-red ray lamp. He had nearly been killed, but he emerged from the ministrations of NHS doctors and nurses (almost) better than ever.

His hospital stay and recuperation were also beneficial in other ways. Naturally, he spent his time of recovery in reading. He read E. P. Thompson's recently published *The Making of the English Working Class*, a classic if controversial account of the origins of working-class radicalism at the dawn of the industrial age, written from a Marxist perspective but linking with broader aspects of the English radical tradition. The book greatly influenced – or perhaps confirmed – Foot's long-standing passion for the historical and literary background of British dissent. He would greatly have appreciated Thompson's judgement of Hazlitt as a steadfast British supporter of French Revolutionary ideals. However, Thompson also shrewdly noted, comparing Hazlitt with the more proletarian William Cobbett, 'there is still the drawl of the patrician Friend of the People'. Thompson adds that Hazlitt's style 'belongs to the polite culture of the essayist'.[25] So, truly, does that of Michael Foot, a patrician Friend of the People as completely as nineteenth-century reformers like Sir Francis Burdett or Admiral Cochrane – and, of course, Hazlitt.

But probably even more important than Thompson's book was Foot's discovery in hospital of another of his father Isaac's passions, the essays of Montaigne.[26] Michael Foot loved their cool, sceptical tone, and the old *politique*'s passion for peace during the turmoil of the French religious civil wars: Montaigne, after all, began writing around the time of the Massacre of St Bartholomew's Day, the butchery of the Huguenots in 1572. Foot enjoyed his rationality and civility, the Swiftian simplicity of his style, the subtlety of his view of human experience (free from the declamatory dogmatism Foot himself often exhibited) – and also a distinct raciness shown in his writing on women's sexuality in the deceptively entitled 'On Some Lines of Virgil'. Montaigne was fascinated by the past, but never in awe of it. Foot now fully understood the great appeal his essays held for the equally sceptical Swift, not to mention some of the Levellers a century earlier. It was a matter on which that great Swiftian Kathleen Williams had instructed him in 1959: in *Debts of Honour* he delighted in the paradox of 'Swift as a militant Montaigne'.[27] Montaigne was the founder of that great celestial genealogy of authors extending from sixteenth-century Bordeaux to Foot's own day, taking in Swift, Hazlitt, Byron and Wells. Foot read Montaigne in a large compendium, *The Complete Works*, translated by Donald M. Frame (Foot's command of French was always slight). His copy is fascinating to look at now, full of pencil annotations with references, many very scholarly, to interpretations of Montaigne and his outlook by writers over the years. Hazlitt's verdict is given especial prominence when he calls Montaigne 'in the truest sense a man of original mind'.

Montaigne, like Swift, was central to Foot's world view, not a part-time hobby but a key to his own value system. Foot treasured Isaac's own annotated copy of John Florio's early translation of Montaigne's *Essais*; apparently a second copy went to the library in Santa Barbara. In 1967 a highlight of a visit to France was seeing Montaigne's château in the Dordogne. More important even than the castle was the important 'Bordeaux copy' of Montaigne's works, in the 1588 edition, and he chased it up in the municipal library. He noted carefully in the margin of the *Complete Works*: 'seen at Bordeaux, 11 August 1967'. Keats's stout Cortez would not have been more excited on his peak in Darien. Since he also read through Byron's *Don Juan* in its entirety – 'the best thing he ever did' – Foot certainly kept his brimming mind active in Hereford hospital. It made him a more complete radical and an even more complete intellectual.

There were many who felt that Foot's accident had changed his personality also, and for the better. Leo Abse, an amateur psychoanalyst as well as the MP for a neighbouring Welsh constituency, claimed that it had a liberating effect on Foot both psychologically and physically, releasing suppressed aggression directed even in part towards Jill.[28] This is hardly a scientific or verifiable opinion. But Abse is certainly correct in saying that, for whatever reason, Foot emerged from the trauma a more effective parliamentarian who commanded the attention of the House in a way he had never done before. The finger-stabbing dogmatist was being replaced by a more amiable and mellow middle-aged man. Opinions on so subjective a matter varied greatly amongst Foot's colleagues, but it seemed that a gentler, older bibliophile made friends now far more readily with unusual Conservatives like Christopher Soames, Ian Gilmour, Julian Critchley, and even Enoch Powell, and was more approachable and less divisive amongst his Labour colleagues. Foot was to play a subtly different role politically from now on, still a rhetorical crusader but also paddling towards the mainstream, and becoming far more that force for unity and comradeship he had always claimed to be. It made him a more constructive political figure.

In the summer of 1964, several important things happened for him. Soon after he left hospital the *Daily Herald*, which in 1961 had been sold to the Mirror Group, metamorphosed into the *Sun*. At this point, with remarkable churlishness and even cruelty, John Beavan, a former editor of the *Herald* and now political adviser to the new management, in effect fired Foot, terminating his long-standing contract with the newspaper as soon as he got out of hospital. It was not an amicable parting after twenty years, but Foot had lost none of his fighting spirit after his accident. The owners wrongly believed he was a freelance writer, and could therefore be dismissed at will. But in fact he was a member of the National Union of Journalists, which had agreements with the press on decent severance pay. After a sharp tussle the Mirror Group Chairman, Cecil King, had to give Foot £5,000 remuneration, which eventually went to pay for a fine new staircase in the Foots' Hampstead house. The entire episode strengthened Foot's resolve to defend the status of the NUJ and its closed shop when the issue came up while he was a minister in 1975. It made him the more determined to win, which he did.

Foot had suffered a severe loss of income nevertheless. But once again his old friend Max Beaverbrook, now well into his eighties and on the verge of death, came to the rescue with remarkable generosity. Keeping the matter quiet while Foot was negotiating his severance arrangements from the *Herald*, Beaverbrook arranged a contract via

Charles Wintour, editor of the *Evening Standard*, that Foot should write book reviews on a long-term basis, with the possibility of some political notes as well.[29] Foot became a regular writer on his old newspaper from then on, and proved himself to be a reviewer of particular brilliance and literary panache. As always his pieces were spiced with references to the past, maritime patriotic as well as radical (e. g. Francis Drake or Nelson), and he kept them up during his time as a very busy minister from 1974 to 1979. His *Standard* reviews were often amongst his most distinguished writing. An early one in 1966 was of Robert Blake's magisterial biography of Disraeli. Foot rightly praised it, but also effectively showed that it underestimated Disraeli's attachment to principle and to radical causes such as industrial and social reform, and to the status, if not exactly the rights, of women. Foot wrote of the 'divine Theodora' in Disraeli's novel *Lothair* with the same tenderness he had shown for Sarah, Duchess of Marlborough.[30] But of course Dizzy, unaccountably a Tory, was always a colourful hero (more so than the puritanical, anti-feminist Gladstone), who provided a dedication for one of Foot's books and a name for his later Tibetan terrier.

Another highly important and pleasant consequence of the crash was a new home. In 1964 Foot and Jill left St John's Wood, where they had lived for a decade, for a new home in Jill's favourite Hampstead. They had had to pay for the Abbey Road house by selling a Renoir amongst other things. This time their finances were more secure, for the dismal reason that Foot received £60,000 compensation from his insurance company for his injuries. The Foots paid £12,000 for a somewhat undeveloped terrace house in Worsley Road. It was a tall, three-storey Victorian building, dating from 1876. At first there was water in the basement and a general need for renovation. But Jill took that in hand, and in time the basement was totally modernized with a kitchen and dining room, and a french window that opened out to a charming, well-cultivated garden where the Foots delighted in having great parties for their political and artistic friends. The basement was further improved in the 1990s following libel damages from the owners of the *Sunday Times*, in which Foot had been accused of being a Soviet spy. On the first floor, one room was for Michael's writing, mainly literary. Another was Jill's shrine to the suffragette movement, full of pamphlets, posters, banners and other artefacts, where she pursued her lifetime's research on the Pankhursts and their colleagues. On the top floor a self-contained apartment was created, where a variety of tenants were to stay, including at various times Hugh and Paul Foot, and the equally bookish, equally dishevelled Scottish Labour MP Donald Dewar. One early guest was Michael's former American girlfriend Connie Ernst, whose husband Michael Bessie, Michael's New York publisher, had left her. Crossman wrote in his diary (26 June 1966) that her two noisy adopted children left Michael and Jill 'utterly exhausted'.

Of course, everywhere in the house there were books, works of literature rather than on politics. Books by poets, essayists or novelists spilled over from every rickety bookcase, each invariably stuffed with Foot's own notes on matters great and small, and sometimes with letters from Brailsford, Cripps or other notables. Works dealing with such political matters as the balance of payments, local government reform or comprehensive schools were much harder to find: Foot's library seemed like the treasure chest of a somewhat unworldly man of letters rather than a working politician. Only in the basement, where copies of newspapers and periodicals were piled high, was there a different emphasis. The house was very much Jill's project, but Michael joined in a very important achievement as well. In the 1970s, remarkably enough, they persuaded the local council to extend the name of nearby Pilgrims Lane to obliterate poor Worsley Road. The Foots and their neighbours therefore had a new address. It was a personal tribute to the history and even the football team of the Foot family's ancestral home of Plymouth. Number 66 Pilgrims Lane became a famous epicentre of Labour politics from then on, with the Gay Hussar, the Soho restaurant where Foot resumed his visits on getting out of hospital, the runner-up.

Michael Foot thus became the Hampstead left-wing intellectual par excellence, in a bastion of what John Vincent once called 'the thin pink line from Fleet Street via Bush House to Golders Green'.[31] Foot loved everything about his cosmopolitan new neighbourhood, with its many pre-war intellectual émigrés from the Nazi regime. There were pleasant strolls on which to take the dog along Parliament Hill Fields and up to Whitestone Pond with its fine views, little bookshops in Flask Walk, Viennese-Jewish delicatessens, avant-garde Continental films at the Everyman cinema, congenial friends living nearby. Foot developed a strong connection, as columnist and book reviewer, with the lively local newspaper the *Hampstead and Highgate Express*, universally known as the *Ham and High*. Politically, Hampstead was an affluent Conservative seat, but it had strong links with the left, and indeed Ben Whitaker won the seat for Labour in 1966. Politicians like Douglas Jay, Anthony Greenwood and Sydney Silverman lived in the area, while Harold Wilson, resident in nearby Hampstead Garden Suburb, sent his sons to the local direct grant school, University College School, as did George Strauss and Silverman amongst others. One irony was that Hugh Gaitskell had also lived nearby, about ten minutes' walk away in Frognal Gardens, but he died over a year before the Foots arrived. Gaitskell was buried in the churchyard of St John's parish church in Church Row, close to the graves of such cultural icons as the actors Sir George du Maurier and Herbert Beerbohm Tree, and the novelist Walter Besant. Gaitskell's widow lived on in Hampstead, and had a distinguished later career at the United Nations and in the House of Lords. But with the Foots there was no contact.

These developments were accompanied by a sad one. On 9 June 1964, very soon after arranging Foot's contract with the *Evening Standard*, Max Beaverbrook died at the age of eighty-five. There was a memorial service in St Paul's cathedral and his ashes were sent back to his native New Brunswick in Canada. Michael Foot was deeply moved by the loss of his devoted old friend and patron, who had sustained and stimulated him for twenty-five years past, and for whom Jill also had the warmest regard. His tribute in *Debts of Honour*, published over twenty years later, is a monument to his affection and near-reverence for one he considered a great man and a beneficent influence 'who liked to stir things up'. His relationship with Beaverbrook brought Foot flak from the left, but he never regretted it.

Foot returned to full-time politics in May 1964, with a general election only a few months away, with articles in *Tribune* denouncing the Douglas-Home government and urging that Labour's election manifesto have a strong emphasis on doing away with the bomb. But he had surely now to devote his efforts to sustaining, not attacking, a Labour Party that was close to returning to power with one of his closest associates from Bevanite days as its leader. He played his part with a campaign biography of Harold Wilson, published by Robert Maxwell's Pergamon Press. It was a picture book of sixty-three photographs and a few Vicky cartoons. Foot contributed about a dozen unremarkable pages, although with a few implied contrasts between Harold Wilson, the man who united the party, and Hugh Gaitskell, the man who divided it. Foot would not wish to be remembered for this work, which Francis Wheen calls 'an embarrassingly reverential doxology'.[32] It no doubt was of some help electorally, though Foot found extracting money from Maxwell, who was also Labour candidate for Buckingham, a great difficulty – a problem many others were to discover in years to come. In October 1964, the last possible date, the general election duly came, and proved especially tense and close. Labour denounced the failures of 'thirteen wasted years', but the case was hard to make in the light of current economic prosperity. Foot himself had a typically uncomplicated campaign in Ebbw Vale, with only one challenger, the much-abused Conservative Sir Brandon Rhys-Williams once again. Foot polled 25,220 votes to his 4,949; his share of the vote soared to 83.6 per cent. But nationally the Conservative vote held up strongly in rural areas (though not in Wales), and Labour only just crept home. It gained in the end an overall majority of only four, with 317 members to the Conservatives' 304 and the Liberals' nine. Still, it was a Labour government again at last.

To his joy, Foot saw old friends in charge of key offices. Apart from Prime Minister Wilson himself, Richard Crossman became Minister of Housing and Local Government, and Barbara Castle went to Overseas Development, though at first outside the Cabinet. Also outside the Cabinet, Jennie Lee became Minister of the Arts, where she proved a brilliant, if scarcely orthodox, success. Old Bevanite friends like J. P. W. Mallalieu and Stephen Swingler also received significant office. The Foot family also progressed. Dingle became Solicitor-General, while Hugh, free from his duties in Cyprus, received the title of Lord Caradon and joined the government as Minister to the United Nations, where he pursued his traditionally pro-Arab outlook in Palestine. In addition, Frank Cousins, Foot's closest trade union friend, became Minister of Technology, and entered Parliament in a by-election in Nuneaton. There was some question that perhaps Michael Foot would break the habit of half a lifetime and join him in government, but he had made it clear that he did not seek or want government office, which would cripple his independence. Indeed, some time in the winter of 1965–66 he was actually offered the Home Office, so Wilson told Tony Benn. But Foot resisted on the grounds that he opposed the government's backing for America over Vietnam.[33]

The Wilson government was overshadowed from the start by the economic background it inherited from the Tories. This was dominated by a massive balance of payments deficit of over £800 million. The key ministers, Harold Wilson, his Chancellor James Callaghan and Secretary of State for Economic Affairs George Brown, immediately decided, only a few hours after taking office, in a Saturday-morning meeting on 17 October in secret conclave with Lord Cromer, the Governor of the Bank of England, that the pound would not be devalued. This decision has provoked intense argument amongst economists ever since. The immediate effects seemed to be almost calamitous: Callaghan's first budget in November 1964 was not viewed favourably in the markets. By the end of the month there had been a tidal wave of selling of sterling and a huge run on the reserves. Disaster was averted only by a package of international assistance, mainly from the United States, amounting to $3,000 million. It was a traumatic start for Wilson and Callaghan: referring to a famous meeting between the Holy Roman Emperor Henry IV and Pope Gregory VII in 1077, the *Economist* declared that the 'Labour government has gone to Canossa'.[34]

Foot tended to be a devaluer, and recalled the Cripps devaluation of 1949, which had been seen as successful, with a positive impact on British exports. But as a non-economist he did not have any particular expertise on the topic. In a special issue of *Tribune* on 4 December devoted to 'The Pound and Politics', he blamed the crisis on the 'fatuity' of international financiers reacting against the fact that the new Labour government was not adopting 'the same imbecile deflationary measures which were adopted after the last British crisis' (in fact the government had had to raise the bank rate to 7 per cent). The answer lay, he claimed, in removing the wealth from foreign speculators/investors, and in a 'vastly extended public ownership, for Socialism on a national and international scale'. Unfortunately for this line of argument, it was precisely through international finance that the rescue operation to prop up the pound had to be mobilized. The strength of the pound and its exchange rate cast a massive cloud over the Labour government from its outset; for the next five years there was a feeling that the Wilson administration never really had the economy, especially the balance of payments, under control. Many other profound unanswered questions faced Foot and the left about government foreign and defence policy, particularly the deepening American involvement in South Vietnam, to which the Wilson government gave moral support, and the looming presence of the supposed nuclear deterrent. There was anxiety, therefore, from the start. But it was still a Labour government after thirteen years of disappointment. There was some evidence that Labour might have recaptured the intellectual and cultural *élan* it had last claimed back in 1945, and the outlook would surely be brighter.

Under the Wilson government Michael Foot was largely an observer, although an important one. In the period 1964–66 it was largely a matter of simple political survival, with the government having such a tiny majority. It threatened to disappear altogether in 1965 when two right-wing, though formerly leftish, backbenchers, Woodrow Wyatt and Desmond Donnelly, threatened to oppose the renationalization of steel. Michael Foot, whose own Ebbw Vale steelworks were always present in his thoughts, flayed them in a Commons speech on 6 May. He attacked the Iron and Steel Board's policy of low investment since denationalization in 1953, and declared it to be 'the most serious, powerful, malicious, vengeful vested interest in the country'. He referred to Donnelly as a 'compulsive traitor'. The latter's speech dismissed Foot's remarks as 'Restoration comedy', but in the end he and Wyatt were prevailed upon to vote with the government, which scraped home by 310 votes to 306.[35] The apostasies of Donnelly, a fleeting Bevanite sympathizer back in 1951, were long remembered. In the second volume of Foot's life of Bevan there were references to his claiming thirty pieces of silver and other allegations that ended up in the courts (see page 268). Meanwhile Foot made threatening noises of his own when the subject of steel nationalization was omitted from the Queen's speech in both 1964 and 1965.

Otherwise, Foot's main role, as pledged to Wilson, was to ensure that the left did not create undue difficulties. In the Commons a new

'Tribune group' was formed, of perhaps forty members, representative of the left. As its name suggested, they included familiar old figures from Bevanite days like Foot and Mikardo. But there were also younger recruits like Stan Orme, a product of the distinctive AEU, who took a different stance from his seniors on key issues like incomes legislation, which he opposed. The Tribune group met weekly on Mondays, but had no settled policy laid down. The editor of the newspaper, Dick Clements, always attended. Foot himself, however, was only occasionally present. At party conference the Wednesday Tribune evenings were always a highlight for the left.

Two particular issues divided the Tribune group: incomes policy and Palestine.[36] On the first, whereas Foot had spoken of the need for a planned incomes policy in the past, most Tribune group MPs were totally opposed to any form of prices and incomes legislation, which would bring with it the threat of legal sanctions in an area traditionally left to voluntary negotiation. Stan Orme recalled, disapprovingly, that Foot was tempted to 'go down the Barbara Castle route' of legislative control. On Palestine, the old instinctive pro-Israeli sympathies were being replaced by concern for the Palestinian Arabs, which emerged strongly during the Six Day War in June 1967. MPs like Orme, Eric Heffer, Will Griffiths, Norman Atkinson, Sid Bidwell and John Mendelson were all favourable to the Palestinian Arabs. Foot himself was still pro-Israeli, but was swayed by his colleagues. He found his mind changing as developments in the Middle East took place, especially the occupation of the West Bank of the Jordan by Israeli troops and settlers after 1967, a process only beginning to be reversed in 2006. On these and other issues Foot tried to use his influence, but in a way that would not create the extreme difficulties for the Wilson government that Attlee and Gaitskell had experienced from the parliamentary left in the past.

On other issues, precarious though the government's position was, Foot felt compelled to speak out. There were alarming developments in the government's overseas policies. In South-East Asia the rapid growth of the American military involvement in South Vietnam, including savage bombing attacks on its peasant population, deeply worried Foot and his colleagues. The Chief of Staff of the US Air Force, General Curtis LeMay, talked of bombing the Vietnamese 'back to the stone age'. By 1968 demonstrations in Britain against American policy in Vietnam rivalled anything achieved by CND. Yet Labour's new Foreign Secretary, Michael Stewart, spoke with astonishing warmth in defending the American military strategy. It was known that there was pressure from the National Security Advisers McGeorge Bundy and Walt Rostow, and others in President Lyndon Johnson's administration, for Britain to send troops, as it had done in Korea fifteen years earlier.[37] Harold Wilson, however, showed a good deal more dexterity in resisting than Tony Blair was to do over Iraq in 2003. Rhodesia was another problem area, with the Labour government appearing to be extraordinarily restrained in allowing Ian Smith's illegal regime to maintain its independence from Britain. Here, as in other Commonwealth areas, Foot and *Tribune* both demanded that British troops be sent to bring down a racist regime, though they surely underestimated the diplomatic and logistical difficulties that this would entail. Talks between Wilson and Ian Smith on HMS *Fearless* in August 1968 (which aroused the keen concern of Hugh Foot, Lord Caradon, Britain's minister at the UN) led nowhere, since Smith disavowed any agreement as soon as he got home. The civil war in Nigeria, between the Ibo people in Biafra and the government in Lagos, was another coming flashpoint. But in each case Foot's was a voice of conscience, but not of authority. What he did maintain was that the solution could only lie within the Labour Party. He thus strongly disapproved of the forlorn intervention of a former CND activist and anti-Vietnam campaigner, Richard Gott, in the Hull North by-election in January 1966. The strong victory by the Labour candidate there, Kevin Macnamara, vindicated Foot's view. It also incidentally lumbered the nation with the cost of the Humber Bridge, which Barbara Castle promised the electors of Hull during the campaign.

There were two grave personal sadnesses at this time. In March 1965 the body of Michael's much-loved older sister Sally was found in the river Lynher, near the family home in Pencrebar. She had had a peculiarly sad life, in which various enterprises involved with horses had gone awry. Latterly she had lapsed into mental difficulties and alcoholism, and it had been difficult to find her a home. She of all the Foots never had much of a life at all. It looked like suicide, although the court returned an open verdict. Michael Foot particularly grieved at the death of a cherished sister, with whom he had had particular bonds of attachment in his childhood and who had first shown him the joys to be found in reading books. Sally had always felt nearest to him of all the family. Then in January 1966 one of his closest friends, Victor Weisz, the cartoonist Vicky, committed suicide with an overdose of sleeping pills. Foot deeply mourned a beloved knight-errant of a friend who, like another wandering Jew, Heinrich Heine, grieved at the wars and persecution that ravaged humanity.[38] The civil war in Nigeria had been the last of them, and it killed poor Vicky. Foot's testament to him in *Debts of Honour* is full of love and compassion for one who was surely what Heine described as 'a soldier in the war for the liberation of humanity'.

After the Hull by-election Labour's poll ratings soared, and Harold Wilson, having struggled for so long with a minuscule majority, called a general election for March 1966. The result was a big swing to Labour and a ninety-seven-seat overall majority. Labour ended up with 364 MPs against the Tories' 253. Its proportion of the votes cast, at 48.1 per cent, was close to the record level of 1951. Michael Foot routinely defeated a Conservative, J. R. Lovill, in Ebbw Vale, by 24,936 votes to 4,352; his proportion of the poll, 85.1 per cent, was his best yet. Naturally he largely concerned himself with campaigning for others, but less conspicuously than before. General elections were now essentially fought on television, where Harold Wilson, with skilful use of his pipe and a deceptively populist style, was a master. Michael Foot, by contrast, despite his experience on *In the News* long before and his brilliance as a communicator through the written word, was not so effective on television. He was essentially a pulpit orator, of unpredictable style and with rolling cadences and rhythms in his sentences that did not go down well with the common man or woman on the sitting-room sofa. He needed much tutoring to cope succinctly with the sharp interrogations of Robin Day and other television interviewers, and never wholly mastered the medium. On the stump, however, he was still marvellous value, better than ever, but essentially in preaching to those already converted.

Labour seemed destined for a solid tenure of power. As much as in 1945 could it be said that they were the masters now. The country's mood was joyous, the long-haired, mini-skirted young revelled in a new age of 'permissiveness'. Journalists wrote of 'swinging London'; Harold Wilson gave the Beatles the MBE. To Foot's great rejoicing England defeated the West Germans to win the football World Cup in July 1966. But by then the political mood had been abruptly transformed. The government had plunged into serious economic difficulties. The second week of July was a time of turmoil. In the long term, it was the most decisive episode in the Wilson government's life, confirming the Prime Minister's famous opinion that a week is a long time in politics. The outcomes of that week were variously that the government decided to ignore American advice and move towards devaluation of the pound, to seek once again membership of the European Common Market, and to withdraw British forces from east of Suez. All of these were in different ways moves to diminish Britain's special relationship, so-called, with the United States, and should therefore have been acceptable to Michael Foot. Each fundamentally recast Britain's role in the post-war world, and suggested a European rather than a transatlantic orientation. A more parochial development in that tumultuous week was the first election of a Welsh nationalist, Gwynfor Evans being elected for Camarthen. This opened up new questions about the integrity of the United Kingdom, and was to spur on demands for devolution, with major consequences for the career of Michael Foot.

But in the short term, it was economic calamities that aroused the greatest concern. Spurred on by a seamen's strike and by serious news about the June trade deficit, there was a huge run on the pound, which fell on 12 July 1966 to its lowest point since November 1964. On 14 July the bank rate was belatedly raised to 7 per cent. George Brown's National Plan for 25 per cent sustained growth over the next six years was in ruins; a statement on expenditure cuts cobbled together on 14 July made the plight of sterling worse. Wilson and his Chancellor Jim Callaghan seemed almost helpless. Wilson's ill-timed departure on a three-day visit to Moscow left behind him a maelstrom of rumour and intrigue: there were said to be plots to depose him as Prime Minister in favour of the emotionally erratic George Brown. Some kind of stability returned only on 20 July, when Wilson announced a huge package of spending cuts, £500 million in all. It was, said the *Economist*, 'the biggest deflationary package in any industrial nation since Keynesian economics began'.[39] A formal vote had, most unusually, been taken in the Cabinet on whether to devalue the pound. The Cabinet voted against by seventeen to six, both Brown and Barbara Castle being in the minority. It was a truly dreadful time for Wilson's team. The self-proclaimed planners had apparently lost all control of the economy. The government never recovered from July 1966. Wilson, who had campaigned on 'Labour's plan for the New Britain' and derided the Tory free-for-all society, said Labour had been 'blown off course'. In reality it was eventually to be blown out of office.

These events had serious implications for the left, and for Michael Foot in particular. They seemed to confirm that, as the Tribune group had always argued, the government's traditional and distinctly unsocialist economic policy, with much use of fiscal techniques and interest rates, was fundamentally flawed. Foot had already joined others in attacking Wilson's attempts to discredit the National Union of Seamen's month-long strike, which had so seriously affected the trade balance. Wilson claimed that the strike was the result of Communist activism by men like the party's Industrial Organizer Bert Ramelson – 'a tightly-knit group of politically-motivated men' – which caused loud protests on the Labour left. But the crisis went much further than that, to the very fundamentals of Labour's approach to the economy. During the turmoil in July one ministerial casualty had been Foot's friend Frank Cousins, who resigned as Minister of Technology when the Cabinet decided to introduce a prices and incomes policy to keep check of domestic demand and inflationary pressures from wages at home. This policy was anathema to most of the Tribune group. Foot headed a number of left-wing backbenchers who wrote privately to Wilson on 2 August in protest about the policy and to demand that the guillotine not be used in debate, to afford them more leeway in making their case. They also raised more fundamental matters, including the rise in defence expenditure under pressure from the Americans, and Britain's attempt to continue an unsustainable policy of keeping sterling as a reserve currency.[40] The severe cuts in public spending announced on 20 July were another keen grievance. The committee stages of the Prices and Incomes Bill in August had many difficult sessions. On a key amendment, twenty-eight Labour MPs abstained,

Foot amongst them. There were calls for the whip to be withdrawn yet again. In the end the new Whip, the emollient John Silkin, managed to find a compromise formula.[41]

For Michael Foot these developments meant that his caution in criticizing the government in the 1964–66 period was replaced by a more familiar attitude. There had been suggestions since the general election about the prospect of his at last entering the government. Wilson had dispatched his Parliamentary Private Secretary, the MP for Jarrow, Ernie Fernyhough, to see whether Foot might consider becoming a replacement for Frank Cousins.[42] But, especially after the Prices and Incomes Bill, that was unthinkable. Foot repeatedly emphasized in the Commons that he was not opposed to an incomes policy in principle, and that he had argued for one in the past as a component of economic planning. But this kind of incomes policy, accompanied by severe deflation, was not acceptable at all. However, no government, Labour or otherwise, could accept the kind of painless, non-deflationary incomes policy that he advocated. In 1966–68, therefore, Foot settled down to his well-practised role as a long-term critic, on the outside and not particularly concerned with looking in, though less intractable than in the past.

It was an increasingly difficult period for the government on the economic front, especially after the rise in oil prices following the Six Day War in June 1967. It culminated in the forced decision to devalue the pound on 18 November 1967, which saw the resignation of Jim Callaghan as Chancellor and his replacement by Roy Jenkins. This inaugurated what Jenkins himself called 'two years of hard slog'. In other respects, the government had considerable achievements to show. Michael Foot's old friend Jennie Lee, now Minister of State for the Arts, could claim credit for an important part of it, with a bold programme to support the arts and, more important still, the launching of the Open University, an innovation some felt was almost comparable to Nye's creation of the National Health Service. Roy Jenkins's enlightened regime at the Home Office before he became Chancellor was also a great landmark, including much libertarian reform with regard to sexual preferences, drugs and in particular freedom of expression in literature and the theatre. These last won the fervent support of Michael, and even more of Jill. Jenkins, indeed, consulted

Foot from time to time in getting his proposals through the Commons. During the years of Tony Blair it was common for survivors of the old left of the sixties to look back nostalgically to the good old days of Harold Wilson's government, with its civilized permissiveness, its bold support for education including especially university education, its support of the welfare state on good egalitarian principles, and a vigorous regional policy to sustain areas of former high unemployment. Despite the devaluation and other crises, economists could place the Wilson years within a supposed 'golden age' prior to the huge inflation in oil and other prices in 1973. Critics of Tony Blair for sending British troops to Iraq in 2003 noted approvingly that Harold Wilson had not caved in to US pressure to do likewise in Vietnam in the sixties. And in the end, despite much protest from the Pentagon and from Asian leaders like Lee Kuan Yew in Singapore, Wilson's government withdrew British forces from east of Suez. It was under Harold Wilson that the sun did indeed finally set on the old British Empire, and rightly so.

But at the time, Labour MPs, by no means all on the left, found much to criticize in government policy. They were not discouraged from doing so under the more tolerant regime operating in the Commons after John Silkin became a disarming Chief Whip, and Douglas Houghton succeeded the acerbic veteran Emanuel Shinwell as Chairman of the parliamentary Labour Party. Generally, the going seemed to be rough before and after devaluation, and the government lost by-election after by-election, not only to the Tories but, alarmingly, to Scottish and Welsh nationalists in Labour's strongest areas. There was low morale in constituency parties, and a worrying loss of party members. The discontent, even demoralization, in the grassroots was to be reflected in the Labour vote falling by almost a million in the 1970 general election.

Amongst Labour MPs, the two main areas of discontent were the domestic aspects of economic policy, especially incomes policy which meant enforced wage restraint, and the support expressed for American policy in Vietnam. These were certainly Michael Foot's priorities. On 26 March 1968 his signature headed a letter from twenty-one Labour MPs to Harold Wilson telling him they could not 'under any circumstances' support incomes legislation in the lobbies. Wilson replied in gentle terms, spelling out the need for income restraint along with other policies such as industrial restructuring and modernization: 'Without an effective policy of this kind there would be literally no other choice than to restrict the level of jobs to that at which workers will not ask for wage increases or where, if they did so ask, employers would not be able to afford to pay them.'[43] Predictably, there was no meeting of minds here.

Two months later an interview with Foot appeared in the *New Left Review*, conducted by Robin Blackburn and Alexander Cockburn.[44] Here, apart from reiterating his opposition to any prices and incomes legislation, he attacked, in wild and windy terms, the entire economic policy of Wilson's government. It should have taken the opportunity in 1964 to re-establish the apparatus of control over capitalism dismantled by the Tories in the 1950s. Instead it 'accepted international financial doctrine' with the deflationary measures of July 1966. Foot wound up in rhetorical and almost utopian terms, upbraiding Labour for its 'undue concentration upon economics'. There ought to be 'a restatement of socialist philosophy which puts economics in the background'. Meanwhile *Tribune* on 5 June included a Socialist Charter published by Labour MPs and trade union leaders. Britain should aim for 'economic independence' through cuts in its arms budget, the mobilizing of privately-owned overseas assets, the control of export capital, and import controls. The solution to Britain's problems lay in 'socialist planning', accompanied by 'an independent foreign policy'.[45] It was hard to reconcile this kind of approach with the notion of Labour as in any sense a party of government. The Labour Cabinet minister and historian Edmund Dell later commented, quite reasonably, that Foot did not explain how a government so totally dependent on foreign borrowing could escape from a desperate dependence on international finance.[46]

There were many other areas of policy which aroused particular protest. Among them were the restriction of immigration, notably Asians from Kenya in 1968, after Callaghan succeeded Jenkins at the Home Office; the failure to remove Ian Smith in Rhodesia; and the civil war in Nigeria. Michael Foot was involved in all of these issues, although in the main there was not much that was distinctive in what he had to say. In the debates on the aftermath of the Arab–Israeli war in 1967, linked to the issue of passage through the Straits of Tiran by

Israeli vessels, Foot was still markedly more sympathetic to the Israelis than were most of the younger Tribune MPs. There was, however, one important dog that did not bark. Despite all the years of campaigning in CND by Foot and others only a short time earlier, the bomb never arose as an issue. In fact, defence policy under Harold Wilson remained virtually identical with that under the Tories: pledges to do away with the separate British nuclear deterrent made at the 1964 general election were quietly dropped. Relations with the Soviet Union did not noticeably improve, despite Wilson's repeated attempts to work with President Kosygin to resolve the situation in Vietnam. But the bomb, so omnipresent to the protesters in 1959–60, now simply did not seem to be a priority, especially since nuclear tests had been formally stopped by the test-ban treaty in Moscow in 1963.

Michael Foot devoted most of his active hours at this time to parliamentary protest. He was no longer editor of *Tribune*, though he was still head of its managerial board. His main journalistic commitment was gentle book reviewing once a week in the *Evening Standard*. He had no major book immediately on hand, although he was making somewhat stately progress on the second volume of his life of Aneurin Bevan, covering the years from 1945. Nor did he hold office in the Labour Party: his bid to become Party Treasurer in October 1967, as the nominee of the TGWU and some other unions and militants in the constituency, ended predictably in heavy defeat by Jim Callaghan, who had made careful preparations with union friends and defeated Foot by roughly two to one. Foot was later to observe: 'Jim does everything on purpose.' So Foot's life was largely an endless concatenation of protest, criticizing the government on almost every area of policy while at the same protesting his fervent enthusiasm for a Labour government being in office.

In some areas of domestic policy he was less aggressive than he might have been. For instance, after Enoch Powell made his inflammatory speeches about immigration in the summer of 1968, talking of, like the ancient Romans, seeing 'the Tiber foaming with much blood' in a way that most people thought racist and highly offensive, Foot actually extended the hand of friendship. He took a very different line from his nephew Paul, who subjected Powell to fierce attacks in a book, *The Rise of Enoch Powell*, at this time.[47] Foot liked Powell for his cerebral approach to politics, his love of learning, and especially his feeling for the use of language. Soon the two men were to collaborate on a variety of issues, including opposition to joining the European Common Market and the manufacture of nuclear weapons. They were to form an unbeatable team in challenging House of Lords reform in 1969. Foot seemed a good deal less shocked about Powell's speeches than other progressives were, and argued that Powell was no kind of racist: in 1959 he had been prominent among those parliamentarians who condemned the undoubtedly racist atrocities in Hola Camp in Kenya, where twelve alleged Mau Mau terrorists, detained by Britain, died after being beaten. Powell himself described Foot as his 'pin-up boy' because 'he speaks beautiful English'. At any rate, from 1968 onwards Michael and Jill would entertain Powell and his wife Pamela to dinner at home in Hampstead, free from journalistic intrusion, to discuss their favourite books and authors, in an atmosphere of sweetness and light. It was one of Michael Foot's more unexpected friendships.

In the late sixties, then, Foot seemed, as so often in the years since 1945, stuck in a backwater of the oppositionist left. He spoke to Richard Crossman, when they met, of his disappointment and disillusion with government policy on a broad front. He had never had the close relationship with Wilson he had enjoyed with Bevan, and found the Prime Minister's paranoia about moles, leaks and conspiracies simply baffling. Yet, quite unexpectedly, Foot was heading erratically towards the mainstream. This was not through close relations with anyone in the Cabinet. His best friend there was Barbara Castle, who became Secretary of State for Employment and Productivity in 1968, but whose approach to incomes policy and trade union reform was not at all what the left would endorse. Foot's lifeline came rather, for the first time in his life, from the trade unions. If anything, the unions had been the enemy in his earlier years, personified by Arthur Deakin of the TGWU, whom he had denounced with such fervour in his *Tribune* columns. He had struck up a friendship with Frank Cousins and his wife, mainly through joint involvement with CND, and Cousins had persuaded his TGWU to prop up *Tribune*'s ever-shaky finances. But after his resignation from the government Cousins was no longer a major player in political life. Foot knew relatively little of the unions: he was a member of the distinctly white-collar National

Union of Journalists, which was a highly untypical body in the TUC. He did not have the innate feel for union attitudes of, for instance, Jim Callaghan. Callaghan was after all at one time a leading official with the Inland Revenue Staff Federation, and instinctively understood the importance for trade unionists of such formalities as the rule book; he felt that neither Wilson nor Barbara Castle, let alone Foot, ever had that kind of understanding.

But Foot now became friendly with the most powerful trade unionist of the day. He got to know Jack Jones, recently appointed General Secretary of the TGWU, the same union as Deakin and Cousins. Jones and Cousins, two imperious personalities, were mutually hostile, and differed fiercely over aspects of running the TGWU. But Foot's relationship with Jones was, if anything, even stronger than that with Cousins, and it also yielded much-needed financial support for *Tribune*. Foot's admiration for Jones was total.[48] He came from Merseyside, where Foot had become a democratic socialist. Though he had worked with Communists within a wider left in the forties, he had some background of industrial syndicalism in the docks, very much the same tradition of industrial democracy which Nye Bevan had imbibed in south Wales as a young man after the publication in 1912 of *The Miners' Next Step* by the miners' agent Noah Ablett and his colleagues, which called for control of the mines by the miners themselves. And Jack Jones had fought with distinction, and been wounded, in the International Brigade in the Spanish Civil War. Jones now reached out to Foot as a credible socialist leader who would defend the unions' cause in the face of threatened legislation to impose legal sanctions on them. The unions were increasingly under fire in the later sixties after unofficial strikes had multiplied, with damaging effect on a frail economy. The role of the seamen's strike in June 1966 in hastening the financial crisis of the following month was fresh in the memory. The Donovan Commission was sitting to examine their relationship with the law, and investigating whether their traditional immunity from civil damages over industrial action, dating from the Trades Disputes Act of the Liberal government of Campbell-Bannerman in 1906, could still be sustained.

In return, Jones greatly admired Foot for his sincerity and idealism, and as a rare example of a genuine socialist. He shared his views, too,

Aneurin Bevan speaking in Ebbw Vale, Michael listening, 1947.

Left Michael Foot MP speaking at a local carnival, 1950.

Right Barbara Castle watching Michael anxiously, *In the News*, BBC Television, 10 February 1951.

Free Speech, ITV, 1954: *left to right*, W.J. Brown, Robert Boothby, Kenneth Adam (chairman), Michael Foot, A.J.P. Taylor.

Michael and Jill at Paddock Cottage, on Beaverbrook's Cherkley estate, near Leatherhead, c.1955.

Out: Joan Vickers defeats a crestfallen Michael at Devonport by a hundred votes in the general election, May 1955.

Out again: Michael dismissed in the annual *Tribune* vs *New Statesman* cricket match, late 1950s.

Passionate Pilgrims: *left to right*, Michael, Isaac, Hugh and Christopher watching Plymouth Argyle play at Home Park, 1958.

In: Michael, Vanessa and Jill, Ebbw Vale by-election, November 1960.

Above Vicky cartoon (early 1960s) of himself and Michael in full spate: the wording reads, 'Dear Michael, I'm sorry I lost my temper last night. Hope to see you soon. Yours, Vicky.'

Right CND en route to Aldermaston: Michael, James Cameron and Michael's step-grandson Jason Lehel, Trafalgar Square, 30 March 1964.

Above The old patron: Michael and Lord Beaverbrook, Capponcina, Italy, 1964.

Right A Welsh Member: cartoon by Glan Williams, *Sunday Citizen*, 17 July 1966.

Below Reflecting on a giant: Michael at the Aneurin Bevan memorial stones, Waun-y-Pound, near Tredegar.

EBBW VALE — LABOUR MAJORITY 20,584 ... MARGINAL ?

Left Keeping in touch with the rank and file: Michael at a Co-Op beauty contest, early 1970s.

Below Voice of the miners: Michael at a Yorkshire miners' demonstration, Doncaster, June 1971.

Marching for the miners, Doncaster, June 1971. *Front row*: Will Paynter (General Secretary, NUM), Owen Briscoe (General Secretary, Yorkshire Miners), Arthur Scargill, Michael Foot and Phil Horbury (Yorkshire miners' official); *back row* includes Dick Kelly MP, Eric Varley and Martin Flannery (a future Labour MP).

Speaking at party conference, Blackpool, October 1973: *left to right*, James Callaghan, Michael, Roy Grantham (General Secretary of APEX), Ian Mikardo, Tony Benn.

on nuclear weapons and Europe. Jones knew that Foot had no specialist knowledge of union matters, but felt that he wanted to be helpful to his members.[49] Foot understood intuitively the threats emerging on the legal side, and the need to secure protection over both collective bargaining and workers' rights. The law should strike out boldly in new directions to defend working people at the workplace as the nature of industrial work changed from the classic assembly-line pattern. This was crucial politically. The Labour Party in the later sixties was very different from that of Attlee's heyday. In particular, even though trade union matters had played little part in the 1964 and 1966 general elections, the unions were assuming a more central role in both national and party affairs as issues of industrial relations moved up the political agenda. Among many previously loyalist unions, such as the TGWU and the AEU, there was a clear swing to the left. Union membership soared to over twelve million. White-collar workers in particular were joining large unions like the Confederation of Health Service Employees (COHSE) and the National Union of Public Employees (NUPE). Women were also becoming unionized in large numbers, while progress was also being made in unions like the Association of Professional, Executive, Clerical and Computer Staff (APEX) among Asian and African workers who had migrated to Britain in the large influx from the Commonwealth in the sixties.

It was, therefore, more essential than ever that the historic Labour alliance of political socialists and trade unionists be kept in being. Michael Foot sensed a historic opportunity here, quite apart from his personal admiration for Jack Jones and his friendship with other union leaders such as Hugh Scanlon of the AEU (whose stance on key issues was by no means identical with that of Jones). The trade unions were manifestly going to be central to the politics of the immediate future. The Donovan Commission eventually reported in 1968 very much in support of the traditional pattern of voluntary labour relations with wage bargaining conducted on a basis of consensus. It emphasized the shift in wage negotiations from corporate national agreements to local decisions taken on the shop floor of each plant, a development of which an old syndicalist like Jack Jones, wedded to industrial democracy, warmly approved.

Foot therefore emerged from the margins of political life as a major figure in the new pattern of politics. Under Jack Jones's tutelage he was moving on from being a patrician progressive, living in a world of humane middle-class intellectuals, to seeing himself as a tribune of the proletariat. To follow E. P. Thompson's analysis in *The Making of the English Working Class*, the Friend of the People was turning into the voice of the worker. William Hazlitt was subtly mutating into William Cobbett.

8

UNION MAN
(1968–1974)

For a quarter of a century after 1945, Britain lived under one-nation unionism. The trade unions stayed within the implicit social contract with the Ministry of Labour worked out with Ernest Bevin when he served under Churchill in 1940. The government listened with respect to the suggestions of the TUC and union leaders. They, in turn, endeavoured to keep their members away from the path of militancy, strikes and industrial disruption. They did not have undue difficulty in doing so. The unions' loyalty to the Labour government in 1945–51, along with the blessings of full employment and a welfare state, saw them prepared to put up with rationing and austerity, a total wage freeze in 1948–50, and the continuance of the wartime Order 1305, which forbade strikes. In effect, real wages fell. The Conservative years after 1951 were also quiet, with no sign of the confrontational attitudes of the 1920s. In 1951 Labour had raised the spectre of Tory class warriors trying to hammer the unions as Winston Churchill had done in 1926. But this was very far from being the case. There was full employment, the welfare state was extended under the Tories, a mood of consumer choice and growing affluence prevailed. Spain to trade unionists in the early sixties meant not passionate, class-conscious memories of Franco and the Civil War, but cheap and cheerful holidays on the Costa Brava. Conservative Ministers of Labour, one after the other, made every effort not to provoke the unions. The tone was set by Walter Monckton, Churchill's Minister of Labour, whose reputation was entirely based on his being an amiable high-class fixer in relation to the TUC as he had formerly been to King Edward VIII, not to mention his role in Foot's own 'Lower than Kemsley' affair. Monckton's relationship with his Labour opposite number, Alfred

Robens, was gentility itself. Macmillan once suavely remarked that the three institutions the Tories would never take on were the Catholic Church, the Brigade of Guards and the National Union of Mineworkers, and all three were left undisturbed.

The unofficial strikes of the early sixties amongst a wide range of industrial workers led to anxious debate amongst free-market Tories about the legal status of the unions. Iain Macleod, one of Monckton's successors, wrote in 1963 that he was 'frankly schizophrenic' about wildcat strikes – but then, without the votes of one and a half million trade unionists and their wives, the Conservatives would never get elected. After mature consideration of all the possible legislative actions that he might take, Macleod elaborately gave his voice in favour of doing nothing.[1] This particular boat need not be rocked. His successors in the Labour department, Edward Heath and John Hare, took the same view. For industrial relations, it meant thirteen peaceful years. It was assumed that under a Labour government from 1964 things would be much the same.

The trade unions were for a long time scarcely any more belligerent. Old militant bodies like the mineworkers were docile, at least at the national level; the last major miners' dispute had been in 1926, at the time of the General Strike. The emergence of Frank Cousins as General Secretary of the TGWU in 1956, after the sudden death of his predecessor Jock Tiffin, suggested a new militancy in the leadership of large unions. A celebrated London bus strike took place in 1958 which saw Macleod and Cousins in fierce confrontation, and the bus drivers duly lost. But there were no alarming consequences, and Macmillan kept up a non-confrontational policy towards the unions. A forceful, comparatively anti-union document like *A Giant's Strength*, written by some Conservative lawyers (including the future Lord Donaldson) in the late fifties, remained essentially academic. From 1960 to 1968 the TUC's General Secretary was George Woodcock, an even more tranquil figure than the supreme apparatchik, Walter Citrine, had been during the war. Woodcock, an intelligent, taciturn man, previously the head of TUC research, wished to preserve the status quo, without any threat to trade unions' privileges and legal immunities, as guaranteed under their Magna Carta, the 1906 Trades Disputes Act. When that appeared to be confirmed by the report of Lord Donovan's Royal Commission in 1968, voluntary collective bargaining seemed to be ensured. After Woodcock moved on to become head of the Commission on Industrial Relations, his replacement in 1969 by the more combative Vic Feather might have suggested a coming crisis. But not yet. In any case, Feather's Bradfordian belligerence was perhaps largely a matter of style: in TUC terms he was very much the establishment figure. There remained legal dangers arising from the 1964 Rookes v. Barnard case, which raised the spectre of individual workers challenging union officials in the courts over industrial action taken in their name. Rookes, a draughtsman at London Airport, had resigned from his union, which operated a closed shop. He sued union officials for conspiracy and won 'exemplary damages' for his dismissal. This appeared to undermine the 1906 Trades Disputes Act.[2] But things had been largely left in abeyance thereafter. The one legislative change in the early Wilson period was the 1965 Trade Disputes Act, which reversed the Rookes v. Barnard decision. It was passed by his Minister of Labour Ray Gunter, otherwise reclining with some equanimity on what he called his 'bed of nails'.

But the new links Michael Foot was building up with Jack Jones and other major union figures from 1969 implied a fundamental change. For the next fifteen or more years, the question of trade union power was to be central to British public life, and it was decisive in making Margaret Thatcher Prime Minister in 1979. As membership soared ever upwards, reaching a peak of thirteen million in 1979, 55.6 per cent of the labour force, union muscle was said by some to be undermining the economy, destroying social peace and (in the famous words of one American Congressman) making Britain as ungovernable as Chile. It set the tone of Michael Foot's political priorities from the late sixties on, giving him, for the first time in his parliamentary career, a clear departmental interest. More remarkably, it meant that this incorrigible rebel, veteran of a hundred rebellions, the scourge of the whips and the critic of party standing orders, was to become a man of government, and thereby to discover, in the phrase of the former French Prime Minister Pierre Mendès-France, that to govern meant to choose.

The new mood of conflict was heralded by, of all people, Barbara Castle, the new Secretary for Employment. Always on the left, she had never been close to the unions, which she viewed with Bevanite detachment, if not actual hostility. The rational appeal of socialist planning was juxtaposed by her against union sectionalism. She was in no way seduced by the power of Jack Jones, and regarded the Donovan Report as a huge missed opportunity. It was a document which contained no philosophic view of industrial relations. She made it her business to supply one. Hence her famous – or notorious – white paper *In Place of Strife*, published in November 1968 (the title was a conscious echo of Bevan's *In Place of Fear*), posited a quite different approach, and generated a new turmoil on the industrial relations front. It proposed many things highly acceptable to union leaders like Jack Jones. It did indeed offer the unions legal guarantees and protection, notably the compulsory registration of unions and a Commission on Industrial Relations (CIR) to spread good practice in the conduct of collective bargaining. This would be given powers to deal with any employer who refused to recognize a trade union, much as suggested to Donovan by the Nuffield College authority on industrial relations, Allan Flanders. However, *In Place of Strife* also made the deeply controversial proposal that the government should be able to intervene, with powers backed up by legal sanctions, in three areas: enforcing the recommendations of the CIR, implementing a 'conciliation pause' in unconstitutional strikes not preceded by adequate joint discussions, and the holding of ballots on strike action when the support of the workers might be in doubt. There was a bad-tempered series of Cabinet meetings in January 1969 when Barbara Castle's policy was sharply criticized by Crossman and Callaghan, the Home Secretary, who had begun life as a union official and could plausibly present himself as the keeper of the cloth cap.

In April, after much debate in Cabinet, Barbara Castle introduced a short Industrial Relations Bill of five clauses. The two key ones threatened possible penal sanctions against the unions, since they gave the government power to impose settlements in inter-union disputes where voluntary agreement could not be reached, and to impose a twenty-eight-day conciliation pause in cases of unconstitutional industrial action. There was uproar. The TUC totally rejected the government's approach, and offered its own brand of mediation and intervention by itself instead. Castle and Wilson now found themselves increasingly isolated in Cabinet, as minister after minister drifted away.

The Welsh Secretary, George Thomas, had been sufficiently stirred by Castle's first version of her Bill to write her a note in Cabinet which began 'Oh, you beautiful doll!!',[3] but other responses were far less printable. The Parliamentary Labour Party, now chaired by Douglas Houghton, a veteran public-service union leader close to Callaghan, seethed with rebellion. A special TUC Congress at Croydon in June rejected the government's proposals overwhelmingly, by nearly eight to one. After angry exchanges with Jack Jones, Hugh Scanlon and other union leaders at 10 Downing Street – 'take your tanks off my lawn, Hughie' – Wilson had to recognize his political weakness and climb down humiliatingly in the face of the new Jones–Scanlon axis of power in the TUC. A virtually meaningless 'solemn and binding' covenant procedure was cobbled together by government and TUC: journalists ridiculed the phantom figure of 'Solomon Binding'. A Labour government had caved in abjectly to union power. At the same time, it was clear that Barbara Castle was a Pandora who had opened an ominous box. The shelf life of Solomon Binding could not be lengthy. Some form of industrial legislation to control the unions, perhaps from a future Tory government carrying out the terms of the right-wing Selsdon Park programme of January 1970, appeared inevitable.

Michael Foot was, of course, totally opposed to the entire philosophy of *In Place of Strife*. He had angry meetings with Barbara Castle, who recognized that his opposition to her proposals was even more implacable than that of others on the parliamentary left. She savaged him for his lack of realism. When he urged that her Bill be delayed until the special TUC Congress, he was compelled to admit that even if the Congress came up with nothing, he would oppose her proposals anyway: 'I told Mike flatly that he had grown soft on a diet of soft options because he never had to choose.'[4] It is a tribute to both of them that the Foot–Castle relationship survived exchanges like these. But Foot was only a bit player in the unfolding drama. The government's key opponent was none other than its own Home Secretary, Jim Callaghan. He led the fight on the NEC and in Cabinet, and in the end faced the Prime Minister down. Roy Jenkins wrote with some awe of Callaghan striding through the crowds in Victoria Station during the crisis, 'with a defiant dignity which made me realize how important a politician he had become'.[5] The future TUC General Secretary Len Murray believed it all showed that Callaghan's informed grasp of industrial relations was 'intuitive', whereas that of Wilson and Castle was 'ideological' and misconceived.[6] With the new links Callaghan had cultivated with the unions before being elected Party Treasurer in 1967, he was too big to be disciplined. Indeed, very shortly his adroit handling of the crisis in Northern Ireland made him the government's single most valuable and effective minister. He never regretted the stand he took over industrial relations in 1969, not even after the 'winter of discontent' ten years on. Contrary to one or two public statements later in his life, he always felt that penal sanctions on trade unionists were counter-productive and illiberal. Until the end of his life Jim Callaghan was always a voluntarist, always a Donovan man.

Michael Foot's role, though, unlike that of Callaghan, lay in the future, through his new alliance with Jack Jones, Clive Jenkins and other union power-brokers. He had a long and cherished legacy to defend. The existing system of voluntary industrial relations had become the prevailing conventional wisdom, and was seminal to old Labour ideas. Almost the first measure to be introduced by the Attlee government in 1946, moved by no less than the Foreign Secretary Ernest Bevin, was a Trade Disputes Act. It restored legislation on the unions' political levy to the situation prior to the Tory measure of 1927 which had imposed 'contracting in' on trade unionists paying the levy. This tradition was broadly endorsed by almost all of the academic authorities in the field, by Otto-Kahn Freund, Allan Flanders and the TUC's industrial adviser Bill Wedderburn. In 1983 the eminent labour historian Henry Phelps-Brown was to publish a subtle volume, *The Origins of Trade Union Power*, which drew a sharp distinction between the voluntarist British tradition of industrial relations and the preference of union leaders in Australia and New Zealand for state action on arbitration, legal liability and the restriction of strikes.[7] The shift in policy implied in Barbara Castle's proposals meant a new role for the law, and a transformation of the balance of social power. The argument gained in passion throughout the strike-torn seventies. The unions seemed to dominate the domestic agenda, and were credited with effectively overthrowing two Prime Ministers, Heath and Callaghan. The union question as variously understood by Castle or Heath meant a fundamental redirection of public policy. It also meant a major redirection for the career of Michael Foot as he was forced to contemplate changing the habits of half a lifetime spent in permanent opposition.

On another issue over which he challenged the government, Foot's role was far more central. This was a curious episode, a proposed reform of the House of Lords devised by Wilson and Crossman in which hardly anyone really believed. It was scarcely even relevant to current politics, since it was impossible to argue that the difficulties into which the government had plunged were in any way due to the House of Lords, even with its eight-hundred-plus hereditary, mainly Tory members. The Parliament Bill proposed creating two categories of peers, non-voting (largely hereditary) and voting. The latter would largely be chosen by the party whips, and would create a huge reservoir of patronage for the Prime Minister and other party leaders. Even Callaghan, the Home Secretary who had to introduce the Bill in the Commons in 1969, had little belief in it, and viewed its defeat without distress.[8] Crossman also viewed the end of his own Bill with equanimity: he later invited Foot to lunch at the Athenaeum so that he could congratulate him on 'scuppering' it. Callaghan's relations with Wilson were in any case glacial at this time, as a result of policy on the unions.[9] The difficulties of constructing a House of Lords that had a measure of independence but was also basically controlled by a democratically-elected Commons plagued the Blair government for almost a decade after 1997. An elected House would indeed be democratic, but also potentially an assembly of party hacks unwilling to play an amending or scrutinizing role. The Blair government dithered over possible answers in the 2001–05 session and did nothing; in 1969 Wilson's could find none.

Michael Foot, the traditional opponent of party discipline, whether through standing orders or the *ukase* of the whips, was a predictable and brilliant critic of such a measure. He was also, of course, a committed abolitionist as far as the Lords was concerned. He led the charge against the Bill on Labour's backbenches during the second reading debate in February 1969. Many of all shades of his party eagerly supported him: another trenchant critic of the Bill was Robert Sheldon, by no means a man of the Labour left, who began the resistance by conducting a lengthy filibuster. But Foot also naturally acquired support from Tories resistant to change to the Constitution and tender towards the hereditary principle. His most effective ally was Enoch Powell, his private dinner-party guest and another natural rebel with high skills of oratory and literacy. Wedgwood-Benn, a strong supporter of the Bill, designated them as Conservatives of the left and the right. Foot's onslaught upon it bore the imprint of Cobbett's past assault on 'The Thing' – his term for the Establishment: 'Think of it! A second Chamber selected by the whips! A seraglio of eunuchs.' Expanding on this interesting metaphor, he declared that, in some national crisis, 'we would hear a falsetto chorus from the political castrati. They would be the final arbiters of our destiny.' There would arise 'a Heath Robinson House of Lords, a contraption which will fall to pieces in any crisis, which will be laughed out of court on such an occasion and which it would be better for us to laugh out of court now'. In the subsequent vote, Foot acted as teller for the Noes: one of those voting with him was his brother Dingle, former Solicitor-General.[10]

The subsequent committee stage of the Parliament (No.2) Bill was a masterclass in the filibuster, with Foot and Powell the outstanding participants. In all, Foot spoke twenty-six times on the Bill between February and mid-April. On 25–26 February he orated through the night. He condemned the Bill as an instrument of patronage, he drew on a range of historical evidence probably lost on many honourable members, he cited an array of past heroes from Aneurin Bevan back to Edmund Burke: 'The British Constitution is an interesting contraption. I hope that is not too Burkeian a statement for a Thomas Paineite like myself to utter.'[11] Since there was an obvious parallel with the Tory creation of peers in 1711, Dean Swift made a predictable entry, with lengthy extracts from his letters to Stella. There was indeed a great deal to ridicule in a Bill that was a parody of democracy. By the start of April it was clear that the measure, assailed on all sides and scarcely defended by a Home Secretary going through the motions of presenting it, was doomed. Throughout, Foot engaged in a torrent of vigorous, if good-humoured, invective. He had a final evening of knockabout fun on 14 April, ridiculing the presence in the legislature of the Anglican bishops: 'The bishops like the shepherds should be watching their flocks. If they did, they might have a visitation from the angels and glory shine all around ... Many bishops have been watching their flocks. It is better that they should be left undisturbed to do so.' He added, on a more philosophical note: 'I approach these matters in an Erastian spirit. I wish to see a subordination of the bishops to the popular electorate. That is one definition of Erastianism.'[12] Three days later, Harold Wilson ended the farce by telling the Commons that the Parliament Bill was being withdrawn so as to give priority to the Industrial Relations Bill. Foot warned him that it would very likely suffer the same fate. Crossman observed of this remark that he agreed with every word of it.

Apart from helping to inflict a sharp defeat on the government, Foot's performances in the debates on Lords reform confirmed his growing command as a parliamentary performer. For observers like Leo Abse they showed how he had developed a wider range of political skills since his enforced stay in Hereford hospital five years earlier. Alan Watkins had observed in the *Spectator* that sketch writers rated Foot (along with Wilson at that time) as the outstanding speaker in the Commons.[13] As with his hero Disraeli long ago, the time had come when they would listen.

Michael Foot's role throughout this period was one of fairly consistent opposition to the Labour government, on the unions, on the reform of the Lords, on Vietnam. On 5 May 1970 he initiated an adjournment debate to warn against an American invasion of Cambodia following the mass atrocities inflicted in Vietnam, and urged the remarkably passive Foreign Secretary, Michael Stewart, to reactivate the 1954 Geneva Conference on Indo-China: sixty-eight MPs, mainly Tribune group and some Liberals, backed him in the division lobby. However, Foot did warmly endorse the government's liberal social policies, especially Roy Jenkins's measures to free books, plays and films from puritanical censorship by the Lord Chamberlain. Jenkins had kept in touch with Foot on these measures, and also tried unsuccessfully to get him, rather than the erratic and unpredictable Leo Abse, to introduce a Bill to reform the laws on homosexuality. But this humane policy showed signs of coming to grief under Jenkins's distinctly non-permissive successor, Jim Callaghan; ever the libertarian, Foot attacked Callaghan's refusal to follow the proposals of the Wootton Report to liberalize the law on the smoking and supply of cannabis.[14] On the other hand, Foot did give warm backing to Calla-ghan's stand in 1969 to remove capital punishment once and for all from the criminal justice system, an aspiration for which he had worked with Victor Gollancz, Arthur Koestler and others over many decades. But on balance, despite the joyous knockabout of the debates on the Parliament Bill, Foot was privately gloomy about the general standing of the government and its broadly non-socialist attitudes. He was scathing about its performance, uncontaminated and undefiled by its failures.

Some wondered about the precise ties that bound him to the Labour Party at all. They might have wondered even more had more attention been paid to a strange speech that Foot made on being invited to address a '*Morning Star* birthday rally' held by the British Communist Party's newspaper in his Ebbw Vale constituency on 4 March 1969.[15] Here he spoke with warmth of the Communist Party and called for the 'sectarian walls' in the socialist movement to be broken down, to secure the triumph of the working class all over the world. He quoted examples, such as France in 1958, of the disasters that could occur if the left allowed itself to be divided, and hailed Marxism as 'a great creed of human liberation' which 'enlarged the empire of the human mind'. Interestingly, among the evils to be fought he listed 'Powellism and all the bestialities of racial discrimination'. It was difficult to rec-oncile outpourings such as this, reminiscent of Cripps in the 1930s, with the anti-Communist, distinctly democratic socialism for which Foot's *Tribune* had stood. It was a throwback to a much younger Foot in Socialist League days, or perhaps to his collaboration with Harry Pollitt in the Russia Today movement during the war. Perhaps at that period a left-wing democratic socialist could reasonably claim common cause with the Communists in the fight against fascism. To take such a view in 1969, when so many distinguished Communists had left the party after its Stalinist intolerance had been openly exposed, seemed barely credible.

A more characteristic performance, perhaps, had come two months earlier when Foot and his parliamentary colleague Eric Heffer took on Tariq Ali and Bob Rowthorne of the underground newspaper *Black Dwarf* in London in what was hailed as the 'debate of the century'.[16] The background was the surge of a youthful grassroots New Left in the constituencies, fanned by the protests against the Vietnam War. British university campuses followed Berkeley and the Sorbonne with 'demos' and sit-ins directed against the 'repressive tolerance' of their institutions during the long hot summer of 1968. But Foot lent no support. In fact, his speech in the debate adopted his most characteristic stance of championing the parliamentary route to socialism. He quoted examples from the past, notably Germany in 1932, to show the dire results of turning away from democracy to direct action: the lesson of CND was that extra-parliamentary activity had its place, but that it should be channelled to achieving socialist change in Parliament. It was a foretaste of the long debate between Foot and Tony Benn during Foot's time as party leader after 1980, and consistent with his views for most of his career. He made little impact on the revolutionaries in his audience, and the meeting became increasingly angry, ending in near uproar. But it did draw a clear distinction between democratic change achieved through consent and persuasion, and the revolutionary Marxism of those on the further left, and helped to place Foot more centrally within Labour's broad church. He received rare praise from *Socialist Commentary*, Rita Hinden's old pro-Gaitskell monthly, which saw his defence of representative government as quite distinct from the 'protest left'.[17] Foot had more contempt for anything remotely Gaitskellite than for almost anything else in politics, but his debating speech was a more convincing performance by far than the clichéd *soi-disant* Marxism offered to the *Morning Star* rally.

In the spring and summer of 1970, things at last seemed to be going better for Wilson's government. Roy Jenkins had presided over a significant improvement in the balance of payments: his 'two years of hard slog' were officially over. In Northern Ireland, Callaghan had shown the smack of firm government not often evident elsewhere, with a series of strong executive decisions. Foot approved of all of them, including the decision to send in troops to protect the Roman Catholic minority. The polls began to move strongly back in Labour's favour, and Wilson called a general election for the sunny month of June 1970. Despite all his manifold grievances in the past six years, Foot had no difficulty in throwing himself into the fray as stump speaker. In Ebbw Vale there was the usual non-contest, with Foot romping home over the Liberal Angus Donaldson with a majority of

17,446 and 72.4 per cent of the vote, and the Conservative and Plaid Cymru candidates losing their deposits.

But elsewhere in Britain, Labour met with a rude awakening. The campaign never got off the ground, and there was much demoralization and indifference at the grassroots. Labour's poll fell by almost a million compared with 1966, while that of the Conservatives rose by 1,700,000; Labour took only 288 seats, against the Conservatives' 330. Edward Heath became Prime Minister, and Wilson and his team departed, later derided on television as 'yesterday's men'. Much was made of events during the campaign, including somewhat unfortuitous bad news on the balance of trade three days before polling day, but the outcome lay in more deep-seated factors. Labour had seldom seemed to be in control of the economy, its strategy for 25 per cent economic growth had not been fulfilled, the planners had shown an inability to plan, thereby creating, in Ben Pimlott's judgement, a permanent void at the heart of the party's ideology.[18] The long, painful decline of Old Labour, with its client support in economic backwaters, council estates and public sector workers, was already under way before the left-wing tide of the seventies. Michael Foot raged furiously at the Labour right for frustrating the socialism which he believed would have guaranteed electoral victory: Roy Jenkins at the Treasury, seen as a latter-day Gaitskell, was a particular *bête noire*. But the electoral results, beyond Ebbw Vale and other traditional but declining working-class citadels, gave little support for Foot's view. Sociology apparently stood in the way of socialism.

It might well have appeared that the bulk of Michael Foot's Commons career was now past. There was not a great deal to show for his two and a half decades of permanent dissent. He was the darling of the parliamentary sketch writers, civilized and amiable, hailed as a writer and orator, 'a wonderful man to have in politics', in the view of *The Times*.[19] But that cut little ice in the real world. If he was to play a role in building socialism in our time, it would have to be a constructive and active one. This was strongly urged upon him by close associates like Jack Jones, anxious that the unions should be strongly defended at the highest level. When the new Parliament assembled in late June, Foot was predictably defeated (133 to sixty-seven) by Roy Jenkins in the contest for the deputy leadership in a simple battle between old left and newish right. But he also stood for the Shadow Cabinet, elected by all Labour MPs, immediately the new Parliament assembled. His campaign was enthusiastically managed by allies like Stan Orme and a young Welsh constituent of Foot's, Neil Kinnock, newly elected for neighbouring Bedwellty. Foot duly came sixth in the poll, with 124 votes. He did so manifestly as the leader of the left: his only possible rival was Tony Benn (formerly Wedgwood-Benn, and an ex-Gaitskellite) but Benn's transition from right wing to left was only now taking place, while in any case he was twelve years Foot's junior, and Labour usually made a virtue of age and experience. Harold Wilson made Foot opposition spokesman on fuel and power. It was by far the most encouraging news that a despondent Parliamentary Labour Party was to hear. Foot's elevation suggested a new surge of political energy at last, and so it proved. So successful was he in this new role that in the following session, in October 1971, he became Shadow Leader of the House, with a wide-ranging brief, from the miners' strikes to Europe. The press for the first time, and almost inconceivably in the light of his career prior to 1970, talked of him as a possible Labour leader. For the man himself, the period 1970–74 marked a decisive transition in his career. At the age of fifty-seven he found himself a coming man, custodian of his party's dreams for the future, the symbol of the old alliance of party and trade unions, the best hope of Labour's rapid return to power.

But, Foot being Foot, his literary interests were never far away even at this pivotal moment in his life. He spent the first period of the opposition years after the 1970 general election writing the second volume of his life of Aneurin Bevan, which he had for long been impatiently urged to complete by Jennie Lee. It finally appeared to much acclaim in mid-1973, published by Reginald Davis-Poynter, a distinctly minor publisher but a good personal friend. It was published in the United States by his old friend Michael Bessie.[20] This time the sales were less impressive than for the first volume, at ten thousand copies, no doubt a reflection of the thirteen years that had passed since Bevan's death. Even so, the volume's 684 pages give ample opportunity for consideration of Foot's remarkable talents as writer, commentator and political historian.

The first 330 pages are the most valuable part of the book, covering

Bevan's almost six years as a Cabinet minister under Attlee, at Health
until the start of 1951 and then the three unhappy months at Labour.
Some of Foot's account has aroused keen controversy, especially his
discussion of the conflict between Bevan and Gaitskell over NHS
charges, and Bevan's subsequent resignation. Foot himself said later,
on many occasions, that he wrote his book before he himself had had
experience of serving in Cabinet, and that it would have been a
different book had he written it after 1974.[21] Even so, it offers a vivid,
if one-sided, view of the history of the Attlee government which
hardly any other biography can match: perhaps only Ben Pimlott's
outstanding biography of Hugh Dalton merits comparison with it.
As noted above, Philip Williams rightly pointed out factual inaccuracies in Foot's treatment of the high politics of 1950–51 and the
formation of the Bevanites,[22] but the overall sweep of Foot's account
has not been equalled by any later author. His account of the years of
opposition after 1951 is less satisfactory. He too often elides Bevan's
views with those of the Bevanite group, when in fact Bevan himself
was often embarrassed by their rebelliousness, and at odds with them
on many issues, especially the bomb. After 1951 the book becomes
seriously distorted by Foot's animus towards Gaitskell. The difficulties
between Gaitskell and Bevan are often exaggerated, and Bevan's urge
for power underplayed. The tortuous internal quarrels of various
groups of Labour MPs are given priority over the large swathes of
issues, especially in domestic policy, over which the party in general
could coalesce. Bevan's socialism is regarded as being the only version
seriously on offer, while the fruitful revisionism associated particularly
with Tony Crosland, and Bevan's reaction to it, are nowhere examined. Foot's own savage breach with Bevan over the bomb is treated
with inevitable delicacy, and the length of the breach between them
is not made clear. Without doubt, Bevan would have been content to
continue working under Gaitskell as Shadow Foreign Secretary. Had
both lived on into the 1960s, Bevan would probably have been a
pragmatic and by no means pro-Soviet Foreign Secretary, a kind of
more ideological Ernie Bevin. But this would not be gleaned by
reading Foot's account.

Even so, the second volume of Foot's biography is as remarkable
an achievement as his first. It is a powerful book which brings out the

charismatic greatness of its subject. Bevan's philosophic originality, his magnetic presence, his towering international stature in the changing diplomatic fluidity of the fifties, are fully evoked. No other writer could have achieved this, especially as Foot's account is stamped on almost every page by his own intimate association with his subject. The final pages, on Bevan's death and the posthumous assessment, are deeply dignified and extremely moving:

> For Socialists, for those of us who heard him speak and talk and argue and who shared his political aspirations, he was the man who did more than any other of his age to keep alive the idea of democratic Socialism. With him, it never lost its power as a revolutionary creed. Others might define it as well or serve it as faithfully. But no one else, for most of us, could give it a vibrant and audacious quality and make it the most ambitious and intelligent and civilized of modern doctrines. He was, as the Speaker of the Indian Parliament said in introducing him to its members during his visit of 1957, a man of passion and compassion; but only his closest friends could know that to the full. The feeling that surged towards him in those months of 1960 cannot be thus explained. For it was not confined to his political friends of his own party; it burst all banks and frontiers. It was, maybe, a sense of national guilt; a belief that he had been cheated of his destiny, that some part of his greatness had been shamefully thrown away; an awareness that he had much to say to our perplexed, polluted world, and that we had listened only fitfully. What the nation mourned was the tragedy which mixed with the brilliance and the genius, and what it did in expiation was to acknowledge his unique place in our history.

Other Labour politicians have written powerful autobiographies: Roy Jenkins's and Denis Healey's have rightly been hailed for their intellectual brilliance. But none has written a work with the passion and panache of Foot's two volumes. Perhaps the only written work that can be compared with it is the two chapters by Michael and by Jill Craigie in an excellent centenary volume on Bevan edited by Geoffrey Goodman in 1997.[23] Foot's biographical masterwork affirms, with unique power, the vibrancy of the values of British democratic socialism. His life of Bevan is not his best book – it lacks the scholarly qualities of *The Pen and the Sword*. But it is his most important book, and his imperishable contribution to the socialist tradition of which his career in public life was a celebration.

It should be added as a postscript that, not unusually in Foot's writing career, the second volume of his life of Bevan led to busy activity in the courts. In a footnote, Foot accused Desmond Donnelly, then a Bevanite of sorts, of leaking secrets from their meetings to right-wing journalists; rather surprisingly, in November 1973 Donnelly sued author and publisher for libel. Foot took the precaution of hiring a prominent Conservative QC (and future Home Secretary), Leon Brittan, as defence counsel, and it was soon found that his account was amply confirmed in the published diaries of Hugh Dalton for 1951. In the end the judges were not troubled, since Donnelly had to withdraw his prosecution. His sad life was by this time in much turmoil, with alcoholism and womanizing playing their part; he had in any case left the Labour Party and lost his Pembrokeshire seat. A few months later, in April 1974, the turbulent career of a gifted man came to an end following an overdose of drugs.[24]

But the main thrust of Foot's career now was manifestly in front-line politics. He was a key member of the Shadow Cabinet, as spokesman on fuel and power. He and Jack Jones were in regular contact, strengthening the ties between the parliamentary party and the unions after the near disaster of *In Place of Strife*. In 1971 they together created the TUC/Labour Party Liaison Committee. It was essentially a forum for the TUC leaders to present their priorities to the NEC and the government. Its dominant personality, Jack Jones, felt that its achievements were modest – it was 'useful' and no more – but it was a means for him to spell out his own views on such matters as an advisory and conciliation service, and the need for the immediate repeal of the Conservatives' new legislation on industrial relations, especially their Trade Union Act of 1979.[25] The Parliamentary Party found such a committee difficult to handle, since matters of high policy tended to bypass the elected Members altogether. Nevertheless, Foot thought it an invaluable means of discovering the wishes of union leaders, and thereafter of trying to satisfy them. This was by no means a straightforward process, since on some matters (such as protection of employment) the unions wanted the state to do more, but on others (such as industrial relations) to do as little as possible. But whatever they wanted, Foot would endeavour to discover it and do his best to oblige. The Liaison Committee was important. Without it, such a vital initiative as Jack Jones's policy in 1975 for a £6 flat-rate pay increase, which rescued the government at a time of overwhelming inflationary pressure, might never have emerged. The committee was also a clear indication of the new stature that Foot had so rapidly built up after the 1970 general election, which was further confirmed when he was elected to the party National Executive in 1972, a body on which he had last served back in 1950. This was another signal of Foot's willingness to assume responsibility: he was elected at the expense of an old, fading ex-Bevanite and journalistic colleague, Tom Driberg, who disappeared to the Lords disguised as Lord Bradwell.[26]

Foot's first reaction to being in the Shadow Cabinet was ironic, with joy strictly confined. Noted for his informality, he expressed private surprise at how disorderly the meetings were, 'at moments slightly raucous or comic', with Wilson exerting little authority. His fellow Shadow Cabinet members were less than impressive, Callaghan 'obdurate', Jenkins 'dour and not very versatile', Crosland 'superciliously amused'. Barbara Castle struck a more cheerful note, being 'chirpy and provocative'. Foot concluded that membership 'will take years off my life and theirs'.[27] He did, however, come to welcome moments of appalling frankness in the Shadow Cabinet, which admitted the general failure of the Wilson years. When Tony Crosland declared in October 1970 that Labour's intention of achieving 3.5 per cent annual economic growth was a total illusion and that 'no one had the foggiest idea of how it was going to be achieved', Foot thought this the most sensible contribution to economic debate anyone in the party had made for many years.[28]

However, whether his own alternative nostrums of more socialist planning, public ownership and redistributive taxation would be any more effective in kick-starting a sluggish economy was debatable in the extreme. They found little support, other than from Barbara Castle and the new convert to radical views, Tony Benn. The latter, spokesman for industry, which dangerously overlapped with Foot's departmental concern with fuel and power, was already developing a different leftish perspective and a divergent vision of socialism which was to make his relationship with Foot a complicated one for the rest of the decade and beyond.

Foot's main role in building up his prestige as leader of the left lay in his performance in the Commons as front-bench spokesman for the opposition. From the start he was remarkably, perhaps unexpectedly, effective. His old oratorical and rhetorical skills, an amalgam of the Oxford Union and the West Country chapels, were allied to an ability to absorb complicated briefs, and to speak easily and spontaneously at a moment's notice with apparently little preparation. As regards his themes, his opportunities were inevitably demarcated by collective responsibility. But his main concerns by far were trade union legislation and Britain's relationship to Europe. Here he spoke with force and freedom in voicing what were thought to be the essential positions of the left. On other hand, it might be noted that another politician asserting pro-union and anti-European views at this time, and with more powerful ultimate effect, was Jim Callaghan, only a year older than Foot. Callaghan had long been somewhat disdainful of the Mantle of Nye, but the prospect of the Mantle of Harold drove him on with new momentum, not checked even by a serious and potentially fatal operation for prostate cancer. Meanwhile, clearly on the party right was Roy Jenkins, still a rising star after success at the Home Office and the Treasury, strongly pro-European and with his own group of distinguished young disciples. Denis Healey and Anthony Crosland were other powerful politicians in that section of the party. Foot seemed to have little in common with any of this trio, and clearly had a variety of challenges with which to contend amongst his unfraternal colleagues.

As spokesman on fuel and power until October 1971, Foot had ample opportunity to pronounce on industrial relations. He had concerns closer to his home base to deal with also, since the coal and steel industries, both central to the economic life of Ebbw Vale, were crucial to the nation's energy supplies. Looming in the near future was a great crisis for Ebbw Vale steelworks, which faced significant closure and layoffs. Foot proved to be both an effective critic of government policy and a cooperative front-bench colleague. Eric Varley, when a trade and industry spokesman, was one who found working with him on the steel industry an easy and harmonious experience.[29] Foot attacked ministers for delaying major investment programmes in the steel plants at Llanwern and Ravenscraig, and the Steel Corporation for apparently considering hiving off key functions to private industry. The hapless target of his attacks was the Secretary of State for Industry, John Davies, translated to party politics from the world of the CBI, who was soon to subside as a minister through a combination of political maladroitness and deteriorating health. His reference to firms which needed state assistance as 'lame ducks' was a massive political error. As a parliamentarian he was simply not remotely in Foot's class.

But fuel and power were soon subsumed in a wider crisis in industrial relations. In 1971 the Heath government passed an Industrial Relations Act of astonishing comprehensiveness. It achieved what Barbara Castle had failed to do in 1969, and put industrial relations within a firm legal framework. It also soon proved to be quite unworkable. The Bill proposed serious inroads into the legal immunities that the unions had enjoyed since 1906. A new set of institutions would be created to administer the system: a registrar of trade unions, a Commission on Industrial Relations, and, most provocative of all, a National Industrial Relations Court, presided over by Sir John Donaldson. It had wide powers to impose fines on unions, to order a return to work, and to discipline shop stewards. The unions reacted with a fury that took the government by surprise. The Secretary for Employment, Robert Carr, had seemed a moderate and non-abrasive figure. The Prime Minister, Edward Heath, was by no means disliked by the TUC, and had shown humanity in handling redundant Rolls-Royce workers. Jack Jones was quite an admirer, and felt that Heath would have made a good Labour Prime Minister in other circumstances, with a stronger grasp of the working-class world than Wilson ever had. But the government's proposals seemed coercive and destructive to the unions, and it was a view that Michael Foot faithfully echoed. He linked them with Heath's corporate measures for a statutory prices and incomes policy as what he saw as anti-union measures. Heath, he alleged, had broken his word, and 'his political honour is besmirched beyond recovery'.[30] Soon the entire world of industry, in key areas such as the transport workers, railwaymen, engineers and electricians, was embroiled in challenging the authority of the government's court. A series of tense nationwide strikes, official and unofficial, followed, driven on by shop stewards and the local industrial muscle of the shop

floor. Five dockers from the TGWU defied the courts and went to
Pentonville prison. In a humiliating episode for the government a
hitherto unknown person called the Official Solicitor released the
'Pentonville Five' on a legal technicality. Well might the question be
asked, 'Who governs Britain?' Lloyd George had told the TUC leaders
in 1919, 'Gentlemen, we are helpless before you.' It seemed much
truer now.

The most critical episode of all was a national strike in January
1972 by the National Union of Mineworkers, the first to be called
since 1926, in support of a 10 per cent wage claim. There were power
blackouts and a state of emergency. A young miners' official called
Arthur Scargill mobilized squads of flying pickets to prevent deliveries
of fuel to power stations, most famously at the Saltley coke depot in
Birmingham. The eventual wage award, by a tribunal chaired by Lord
Wilberforce, conceded the miners' demands virtually in full. The Tory
government had suffered a massive defeat, their pay and prices policy
in ruins. For Foot, who spoke with power and passion on behalf of
the miners, some of whom were his constituents, these events illustrated the dangers into which the Act of 1971 had plunged the union
movement. A fundamental revision of labour law was now essential to
restore the social balance and provide the unions with the legislative
protection they had long felt was secure. Ironically, Labour's front-
bench spokesman on labour matters was Reg Prentice, regarded by
Jack Jones and Hugh Scanlon as distinctly more right-wing than Heath
himself, and a strong opponent of miners' and other strikes. In time
Prentice was to leave the Labour Party altogether and to serve as a
Conservative minister under Mrs Thatcher. For the unions, he would
never do. It was clear that they needed a far more positive and sympathetic voice in their defence, and that could only mean Michael Foot.[31]

Europe was an issue that aroused even more passion in Foot's
breast. Heath was strongly pro-European, on good terms with the
French President Georges Pompidou, and in 1972 negotiations were
successfully concluded with the Common Market countries about the
terms of British membership. The resultant European Communities
Bill led to a titanic struggle, in which Foot was perhaps the most
formidable of the Labour opponents. Indeed, for years to come, well
after his party leadership ended in 1983, opposition to membership of

the European Union was a central, driving theme in Foot's career. Even more than his opposition to the bomb, anti-Europeanism was his most strongly held political position. Only much later, after Neil Kinnock had wrenched Labour's outlook into pro-European directions (later still Kinnock was to become an EU Commissioner), did Foot discover the virtues of Britain's being in Europe.

Precisely why Foot should have been so vehement on the subject of Europe needs examination. He was not a natural isolationist, fearful of the influence of the Continent, as might be said of Douglas Jay or Peter Shore. He never went in for the Churchillian note of the latter, prepared to fight Brussels on the beaches. Foot's influential tutor at Wadham, Russell Bretherton, had been, at the Board of Trade in 1961, a major figure in the British negotiations over entering the EEC. And Foot's culture was distinctly European. His revered authors included Montaigne, Heine and Stendhal in the past, and Ignazio Silone in more recent times. Also, as noted above, in his early years in Parliament after 1945 he was a strong advocate of a united Europe, and frequently wrote and spoke of the merits of the notion of European federalism. Admittedly, that idea was commonly linked with the idea of a European 'third force' which might wean Britain away from a subservient dependence on the United States, but a man who took part in the inaugural meeting of western European nations at The Hague in 1948, in defiance of the party whips, was clearly a potential convert to Europeanism. He was also well aware of the pro-Europeanism of all the Continental socialist parties and their wish to have British Labour join them. His particular heroes included men like Willy Brandt and François Mitterrand, both strong federalists.[32] Nor was anti-Europeanism an article of faith on the Labour left at this time. Admittedly Nye Bevan had been suspicious of joining Europe, and might have welcomed Gaitskell's bizarre speech arguing against British membership in 1962. But amongst Foot's closer associates in Parliament, Eric Heffer was one who embraced the idea of Europe and might wrote forcefully to Foot to remind him of the fact.[33]

For all that, Foot's opposition to Europe was unshakeable. When Roy Jenkins, who was as adamant in his pro-Europeanism, tried to persuade Foot over lunch in Brooks' Club that the European Communities Bill should not be defeated, he found him totally inflexible. Foot was content to make common cause with his old comrade Enoch Powell, about whom, Jenkins commented, 'he was nearly as starry-eyed as he had been about Beaverbrook'.[34] No doubt Jenkins's own patrician style, so removed from the Welsh valleys whence he sprang, did not help either. For Foot, as for Benn and many others on the left, keeping Britain out of the embrace of the bureaucracy of Brussels was a passion, a matter of faith. Here the remnants of the old Bevanites, Barbara Castle, Ian Mikardo and others, marched with him, resolute for a better yesterday.

Why was this? Certainly in part Foot opposed Europe because he was a socialist. Europe was a capitalist cartel, a 'rich man's club', as he told the voters of Ebbw Vale, that would take powers of economic management away from the British government and from domestic agencies like British Steel Corporation, and make socialist planning in Britain impossible. The problems of the British steel industry he attributed to competition and pressure from steel from the Continent – though that would surely remain whether Britain joined Europe or not. He objected more generally to the rules governing European policy on steel and other industries, to the threat to proper regional policies in areas such as south Wales, and, of course, to the ending of cheap food, the great triumph of one of his political heroes, Richard Cobden, in 1846. Free trade had always been a central tenet of Foot in his Liberal days, and he never forgot it.[35]

But Foot's basic objection to Europe lay not in his being a socialist but in his being a parliamentarian. Throughout, his fundamental antagonism to Britain joining the Common Market lay in the fact that it undermined the sovereignty of Parliament, the very foundation of Britain's constitution, and diverted control away to institutions overseas over which the British electors would have no control. It was 'the most deliberate proposal for curtailing the powers of the House that had ever been put before Members of Parliament', and much reference was made to parliamentary heroes past, John Pym, John Hampden and Algernon Sidney. British electors could overthrow the Heath government at the polls – and Foot hoped that the issue of Europe would provide an early opportunity for them to do so. But they could never touch the Commissioners of Brussels. With his familiar ally Enoch Powell, he used all his powers of debate and dialectic, all his knowledge of the intricacies of parliamentary procedure, to prevent the catastrophe of Britain entering Europe ever happening, and to try to ensure that Parliament could not bind its successors on Europe.[36] There was an early indication of the crisis to come when a preliminary vote, a declaration of intent, on 28 October 1971, saw the Heath government triumph, after a six-day debate, by a large majority of 112. The Labour policy was to vote against, not on broad principle but because the terms of the agreement were unacceptable (which left open the prospect of their being renegotiated later). Heath's victory was due to sixty-nine Labour MPs, headed by Roy Jenkins, defying the whip and voting with the Conservatives (who were unwhipped). A further twenty abstained. The thirty-nine Conservatives, including Enoch Powell, who voted with Labour were thus easily cancelled out. There was enormous tension in the Labour ranks from that time onwards. One or two senior figures amongst the sixty-nine, such as George Thomson and Cledwyn Hughes, found that they were ruled out ever again as possible members of a Labour Cabinet.

The European Communities Bill limped through the Committee and Report stages throughout 1972. Foot, as over the Parliament Bill in 1969, was a dominant figure in debate, filibustering to the end. He intervened in debate forty-three times in nine days in March 1972. His interventions in Committee between March and July 1972 totalled 112 in all, many of them on technical issues of parliamentary procedure, criticizing restrictions imposed on the debates by the Chairman of Ways and Means.[37] As before, his opposing minister was the hapless John Davies, transferred from Industry to become Chancellor of the Duchy of Lancaster, with responsibility for Europe, and no more successful there. Outside the House, Foot acted in concert with a variety of opponents of the Bill, ranging from an old Labour maverick like Raymond Blackburn to a dissident Conservative like John Biffen, to give Parliament powers to determine the operation of European rules, to redefine the relationship with the EU Commissioners and their directives, and to ensure that Parliament's sovereignty could not be fettered in the future. The Secretary of State for the Environment Geoffrey Rippon, who had negotiated the entry terms, insisted disingenuously that membership of the Common Market would leave Parliament's authority and the rule of British law quite unaffected, and this claim was vehemently attacked. 'What a wonderful fight you are making,' Raymond Blackburn wrote admiringly to Foot.[38] Foot's fundamental hope was that the government should be defeated, and that the subsequent general election should be used as a means of overturning membership of the Common Market. Tony Benn's original proposal for a referendum was unacceptable to a stickler for old constitutional ways like Michael Foot.

But in the end, after the Bill got home on third reading by 301 votes to 284 in July 1972, making British membership of the Common Market inevitable on 1 January 1973, Foot had to go along with the eventual narrow majority on Labour's NEC to commit the party to a referendum after it regained office. This, it was hoped, would repair the deep rift in Labour ranks dating from the initial vote in October 1971. It was clear that for Foot, whatever the Shadow Cabinet consensus on other issues such as trade union legislation, the battle against membership of Europe would go on. To him it, even more than the Tory Party, represented the ultimate obstacle to a socialist Britain. Europe would bring in insidious capitalism by the back door, just as Mrs Thatcher was to see the then President of the European Commission Jacques Delors doing for socialism a decade later. Entry into the EEC would lead inevitably, as the French President Georges Pompidou openly acknowledged, to further attacks on British sovereignty, such as an Economic and Currency Union. In the event of such a union the British government, which had so recently floated exchange rates, would henceforth be cabined and confined by fixed rates, and unable to defend British interests as it saw fit. Foot compared joining the EEC to the shame of Munich. Like his old enemy Gaitskell he would fight and fight again to save the Parliament he loved. There would be no concessions, no acceptance of holding European elections now or ever, no agreement to send Labour delegates to attend what Stan Orme called 'the nonsense in Strasbourg'.[39] But for Foot, this essentially negative campaign, in embryo the start of the party schism which saw the SDP come into being in 1981, had its positive side. He was still only a departmental spokesman. His bid to become deputy leader in 1972 failed again, well beaten this time at the hands of the singularly grey figure of Ted Short, whom Wilson supported. But Europe was changing all that. It confirmed that, for the Labour left and indeed an increasing number in the party centre as well, Foot was in fact a leader, the protector of their liberties, the champion of socialism in one country.

These years of tension over the unions and Europe added excitement to Michael and Jill's domestic life in their leafy, ill-paved Hampstead road, not yet rechristened as Pilgrims Lane. They enjoyed a rich and entertaining social life with a circle of mainly Hampstead intellectuals, the historian A. J. P. Taylor, journalists like Alan Brien, Milton Shulman of the *Standard*, Ian Aitken of the *Guardian*, the former Labour MP for Hampstead Ben Whitaker and his wife Janet. The Foots' social life was colourful and fulfilling, with a remarkable array of political and arts personalities coming to their dinner parties. One whom Jill got to know well was the American film director Stanley Kubrick. The Foots greatly admired his 1964 fantasy of a nuclear world, *Dr Strangelove*, which not only enraged the Pentagon but later received the accolade of providing a title for one of Michael's books. But Jill also looked beyond Pilgrims Lane. She became increasingly fascinated by Michael's prominence in front-line politics, and was even led to speculate that he might rise higher still in political life: if journalists mentioned Michael's age as he moved into his sixties, she might respond that Gladstone became Prime Minister at the age of eighty-two. Their home was increasingly comfortable as Jill redesigned and modernized it, the basement area especially. A few yards away was Hampstead Heath, where Foot's morning walks with his terrier Vanessa became a familiar feature of the social scene.

Jill herself still found opportunities for her professional talents. In 1967 she made a controversial film for television, *Who are the Vandals?*, a 'guilty men'-style title suggested by Michael. It was a fierce attack on Camden Borough Council's policy of rehousing and building tower blocks of flats; the inspiration for it came from Lewis Mumford's prophetic *Culture of Cities* (1938), expanded in 1961 into *The City in History*, invariably major texts for Jill. In the course of making the film she developed a close and affectionate friendship with a much younger architect, Tom Hancock, who found her humane vision of city planning inspirational. Elsewhere, she also found deep satisfaction in her research on the suffragette movement: she focused especially on the particular role of Christabel Pankhurst, whom she treated with a near-religious and certainly uncritical zeal. Michael hoped that Jill's work would materialize in a book, but she was not known as a writer, her skills being visual rather than literary, and early discussions with Hutchinson about a contract led nowhere. More widely, Jill was a major figure in the promotion of women's writing and biographies of women: one beneficiary of her encouragement was the distinguished author and former mistress of H. G. Wells, Rebecca West, to whom both the Foots became devoted, and whose autobiography Jill in time managed to have published by Virago Press.[40]

An important feature of the Foots' calendar was their regular fortnight's holiday in Venice every Easter, or sometimes in September. This was striking in itself, because Foot was never a great traveller. He had long given up visiting America, and he also kept away from all the Communist bloc countries after the war, apart from one trip to Poland. He refused to go to Yugoslavia after Tito imprisoned Djilas. But, until they discovered the rival charms of the walled city of Dubrovnik in Croatia in the early 1980s, Venice held for both Michael and Jill a unique romantic fascination. It was one of Foot's many counts against Hugh Gaitskell that, according to their mutual friend the scholar and writer Maurice Bowra, he disliked the city. Michael and Jill loved its cultural ambience, not only its incomparable art and architecture but also its role as a cradle of baroque music and opera, and in the world of letters. Michael also admired the political traditions of the city. It was historically anti-papist and secular, he believed: the dominant building there was the Doge's Palace rather than a church. Michael and Jill also treasured what Venice had meant to them both since the early 1950s: Michael would read passages about the Serenissima from his beloved authors to underline for Jill its significance for him. He was always entranced by the sensuousness and warmth of the city, a matchless historic jewel which had excited the passion of Byron, Hazlitt, Stendhal, de Musset, Heine, Ruskin, Browning and Proust amongst others of Foot's favourite authors, of Rossini, Verdi and Wagner amongst composers, and Turner amongst foreign painters. Byron's vision of Venice particularly captivated Foot. He felt that Byron 'had put Venice on the map' and introduced Turner to it as a theme for his painting.[41] Byron, Foot believed, had fundamentally changed the way people looked at Venice, and thereby reclaimed it for all humanity:

My only Venice – this is breath!
Thy breeze, thine Adrian sea-breeze, how it fans my face
The very winds feel native to my veins
And cool them into calmness.

Foot's lyrical account of Venice is highly charged, physical, almost sexual in its intensity. He wrote repeatedly of the city's unique power of seduction and how admirers should swoon before it: 'Venice demands from her lovers absolute, hyperbolic submission.'

The place of Venice in Foot's imagination confirms what the world already knew: that he was a romantic, passionate, sensual man. It was this quality that gave wings to his speeches and attracted Jill to him in the first place. But it also led their marriage, if only briefly, into its one moment of crisis. Both Jill and Michael were susceptible to members of the opposite sex, and attractive to them. Jill, as we have seen, had many affairs in her earlier life, and encouraged a variety of talented admirers both in the arts and film worlds. She always appealed to men (not least Welsh men like Bevan or Kinnock) through her rapt and sensitive attention to what they said and felt. Physically, she could charm them at any age of her life. Like other men married to beautiful women, Michael took this as a compliment to his own good taste, and perhaps good fortune. He himself was always susceptible to attractive women, without regard to their politics. His friendship with the upper-class right-wing *saloniste* Lady Pamela Berry, married to Lord Hartwell of the *Daily Telegraph*, the nephew of Foot's old adversary in the courts, Lord Kemsley, aroused Jill's fleeting jealousy. His affections could straddle the class divide. His manner towards women was always out-going and charming, even flirtatious, right through his life. A friend in Dubrovnik observed that 'Michael made you feel happy to be a woman.'[42]

But the Foots remained a strong partnership, whose unshakeable devotion was remarkable in the demanding world of high politics. During their marriage Jill remained utterly faithful to Michael, and instinctively loyal. Michael was no less attached to Jill. Then, in 1971 there came a major exception. Michael became attracted to a twenty-four-year-old, sexually highly charged black woman, and they had an affair. Of course, it caused a serious crisis in his relationship with Jill, not least because it involved significant loans of money to the other woman to pay off some of her bills. There was talk of ending sexual relations, even a divorce, and Jill went to Venice on her own. It took months for matters to be disentangled. Paul Foot (himself married three times) was at one period called in to mediate between his favourite uncle and aunt. But the Foots' marriage was too strong to be uprooted even by a personal crisis of this kind, which, after all, is common enough even in the longest-lasting marriages. By the spring of 1972 the affair was over, leaving the third party unhappy and bereft. Thereafter the renewed strength of the links that bound Michael and Jill reflected credit on both, especially on Jill's capacity to forgive. Michael's passionate romanticism henceforth found its outlet in his books, where it most comfortably and naturally belonged.

In September 1973 Michael and Jill went on an important journey to Michael's favourite country, India, which he had passionately admired since his Oxford days but had not previously visited. They went with a somewhat curiously assorted parliamentary delegation including Jennie Lee and a Labour MP, Michael English, whom Foot found rather tedious company.[43] They travelled widely over three weeks, ranging as far north as Kashmir (where Foot strongly pressed the claims of India against Pakistan). Everywhere they were entranced by the colour and excitement of the subcontinent, and Jill was thrilled by first-hand contact with the thriving Indian film industry, although they also observed the widespread poverty, which indeed stares any visitor to India in the face from the moment of their arrival. The most important aspect of the trip, though, was that for the first time Foot met the Prime Minister Indira Gandhi, daughter of his old hero Pandit Nehru. She had written with much warmth to him of Aneurin Bevan when explaining her inability to attend the unveiling of his memorial at Waun-y-Pound in 1972.[44] Foot was fascinated by her style of leadership, and entranced by her vision of a secular and socialist India. His relationship with her became perhaps his closest political association since the death of Bevan, and his attachment to her and to the Congress was to be no less emotional and uncritical. Already India was engaged in much external dispute, especially after the intervention of the Indian army in Pakistan's civil war in 1971, which saw East Pakistan become the independent state of Bangladesh. When serious internal religious and political troubles rose up in India shortly afterwards, leading to a state of emergency and arbitrary action against dissidents by Mrs Gandhi, Foot was her foremost defender.

Soon after they returned from India, Michael and Jill sensed a significant change of scene in the political world. The Heath government was lurching from crisis to crisis. Another national miners' strike approached, against a background of a world energy crisis following OPEC's refusal to ship oil to countries that supported Israel. In February 1974 the strike duly began, solid in all coalfields, moderate and militant alike. A nationwide three-day week had been imposed after the miners' overtime ban, and the country seemed to be approaching near-chaos: the pressure drove Sir William Armstrong, Heath's head of the Civil Service, into a nervous breakdown. Heath believed that the country favoured a strong response to the unions, and that an early election could be called on the slogan 'Who governs Britain?' On 28 February 1974, a precious week or two late in the view of some close advisers of the Prime Minister,[45] it duly took place. Labour had not anticipated the election with enthusiasm after its internal divisions since 1970, and Harold Wilson seemed to expect, and even to welcome the prospect of, a defeat. But Heath's gamble failed. Labour polled only 37.9 per cent of the vote, and their national tally of votes was 220,000 below that of the Conservatives, but they gained enough seats to end up very narrowly as the largest party, with 301 seats against the Conservatives' 297. David Owen defeated Joan Vickers in Devonport. The Liberals held the balance of power with a mere fourteen seats, but this masked a huge surge in their vote, to 19.3 per cent: this was really the reason for Heath's defeat, not Labour's challenge.

In Ebbw Vale there was actually a 1 per cent swing from Labour to the Liberal candidate, Angus Donaldson. Foot's share of the vote fell below 70 per cent in a general election for the first time, even though his majority of 15,664 was still beyond challenge. A major reason for this slight decline was the deep concern about the industrial future of the valley. It had been announced by the Steel Board in 1972 that iron and steel making would end at the Ebbw Vale works in 1975–77, with the loss of 3,300 jobs, and that the hot strip mill would close in 1978–79, with the loss of a further 1,300 jobs. That would leave only around 4,500 jobs. Labour had announced that an inquiry would take place before any closures or redundancies took place, but there were no grounds for optimism. The *Guardian*'s Welsh correspondent Ann Clwyd (a future chairperson of the PLP) wrote of this sombre local background to the election campaigns in the Gwent valleys.[46]

The next government would be a minority one in a hung Parliament. After a tense few days the Liberal leader, Jeremy Thorpe, was forced by his party rank and file to decline Heath's offer of a coalition with the Conservatives. On the Labour side, Callaghan had assumed control with the new stature he had gained since 1969. He told Wilson to refrain from any comment or intervention, and to leave the Tories, in Kennedy's language, 'hanging slowly, slowly in the wind'.[47] This strategy paid off. So, almost against his will, Harold Wilson became Prime Minister for the third time. He headed a powerful team on paper, with Callaghan as Foreign Secretary, Healey as Chancellor of the Exchequer, and Jenkins as Home Secretary as the main appointments. There were other very able ministers too – Tony Benn, Peter Shore, Harold Lever, Shirley Williams. In more stable times it might have been regarded as a ministry of all the talents, with a high proportion of Oxford graduates. It was on balance a right-of-centre Labour government, but with Barbara Castle at Social Services and Benn at Trade and Industry there were also important anti-European left-wingers as part of Wilson's traditional policy of equilibrium.

But there was another left-winger more central to the government's future than either of them. Good relations with the trade unions were absolutely essential to the government's having any future at all. There had been much trumpeting about the 'social contract' negotiated in 1973 between the party leadership, mainly through Wilson and Callaghan, and the TUC, under which a broad agreement was set out between sympathetic government policies and trade union self-restraint. This corporate approach would determine the way ahead on every front. The immediate government agenda included the rapid repeal of the Tories' industrial relations legislation, creating new legal protection for individual workers in unions, establishing new advisory and conciliation machinery and, most urgent in March 1974, ending the huge crisis of the miners' strike, which threatened to cripple the economy. All these could not conceivably be handled by the shadow spokesman on employment, Reg Prentice, who had long been regarded by the unions as an unregenerate right-winger or worse. He was eventually to cross the floor and join the Tories. Immediately after the election, therefore, Jack Jones saw Wilson and told him that Michael Foot would be the ideal, perhaps the only, choice as Secretary of State for Employment.[48] Foot, with his ties to the unions now central to his reputation, was eager to confront the challenge. At the Privy Council with the Queen at which the new Cabinet was sworn in, Barbara Castle noted that 'it was comical to see Mike balancing on one knee'.[49]

Almost thirty years after he first entered Parliament, Michael Foot was to serve in government, and in perhaps the most demanding portfolio of all. He liked to quote from a favourite novel, Joseph Conrad's *Typhoon*: 'Always facing it, Captain MacWhirr. That's the way to get through' (see page 319). In learning about the exercise of power, Foot was a mature student. But now, for the first time in his life, he was to pay heed to the instruction given to MacWhirr – though not to his subsequent irresolute behaviour – and to face the elements unflinchingly in the very eye of the storm.

9

SOCIAL CONTRACT
(1974–1976)

'We wait with an unusual degree of expectation,' said Robert Carr, the Conservative Shadow Chancellor, on 18 March 1974, immediately before Foot's first appearance at the dispatch box as a Cabinet minister.[1] Carr was very far from being alone. Michael Foot as a member of government was the most unknown of unknown quantities. He had never run anything more grandiose than the editorial board of *Tribune*. He had no experience of holding office anywhere; local government was a world unknown to him. He was widely regarded as an ornament to the House, its finest man of letters, certainly one of its most distinguished intellectuals. Francis Boyd in the *Guardian* hailed him on his first day in post as a brilliant journalist, a superb communicator, and a faithful parliamentarian with a principled background of Cromwellian Liberal nonconformity. He recognized, however, that Foot would have to reach out beyond addressing 'our people' if the government was to succeed. But his administrative and executive skills were unknown. Harold Wilson's senior policy adviser Bernard Donoughue noted that, facing his first ministerial job at the age of sixty, Foot seemed 'the most nervous' of Wilson's team.[2] He neither looked nor sounded like a conventional member of government. His very style suggested protest, not power, and a zeal for permanent opposition. This most natural and unaffected of men resembled a dilettante of bohemian inclination unexpectedly summoned to arms from the cafés and pubs of Fitzrovia. His clothes were often shapeless, even shabby, he favoured pullovers, sometimes with holes in the elbows, his hair was long and untidy. Photographs abounded of his shambling walks around Hampstead Heath in pursuit of his dog: the press would later cruelly christen him 'Worzel Gummidge' after the scarecrow in a children's story made famous on television. If Foot's emergence in government aroused curiosity in many quarters, in some it aroused alarm. Colin Wallace was one of the more extreme of the so-called 'barmy army' working for MI5 in the early 1970s, and in effect reporting privately to their masters about Labour ministers. He listed Foot, along with Tony Benn, Ian Mikardo, Eric Heffer, Judith Hart, Tom Driberg, Barbara Castle and even, astonishingly enough, David Owen, as 'Labour MPs who are believed to be Communists and who hold positions of influence'.[3] Even Peter Wright, in full *Spycatcher* mode, did not go quite that far.

Foot's speeches were also a potential hazard. They were full of intellectual self-confidence and rich with literary reference, to a degree that inspired awe amongst new MPs. His performances were often of rhetorical brilliance but, delivered without notes and with a rhythm and pace all his own, seemed to be made up almost as he went along. Barbara Castle had noted, somewhat enviously, that the preliminary to Foot's leading off for the opposition in a major debate was a casual stroll in the park.[4] This had been an effective strategy on the opposition front bench, when his reputation as a politician rose sharply. But the demands of government, including the need for the most precise statements of intent and policy, were far more searching. Foot's penchant for shooting from the hip with unpremeditated abuse could be a problem for the front bench. This emerged very early on when, on 7 May 1974, he made a sharp personal attack on Sir John Donaldson, the one and only President of the National Industrial Court, for his 'trigger-happy judicial finger'. Donaldson had been bitterly attacked by Labour for repeated decisions against the trade unions since 1971, and 181 Labour MPs had signed a Commons motion for his dismissal. It was also noted that he had been an active partisan Conservative in his earlier years, and was the part-author of an anti-union tract. However, protests about Foot's comments came from the Lord Chief Justice, Lord Widgery. Harold Wilson, while reminding Widgery of the injudicious nature of some of Donaldson's past remarks, also pledged to ask his minister 'not to repeat his observations about the judges any further'. Foot was persuaded to publish a retraction, and did not err in this direction again. Wilson and Callaghan, however, were to inflict a more serious revenge on Donaldson by denying him promotion to the Court of Appeal.[5]

Foot's very mode of arrival on 5 March, his first day at the Department of Employment, located unusually in St James's Square, was unconventional. He came not in a ministerial limousine but in a small car driven by his private secretary, Roger Dawe. His usual preference was for something even more populist, namely the number 24 bus, which he caught at the end of his Hampstead road and which eventually got him to Parliament Square. One of the advantages of this form of transport was that it afforded ample opportunity for reading. Another was that it might give him the chance of historical discussion with a near neighbour and fellow-traveller on the number 24, the historian Eric Hobsbawm.[6] In those days, less obsessed with issues of personal security, no one seemed to mind very much. In due time Foot did have his official minister's car, with a woman driver, Winnie Dabin, with whom he had an excellent relationship.

Foot did at least start with a strong ministerial team. He had three ministers to help him, and would have regular meetings with them at 9.30 every morning. Albert Booth, his Minister of State, had been in the Tribune group since his election in 1966. He had the political problem of being a near-pacifist member of CND who represented Barrow-in-Furness, where nuclear submarines were made. But his service as Chairman of the Select Committee on Statutory Instruments in 1970–74, dealing with delegated legislation, had shown his command of detail. Not all the civil servants in the department were impressed by Booth's intellectual qualities, and he did not cut a great figure when he succeeded Foot as Secretary of State in 1976, although it should be said in fairness that the department was shrinking by then. But Booth was well-liked and doggedly loyal: he also had an immense knowledge of trade union practices. It was he who largely handled the enormously complex Employment Protection Bill during the long committee stages in 1975, and with great success.[7] Foot himself was by no means a natural master of detail. His later PPS John Evans saw him as a 'broad brush man', a view confirmed by two very different witnesses, Jim Callaghan's adviser Tom McNally and the civil servant Sir Michael Quinlan, in relation to devolution.[8] Booth's skilful work enabled Foot to focus more generally on 'the vision thing'.

Harold Walker was perhaps the best of Foot's aides, even though he never rose above the rank of under-secretary. A cheery Yorkshireman and trade unionist, he had served at Employment in 1968–70, in the days of Barbara Castle, and his performances in the House were considered to be impressive both by civil servants and by government colleagues like Stan Orme. He particularly took up the burden in the discussion of the Health and Safety Bill.[9] Foot's third aide was a former PPS to Barbara Castle, John Fraser, a London MP and a solicitor by profession. He covered legal matters, including EEC issues like redundancies, equal pay and the Work Permit Scheme. Foot also encouraged him to pursue issues like race and sex equality. Fraser was seen as 'a nice guy'. For him, Foot was 'the friendliest and most unpretentious but inspiring person I have worked with', whose accessibility and good humour enabled his team to work well and confidently.[10]

Foot also had need of a Parliamentary Private Secretary to enable him to keep in touch with the parliamentary party. At first he gave this (unpaid) position to Neil Kinnock, the youthful Member for Bedwellty who had impressed him in opposition during debates on industrial relations. But Kinnock had little inclination for so shadowy a position; he never seemed to materialize in this role, not even in the Commons parking space assigned to him, and he eventually resigned.[11] A year later, Foot asked Caerwyn Roderick, a pleasant Welsh neighbour who sat for Brecon and Radnor, a former member of CND and a warm admirer, to assume the role. He was to serve Foot as PPS until March 1979, with diligence and frankness. He gave Foot full warning of the disillusion of trade union MPs prior to the 'winter of discontent', and considered his warnings, which Foot largely disregarded, to have been thoroughly justified by events.[12]

Foot had no special advisers of the kind spawned by the Blair years after 1997, although other ministers did have such people to help them on policy and political contacts: Tony Benn at Industry had Frances Morrell and Francis Cripps, and Barbara Castle had Jack Straw. Foot did try to enlist one expert adviser, Bill Wedderburn, Professor of Industrial and Commercial Law at the London School of Economics. Wedderburn was an outstanding authority on labour law; he was a man of the Marxisant left, a former member of CND and an admirer of Michael Foot. But he was a part-time adviser to the TUC, and was helping them to draft legislation to nullify what the Tories had done, and he also wished to retain his chair at the LSE. Reluctantly, he

declined Foot's offer, although his influence, mainly through his discussions with lawyers and civil servants, was very important on Foot's
policies over the next two years. Wedderburn's prolific publications,
notably *The Workers and the Law* (1975), gave academic weight to the new
legislation.[13] In 1976 Foot was to make a different kind of appointment,
bringing in his old friend and *Tribune* workmate Elizabeth Thomas to
help him as Lord President of the Council. But she was to play a more
personally supportive, office-bound role.[14] In 1974 the nearest thing
Foot had to a personal confidante was his deeply loyal, though outspoken, secretary Una Cooze, who had served him since 1966.

It was a good team on balance, bound together by genuine loyalty.
Foot respected them all, and they certainly responded to his mode of
leadership. Indeed Albert Booth and John Fraser tried, though with
little success, to get him to work less hard.[15] He seemed to take on
parliamentary burdens far in excess of what might be required of a
government minister. There was another quality that Foot brought to
his team: he made their lives fun. He was always full of teasing humour,
sociable and highly accessible. Work at the Department of Employment
was extremely tough, but it was also enlivened by parties, receptions
and private drinks sessions that made working for Foot a pleasure as
well as a privilege. It was a style that he carried on when he became
Lord President in 1976, a routine much appreciated by his staff, especially as the weekend drew near.[16] Ray Gunter had called his Employment department a 'bed of nails'. Under Michael Foot the work was
more grinding, but the experience less painful.

The civil servants at the department awaited Foot's arrival with
unusual expectation, even apprehension. They wanted businesslike,
orderly command, and they were unlikely to get it. There was an
underlying awkwardness, in that their role would be to repeal all the
industrial relations legislation they had themselves so laboriously put
together under the Conservatives. Even the strictly non-partisan Civil
Service might find that standing on their heads would create some
difficulty. But in fact their experience of their unorthodox minister
was to be almost uniformly excellent. The one possible exception
was Conrad Heron, the Permanent Secretary. He offered Foot his
resignation at the outset, since he was being asked to demolish his
own committed work at Employment under William Whitelaw. Foot

rejected his resignation, but in fact Heron did soon leave Employment and moved to work at Social Security for Barbara Castle, with whom he had an excellent, sociable relationship. Heron, however, was to tell her, somewhat disloyally, about his reservations about working under Foot, whom he found charming but under-prepared and simplistic: 'His only policy is to find out what the unions want.' He also doubted whether Foot would stay the course, or would find some reason for resigning. Heron was quite wrong, and it was perhaps as well that he and Foot parted company so swiftly.[17]

He was succeeded by the previous Deputy Secretary, Kenneth Barnes, with whom Foot had a good relationship. Barnes recalled Foot telling him not to read Churchill's life of Marlborough on his summer holidays, and giving him a new edition of *Gulliver's Travels* instead. Roy Hattersley noted admiringly that when in 1977 Callaghan wanted to move Barnes from the Department of Employment because he was too pro-union in his sympathies, Foot resisted the move, and Barnes stayed.[18] This showed that Foot could be as fiercely loyal to his former civil servants as to his present ones. Personal generosity of this kind was a strong feature of Michael Foot's conduct throughout his career. With the Deputy Secretary Donald Derx, a cheerful man of broadly Labour sympathies brought up on a council housing estate, Foot had the best of relationships. Derx uncomplainingly unscrambled all the legislation he had himself put together under the Conservatives, and became a huge admirer of Foot in all aspects: 'I count myself lucky to have served someone who had positive aims, definite ideas on how to secure them, and a generous spirit.'[19] When the Conservatives came back to office in 1979 Derx soon quarrelled with Mrs Thatcher's ideological quirks. His career did not progress, and he left the Civil Service early for life on the Continent.

Another civil servant who became very close to Foot was his Principal Private Secretary, Roger Dawe. They met under the best of auspices, since Dawe, like Foot, hailed from Plymouth, and had a similar background of Cornish Methodist ancestry. The Foots had been family heroes in his youth. Dawe even shared an enthusiasm for Plymouth Argyle Football Club, and went with his minister several times to see matches at Home Park. He found Foot affable and courteous, highly intelligent, and caring for his officials. Foot, he felt, 'built up mutual confidence'. Like all civil servants, Dawe valued the fact that Foot spoke well and strongly in defence of departmental policy in Cabinet, despite all the formidable political talents who confronted him there. With Whitelaw and Foot as successive ministers, he felt that the Department of Employment 'climbed up the Whitehall ladder' in importance. Dawe also saw Foot as preserving his independence from the unions on key aspects of industrial relations policy, including on picketing. In 2000 he retired from the Civil Service, and in his farewell speech he observed that if Sue Lawley asked him on *Desert Island Discs* what he would like to take to his mythical island, his answer would be no less than Michael Foot. Dawe's unusual selection did both men credit.[20]

There were other able civil servants at the Department of Employment, very bright and very young. Douglas Smith, later the head of the Advisory, Conciliation and Arbitration Service (ACAS), had previously been Barbara Castle's Private Secretary, and she made unsuccessful efforts to poach him for the Department of Health and Social Security to help with industrial disputes there. Jennifer Bacon, Foot's Principal Secretary, was still in her twenties: she was to be head of the private office under Albert Booth, and twenty years later was to head the Health and Safety Executive, set up by Foot's legislation of 1974.

One other civil servant of importance was the Press Officer Keith McDowall, an able man who was the former industrial correspondent of the *Daily Mail*. He had formerly worked with Willie Whitelaw at Employment, and got on well with him. McDowall had an interesting and influential role, acting at the interface of the Civil Service and the press. He was to be the first official called into Foot's office when he began as a minister. Interestingly, had McDowall not been appointed to Employment, Foot's Press Officer would have been Bernard Ingham, later to be closely associated with Margaret Thatcher. According to Ingham's biographer Robert Harris, Foot toyed with the idea of taking on Ingham. But when he asked Peter Jenkins of the *Guardian* about him at a dinner party the response was not enthusiastic, and the idea was dropped. With Foot's journalistic background, he and McDowall had a particularly close and friendly relationship. For his part, McDowall liked Foot very much personally, but he found him less impressive than others did. He thought his casualness as a minister was a weakness: 'He was impossible to write a speech for'[21] – not that Foot often requested that service.

By 1976 the Department of Employment was perhaps less stimulating for its employees. Its programme of action was being exhausted, and it was losing authority in many directions. With the Manpower Services Commission taking over many of its powers, the creation of ACAS to arbitrate in industrial disputes, training going to the Training Services Agency, and the Health and Safety Commission to administer working conditions, Foot was presiding over a shrinking empire, and his staff had less to do. The powerful Ministry of Labour over which Ernest Bevin had massively presided during the war was being hived off and becoming a shadow of its former self. Under Foot's successor Albert Booth, a far less imposing minister, the process of downsizing went further still. On the other hand, everyone recognized the magnitude of the task confronting the Department of Employment in 1974. There was a state of crisis when Foot began there, in the aftermath of Heath's labour legislation, the confrontation with the unions, and the trauma of the three-day week. In eventually taking some of the heat out of industrial relations, Foot performed a vital service.

Some civil servants might have had their reservations about Foot's performance as a minister. One or two felt that, unlike Callaghan or Healey, he never learned how to run a department, and that as a result things could get out of control. But in general officials found Foot's informal, almost post-modern style as Secretary for Employment attractive and refreshing. They liked the volumes of Rousseau, Montesquieu and Montaigne on the minister's office shelves. They liked his sneaking off from all his hard grind to write the odd book review for the *Observer* or the *Standard*, and the bottles which emerged from his drinks cabinet at unexpected times. They were amused by his habit of leaving a television on in his office with the sound turned down during Test matches. Serious discussions on complex legislative issues would be interrupted by cries of 'He's got him!'

The extent to which Foot's domestic life impinged on his official duties was somewhat less straightforward. One regular visitor to the Secretary of State's office was his dog Vanessa, who needed the occasional walk around St James's Park by ministerial aides. Vanessa was universally popular in Whitehall, the other Foot female, Jill, rather less so. Some civil servants found it difficult that she sometimes entered the office unannounced, insisting on seeing Michael. Keith McDowall found her 'prickly' and sometimes naggy towards Michael: she was 'at him all the time' on equal pay and women's issues generally. Women officials felt that she did not take enough trouble to make her husband presentable in public – a dinner jacket he once wore was 'awful'. Jill's manner seems to have aroused the particular wrath of some of Michael's associates. One Cabinet colleague saw her as snobbish, with little understanding of how ordinary people lived. A junior minister thought she had 'no nerve ends', and 'behaved like the wife of a Roman emperor'. Another felt she tended to speak with too loud a voice on political issues when dining with Michael, Caerwyn Roderick and Stan Orme at the Grand Paradiso restaurant near Victoria station.[22] But the role of a political spouse, frequently in the spotlight yet having to keep one's distance, is notoriously difficult to carry off, as Cherie Blair and many others before and since Jill Craigie have found. Jill's assertiveness in pushing her views was central to her attractive personality. Her broad supportiveness and pride in her husband's growing stature as a major politician were beyond dispute, and her overall influence was a positive one.

Whether Foot was on balance an effective minister was a question which produced a wide range of answers. People who worked closely with him, like Donald Derx and Roger Dawe, were very positive. Andrew Graham, who worked with the Prime Minister on economic policy, thought Foot 'had absolutely no idea how to run a department or how to take decisions', though he recognized his importance in getting the unions to observe wage restraint.[23] Foot tended to be needlessly provocative with employers: Edmund Dell records him on 17 June 1974 interrupting Campbell Adamson and other CBI leaders with debating points.[24] But he did make an excellent impression on trade unionists who came to see him. Muriel Turner, Assistant General Secretary of the Association of Scientific, Technical and Management Staffs (ASTMS), found him both capable and very friendly. She noted that he would always see trade union visitors on his own without any civil servants present, the only minister other than Shirley Williams to do so, and that he delivered results.[25]

He struck the right note at the start, and the reputation stayed with him. His very first ministerial speech in the debate on the address on 18 March, greeted with such anticipation by Robert Carr as noted, aroused trepidation amongst Derx, Barnes, Dawe, McDowall and others in the office. Civil servants were used to their ministers working from a carefully prepared text when they spoke in the House. They would sit on side benches in the Commons chamber 'checking against delivery'. This time there was nothing whatsoever to check.[26] Foot had prepared his observations quite privately during a leisurely walk around the lake in St James's Park. He spoke without any visible notes. And he was brilliant. He tore apart the Conservatives' legacy of industrial legislation, their battery of boards, their commissions and courts, and especially their statutory controls on incomes, which he saw as 'a cancerous growth'. He dealt genially but devastatingly with Carr, author of the previous government's Industrial Relations Act: 'Never was a father so impassive in the face of the prospective slaughter of his pride and joy.' Regarding Edward Heath's charge that he was throwing the pay relativities report out of the window, he said: 'As far as I can recall I have not been guilty of a single act of defenestration since I have been in office.' On incomes policy, he deplored how 'the well-to-do or – even more offensively perhaps – the truly wealthy have been inclined to threaten sanctions or preach sermons to people who have to fight every day of their lives to keep their heads above the inflationary flood . . . Nothing can be more absurd than the spectacle of a few fat men exhorting all the thin ones to tighten their belts.'

He crisply spelled out the heads of the new government proposals, which included repealing the Act of 1971, and examining the distribution of incomes through a royal commission (chaired in the event by the Labour MP Jack Diamond): 'I am sure that my right hon. friend the Chancellor of the Exchequer will not mind even if I anticipate his budget statement, at least if I do it in verse:

> Oh that in England there might be
> A duty on hypocrisy
> A tax on humbug, an excise
> On solemn plausibilities.'

He ended joyously, hilariously, with apposite quotes from his ancestral hero Oliver Cromwell on 'self-denying ordinances which he suspected might have been tampered with by Cavalier hands in the Treasury'.[27]

The press reaction on all sides was ecstatic. Norman Shrapnel in the *Guardian* hailed it as 'the most dazzling parliamentary performance in living memory': 'By turn Mr Foot was sparkling, knockabout comedian, grave statesman, brilliant conjurer with a dispatch box full of tricks.'[28] The *Sunday Times* commented that 'the one-time Devonport reject has emerged as the superstar of the new Labour Cabinet . . . The extent of Foot's triumph is hard to overestimate.' The Tory opposition was sufficiently stunned that its motion of no confidence was summarily withdrawn.

At the very outset, therefore, he imposed himself on his new department and on the House. But clearly a far more formal text would be required from a minister presenting government policy. Foot thus resorted to a technique of composing his own speeches as before, but of including a solid Civil Service statement *en bloc* during its course. The opposition spokesman, James Prior, noted that the different parts of Foot's speeches would be indicated by a change of spectacles. Another pair would be required to read out the Civil Service material – which would also tend to make the speech much duller.[29]

But the criterion for measuring Foot's achievement as a minister lay not in debating triumphs but in policy. This meant, first and last, policy towards the unions. Labour's election manifesto had clearly set out a range of measures to strengthen the legal and industrial status of the unions, as laid down in the 'social contract' negotiated by Labour with the TUC during the opposition years. Foot's task was to implement this in full, and as a leading advocate of the Contract he did so with enthusiasm.[30]

One curious feature was that the Department of Employment under Michael Foot did not seem to be primarily concerned with employment, any more than it had been under Barbara Castle. Never greatly interested in the minutiae of economics, Foot did not spend undue time in discussing strategies of pump-priming or job creation. Economists were heard to complain that he never saw them to consider proposals for combating unemployment, or the consequences for the economy of the oil-price explosion in 1973. Things, they felt, were significantly different when James Prior went to the Employment Department under Mrs Thatcher after 1979. On 18 September 1975, however, Foot did bring to the Cabinet a set of proposals, costing £70 million in all, to alleviate the growing unemployment (forecast to reach 1.2 million by Christmas, but, Foot believed, more likely to rise to 1.5 million). These comprised a recruitment subsidy of £5 per head per week to encourage public sector employers to take on school leavers, a £30 million job-creation scheme proposed by the Manpower Services Commission, an increased adult training allowance, the extension of the Employment Subsidy Scheme at a cost of £7.5 million, and an enhanced Employment Transfer Scheme. To these could be added further public expenditure through more building activity on government and trading estates, and the acceleration of major capital projects. It was Foot's responsibility to take these proposals forward, insufficient though he recognized them to be. The Cabinet, however, brushed aside his suggestion that there should be encouragement for businesses and individuals to 'buy British'. At the end of 1974 Foot was also centrally involved in providing government backing for a redundancy scheme to car workers at the beleaguered Chrysler UK, and in warding off the threatened closure of the Linwood car and steel plant in Scotland.[31]

Foot's holy grail was always to succeed in recasting the framework of industrial law. Here, against a background of global economic crisis and massively rising wage and price inflation, he was under intense pressure. In the 1970s trade unions and industrial disputes were at the very forefront of the public stage in a way inconceivable to people thirty years later. Every newspaper had a labour editor, commonly someone like Geoffrey Goodman or Keith Harper who was sympathetic to the unions and whose copy would usually make or dominate the front pages. Nor were they necessarily typical products of Grub Street. Some labour specialists were to achieve high scholarly acclaim, as Eric Wigham of *The Times* and Robert Taylor of the *Financial Times* were to do. Throughout that wearisome decade, lugubrious labour correspondents would front up television news bulletins on BBC or ITV with lengthy accounts of the latest strike, walkout or wage dispute. Cliché-ridden accounts would tell the miserable viewers, wondering whether electricity, trains or water supplies would next come to a grinding halt, that the '*dispúte*' (American pronunciation preferred) was now 'escalating into a confrontation', but that 'at the

end of the day the government would have to govern'. Foot, therefore, was undertaking a peculiarly sensitive job, with a high degree of
visibility.

From the start he faced pressure from trade unionists, from Jack
Jones down, with their huge expectations that the Labour manifesto
would be carried out and a battery of Tory laws demolished. The
nature of Foot's response to all this was much contested. Some regarded
him as a pushover in the hands of the Emperor Jones. This was the
view held in many quarters, and not only in the right-wing sectors of
the press. Keith McDowall felt that Foot's understandable pro-union
sympathies went too far: he was 'a soft touch'. Somewhat surprisingly
this was also the view, late in his life, of Len Murray, who in 1973
succeeded Vic Feather as General Secretary of the TUC. He saw Foot
as an intellectual and an orator, with no strong grasp of the technicalities
of trade union matters; he was a 'catspaw' for Jack Jones.[32] Whether
this represented Murray's view in the period 1974–76 is debatable,
since he appeared to show confidence in the Secretary then. In fact, it
was not at all true that Foot gave way in Pavlovian fashion to whatever
the unions demanded. In any case, it was not always clear that the
unions themselves knew what they wanted, since they were traditionally wary of legislation and the courts – with some reason, as the case
of Rookes v. Barnard had shown. As will be seen, on many key issues,
including picketing and redundancies, Foot stood firm and did not
give the unions what they wanted. He was also prepared, if unwillingly,
to operate what came very close to being a statutory incomes policy,
anathema to the unions and previously to himself.

Jack Jones, the unions' main voice, was not an easy man to deal
with. Many in government saw him as imperious and less approachable
than his ally, the engineers' leader Hugh Scanlon: Eric Varley saw him
as a 'prima donna', while Stan Orme found him 'prickly' and 'with
no small talk'.[33] But Jones was deeply loyal to the principle of a social
contract. He was even prepared to give Scanlon a public dressing-down
when he intransigently (as Jones thought) resisted TUC proposals to
curb wage claims in return for increases in pensions, a freeze on council
rents, curbs on prices and the winding up of the Pay Board. He
opposed Scanlon when his AEU came before the Industrial Relations
Court for unlawful strike action, from which they were rescued by a

£65,000 donation from an evidently wealthy but unknown source.[34] The evidence suggests that Jones and Foot formed a strong, and not unequal, partnership. Jones respected both Foot's intellect and his socialist commitment. In revising employment law, Foot was 'a worried and often flustered man',[35] but he made good use of experts like Professor Wedderburn, and managed to transform the balance of practice and rights in the conduct of industrial relations in an astonishingly short period. Some of his legacy survived even the ravages wrought by the Thatcher government. The bypassing of his measures and the political marginalization of the trade unions by the Blair government after 1997 was much to Foot's distaste. Indeed, a trade unionist of a different political stamp, the future Prime Minister Jim Callaghan, objected quite as strongly as Foot did.

Cabinet ministers think they have done uncommonly well if they get one major Bill through in a parliamentary session. In just two sessions in 1974–76, Michael Foot passed no fewer than six – Health and Safety at Work and the Trade Unions and Labour Relations Act (TULRA) in 1974, ACAS, the Employment Protection Act and the Sex Discrimination Act in 1975, and the TULRA Amendment Act in 1976. The Race Relations Act, which had obvious employment implications, followed from the Home Office soon after Foot changed jobs. All this was at a time when Labour was governing with a tiny majority or none at all. In addition, Foot was heavily involved in wages strategy with Denis Healey and the unions, in prices and incomes policy with Shirley Williams, and an array of other things ranging from entry into Europe to the publication of the diaries of Richard Crossman, who died in April 1974. For a man in his sixties, indeed of any age, not least a man laid low for a time in 1975 by a serious operation, it was an extraordinary record. Many felt it was the most distinguished and altruistic phase of a principled political career.

But before he began legislative work at all, Foot had to deal with an immediate crisis. It was his role, in partnership with Eric Varley, Secretary of State for Energy, to settle the miners' strike. This he did in his first three days in office, on 5–7 March. The three main NUM officers, Joe Gormley (President), Lawrence Daly (Secretary) and Mick McGahey (Vice-President), called in at St James's Square for summit diplomacy at 2 p.m. on 5 March, almost as soon as Foot arrived there.

He told them that free collective bargaining was being restored.[36] The strike was then brought to a speedy end, entirely on the miners' terms. In effect, Foot kept his distance from the pay negotiations: the National Coal Board was instructed to negotiate an immediate settlement, and the Pay Board agreed that the issue of pay relativities through comparison with other occupations be bypassed. On 7 March the NUM agreed to terms that would raise basic wage rates to £45 a week for face workers, £36 for other underground workers, and £32 for surface workers. It was a settlement costing £108,500,000, an increase of 32 per cent on the existing wage bill. Threshold agreements implemented automatically on the lines of the Pay Code set up under Heath's legislation would add a little more. On behalf of the Cabinet, Wilson formally congratulated Foot and Varley for their part in settling matters so rapidly. The Cabinet looked forward to a speedy end to Heath's Pay Board: in fact it was wound up in July, after a somewhat edgy correspondence between Foot and the Board's Chairman, Sir Frank Figgures.[37]

The resolution of the miners' strike was pragmatic and hopeful, with long-term implications. Foot himself admitted in Cabinet that the deal 'would inevitably have an effect on the general prospect for pay settlements, which was already disturbing'. Inflation was rising sharply: by the end of 1974, earnings would be 19–20 per cent higher than a year earlier, and prices 15 per cent higher. Referring to the staged pay rises of the Tory legislation, he added: 'The fact that the Stage 3 limit had been lifted for mineworkers did not mean that it had been lifted for all other claims.' Varley added that the settlement would make the NCB's deficit in 1974–75 rise to some £400 million.[38] Ministers questioned the value of the TUC's promise that the miners would be regarded as a special case, with no knock-on effect. Still, Foot's solution was surely the right one, and was endorsed by the Chancellor, Denis Healey. The miners had been shown in the Wilberforce Inquiry to have slipped down the wages table. Their union's current President, Joe Gormley, was a Labour loyalist from the moderate Lancashire coalfield, and no enthusiast for industrial action. The government could not grapple with the immense challenges of inflation, following huge oil-price rises, with a standstill in production in what was still a major industry and a prime source of energy. The country breathed a sigh of relief as the miners returned to work, with Foot a short-term hero.

The Department embarked upon its legislative programme at a furious pace. First up was the Health and Safety at Work Bill, a relatively uncontentious measure. It was based on a committee headed by the former Labour MP and Chairman of the National Coal Board Lord Robens, set up under the Conservative government. In May 1973 Robert Carr had announced that the Conservatives would implement the Robens proposals virtually in full, which meant setting up a tripartite health and safety authority. Harold Walker handled most of the detail as the Bill sped through committee. The main change Labour added was to ensure that employers would consult with union representatives on working conditions; indeed the entire consultation process was tilted somewhat in the unions' direction, as befitted a measure governed by the 'social contract'. Walker declared that the Robens proposals had been too permissive in tone. There were one or two difficulties in individual cases. Applying the Act to agricultural workers was one, and this was added to the Bill after the October 1974 general election. There was also ironing-out to be done over the miners, who preferred their own Mines and Quarry Inspectorate. After brief Cabinet debate on 9 May the Alkali Inspectorate, previously a separate system for chemical workers, was absorbed to ensure a fully integrated system of inspection.[39] But the Bill was all happily through in the summer. To Foot, mindful of past workplace disasters, it was a deeply satisfying achievement. In the House he quoted the Gresford mining tragedy in north Wales in 1934, when 266 men had died, as an example of the horrors that had existed under the previous order. His department had shown that it could work well and decisively. Indeed, the Health and Safety Bill actually added to its powers, by transferring certain functions from the Department of the Environment. In the House he spoke cheerfully of Lord Robens's inquiry – 'perhaps he does not still hold the same high place on the pedestal in the Socialist Pantheon which was once his'.[40] Somehow, Hazlitt, Burke and Paine were all squeezed into Foot's observations. But the Health and Safety Bill itself he hailed as a powerful affirmation of three socialist principles. It mobilized the power of the state for a great cause, it meant the active participation of working people, and it empowered

ministers to give leadership. In 1995–2000, the Director-General of
the Health and Safety executive was to be Jennifer Bacon, who had
been Foot's Principal Secretary at the time it was set up.

The Trade Union and Labour Relations Act (TULRA), introduced
at the start of May, was more contentious. Drafted in rough outline
by Booth and Fraser, it completely overturned Heath's Act of 1971.
All the apparatus of that measure – the National Industrial Relations
Court, the Commission on Industrial Relations, the registry of union
and employers' associations – would disappear. The concept of 'unfair
dismissal' would vanish, and unions would no longer be open to civil
action for damages in connection with trade disputes. The idea of
'unfair industrial action' would also disappear, and the unions would
regain their previous immunity from civil claims for damages. Foot
himself wanted to call his measure 'the Workers' Rights Bill', but the
Civil Service forced him, reluctantly, to change his mind.[41] It was not
simply a union-pleasing Bill, devised as a sop to Jack Jones. Indeed,
Foot explained in *Tribune* that the government had refrained from
adopting the TUC General Council's draft Bill because this massive
document, of perhaps seventy clauses, would take too much time to
get through Parliament. One tricky issue was that the TUC wanted
to preserve the unfair dismissals protection part of the 1971 Act while
demolishing the rest of it.[42] Much of Foot's Bill was almost uncontro-
versial, and he hoped that it would reach the statute book very soon.
At an early Cabinet on 28 March, Harold Wilson had emphasized the
certainty of an early general election, and the need to clear up matters
regarded as being of particular electoral importance such as trade union
legislation and housing finance: 'It was highly desirable that the legislation repealing the Industrial Relations Act should have reached the
Statute Book before a general election took place.'[43] In fact, TULRA
became law in September.

Several of the provisions wanted by the TUC were omitted, including stronger legal protection for pickets, an end to conscientious
objection to union membership for religious and other minorities (a
clause on which the libertarian Foot was particularly keen), and
a reinstatement of compensation for unfair dismissal. The Cabinet
did not accede to two major demands by the TUC. One was to deny
the right of strike pickets to stop vehicles on public highways (some-

thing much opposed by the police), an issue which was deferred for
further consideration.[44] The other, agreed to on 25 April against Foot's
wishes, was the setting-up of machinery for appeals to a special tribunal
by union members against unreasonable expulsion or exclusion from
a union: 'The government had made numerous concessions to the
unions and the time had come to see what the unions had to offer in
return. By including this provision in the present Bill the government
would demonstrate that they were not instruments of the TUC but
were taking their decisions on grounds of public interest.'[45] Foot's Bill
was generally well received, even in some Conservative circles. *The
Times* pointed out that it was fundamentally a conservative measure,
restoring the legal situation regarding the unions to what it had been
prior to 1971.[46] The Lord of Appeal, Lord Scarman, was to give a
strong endorsement of Foot's Bill in 1979. He declared that it restored
what had really been Parliament's intention when Campbell-
Bannerman's Liberal government enacted the Bill of 1906 – but it was
'stronger and clearer than it was then'.[47] To do that, Foot's measure
had to go back in time, not just to repeal the Conservative Act of 1971
but also to reaffirm the principles of the Act of 1906, and even of
Gladstone and Disraeli's legislation of 1871–75. Without this the
unions would have had no protection under the common law against
charges relating to breach of contract, conspiracy or intimidation.
Foot's Bill thus achieved a much fairer legal balance between unions
and employers. But it did so not through revolutionary change in the
jurisprudence, but by judicious turning back of the clock.

There were some elements of controversy during the passage of
the Bill, relating to legal protection for those arbitrarily or unreasonably
excluded or expelled from a trade union. During July, the House of
Lords passed five amendments which the Commons upheld, by majorities varying from six to eleven, despite the fury of Foot's invective
against the unelected upper house. The key one was Amendment
Seven, which prevented the Bill from giving legal immunity to unions
when they persuaded members to break a contract.[48] Other amendments sought to protect workers from arbitrary expulsion or exclusion
from a union, for example over closed shop arrangements, to tighten
up union rule book provisions, and to limit the power of British unions
to 'black' goods or otherwise assist with strikes in other countries. Foot

was advised that he had no choice but to accept these setbacks. This meant that a substantial amending Bill to TULRA would have to be introduced at some time in the future. But his Bill went through nevertheless, and a much fairer climate in industrial relations seemed to have emerged. Professor Wedderburn noted that, although not understood at the time, the Bill helpfully removed the need for trade unions, uniquely, to have to conform to certain 'guiding principles' in their behaviour.[49] It was certainly different from what Labour had tried to do during Wilson's previous government. Michael Foot christened TULRA in his own affectionate way. He called it 'In Place of Barbara'.[50]

The next proposal from the department's legislative machine was the setting-up of an Advisory and Conciliation Service (ACAS) for the handling of industrial disputes. This was the particular project of Jack Jones. But first there was an essential political interlude. Wilson could hardly continue in office as a minority Prime Minister dependent on the unpredictable votes of Scottish and Welsh Nationalists. Foot and Crosland were amongst ministers who had urged an even earlier election, perhaps in June 1974, while Callaghan counselled delay. The Conservatives exerted no pressure, since Heath's leadership appeared so beleaguered. The polls suggested that opinion was moving Labour's way, not least because of Foot's work at Employment. So a general election was called for October 1974. Foot naturally took a key part in Labour's election campaign, which saw the party and the unions working in close partnership, as never before since 1945. The *Times* correspondent praised him as 'one of the last of a dying tradition of great political orators', and 'the Bringer of the Only True Socialism'.[51] He declared total opposition to pay controls, but asserted that recent wage settlements, for instance for construction and engineering workers, were not excessive. Heath's claims of 40 per cent wage increases were swept aside as 'statistical bosh'. Foot was also anxious to make clear that the government was not engaged in any craven surrender to trade union power.[52] He was used indirectly as a covert mediator by Wilson in an industrial dispute by ITN journalists which Labour felt was harming coverage of their election campaign, but which nevertheless continued during its course.[53]

Foot had a thoroughly good election, with positive press reaction.

He swept home in Ebbw Vale as usual, this time with an increased majority of over eighteen thousand and an improved share of the poll at 74.1 per cent, despite the looming cloud of the closure of the local steelworks. But nationally Labour's results were much less satisfactory. It was a dull campaign, most of the partisan ammunition having been expended in February. Although the Tory vote fell by 1,400,000, partly as a result of Heath's lacklustre campaign, Labour gained only a 2 per cent swing compared with February, and won only eighteen additional seats. The outcome thus left Wilson with 319 seats against the Conservatives' 277, and an overall majority of only three. It was almost a hung Parliament, with Labour likely to be dependent on a miscellany of eleven Scottish Nationalists, three Plaid Cymru and a few assorted Northern Irishmen (including amongst the Unionists Enoch Powell, who had recommended voters to support Labour in February 1974 because of its policy on Europe). Foot's projected legislation would not face an easy ride in a finely balanced House.

However, the immediate legislative aftermath, the setting-up of the Advisory and Conciliation Service, was again relatively pain-free for Foot's busy department. Jack Jones rightly observed that 'it was my baby'.[54] A nine-person tripartite body would be set up, three members appointed by the TUC, three by the CBI and three others with experience of industrial relations. The Employment Secretary would retain the power to appoint committees of inquiry for serious disputes that ACAS could not solve. Jim Mortimer, a left-wing former trade unionist, currently Personnel Director of London Transport, would be appointed the first Chairman at the start of September 1975. The Service won its spurs a month later by sorting out a difficult strike of road haulage drivers in Scotland. Foot reassured the Cabinet about Jack Jones's satisfaction with the way things were proceeding, a sign of the times.[55]

ACAS, which received statutory powers in 1975, was to prove one of Foot's measures that stood the test of time. During the Thatcher years it survived attacks on its powers both from the government and from judges. It arose because it was widely felt, by many employers as well as trade unions, that existing procedures were unsatisfactory in that the impartiality, and hence the credibility, of the arbitration and conciliation services offered by the Department of Employment was in doubt. With its tripartite controlling body, ACAS was apparently bringing the state directly into the conduct of industrial relations. In fact, Paul Davies and Mark Freedland argue convincingly that it was designed to achieve the exact opposite, namely to create an impartial body in which both sides of industry could feel confidence, as under the old Ministry of Labour in Ernie Bevin's days.[56] Time was to show that the powers of ACAS were far less robust than contemporaries hoped or feared. The Grunwick case in 1976 showed how an unscrupulous employer, in that case the owner of a photo-processing works, could simply evade the recommendations of ACAS (by with-holding the names and addresses of his, mainly Asian, employees). The Law Lords gave him every help by upholding his case.

ACAS remained busily useful, including throughout the Thatcher and Major periods, but Jim Mortimer had to confess in 1980 that his Service could do little more than attempt to persuade, since it lacked any legal or statutory powers of compulsion or regulation to enforce a settlement. The TUC had asked, for example, that ACAS be given powers to make employers pay the 'going rate' to their workers, but that did not happen. This weakness of enforcement powers was indeed to apply to a number of Foot's measures. Unions received some greater powers, but so did the courts, notably over issues involving 'contempt of court'. Apparently sound and fair-minded in conception, some of the legislation lacked teeth. Anti-union employers like George Ward at Grunwick and Eddie Shah in the print industry, the founder in 1986 of the *Today* newspaper, backed by sympathetic judges, could ride roughshod over them.[57]

The Employment Protection Bill introduced in March 1975 was much bigger and more controversial: it was the most wide-ranging and complicated of all the items on Foot's agenda of legislation. It owed much to the proposals put forward by Len Murray and Jack Jones on behalf of the TUC, and was considered by many Conservatives to be an extreme instance of the government surrendering to union pressure. Some quoted Harold Wilson's remark about Edward Heath's negotiations over Britain's entry into Europe – 'rolling on his back like a spaniel'. This was an exaggerated view, and the degree of Foot's submissiveness was overstated. The Bill was taken through committee almost single-handedly by Albert Booth, who did so with much shrewdness and patience in a House where he had the barest of majorities behind him. He himself boldly tried to rewrite passages of the Bill which did not appear to him to make sense. At a party afterwards to celebrate the passage of the Bill, Booth was given a present by his minister which always bore a particular symbolism – a copy of *Gulliver's Travels*.[58]

Like TULRA in the previous session, the Employment Protection Bill aimed to improve free collective bargaining. But while TULRA had done this by removing state intervention, the Employment Protection Bill did so by bringing it back in, by guaranteeing the rights of workers. It therefore mirrored the historic doubts and debates among union leaders, going back to the 1906 Act, as to whether labour law should embody a positive role for the state in industrial relations or not. It created a legal protection of the right of workers to join unions, and a 'recognition procedure' to make employers negotiate with union representatives. Employers would have to be more forthcoming in disclosing information to shop stewards and union officials; workers would be given a statutory right to reinstatement if ACAS found they had been unfairly dismissed; employers would no longer be able to punish workers for shop-floor misdemeanours by deductions from their pay packets. It also protected workers over a variety of other issues, including the insolvency of the employer, guaranteed payments when on short time, rights of maternity payment and the right of mothers to return to a job after childbirth, and the right to a written statement giving reasons for dismissal. The main arbitrating body to decide whether legislation was being complied with would be the Central Arbitration Committee, which Davies and Freedland judged to be 'probably the most successful and innovative of the institutions established by the Employment Protection Act'.[59]

The Employment Protection Bill was a measure which contained many positive features. It could be said to locate the unions within the legal system on a modern basis for the first time. It extended to the wage-earner much of the legal protection enjoyed by the salary-earner. But it also proved to have its limitations, and was capable of being bypassed through the instrumentation of the law. The unions in many cases were reluctant to use the force of positive law in defiance of their historic traditions, and preferred to rely on their own power at a time when union membership was reaching a new peak of close to thirteen million. Of these, only about fifty thousand additional workers gained access to collective bargaining through the Act of 1975. It was union muscle, not the law, that was the dominant factor in this new surge in membership and in power.

It is important too to note what was left out of the Bill. In particular, after renewed debate in Cabinet, the TUC again failed to win the right for pickets in industrial disputes to stop vehicles entering places of work. They wanted properly identified official pickets to be allowed to 'obstruct' the highway for a reasonable period in a non-violent manner, communicating with the drivers of vehicles and trying to persuade them not to cross picket lines outside factories. Foot himself had accepted this, but was overborne by a combination of the Home Office and the police, who felt it would be impossible to administer and would quite possibly lead to violence. In Cabinet on 9 October 1975, Roy Jenkins defended the police objection that Foot had proposed to give pickets equal authority on the public highway to themselves. Jenkins's view was backed, less vigorously, by the Lord Chancellor, Lord Elwyn-Jones, who argued that it would not be to the benefit of the pickets themselves. It was decided that Foot should resume discussions between the police and the TUC on satisfactory guidelines on picketing.[60]

Another point was that the Bill contained no provision about forms of industrial democracy. This was a controversial issue which divided ministers. Foot argued in Cabinet on 19 June 1975 against having an independent inquiry into the subject, since it might alienate the trade unions, whose cooperation was essential.[61] But the prevailing view was that the unions, who had shown so little interest in serving on the boards of companies or nationalized industries prior to the era of Jack Jones, could hardly have the final say. A committee of inquiry was eventually set up, chaired by the Oxford historian Alan Bullock. Its proposals in late 1976, the so-called '2x + y formula' for equal representation from unions and shareholders plus some independents, strongly favoured by Jack Jones, who backed the idea of worker directors, were to founder in the face of opposition from Shirley Williams, Edmund Dell and other ministers who saw it as too great a surrender to unreconstructed trade unions. On another issue, 'a rare rebuff' to the TUC was noted by Paul Routledge, the industrial correspondent of *The Times*. Foot had rejected a TUC proposal to give the Department of Employment power to veto redundancies and even to subsidize temporarily ailing companies to save jobs. Employers wishing to reduce their labour force would have to gain the approval of the department. This bold proposal, of uncertain financial impact, Foot rightly said would be unprecedented.[62]

Most important of all was the contentious issue of the closed shop, where employment rested on membership of a named union, and cases where workers might be deprived of their employment by union practices. Much controversy had been raised by the case of the so-called 'Ferrybridge Six', a group of power-station workers in Leeds dismissed by the Central Electricity Generating Boad for failing to join a specified union under a closed shop agreement. Foot's opponents attacked him for 'callous treatment', since the dismissed men could even be refused unemployment benefit as a result. In the end, this difficult issue was postponed for further deliberation until an amended TULRA was introduced in 1976. Foot had originally supported a TUC proposal to cooperate with the government in setting up voluntary procedures to monitor the closed shop.[63] The National Union of Journalists, of which Foot was a long-time member, was particularly zealous on this issue. But the TUC had been opposed in Cabinet discussions by the Lord Chancellor, who pointed out that the Donovan Commission had gone further than the TUC proposed to do. The TUC scheme, Elwyn-Jones observed, would include no power to award compensation or to enforce compliance: 'If the government retreated from this principle in the face of trades union pressure, its action would be difficult to explain in Parliament and its credibility would come into question.' Roy Jenkins, the Home Secretary, backed this view with more vehemence: 'A threat to deprive a man of his livelihood involved a fundamental question of human rights. The government could not justify reliance on voluntary procedures to deal with these cases any more than with cases of discrimination on grounds of sex or race.' He concluded that 'if the government gave up these safeguards merely because the TUC disliked them it would not only seem wrong; it would be wrong'. Unusually, Jenkins's name is identified with his intervention in the Cabinet minutes, to illustrate the force attached to it. In the end his view, supported by the majority of ministers, prevailed.[64] Foot's Employment Protection Act got through safely at the end of the 1974–75 session, and was hailed by the unions as another Magna Carta, almost comparable to that of 1906. But for all its many merits it soon proved to have serious limitations, while the issue of the closed shop remained for all the interested parties, in politics and in industry, to be fought another day.

The Department's other new measure in 1975 was consensual and straightforward, the Sex Discrimination Act, warmly supported of course by that doughty feminist Jill Craigie. Here again the law was being introduced directly into matters of employment, since the Act forbade dismissal of workers on grounds of sexual discrimination. It came into full force at the end of 1975, on the same date as the full implementation of the Equal Pay Act of 1970. There could be little problem here, least of all from the Conservatives, who had just elected a woman, Margaret Thatcher, as their party leader for the first time. But simultaneously there arose the controversy by which Foot's time at the Department of Employment would be best remembered, the celebrated struggle over the closed shop. This raised major questions not only about Foot's qualities as a parliamentarian and his priorities as a Cabinet minister, but also about his lifelong commitment to journalism and the principle of a free press. This had been sacrosanct for Swift, Cobbett and Hazlitt in the past, and an article of faith for Foot in his various previous incarnations as columnist and editor. The nature and substance of this commitment were now to be put sharply to the test.

The question of the closed shop, and the problems it presented to employees as well as employers where it existed, had been brought up in previous measures, as has been seen. It had been left on one side in TULRA and the Employment Protection Act because of the controversies it aroused, including among ministers. But in 1975 it could no longer be avoided. The closed shop only affected a minority of workers, but it was growing as an institution: by the end of the decade, 23 per cent of the workforce were included, compared with 16 per cent a decade earlier.[65] It should be added that many employers were also inclined to favour the closed shop, since it made discussing labour relations with the unions that much more straightforward. A particular flashpoint was the newspaper industry. In fact the main problems concerned the print unions like the National Society of Operative Printers and Assistants (NATSOPA). Most attention, however, focused on the high-visibility National Union of Journalists, of which Foot had been for thirty-five years a fully-paid-up member. It was a small, somewhat maverick, union of twenty-eight thousand members, at odds with its rival, the smaller Institute of Journalists; its General Secretary, Kenneth Morgan (not the present author), was a moderate. Indeed, one of Foot's arguments was that if Morgan were not backed, it would discredit moderate union leaders everywhere, and hand the initiative over to extremists. But the NUJ did operate a post-entry closed shop, which meant that contributions to journalism from outside the unionized profession might disappear. There was a particular issue in an ongoing trade dispute when the union, in pursuit of a pay claim, refused to handle copy in provincial newspapers that was not submitted by a union member. Conservatives denounced this as a threat to a free press. The NUJ's role thus led to a prolonged crisis, unique in its history, that lasted for almost the whole of Foot's remaining time at the Department of Employment.

Immediately after the general election in October 1974, Foot brought forward a Bill to amend TULRA and permit the closed shop. It was an issue with which he was very personally identified. His bitterest enemy, the *Observer* columnist Nora Beloff, observed of him (in a book described by Lord Goodman's biographer Brian Brivati as 'deranged'): 'only a man of Foot's stubbornness, dedication and political acumen could have driven [the Bill] through against so much opposition inside and outside the Cabinet'.[66] A wide range of critics rose up against him, among them his brother Dingle, on libertarian grounds. Almost a hundred distinguished writers and academics wrote a letter of protest to *The Times Literary Supplement* against the closed shop proposals: among them were prestigious scholars like Isaiah Berlin, Hugh Trevor-Roper and C. V. Wedgwood. Within the Cabinet, Foot's proposals were strongly attacked by Roy Jenkins and Shirley Williams. Jenkins described them as 'an over-hanging menace' inimical to a free press: 'In his pantheon the dead Lord Beaverbrook had been replaced by the living Jack Jones.' Shirley Williams was vocal in Cabinet, and talked of resignation. A group of Labour MPs from the right-wing Manifesto Group, including David Marquand, John Mackintosh, John Grant, Brian Walden, John Dickson Mabon and Bryan Magee, saw Foot privately to demand the affirmation of the rights of individual journalists to protection under the Common Law. The exchanges were often bad-tempered, and some of those present doubted whether Foot was familiar with the details of his own Bill.[67] In Foot's own circle of friends, the *Guardian* journalist Ian Aitken (once his possible step-son-in-law), a member of the NUJ, nevertheless felt uneasy about the freedoms of his own profession. Foot was also told of the position of workers other than journalists. Paul Nicholson of the Committee of Employees' Organizations told Foot: 'Most workers who object to the closed shop have less opportunity to make their case public than journalists . . . You do not seem to have any respect whatever for the integrity of those who oppose your legislation about closed shops.'[68]

The most prominent adversaries that Foot had to face, however, were the newspaper owners and editors, headed by Sir Denis Hamilton, chairman of Times Publications, and three editors, David Astor of the *Observer*, Harold Evans of the *Sunday Times*, and Frederick Fisher of the *Financial Times*. Operating somewhat on a track of his own was Alastair Hetherington, editor of the pro-Labour *Guardian*, who attacked the proposed dismissal without compensation of anyone who refused to join a union, and the removal of 'reasonable grounds' exemptions. He argued that the Bill would give leverage to NUJ militants.[69] But he was a frail reed for the employers' side, pro-Labour and liable to drop away. The main controversy centred on whether newspaper editors should be compelled to join unions, or whether this would compromise their powers of free expression. Perhaps unwisely, the Editors' Guild (forerunner of the Society of Editors) brought in Lord Goodman as their spokesman and representative. He was an old friend of Cabinet ministers, and had given Foot legal advice on *Tribune* matters back in the 1950s, as well as acting as Harold Wilson's lawyer in difficult personal cases involving his secretary Marcia Williams. He had also been close to Richard Crossman and George Wigg, and closer still to Jennie Lee, whom he had wanted to marry. But Goodman's relationship to the proprietors was always unclear, while in any case his own skills as a master backstairs fixer who dealt with the establishment were far less applicable to a high-visibility political question like the press and the closed shop.[70]

In the autumn of 1975 the Bill was beached in the House of Lords. In Cabinet Foot urged the use of the Parliament Act to restore the original Bill, but this was hardly practical politics, so tiny was the government majority. Instead it was decided to consider possible movement on amendments put down by Goodman.[71] Discussions between Foot and the editors then began on 19 November 1974, in his offices in St James's Square. From the start it was clear that the initiative lay with Foot. It was an issue on which he was very determined to win: he had a warm regard for the NUJ, and well recalled how his union had backed him and secured his severance pay when he was sacked without warning by the *Sun* in 1964. He also knew the facts of the case intimately. He was 'far better prepared than we were', David Astor was to declare ruefully.[72] The truth was that Foot's mind was far clearer and his objectives more easily defined. Some of his departmental officials, notably Jennifer Bacon, were also powerfully effective in championing the cause of the rights of workers, journalists included.[73] By contrast the editors were a miscellaneous crew, and Goodman an uncertain captain of them. Having Wilson's former Press Secretary Trevor Lloyd Hughes to run a public campaign did not help the editors' cause. By the end of January 1975 Hetherington of the *Guardian* had in effect signed a peace pact with Foot, and his Bill went through the Commons.[74]

The editors now gave up hope of altering the main lines of Foot's legislation, and concentrated instead on a voluntary press charter drafted by Kenneth Morgan and Alastair Hetherington, with help from Lord Houghton, to be embodied in the amended TULRA that Foot now proposed. This charter was voted down by NUJ members, and once again Foot found himself attacked in a letter in *The Times Literary Supplement*. The signatories this time included writers like Arthur Koestler, J. B. Priestley, Jacquetta Hawkes and Rebecca West, all old comrades-in-arms on the left. Their main lifeline lay in the uncertain forum of the House of Lords, where Lord Goodman put forward a series of amendments drafted by the judge Leonard Hoffman. But Goodman had undercut his own position by reaching agreement with Foot privately on some issues.[75] For the Conservatives Lord Hailsham, their leader in the Lords, was often exasperated by Goodman's tactics, and the new party leader, Margaret Thatcher, refused to offer official party assistance by use of the Conservative whip in the Lords. In Cabinet, Shirley Williams continued to protest, with support from Harold Lever and Reg Prentice. Roy Jenkins suggested a possible compromise on the basis of proposals drawn up by his special adviser Anthony Lestor. But most ministers were content to let Foot's Bill progress. Callaghan, Healey and Crosland refused to obstruct it, while Roy Hattersley, a centre-right figure and a frequent journalist, gave Foot his support.[76]

The Bill shuttled to and fro between the two Houses in November 1975; amendments moved by Lord Hailsham in the Lords to enforce the proposed code of conduct by law and to add that breaches in the press charter were 'contrary to public policy' were rejected by the Cabinet. By now the press code had been endorsed by the NUJ membership. The Lords were effectively conceding that the Bill would become law in the next session. On 21 January 1976 the government's additional proposals on press freedom to be added to TULRA mark two were passed by the Commons by the comfortable margin of forty-five.[77] Goodman's final proposal was that the press charter, which he saw as brought forward by the government but drawn up by the NUJ, be dropped from the Bill altogether. But this was defeated, and the Bill finally got the royal assent on 25 March 1976. The Trade Union and Labour Relations (Amendment) Act thus became law. It featured a lengthy clause headed 'Charter on freedom of the press'.[78] By this time Foot was actively campaigning for the leadership of the Labour Party after Wilson's announced resignation, his prestige higher than ever.

Foot could view the outcome of the closed shop debate with much satisfaction. He had comprehensively out-argued his opponents, and a subsequent book on the affair, Nora Beloff's *Freedom Under Foot: The Battle Over the Closed Shop in British Journalism*, was too intemperate and inaccurate to make much impression. Foot had been able to show that the issue was really about the rights of trade unionists and their immunity from actions in restraint of trade as understood since 1871, not the freedom of journalists to think, write or publish what they chose. Parliament was debating the imposition on journalists of the restrictions of the 1971 Act, which applied to no other group of workers. Now journalists would have the same freedoms as other workers to protect their professional status and skills, in negotiation with their employers, free from the intervention of the judges. Their rights of free speech would remain undiminished. Foot was also able to tell the Conservative MP Ian Gow that closed shop arrangements would be applied with much flexibility, and in any case covered only a small minority of workers.[79] The editors had cut unimpressive figures, detached from their journalists, finding it difficult to maintain a common front. They had failed to demonstrate exactly how their own professional freedom would be undermined by either their joining a union or their employees doing so through a closed shop. The half-hearted response of Mrs Thatcher and the Conservatives to the editors' plight suggested an unreality in their position. Throughout a tricky passage of play, Michael Foot had managed to confirm both his effectiveness as an adroit minister and, through the adoption of a press charter which affirmed the right to free comment, his lifelong commitment to free speech. In his confrontation with the newspapers, Foot was much the best communicator of them all.

The passage of the short TULRA Amendment Act, which also included a stronger provision on freedom from actions for tort in pursuance of a trade dispute, completed a remarkable battery of legislation. At the time the Act aroused much press comment about the menace of trade union power and the empire of 'the Emperor Jones'. In fact it was essentially a restoration of the balance between the two sides of industry after the problems caused by the Act of 1971. The law was certainly amended in ways favourable to the unions, but many of their key points were not conceded, and the enforcement of many of the measures proved difficult afterwards. In the later 1970s the atmosphere of legislative conflict passed away, and the Department of Employment moved into a quieter and more functional role. As Lord Scarman observed, its work had made the legal framework for industrial relations significantly clearer. Even at the time, on 12 January 1976, the Conservative shadow spokesman, the studiously moderate James Prior, was able to tell his party that TULRA had been accepted as the 'basis for labour law'. In formulating any Tory response he 'counselled a cautious, considered approach', not least because millions of trade unionists voted for his party.[80] After the election of the Thatcher government in May 1979, much of Foot's legislation was swept away. But that was less because of its intrinsic weaknesses than because of the failings of the leaders of the unions themselves, especially following the retirement of Jack Jones in 1977. The 'winter of discontent' of 1978–79, while often exaggerated in the right-wing media, did highlight major problems in the calling and conduct of strikes, and in the powers of central government. A Labour government, headed by the only trade unionist ever to become Prime Minister, was helpless, and the machinery of government ground to a halt. Foot's legislation should have laid the foundations of long-term industrial consensus, not of class war. Thirty years on, moderate union leaders like David Lea, John Monks and Brendan Barber recalled the Foot years as a golden age which redressed the social balance, but to which a market-orientated, managerial New Labour showed no inclination to return.

His union legislation showed how indispensable Michael Foot had become to the government. He was at the heart of every crisis. It was Foot who led off for the government on the nationalization of the aircraft- and ship-building industries. It was this that led the then Shadow Industry Secretary Michael Heseltine to engage later in the extraordinary charade of seizing the mace in the House of Commons chamber and brandishing it at Labour MPs who were celebrating winning the crucial vote by singing 'The Red Flag'. Foot, who disliked Heseltine, said that it was much the best thing he ever did. It was also Foot who brought forward the Dock Work Regulation Bill at the behest of Jack Jones, who needed it for his own credibility within the TGWU. This would seek to combat the effects of containerization and the growth of non-scheme ports, thus continuing the fight against casual employment and the threat of port closures. It aimed to extend the 1947 Dock Labour Scheme which Foot had strongly supported when MP for Devonport, but was emasculated by hostile amendments in the Lords, a process assisted (strangely enough) by private advice from Vic Feather, former Secretary of the TUC.

But much the most serious problem confronting the government was inflation. It continued to soar throughout 1974, with wage settlements reaching a level of increase of over 28 per cent. By January 1975 Peter Jenkins in the *Guardian* was writing of how the Chancellor of the Exchequer Denis Healey's 'chilling' assessment of the economy had influenced Foot, 'who no longer disguises from himself or others the extreme seriousness of the wages problem'.[81] The key relationship in the government, therefore, was that between Healey and Foot, who were in constant negotiation with the union leaders about ways of controlling wages without the coercive powers of legal sanctions. Healey and Foot were hardly a natural pairing. They had been in disagreement over virtually every aspect of policy over the last twenty years. Healey, a Gaitskellite and pragmatically pro-Europe, had been Defence Secretary between 1964 and 1970, operating a policy in which the British nuclear deterrent, as renegotiated by Macmillan with Kennedy at Bermuda, had survived unscathed. It would be difficult to find a set of policy positions with which Foot disagreed more comprehensively. Television programmes on the bomb had featured Healey shouting at him, 'Stop mucking about with debating points, Michael.'

However, confronted with the realities of trying to produce an anti-inflation policy, they got on remarkably well. They were both bookish intellectuals, though of different kinds, fellow members of the Byron Society. Foot admired Healey's great intellectual power; Healey was impressed by Foot's loyalty.[82] In detailed discussions with the unions on wage claims Foot played little part, but he was important in overall strategy and in selling the alleged success of government policy to the public, or more particularly to Labour Party members. One of his major triumphs was in persuading a very doubtful Jack Jones that Healey was someone with whom he could do business. Foot had to strike a difficult balance. In June 1975 he was condemning a pay claim of up to 33 per cent from the railwaymen (British Rail's offer of 27.5 per cent had been rejected). A rail strike 'would be a catastrophe for us all', declared Foot.[83] On the other hand, at this very time there was a threat that the Cabinet might have to bring in statutory powers to enforce wage restraint, something to which Foot was fundamentally hostile, and over which his friend Eric Heffer resigned as Minister of State at the mere threat of their being introduced. Foot still pinned his hopes on the power of reason.

The other partnership in which Foot was deeply involved was with Shirley Williams over a prices and incomes policy. As Minister for Consumer Affairs, Williams had to work closely with the Department of Employment – she was 'prices' and Foot was 'incomes'. Here again, the two ministers had had little enough to do with each other before, but worked together excellently. This was especially true of the negotiations they had with the Economic Committee of the TUC and with CBI representatives in the tense days of early July 1975, leading up to the acceptance of Jack Jones's £6 flat-rate pay limit. Williams admired the way in which Foot's work for the government's broad economic objectives was combined with social concern, notably for the low-paid. She found his literary approach to life appealing; she also felt him to be fundamentally a 'radical', an anti-statist liberal in 1975 as in his student days. Foot himself, with his penchant for intelligent women, formed a strong bond with her. Williams's defection to the Social Democrats in 1981 was the one which Foot most regretted, and which he worked hardest to try to avert.[84]

For over a year the government allowed the voluntary method of wage restraint to take its course. The TUC had offered guidance to unions in a document that Foot called 'highly intelligent', which emphasized the need for maintaining rather than increasing real incomes, and to stick to a twelve-month rule for pay increases.[85] By the summer of 1975, however, this policy was manifestly collapsing, and new initiatives were urgently needed. Wage settlements were rising to over 30 per cent, the balance of payments was lurching into huge deficit, the value of the pound was falling relentlessly, unemployment was the highest since 1940. Economists spoke of 'stagflation', economic recession and price inflation at one and the same time. Government ministers were at odds on the way forward. Reg Prentice delivered some sharp criticisms of the unions' lack of responsibility. Foot tore into him for his 'economic illiteracy' – and for his use of the verb 'to welsh', which, rather quaintly, he took to be an insult to constituents in Ebbw Vale and elsewhere.[86]

But clearly some immediate way had to be found to curb wage settlements. On 20 June 1975 Healey gave the Cabinet a deeply sombre account of the nation's economic position. He spoke of imminent threats to sterling, and possible cuts of £1,000 million in public expenditure, with unemployment rising to two million as a result. He still hoped that a voluntary system of wage negotiation could be preserved, a view echoed by Harold Lever, but there were now serious proposals within the Treasury for a statutory policy to avoid both massive expenditure cuts and an unacceptable fall in living standards. Foot had from the start of the government declared his total opposition to a statutory policy, and it was known that he regarded it as a resigning matter. When proposals advanced further, Foot saw Wilson privately at 9 a.m. before the Cabinet meeting on 20 June, telling the Prime Minister that he would resign. He acknowledged the vital need for an incomes policy, but believed it should be voluntary, and never enforced by law, which 'would almost certainly lead to serious industrial disputes'. Almost any other resignation would have been more bearable to Wilson. He persuaded Foot to defer a decision, and then, influenced by a paper from Bernard Donoughue and his Private Secretary Kenneth Stowe, dropped the idea of a statutory policy. The Cabinet decided to continue talks with the TUC on voluntary guidelines for pay increases of 10 per cent, a level which economists considered to be more than the economy could bear. (Foot himself had suggested in Cabinet that 15 per cent would be 'a more reasonable target'.)[87]

Meeting followed meeting: Healey with Len Murray and his assistant David Lea, Foot with Jack Jones, key sessions of leading ministers in the MISC committee of the Cabinet. Healey was told by Gordon Richardson, Governor of the Bank of England, that sterling was collapsing. There were threats to withdraw from sterling by holders in oil-rich Nigeria and Kuwait. Eventually, with government policy at a near impasse, Jack Jones agreed to endorse a proposal for a flat-rate £6 weekly pay increase, a single cash sum, not a percentage. It was a major concession by Jones, who had favoured £8. But it was to haul the government back from the brink of economic collapse.

Wilson's proposals on 22 July to put this policy into practice included the prospect of reserve powers which, if applied by regulation in particular cases, would make it illegal for an employer to exceed the £6 pay limit. This virtually amounted to a reversion to a statutory policy. Foot had to concede as much before the Commons, in what Ian Aitken called 'a painful and sometimes embarrassing performance' (a description for which he was afterwards fiercely rebuked by Jill Craigie). In response to a Tory interruption, Foot admitted that if a statutory policy were introduced, 'I would hardly be the person to do it'. In fact he had argued strongly against reserve powers being included during a long, lunchless Cabinet meeting on 10 July. It would lead,

he had said, 'to the destruction of the government' by creating difficulties in Parliament and in relations with the unions. When Roy
Jenkins called for a strong statutory policy, Foot asked him, 'Are you
suggesting putting people into prison?' But a few days later Ian Aitken
(who was kept unusually well-informed on these matters) wrote that
the proposals for reserve powers had dropped into a 'legislative limbo',
and that this was 'a clear victory for Mr Foot'.[88]

Henceforth, the centrepiece of the government's anti-inflation
policy was Jack Jones's £6 a week pay limit. It would involve an
enormous amount of monitoring by the Department of Employment,
working with the TUC. The measure was not as powerful in reducing
inflation as the Treasury had hoped, since in 1976 the retail price index
fell only from 25 per cent to 15 per cent, not to the hoped-for 10 per
cent. But it was the only show in town. It was also powerfully egalitarian, since it would inevitably erode wage differentials. It had been
a close-run thing, but Foot's resignation was never again to be on the
agenda. On the other hand, the fact that Wilson had been forced
abruptly to reverse policy on incomes showed how absolutely indispensable Foot had become.

Foot not only accepted a difficult compromise, he sold it to the
Labour faithful with incomparable panache. At the Labour Party conference on 29 September he produced an extraordinary oratorical
performance to win over the delegates on economic policy. Keith
Harper in the *Guardian* called it 'an actor-manager's tour de force',
'full of meaty phrases and literary allusions' which 'kept his audience
enthralled'. Hugh Noyes in *The Times* described it as 'a glorious performance which mesmerized his audience'. The same newspaper's
political correspondent, George Clark, thought it 'surpassed all the
others in its oratory and sincerity'.[89] In his speech, Foot dwelled with
pride on the government's achievements in its last year and a half in
office: stopping the miners' strike, repealing the Industrial Relations
Act of 1971, TULRA and the Employment Protection Bill, the introduction of ACAS. He pointed out, as he had done before, the absurdity
of claiming to plan for investment, health or housing, while having no
plan whatsoever for wages policy. He concluded with great power, in
a peroration that Barbara Castle wrote almost reduced her to tears by
its 'emotional voltage' and passionate sincerity:

We face an economic typhoon of unparalleled ferocity, the worst the world has seen since the 1930s. Joseph Conrad once wrote a book called *Typhoon*, and at the end he told people how to deal with it. He said, 'Always facing it, Captain MacWhirr, that's the way to get through.' Always facing it, that's the way we have got to solve this problem. We do not want a Labour movement that tries to dodge it, we do not want people in a Labour Cabinet to try to dodge it. We want people who are prepared to show how they are going to face it, and we need the united support of the Labour movement to achieve it. I am asking this movement to exert itself as it has never done before, to show the qualities which we have, the socialist imagination that exists in our movement, the readiness to reforge the alliance, stronger than ever, between the government and the trade unions, and above all to show the supreme quality in politics, the red flame of socialist courage . . .

In the emotional aftermath, conference rejected two motions from the engineers' union to reject any kind of statutory wage policy and any government interference in wage bargaining machinery. Foot's speech was strong on rhetoric, but negligible on economic analysis. It was essentially an emotional appeal for unity. But it worked, and was a massive confidence-booster for the government. No one but Michael Foot could have managed it. It was a sign of changing perspectives. Foot's declaration, so very different in tone from most of what he had been saying in the previous thirty years, annoyed many on the left. Several delegates from the NEC refused to join in the standing ovation afterwards, including Tony Benn, Ian Mikardo, Frank Allaun, Judith Hart, Renee Short and Lena Jeger. There was a massive row over wages policy at a subsequent *Tribune* meeting between an incensed Jack Jones and Mikardo.[90] But from that time there was no more consistent advocate of the government's attempt to promote economic recovery through controls on wages than that veteran champion of free collective bargaining, Michael Foot.

By now, his resignation threat over statutory wage control proposals apart, Foot was the very model of collective responsibility. He was felt by colleagues to be far more loyal in that respect than Tony Benn, whom one of them later called 'treachery incarnate'. Yet Foot insisted that he remained the unmuzzled left-winger he had always been. One sign of this was a group of left-wing ministers who met regularly to dine together – Foot, Barbara Castle, Benn, Peter Shore, John Silkin and Judith Hart, their spouses and also the economist Thomas Balogh – and discuss matters of common interest. They met sometimes in a private room at Locket's fish restaurant near Westminster, sometimes at each other's homes.[91] Jill was a regular hostess at the Foots' home. On one of these occasions Caroline Benn actually fell asleep, and was gently borne home by her husband. These evenings were given the extraordinarily staid title 'the husbands and wives dinners', but the closed circle of their participants was obvious to all. These were important forums for discussing policy from a left perspective, and continued to be held until the fall of the Callaghan government in 1979. They were also ways of letting off ideological steam. John Silkin observed to Barbara Castle when they found Roy Jenkins and Reg Prentice also dining at Locket's, 'I can't bear these right-wingers. They are arrogant, selfish and . . .' Castle helpfully added the adjective 'insensitive'.[92]

At times the group could rouse itself to collective action, notably when Harold Wilson chose to remove a left-wing minister, Judith Hart, from the Department of Overseas Development and replace her with Reg Prentice, who was distinctly on the right and with whom Foot had clashed in Cabinet, but who had the backing of Roy Jenkins. Foot, Castle and Benn saw Wilson close to midnight on 10 June to protest, and demanded Hart's reinstatement. Foot shouted about 'poor Judith's blood being on the carpet'.[93] But Hart departed just the same, declining the offer of Transport, and went to the back benches. In fact these dinner meetings were not at all private conclaves of like-minded dissidents. They were frequently marked by sharp disputes between Foot and Benn, notably over wages policy. Benn believed that Wilson, and later Callaghan, were kept fully informed of these occasions, and that they were a part of Foot's shoring up of the leadership.[94] Foot had written extensively about Bevan's challenging of the Attlee government from the left and his eventual resignation in 1951, but he had no intention of repeating the exercise himself. He did, however, argue strongly against any idea of Wilson removing Benn from the Cabinet, not out of personal affection for Benn, but because it would upset many of the unions at a time when relations with the government were particularly fragile. The eventual outcome, with Benn moving from Industry to Energy that same day and suffering a perceived loss of prestige, was one Foot felt was satisfactory.

One quite different test of Foot's view of collective Cabinet responsibility arose in the autumn of 1975. He had known that Richard Crossman, who had died of cancer the previous year, had dictated, almost every night, full diaries of the Cabinets he attended. Foot strongly disapproved of the practice, which he regarded as a disservice both to responsible government on grounds of trust, and to history on grounds of accuracy. He equally disapproved of Barbara Castle and Tony Benn for doing the same later on, as he indicated in a famous review of the first volume of Castle's diaries in 1980.[95] However, he had agreed in 1973, as Crossman's health deteriorated, to act as one of his literary executors, and the issue of publication would clearly come up. The Cabinet Secretary, Sir John Hunt, actually suggested in March 1974 that Foot should stand down as Crossman's executor because it would clash with the principle of confidentiality to be observed by a Cabinet minister, but Foot stoutly declined. By the autumn of 1974 the Nuffield College, Oxford, academic Dr Janet Morgan had prepared the diaries for publication, and a contract was agreed with the publisher Jonathan Cape. The manuscript was then sent to Sir John Hunt, who simply rejected the idea of publication at all on the grounds that it would erode the idea of collective Cabinet responsibility by revealing differences between ministers, and other sources of contention. However, the executors decided to go ahead with publication, and to authorize the preliminary serialization of extracts in the *Sunday Times*.

Apart from considerations of the 'right to know', this was certainly in line with Crossman's own wishes on scholarly grounds to reveal the working of modern Cabinet government. He had already touched on this theme in his famous introduction to the 1963 edition of Bagehot's *English Constitution* of 1866.[96] Crossman believed that a record of Wilson's administration would confirm the view that Cabinet government, as interpreted by Bagehot, had been transformed into prime ministerial government; indeed, the Cabinet was joining the monarchy and the Lords as a 'dignified' part of the current constitution. John Mackintosh, a Labour MP who amplified this interpretation in a classic account of

The British Cabinet (1962), saw the process of prime ministerial rule as beginning with Lloyd George in 1916. Historians and political scientists had joined in a lively and fruitful debate on the subject from the mid-1960s.

There was now a vigorous tussle in the courts. The Secretary of the Cabinet and the government itself through the Attorney-General, Sam Silkin, strove to prevent the publication of Crossman's diaries. Silkin did not invoke the Official Secrets Act, that powerful barrier to free enquiry, but turned instead to an arcane Victorian law protecting official confidentiality. It was alleged (wrongly) that Silkin's behaviour was a case of a supposedly independent Attorney-General, embodying the public interest as the law officer of the Crown, acting under political pressure from the Cabinet. He was to be accused of the same offence in 1977 when refusing to take action, namely in not pressing on with the relator case of Gouriet v. the United Postal Workers, when a trade union declined to handle South African mail. Silkin was to be sharply criticized by the Master of the Rolls, Lord Denning, although his view that he was ultimately accountable to Parliament, not to the courts, was upheld in the Lords. Both cases indicated the problems of the Attorney-General's fulfilling at the same time both a legal and a political role, and the difficulties this created in entrenching the rule of law. The Crossman diaries case came before the Lord Chief Justice, Lord Widgery, in July 1974.

Foot's role was an awkward and paradoxical one. As a Cabinet minister, he was committed to previous practice as a basis of collective responsibility. He disapproved of the habit of ministers keeping diaries anyway, let alone of publishing them in the newspapers. Yet he found himself in conflict with his own government's law officer, Sam Silkin. There was a real prospect of Foot, busy at the time with major trade union legislation, appearing before Widgery in the high court. On the other hand, his every instinct was for the freedom to publish and to roll back official censorship; after all, at the time Crossman was dictating his diaries, the fifty-year rule operated, which meant that historians could not examine the public archive subsequent to Asquith's government, which ended in 1916. In the 1970s it became a thirty-year rule, and that was still the case in 2006, although it had been healthily modified by the Freedom of Information Act (2000). Foot had earlier refused, quite rightly, to sign a pledge, as recommended by Lord Radcliffe as Chairman of the Committtee of the Privy Council on ministerial memoirs, that no minister should publish any memoirs for fifteen years after being in office. Benn, Jenkins and Barbara Castle joined him in this. At the meeting of Crossman's executors and the diaries' publisher, Foot 'was prepared to accept the risk and bare his breast for the dagger'. In fact he did not have to, since Lord Widgery, in a distinctly curious judgement published on 1 October 1974, decided to allow publication on the grounds that 'much of the action is up to ten years old'. The outcome appears to have been satisfactory for Harold Wilson, who was contemplating publishing his own lucrative memoirs in due time.

The extracts appeared in the *Sunday Times* in the new year, and Crossman's four classic volumes, brilliantly edited by Dr Janet Morgan and covering the major span of Crossman's career, as backbencher as well as minister, from 1951 to 1970, were published between 1975 and 1981.[97] Foot has sometimes been criticized over the false position in which he placed himself. But his instinct was surely right. Plenty of previous ministers had published their diaries, notably Hugh Dalton only a few years after leaving office. Ministers and Prime Ministers had been cavalier in deciding whether documents in their possession were in the public domain or were private material belonging to them as individuals – Lloyd George's and Churchill's war memoirs being the most obvious examples. Foot's impulse to challenge official censorship so as to allow material into the public domain, just as Hansard itself had fought to be published a century and a half before, was a tribute both to his instincts and to his sense of history. The Crossman diaries, like all such sources, are flawed and governed by the diarist's personal perspective. But they are also an enormous aid to historical enquiry and public understanding. Scholars may feel gratified that a politician as libertarian as Michael Foot was a key figure in these events. He helped to ensure that a firm blow was struck against the British curse of official secrecy, the psychological backdrop to its unwritten constitution, based on convention, custom, informality and social conservatism.

These were complicated and troubled times for Michael Foot, at home and abroad. There was the huge controversy over Britain's membership of the European Economic Community to be resolved, with Foot known as the Cabinet's most forthright anti-European. But before that there was a crisis much nearer home, in his own constituency. In February 1975 the long-anticipated but still traumatic closure of most of the Ebbw Vale steelworks, the hub of the valley's economy, took place. The minister and his government had done what they could in a lost cause. In November 1972 Foot had been putting pressure on Lord Melchett, who had made proposals to downsize the plant, to retain most of the work at the south end of the plant. The Wilson government set up an inquiry under the former Labour minister Lord Beswick, but he reported in February 1975 that the closures should go ahead as planned. That meant that over 3,500 jobs would go in the near future – three hundred from the A blast furnace in April 1975, seven hundred from the C blast furnace in July, 1,300 from the open hearth shop and slabbing mill in March–September 1977, and a final 1,300 from the hot strip mill in March 1978. Eventually, 4,600 jobs would be lost in all. The government announced that £12.6 million would be additionally allocated as follows: £5.5 million to develop water and sewerage facilities, £2.5 million to clear derelict land, £2.3 million for new, government-assisted, advance factories, and £2.3 million to the local council for additional industrial sites. The Welsh Office said that 1,950 new jobs were currently in the pipeline. But that would inevitably take time, and the closures were a body blow for an already declining area. Shutting down a steelworks inevitably caused more layoffs and closures than a coalmine would.[98]

Foot, bravely but perhaps unwisely, decided to bear the burden directly himself. When he went down to his constituency with John Morris, Secretary of State for Wales, and Caerwyn Roderick on 7 February, he faced a reception unique in his thirty-two years as Ebbw Vale's MP. A demonstration of two thousand angry steelworkers in Ebbw Vale Civic Centre shouted abuse at him. It was eight minutes before the crowd would even let him speak. At the same time, six thousand local steelworkers took part in a one-day protest strike. People shouted out, quite unfairly and wrongly, that it would not have happened if Nye Bevan had been alive. Foot left, pale and shaken.[99] The following day he had another difficult, though less hostile, meeting at the Ebbw Vale leisure centre. The occasion could have been even more disastrous, since John Morris narrowly escaped death in a car crash on the M4 on his way back to London. Both in Ebbw Vale and in an angry debate at Westminster, it was Foot who took the full force of his passionately angry constituents.[100]

He made immense efforts to bring new jobs to his stricken valley. A few days later, the first fruits were announced. With government assistance, a total of 550 jobs would come from a BSC factory making coated steel products, and a further 350 eventually from a Grundy plant manufacturing stainless steel car silencers. A Colorcoat plant to make wide-coated steel strip would employ a further two hundred in 1977. But much more was needed, and local men, used to doing 'proper' work in a steel plant, were critical of the 'marshmallow' jobs in light industries due to come in, including the making of fur coats. It was a slow and partial recovery, but there was one hugely symbolic development, originating as it happened from Foot's strong contacts with India.[101] He persuaded a British-based Indian industrialist, Swraj Paul, Chairman of National Gas Tubes, to invest in the constituency by setting up the most advanced spiral weld steelmill in Europe, with the aid of funding from the British government and the EEC – Foot, an arch anti-European, was fully prepared to receive money from Europe for a good cause. Swraj Paul (later Lord Paul) had earlier helped to arrange Foot's first visit to India in 1973, and his giving the Krishna Menon Lecture, in honour of the old socialist guru of the thirties, in November 1976. Foot, 'a man who inspires trust through his integrity', was always a hero to him.[102] Swraj Paul's plant was opened on 22 November 1978 by no less a person than Mrs Gandhi. The Ebbw Vale economy continued to limp along.[103] The Garden Festival of Wales, on the site of the former steelworks in 1992, did not create many new jobs, while in 2001 the Corus company, which now owned what was left of the steelworks, virtually closed it down. Nevertheless, it was a characteristically courageous effort by Foot. A steelworkers' leader later considered that closing the works had been inevitable ever since the Llanwern works was opened on the coast in 1962.[104] In difficult circumstances, ones that Bevan had never had to face, Foot took the flak, worked hard to repair some of the damage, and soon recovered his local esteem.

Europe was the big problem overshadowing Harold Wilson's government from the start. Jim Callaghan, the Foreign Secretary, spent many months before and after the October 1974 general election purportedly 'renegotiating' Britain's terms of entry into the EEC. There was a good deal of scepticism about the practicality of this, including from Callaghan's great ally Helmut Schmidt, the German Chancellor, but he did achieve some improvements, notably over the admission of Commonwealth produce such as New Zealand dairy products to markets within the EEC, and also over Community budget payments. On the other hand, Callaghan had said early on that he was 'negotiating for success', and the relationship of Britain to the EEC remained much the same despite his efforts.[105] After much debate, Foot had reluctantly gone along with Benn's proposal that a referendum on the question of Britain's membership of the EEC should be held, and he, Benn and Peter Shore wrote to Wilson on 27 November 1974 asking for one, with ministers being given the right to differ in public. Wilson replied firmly that this must be a collective Cabinet decision after the renegotiations of the terms of entry were concluded, and that until it was agreed ministers should not air their own personal views. Benn responded by claiming his own fidelity to the manifesto. In a milder letter to Wilson on 3 January 1975, Foot wrote that it was wrong to assume British approval on three key issues – the weakening of the British veto, direct elections for the European Assembly, and the terms for a monetary and economic union. The communiqué of the recent European summit meeting, he argued, had 'altered the position which prevailed before'.[106]

Eventually, at a marathon session on 17–18 March, the Cabinet endorsed the terms renegotiated by Callaghan for remaining within the EEC by sixteen votes to seven. There would be a referendum on 5 June 1975 to confirm or reject British EEC membership, and during the campaign ministers would have the freedom to 'agree to differ', as Liberal ministers in the National Government (including Isaac Foot) had done over imperial preference back in 1932. The Cabinet minority of seven were Foot, Benn, Castle and Shore (who was especially vehement), along with three less powerful figures, John Silkin, Eric Varley and Willie Ross, the Scottish Secretary (the last two being far more even-handed in their views). The contributions of all seven are recorded by name in the minutes. For his part, Foot was implacable in resisting what he saw as a sacrifice of British parliamentary sovereignty. Benn records him as saying 'We shall dismember Parliament and the UK.' A pro-European colleague, Edmund Dell, wrote later that 'it sometimes seemed that extracting Britain from entanglement with the EEC had become his predominant ambition to which every other policy objective should, if necessary, be sacrificed'.[107] The bare bones of the Cabinet minute give Foot's key arguments:

> The consequences of withdrawal from the EEC had been exaggerated: he did not accept that Britain's problems could be solved only by our accepting an alien system whose legislative basis – the European Communities Act 1972 – it was not proposed to change. Policies which had stood Britain in good stead, for example on agriculture and the Commonwealth, had already been destroyed by attempts over the last decade to join the EEC. Continued membership would lead to the dismembering of the United Kingdom, and of the authority of Parliament which had already lost much of its power in EEC affairs. If we remained in the Community the seat of power would lie in future in permanent coalition in Brussels.[108]

At Labour's special conference in Islington's Sobell Hall on 26 April, Foot struck a note of evangelical patriotism, citing the Putney Debates and Nye Bevan along the way: 'I say to our great country, "Don't be afraid of those who tell us that we cannot run our own affairs, that we have not the ingenuity to mobilize our resources and overcome our economic problems."' The anti-Marketeers won the vote on EEC membership taken in the hall, and in Benn's view also the argument, after Foot's 'brilliant' speech.[109]

In fact Foot played a limited part in the 'No' campaign because, quite unexpectedly, he was rushed to the Royal Free hospital immediately after this conference for an emergency operation. At first cancer had been feared, but he soon recovered – sufficiently to mount a successful libel action against Linda Lee-Potter of the *Daily Mail*, who had spitefully and inaccurately suggested that he was receiving private treatment under the NHS. Foot was able to speak at a few meetings, including one spectacular oratorical performance with the Conservative John Biffen. But it was Benn, Castle and Shore who led the attack for the 'Noes'.

The outcome of the referendum was a massive victory for the 'Yes'

campaign, with seventeen and a half million votes in favour to eight
and a half million against. Edward Heath proved to be a strong performer for the 'Yes' campaign, as was Roy Jenkins: only the fringe
areas of the Scottish Western Isles and the Shetlands showed a 'No'
majority. The campaign was hardly a proper debate on the political or
economic issues at stake, and the 'Yes' vote was no doubt swayed by
industrial funding, along with the fact that it was supported by every
national newspaper. But at that time, with membership of Europe
being presented as being primarily of economic benefit to an ailing
British economy, and no mention being made of federal superstates or
anything of the kind, public opinion was manifestly in favour. Foot
remained implacably opposed, however. He kept up the fight to question all EEC directives, to limit the controls exercised by Brussels,
and to keep at bay any proposal for direct election to the European
Assembly.[110] The referendum was not his finest hour. He was not at
all a natural isolationist or xenophobe, as some of his fellow 'No'
campaigners seemed to be. At least, however, he accepted the verdict
with better grace than other, more extreme Labour anti-Europeans
such as Shore or Douglas Jay, and felt able to move on. He made
no attempt to interfere with John Fraser's work on directives for
redundancies and equal pay at EEC ministers' meetings on social affairs.
These and the economic rescue of Ebbw Vale showed that even the
Brussels bureaucrats had their uses.

In the spring of 1976, Foot seemed to be entering a more tranquil
phase. His trade union legislation had got through, more or less, and
the Department of Employment was operating at a less hectic pace as
some of its activities were hived off to ACAS, the Manpower Service
Commission and other bodies. Not too many scars had been left
by Europe. On issues like the financial crisis in the car firm Chrysler
(UK) and the Public Expenditure White Paper he played an emollient
role. Then, to general astonishment, on 16 March Harold Wilson
announced that, after precisely eight years in office, he was going to
retire from the premiership, almost certainly on health grounds. Jim
Callaghan alone of the leading contenders to succeed him had been
told beforehand, and could prepare the ground.[111] For Foot, as for
almost everyone else, Wilson's announcement came as a great shock.

Clearly, though, Foot was obliged to campaign for the party leadership as the main challenger from the left. The odds were against him – the press thought that out of 319 Labour MPs, only around 127 were on the left. But Foot had performed strongly in office, and could well pick up votes from the centre-right as well. There were six candidates nominated: Callaghan, Crosland, Healey and Jenkins on the right, Foot and Benn on the left. Callaghan was the clear favourite, with Jenkins certain to have strong but small support from the pro-European Manifesto Group. On the left, Benn would have the support of the most socialist elements, including some from the Tribune group. Foot's chances were believed to be strong by Peter Jenkins in the *Guardian*. On the other hand, Jenkins's assessment of Foot's qualities was scathing: he was 'almost totally ignorant of economics' and essentially a romantic. His knowledge of foreign affairs was also said to be slight: he was interested in Spain, although he had never been there, 'he knows Venice extremely well and James Cameron has told him some plain tales of India'.[112] Here, as elsewhere, though, Jenkins's balance deserted him.

Foot campaigned in his usual relaxed fashion, leaving the ward-heeling to be done by Eric Heffer, Albert Booth and his young protégé Neil Kinnock.[113] On 25 March it emerged that Foot had headed the poll on the first ballot, with ninety votes to Callaghan's eighty-four and Jenkins's fifty-six. Benn polled thirty-seven, and promptly announced his withdrawal and his support for Foot. Crosland also withdrew, with a somewhat humiliating seventeen votes; Healey polled thirty, but decided to stay in. In the second ballot, Callaghan drew ahead with 141 votes to Foot's 133 and Healey's thirty-eight. Clearly the eliminated Healey's votes would almost all go to Callaghan, but even so Foot's poll was remarkably strong. On 5 April the third ballot showed Callaghan polling 176 votes to Foot's 137. Foot had probably done better than was expected by even his most hopeful supporters. He even received one or two right-wing votes – from Douglas Jay because of a shared antipathy to Europe, and Brian Walden, soon to leave Parliament, who voted for Foot because he was 'a man of principle'.[114] Foot's political reputation was continuing to rise, as it had done ever since the 1970 election. He enhanced it further with a wonderfully entertaining, noteless speech to the parliamentary party after the result was announced. Barbara Castle, who had strongly backed him, observed, 'I thought as I listened what a joy it was to have a touch of quality brought back into our political dialogue. Mike is the only one to give it to us since Nye died.'[115] Even the top of the famous greasy pole seemed not hopelessly unattainable now. The question of age could not be raised because Foot, at sixty-three, was actually sixteen months younger than Callaghan. George Hutchinson wrote, in somewhat exaggerated terms, in *The Times* that Foot, 'the supreme political pamphleteer of his day and generation, orator, biographer and romantic', had taken a big stride forward: 'The Foot philosophy is in the ascendant.'[116]

Callaghan's Cabinet-making demonstrated Foot's new authority. He became in effect Deputy Prime Minister, and moved to become Lord President of the Council and Leader of the House. Jack Jones regretted this, as Foot had been the best friend in government the unions had ever had. But Foot, who would have been prepared to stay on at Employment, sensed that leading the House would be crucial at a time when the government's majority had disappeared after the death of a health minister, Brian O'Malley, and the defection of John Stonehouse to Australia in mysterious (indeed criminal) circumstances, after faking his suicide following an investigation into his financial affairs. There would be much interest for him in constitutional reform, notably Scottish and Welsh devolution, which the government was pledged to introduce after the report of the Kilbrandon Commission on the subject. The greatest interest lay in the composition of Callaghan's Cabinet more generally, since Denis Healey was staying on at the Treasury and Roy Jenkins leaving Westminster to become a European Commissioner.

Foot had three main demands or requests which he put to Callaghan in a private meeting on 5 April.[117] He succeeded with two of them. He ensured that Jenkins, immensely pro-Europe as he was, would never go to the Foreign Office, though in this case Foot and Callaghan were of one mind anyhow; Tony Crosland, much cooler over Europe, went there instead. Foot also secured a promise that his loyal colleague Albert Booth would succeed him at Employment. The third, however, was the most symbolic of all, and here he failed. Callaghan, predictably in view of many past conflicts, decided to sack Barbara Castle. She was mortified, but also disappointed that Foot had not insisted that she should stay in office, as she made clear to journalists afterwards. During the election campaign Jill Craigie, sitting next to Castle on a sofa, had whispered, 'Mike won't let Jim be nasty to you.' Most certainly Foot pleaded her case strongly – '*Barbara should not go*' is recorded in Callaghan's private diary account of their conversation – but the new Prime Minister was clearly adamant. Foot equally obviously did not regard Castle's fate as a resigning matter, unlike political issues such as a statutory incomes policy. He recognized the long antagonism between Callaghan and Castle, going back to the time when Callaghan was shadow colonial spokesman in the late fifties, and Castle had harried him unmercifully on behalf of the union of Cyprus with Greece, rather than Labour's favoured position of territorial independence for the island. After her sacking Castle found Foot 'sorry but not desolate'. For all his regard and affection for his old comrade, he could joke years later that when she left office, 'Barbara thought the whole world would come to an end'.[118]

Foot and Callaghan, drawn from quite different wings of the party, were now pledged to be in indissoluble partnership. Without Foot in high office, the government's precarious alliance with the unions, facing huge new pressures as massive economic clouds rolled up, would fail almost at once. His reluctant desertion of Barbara was thus a signal of his authority as a political leader, gained almost by stealth. But it was also a recognition that the priorities of the old Labour past, based on protest and suspicion of the facts of life when in office, would have to be subordinated. For Michael Foot, veteran of Bevanism, *Tribune* and CND, who had once entertained the young Barbara Betts in her Bloomsbury flat with readings from *Das Kapital*, but now responsible minister and practitioner in the uses of power, it was goodbye to all that.

10

HOUSE AND PARTY LEADER
(1976–1980)

Michael Foot surveyed his changed world from an office of faded Victorian splendour with a bay window looking out on Horse Guards Parade. He moved from St James's Square to 68 Whitehall, at the heart of government: he had access to number 10 directly through a connecting door later made famous in the television series *Yes, Prime Minister*.[1] His new role as Lord President and Leader of the House was remarkably flexible and unstructured. To a degree, the job would be what he made of it. It was perhaps a role more appropriate for a free spirit like Foot than undertaking a heavy and formal departmental responsibility. He had only a handful of, mainly junior, officials to help him, unlike the large Civil Service machine he had had to assist and advise him at the Department of Employment. Much of his briefing came from the Cabinet Office next door at number 70, which also, of course, gave advice to 10 Downing Street, and thereby enabled the Prime Minister and his party deputy to say identical things. For Foot's position was to be strengthened later in the year, on 21 October, when he defeated Shirley Williams in a little-noticed contest for the deputy leadership by 166 votes to 128. Callaghan had supported him.

It emerged at once that leading the House of Commons had its decidedly social side, especially as the political parties were so finely balanced and the government's fate rested on a miscellany of small groupings. The nationalist minorities in Scotland and Wales, and Unionists in Northern Ireland, had to be conciliated with a variety of concessions – a pipeline here, compensation for retired quarrymen there. John Biffen, a Conservative Leader of the House in the 1980s, called it 'a very drinks kind of job'. So it was, with Foot an active and genial host.[2] Compared with an earlier Lord President, his old bugbear

Herbert Morrison, Foot was a far more flexible and accessible, if also more disorganized, operator.

He had a large number of major responsibilities in his new role. His Private Secretary's initial memorandum of 8 April 1976 ran to eight pages and listed twenty-four separate items.[3] The Lord President bore overall responsibility for the government's legislative programme, and had formal relationships with the opposition leaders and with all Members of Parliament. It was a priority of Foot's to ensure, along with the Chief Whip Michael Cocks, that the government had sufficient votes to survive. He also had to arrange, with Cocks's Private Secretary Freddie Warren, the business of the House, to make parliamentary statements and answer questions on a wide-ranging and unpredictable number of issues. His very first formal debate on the adjournment ranged, in his Private Secretary Clive Saville's words, from 'the iniquity of VAT on yachts to the fate of the New York dressed turkey'. His role also covered domestic Commons matters (such as the huge £500,000 deficit in the catering budget), Members' pay and pensions, and arrangements for party political broadcasting. All these were unpredictable issues, especially in a hung Parliament.

In addition to these shifting and varied tasks there were his formal duties on the Privy Council as Lord President, advised in this area, though never on political matters, by the Clerk to the Privy Council, Neville Leigh. The Privy Council was a dignified but still functional part of the constitution which met about once a month to approve Orders in Council, grant Royal Charters, prick Sheriffs and the like. This meant that Foot was in regular contact with the Queen, and he would travel down to Windsor each month by car with Neville Leigh, a somewhat formal character who may or may not have appreciated having Foot's dog Vanessa on the back seat for company. Foot's very first Privy Council featured the swearing-in of the New Zealand Prime Minister, who had to fly all the way from Wellington for the ceremony.[4]

Foot was a known republican, and declared himself as such in the House on more than one occasion, to the anger of traditionally-minded Tories. It was commented that he never attended the Trooping of the Colour since he was temperamentally unsympathetic to both the army and the monarchy. But in fact he and Queen Elizabeth got on remarkably well.[5] He made an effort to be neatly dressed for their meetings, and treated the Queen with his habitual courtesy towards all women. He liked her, and pronounced her to be, like Jack Jones, 'highly intelligent'. They had at least two points in common. They shared an interest in political and constitutional history; it may be surmised that the Queen was treated to frequent discourses on the reign of Queen Anne. Also, they both liked dogs: Foot's terrier Vanessa (shortly to be joined by Roxana, another Swiftian name) and the Queen's corgis provided a strong bond. Foot was required, under formal 'Procedure for Ministers', to give attendance at the Privy Council priority over all other business. On the one occasion he failed to do so, because of a crucial meeting of Labour's National Executive to discuss 'entryism' by the far left or Trotskyists into the party, he went to much trouble in writing out a three- or four-page letter, beginning 'Madam, with my humble duty', explaining why the NEC had to take priority (unfortunately this letter cannot now be traced in the royal archives). By contrast, Foot had little time for the Duke of Edinburgh, whom he regarded as a hopeless reactionary. He was, however, quite a favourite of the Queen Mother, who called him 'Michael' and later even complimented him on his notorious 'donkey jacket'.[6]

The personal chemistry between Foot and the Queen was always good. On one occasion, when the topic under discussion was the appointment of a chaplain to his old Oxford college, Wadham, he went on at such length that the Queen had gently to suggest that they move on to other business. A spectacular issue arose in the summer of 1981, when Foot was leader of the opposition. The Queen indicated her irritation with King Juan Carlos of Spain, who had objected to the Prince and Princess of Wales calling in at Gibraltar aboard the royal yacht during their honeymoon. 'After all,' declared the Queen, 'it's my son, my yacht and my dockyard.' After a period of silence, Foot burst out enthusiastically, 'Your Majesty, Queen Elizabeth I could not have put it better.' When his Labour colleague Roy Hattersley expressed some surprise to Foot as they left, Foot replied, as if no further explanation was necessary, 'She was standing up for England.'[7]

Foot had one important ministerial colleague, his Minister of State John Smith, appointed to handle constitutional matters and particularly the forthcoming Bills on Scottish and Welsh devolution. Smith and Foot had not previously been close: Smith was a Callaghan supporter, and was viewed by the Prime Minister as one of three bright young men (along with Roy Hattersley and David Owen) who could make a future leader. He had previously been cool on devolution, but his legal expertise and high intelligence made him an invaluable support for Foot in handling business in the House: indeed, since his minister was never a detail man, Smith took the various Devolution Bills through the long committee stages himself, almost single-handed. He was a convivial man, and he and Foot struck up the best of relationships, often with the assistance of a glass of whisky. Smith remained Minister of State until almost the end of the government, when he was succeeded by a peeress, Alma, Lady Birk.[8] Caerwyn Roderick remained Foot's knowledgeable and amiable PPS. His only other political support in his new role was the appointment as special adviser of Elizabeth Thomas, an old flame and long-time aide on *Tribune* who fulfilled a number of party duties in the office, including at times the thankless task of writing Foot's effectively non-scripted speeches. She was punctilious in keeping the government and party lines quite distinct.[9] Elizabeth was a constantly reassuring presence, but for the support a minister would normally expect to receive from his department, Foot was thrust onto his own resources. The Cabinet Office would brief him on formal matters, but on other questions, such as the IMF crisis of 1976 or incomes policy, the Lord President had to look elsewhere for guidance. His job was a somewhat lonely one, but on the whole Foot, a self-contained operator who invariably met visitors to the department on his own without civil servants present, preferred it that way.

Foot's Civil Service staff in his private office was small and junior. He had two relatively young high-flyers, recruited from Education and the Inland Revenue, a Parliamentary Clerk, a Diary Secretary and a couple of clerk/typists. His Private Secretary was Clive Saville, an able young graduate of University College, Swansea. There was also a separate Civil Service directorate for the Constitutional Unit, headed by John Garlick, Second Permanent Secretary of the Cabinet Office, and, most importantly, Michael Quinlan.[10] An interesting appointment was Jacqui Lait, a young Scottish woman, one of two Press Officers who ran the government information service for the Privy Council, working mainly with John Smith. She was to become a Conservative

MP in 1992 and a junior minister, but she recalled working with Foot with great affection. One instance was his courtesy in giving her a lift in his car to Paddington station and carrying her case down the platform when she was late for a train due to take her (as Foot knew) to a Conservative conference in Oxford. She felt comfortable working with him. Foot's methods of work, 'a process of osmosis', were chaotic, and he seldom used notes for his speeches. But he was always honest and open: 'You knew he was reliable.'[11]

Much the most important adviser, by common consent, was Freddie Warren, Private Secretary to the government Chief Whip. Located in 12 Downing Street, he was a vital player in keeping government business up and running: he was, in his own bluff person, 'the usual channels', the permanent link between government and opposition whips, in this case Michael Cocks and Humphrey Atkins. He might get a guillotine motion drafted or negotiate the duration of a debate. He was also an ebullient, highly eccentric personality, unpredictable in mood and with a formidable capacity for whisky. Simon Hoggart well described him as 'a strange combination of technocrat and court jester'. Warren and his secretary Mabel Dodd ('Freddie and Doddy') were a legendary duo throughout Whitehall. He would have shouting matches with the combustible Chief Whip Michael Cocks, and even on occasion with Michael Foot – who, uncharacteristically, would sometimes shout back. But Foot realized that Warren, with his intense institutional loyalty and unique knowledge of parliamentary procedure and detail, was one of those officials indispensable to the operations of government, comparable with Ken Stowe in the Prime Minister's private office. One of Warren's colleagues also observed, 'He knew where all the bodies were buried.'[12]

The civil servants became happily attuned to Foot's weekly routine, both regular and irregular. Every Monday there would be a session with Michael Cocks; every Wednesday there would be talks with Freddie Warren about next week's business; every Thursday Foot and a private secretary would walk from 68 to 70 Whitehall, then through 10 and 11 Downing Street via internal corridors to see Warren and Cocks together at number 12.[13] But there was also Foot the free spirit, the man who hated being addressed as 'Lord President' (his Private Secretary called him 'Mr Foot'). As before, his dog Vanessa would accompany him to his office. As before, a television might be left on with the sound turned down during Test matches. Foot's book-reviewing, notably for the *Observer*, and writing of articles always claimed some of his time. In November 1977, with the minority government immured in devolution and other problems, Foot found time to write a full-page article in the *Evening Standard* on his cherished authors and the joys of reading. His desk and shelves were piled with books, all of them non-political. One of his secretaries learned how to spell names like 'Montesquieu'.[14] On occasion, Foot would simply take time off to wander about the bookshops of Charing Cross Road: on at least one such expedition he returned triumphantly with a copy of a Stendhal novel he had not previously read. Staff in his office would be given presents of books, sometimes books written by the Lord President himself. A woman secretary received a heavily inscribed copy of his life of Nye Bevan. Foot always generated warmth in the people around him.[15]

But his methods of work were chaotic, and civil servants often had to hunt around to find where he was. One aide, who greatly liked him, said, 'You could never have had him as a junior minister.' The pressure of routine business was evidently less in those days than it has since become, as was the obsession with personal security. As at Employment, work in the office could be fun, particularly late on Friday afternoons as the freedom of the weekend beckoned, or when the passing of some crisis was being celebrated. Women staff like Elizabeth Thomas, Vivian Williams and Jacqui Lait provided the food, while the minister obliged with decent white wine, French or Italian. Foot was always a popular figure at these events. Occasionally some criticism was directed towards Jill, who could make patronizing remarks about the food, and who was also thought to take insufficient trouble in making sure that Michael turned up for work in a respect-able, stain-free suit.[16]

The main colleagues who worked with Foot were, of course, the Cabinet ministers. Among them he was in general a popular and much-respected figure: his most difficult relationship was probably with Tony Benn. Foot was number two in the pecking order (confirmed when he formally replaced Ted Short as deputy leader in October 1976), and in Cabinet he sat next to Callaghan. His relationship with the Prime

Minister was strong and unbreakable. Foot's loyalty and absolute refusal to engage in left-wing conspiracies against his leader were unqualified. The two men would meet before Cabinet to sort out their joint attitudes to issues, and Foot's conduct in Cabinet was always totally supportive in every respect – to a degree that aroused some concern from old colleagues on the left like Barbara Castle, who felt he 'fawned' towards the Prime Minister. In 1977, when Foot refused to criticize the Home Secretary Merlyn Rees for deporting two radical American journalists, Philip Agee and Mark Hosenball, for publishing details about GCHQ, the government's secret intelligence listening post at Cheltenham, Benn attacked him as 'an extinct volcano' who refused to 'fight for anything [in] particular'.[17] Potentially awkward topics like nuclear weapons were never to intrude into Cabinet business. Foot sat on the Defence and Overseas Policy Committee of the Cabinet, but this did not handle nuclear weapons policy. In 1978–79 the use of Polaris, Trident or Cruise missiles was never raised in Cabinet by Foot, or indeed by anybody else. On one occasion the Prime Minister's adviser Tom McNally had the entertaining experience of seeing Foot brief members of CND, with some aplomb, on the government's approach to nuclear weapons. Even during highly contentious discussions, as on the IMF loan in December 1976 or the problems with the unions during the 'winter of discontent', Foot, while arguing his case with due vigour, never made any fundamental difficulties for the government. Equally, he went to some lengths to protect Benn when it appeared likely that his free-wheeling behaviour might lead Callaghan to dismiss him. Foot's fundamental role was to ensure that the Labour government kept together, in partnership with the unions, until the blessings of North Sea oil came on stream – at the end of the decade, it was hoped – and the nation's balance of payments would be transformed.[18]

Foot's relationship with Callaghan was an odd one. They were both men of 1945, and had been temporarily associated in the Keep Left movement in 1947. But they had radically diverged during Labour's civil wars in the 1950s. Callaghan had not particularly liked Gaitskell, whom he saw as an Oxford intellectual prone to patronize him, but he agreed with his views on the bomb, multilateralism and the centrality of NATO. Foot, of course, was a veteran Bevanite, unilateralist and founder member of CND. The two were never close friends: Tom McCaffrey, who worked as Press Officer for both men and greatly admired both of them, said they were 'not best buddies'.[19] Neither ever invited the other to his home: Michael and Jill never visited Callaghan's Sussex farm. But as a working relationship, that between Callaghan and Foot could not have been bettered. Each was resolutely loyal to the other: when he went to the Lords in 1987, Callaghan was to say that of all the people he had worked with, he would most like to work again with Michael Foot. He was much gratified when Foot became deputy leader. In a private note written during his retirement he wrote most warmly of Foot as 'a great Englishman of the libertarian left'.[20] There was another bond between them, too – a shared ancestral patriotism based on the Royal Navy and the freedom of the open sea. Callaghan was a Portsmouth boy, the son of a sailor who served on the royal yacht and fought at the Battle of Jutland. He himself served during the war on HMS *Elizabeth*, Beatty's flagship after Jutland, and acted as an Admiralty minister under Attlee. The beguiling sound of the 'Pompey Chimes', the musical chant of Portsmouth FC's supporters at their home ground of Fratton Park, was as emotionally powerful for Jim Callaghan as were Plymouth, the Armada and the throbbing beat of Drake's Drum for Michael Foot. When it came to using the power of the Royal Navy to defend British subjects in the Falklands in 1982 against the fascist junta in Buenos Aires, the two old naval patriots stood instinctively shoulder to shoulder.

With Chancellor of the Exchequer Denis Healey and Shirley Williams (now moved to Education) Foot retained a strong relationship too, as both fully acknowledged in later years.[21] He also showed generosity to Roy Hattersley when he defended his short-lived Prices and Consumer Protection department from the Prime Minister's wrath,[22] while his performance as Leader of the House was thought to be incomparably skilful. The generally civilized tone of his role in Cabinet is captured in a letter to Tony Crosland. When the Foreign Secretary pointed out that a lunch with the Russian Ambassador should have been cleared with the Foreign Office first, Foot replied:

My lunch with the Soviet Ambassador was a less sinister or convivial occasion than might have been supposed. We spent

more time than probably either of us would have wished discussing the difficulties of appreciating Pushkin in translation, the
comparative claims of Turgenev and Oscar Wilde to have written the wittiest of all plays, the role of M. Maisky (an old
friend of mine) in the Second World War, and many varied and
comparable topics . . . When I accepted the invitation to go to
the Embassy . . . I had no idea it would lead to the unrestrained
carousals detailed above.

He concluded, 'I did not, I fear, learn much except from the glimpse
into the world of the single-minded pursuit of pleasure which must
be the daily lot of the Foreign Secretary.'[23]

Such diversions aside, Foot was now to encounter crisis after crisis.
There was a huge parliamentary storm on 26 May 1976 when the
Speaker, George Thomas, no friend of his old party, declared that the
Aircraft and Shipbuilding Industries Bill was a hybrid measure that did
not deal equally with every shipyard concerned. Foot then used a
procedural motion to overrule him. He and Thomas were to have
furious rows on the matter at the end of each session. The next day
there was an even bigger row when, after a tied vote 303–303, the
government managed a majority of just one, 304–303, on the main
motion on the Bill. Even this was a relief, since two Labour backbenchers, John Mackintosh and Brian Walden, had threatened to
abstain. Amid extraordinary confusion, a government whip, Tom
Pendry, was recorded as having voted in the second division but not in
the first: there was a dispute about whether a 'pairing' agreement had
been broken, and Labour's Willie Hamilton complained that the
Serjeant-at-Arms, responsible for keeping order in the House, had used
foul language. Foot was involved in heated exchanges with the Tories:
the Liberal leader, Jo Grimond, twitted him for heavy-handed imposition of the whip after having argued for free votes in his pamphlet
Parliament in Danger back in 1959. Michael Heseltine later observed,
'It is curious how often the greatest self-styled champions of the constitution prove the most willing to indulge in ruthless suppression of
those rights when they conflict with their narrower objectives.'[24]

Throughout the long and extremely hot summer of 1976 Foot was
again heavily involved with the Chancellor Denis Healey and Jack
Jones in the grind of ensuring another year of anti-inflationary wage

restraint: Foot's role, of course, was the indirect but crucial one of trying to win the agreement of the TUC. Back in March, when still at Employment, he had warned Healey that the TUC would have great difficulty in finding an acceptable successor to Jones's £6 pay limit, and hoped for some extra pump-priming of the construction industry and private house-building to help reduce unemployment.[25] With the assistance of Len Murray, Healey managed to win the unions over to a wage settlement for 1976–77, presented as 3 per cent plus tax concessions, and this was endorsed by a special TUC conference in June. Foot wrote a very warm letter of congratulation to Healey afterwards, rightly describing it as 'a Herculean feat on your part, a sustained piece of intellectual argument with those who are born arguers themselves'.[26] Intense Cabinet debates followed about the scale of public expenditure cuts. Divisions among ministers emerged, roughly similar to those that appeared during the IMF crisis in December 1976, with Foot and Benn heading a left-wing group opposed to major cuts. In the end, a programme of £1 billion of cuts was announced, with a further £1 billion to be raised via a surcharge on employers' National Insurance contributions, broadly in line with the Treasury's views.

After a relatively stable August, however, further economic troubles welled up in September, with the pound, notionally valued at $2.40, falling rapidly to a level of under $1.60, and Healey having to raise the minimum lending rate to a record 13 per cent. There was a huge slump in international confidence in the state of the economy, the balance of payments and the strength of the pound. Massive financial support would have to be found to prevent the country seemingly going bankrupt. The most damaging image was that of the Chancellor having to cancel a projected trip to meet the International Monetary Fund representatives in Manila and scurry back from Heathrow airport on 30 September to save a collapsing pound. Healey wrote in his diary, 'Beautiful day, sterling going down.'[27] He was also persuaded to attend the Labour Party conference at Blackpool, where he was shouted at for his pains by left-wing delegates. In return, he heaped scorn on his critics, prisoners of illusion, who wanted to stop the world and get off. For once, Foot played no part. The most spectacular contribution came in a conference speech from Callaghan, who, in a passage written by his son-in-law Peter Jay, the financial journalist and future

Ambassador to Washington, informed his stunned audience that it was not possible to spend your way out of a depression. Healey wryly told the present writer years later that the moral was 'Never have a speech written by your son-in-law.' Inflation, not unemployment, was henceforth to be identified as the major evil to be confronted. A generation of Keynesian finance seemed about to be overturned. The government in which Foot was second in command appeared likely to bury the basic, uncomplicated economic tenets in which he had believed all his adult life.

If this was a whirlwind deferred, Foot flew with Jill straight into one of his own creation in India. He went there in October 1976 at the invitation of Swraj Paul and others.[28] He visited different parts of the country from Kashmir to Bombay, and delivered the Krishna Menon Memorial Lecture in New Delhi on 5 November. India was Foot's favourite foreign country: he had been enrolled, along with the Conservative MP Reginald Maudling, as a Vice-President of an all-party British Indian Association a year earlier. Central to his view of India was his passionate admiration for the Nehru dynasty, including the Congress Prime Minister, Indira Gandhi. November 1976, however, was a bad time to sing her praises. Following direct action by dissident groups, notably what were termed 'Sikh extremists', Mrs Gandhi had declared a State of Emergency in 1975. This democratic paradigm amongst the emerging nations now saw government increasingly run by 'committed' judges and civil servants, opposition leaders thrown into jail, press censorship imposed partly through cutting off electricity supplies to the main Delhi newspapers, and around 110,000 people thrown into prison without trial. When the courts condemned Mrs Gandhi for unconstitutional conduct and sought to deny her public office, she tampered with the constitution by passing legislation to deny the Supreme Court powers of judicial review. By the time Foot arrived India was in a state of turmoil, with some shocking cases of malpractice, including the imprisonment of the Socialist Party leader George Fernandes, and stories of prisoners appearing in court in chains. Even more disturbing, Indira's son Sanjay (who held no elected position in government) began a programme of sterilization, and used financial and other methods of enforcing vasectomies. There was an outcry from socialist circles around the world, including Britain.

Foot had been cautioned by the Foreign Office not to embroil himself in the internal conflicts in India. In fact, he did the complete opposite. Following an official lunch with Indira Gandhi, he declared robustly that the Emergency was entirely justified in the light of the seditious threats faced by the Indian democracy. Foot was a great hero in India, and his support for the State of Emergency, delivered without qualification or reservation, caused shock and anger. Some years later the historian E. P. Thompson would write that the news that Foot had endorsed the Gandhi regime was 'devastating'; at that time her only supporters were the Indian Communists, 'perhaps the most slavish and unreconstructed Stalinist CP in the world'.[29]

India, the beacon of hope for progressives everywhere, had apparently turned into something approaching an authoritarian tyranny. The historian Professor Judith Brown described Mrs Gandhi at this time as 'isolating herself from the harsh realities of public dissent and fear, and probably from the truth about the acts of oppression and the destruction of personal liberty and integrity done in the name of her government'. The Indian historian Ramachandra Guha has added that the decline in Pandit Nehru's reputation after his death was partly due to the misdeeds of his daughter: 'His Congress was a decentralized, democratic organization, her Congress was a one-woman show,' which Indira Gandhi converted into a corrupt 'family business'. Foot kept up his close connections with India, and later on in *Dr Strangelove, I Presume?* (1999) he appeared very mildly to admit that he might have gone too far in his support of Mrs Gandhi at this time.[30] But he defended her by claiming that without the measures she took, the Indian state might have dissolved. He said she listened carefully to the concerns he had privately expressed – and had satisfied them, evidently. At an India League reception in London on 6 January 1977 he renewed his strong support for Mrs Gandhi's regime, and denounced criticism of her from Bernard Levin in the London press as a 'monstrous lie'. He also regarded it as a cause for praise that she had belatedly offered to hold a general election after all in 1977 – in which, to the great surprise of the Congress, she was heavily defeated despite much government pressure on voters. Foot also praised her, somewhat surprisingly, for accepting the verdict of the electorate and resigning office. He continued to support the Congress campaign against what were thought of as terrorist minorities. Thus in the early and mid 1980s he was involved with Indira's successor as Prime Minister, her son Rajiv, in trying to get the Thatcher government to take action against Sikh militant groups operating from Britain.[31]

Foot's view of India was idealistic. But several Indian friends such as the old *Tribune* cartoonist Abu thought that with his defence of Mrs Gandhi he had blundered, on the basis of one-sided and limited information, and out of blind loyalty to the Nehrus, whom he seemed to regard as incapable of error. He was strongly attacked by old comrades like James and Moni Cameron, and Frank Cousins. Moni Cameron was disturbed that Foot's speech in London on India's Republic Day in February 1976 failed to condemn 'so much indefensible repression', though they remained good friends. Foot had the particular embarrassment of meeting George Fernandes at the 1977 Labour Party conference, and listening to protests from the Secretary of the Socialist Party of India, Mehar Chand Yadev. His radicalism had seemingly lost its sheen through his impulsive intervention in Indian affairs. In the *Times of India* he had strongly denied that India was a dictatorship at a time when it was manifestly, for the moment at least, a one-party state.[32] It seemed strange to many of his admirers that the disciple of Hazlitt, Byron and Heine should seek to justify the suspension of democratic freedoms and the rule of law for the sake of *raisons d'état*. To that degree the visit of Mrs Gandhi to open Swraj Paul's steelworks in Ebbw Vale in November 1978[33] was less an honour than an embarrassment.

Foot returned from India to a mighty crisis at home that would define the entire course of the Callaghan government. By November 1976, negotiations were well under way with the International Monetary Fund to try to bail out the British economy. All other approaches had failed, including private initiatives by Callaghan to try to get assistance from the United States or from his friend Helmut Schmidt in Germany. The question was what terms, in other words what scale of public expenditure cuts, would accompany an IMF loan. Cabinet ministers with long memories, including Callaghan and Foot, talked gloomily of Ramsay MacDonald in 1931, when Labour had been divided and forced out of office amidst a financial and political catastrophe. From 23 November until the resolution of the crisis on

14 December Callaghan held a series of almost daily exhaustive Cabinets to consider the cuts proposed by the IMF.[34] There were four groups amongst ministers: the Treasury view, represented by Healey, Edmund Dell, Joel Barnett and Reg Prentice; a social democratic group of Keynesian expansionists, headed by Tony Crosland and including Shirley Williams, Harold Lever, Fred Mulley, William Rodgers and the newly promoted Secretary for Prices and Consumer Protection Roy Hattersley; Callaghan himself, keeping his own counsel, but with ministers who would follow his lead, Merlyn Rees, Lord Elwyn-Jones, Fred Peart, Eric Varley, Roy Mason, John Morris and Bruce Millan; and a left-wing group of Benn, Foot, John Silkin, Peter Shore, Albert Booth and Stan Orme. The debate went on and on about the level and type of cuts which might be acceptable. The left-wing group tended to endorse the 'alternative economic strategy' of no or few cuts, and a near-siege economy including import controls. Foot went along with this.

However, the left group of ministers was less unified than it seemed. Silkin, Booth, Shore and (more doubtfully) Orme were essentially Foot men rather than Bennites. Foot wanted the very minimum of cuts, but he also wanted to keep the government together, and the party unified at a time of economic peril. He intervened infrequently in the Cabinet discussions: he was not a specialist economist, and lacked the authority of Crosland or Shore. But his was also an important influence: the fact that he kept no diary has swayed some of the historians of the IMF crisis, perhaps unduly influenced by the diaries of Edmund Dell and Tony Benn, whose roles in the crisis were ultimately not decisive. Callaghan, with much skill, kept his views to himself as the discussion ground on and the terms demanded by the IMF were exhaustively investigated. Finally, on 2 December, Healey proposed cuts which he believed the IMF would accept – £1 billion in public sector borrowing requirement for 1977–78, plus the raising of £500 million from the sale of Burmah Oil shares, and other cuts of £1.5 billion for 1978–79. It was impossible to argue that this was another 1931, and Callaghan, as arranged, declared his support for the Treasury team. He had told Crosland on a flight back from a European finance ministers' meeting in the Netherlands that a modified IMF loan would be the best solution, and that he would be backing Healey.

In effect he was urging Crosland, a strong Keynesian, to do the same, and Crosland did so, with immense reluctance.[35]

Roy Hattersley, at forty-four the youngest member of the Cabinet, was the last minister to fall into line. His later judgement was that Foot's final intervention in Cabinet, urging them all to pull together for the sake of the Labour movement, was a decisive moment. Tom McNally, Callaghan's shrewd political adviser, saw the group of right-wing Keynesian ministers – Crosland, Hattersley, Williams – as fundamentally more inflexible than those on the left.[36] Foot spoke with deep feeling in Cabinet on 2 December, his first intervention for many days. According to Callaghan's diary, he told the Prime Minister that the proposed cuts of £2 billion, which would mean reductions in unemployment and other social benefits, along with a rise in unemployment to 1.75 million, were unacceptable. They risked creating a huge split in the party and a breach with the trade unions: 'There was a whiff of 1931 in the air.' But his alternative proposals were almost a cry of hopelessness: 'Go back to the IMF with a different package, propose a few cuts . . . plus the protection of the exchange rate as Tony Benn suggested.' After further debate, however, Foot was content to insist on it being recorded that the decision was the view of only a majority of the Cabinet, and that judgement be deferred until the details of the final package were known. In effect, Foot and his friends had given way to the Treasury.[37] At a meeting of a group of five left-wing ministers on 6 December, Foot made it clear that he would not be resigning. In the light of this, Silkin, Shore and Booth, together with Orme after some hesitation, also took this view. The next morning, when Callaghan lost his temper about possible Cabinet resignations (almost certainly a prearranged tantrum), Foot at once intervened to smooth things over as a loyal deputy should.[38]

After that, negotiations with the IMF moved rapidly. Social benefits did not suffer; the defence budget did. The parliamentary party, almost punch-drunk, accepted the terms with something like relief. A week later the IMF crisis was over, a great triumph of political management for Callaghan. There had been no 1931 after all; the cuts were severe but manageable; unlike 1931, social benefits had been protected. Thereafter, the economy entered upon eighteen months of remarkable stability, and the paying-off of the IMF loan (Denis Healey's famous

'Sod Off Day') was soon achieved, with the balance of payments again in surplus and the pound rising in value to $US1.90, higher than Healey wanted, in fact. It turned out that, as many had forecast, the Treasury's predicted statistics were far too pessimistic. In 1977–78 the Public Sector Borrowing Requirement proved to be only £8.5 billion, rather than the £10.5 billion estimated by the Treasury mandarins. But within Callaghan's Cabinet, the centre had held. Michael Foot, one of the less heralded players in the drama, was important in ensuring that it had. Indeed, the Chief Secretary to the Treasury, Joel Barnett, who was responsible for ensuring that the public expenditure cuts following the IMF settlement were actually carried out, was struck by Foot's making no difficulty at all over any of them. He showed himself to be, thought Barnett, 'a realist'.[39]

Early in 1977 the government moved from a financial crisis to a political one. Labour was a minority government, dependent on small splinter groups of MPs, and simply had no reliable majority. Unusually, it seemed that their continuing in office might depend on the course of any one debate. This gave ample scope for Foot's powers of rhetoric and abuse of the Tory enemy. A particular foe was Norman Tebbit, a rising Conservative and a dangerous opponent on union matters since he was that *rara avis*, a working-class Tory and, what is more, a former trade union activist in BALPA, the British Airline Pilots' Association. He attacked Foot strongly over the dismissal of the so-called Ferry-bridge Six, power-station workers who had lost their jobs after refusing to join a closed shop and were then denied unemployment benefit. On 1 November 1975, he denounced this as 'pure undiluted fascism' which left Foot 'exposed as a bitter enemy of freedom and liberty'. In retaliation, in the debate on the Queen's Speech on 30 November Foot replied in kind, referring to Tebbit as 'the most studiously offensive member of the House. He does not even have to rise to his feet to sustain his reputation.' On a later, more famous occasion he dismissed Tebbit as 'a semi-house-trained polecat'. Tebbit commented in his memoirs that he never recalled sharing a conversation with Foot: 'He was always too securely wrapped up in the armour of self-righteousness – the uniform of the arrogant middle-class intellectuals.' However, the bad blood between the two could be diluted. Years later, when he went to the House of Lords, Tebbit actually negotiated with Garter King of Arms that his coat of arms should include a polecat, a choice that reflects well on his sense of humour.[40]

Things reached a climax on 17 March 1977, when Callaghan learned that all the variegated opposition parties would unite against the government in a no confidence vote. After recent by-election defeats and Tony Crosland's death, that meant that the government would lose. So Labour had no alternative but to abstain, allowing a Conservative motion on public expenditure cuts to be carried by 293 to none. The Conservative leader Margaret Thatcher then announced that the Conservatives were tabling a motion of no confidence for 23 March, which the government could be expected to lose, thus triggering a general election. With devolution in the melting pot, neither the Scottish nor the Welsh Nationalist MPs could be relied upon to support Labour. Approaches were made to the ten Ulster Unionist MPs, and Foot held talks with their spokesmen James Molyneaux and Enoch Powell about possibly increasing Northern Irish parliamentary representation at Westminster, but nothing conclusive emerged from this. The Irish Secretary, Roy Mason, had relatively poor relations with the Ulster Unionists, and virtually glacial ones with Gerry Fitt and the Catholic SDLP. Foot told him that the government could not go back on the idea of a Speaker's Conference to consider Northern Ireland's representation in Westminster, nor offer proportional representation (in the form of a single transferable vote) for the European elections in Northern Ireland to please the Catholic SDLP.[41] Foot's own relations with the various groups in Northern Ireland were much better, given his friendships with both Gerry Fitt of the SDLP and Enoch Powell amongst the Unionists. His standing in the Province was such that he would have been sent to the Northern Ireland Office had Labour won the general election in 1979.[42] But for the moment there was nothing positive he could offer.

However, there was one possible lifeline for the beleaguered Callaghan government, and it was Michael Foot who went some way towards supplying it. The only remaining alternative to parliamentary defeat was a pact with the thirteen Liberals, now under the shrewd tactical leadership of David Steel, who had taken over from Jo Grimond in 1976. They were a mixed lot ideologically, but most were not too distant from Labour, including Steel himself. Foot was not the first to establish contact with the Liberals: that seems to have arisen from meetings between two redoubtable products of the Aberystwyth University law school, Cledwyn Hughes, Chairman of the Parliamentary Labour Party, and the Liberal MP Emlyn Hooson. But Foot, who knew both well as fellow Welsh Members, gave them ample encouragement, and on 18 March Callaghan asked him and Hughes to make formal overtures to David Steel.[43] After further desperate telephone diplomacy over the weekend, on Monday, 21 March 1977 Steel made his offer to Callaghan about a possible pact. His first approach was unpromising, since Callaghan was much angered by the terms contained in Steel's letter, which seemed to conflict with the government's authority over policy, and furiously threw it to the floor. But others, including Kenneth Stowe, his Private Secretary, and his Press Officer Tom McCaffrey retrieved it and persuaded him to calm down. Callaghan and Steel had a very friendly meeting later that day. At some stage there seems even to have been a suggestion that Steel might join the government.[44] The next day Foot had two pivotal meetings with Steel, at 12.30 p. m. and 6 p. m., which went well, even on the touchy subject of Europe.[45] That evening it was clear that a Lib–Lab pact had been born.

There were four policy proposals contained in the pact. There would be a consultative committee between the two parties, to which any major departmental Bill would be referred: Foot would chair this. There would be regular meetings between Healey and the Liberals' economic spokesman, John Pardoe – meetings which turned out to be noisily combustible. There would be rapid progress on Welsh and Scottish devolution, which would be separated into two measures, not one. On Europe, the most difficult problem, it was agreed that there would eventually be direct elections to the European Parliament, with the voting system, PR or otherwise, to be decided later.[46] In the event, on a free vote, Foot was to support PR, which however a majority in the Commons rejected.[47] On the morning of 23 March, before the no-confidence debate, the Cabinet discussed whether to accept the pact. Foot, according to Tony Benn's diary, looked pale and drawn. But Callaghan put the case for a pact with great power. Healey endorsed what he said, and observed that a deal with 'Nats and nutters' was the only alternative. In the end, the Cabinet endorsed the pact by twenty to four, the dissentients being Shore, Benn, Orme and, surprisingly, Bruce Millan, the Scottish Secretary. Another left-winger, Albert Booth, had been persuaded by Foot to vote with the majority. Foot himself spoke firmly for it, saying the government could emerge stronger and stay in power longer. Callaghan's personal note on the Cabinet meeting included the entry: '*Foot*. Get 18 months agreement with Liberals. Healey too cautious.'[48] Later that day, the government won the no-confidence vote by 322 votes to 298. All thirteen Liberals voted for the government, David Steel talking of the need for 'stability', and three Ulster Unionists (including Enoch Powell) abstained. The Scottish Nationalists and (more surprisingly) Plaid Cymru voted with the Conservatives. In his winding-up speech, Foot had stoutly defended the pact: there was 'no question of coalition'. The political crisis, like the economic one, was over for the time being.

The Callaghan government thus had an assured lease of life. The prospect of defeat in the Commons in the near future had disappeared. Callaghan and Steel built up a good, father-and-son-type, relationship. The pact proved to be much to Labour's advantage, since it had conceded little of substance on policy. The Liberals gained an improvement in status – along with the promise of government soft-pedalling on tricky issues, of which the most delicate was a possible inquiry into the behaviour of the party's former leader, Jeremy Thorpe, who had been forced to resign after a scandal involving homosexuality, blackmail and conspiracy to murder. For Michael Foot, it was an important turning of the ways. Tony Benn was furious with him, and considered that Foot had broken his word. At dinner with Foot on Sunday, 20 March Foot had referred only to a pact with the Ulster Unionists, not the Liberals. Benn wrote in his diary: 'Jim and Michael have negotiated something absolutely contrary to what Michael told me on Sunday night.' The rift between the two, as putative leaders of the left, began at this point. The sons of two earlier eminent Liberal MPs now clashed fundamentally.[49] But Foot had no regrets. It had been a case of political necessity and simple parliamentary arithmetic. He was a socialist, not a Liberal. But he was not an anti-Liberal either – how could he be, with his political and family background? The disciple of Lloyd George, the protégé of Beaverbrook and the good friend of Enoch Powell was hardly tribal in his political associations, for all his vehement socialism. On most current issues, Europe aside, there was little enough policy difference between him and Steel. Public ownership had been left out of the pact entirely. During their discussion the Liberal leader noted the political strength of Foot, and how Callaghan tended to defer to him.

From the start, Michael Foot was the man who gave the Lib–Lab pact its essential dynamism, who chaired the key inter-party committees, who saw Steel regularly in one-on-one meetings, and who was, in Steel's words, 'the front man' throughout.[50] Foot wanted the pact to go on and on – he greeted the Liberals' decision to end it in the summer of 1978 with dismay. It was a fudge, but an essential one to retrieve what was left of Foot's democratic socialist mission. His break with his family's ancestral Liberalism back in 1934 had caused a shock at the time. But he was also a key player in breathing new life, if only briefly, into the noble pre-1914 cause of the Progressive Alliance between the Liberal and Labour parties.

Michael Foot's career at this time was concerned with more than ministerial fixes. It was also absorbed by a major legislative issue of fundamental importance, that of devolution for Scotland and Wales.[51] Devolution had been on the political agenda since the nationalist by-election successes in the later 1960s. In Wales, Gwynfor Evans had won Carmarthen for Plaid Cymru in 1966, and the party had polled astonishingly strongly in Rhondda East and Caerphilly, two apparently impregnable Labour citadels. The veteran Labour MP James Griffiths had been persuaded to stay on in the House until 1970 lest a Welsh nationalist threaten his Llanelli constituency, with its many Welsh-speaking voters. Ebbw Vale, in anglicized Gwent, was not vulnerable to a nationalist challenge, but even there Plaid Cymru, as a non-Tory alternative to Labour, had made headway on the local authority in Rhymney, the most Welsh part of the constituency. In Scotland, the Scottish Nationalists in the person of Winnie Ewing had won Hamilton in 1967, in 1970 they won the Western Isles, and in 1973 in another by-election Margo MacDonald won the rock-solid Labour seat of Glasgow, Govan. Their tally of seats had risen to eleven in the October 1974 general election: Plaid Cymru had three, all in rural Wales. After forty years of unionism and basically two-party politics, a political transformation seemed to be at hand.

This caused panic in Transport House, and indeed in Labour's Welsh headquarters in Charles Street, Cardiff, too. If they lost their Scottish and Welsh heartlands, fundamental to their vote since 1918, no Labour government could ever be elected at all. Harold Wilson, much concerned, had appointed a Royal Commission in 1968 to examine devolution and the structure of the constitution generally, under the chairmanship of Geoffrey Crowther. When Crowther died he was succeeded by Lord Kilbrandon, whose commission produced two reports in 1973. A majority proposed an elected Scottish Parliament in Edinburgh with primary legislative powers, and an elected Welsh Assembly in Cardiff which would have only executive powers in spending a block grant from Whitehall on domestic areas of policy.

The government was divided in its views. Some members of the Cabinet were strongly hostile, notably Willie Ross, the Secretary of State for Scotland. Major figures like Callaghan, Healey and Crosland were scarcely even lukewarm. Others, like William Rodgers, Member for Stockton-on-Tees, tended to oppose proposals that might give advantages to Scotland and Wales, for example in regional assistance, over regions like the north-east of England. But political circumstances made proposals for devolution inevitable: the relevant minister at the time, the Lord President, Ted Short, a laconic man, seemed to feel that achieving devolution might give him his niche in history.[52] The government published a White Paper, *Democracy and Devolution*, in September 1974, just before the general election, committing itself to the Kilbrandon proposals, without a reduction in either Scottish or Welsh representation at Westminster. It was now poised to bring a joint Scottish and Welsh Bill before Parliament. The minister responsible for this massive departure from a thousand years of governmental centralization in Britain was now Michael Foot.

Devolution was not an issue to which he had devoted any attention earlier in his career. His hero, Aneurin Bevan, had been strongly centralist, on the grounds that socialist policies should be implemented equally in all parts of the kingdom. Bevan was a nationalizer, most obviously in the case of the National Health Service, where the hospitals had been taken out of the hands of the local authorities to be centrally administered. Constitutionally, he was a unionist who despised any concession to nationalism. He had spoken in the Commons during the first 'Welsh day' debate in 1944 against the notion of having such a day at all. He had also attacked the proposal to have a Welsh Secretary of State, which first appeared in Labour's manifesto in 1959.[53] There is no evidence that Michael Foot, for all his one-time Liberalism, differed from this view; indeed he had attacked the idea of devolution as divisive in the *Daily Herald*.[54] Certainly, devolutionist views would not bring him any votes in Ebbw Vale. No pronouncement of his on devolution in Parliament can be detected prior to 1970.

However, he responded positively to the evidence of sympathy for devolution in Wales and more especially Scotland in the early 1970s: it could be recalled that old Labour heroes like Keir Hardie and George Lansbury had supported devolution and the idea of localized democracy, as against the bureaucratic centralism of the German SPD.[55] A historically minded socialist like Foot could argue that Labour was coming home, returning to its own philosophical traditions: the Fabians had championed municipal socialism, and the Independent Labour Party, with its various Scottish and Welsh supporters, was devolutionist. His first thought was to call his two Bills 'Home Rule' Bills, with echoes of Gladstone's crusade for Irish self-government, but the Cabinet overruled him. While Scotland was clearly the more enthusiastic for devolution, Foot also had enormous enthusiasm for the Welsh people, not only their instinctive socialism and egalitarianism, but also their vibrant culture and enthusiasm for their language. In later years he was to listen with rapt enthusiasm when the present author and Foot's housekeepers conversed in Welsh. Jill Craigie was even more pro-Welsh than Michael. They might both have reflected on Nye Bevan's observation – 'The Welsh are good, boy, but they're not that good.' The notion of pluralism and a multicultural identity was naturally appealing to Foot. Therefore he took over the entire idea of devolution with all the zeal of a convert. It was an important development. Even if devolution failed in his own time in government, Foot did launch a great debate about participatory democracy in Britain. Two decades later the Blair government was to pursue this much more systematically, and devolution was pushed through and ratified in referendums in both Scotland and Wales in 1997. The concept of a United Kingdom was then transformed for ever.

To prepare legislation, Foot had set up a major Constitutional Unit of the Cabinet Office within his remit as Lord President. It was a self-contained unit of around thirty civil servants, chaired by Sir John Garlick. There were three Under-Secretaries: Michael Quinlan (who dealt with social and constitutional aspects), Stuart Scott-Whyte (economic aspects) and Gordon Gammie (legal aspects).[56] The most powerful of these was Quinlan, whose role was to shape and coordinate legislation, and of course to direct matters with Michael Foot. John Smith, the Minister of State, would take devolution in Commons committee, but devolution would ultimately be the responsibility of the Lord President.

Quinlan and Foot did not have a straightforward relationship. Quinlan liked Foot personally, as a cultured and intelligent man, even if he thought he was 'not a natural minister', and Foot had a high regard for Quinlan's abilities. Foot showed 'patience and kindness', Quinlan felt, when the Devolution Bill was going through the House – and indeed a good deal of personal resilience when he suffered from an unpleasant attack of shingles at the time. But the Civil Service machine was in many ways going through the motions, without commitment. Quinlan himself was not in sympathy with the Devolution Bill on which he worked. He felt that the entire exercise showed 'Whitehall working well without conviction'.[57] John Morris, Secretary of State for Wales, observed that 'the whole of Whitehall was against devolution', as was graphically shown during a civil servants' gathering at Sunningdale.[58] One of those present believed, with good reason, that the Devolution Bill on which he worked in 1976–77 was a great mess, and far too complicated. Another thought the Bill was 'constipated', and would never have worked.[59] The Cabinet Committee on devolution, chaired by Shirley Williams, the civil servants saw as basically 'an instrument for moaning'. The Welsh proposals, half-hearted as they were, were especially confusing, despite the Herculean efforts to make sense of them by the government's legal adviser, Gwilym Prys-Davies. Quinlan moved on in February 1977, to the Department of Defence. He had been scheduled to go in December 1976, but the position of the Bill in the Commons was too delicate at that stage. It may be guessed that he left the Constitutional Unit in a mood of some relief.

More surprisingly, perhaps, certain civil servants felt that Foot himself had no great enthusiasm for the Bill either. This was a view shared by Tony Benn, who thought Foot was 'bored' by devolution. Certainly it was not a topic to which he had given his mind before, and he was far less involved in it than he had been in defending the trade unions with his labour legislation in 1974–76. The Secretary of the Cabinet, John Hunt, felt that Foot, as chairman of committees at least, tended to rely unduly on his brief – though it should be said that Hunt sprayed around criticisms of other ministers too, including Rees, Owen, Shore and Shirley Williams.[60] Many of the official meetings on aspects of devolution seemed to Foot to be extremely boring – perhaps because they were. During such meetings the television set in the Lord President's office seemed to be switched on a great deal, covering events in the 1976 Test series between England and the West Indies.[61] Meetings on such matters as the possible tax-raising powers of the Scottish Assembly tended to be interrupted by the Secretary of State shouting out excitedly at the fall of a wicket. Cabinet committees on the Devolution Bill were complicated and immensely tedious: ministers were unenthusiastic about serving on them. Foot approached the devolution measure with the broadest of brushes. Many of its aspects were highly arcane or legalistic. It is not evident that he made any intellectual imprint on the Bill. On the other hand, he showed much persistence and great loyalty to the Celtic nations in pressing ahead with the Bill despite immense discouragement. Much of his work on behalf of devolution was at the level of private parliamentary discussions and arm-twisting, activities of which the civil servants would have been unaware. Even if Foot was not always intellectually engaged, he certainly was emotionally engaged, and prepared to take on all comers in defending his Bill.

The Scottish and Welsh Devolution Bill made very faltering progress in that hung Parliament. The Scottish Bill was especially long and needlessly complicated, the result of lengthy discussions between the Constitutional Unit and the Scottish Office over the precise boundaries, and what powers should be retained by the Scottish Office. The logical answer, that it had no reason to continue in being, was not offered at this stage. There were still turf wars between Quinlan and the senior Civil Service draughtsman, Henry Rose, who was 'rather peppery'.[62]

Whatever the arguments behind the scenes, in the Commons

chamber things were worse still. Both Labour and the Conservatives were divided on the question of devolution, while the Liberals and nationalists tended to argue that the Bill was far too weak. There was much opposition to Foot's measure within the Labour Party, especially from English MPs in regions such as the north-east and north-west. One opponent was Eric Heffer, a Liverpool MP and a close associate of Michael Foot: MPs on both the left and the right were resistant. A number of Scottish Labour MPs were hostile to devolution, among them Robin Cook and Tam Dalyell; the latter posed his famous, and logically unanswerable, 'West Lothian question' about why Scottish MPs would be able to vote on English questions after devolution, whereas Scottish matters would be kept free of English interference. Thirty years on, the Blair government had no answer. Lord Irvine, the dynamic architect of the devolution settlement of 1997–99, memorably observed that the best way of dealing with the West Lothian question was not to ask it at all.

In Wales, five south Wales Labour MPs opposed devolution, which they saw as damaging to British domestic policy-making and in any case a sop to nationalists, who spoke Welsh, which none of them did. The five included some close friends of Michael Foot such as Leo Abse, the Member for Pontypool and a fierce critic of the motives of advocates of devolution in parts of rural, Welsh-speaking Wales. More serious was the defection of Foot's young friend, political neighbour and protégé Neil Kinnock, whom Michael and Jill both saw as a future Nye Bevan. Kinnock blankly declared 'I am a Unionist,' cited Bevan in his support (correctly so), and opposed devolution at every opportunity. His wife Glenys, a friend of Jill and a Welsh-speaker from Holyhead, Anglesey, had a ferocious animosity towards the local Plaid Cymru activists there.[63] The Foots' relations with the Kinnocks remained astonishingly amicable despite this serious political rift, which does much credit to all four of them.

The second reading of the Devolution Bill was passed comfortably on 13 December 1976, by 294 votes to 249. Ten Labour MPs voted against it, and another forty-five abstained or were paired. Five Conservatives voted for the Bill, while forty-two abstained or were paired, including the party leader Edward Heath. The Liberals voted for it, of course, but David Steel threatened that they would oppose it in committee unless the government granted PR in Scottish and Welsh elections, and gave the Scottish Parliament powers to raise revenue through taxes. The committee stage was bumpy throughout. On 10 February 1977 the government was forced to accept an amendment by Leo Abse, signed by eighty Labour MPs, for referendums in both Scotland and Wales before devolution came into operation. This meant that the fourteen nationalists would be likely to vote against the Bill. Foot now had to consider imposing a guillotine to curtail debate in order to get the Bill through – something which was always anathema to him, and which he had persistently opposed as a backbencher himself. But on 22 February the guillotine motion was defeated by 312 to 283, with twenty-two Labour MPs voting against, and another twenty-three abstaining. Michael Quinlan's office staff held a sweepstake on the likely majority against the motion.[64] He did not prophesy twenty-nine as the figure, but was certain that it would be lost. The defeat was a considerable setback for Labour's programme, and left John Smith in particular in a mood of some depression. But eventually Foot announced in July that the government would try again, with two separate Bills this time, a proposition against which he had previously argued with much fervour. The Liberals complained, not least because this pushed their vision of a federal Britain very far into an undiscernible future, but they had no choice but to agree.

On 14 and 15 November 1977 the two separate Bills for Scotland and Wales passed their second reading in the Commons, with only sixteen of the forty-five Labour dissentients of February withholding their votes. But there were still shoals ahead. There was much animation in the lobbies and in Annie's Bar, notably amongst the convivial Scottish Nationalist MPs. For them, wrote the equally convivial political commentator Alan Watkins, every night was Burns Night.[65] On 25 January 1978 (which actually was Burns Night) a potentially disastrous amendment was carried against the government. It was the work of George Cunningham, a Scottish Labour MP who sat for an Islington seat in London, and laid down that devolution would be carried only if 40 per cent of the voters on the electoral register supported it, rather than a simple majority of those who voted. It was carried by 166 to 151, with the Conservatives abstaining. This proposal, which became Section 85(2) of the Scotland Act, made the hurdle for achieving devolution much higher – indeed, in Wales quite impossibly higher. The most that could be argued, as Foot did, was that the referendum was advisory and not mandatory – the Secretary of State was required to lay down an order to repeal the decision if the vote in favour of devolution was below 40 per cent of those on the register, an aspect which Foot was to focus on in the last stages of the Callaghan government.[66] In early May 1978 the two Devolution Bills were carried, and they received the royal assent on 31 July. Some Welsh Members sang their national anthem 'Yr Hen Wlad fy Nhadau'. It was indeed a constitutional landmark.

But it was likely to be a token one only. The referendums were eventually scheduled for St David's Day, 1 March 1979. By that time the government was to be engulfed in widespread industrial disputes which transcended the particular issues posed in the referendums. Locked-up schools and hospital wards, overflowing dustbins and unburied dead, the result of industrial action by the unions, overshadowed the minutiae of devolution. The government could not look forward to the result of the votes with any confidence. Polls showed that the cause was hopelessly lost in Wales, which had much the weaker urge for nationalism or separatism – after all, unlike Scotland, there had never been a Welsh state, and the various princedoms had been conquered by the English as long ago as 1283. Wales was never to establish a National Convention as Scotland was to do; there was little sense of Welsh citizenship. Michael Foot, therefore, had battled on, like Bunyan's pilgrim, against all discouragement. The Prime Minister, Jim Callaghan, showed no enthusiasm for devolution, and did nothing to campaign in either nation. Nor did ministers, either on the right or the left. The Chancellor Denis Healey and the Home Secretary Merlyn Rees, a Welshman, were no less tepid; Tony Benn, the great supporter of democratic participation, was relatively silent. Only the constituencies of the Scots and the Welsh were enthusiastic, and as has been seen, only some of them. Cledwyn Hughes wrote warmly in his diary of Foot's dedication to the cause:

> He has made a greater effort to understand us, and to meet Welsh aspirations than any other non-Welsh politician I have ever known. He has stood up to cruel attacks which would have

> daunted lesser men. Foot has won an honourable place in Welsh
> history whatever may come of this Bill.[67]

So he had, but it was manifestly a losing cause. Foot was to see his
project finally meet with victory in September 1997, triumphantly so
in Scotland, by the tiniest of margins in Wales. But at the time of the
Callaghan government devolution was largely seen, even in Scotland
and Wales, as a political distraction, an irrelevance at a time when the
country as a whole was facing crushing economic difficulties. Foot's
Bills were a testimony to his idealism, but not to his political judgement. Whatever his future place in history, in the context of the 1970s,
through no fault of his own, he was contributing to a debate that
further weakened a struggling government, and in the end contributed
directly to its fall from power.

In the summer of 1978, things were going much better for the
Callaghan government. The balance of payments and the value of the
pound had shown a steady improvement for the past eighteen months;
the trauma of the IMF crisis seemed very distant. The judgement of
Callaghan and Foot at that time had been fully vindicated. Callaghan
had grown in authority, and was widely endorsed as Prime Minister.
There was an encouraging record of economic recovery and new
initiatives of his own, such as the Ruskin Speech in October 1976 on
educational standards. The Prime Minister had added to his prestige
in foreign policy as a mediator between President Carter of the United
States and the Europeans, especially Helmut Schmidt, Chancellor of
Germany. His advice had been crucial in helping Carter to conclude
the Camp David Agreement between Egypt and Israel, which was
signed in September. In the peace of his Sussex farm during the month
of August, therefore, Callaghan meditated calling an early general
election in October. There was a strong reason for it, since the Liberals
had called an end to the Lib–Lab pact, which many of them had always
disliked, and the government's continuance in office was no longer
guaranteed. In fact the precariousness of Labour's position as a minority
government was even more pronounced, after a sequence of surprising
by-election defeats. There was a long-standing election team at the
ready, chaired by Derek Gladwin of the General and Municipal
Workers' Union (GMWU). Foot was a member of it.[68]

After discussing matters in a general way with TUC leaders, Calla-ghan consulted four key ministerial colleagues – the wrong four, in the view of Roy Hattersley. These were the Chancellor Denis Healey, the Foreign Secretary David Owen, the Home Secretary Merlyn Rees, and his trusty deputy Michael Foot. Healey gave no clear view, but felt there was no immediate financial reason for having an early poll. No new crises appeared to be around the corner. Owen was against, because of upcoming initiatives proposed to take on Rhodesia with the US Secretary of State, Cyrus Vance. Rees was opposed on grounds of general caution.

But Michael Foot was the most opposed of all.[69] He had pressed the case for carrying on through the winter as early as a meeting of the 'inner group' of ministers, including Callaghan, Healey and Rees, on 25 July. He then offered a series of arguments to Callaghan when he rang him at home during Sunday lunch on the August bank holiday weekend. Foot wanted to carry on with negotiations with friendly union leaders like David Basnett of the GMWU and Clive Jenkins of ASTMS, the more so as Jack Jones had retired as Secretary of the TGWU and had been succeeded by a Welsh former shop steward, Moss Evans. Evans commanded far less authority within a union in which Jones had promoted a more decentralized and pluralist structure. Foot was also in touch with MPs in marginal constituencies who were apprehensive. His fundamental point was that Labour had a mandate for a five-year Parliament, and that it should stay in office as long as possible to carry out its programme and await the benevolent advent of North Sea oil (even though any significant impact of oil on the balance of payments would not occur until after the next general election). It could carry on because the negotiations with the Ulster Unionists over increasing Northern Irish representation meant that there was a kind of 'Labour–Unionist pact' to replace the defunct Lib–Lab pact. Enoch Powell was not going to rock the boat. Callaghan was told by his Private Secretary, Kenneth Stowe, that Powell had called on his old friend Michael Foot on 3 August to say that the Unionists would not feel it right to bring down the government with the Northern Ireland Representation of the People Bill due to be included in the Queen's Speech. These were all matters of political calculation. But Bernard Donoughue felt it might also simply have been a case, with Foot as with Rees and Harold Lever, of an older man preferring to hang on. When he returned from a talk with Callaghan, Foot was overjoyed – 'We've won, we've won.'[70]

Callaghan was swayed by the views of his four senior Cabinet colleagues, even though almost every other minister, from Edmund Dell on the right to Tony Benn on the left, urged an early election. Only Eric Varley and Harold Lever amongst the others agreed with the arguments for delay. In a messy and unsatisfactory way, in which his customary political skills seemed to desert him, Callaghan then irritated the TUC Congress in early September with an unclear, almost frivolous speech in which he sang an old music-hall song, 'There was I, waiting at the church'. He did not, however, declare himself to be for or against an early election, although most commentators still assumed there would be one. Then he astounded the Cabinet and his own Political Office on 7 September by telling them there would be no autumn election, and that he had written to the Queen to tell her so. His calculation, based on his reading of psephological data, was that an early election would at best lead to another hung Parliament, with the findings of the polls particularly worrying for the pivotal West Midlands constituencies. There was, indeed, a good deal to be said for this analysis, even though it led to a sharp quarrel with Labour's private pollster, Bob Worcester of MORI. Significantly, Michael Foot had been the first to know. Callaghan had told him as early as 29 August that there would be no autumn election. Denis Healey and Callaghan's Press Officer Tom McCaffrey were told that he would make a statement on 7 September, but Callaghan did not say what it might contain. There could have been no stronger indication of Foot's absolute indispensability for the government's remaining in office.[71]

But the decision, and even more the unsatisfactory way in which it was announced, led to dismay and even demoralization in Labour's ranks. The finger of blame was pointed at over-cautious machine politicians, notably Michael Foot. The polls soon afterwards showed a Labour lead of 4 per cent, though its duration was very short-lived. The prevailing judgement later on was that Callaghan's caution or cowardice in not going to the polls had been the origin of Labour's defeat by Margaret Thatcher in May 1979. Neil Kinnock argued forcefully to Callaghan that the decision not to hold an election was a huge strategic mistake, since it left the government totally at the mercy of the nationalists and other small groups as soon as the Scottish and Welsh referendums were held on 1 March 1979. Callaghan's view can certainly be defended from the polling evidence available to him. All politicians naturally prefer to stay in office if the alternative is a possible or probable defeat. But the remaining period of the Callaghan government was one of continuous and demoralizing crisis.

By November, it was clear that a further year of wage restraint would be almost impossible. Angry exchanges at the party conference in October had confirmed the fact. In particular, low-paid public sector workers, who had in effect enjoyed no pay rise at all for three years, were deeply angry. As after any pay pause, of however long a duration, the dam was likely to burst. Callaghan's unexpected declaration in a radio interview in favour of a 5 per cent norm for wage increases (both Foot and Healey would have favoured 10 per cent) proved to be a major strategic blunder, and added significantly to the alienation of the unions. In fact it was far better-off workers like lorry drivers who led the way in strike action. A seven-week strike by TGWU workers at Ford Motors in October and November saw the pay norms shattered, with a pay rise of 17 per cent agreed with the employers. This was followed by another serious strike, by tanker drivers of four of the five main oil companies. The 'Neddy Six' of the TUC who sat on the National Economic Development Council seemed unable to exert control: key union leaders such as Alan Fisher of NUPE appeared oblivious to the need for any wage control at all.

The TUC General Council on 14 November failed to endorse its own proposals for 'Collective Bargaining, Costs and Prices'. Three supporters of the document failed to vote for it for a variety of reasons. Sid Weighell of the NUR, the railwaymen's union, was absent doing a broadcast. Bill Sirs, the distinctly right-wing leader of the steelworkers, actually voted against it because he did not wish to commit his union at that stage. Worse still, the TGWU's Moss Evans, who had appended his signature to the document, was not present since he was enjoying a pre-booked holiday in sunny Malta. The Chairman, Tom Jackson of the postal workers, another supporter of the document, refused to use his casting vote, and the result was a fourteen–fourteen tied vote, which meant the motion failed. There could hardly have been a clearer demonstration of incompetence and irresponsibility by the union leaders.[72]

By the end of the year there was a growing torrent of strikes, variously by oil tanker drivers, road haulage drivers, British Leyland production workers, water and sewage workers (whose industrial muscle had not hitherto been appreciated) and a wide miscellany of local authority manual workers. The government seemed unable to offer a lead. It was decided not to make the Ford settlement an issue of confidence by putting forward a motion in the Commons, as David Owen wanted – both Callaghan and Foot argued against. A number of Tribune group members argued against the government's pay restraint policy and abstained on the vote; among them was the future Deputy Prime Minister John Prescott. The government was defeated by 285 votes to 279, and financial penalties on Ford had to be withdrawn. Labour's problems were made worse by a series of quite unexpected political miscalculations by the normally shrewd Prime Minister. There followed in turn his almost off-the-cuff advocacy of a 5 per cent pay norm, without consulting the TUC, and then his unguarded words (perhaps significantly to a young woman journalist whose question irritated him) on returning to his frozen country suntanned from an international conference in Guadeloupe in January 1979. In disputing the view that there was chaos in the land, he used words which were translated in the popular press as 'Crisis, what crisis?' Callaghan shares slumped accordingly.

In January 1979 it looked as if there was indeed something close to industrial chaos as public sector workers stopped work. Hospital patients were unattended; vital anti-cancer drugs piled up on quaysides; schools were closed by striking caretakers or cooks; ambulances did not run; frozen roads were ungritted; dustbins were not emptied for weeks on end; on 21 January some gravediggers in Liverpool actually refused to bury the dead. Callaghan, a great patriot and also an old union stalwart seemingly betrayed by his own comrades, was in despair, the government machine in a state of total inertia. In later years he would say sadly, 'I let the country down.'[73] In February there was a slow return to work, and a 'Valentine's Day concordat' was cobbled together with the TUC on 14 February. But industry and public services appeared to be in chaos, the Labour Party incapable of disciplining the unions, and Britain seemingly facing its darkest hour since the war, unruly, near bankruptcy, 'as ungovernable as Chile', in the excited words of one American politician. Titles of books on recent British history at this time commonly included works like 'decline' or 'eclipse'.

Throughout this so-called 'winter of discontent' Michael Foot was a heroic but unavailing figure trying to stave off disaster. It was debatable whether he had anything new to offer now as an executive minister. Tom McNally believed that with the change of union leadership since the retirement of Jones and Scanlon, Foot no longer had any special status as a link to the unions. Bernard Donoughue suggested to Callaghan that he might refresh his government with a reshuffle, and appoint Foot as a libertarian Home Secretary.[74] This was an interesting thought, but in fact Callaghan made no changes other than replacing the Paymaster-General Edmund Dell when he took up a post in the City. Foot was eventually earmarked for a future move to the Northern Ireland Office. The government otherwise ground on somewhat fatalistically, with no innovations in sight: new policies suggested by the Prime Minister's think-tank, such as the sale of council houses, were deemed far too daring and unacceptable to the left. Foot slogged on as before in November and December 1978, spending much time in talks with union leaders. He urged upon them the government's commitment to a voluntary approach to wage bargaining through unfettered collective bargaining, to be underpinned by the unions showing moderation, restraint and loyalty to the Labour movement. He had more than one fierce row with Moss Evans, who like many union leaders seemed almost oblivious to the facts of escalating inflation.[75]

But in the end Foot too was caught up in the *anomie* of the administrative machine in January 1979 when, for days on end, government seemed to come to a halt. In a Cabinet meeting of 15 January he threw his weight against the calling of a state of emergency, including the use of troops to keep supplies flowing; this was in any case the majority view amongst despairing ministers. Foot took the opportunity to remind his colleagues that hundreds of thousands of trade unionists believed they had a just cause. He opposed any thought of changing trade union law. Secondary picketing, a major feature of all the strikes, was allowed under the Trade Disputes Act of 1906, the unions' Magna

Carta.[76] The government seemed to be drifting, its lease of office fast running out. Callaghan had a meeting with Foot, Healey, Varley and Booth on 22 January to consider ways of regaining the initiative, but it yielded nothing of substance. Foot made his usual spirited defence of government policy in the Commons debate on the Queen's Speech on 25 January. He admitted that they had considered imposing a state of emergency before Christmas, and would have sought to do so if the strikes then had gone on for forty-eight hours longer. Under the Tories, he said, there would have been no free collective bargaining, while their industrial proposals would have given great impetus to both secondary picketing and the spread of the closed shop.[77] Labour MPs had some oratory to cheer, but the overall mood was fatalistic, even after the strikers began to drift back to work in February. In Bernard Donoughue's vivid words, 'It was like being on board the sinking *Titanic* without the music.' Number 10 was enveloped in 'a sort of quiet despair'.[78]

The only area which brought Foot good cheer was the progress made over the Public Lending Right Bill, designed to offer some recompense to authors of books borrowed from public libraries. He had worked hard on this with the writers Brigid Brophy and Maureen Duffy of the Society of Authors after it had been 'talked out' by both Tory and Labour backbenchers in 1977. Elizabeth Thomas was also an important influence. The Bill was reintroduced at the end of 1978 and, through the calm guidance of John Smith, made it through the Commons swiftly a second time, and then the Lords, receiving the royal assent on 6 March 1979. The scheme proved to be a great success. The literary world, most appropriately for Michael Foot, was thus a beneficiary of his work in the Callaghan government, which was otherwise running into the sands.

Another serious crisis emerged on 1 March, when the referendums took place on Foot's Devolution Bills. In Wales the defeat was overwhelming, about four to one: only 11.8 per cent of the total electorate favoured it. Welsh devolution therefore disappeared as an issue. The Scottish referendum actually showed a majority for devolution, though by a narrow vote on a fairly low poll of 63 per cent. But only 32.85 per cent of the total Scottish electorate voted 'Yes', well below the 40 per cent stipulated by the Cunningham amendment, and that meant that devolution would lapse there too, unless the Lord President used his delaying powers by introducing a repeal order. The eleven Scottish Nationalist MPs then declared that they would vote against the government if it did not proceed with devolution: Callaghan was to deride this as 'turkeys voting for an early Christmas', but it did mean that the government could almost certainly be defeated in any Commons vote.

Foot was characteristically busy in negotiations to try to find a compromise. He was the only leading minister who actually believed in devolution, and was anxious to salvage something from the debris.[79] He argued that the referendums were consultative, not mandatory: ministers still retained some initiative, and the last act had not necessarily been played out. On Sunday, 4 March he rang Callaghan with an ingenious strategy for survival. Through this, the Commencement Order for the Scotland Act would be delayed, and would not be implemented until the start of the next parliamentary session in October, by which time the electorate would have been given an opportunity to consider the matter afresh. This became known as 'the Frankenstein solution', and only someone with Foot's encyclopaedic knowledge of parliamentary practice and procedure would have offered it. Although Callaghan received the idea without enthusiasm, Foot brought it up formally at a meeting of ministers on 5 March: he argued for delaying the Commencement Order, but putting forward a vote of confidence, in which the SNP would be politically obliged to support the government. Callaghan was negative. The plan was too convoluted, and he recalled the charges of gerrymandering made against him in 1969 when he delayed the redistribution of constituency boundaries for purely party reasons. The Scotland Act could not be forced through the House, but Callaghan then went off for private talks with David Steel to check out the Liberal attitude. On 8 March Foot returned to the charge in full Cabinet, arguing that rejecting the Scotland Act because of the referendum vote would merely be playing into the hands of the Scottish Nationalists.[80] But Callaghan again seemed fatalistic, and unable to respond to what he felt was an over-subtle policy which ordinary electors would not understand. On 15 March Foot took time off in Cabinet to call for the repeal of the Official Secrets Act, almost as a relaxation.[81]

Foot's last throw was on the evening of 21 March, after all other initiatives had failed, when he suggested that all-party talks be held and Repeal Orders be debated in the week beginning 7 May.[82] He argued that this offered a chance to take the initiative out of the hands of either the Tories or the Scottish Nationalists. Callaghan did not appear unsympathetic to Foot's ingenuity this time, but he rang Foot at home at 11.30 p.m. ('a late hour for him', wrote Foot) saying that it would not be right to proceed in this way.[83] Foot did not argue. The next morning, 22 March, apparently deliberately, Callaghan found time to see Foot on the upstairs landing of 10 Downing Street for only a minute or two before the morning Cabinet, and told him that the matter should be dropped. Effectively Foot was being told he was being too clever by half.

Foot wrote later, 'It seemed to me then . . . that his patience had suddenly snapped. He wanted to invite the election and the decision that would lead to it. It was in my opinion a considerable error.'[84] But in Cabinet Callaghan had his way: Roy Hattersley, who had some sympathy with Foot's ideas, felt the Prime Minister had decided to 'play the noble Roman' and await his fate.[85] A Tory motion of no confidence would now be debated on 28 March, and frantic discussions went on with Plaid Cymru, Ulster Unionists and other minority groups to try to stave off defeat. Every single vote was vital. On 26 March Callaghan urged at a meeting with Foot, Healey, Rees and Michael Cocks, the Chief Whip, that no further negotiations should take place with the smaller parties, but on this occasion he was overborne by his colleagues: Foot defended his discussions with the three Plaid Cymru MPs about a Bill to compensate slate quarrymen who were victims of silicosis – such talks were in no way 'discreditable'.[86] In the end the Plaid Cymru MPs did agree to support the government: it would be difficult for any Welsh MP to be seen to be levering the Tories into power. So also did two Scottish Labour MPs and two Ulster Unionists, safely shepherded through the lobbies by Hattersley. It would go right down to the wire.

In the end the government was sunk by two other factors – the fatal illness of a Labour MP, Sir Alfred Broughton, who was physically unable to come to vote, and the decision of Gerry Fitt of the normally pro-Labour SDLP to abstain, along with his Republican colleague Frank Maguire, a Fermanagh publican who made a rare journey across the Irish Sea to 'abstain in person'. Foot later came up with a number of subtle tactical scenarios which might perhaps have enabled defeat to be staved off by a vote or two.[87] The Tories' confidence motion could have been challenged by a government variant of it which would have left them isolated against all the other parties. Shirley Williams agreed with Foot's suggestion that the SNP might have been conciliated by the offer of any early date for the debate on the Repeal Order. But as for Callaghan, 'for one reason and another, many of them perfectly creditable, his patience *had* snapped'.[88] Foot himself made a brilliant and sparkling, if rambling, final speech to wind up the debate. It had little enough substance, but plenty of debating ammunition trained on the various opposition groups. The SNP were compared with the gladiators of ancient Rome addressing their Emperor: 'We who are about to die salute you.' He satirized David Steel, 'the boy David', for having 'passed from rising hope to elder statesman without any intervening period whatsoever'.[89] (When the Liberals' David Alton won a by-election in Liverpool from Labour the next day, Steel greeted Foot cheerfully, 'How's Goliath this morning?') But in the division the government met with defeat by just one vote, 311 to 310. For the first time since MacDonald in 1924, a government had fallen as the result of a defeat in a vote in the House of Commons. In view of Foot's extraordinary and selfless labours over the past two years, it was bitterly ironic that the government had in the end fallen not as a result of wars or even strikes, but because of 'ploughing the sands', the term the old Gladstonians had applied to pressing on with Irish home rule. In Foot's case it was the product of the thankless pursuit of Scottish devolution which had brought its main advocate down. To quote his old friend A. J. P. Taylor once again, it was one of history's 'curious twists'.

After his defeat in the Commons, Callaghan announced a general election. He then had a summit meeting with Foot, Healey, Merlyn Rees and the Whip, Michael Cocks: the election was called for 3 May. The campaign was preceded by difficult exchanges on the NEC, a harbinger of things to come, about the party manifesto. Here Callaghan, supported by Healey and usually Foot, refused to accept a series of radical socialist proposals from Benn, Heffer, Frank Allaun and others. One change that was endorsed was a proposal to abolish the House of Lords, supported by eleven votes to four, the majority on this occasion including Michael Foot.[90] But Callaghan issued a straight leader's veto, in a way that gave momentum to pressure for more grassroots democracy within the party, and more control for the left. There had been debate previously on the abolition of Clause Four. Now Clause Five, the drafting of the manifesto jointly by the National Executive and the party leadership, was equally under fire. Whatever the results of the election, the Labour Party would be racked with tension and crisis.

The five-week election campaign was desultory and disappointing. Labour focused heavily on Callaghan's personal popularity; he was projected as the custodian of one-nation values, a kind of Labour Disraeli. Margaret Thatcher was written off as an extremist, and perhaps in some quarters as a woman (Foot strongly disapproved of this, though he objected to her on almost all other grounds). Callaghan spoke of Labour creating a just, unified, cooperative society, and adopted a slogan of 'Fairness for All'. His press conferences, at which he was usually flanked by Healey, Hattersley and Shirley Williams, followed this line. Michael Foot made virtually no appearances there, or on television broadcasts. He was still thought of as an agitator who might scare the horses, not to mention the voters. His forte was, famously, nationwide stump speaking, and he threw himself into it with his usual gusto in a variety of industrial towns. He was clearly recognized now as one of Labour's strongest electoral assets amongst its own people, nationally celebrated and the darling of the parliamentary left. On *The World at One* on BBC radio he declared that voting Labour meant voting for an increasingly socialist Britain, more planning and a more democratic society. He launched a fierce broadside on Lord Justice Denning, who had said, in distinctly confused fashion, that the trade unions were almost above the law.[91] Foot's personal contest in Ebbw Vale, as always, presented no problems: he finished up with a majority of 16,091 over the Conservative Geoffrey Inkin, a substantial Monmouthshire farmer, with the Liberal and Plaid Cymru candidates losing their deposits. Foot's share of the poll fell slightly, to 69.1 per cent. Even in Ebbw Vale there were detectable, in minuscule form, the green shoots of Tory advance.

Nationally there was a predictable decline in Labour's vote. Callaghan never expected to win: he made a famous remark to Bernard

Donoughue towards the end of the campaign about the sea-change he observed in politics, whatever the politicians did: 'I suspect there is now such a sea-change – and it is for Mrs Thatcher.'[92] Labour's vote fell to 36.9 per cent, the party's worst result since 1931. The Conservatives ended up with 339 seats, Labour with 269. The Liberals won just eleven: the Lib–Lab pact had evidently done them no favours. Old Labour's last throw had failed. Jim Callaghan went back to his Sussex farm. For Michael Foot it was not all bad news: had Labour won he would have become Secretary of State for Northern Ireland, a bed of nails more painful than Employment had ever been.

Now he returned to the familiar pastures of opposition. A brief parliamentary session followed. There was a brisk passage of arms between Foot and Tony Benn when the latter announced that he was not going to stand for the Shadow Cabinet, but would campaign in the country instead. Foot thought this disloyal. Then there was a holiday in Venice for him and Jill to lick their wounds. And time to write another book.

Jim Callaghan, probably unwisely, decided to continue for a time as party leader. He remained, with Michael Foot as his deputy, for a further seventeen months, until October 1980. It is difficult to find a more dismal and depressing time in the history of the Labour Party. It was a period of almost unrelieved internal quarrelling. Callaghan argued, in somewhat illogical cricketing terminology, that he was 'taking the shine off the ball for Denis'. In fact he had the mortification of seeing almost the whole of his team, Michael Foot excepted, throw their wickets away.

In this depressing period, by far Foot's most enjoyable experience was writing and publishing another book, *Debts of Honour*, published again by his friend Reg Davis-Poynter in 1980. Much of it had been published in one form or another long before, in book reviews or brief essays. But it is still an enchanting volume, revealing of Foot's style and of his friends and heroes past and present. His heroes are literary and political, though it is clear that for Foot the categories merge into one common stream of aspiration. Of the fourteen people covered, the majority are dealt with in brief, affectionate sketches – Brailsford, Russell, Silone, Vicky and Randolph Churchill; Defoe, Paine and Hazlitt. The essay on Silone is particularly sensitive on his ideology as an ex-Communist, now treated in sympathetic detachment, on the lines of the post-war collection *The God that Failed*. There is a whimsical piece on Sarah, Duchess of Marlborough, put in as an afterthought to please Jill, who had complained that it was a book without a woman. It is interesting that he chose not to write about a suffragette – indeed he never did.[93]

The remaining four pieces are of more substance. His already celebrated essay on his father, previously published in both the *Evening Standard* and the *Daily Telegraph*, leads off: Isaac's personality and whims, especially as a bibliophile, set the tone for the book as a whole. The section devoted to Benjamin Disraeli, 'the good Tory', is largely a perceptive account of themes in his novels, although Foot also takes some time to defend Disraeli's principled radicalism in social matters and feminism from the charges made in Robert Blake's 1966 biography. Disraeli's institutional conservatism, and even more his imperialism, are ignored entirely. In much the most scholarly essay, a brilliantly written sketch, Dean Swift is treated in the round as essayist, satirist and (to a degree) as lover, and the opportunity is taken to dress down critics, mainly on the right, from Dr Johnson to right-wing Oxford dons in the 1970s. But the commanding essay is that on Lord Beaverbrook, 'The Case for Beelzebub'.[94] It includes much fascinating material on Foot's early acquaintance with his old master, from the time he joined the *Evening Standard* in the later 1930s. It is also totally uncritical, suffused with affection and gratitude towards one whom Foot still insisted was a genuine radical. No mention of, say, Munich, Empire or the election of 1945. He dwelled instead on his hero's unlikely friendships with men of the left like H. G. Wells and A. J. P. Taylor. Of Beaverbrook's personality, he wrote:

> It is to his humour we must always return. 'If Max gets to heaven,' wrote H. G. Wells, 'he won't last long. He'll be chucked out for trying to pull off a merger between Heaven and Hell . . . after having secured a controlling interest in key subsidiary companies in both places, of course.' But the merger had already taken place under his roof; a mixture of Heaven and Hell was what it could be like but, after some moments of Miltonic doubt about the outcome, it was usually Heaven which triumphed in that combat, and a Heaven too which no Calvinist

could recognize, one which was always liable to dissolve in laughter. Even at the gravest moment the chance of such a beneficent explosion would reappear, and the House of Rimmon might resound to the healing strains of 'The Red Flag', led, say, by another companion, treasured for company alone, say Stanley Morison of *The Times*, ex-jailbird, ex-pacifist, militant Catholic and, as far as I can recall, a light baritone . . . Not all the paroxysms of anger, of urgency, of frustration could shake those walls as the laughter did, and there was in it no vein of pretence or hysteria but rather a rich comic view of the human species. It could be called Dickensian or Chaplinesque were it not for the fact that Dickens and Chaplin, along with the Co-op or Covent Garden or the British Council, were listed among his absurd *bêtes noires*, and were it not that he lacked the last full measure of compassion which only the greatest comedians have. Anyhow, Beaverbrook's was a volcano of laughter which went on erupting till the end. No one who ever lodged beneath that Vesuvius will ever forget.

This was the fullest version yet of an unbreakable attachment, but many on the left still found Foot's view of his old patron hard to defend or even understand.

The book was widely commended by reviewers, with A. J. P. Taylor and Bernard Crick especially enthusiastic. It also had an inspirational effect on an idealistic young trainee barrister, Tony Blair. There is much in it for Foot's biographer, but mainly on his earlier years. His studies are either of dead authors or of people he first got to know in the 1930s. None of them had been active in recent Labour politics – because Foot, now in his mid-sixties, considered that his role in active politics was far from over.

That role mainly consisted in 1979–80 of trying to act as a stabilizing force, as Labour attempted to recover from the trauma of the seventies and the sense of failure or betrayal that decade left. The party was in fact in growing turmoil. From the late seventies a powerful grassroots movement on the left had been making headway amongst both the constituency parties and the unions. The winter of discontent and the revolt of the public sector workers had given it more headway. The main agency for protest was the Campaign for Labour Party Democracy (CLPD), founded in the early seventies by a young émigré

Czech, Vladimir Dederer. It argued that the failures of Labour in the seventies were the result of the lack of internal party democracy: Tony Benn and others on the Labour left who had pushed the cause of 'participation' enthusiastically took up the movement's demands, somewhat on the lines of critics amongst the left of the ILP before 1914.

There were three demands in particular: there should be mandatory reselection of MPs by constituency parties, rather than leaving them as virtual representatives for life; the party manifesto should be the work of the National Executive alone, rather than being written jointly by ministers, and subject to the party leader's veto if he wished to exercise it (as many believed Callaghan had done in April 1979); and the leader should be elected not by fellow MPs alone, but through an 'electoral college' with a heavy preponderance for the block votes of the trade unions, with constituency parties and associated socialist organizations receiving agreed smaller percentages.[95] Many in the party were alarmed by these proposals, seeing them either as basically anti-democratic or as calculated sops to the far left in constituency parties. Yet many in the party centre and right also recognized how stale, elitist and out of touch the leadership had become during the Wilson and Callaghan era, how party membership was falling inexorably, and how many local parties in inner cities were tiny, decaying or perhaps corrupt rumps, ripe for entryism by Trotskyists or others, the depressing remnants of what in 1945 had been a mighty mass party. The state of the party in the London dockside constituency of Bermondsey was sometimes mentioned as an illustration.

All these disputes surged to the fore at a venomous party conference in Brighton in October 1979. As luck had it, the Chairman was the veteran Frank Allaun, a former Communist and a bitter opponent of Callaghan and Healey. Callaghan was subjected to the most savage attack from the left, as the guilty man who had blocked socialism and been the cause of electoral defeat. A defeated left-wing former MP, Tom Litterick, complained angrily how 'Jim had fixed it' for him. The most ferocious attack of all on the party leader came, astonishingly, from the party General Secretary, Ron Hayward: 'I come not to praise Callaghan but to bury him [loud applause].' He wished that a Labour Prime Minister could act in Labour's interests the way that Tory Prime Ministers did for their people. A class-war rant from Derek Hatton of

Liverpool City Council heralded the appearance of Militant Tendency, already a presence in such places as Liverpool, Walton, and Brighton, Kemptown. In plenary session the proposals for reselection or deselection of MPs and the writing of the manifesto were passed by conference with large majorities. Only on the question of an electoral college to appoint the leader was there some breathing space. The proposal was left to a committee of inquiry to work out the balance between the different segments of the party, though the committee's composition left no doubt as to the outcome. Only Callaghan, Foot, David Basnett of the General and Municipal Workers and Terry Duffy, President of the engineers' union, were of the mainstream, with Benn, Norman Atkinson, Frank Allaun, Jo Richardson, Joan Lestor, Eric Heffer and perhaps Moss Evans likely to be on the left. A left-wing steamroller seemed irresistible, and Benn and his supporters were joyous.

Michael Foot, by contrast, was disconsolate. His main conference speech had been on unemployment. He told the delegates, 'It is easy to say that all you have to do is to obey Conference's decisions. Sometimes Conference asks for contradictory things.'[96] His view of the Labour Party was of a pluralist, tolerant body which strove to keep a balance between its different sections. As for the demands of the CLPD, basically he opposed them all. He felt that reselection would make MPs the creatures of highly unrepresentative management committees on the far left. His model was always of Members as independent spirits, as Edmund Burke had proclaimed to his electors in Bristol in 1780. On the manifesto, he thought the right balance had already been achieved, signifying the equal status of the NEC and the leadership as policy-makers, the kind of equipoise achieved in the original party constitution of Arthur Henderson and Sidney Webb back in 1918. On the electoral college, he reluctantly conceded that the party as a whole might be offered some element of participation in the choice of party leader, but the party in Parliament could not have a leader imposed on them by unelected and perhaps unrepresentative elements outside.[97]

Foot's essential view, then and always, was that socialism could only come through persuasion and the constitutional approach. The only acceptable version of socialism for Michael Foot was parliamentary socialism, and the independence of the Labour Party's representatives in the House of Commons was inviolable. Marches, demonstrations, even strikes would be important but subordinate tactics, to strengthen the resolve of democratic socialists at Westminster. He did not accept any form of dragooning Labour MPs or local councillors into mindless loyalism, and had always seen the purges of comrades as McCarthyite witch-hunts. Of course, he had some experience of this himself in the Bevanite past. When in 1975 the National Executive had before it a report by Reg Underhill, former National Party Agent, on the infiltration of local parties by Trotskyists and other 'entryists', Foot was foremost amongst those who strove to bury it. He cited the historic judgement of Clem Attlee that there had always been Marxists in the Labour Party, and declared that there should be no witch-hunt.[98] Soon the same issue – and the same entryists – was to re-emerge with the rise of Militant Tendency. By then, experience had forced Foot to think again.

This made him an obvious target for the far left. His attempts to defend Callaghan's view at the 1979 party conference were shouted down by constituency delegates. The commission of inquiry due to report to party conference about the best composition for an electoral college lumbered on. The argument reached its climax on 13–15 June 1980 in an elegant country house near Bishop's Stortford in Hertfordshire belonging to the ASTMS union of Clive Jenkins. There was a major row over reselection, but the conference decision was reaffirmed by seven votes to six. On the crucial issue of the electoral college, the CLPD argued for 50 per cent for the unions, and 25 per cent each for the constituency parties and the MPs.[99] In the end, the precise proportions were left to be determined at a special conference at Wembley in January 1981. At Bishop's Stortford, Foot proposed sticking to the status quo, but he was defeated by nine votes to three, his only supporters being Callaghan and the engineers' leader Terry Duffy.[100] Callaghan made it clear that he totally disapproved of the change, but to the disappointment of many MPs he gave up the fight. William Rodgers, Shirley Williams and David Owen turned on their old leader and accused him of betrayal; the germ of a new political alignment could already be seen.

This was a totally dispiriting time for the party. At this period the Thatcher government was deeply unpopular, with rising unemployment and the severe erosion of manufacturing industry under the impact of monetarist economic theories. There were marches, in many of which Foot participated, on behalf of the right to work. But the Labour Party seemed almost oblivious to all this, obsessed with its own internal arguments about machinery. Callaghan was to plead with conference delegates on 30 September 1980, 'For pity's sake, stop arguing,' but in vain.

Michael Foot was not a major player in these bitter controversies. His only conference contribution of note was introducing the party statement on 'Trade and Industry' on the first morning, 29 September. By his standards it was a low-key affair. He remained a deeply respected voice of the left, as was confirmed when he resumed his role as speaker and marcher in a revival of the Campaign for Nuclear Disarmament in the summer of 1980. This followed proposals to renew the British nuclear deterrent, including the stationing of American Cruise missiles on British soil. They had emerged in the last stages of the Callaghan government, of which Foot had been a key member. But he fought desperately to avoid a party split: like Bevan in days of yore, he spoke of the urge for unity in the Labour movement, though it seemed scarcely visible now. After the party conference, with all its defeats for the leadership on issues of policy and organization, Callaghan's resignation seemed inevitable. Ironically, many on the left who had been venomously condemning the leader for years past now begged him to stay, since the alternative appeared to be the succession of Denis Healey, an abrasive representative of the party right. On 14 October Michael Foot, far more consistently and honourably, made a public appeal to Callaghan to stay.[101] But the next day his resignation was announced. The party would elect a new leader in November.

Whether Michael Foot would be involved in the leadership contest was eagerly debated. It seemed highly unlikely that he would stand. Healey was a clear front-runner. Foot had shown no instinct or taste for leadership before. He had first become a minister late in his political life, and he was now sixty-seven years of age. He looked even older. His own wish was for a quieter and more bookish life. But there were other factors at work. The leadership election would be fought in the old style, with MPs alone voting. Leftish union leaders such as Clive Jenkins begged Foot to stand, to save the movement. Left-wing MPs represented by Stuart Holland, the Member for Vauxhall, added pleas of their own; Peter Shore, Holland wrote, had failed to commit himself to conference resolutions either to leave the Common Market or to renounce nuclear weapons, and was not therefore a proper standard-bearer of the left.[102] Others, not at all on the left, feared for party unity if Healey, seen to be abrasive and aloof, and felt to be on the far right, were elected.[103] At the very least Foot would prevent the party from tearing itself apart.

During his visit to Dublin to give his famous lecture on Swift in St Patrick's cathedral on Saturday, 18 October, Foot's telephone was busy with callers begging him to run. He returned to Hampstead on the Sunday evening, to a dinner gathering arranged by Jill. She had ambitions for her husband in the twilight of his career, and some believed her influence might have been decisive. Foot always disputed this, but encouraged speculation by saying that if he didn't stand, 'Jill will never forgive me.' During that weekend Eric Varley had dinner in Pontypool with its MP Leo Abse, who predicted that Jill would get Michael to stand.[104] As *Tribune*'s editor Dick Clements left the Foots' home and walked down Pilgrims Lane early that evening he caught sight of Clive Jenkins coming the other way, bearing flowers (believed to be fuchsias).[105] Floral tributes meant that something was clearly up. The gathering included several union leaders: Clive Jenkins, Moss Evans, Bill Keys of SOGAT and the young miners' militant Arthur Scargill. Even David Basnett, far from being on the left, would support Foot as a caretaker leader. They were pushing at an open door. Foot had already phoned Stan Orme from Dublin to say that he had decided to stand.[106] The day before, he had rung the *Observer*'s political correspondent, Alan Watkins, to give him the same message. This news was duly reported on the *Observer* front page the next day.[107] On the afternoon of Monday, 20 October, Foot announced his candidature. This was perfectly acceptable to the supporters of Tony Benn, who felt his time would soon come in a 'real contest' with an electoral college. The left-wing Geoff Bish of party headquarters proposed, 'If Foot stands, we vote; if not, we boycott.'[108] Far more upset was Peter Shore, who had anticipated being the main standard-bearer of the left, since he had understood that Foot would never take part.[109] The truth was that Shore's credentials as a left-winger lay in his being anti-Europe, and not much else.

Foot brilliantly seized an early opportunity to make his mark, in a Commons debate on unemployment on 29 October. He had the House in stitches as he tore apart the Secretary for Industry, Sir Keith Joseph:

> I should not like to miss out the Secretary of State for Industry, who has had a tremendous effect on the government and our politics generally. As I see the right hon. gentleman walking round the country, looking puzzled, forlorn and wondering what has happened, I try to remember what he reminds me of. The other day I hit on it.
>
> In my youth quite a long time ago, when I lived in Plymouth, every Saturday night I used to go to the Palace Theatre. My favourite act was a magician-conjuror who used to have sitting at the back of the audience a man dressed as a prominent alderman. The magician-conjuror used to say that he wanted a beautiful watch from a member of the audience. He would go up to the alderman and eventually take from him a marvellous gold watch. He would bring it back to the stage, enfold it in a beautiful red handkerchief, place it on the table in front of us, take out his mallet, hit the watch and smash it to smithereens. [Geoffrey Howe, Chancellor of the Exchequer, recalled how Foot struck the dispatch box sharply at this point.] Then on his countenance would come exactly the puzzled look of the Secretary of State for Industry. He would step to the front of the stage and say, 'I am very sorry. I have forgotten the rest of the trick.' It does not work. Lest any objector should suggest that the act at the Palace Theatre was only a trick, I should assure the House that the magician-conjuror used to come on at the end and say, 'I am sorry. I have still forgotten the trick.'

He was able to pull Healey's leg in genial fashion as well. Meanwhile Healey's own speech, handicapped by a heavy cold, was wooden, and he sounded unexpectedly nervous.[110]

In the contest among MPs it was obvious that Foot was a strong runner. There were four candidates nominated: Healey, Foot, John Silkin and Peter Shore, the latter two of the soft left in broad terms. Foot himself seemed to make little effort to campaign: a supporter described his performance as 'bloody awful'.[111] His own view was that Denis Healey was certain to get it. But his campaign, led by one or two senior figures like Stan Orme, was vigorously conducted by three backbenchers, Neil Kinnock, Peter Snape and Jim Marshall, and made some headway across the party. Kinnock had initially felt that a Foot victory was impossible and that he would lose by anything between eight and sixteen votes, but he changed his view after analysing weaknesses in the potential Healey vote. There were other factors at work to help Foot on his way. As noted, Healey's right-wing views and abrasive manner, including a talent for abuse, caused several on the centre-right to have doubts about him. He was said to show 'uncharacteristic reticence' during the leadership campaign for precisely this reason. At least one centrist MP, Phillip Whitehead, voted for Foot after Healey's incomprehensible refusal to set out a manifesto in the *Guardian* as Foot, Silkin and Shore had done.[112] Healey was thus open to criticism for being both too aggressive and not aggressive enough. He had a falling-out with some important supporters, notably William Rodgers and David Owen. Three MPs, Jeffrey Thomas (an alcoholic who sat for neighbouring Abertillery, whom Foot particularly disliked), Tom Ellis and Neville Sanderson, all later to join the SDP, are known to have voted for Foot in the belief that his left-wing views and lack of capacity to lead would destroy the Labour Party all the more quickly. Healey wrote in his memoirs that 'several' did this as a wrecking move. Ivor Crewe and Anthony King, in their authoritative *SDP: The Birth, Life and Death of the Social Democratic Party* (1995), traced at least five who did so.[113] One alleged oddity was that Harold Wilson told Healey that he voted for him on the first ballot, but for Foot on the second. At any rate, these eccentric votes just made the difference.

On the first ballot, announced on 4 November, Healey polled less well than his campaign managers Eric Varley and Barry Jones had expected, with only 112 votes against eighty-three for Foot, thirty-eight for Silkin and thirty-two for Shore. The last two dropped out, declaring their support for Foot. The potential Healey vote was then marginally whittled down: Neil Kinnock's persuasiveness won over Barry Sheerman, for instance. After the second ballot it was announced on 10 November, to widespread astonishment, that Foot had won with 139 votes against 129 for Healey. Foot made a generous acceptance speech, with much predictable reference to the eternal wisdom of Nye Bevan. One of Healey's strong supporters, Giles Radice, thought the result was 'catastrophic' – 'the last fling of a vain old "Bollinger Bolshevik"'.[114] David Owen, perhaps psychologically already half out of the party, felt that with his views on NATO, defence and Europe, Foot's victory was 'something only for nightmares'.[115] In the *Guardian*, Ian Aitken emphasized how dramatic a result this was. Foot was the first left-wing revivalist to be elected to lead the party since Keir Hardie.[116] He confirmed this reputation by saying that his first action as leader would be to take part in a protest march against unemployment in Liverpool, the city where he had first become a socialist. Party members, not all on the far left, wrote of their unbridled joy. In Oxford, Councillor Olive Gibbs, a stalwart of CND, wrote, 'What a magnificent victory for Socialism and commonsense it is . . . I feel a pride I haven't felt for years in being a member of the Labour Party.' Bruce Grocott, a former MP and a future Labour Chief Whip in the Lords, wrote, 'Absolutely delighted – I always thought in politics the good guys lost.' David Stoddart, MP for Swindon, wrote ecstatically, 'Dreams seldom come true – mine did tonight!' Spike Milligan of the 'Goons' wrote in characteristic vein, 'Don't forget dinner at No.10 and I don't want Jill using old Harold Wilson recipes . . .' A more weighty correspondent was Tony Benn – 'a historic victory which will put new heart back into the party'.[117]

Michael Foot's rise to become Labour's leader was far from premeditated. It could never have been predicted until the previous year or two. Even compared to predecessors like Hardie or George Lansbury, he had never been educated in the kind of political experiences that would have helped him to mobilize a great political party. The words 'Foot' and 'leader' hardly seemed to go together. But it was a natural outcome of decisions Foot had successively made since he first took Cabinet office under Wilson, and then served as Callaghan's deputy. He had shown unexpected skills as a minister, in a way that impressed the wider public, if not always the civil servants who saw him at close quarters. At every stage – the IMF crisis, the pact with the Liberals, the winter of discontent – the solidarity of the government and the movement had been decisive for him. When the Callaghan government fell from power, Foot was one of the relatively few ministers whose reputation had risen since being in office. As Leader of the House he had won golden opinions from colleagues as varied as Shirley

Williams, Owen, Healey, Rees, Varley, Hattersley and Orme. Gerald Kaufman, often a critic later on, thought his performance had been uniformly excellent.[118] In opposition since May 1979 he had battled for loyalty and unity without shedding his credentials as a man of the left.

Michael Foot as a possible Prime Minister was not on anyone's radar screen in November 1980. But Foot as a credible, even inspiring, leader of the opposition, binding the forces of progressivism and protest together in a mood of solidarity and fraternity, was perfectly possible. Here was a cultured leader and a commanding orator with values and ideas, and also a patriot who saw himself as the natural heir of great popular movements rooted in Britain's past. Whether these were values and ideas relevant only to that past, whether they could be reclaimed to revive a declining Labour Party, indeed whether democratic social-ism in any form, Bevanite or even Gaitskellite, had a future in a post-imperial, post-industrial society, remained to be seen. Michael Foot's experiment with power would be put to the severest of tests. But as a group of happy comrades, headed by Foot and Kinnock, went off to the Gay Hussar that evening, celebrating victory, and the merry refrain of 'Avanti Populo' and 'The Red Flag' rang down Greek Street, hope was for the moment reawakened. Seen from Soho Square at midnight, the political weather forecast was 'Faint in the East behold the dawn appear.'

11

TWO KINDS OF SOCIALISM
(1980—1983)

The Labour Party has always had problems with the idea of leadership.[1] It used to think of itself as a socialist party, a body which exalts collectivity and the general will and plays down the role of individuals. 'The goal is nothing, the movement is everything,' the German SPD theorist Eduard Bernstein would proclaim. Labour has also prided itself on being a democratic party, confirmed in the 1918 constitution, where power lies in the grassroots, not in a triumphalist leader surveying his forces from his pedestal. Caesarism was for the Tories, not the people's party or what Arthur Henderson called 'this great movement of ours'. The first person to lead the Labour Party was called its 'Chairman': he was Keir Hardie, a great evangelist and crusader for whom, wrote his colleague and fellow socialist Bruce Glasier, leadership of the party was 'a seat of misery'. The first man to be called party leader, Ramsay MacDonald, in 1922, gave leadership a bad name for ever through his secret manoeuvres in 1931 when he deserted his colleagues and formed a so-called National Government with the Conservatives and Liberals. All subsequent Labour leaders, from George Lansbury in the thirties to Neil Kinnock in the eighties, would regard it as an article of faith that 'I will never be another Ramsay MacDonald.'

Successive post-war leaders – Attlee to some extent, Gaitskell, Wilson and Callaghan – were attacked at various times, largely from the left, for being too dictatorial and for ignoring, or even betraying, the rank and file membership. There is nothing more ironic in Labour's history than when in 1996 Tony Blair, a more assertive leader than the party had ever known after his victory over abolishing Clause Four of the Labour constitution, pointed across the Commons chamber and told the Prime Minister, John Major, 'You follow your party, I lead mine.' After Winston Churchill, 'Supermac' Macmillan and the Iron Maiden, such a claim was role reversal indeed.

Michael Foot shared in full this traditional Labour suspicion of leadership. He was the natural heir of Hardie and Lansbury, if not quite of the firebrand Jimmy Maxton of the ILP. His historical models were the great rebels – the Levellers, Wilkes, Fox, the Chartists, the suffragettes, not to mention Benjamin Disraeli in his younger days. Like his idol Nye Bevan's, much of Foot's career had been a battle with the whips and successive leaders against the constraints of party discipline. He had championed the freedoms of individual MPs with a consistency few had shown since the famous declaration of independence delivered by Edmund Burke (one of Foot's heroes) in the reign of George III in 1780. Foot's line on his election as leader precisely two hundred years later was one of tolerance and pluralism. There would be no witch-hunts either of right-wing potential defectors at Westminster or of Trotskyist militants in the constituency parties. All would be comprehended within the big tent of the broadest of broad churches, to carry on the good fight for socialism in our time.

But Foot's prejudice against leadership, and against seeming to act like a leader himself, was the root cause of many of his problems. Even close allies like Geoffrey Goodman felt that leadership did not come naturally to him. Several colleagues believed he did not have either the disposition or the political (or perhaps temperamental) equipment to be a leader. Eric Varley thought his election a 'serious mistake'. Roy Hattersley could not understand why he sought to be a second-class Nye Bevan when he could be a first-class Michael Foot. Gerald Kaufman, shadow environment spokesman, felt that Foot was far too easily bullied by the left. When Kaufman urged that council house rents should be allowed to rise, Foot refused to change the policy after fierce pressure from the extreme hard-left NEC member Frank Allaun. Foot also allowed Tony Benn too much scope, Kaufman thought, as Chairman of the Home Policy Committee in 1980–82. Foot was too emollient, too vague, perhaps simply too nice. People who worked with him repeatedly, and rightly, called him 'a lovely man'. Geoffrey Goodman has written of him as 'almost too gentle a human being to be thrown into the snakepit of normal political life'. He was a man who 'loathes cultivating enemies'. Foot's personal generosity towards colleagues and staff was legendary, but in politics, like sport, nice guys tend to come last.[2] When Labour lost the general election of 1983, a decisive factor cited by the voters in poll after poll was Michael Foot's qualities as a leader. Compared with the abrasive, authoritarian image of Mrs Thatcher, who was admired as a leader if not widely liked, he always ended up far behind.

Whether this kind of analysis misinterpreted the nature of leadership, indeed what sort of leadership Foot might be expected to offer – disciplinary, ideological, moral or whatever – will be considered later. To assume that Denis Healey would have been a more effective leader, as right-wing Labour writers have been wont to do, begs too many questions. Many MPs who were far from radical voted for Foot in 1980 because they felt that he alone could keep the party together, whereas Healey's more aggressive approach would perhaps have shattered it for all time. It can also be argued that the state of the Labour Party in 1980–83 was such, especially with the far-left tide in the constituencies and the attitude of several major trade union leaders, emboldened by their influence in the seventies, that no conceivable leader could have turned it around. Foot at least kept the ship afloat, even if it was listing and badly holed. After the catastrophic defeat in 1983 (which nevertheless was a better performance than the Conservatives were to manage in 1997, 2001 or 2005) there was a new mood for unity, and electoral recovery eventually followed. Nevertheless, for the whole of his two and a half years as Labour's leader, Michael Foot's role and standing were a constant source of anxiety.

He started off with a very small staff: no smack of Blairite presidential style here. The key appointment was Tom McCaffrey, who became Foot's Press Officer, having played the same role for Callaghan during his premiership with great success. He was no Alastair Campbell spin-merchant, but a professional civil servant who, broadly, gave the unvarnished facts and was fully trusted by journalists and the media. He much liked Foot, admired his journalistic skills, and found him 'perfect' professionally in working on press statements and handling press conferences. He and Foot were often left beleaguered during the 1983 general election campaign, when the party organizers left the leader stranded in some remote and unhelpful part of the country with, as

McCaffrey put it afterwards, 'an entourage of one', namely himself. In drawing up the notorious party manifesto of 1983, the so-called 'longest suicide note in history', McCaffrey was no more than a spectator.[3] In 1982 he was given an assistant, the young Francis Beckett, who had formerly worked for the farmworkers' union and was the son of a famous former left-wing MP who in the 1930s had turned to Oswald Mosley's New Party. He was promptly drafted to run a key by-election at Darlington, which Labour won.[4]

Dick Clements was brought in from editing *Tribune* to run the Political Office. He dealt there primarily with the party, and had a far narrower remit than his predecessor Tom McNally had under Callaghan, when he was encouraged to range far and wide on issues of policy and strategy. Clements was widely liked, but some felt he was too gentle and insufficiently ruthless to perform his role with success. It should be said that, given the crises of his time with Foot, notably the long-running saga of Peter Tatchell and the Bermondsey by-election (see pages 420–5), his task was virtually hopeless. A charming and deeply loyal man, Clements never lost his sense of humour. After the 1983 debacle he was heard to comment, 'At least we didn't peak too early.'[5] By Clements's side, also from *Tribune*, was the ever-faithful Elizabeth Thomas, who continued as Foot's personal assistant and helped with speechwriting, so far as that was possible. Then there was a young woman, Sue Nye, shortly to marry an economist, Gavyn Davies, who had worked in Callaghan's private office during his premiership. Once a civil servant, she became a paid employee of the Labour Party from that time on. She had met Foot during his time at Employment, and warmly backed his leadership campaigns both in 1976 and 1980. She acted with McCaffrey on press communications, but increasingly ran major aspects of the office. During the darker days of the 1983 campaign she was often at Foot's side, or rather at the side of Foot and his dog Vanessa. On one occasion she and Michael braved the wrath of angry fox-hunters. Sue Nye remained a major official in Labour's ranks at the highest level, working particularly closely with Gordon Brown. Under Tony Blair she ran Brown's office. One of her frequent duties even as late as 2006 was to put Michael Foot through for telephone conversations with the Chancellor of the Exchequer, which both enjoyed as renewing the links between the generations of democratic socialists.[6]

McCaffrey, Clements, Elizabeth Thomas and Sue Nye worked alongside the endlessly loyal Una Cooze – rightly called by Nye 'Michael's conscience' as well as his secretary. She had occasional assistance from her friend Sheila Noble, from the *Tribune* offices. That was all Foot's private staff consisted of. It was an indefatigable thin red line, but nowhere near enough to help the leader impose his authority on the party and the country. It was almost impossible for him to spell out the main lines of policy that should be followed, or to give the party and the movement a sense of direction or of priorities.

His PPS was the first appointment he made, John Evans, MP for Newton and then St Helens North after 1983, later Lord Evans of Parkside (Caerwyn Roderick had lost his Brecon and Radnor seat in the general election). Evans was a man of the soft left, a supporter of CND who had voted for John Silkin in the recent leadership election, and was surprised, though thrilled, to be approached by Foot afterwards. A trade unionist of much shrewdness, he was to become an important aide for his leader, passing on gossip, acting as link with union leaders like Ron Todd of the TGWU, protecting Foot from tiresome backbenchers like Arthur Lewis, a regular correspondent who tried to pester him. He was a staunch ally in the battle against Militant in 1981–82, while at a different level of party activities his membership of the Party Conference Arrangements Committee, under its highly knowledgeable Chairman Derek Gladwin, made him helpful in exercising the arcane skills of handling composite resolutions. Evans got onto the National Executive in 1982, which meant that Foot gained a majority of one. In the undercover skirmishes against the hard left that occupied so much time and nervous tension during Foot's period as leader, John Evans was an unheralded comrade who stood firm in crisis after crisis, and eventually helped John Golding of the Post Office engineers' union and others to win the day.[7]

As for policy advisers, in contrast with the range of advice available to Kinnock, Smith and Blair after 1983, Foot had just one, the economist Henry Neuberger, seconded from the Treasury in 1981 to work as his economics adviser.[8] He was a gifted man with a wide range of interests, including economic modelling and the plight of the low-paid. He argued the case for a Cost Effectiveness rather than a Cost Benefit form of analysis. He used his influence with Foot to try to recreate some form of incomes policy, and had a free run in the leader's office on economic policy-making. Foot seems to have believed that the next Labour government could try to resurrect the social contract with the unions that had operated during the time of Jack Jones's heyday, and many of his speeches contain hints in that direction.

Neuberger's main dealings were not with Foot but with the Treasury team, headed by Peter Shore and also including Robert Sheldon, Robin Cook and Jack Straw, in producing an Alternative Economic Strategy. This included a commitment to reflation, planning agreements, more public ownership, price controls and a measure of industrial democracy, much as the left were arguing for at that time. He did not spend a great amount of time with Foot, in large measure because the leader never had any great interest in the minutiae of economic policy, compared with his concern with Europe and defence. It may be surmised that Neuberger did not find his time as adviser to the Labour leader particularly rewarding. He stayed on for a time as adviser to Neil Kinnock after 1983, and wrote important papers on the low-paid and a national minimum wage. But Neuberger seems to have been unhappy with a movement towards a more market-orientated approach to Labour's economic policy and the abandonment of large-scale government intervention. Neil Kinnock saw him as 'stuck with the Alternative Economic Policy'.[9] In 1987 he was effectively replaced as economic adviser by John Eatwell, and he moved to work for Bryan Gould, the shadow economics spokesman, only to differ from the strongly anti-European line adopted by Gould (who was a New Zealander). He moved back to the Civil Service in 1990, then served at the Central Statistical Office and as head of the Economic Assessment and Strategy division, but died young in 1998. On balance, Neuberger's experience was not a tribute to policy-making by the leadership in the Foot era.

Foot's leadership method was distinctive, idiosyncratic and highly personal. It was directed mainly towards the party and to keeping it together. He was always available to backbenchers, and often a cheery figure in the Commons tea room. He once had a friendly chat with a junior whip, Norman Hogg, backing up his view of the importance of adjournment debates – after all, Neville Chamberlain had fallen in 1940 after such a debate.[10] He also liked to have lunch with fellow

MPs on the 'Welsh table'. His previously close relations with union leaders remained, notably with Clive Jenkins of ASTMS, but it was the Treasury team which was required to cope with the Sisyphean burden of devising a wages and prices policy. As before, Foot took advice from an immense range of colleagues and friends, including many journalists, almost in a mood of serendipity. While he took the Socialist International, drawn from socialist parties worldwide, very seriously, his focus was almost entirely directed inwards towards Britain itself. There was no serious discussion of issues within the European Union, because Labour policy was that Britain should leave it.

Another striking feature of the Foot leadership was that he made virtually no formal visits abroad. The only exception was to the Soviet Union in September 1981, his first trip there since 1937. On this occasion he and Denis Healey, his Shadow Foreign Secretary, had talks in Moscow with President Brezhnev about Russian SS20 missiles and ways of restarting the SALT disarmament talks on arms limitation which had made some headway during the Callaghan premiership. Brezhnev's offer to withdraw some SS20s threatening central European targets greatly excited Foot. But nothing came of it, partly perhaps because of Brezhnev's growing senility. When Foot and Healey entered the room in the Kremlin, the Soviet President's initial question was, 'Who are these people?'[11] Predictably perhaps, Foot never went to the United States, nor did he show any sign of wishing to. At the invitation of the Yugoslav government he went on his first visit to Dubrovnik in 1982, and was immensely to enjoy holidays there from then on. That first visit was not wholly successful, since photographs of Foot in bathing trunks were sent to the newspapers, which did not enhance his sense of dignity. Foot also paid a visit to Northern Ireland in February 1982 with the shadow ministers Judith Hart and Don Concannon, with the intention of getting away from endless security issues and discussing jobs and employment.[12] But the general impression was of a well-meaning and cultured man intent mainly on keeping the party together rather than on playing the international statesman or setting out an agenda which he would take up as a future Prime Minister.

Foot's style and even his personal appearance were used against him. He often appeared in public looking unkempt and even shabby.

The shambling walks on Hampstead Heath with his dog, waving his stick, did not suggest the leader of the nation. His air of eccentric, donnish absent-mindedness, perhaps at the expense of hygiene at times, could be astonishing or endearing, according to taste. When they flew together to a meeting of the Socialist International, an aide, David Lipsey, was surprised to find Foot at the airport with scant luggage and no money at all. All he had with him was a volume on Hazlitt, which he proceeded to read throughout the flight.[13] He improved his performances on television in interviews with sharp interrogators like Robin Day and Brian Walden, a former parliamentary colleague, but still tended to orate in unstructured fashion rather than give the brisk, concise comments that an interview demanded. In Parliament, colleagues felt that he should have run rings round Mrs Thatcher in debate, given his intellectual superiority and Callaghan's earlier domination of her, but his natural courtesy towards women held him back. In any case, she gained considerably in confidence as her premiership went on. He also had some sheer bad luck. He was short-sighted, with a very poor left eye, and had difficulty in reading speeches from a lectern; John Evans, his PPS, had to arrange a 'secure room' where Foot could have a quiet half-hour's meditation before making a speech.[14]

It was his bad eyesight which may have led to an immediate mishap on 12 November 1980, forty-eight hours after being elected party leader, when he stumbled down some stairs in the Commons and broke a bone in his ankle. His first major appearance on the opposition front bench on 14 November saw Foot in a wheelchair, to which he was confined for some time. On that occasion his physical disability did not stop him from being fiercely attacked from the Conservative benches for the unruly behaviour of some Labour backbenchers the previous evening, when 'The Red Flag' was sung and it was claimed that blows were struck. This had followed justified Labour anger at Secretary of State for the Environment Michael Heseltine's distinctly improper method of announcing through a written answer a rise in council house rents of up to £3 a week, an announcement which the Speaker later got him to withdraw. Fred Emery in The Times said Heseltine should not have made explosive documents public through the subterfuge of a written parliamentary answer – it was a 'rupture of civility'.[15] But events like these did give the impression of a Labour

Party in disarray, with its stricken leader unable to exert any kind of control.

Foot's style came most under attack after a tragicomic episode in November 1981 when he appeared at the Cenotaph on Remembrance Day for the first time, with Mrs Thatcher and the Liberal leader David Steel, wearing a short blue-green overcoat. It became hallowed in legend as a 'donkey jacket'.[16] It looked like a dufflecoat, of the kind familiar on Aldermaston marches. Walter Johnson, Labour MP for Derby South, a former government whip and an ex-serviceman, attacked his leader publicly for turning out looking like an 'unemployed navvy'. Foot was also accused of looking around during the ceremony. (In fact he was a deeply courteous person, with immense respect for men who had given their lives fighting against fascism. He was always nervously restless, and no discourtesy towards the dead was intended.) He was also criticized for allegedly dropping the Labour wreath on the Cenotaph 'as if putting out the rubbish'. The *Evening Standard*, which he had once edited, described him as wearing 'an unbuttoned green duffle-coat, plaid tie and brown shoes'. The *Guardian*, more sympathetically, commented that he should not have turned up 'looking as if he had just completed his Sunday constitutional on Hampstead Heath', though it also noted that in his former job he had understandably refused to wear the set garb for the Lord President of the Council – 'dark blue cloth, single-breasted coatee with a staid collar and nine gilt buttons with white Kerseymere breeches, white silk hose and a sword'.

The criticism of Foot's appearance was particularly upsetting to Jill, who had recently bought his new overcoat and had taken care that her unpredictable husband wore a smart suit and tie. It attracted unhelpful publicity at a time when Labour was struggling in the polls. People wrote to Foot, thoughtfully or ironically sending him donations of banknotes or vouchers for suits at Marks & Spencer. The tailor 'Herbie Frogg' of 16 Savile Row wrote privately to him suggesting he consider 'the possibility of changing his public image' and inviting his custom. Foot replied amiably that he would try to drop in at their Jermyn Street branch 'in the near future'. The entire episode was absurd, but sadly it became one of the defining images of Foot's period in charge, suggesting someone who lacked the dignity or the sense of occasion to lead the nation. The Cenotaph donkey jacket proved to be a more troublesome garment than the Mantle of Nye ever was. Foot did, however, have one appreciative admirer of his attire. The Queen Mother came up to him in the Foreign Office after the ceremony and said, 'Oh, hello, Michael. That's a smart sensible coat for a day like this.' Foot later reflected to a *Guardian* journalist, 'Which it was, and d'you know, I'd far rather take the Queen Mother's opinion than that dreadful woman Thatcher's.'

In time, Foot and his admirers were perfectly happy to take the Cenotaph episode on board as part of his personal legend. When on 23 July 1998, his eighty-fifth birthday, a portrait of him by the Welsh artist Graham Jones was unveiled in Westminster, it was seen to general joy that he was depicted for all time in the famous green 'donkey jacket', as planned by Jill and cross-party friends like the Conservative MP Sir Patrick Cormack. Foot is shown against the congenial background of Waun-y-Pound mountain above Tredegar, the memorial site of Aneurin Bevan, looking down on his beloved valleys, the Rhymney, the Sirhowy and especially Ebbw Vale.

The main problem facing Foot, however, concerned neither his clothing nor his deportment, but something far more serious. This was the evidence of a massive rift in his party, with leading figures on the right appalled by the left-wing tide in the constituencies. William Rodgers, Shirley Williams and David Owen had all protested during Callaghan's last year against the surrender to the left over deselection, the drafting of the party manifesto and the composition of the electoral college. They believed that the very democracy of the Labour Party was under threat. The party's policy showed major lurches to the left, including withdrawing from Europe, cutting links with NATO over nuclear defence policies, mass nationalization and centralized planning agreements, which were a radical departure from the humane, broad-church social democracy in which these MPs had grown up under Attlee and Gaitskell. In the phrase of the time, 'This was not the party I joined.' Owen and Rodgers had written to Foot after the council rents disturbance in the Commons on 12 November, complaining of Labour MPs' behaviour and openly accusing the party of connivance, trying to exploit council rent rises for opportunistic reasons. Meanwhile Shirley Williams, who had lost her Stevenage seat at the general election, but who was generally thought to be more likely than Owen to remain in the party, caused a stir on 28 November, telling her former constituents that unless the left-wing policies adopted at the party conference were dropped, she could not stand as a Labour candidate at a subsequent general election.[17]

When the parliamentary party regrouped after the leadership election, David Owen refused to stand for the Shadow Cabinet. But William Rodgers was elected in a contest which saw Roy Hattersley top the poll with 143 votes, and Neil Kinnock, with ninety votes, elected for the first time with the lowest total of the successful candidates. Foot and Rodgers never got on. Rodgers was, after all, not only a strong multilateralist in defence policy, but had also been the organizer of the pro-Gaitskell Campaign for Democratic Socialism twenty years earlier. He refused a succession of Shadow Cabinet offers, including Health, Social Security, Regional Policy and Northern Ireland; meetings with Foot were inconclusive. In the end, even though he of all the major dissidents was the most anxious to stay in the party, Rodgers withdrew altogether, and Tony Benn, who had the next highest tally of votes, replaced him on the Shadow Cabinet. Elsewhere, Foot worked desperately to conciliate the right and called for tolerance all round. His Shadow Cabinet was distinctly 'Healeyite', perhaps by seven to five. He retained allies like Shore, Silkin, Orme and Booth, though all of them were soft-left Tribunites, and he was under fire from Heffer and Reg Race, Member for Wood Green, on the further left for favouring the other side. Always he pledged himself to work for unity. He denied that he had been 'soft on the unions' when he was a minister, and while totally opposed to remaining in Europe, assured pro-European colleagues that they had ample opportunity to stay in the party and argue their case.

It was known that Roy Jenkins, who had returned to British politics in 1981 after his four-year term as President of the European Commission, was thinking about a new political formation of the centre to combat what he saw as the extremism both of the Thatcherite right and of the Bennite or militant left. His Dimbleby Lecture, delivered at the BBC in November 1979, 'Home Thoughts from Abroad', had evoked this idea, with its echoing of Yeats's famous passage about the centre being unable to hold: 'The best lack all conviction while the worst/Are full of passionate intensity'. Jenkins was in close touch with Labour figures like Rodgers and David Marquand, former MP for Ashfield and a leading intellectual, in pursuit of this modest centrist ideal. Foot was understandably terrified of a mass defection, and devoted much time to intense discussions with colleagues he regarded as vital to the party's future, especially Shirley Williams, but also the Labour MP for Woolwich East, John Cartwright. Williams, Owen and Rodgers were now commonly referred to in the press as 'the Gang of Three'.

The conference to decide the composition of the electoral college was held at Wembley Conference Centre on 25 January 1981. It included the same membership as the annual party conference, and was a dreadful occasion in every respect, with vitriolic bitterness among many delegates towards the party right. Figures like David Owen and Robert Maclennan, Member for Caithness and Sutherland, were jeered at. An USDAW (shopworkers' union) motion was carried, allotting 40 per cent of the votes to the unions and 30 per cent each to MPs and the constituency parties, as against a GMWU motion which would give MPs 50 per cent, with 25 per cent each for the unions and the constituencies. The AEU, committed to MPs having a majority in the electoral college, hobbled itself through muddle-headedness, while USDAW was far from being a natural ally of the left. It had been anticipated that Foot would make a strong speech, appealing for support for the GMWU motion, but for reasons that are not clear, he remained silent in the main debate. Michael White in the *Guardian* thought he 'looked like someone who wished he had stuck to book reviewing'. He went on: 'Mr Foot seemed disinclined to dissipate his moral authority with a major reproach and settled, instead, for slapping them on the wrist with a limp anecdote.' This referred to Foot's tame closing remarks, in which he quoted Keir Hardie and the Pankhursts, and implored delegates to stay together and 'fight the real enemy'. Peter Jenkins, shortly to join the SDP himself, wrote in the same newspaper that Foot's authority had been destroyed at Wembley, and that it had sunk to the record low for an opposition leader achieved by Heath back in 1967.[18]

Within the next three weeks a major Labour split took place. Foot had no great affection for either William Rodgers or David Owen, though he wanted them to stay in the party. Both men had a low opinion of him. Foot regarded Owen as a nuclear warrior of hard-line views. Memorably, he quoted a remark by the glamorous Hollywood film star Zsa Zsa Gabor in this connection: 'Most men who are macho aren't mucho.'[19] Foot did devote much time, however, to trying to persuade Shirley Williams to remain. He had an immense regard for her, both as a Cabinet colleague and as the daughter of the famous feminist Vera Brittain. She was a popular politician, important in Labour's appeal to the wider public. He appealed to her to stay on grounds of loyalty, and told her that her leaving would destroy the party. He promised that there would be no revenge on the party right, that he would keep the balance as leader, and that she could stay and fight her corner on Europe, the bomb, party democracy and everything else. But Shirley Williams at no time detected a feeling that the party was going to change on any of these issues. She was implacably hostile to anti-democratic pressures by left-wing constituency management committees over reselection and writing the party manifesto, after 'entryism' within the party which Foot had made no effort to check. She was also astonished that Hattersley, Shore and others of the party mainstream had been prepared to accept an electoral college on such a basis. Nor could she detect any change of mind on Europe. Foot saw in the EU a profound threat to parliamentary sovereignty and the British constitution as it had existed over the centuries, and regarded her as prepared to surrender it. She saw him as very British, with no real internationalist view or concern for global issues of development. He had travelled little: he had never, for example, gone to the Anglo–German conversations of political journalists and intellectuals held at Königswinter on the Rhine, launched in 1950, while she had. She had been to the Soviet Union in 1969, while he had not gone there at all between 1937 and 1981. There was no meeting of minds. Nor did Foot's deputy leader Denis Healey offer any help. He stayed strangely aloof from these matters even though he was regarded as a potential saviour of the party by followers like Giles Radice.[20]

In any case, Shirley Williams was no longer in Parliament and was meditating on her political options with academic friends like Anthony King and Ivor Crewe. She had expressed her concern about Marxist extremists taking over the Labour Party: she compared the situation, hyperbolically, to the Nazi seizure of power in 1933. On the morning of 26 January 1981, the day after the Wembley conference, what came to be known as the Limehouse Declaration was proclaimed by Rodgers, Owen, Williams and also Roy Jenkins outside Owen's home in the East End of London: it outlined a new political initiative for moderates everywhere, not solely confined to Labour defectors. Foot and Healey had a final meeting with Rodgers, Owen and Williams at the Commons on 2 February, but no minds were changed. On 9 February Williams announced her resignation from the NEC. On 26 March a new party was born, to be called the Social Democratic Party, or SDP.[21] In all, twenty-eight Labour MPs and one Conservative MP were to join it in 1981–82, as well as notables such as Roy Jenkins and Shirley Williams who were outside Parliament. The political landscape seemed utterly transformed. The threat from the new party to Labour was illustrated in July when Roy Jenkins, running for the SDP, came close to defeating Labour's leftish candidate Doug Hoyle in a by-election in the traditional industrial bastion of Warrington.

The defection of Shirley Williams, along with the formation of the SDP, was a massive blow to Michael Foot. It coloured the whole of his period as leader. It imposed the stigma of decline and decay upon the Labour Party, the more so as the new SDP seemed to make rapid progress, including in by-elections, and was touted in the press as a rising force simply because of its novelty. Britain appeared to have genuine three-party (or perhaps four-party) politics for the first time since Isaac Foot's heyday in 1929. From then on, Foot's prospects of coming anywhere near winning power seemed to disappear. In January, before the Wembley conference, Mrs Thatcher's unpopularity had given Labour a lead of 13 per cent in the opinion polls. A month later, the Tories were just ahead. The most Foot could hope for was to work with the remainder of his party (much the largest part, after all) to ensure that it remained forward-looking and democratic. The priority now was to enable Labour to retain its balance as a broad social democratic movement, linked to the unions but trying to push out far beyond its old constituency, as it had done in 1945 and 1966.

There were many difficulties. One was that Jim Mortimer, previously of ACAS, proved a poor choice as Ron Hayward's successor as Party Secretary. He did not have the political background to make a success of so sensitive a post, while in any case, as a man of the left, he was unsympathetic to moves to discipline Militant Tendency or any other far-left group within the party. Throughout his time as leader, Foot could not always rely on the apparatchiks in Walworth Road, the party's new headquarters, some of whom, like the Policy Director Geoff Bish, were well-known Bennites. That merely intensified the strain of Foot's constant struggle to defeat the doctrinaire militants of the far left, many of them young, with no sense of the historic Labour tradition that meant so much to a man like Foot. In turn that meant an unending conflict between the contending socialist visions held by Michael Foot and Tony Benn, two kinds of socialism, in the struggle between which tormented the party thenceforth.

The relationship between Foot and Benn, the two outstanding and charismatic exponents of left-wing socialism, had never been a straightforward one. They were both children of Edwardian progressivism. William Wedgwood Benn, Tony Benn's father, had been a left-wing Liberal MP and ally of the radical Dr Christopher Addison before and after 1914, who had then joined Labour in the mid-1920s and served in the governments of both Ramsay MacDonald and Attlee. But beyond that, Benn and Foot had found cooperation tortuous. In the fifties and sixties, while Foot was frequently a rebel and critic, Benn had been first close to Gaitskell and then a centrist, pro-Europe, pro-NATO Postmaster-General and Minister of Technology under Harold Wilson. He regarded Foot, during the parliamentary debates on the reform of the House of Lords in 1969, as 'a conservative of the left'.[22] After the 1970 general election, as has been seen, Benn changed his standpoint very radically, and became a voice for all the main demands of the left. He and Foot were part of the left group of ministers during the governments of 1974–79, and participants in the 'husbands and wives dinners'. Foot had put pressure on Wilson not to remove Benn from his Cabinet in 1975, and did the same under Callaghan.

However, they were never close, and increasingly their paths diverged. Foot thought Benn was fundamentally disloyal, both in his leaks about Cabinet discussions to the press and in his disavowal of collective responsibility. Benn, who was in awe of Foot's literacy and was himself unfamiliar with the works of Swift, Hazlitt and the rest, felt that Foot 'repudiated himself' in his political attitude over time. He believed that the substance of the talks at the 'husbands and wives dinners' was relayed back to the leadership: they were nothing but 'licensed dinners'. Foot was also seen as less vigorous than he might have been in the 'No' campaign on Europe. In the IMF crisis Benn felt that Foot was always prepared to give way ultimately, and was really 'a Callaghanite'. Foot, he thought, was a conservative on internal democratization of the Labour Party, and agreed to an electoral college coming into being on the understanding that it would never be used.[23] Benn did not stand in the leadership contest in November 1980, in the belief that Foot, who was twelve years older than him, would only be a temporary leader if he won, and Benn supporters like Alan Fisher of NUPE were sure that their man would make it next time. Benn came to be supported by an enormous variety of far-left radicals in a myriad of pressure groups and protest movements. But it should be noted that his supporters also included prominent members of the Blair governments after 1997, including Patricia Hewitt, Margaret Beckett, Alan Milburn, Stephen Byers, Margaret Hodge and many others; his secretary in Bristol South-East, Dawn Primarolo, later became Paymaster-General. Tony Benn embodied the aspirations of many idealistic younger socialists. Whereas Michael Foot was the honoured icon of a passing generation, Benn was truly a representative of a new Labour, even though ideologically light years away from that creed as interpreted after 1997.

From the start, colleagues noted an edginess between Foot and Benn; nor did Caroline Benn and Jill Craigie share the same enthusiasms. It was the 1647 Putney Debates once again, save that it was the leader who took his cue from the Levellers, while it was Benn the rebel who seemed the more Cromwellian. Foot profoundly distrusted his younger colleague, and his suspicions were widely shared on the Labour front bench. Row followed row. The biggest of all arose in April 1981, when Benn announced that he would challenge Denis Healey in the election for deputy leader. The deputy leadership was really a trivial post, invented to placate Herbert Morrison in the 1950s by giving him a seat on the NEC after defeat in the constituency section elections, but clearly a contest between these two major figures would plunge the party into a massive internal division. Foot spent over an hour with Benn pleading with him not to stand, and his view was reinforced by Judith Hart and John Silkin, but to no avail. A complication which might save the leadership was that John Silkin, a distinctly soft-left Tribunite, also entered the contest, and would clearly peel off some of the left-wing vote. Benn then tried Foot's patience further on 20 May by leading seventy-four left-wing Labour MPs into voting against the government on the defence vote on the grounds of their hostility to nuclear weapons, thereby upstaging a possible Tory backbench revolt. Benn was joined by several Tribunites, including Jack Straw, Robin Cook, Jeff Rooker and Frank Field, all of them greatly to change their positions later on.[24]

The main battleground was the National Executive, which was now in the hands of the Bennites. Fifteen of the twenty-nine places were held by the hard left, and Foot found it difficult to get the other fourteen – eight 'soft left' and six on the right – to act together. The pressure placed on individual MPs by left-wing militants in constituency parties led to furious arguments. Stanley Clinton Davis, the MP for Hackney Central, who had voted for Foot in the leadership election in 1980, was one early target of local pressure, though he was in fact reselected. In the end only eight Labour MPs were to lose their seats in 1983 because of mandatory reselection, the best-known being the former Cabinet minister Fred Mulley in Sheffield, Park; but in many other places the procedures led to disputes and bad blood.[25] There was journalists' talk of 'bedsit Trots', young Marxists who infiltrated small and decaying constituency parties in the inner cities and virtually took them over; *Private Eye* immortalized them in the shambling class warrior 'Dave Spart'. Other popular villains with walk-on parts were further-education lecturers in sociology, what Peter Jenkins in the *Guardian* called the 'lumpen-polytechnic', to be carefully distinguished from genuine university scholars. On 27 May Benn was part of a fifteen to nine majority on the NEC insisting that all MPs should have to go through reselection procedures. It was noted, though, that Foot now had with him a powerful young supporter in Neil Kinnock, no enthusiast for Benn. When Foot and Benn both addressed the TUC People's March for Jobs on 31 May, it was observed that they did not address a word to each other.[26] Then there came a dramatic scene in the Shadow Cabinet on 3 June. Foot read out a twenty-five-page prepared statement, attacking Benn for repeated disloyalty, and denying that Labour was dragging its feet on economic or defence policy, or Europe or Northern Ireland either. There had to be trust between colleagues: 'There can't be one rule for Tony and another for everybody else.'[27] He urged Benn to fight him for the leadership, but the gauntlet was not picked up. One member of the Shadow Cabinet thought this showed Benn to be 'a bit of a coward', and that his conduct generally was disgraceful. Other colleagues were less flattering.[28] Joyce Gould, a leading party organizer, thought him 'a different breed of oppositionist' from Foot, and with no firm principles.[29] In his diary Benn noted that the atmosphere towards him was 'poisonous',[30] but he does not speculate as to why that might have been.

Two days later, with MPs prepared for a disciplinary 'crackdown' by Foot in the face of Benn's disobedience, Benn went to hospital for urgent medical examination after suffering pains in his legs, and the personal insults temporarily tailed off. But the tension continued all summer as Healey and Benn supporters campaigned for votes in the deputy leadership election. Benn's campaign was largely run through the Rank and File Mobilizing Committee, in which a young militant, Jon Lansman, was a key influence, and which had strong backing from the mainly Trotskyite Outside Left movement: for them the quintessential objective was the destruction of Healey's career. Polls, however, showed that Healey was overwhelmingly the choice of Labour Party supporters, and of voters generally. Eventually, to Foot's huge relief, the result declared at party conference on 24 September showed that Healey had scraped home on a second ballot by less than 1 per cent, 50.426 per cent to 49.574 per cent. This was, of course, conducted under the new electoral arrangements, the first time they were used. Healey had clear majorities in the parliamentary party and the trade unions, but in the constituency parties Benn had a majority of five to one.

It was the closest of close-run things. Yet in retrospect it marked a turning of the tide. The vote was in some ways misleading. It showed up the inadequacy of union 'consultation' of members. The result was as close as it was in part because of malpractices by some trade union executives, notably those of the TGWU, who threw all their million-plus votes behind Benn despite having no mandate from their branches to do so. Their vote, which saw Healey apparently take 52.2 per cent of branches to Benn's 24.6 per cent, was a total shambles from start to finish. Unions which held ballots, such as NUPE with its left-wing leadership, invariably found that their members preferred Healey: this was particularly the case among women. Benn's majority in a union like ACATT was boosted by the votes of Communists. Benn was only defeated because Foot and Kinnock managed to mobilize the softer left, MPs like Stan Orme, Albert Booth and Joan Lestor, who all voted for Silkin on the first ballot but abstained on the second. An associate of Benn, Doug Hoyle, was persuaded to follow this course after intense personal pressure from Orme.

Healey thus scraped home against a background of the most bitter internal infighting, and indeed actual fighting in a Brighton hotel washroom, in which Kinnock was reportedly a combatant. Even so, Foot's preferred candidate (he did not vote himself) had got home, just, and things began to get a little easier. The rejection of Benn's methods and style, appealing to all left-wing dissenters without discrimination, by the older ex-Bevanite left, and by some key allies in the unions, gradually saw a change of mood, and was to prove important as Labour slowly recovered during the Thatcher years. The debate amongst the soft left was pivotal – at the *Tribune* rally at the party conference, Neil Kinnock was both cheered and booed by the membership for the role he had played. As in the past, there were somewhat pathetic evocations of the memory of Nye and his cry for unity. Outside the bitter, internecine world of Labour infighting, all the opinion polls showed that Healey's victory was popular with the voters, and much more likely to make the party electable.

The Brighton conference saw other setbacks for Benn, as important as the result of the election for the deputy leadership. Norman Atkinson, one of his most vehement supporters, was defeated as Treasurer by Eric Varley, a Healey supporter. In the elections for the National Executive, five Bennites were defeated: Atkinson (dumped by his own union, the AEU, which was shifting to the right), Margaret Beckett, Renee Short, the recently elected Bernard Dix of NUPE, and Charlie Kelly of UCATT. In their place came Eric Varley, Gwyneth Dunwoody, Shirley Summerskill, Roy Evans (of the iron and steelworkers) and David Williams (COHSE), all on the right. The Executive was being slowly reconstituted by a formidable operator, the self-styled 'hammer of the left' from the postal engineers, John Golding MP.[31] Foot brought the conference to its feet with a closing speech in which he referred to himself as 'an inveterate and incurable peacemonger'. But he also talked a good deal about multilateral approaches to disarmament. Peter Jenkins of the *Guardian*, invariably scathing on everything about Foot, from his speeches to his suits, observed that 'after a year of vacillation and ineffectiveness' Foot had 'slapped down Benn with an olive branch'.[32]

But there was still no ceasefire. Conference defeated the leadership over the NEC's having sole control in writing the party manifesto (the consequences of which were shown to disastrous effect in the 1983 general election). Foot then put some effort into trying to persuade Benn to run for the Shadow Cabinet elections, but also to accept the principle of collective responsibility. Benn refused, because he declined to be gagged. With remarkable tolerance, Foot made him spokesman on energy. But he was then badly let down in a debate on nationalized industries on 10 November. Winding up for the opposition, Benn, after speaking well in orthodox fashion on Labour's opposition to selling off part of the oil industry, then declared without prior warning that Labour favoured renationalization of the assets of the industry, without compensation. This was a bombshell on which the then Secretary of State for Energy Nigel Lawson immediately fastened, and Benn's totally unauthorized response made matters worse.[33] At an angry PLP meeting Foot denounced Benn's remarks as 'misleading and offensive', and relations between the two reached a still more glacial level. This was the same week in which Foot had had his troubles at the Cenotaph. Nevertheless, the beleaguered leader, with his hatred of witch-hunts, was showing distinct signs of beginning to lead, as the battle with Benn moved on to become the battle for Bermondsey.

The long-running cold war between Michael Foot and Tony Benn, the two most gifted voices of the left, had obvious personal aspects. There were antagonisms that went back years. Many private issues, great and small, were involved. Foot's essay 'Brother Tony' in his book *Loyalists and Loners* (1986) shows a controlled bitterness towards one whom he regards as very much a wilful 'loner', and not a team player at all. He writes that Benn fell out with virtually every colleague he ever had to work with.[34] However, underlying these skirmishes was something more interesting, namely a major ideological debate about what the Labour Party was, and indeed what British socialism had become in the last quarter of the twentieth century. Neither Foot nor Benn was a political theorist, but their rival philosophies can be gleaned from their publications at this time. Foot's viewpoint was set out most clearly in a pamphlet published by the *Observer* in December 1981, *My Kind of Socialism*. Benn's had appeared at much more length, especially in two books, *Arguments for Democracy* (1978) and *Arguments for Socialism* (1981). When all the personal backbiting is set aside, their two kinds of socialism are well worth consideration.

Foot's pamphlet is not long, a mere ten thousand words. Some of it is taken up with his familiar range of historical and literary quotations, featuring Oliver Goldsmith, the inevitable Hazlitt and Alexander Herzen among others. Nevertheless, it is the most substantial written elaboration of his socialist principles that Foot ever produced. His books were treatises on literary ideas, not political ones, other than his life of Bevan, in which Foot's own ideology emerges vicariously through his hero. A key quotation in his 1981 pamphlet is from Ignazio Silone, one of his favourites: 'Every means tends to become an end.'[35] Foot's pamphlet is entirely about means. That means is Parliament, placed almost romantically in centre stage in the very first sentences: 'Why Parliament? Can those old arthritic limbs still move as the nation needs? Why parliamentary democracy? Why should democratic socialists . . . continue to assert their faith in the supremacy of Parliament?' Nothing is said about local government or devolution. Foot wrote warmly of the demands of the unions in the early 1970s, but they needed the Labour Party in Parliament to put them into effect. The sometimes unlawful extra-parliamentary activities of the Chartists or the suffragettes in years past arose from the fact that in those times there was no alternative. R. H. Tawney, the prophet of socialism as equality who was once the cherished philosopher of the Gaitskellite right, is cited from 1953: 'It is not certain, though it is probable, that Socialism can in England be achieved by the methods proper to democracy. *It is certain that it cannot be achieved by any other.*' (Foot's italics.)

The most effective part of Foot's argument is at the end. He takes issue with Bennite demands that the parliamentary party be subordinated to the wishes of the delegates at the annual party conference, through reselection and other means. Foot denied that this was necessary. The party in Parliament had not betrayed the faith: he drew on his own experience of the Callaghan government to show how it had taken up socialist issues, nationalizing aircraft- and ship-building, abolishing tied cottages and the like. But his basic argument is an essay in tolerance and pluralism, even divided sovereignty. Twin sovereign bodies had been created in the party's 1918 constitution: the annual conference and the parliamentary party: 'Neither will bend the knee to the other', wrote Foot. But then, neither need do so if party debates were conducted in a spirit of comradeship rather than doctrinaire zealotry. He was echoing Keir Hardie, who had called back in 1907 for 'free play between the sections'.[36] Foot's view of the Labour Party was an organic one, as a pluralist popular movement which exerted pressure at a variety of points. Implicitly, he echoed the argument in Aristotle's *Politics*: 'A polis, advancing in unity, will cease to be a polis . . . It is as if you were to turn a harmony into mere unison, or to reduce a theme to a single beat. A polis is an aggregate of many members.' So too was a great party, and its life force depended on what Tawney had called 'the elementary decencies' of parliamentary government.[37]

Foot's view of socialism was parliamentary and Aristotelian. Benn's was populist yet in some ways Platonic. In themselves as multi-faceted as Foot's, his books, and even more his tactics, lent themselves to the discipline of the guardian class as outlined in Plato's *Republic*. His *Arguments for Socialism* begin with some comments on historical strands, of which the most important is Christianity, but his vision lacked the historical grounding of Foot's. However, while the socialist theme peters out some time after the Levellers, Benn certainly does focus on major contemporary issues, particularly energy resources (especially nuclear energy and oil), Europe, and democracy and open government. His vision of a socialist Britain was futuristic. Foot, on the other hand, offered no blueprint of what a socialist Britain might actually look like, other than some more 1945-type nationalization and planning policies to combat unemployment, alongside a reinforced welfare state. Benn's enemy is the corporate multinational capitalism which had grown up since 1945. Unlike Foot, he did acknowledge that Keynesian economics had run its course by the 1970s, and that the kind of management model endorsed by Tony Crosland in *The Future of Socialism* (1956) was out of date. But his focus, unlike Foot's, is on ends rather than means. Some of his incidental proposals on open government, for instance, were distinctly prophetic, and were to see partial fulfilment under Tony Blair's government via its Freedom of Information and Data Protection Acts.[38] But Benn's designated ends, and his apparent lack of fussiness at the miscellaneous forces enlisted to promote his objectives, weakened his cause.

Benn tried to be at one and the same time a technocrat and a populist. He advocated both centralism and localism, a kind of mixture between Jean Monnet and Jean-Jacques Rousseau, the planner and the philosopher. While always stimulating, he was often inconsistent. Thus he saw the annual party conference, dominated by the union block vote, as the authentic voice of party democracy, yet consistently opposed the principle of one member one vote. He had much more ministerial experience than Foot. He had been a pro-NATO, pro-European Minister of Technology in the 1960s. In the second Wilson government he advocated a massive increase in nationalization and corporate planning agreements with the rest of major industry. Yet he also praised the Upper Clyde Shipyards work-in of August 1971, following the Heath government's refusal to bail the company out with a £7 million loan, and strongly supported workers' cooperatives such as he had himself encouraged as a minister in 1974–75, at Meriden motorcycles, Kirkby Mechanical Engineering and the *Scottish Daily News*, ignoring the fact that every single one had been a financial and managerial failure. He made scant effort to relate improved industrial efficiency to the larger role he foresaw for the trade unions (or rather their shop stewards): towards them he was uncritical (as Foot often was too), and ignored such matters as their antiquated attitude towards work practices or job demarcation, the prevalence of inter-union disputes, and their resistance to being involved in the management of industry, compared with the very different view taken by German, Dutch or Swedish workers. Deep-seated weaknesses in the British economy were traced to the malign role of foreign capital, not to internal weaknesses of productivity or rising wage inflation. Benn's argument gradually dissolves into a series of fragments. Much the most interesting parts of his books relate to democracy rather than to socialism, an idea in which the author gradually loses interest.

Politically, for Benn the Labour Party is an important instrument of change. But it is an organization given its life force by socialist true believers in 'the party nationally'. His book *Arguments for Democracy* (1981) is marked throughout by a deep suspicion of the idea of leadership, quite apart from the perceived errors of individual leaders such as Callaghan. Labour MPs, he writes, should be mandated to carry out decisions taken by the membership. If they did not do so, they should be deselected. The party leader and Cabinet (or Shadow Cabinet) members should then be controlled by Labour MPs, who should elect them and determine the portfolios which they would be allocated, following directives from party members. Despite this chilling iron discipline throughout the party hierarchy, Benn nevertheless calls for a spirit of tolerance within the movement, although this is not to be extended to any dissent from the manifesto. However, 'anyone dissatisfied with any NEC vote should seek to have it reversed at the next meeting. This is the democratic way to act.'[39] It reads more like a recipe for permanent civil war.

Unlike Aneurin Bevan, who drew a sharp distinction between democratic and undemocratic visions of socialism, and usually refused to conflate totally opposed forms of socialist belief, Benn endorsed dissidents of all kinds. Whereas Foot (eventually) turned against 'entryism' by Trotskyists and others, Benn welcomed it because it brought in 'good socialists'. This meant paying less attention to what their objectives actually were – syndicalism, the recognition of Sinn Fein, animal rights, liberation theology or whatever – and trying to argue that small groups of infiltrating ideologues in the constituencies added up to a broad democracy. He had none of Foot's distaste for 'infantile leftism', in Lenin's famous phrase. Benn's 'arguments for socialism' were undermined by the collapse of traditional forms of public intervention in the new global economy. Neither his planning agreements nor his workers' co-ops showed any signs of working, let alone of bringing down inflation or creating viable jobs. Benn's 'arguments for democracy' were undermined by the selective terms in which he interpreted it. Both his lines of argument were central targets for Michael Foot as he strove to educate as well as to lead his party.

The Foot and Benn conceptions of socialism and the Labour Party, while both untidy and often vague, were basically incompatible. Arguably, they were both fundamentally flawed. They were also, in the view of New Labour enthusiasts in the 1990s, fundamentally dated. To Peter Mandelson and Roger Liddle in *The Blair Revolution* (1996), or Philip Gould in *The Unfinished Revolution* (1999), both Foot and Benn were products of an anachronistic, ill-defined Old Labour from which the party had 'moved on'.[40] Tony Blair vaulted above and beyond both Foot and Benn, with the modernizing of the 'Third Way' – not the 'Middle Way' of Foot's colleagues during the Attlee government, but a post-modern creed set in a totally different continuum, which argued that Labour should base its values and ideas on quite other foundations than those which had gone before. Foot and Benn were lumped together by the Blairite managerialists not only with each other, but also with Attlee, Gaitskell and Bevan, so at least they were in good company.

In the Labour Party between 1980 and 1983, members had to choose between two contending visions, set against a background of long-term systemic decline. Foot's commitment was to Parliament and the formal processes of democracy. Benn's was to Parliament as simply one forum for protest in a world where corporate capitalism is incompatible with democracy, and forms the main threat to a civilized life. Foot's commitment was to a strong, radical Labour Party, bound by strong internal loyalties from the grassroots to Westminster. During his most quarrelsome Bevanite days, he claimed always to have sustained the party. Even CND, to which he was passionately committed, he never saw as anything other than a pressure group out to convert his comrades. Benn, by contrast, regarded a fundamental restructuring of the party by socialists in the grassroots, and the discipline they imposed, as essential. Even heavy electoral defeats like those of 1979 and 1983 were only temporary setbacks as the cause advanced; two steps backwards but, in the fullness of time, three steps forward. Benn's optimism seemed without limit; when he visited Crosby during the by-election in November 1981, he actually forecast a Labour victory in a contest eventually won by Shirley Williams for the SDP, with Labour losing its deposit. Foot's Labour Party was still the classic Labour alliance, the grand old partnership with the trade unions as originally created by Keir Hardie. It was still 'this great movement of ours'. Benn's was more of a fluid popular front, where the official Labour leadership would rapidly be superseded. His socialism in 1979 was akin to what Foot's had been in his Socialist League days in 1937. Foot's party was the classic broad church, where a variety of belief systems and movements could contend within the broad flapping tent of the Labour tabernacle. Benn's party was the priesthood of all believers, an extension of the Congregationalism of his father and his forebears, with groups like Militant as the new Anabaptists. Foot, he believed, had become a conventional mainstream figure and the 'prisoner of the right'.

Foot's socialism is evolutionary, and grows out of a sense of historic identity. It is an outgrowth of the radical Liberalism in which he had been brought up. It is fundamentally based on his own idiosyncratic sense of history. Benn's, by contrast, is not really historical at all, despite some observations on the Levellers or the Chartists. It is curiously abstract, focusing on structures and mechanics, and unrelated to the political antecedents. Foot's socialism is literary, cultural and humane, drawing heavily on traditions of protest and demands for democratic change from the time of the French Revolution. When he addressed mass marches on the meaning of socialism, Hazlitt and Byron were at his shoulder. He conveyed a vision of warmth and solidarity. Benn's socialism is neither literary nor cultural. His bleak analysis seems on paper peculiarly mechanical, even bloodless, curiously lacking in humanity for so personally charming and cultured a man. No non-political author intrudes onto his pages, other than an interesting passage from H. G. Wells reflecting on the importance of Christ's crucifixion.[41] Foot sees British socialism as the custodian of a culture. Benn sees it as a weapon to be mobilized for social transformation.

As exponents of socialist theory, neither Foot nor Benn is significant, though Foot is much the more comfortable with Tawney. Neither begins to define socialism or to describe what a socialist society might actually be like. Both pay tribute to the inspiration of Marx, whose role in British socialist thought had been virtually ignored during the Cold War years. Even if neither was seriously a Marxist socialist, Marx had been an influence on both over the years. Both adopted Marx's view of historic necessity and the centrality of class. Foot, as we have seen, spent time reading through the Marxian dialectic in his Socialist League days, and instructed Barbara Betts in the fundamentals of Marx's message. Benn discovered Marx much later in life, and first read *The Communist Manifesto* in his fifties. But, as befits that versatile ideological genius, the Marx to whom each pays homage is distinct and drawn from different contexts. Foot's Marx is the Marx of the years after *Das Kapital* (1867). These saw his attack on Bakunin's anarchism at the Hague Socialist International in 1872, and his authorship of the German SPD's Gotha Programme critique of 1875, which provided inspiration for young radicals like Karl Kautsky in the German Social Democrats, despite his criticizing many features of the Programme itself. Marx here came to acknowledge that the socialist revolution could eventually be achieved by parliamentary means, through the dynamic energy of universal suffrage. Foot himself had responded warmly to John Strachey's *Contemporary Capitalism* (1956), in which the Labour Party was identified as the instrument in Britain embodying Marx's later view of democracy, one which had made violent class conflict unnecessary. Tony Benn's Marx is a much earlier Marx, the revolutionary itinerant author of *The Communist Manifesto* of 1848, passionately condemning the economic slavery of the proletariat, and looking forward to the overthrow of capitalism in favour of a utopian, classless society, whose specific features are nowhere described. It is this almost metaphysical Marx whom Benn evokes, linking him with earlier mystics in a way reminiscent of William Morris's *Dream of John Ball* (1886), set during the Peasants' Revolt of 1381. Foot and Benn each created his own personal Marx, as what the French call a *lieu de mémoire*, part real, part legend, part history, part memory.

Ultimately, both Foot and Benn seemed profoundly English, each a patrician rooted in his time. Indeed, there was an insularity about both, since each, in time, was strongly dismissive of the European Union, and they came together in condemning its threat to parliamentary sovereignty and the British constitution. In supporting CND, both Foot and Benn were calling for an independent British foreign policy, and a weakening, if not an abandonment, of overseas alliances. Both were products of a native radical tradition imbibed from their Liberal fathers. Neither had many close associations with Continental or Third World socialists. Foot did at least find kinship with the more intellectual European socialist leaders – Léon Blum, Willy Brandt, François Mitterrand. Benn thought all of them far too revisionist, and claimed to find his allies rather in eastern Europe, or perhaps Third World rebels in Latin America. Neither was pro-American. Despite Benn's having an articulate and gifted American wife, the United States, whose capitalism he saw as in fundamental crisis, had little to attract him, and he found many of its characteristics deeply distasteful. Whereas Foot had once been excited by Franklin Roosevelt's New Deal, to Benn it had been an economic contradiction which demonstrated the futility of Keynesian capitalist economics.

And yet both Foot and Benn, English to the core, looked like outsiders in British politics too. Both stood outside the mainstream; neither was a party regular, not even Foot when he became leader. Neither could be seen as a central integrating figure in the Labour movement on the model of Henderson, Morrison or Callaghan. Each claimed the Levellers as ancestors (though Foot, confusingly, also paid ancestral tribute to Oliver Cromwell). But perhaps their true historical habitat, if anywhere, was rather the French Enlightenment, with its varied philosophical strands. Foot versus Benn was, by extension, Voltaire versus Rousseau, even if Foot's attacks on his rival were a good deal more rational than Voltaire's on Rousseau in his vituperative pamphlet *Sentiment des citoyens* (1764). Just as the two French *philosophes* lie near each other in death in silent dialectic in the distinctly secular Paris Pantheon, so the two ageing icons of the Labour left exchanged muffled broadsides between Hampstead and Holland Park. Almost romantically, Foot upheld the British Parliament as the true champion of free thought and the rule of law, what Lloyd George had called 'the great assize of the people'. Benn advanced the Rousseau-esque general will, the impulses of citizens born free who would create a wider freedom within a contrived collectivity. It should be said that Foot had from time to time written enthusiastically about Rousseau, and liked to quote his friend A. J. P. Taylor, who claimed that 'Rousseau was the man who invented democracy.' It might be added, however, that on his only visit to England, in 1766, Rousseau, unlike Voltaire or Monte-squieu, found the country distinctly unappealing and not at all demo-cratic. But in any case Foot's main interest lay in Rousseau's literary not his political writings – the *Confessions*, with their enthusiasm for 'bringing women into the game', not the ambiguous doctrines of the *Social Contract*. Barbara Castle had shrewdly noted the basic rationalism of the 'collective Foot type', but it was directed towards a model of free thought shaped by institutions and culture over the centuries, not a metaphysical notion of a general will. Benn's vision, like Rousseau's, aimed at forcing men (and women) to be free. Foot's, like Voltaire's, celebrated tolerance and open government, alongside unremitting enmity towards modern versions of *l'Infame*. For him, freedom always came from within.

The bitter argument between these different approaches dragged on into 1982. Benn was losing ground in tactical skirmishing in the National Executive, and Foot seemed to have made progress since the 1981 party conference. On the other hand, in what remained of the Labour Party throughout the country, Militant Tendency, linked with other far-left fragments, was becoming ever more vocal, and putting pressure on local parties and centre-right MPs due for reselec-tion. Then a totally different issue emerged, which put the contention between Foot and Benn in the background, and at least for the moment put Foot's leadership of the party in a quite dramatic new light.

On 2 April 1982 Argentine forces invaded without warning the British territory of the Falkland Islands in the South Atlantic. Their tiny British population of just over a thousand, mainly farmers, was thrust under enemy occupation. The diplomatic conflict between British and Argentine governments over sovereignty of the 'Malvinas', as the islands were known in Buenos Aires, had been active for some years. In 1977 a British vessel, the *Endurance*, was sent to Falkland waters when it was feared that Argentina might attempt an invasion, and Prime Minister Callaghan sent firm messages privately to the Argentine government warning them not to take military action.[42] Foot warmly approved of Callaghan's handling of the issue. The Argentine government dropped its belligerent posture, and the threat of war died away. However, under the Thatcher government there were ministerial talks over a diplomatic compromise, with Nicholas

Ridley sent to Buenos Aires to consider possible 'lease-back' arrangements. Then the withdrawal of the *Endurance* from the region gave a signal which the Argentine government interpreted as indicating that the British government was drawing back from a confrontation. On 2 April the invasion of the Falklands, with the detention of its Governor Sir Rex Hunt, appeared to be the consequence.

British public opinion, which had known virtually nothing of the distant Falklands previously, except perhaps the appeal of its postage stamps to philatelists, was outraged. Newspapers raged in patriotic fury at this assault on a tiny British outpost by a fascist government headed by General Leopoldo Galtieri. Parliament was recalled for emergency session on a Saturday, 3 April. But no one reacted with greater passion than that famous 'inveterate peacemonger', the pillar of CND and many other neo-pacifist organizations, Michael Foot. He was, of course, no pacifist – how could the co-author of *Guilty Men* ever be seen as such? Although totally opposed to the use of nuclear weapons, he had backed the Foreign Secretary David Owen in Cabinet in 1978 when it was suggested that Britain send troops to Rhodesia to enforce a military solution upon the Ian Smith government during the critical years of the UDI. But the sheer spontaneous force of Foot's reaction to the Falklands invasion rocked his party and the country. The Prime Minister, often hailed as 'the Iron Maiden', was shaken to the core.[43]

Foot's speech, perhaps his last great parliamentary performance, galvanized the nation as much as the spectacle of Arthur Greenwood 'speaking for England' had done in 1939. He was adamant that the Falklanders should be defended and liberated. He poured scorn in 'guilty men' style on the role of the Foreign Office, where indeed the Foreign Secretary Lord Carrington and two ministerial colleagues were shortly to resign:

> The Falkland Islanders have been betrayed. The responsibility for the betrayal rests with the government. The government must now prove by deeds – they will never be able to do it by words – that they are not responsible for the betrayal and cannot be faced with that charge. That is the charge, I believe, that lies against them. Even though the position and circumstances of the people who live in the Falkland Islands are uppermost in

our minds – it would be outrageous if that were not the case –
there is the longer-term interest to ensure that foul and brutal
aggression does not succeed in our world. If it does, there will
be a danger not merely to the Falkland Islands but to people all
over this dangerous planet.

While Mrs Thatcher appeared strangely halting and subdued, Foot's
fiery utterances won massive acclaim on the Conservative benches.
Edward du Cann congratulated him on his speech; Patrick Cormack
praised him strongly – 'For once he spoke for Britain.' The Labour
benches were somewhat stunned. Denis Healey was away in Greece,
and had also been ill. Foot had not consulted him beforehand: it
emerged that for once he was a good deal less hawkish than his leader.
Colleagues like Hattersley, Varley and Kaufman were astonished, but
also delighted. On the left, there were protests from Tony Benn, who
urged the country not to give way to generals and admirals and their
backers in the media, and from others including Ian Mikardo. One of
Foot's closest friends, James Cameron, wrote of his surprise: 'I am so
aghast at the Falklands shambles that I expect you to be as intemperate
as I.' Tam Dalyell criticized Foot's belligerence in a parliamentary party
meeting, whereupon his leader snapped back at him, with rare ferocity,
'I know a fascist when I see one.'[44] Foot was also attacked by the
left-wing editor of *Tribune*, Chris Mullin, but ignored it.

Foot's response to the crisis was unpremeditated and highly personal. The day before the invasion of the Falklands he had heard about
the possibility of it at a meeting of the Socialist International in France.
François Mitterrand had pledged to him that the French socialists
would strongly support Britain in resisting an attack. Labour had in
any case been contemplating what its policy should be for smaller,
contested territories like the Falklands, Belize, Malta and especially
Gibraltar, which caused difficulties with Spanish socialist comrades.[45]
Most of Foot's close colleagues, including Neil Kinnock, gave him
strong support, as did old friends at the naval base in Plymouth. He
continued to utter belligerent noises. On 14 April he strongly backed
the British task force being sent to the South Atlantic, though he
combined this with trying to pursue 'peaceful methods of solution' at
the United Nations. When Labour dissidents objected, he wryly
observed that 'they were putting too great a strain on the good nature

of General Galtieri'. The friendly *Guardian* wrote that for a second time Foot 'stole the show' through force of oratory and command of language.[46]

By 27 April, however, Foot was striking a more balanced, or perhaps equivocal, note, after pressure from Healey and Shadow Cabinet colleagues. He was now asking Mrs Thatcher to accede to a request from Javier Pérez de Cuéllar, the Peruvian Secretary-General of the UN, to desist from an escalation of military action. Britain, he said, should make sure it kept worldwide support by maintaining its allegiance to the UN Charter. The consensual mood had gone, and there were angry exchanges now with Mrs Thatcher, she and Foot each claiming the other was putting British lives at risk. Peter Jenkins, writing in the *Guardian* and on the verge of joining the SDP, noted how Foot the peacemonger had 'draped himself in the Union Jack', but that Foot and Healey were showing signs of abandoning Mrs Thatcher and finding a bolt-hole in 'that warren of lost causes, the United Nations'.[47] One factor was that Healey and others of the party right had a clearer understanding than Foot of the military risks involved, and saw that much would depend on technological assistance from American early-warning systems.

Once the war began, though, Foot was strong in supporting the British cause. Denis Healey's excellent biographer Edward Pearce is scathing about Foot's attitude: 'The man content with the bombing of Belgrade [in 1999] could have no difficulties over the Falklands. Hazlitt would have been ashamed of him.' Foot called this view simple appeasement; he also disputed the interpretation of Hazlitt.[48] In the most controversial episode of the war, the sinking of the Argentine cruiser the *Belgrano* with many hundreds of lives lost, Foot gave the action astonishingly belligerent support which he always refused to disavow later on. His argument was that even if the *Belgrano* was sailing away from the battle zone, it might have reversed course and wreaked death and destruction on British soldiers in the way that was done to the British ship the *Sir Galahad*. That is to say, it was a preventive strike, like the invasion of Iraq in 2003. He ignored an adjournment vote on 20 May, when thirty-three Labour MPs disobeyed the whips and voted against the government on the Falklands issue; they were nearly all from the harder left: Benn, Frank Allaun, Norman Atkinson,

Bob Cryer, Joan Maynard, Reg Race and Dennis Skinner among others, but also included Judith Hart and Ian Mikardo from the old Bevanite left, and one frequent ally, Leo Abse.[49] It should be noted that unease about the sinking of the *Belgrano* was very far from confined to the hard left. The most powerful critic was Tam Dalyell, who had been a Callaghan supporter. Concern was voiced higher up the party, notably by Denis Healey. Foot later noted in a book published after the 1983 general election that he and Healey came to an agreement not to mention the *Belgrano* during the campaign.[50]

The one precaution that he took was to decline the offer of sharing military intelligence with the government, an offer which the Liberal leader David Steel accepted. Foot would support the government, but would not be embraced by them. It was a view supported by Neil Kinnock, who said it would 'not have secured the cause of parliamentary accountability or, accordingly, the public interest'.[51] But right until the war's ending on 14 June, after the capture of the islands' capital Port Stanley by British forces, Foot was consistent in his belief in the rightness of the task force being sent and the war being fought to the end. Some thought it was Foot's finest hour as leader. It certainly shows him as courageous and determined to take a moral stand, whatever view is taken of the Falklands War, about which friends of Denis Healey had doubts from the start. But, sadly for the Labour Party, the Falklands war was not at all its finest hour. The jingoism of wartime seldom helps a party of the left, whether in the Boer War or the Suez crisis, nor did the bloody aftermath of Iraq do anything but undermine Labour in 2005–07. In 1982–83 Labour's standing in the polls slumped, the Social Democrat challenge to the Tories withered away, and Mrs Thatcher reinforced her control over her own ranks. Foot's role during the Falklands War had perhaps increased his public credibility, but it had also made a Conservative victory at the next election all the more certain. All that was left was to call for a Committee of Inquiry into the origins of the war and the government policy that led up to it. In that same year one was indeed set up, under the chairmanship of Lord Franks. After the invasion of Iraq in 2003, Foot was to call for a similar inquiry into the origins of that war, its legality and the relationship of the government to the security services. The terms of reference of the Hutton Inquiry into Iraq were limited solely to the circumstances surrounding the death of Dr David Kelly. But Hutton and Franks had one thing in common. Each was a total whitewash.

Nor was the Falklands issue much to Foot's advantage in the continuing battle with the left for control of the Labour Party. This was taking place at two levels. Within the party, Foot was gaining a much greater semblance of control. He had broad support in the parliamentary party and the Shadow Cabinet, even though strong doubts remained about his credibility as leader. Colleagues noted his preference for marches and 'demos', and how most of his weekends seemed to be spent this way, rallying the faithful in some of the unions and amongst the left, but having a negative impact on the electorate as a whole.

Foot's main interests focused on unemployment and unilateral nuclear disarmament. Monetarist policies had led to unemployment rising by 300,000 since November 1981, manufacturing output had fallen by 16 per cent and taxes had risen by over 6 per cent. That meant frequent appearances on Marches for Jobs to denounce Thatcherite monetarism, alongside demonstrations on behalf of CND, which enjoyed a new lease of life after 1979. For Foot these were basically moral issues, to be supported on principle without regard to what the opinion polls said. On 3 September 1982 he told a peace and disarmament rally at Bristol that a Labour government would unilaterally scrap Trident and Cruise missiles, and 'the so-called independent nuclear deterrent', *en bloc*. He used a public lecture in Cardiff ('Byron and the Bomb') to press home what he saw as the message he was given by Brezhnev during his visit to Moscow in 1981 – that the Russians were likely to remove all their SS20 missiles threatening central Europe, provided that the Americans never introduced Cruise missiles or Pershings into western Europe again. There was criticism that he used his power as leader to take revenge on multilateralists. Thus at the end of 1981 the unilateralist John Silkin replaced Brynmor John as defence spokesman, while Peter Archer replaced John Morris as Shadow Attorney-General: Brynmor John and Morris were both multilateralists, and in the Healey camp. Foot wrote a compelling article on the dangers of nuclear proliferation in *The Times* in December 1982, headed 'Why *The Times* is Wrong'. His argument was certainly placed in far broader context than the conventional Atlanticism of *The Times*, effectively citing not only the views of eminent scientists like Lord Zuckerman, but even the public apprehensions of President Reagan about a nuclear accident that could annihilate mankind. Nearer home, Foot made his enthusiasm plain for the women demonstrators against American Cruise missiles at Greenham Common in Berkshire – a cause that Jill also strongly supported, on feminist as well as anti-nuclear grounds. He was urged not to be too vocal in this connection, since the miscellaneous, if courageous, women involved were believed to be electorally unpopular. But on Boxing Day 1982 Michael, Jill and their latest dog, Dizzy, a Tibetan terrier, turned up amongst the Greenham Common women and gave them Christmas presents.[52]

On the whole, things were going much better for him within the party by this time. In the TUC David Basnett of the GMB was showing signs of shoring up support, in cooperation with the distinctly mercurial Clive Jenkins of ASTMS. On the National Executive, Tony Benn was gradually being sidelined, in some measure because of the stern policy of retribution against his followers (a 'witch-hunt', in the view of the left) led by that fixer extraordinary John Golding, Foot's extremely tough right-wing ally from the Post Office Engineers' Union. 'Benn's star is no longer in the ascendant,' wrote Keith Harper in the *Guardian*.[53] Foot showed signs of being alarmed at the extent of the right-led purge, and tried to have an old comrade, Eric Heffer, appointed as Chairman of the NEC Home Policy Committee, where he had hoped to follow Benn. But John Golding and his friends were unflinching. A major factor here was the ignoring of the views of NUR members by Sid Weighell, the railwaymen's union leader, in failing to vote for the miners' nominee, Eric Clarke. Ignoring the niceties of democratic processes came as naturally to the Labour right as it did to the left. On 27 October a series of votes for the chairmen of NEC committees saw all the hard left eliminated from the list of names put forward by Jim Mortimer, the General Secretary. The hallowed left-wing names of Tony Benn, Judith Hart, Dennis Skinner, Audrey Wise and Frank Allaun, along with Lawrence Coates of the neo-Trotskyist Young Socialists, were all purged as committee chairmen. Benn was replaced as Chairman of the key Home Policy Committee by John Golding himself, to make sure that nothing was left to chance. Party loyalists noted that the Tory lead over Labour in the polls had been cut from 12 per cent to 4 per cent (41 per cent to 37 per cent), with the Liberals and Social Democrats added together coming a poor third with 19 per cent.[54]

As a leader trying to control and manage his party, Foot was thus showing some real success in key institutions at various levels. He was winning the internal dialectic with Benn. There were also promising new recruits coming into the party. One who impressed Foot was an articulate and attractive young barrister, Tony Blair, who unsuccessfully fought the Beaconsfield by-election in May 1982. Blair was passionately inspired by reading Foot's book *Debts of Honour* two months after Beaconsfield. The following week, on 28 July, he sent Foot an emotional, handwritten twenty-two-page letter:

> The first thing that struck me about *D[ebts] of H[onour]* was the prison of ignorance which my generation has constructed for itself. How many of us have read Hazlitt, Paine, Brailsford or even Swift (apart from *Gulliver's Travels*) in the original? . . .What is startling to me, reading *D of H*, is that your creditors have something so enduring and enriching to say. I actually want to go out and explore these people first hand. It has shown me how narrow is our source of modern political inspiration. Look at Thatcher and Tebbit and how they almost take pride in the rigid populism of their political thought. There is a new and profoundly unpleasant Tory abroad – the Tory party is now increasingly given over to the worst of petty bourgeois sentiments – the thought that there is something clever in cynicism; realistic in selfishness; and the granting of legitimacy to the barbaric idea of the survival of the fittest. Even in our own party (though to a much lesser degree) there is a tendency against letting the mind roam free. In this I can't help feeling the continual association of Marxism with Socialism is to blame . . . For me at university, left-wing politics was Marx, and the liberal tradition was either scorned or analysed only in terms of its influence on Marx. It is so abundantly plain to me when I read *D of H* that there is a treasure trove of ideas that I never imagined existed. We need to recover the searching radicalism of these people.

Blair was impressed too by the variety of Foot's heroes, 'not least of all, your father. It was as much about your politics as theirs. There was hope and vigour and something irrepressibly optimistic that struck a deep chord in me.' He concluded that the salvation of the Labour Party could only come through 'the spirit of *D of H*'. To this end, he urged Foot to drive Militant out, and to appeal to 'a sense of purpose in the party' on the basis of its programmes for creating jobs and preventing nuclear annihilation. On this basis, Blair apparently believed, Foot would surely win the next election. He quoted a friend of the poet Gerard Manley Hopkins who once wrote: 'If I were not your friend I would wish to be the friend of the man who wrote your poetry.' Blair added emotionally, 'I feel the same about *D of H*.'

Foot remained much impressed by this idealistic, perhaps naïve, young man. In April 1983 he threw his influence behind Tony Blair when the nomination for the safe Labour constituency of Sedgefield in County Durham came up – although a factor was the wish of Foot and many others to prevent the nomination of an erratic Bennite, Les Huckfield.[55] A talented young Scotsman, Gordon Brown, also carried Foot's good wishes when his search for a constituency ended in nomination for the safe seat of Dunfermline East in 1983. Brown had battled with some success on the Scottish Labour Party Executive to defend Foot against hard-left critics like George Galloway. Within the confines of Labour's tabernacle, the mood was somewhat better.

However, Foot's attempt to make a personal impact on opinion in the country at large was manifestly not succeeding, despite Mrs Thatcher's low standing until she was given a boost by the jingoism of the Falklands War. This was partly because Foot was not perceived as a likely or even a credible Prime Minister. If he was not electable, then in the current presidential mode of politics, in contrast to Attlee's day, neither was his party. But Foot's problems were largely the result of the continued party disarray, which would have defeated any leader at that time.

The main cause of this was Militant Tendency.[56] This tiny group, whose guru was Ted Grant, originally of the Revolutionary Socialist League in Liverpool in 1955, had the aim of capturing the Labour Party for the cause of revolutionary socialism. Rival protest movements like the Trotskyists were treated with contempt. The Militant Tendency first made progress after the creation of its propagandist newspaper *Militant* in 1964, with Peter Taafe as editor. They captured the place reserved for the Young Socialists on Labour's NEC, and by 1970 could claim perhaps two hundred activist members. They kept their distance from the sharp shift to the left in the late seventies, and had little contact with the various Bennite groups in the constituency parties. They made their base in Liverpool, which in the 1970s was an old, decaying industrial city. When Labour won a majority on the city council in 1983, for the first time in ten years, of the fifty-one Labour councillors elected, sixteen were identified with Militant, including the self-publicist figure of Derek Hatton. Even if formal membership of the group remained very small, there were signs of it extending its influence across the country; in London 'Red Ted' Knight, the leader of Lambeth Council, was a prominent figure.

Growing anxiety about Militant's role after 1979 was far from confined to the party's right. Until his election as leader, Michael Foot had stoutly resisted inquiries into, or purges of, left-wing dissident elements; he had fought hard against their being directed towards himself in the fifties. He had been mainly responsible for the Underhill Report on 'entryism' being shelved in 1975–76, and had hitherto refused to use what would have been a casting vote on a finely-balanced NEC to drive Trotskyists out of the party. When the Organization Committee chaired by Eric Heffer took no action on this issue, Foot did not respond. But he was now under attack for being 'indecisive and content to drift'. Some journalists were far more ferocious. Peter Jenkins in the *Guardian* compared the Wembley Conference with Munich, and Foot's walking stick with Chamberlain's umbrella.[57]

Things could not go on like that. In November 1981 Foot decided to forswear the habits of a lifetime and to take disciplinary action. He was strongly backed by Neil Kinnock, who saw Militant as endorsing Lenin's programme of 'democratic centralism'. On 9 December Foot managed to get the agreement of a ten–nine majority of the Organizational Sub-Committee to have a full investigation into the activities of Militant. It would be conducted by the Party General Secretary, Ron Hayward, and the National Agent, David Hughes. A fudge proposed by Eric Heffer was defeated by ten to nine. In other moves, the wealthy globetrotting International Socialist Tariq Ali was refused membership of the party, while Joan Lestor, a sentimental soft-left figure, now strongly condemned Benn. He responded with the astonishing and baseless charge that Foot was contemplating a coalition with the Liberals and the Social Democrats; memories of the 1977 pact evidently had a long life. On 17 December, by the surprisingly large majority of nineteen votes to ten, the inquiry into Militant was confirmed by the NEC, and Hayward and Hughes began work.[58]

The issue of Militant overlapped with a quite distinct matter, the problem of selecting a Labour candidate for the decaying London dockside constituency of Bermondsey. There was constant trouble over the operations of the far left, whether called Militant or not, in a variety of constituencies, including some in Liverpool, notably Wavertree, where Derek Hatton of Militant sought the parliamentary nomination. In February 1982 there was actually a Militant member formally nominated as Labour candidate, Pat Wall in Bradford North, after the sitting member, Ben Ford, had been deselected by his local party; Bob Clay, another Militant member, was to follow by being nominated for Sunderland North in July.[59]

A particularly bad, if unlikely, case was in the Home Counties constituency of Hemel Hempstead, also in July. Here Robin Corbett, who had been the sitting MP until 1979, and who sought renomination, was under attack from militants in the constituency party because he had voted for John Silkin rather than Benn in the deputy leadership election. Even though nine out of twelve constituency branches voted for Corbett in the nomination process, he was left off the shortlist as a result of hard-left pressure, and Paul Boateng of the Greater London Authority was put forward instead. It was said of Boateng that 'his strong ambition to get into Parliament has stifled his principles'. Foot was told about this, and the intimidation and shouting down of pro-Corbett delegates. But since the authorized members of the local party confirmed the wholly undemocratic nomination procedures by fifty-four to thirty-seven, he felt there was nothing he could do. In the event Boateng proved an unpopular candidate and came in third in the 1983 general election, whereas Corbett found another, much safer constituency in Birmingham, Erdington, and was comfortably elected. Boateng, however, later moved sharply rightwards, as many ex-Bennites did, and became a Treasury minister under Tony Blair.[60]

But Bermondsey was by far the most notorious case. Here the

party was moribund, and Bob Mellish's resignation as MP was anticipated, since he had been offered a post as Vice-Chairman of the
Docklands Urban Development Corporation by Michael Heseltine in
February 1980. This would trigger a by-election. Key members of the
local party, the so-called 'Bermondsey Mafia', headed by John
O'Grady, leader of Southwark Council, were in open warfare with
younger militants in the constituency. The Roman Catholic Church
was a major, if divisive, factor in an area with strong Irish representation. A young Australian emigrant, a prominent figure in the homosexual world, Peter Tatchell, had moved into the constituency in
late 1978, and was adopted as prospective Labour candidate by the
constituency party in mid-1981, defeating a former Labour Tribunite
MP, Arthur Latham, by thirty-seven votes to thirty.[61]

From the start, Tatchell was highly controversial. Apart from his
unusual background for a candidate for a working-class London constituency, he had written an article in a party tract, *London Labour
Briefing*, in which he called for a 'tent city' to be set up in the grounds
of County Hall, a sit-down in Parliament Square, and 'a siege of
Parliament' on behalf of the unemployed, and advocated 'new, more
militant forms of extra-parliamentary opposition'. Tatchell behaved
with dignity when the press attacked him as a homosexual and a
draft-dodger in Australia, and survived some element of physical threat.
There was a scurrilous doorstep campaign by local Liberals, who presented their candidate, Simon Hughes, as 'the Straight Choice' (in
2006, when running for the Liberal Democrat party leadership, Hughes
revealed that he too had been an active homosexual). The atmosphere
in general was unsavoury. Nevertheless, as a Labour candidate trying
to appeal to the traditional electors of Bermondsey, many of whom
were Catholic, let alone to the electorate more widely, Tatchell
appeared an unelectable choice.

Foot was incandescent at the selection of Tatchell, and in the
Commons on 3 December, perhaps unwisely, declared that he would
never be endorsed as a candidate. What made matters worse was that
by a slip of the tongue, perhaps reflecting the pressure he was under,
Foot actually said 'member' instead of 'candidate'. In any event, whatever he meant to say, he was in error. It was the NEC, not the leader,
which could debar prospective parliamentary candidates, and then only

if there had been procedural irregularities. At an uneasy meeting with Tatchell in the Commons on 7 December, Foot told him that his *London Labour Briefing* article was clearly anti-parliamentary, not merely extra-parliamentary, and asked him to stand down. That afternoon the NEC passed by twelve to seven a motion proposed by John Golding and seconded by Denis Healey that Tatchell's candidature should not be endorsed. Foot observed that Tatchell would be 'an electoral disaster'. A few days later the NEC narrowly carried, by fifteen to fourteen, a motion refusing to let Tatchell put his case in person, with Neil Kinnock strongly backing Foot, but three soft-left members, Joan Lestor, Judith Hart and Alex Kitson, voting against him. Bob Mellish, after a talk with Foot, said that he would not be resigning as an MP after all. It was then that the committee of inquiry into Militant headed by Ron Hayward and David Hughes was set up.[62]

Matters were far from straightforward. Tatchell had apparently been selected correctly, and he was not a member of Militant Tendency. In any case, Militant claimed it was no more than a legally published newspaper, and did not have members as such. The distinction between what Tatchell wrote and what many others, including Michael Foot in the past, had said about the relation of parliamentary and extra-parliamentary activity was not easy to define. Tatchell had not advocated violence. Foot's attitude looked like an attack on Tatchell's right of free speech in response to what was undeniably a very minor publication indeed. Tatchell, in two effective articles in the *Observer* on 10 and 17 January 1982, cited technically unlawful activities which the Labour Party had supported at the time – Poplar's Poor Rate rebellion in 1921 and, in the very recent past, the actions of Labour councillors in Clay Cross, Derbyshire, who were surcharged after refusing to implement the Conservative Housing Finance Act in 1972 because of the severe impact on the rents paid by working-class people. The real illegality, Tatchell argued, came from the capitalist classes seeking to bludgeon the socialist left and the working class in general. Foot received a torrent of letters of bitter protest from left-wingers in the constituency parties, including the future MP Kate Hoey from Dulwich. 'You, comrade, are a walking disaster', wrote one fraternal member.[63] Foot also had a pained letter from a colleague on the soft left, Joan Lestor, who pointed out that Tatchell was not a

Militant: 'Michael, your position is crucial. You can't be seen to be censoring a guy like Tatchell – it is not in keeping with your whole history in the Movement. It will be seen as sacrificing someone that the Movement will one day need in order to placate those that many feel we can do without.'[64] This view was predictably echoed by Eric Heffer and Ian Mikardo, while Tony Benn was passionately angry.

The situation in Bermondsey went from bad to worse. In the May 1982 local elections, three old Labour opponents of Tatchell ran for the Riverside ward as 'Independent Labour and Tenants' candidates', with the support not only of Southwark Council leader O'Grady but also of Bob Mellish, the sitting Labour MP. Labour's vote fell to 22 per cent. Mellish was then expelled from the Labour Party, only promptly to break his word and announce in August that he was taking up his new post with the Docklands Urban Development Corporation after all, which would mean a by-election.[65] Since it was known that the SDP/Liberal support in Bermondsey was growing, the difficulty for Labour was considerable, and Foot seemingly helpless. Tatchell was eventually overwhelmingly re-endorsed in a reconvened nomination meeting on 9 January 1983. Foot sent a written formal confirmation, and the NEC approved it. The most Foot could do now was to delay the by-election as long as possible.

However, his campaign against Militant received a strong boost in July, when the Hayward–Hughes report finally appeared. It got around the difficulty of disciplining a movement that claimed not to exist by proposing a 'Register of Non-Affiliated Groups', all of which had to be compatible with Clause 2 of the party constitution, defining the basis of membership and affiliation. Foot threw all his authority behind this report; the Tribune group of MPs backed him by thirty-nine to twenty-seven. Foot's lengthy statement in *Labour Weekly* on 10 September fiercely attacked Militant for democratic centralism, entryism and using the democratic machinery of the Labour Party to undermine that democracy. At party conference the sins of Militant were spelled out, and a motion to endorse the register was overwhelmingly carried, 5,087,000 to 1,851,000, with all the big unions in favour.[66]

Foot made a powerful intervention, drawing a distinction between the Bennite left and dissenting movements with which he himself had been involved earlier in his career:

I also agree with the proposition that those who wish to present particular views to the party have a right not only to argue their case – Marxist ideas, if you like, Marxist ideas have always been a matter for debate in our labour movement as they have been in the labour movements of the Continent of Europe and elsewhere – but that all such ideas are to be debated in our party, and that anybody who said we should suppress them would perhaps be suppressing the very ideas of the future. I am absolutely opposed to that. But when people say to me that Militant Tendency are just like Stafford Cripps or Aneurin Bevan, or the Salvation Army . . . it is not like that at all. It is very different. There was no secret conspiracy with Stafford Cripps or Aneurin Bevan: they wanted everybody to know what they were doing. [Applause.] There were no false colours about the way in which they went about propagating their views. They were accused of trying to form a party within a party, but it was not true. It was not true, but in this case it is true, and that is a big difference.

These observations were greeted by delegates with loud applause, but what the effects of this decision would be was unclear. Foot hoped that people 'linked with Militant' would be deterred, but who they were seemed almost impossible to define. In the end, only five people were actually be expelled from the Labour Party: the known editorial board of *Militant*, Peter Taafe, Ted Grant, Lynne Walsh, Clare Doyle and Keith Dickinson. It was a token gesture and no more. Even expelling the five was difficult. The only clear grounds for expulsion from the party were working for a candidate opposed to a Labour candidate, and none of them had done that: the Militant moles had all been burrowing away from within. Foot had a report prepared on the legal aspects of expulsion by John Smith's old university friend Derry Irvine, with the actual drafting done by his junior, Tony Blair, setting out the reasons for taking action, but also spelling out the legal difficulties. The five Militants challenged the party in the High Court over their expulsion. They had a strong case, and eventually lost, so Irvine believed, simply on a legal technicality. The National Executive confirmed the expulsion of these five – but only these five – from the party by nineteen to nine on 24 February 1983, the day before the Bermondsey by-election.[67]

Militant in general, and Bermondsey in particular, had done colossal harm to Foot's leadership. A by-election in the neighbouring constituency of Peckham in October 1982, won by Harriet Harman, saw a large fall in the Labour majority. The dénouement came when the Bermondsey by-election eventually took place, on 25 February 1983. There was a row beforehand between Tatchell's supporters and Labour's National Agent David Hughes, when Hughes demanded that election literature should not be printed by Cambridge Heath Press, with which Militant was linked. Jim Mortimer had to order the local party to obey. The press printed a highly embarrassing photograph of Foot welcoming Tatchell at the House of Commons. There was talk of strong opposition to the candidate in Southwark's union branches and Labour clubs. In the event, the Labour campaign was a catastrophe. With a 44 per cent swing from Labour, at a time when the now formal Liberal-SDP Alliance was trailing in the polls nationally, Simon Hughes (Liberal) won the seat with a 9,319 majority.[68] A leftish figure, Hughes was to hold the seat comfortably beyond the 2005 general election. Peter Tatchell disappeared from Labour politics for ever, though not from public controversy, especially over gay rights. Foot had fought with courage and determination to hold his ground in Bermondsey. But his early tactical errors, plus the wider feebleness of grassroots Labour in such a constituency, made his task hopeless. Comments on air by colleagues like Gerald Kaufman were less than helpful. Paradoxically, one of the few to urge loyal support for Foot as leader was Tony Benn.

Buoyed up by Labour's disasters, Margaret Thatcher called a general election for 9 June 1983. It was a challenge which the party had long been dreading. Foot knew that Labour was bound to lose.[69] People on his staff were not optimistic, but would be shocked at the scale of the defeat. Of course, morale and organization in the constituencies were in much disarray after all the troubles associated with Benn, Militant and the hard left. Demography was cutting away the sociological base of Old Labour, with the shrinking of manufacturing and the drift to the suburbs or outlying communities leaving just client groups like council house tenants and local government employees. Centrally, Labour began private opinion polling again at the start of 1983, through Robert Worcester's MORI, which had been used by

Wilson and (less happily) Callaghan in the 1970s, but which stopped being used after the defeat in 1979. This may have been partly for financial reasons, with Labour facing large debts after the cost of establishing their new headquarters in Walworth Road, where rents and rates were £250,000 a year higher than in Transport House. But it was also partly because the left, who dominated the NEC after the 1979 election, did not really believe in polls, and felt they were merely a consumerist attempt to emulate the meretricious approach of the Tories. When Worcester did start his polling in February 1983, and told Norman Atkinson, the left-wing Party Treasurer and MP for Tottenham, that Labour had the support of only 26 per cent of the public, 14 per cent behind the Tories, Atkinson was extremely angry.[70] Foot himself at first took little interest in polls, an attitude he shared with Aneurin Bevan: psephology was for Oxford dons, not the real world. But he had become more interested in polling after 1979, as a guide to what the electors were thinking. On the other hand, since his own two main priorities, trade union policy and unilateral disarmament, were negatives with the voters, Foot's response to MORI's information was limited.

What all the evidence did show was that apart from a general lack of confidence in Labour handling the nation's problems, there was also a massive lack of confidence in Michael Foot. He was thought to be neither competent in making and carrying out policy, nor in control of his party. In 1981 only 18 per cent of the electorate were satisfied with his performance as leader, and things hardly improved thereafter. MORI's private poll for Labour on 16 May 1983, three weeks before polling, showed Foot's satisfaction level running at 'very well' 6 per cent, 'fairly well' 21 per cent, 'not very well' 27 per cent, and 'not at all well' the highest of all with 39 per cent.[71] Nor did he show up well on television, as opposed to his sparkling performances as a mass orator: in an interview on *Weekend World* with Brian Walden, Foot appeared rambling. At the start of 1983 there had been much disaffection with his leadership amongst Labour MPs, voiced by Members like Jeff Rooker, Dale Campbell-Savours and Robert Kilroy-Silk, and also the more senior figure of Gerald Kaufman. There was talk of getting Denis Healey moved in as Labour's leader to fight the next general election. After the Bermondsey disaster, the stream of criticism was turning into a torrent.

Left Cabinet minister: Michael leaving number 10 after a crucial Cabinet meeting on whether to join the Common Market, 18 March 1975.

Below With Indira Gandhi in New Delhi, December 1976.

Speaking at a Labour Party/TUC Rally against Racialism, Trafalgar Square, 21 November 1976: those on the platform include Len Murray (General Secretary, TUC), Tom Jackson (General Secretary, Union of Postal Workers), Merlyn Rees (Home Secretary) and Joan Lestor MP.

Battling for Devolution: cartoon by Garland, *Daily Telegraph*, 1977.

Prime Minister and Deputy: on the platform with Jim Callaghan, party conference,
5 October 1977.

Union man: with Jack Jones of the Transport Workers at Jones's leaving party,
Royal Festival Hall, 20 February 1978.

Left Michael arriving at St Patrick's cathedral, Dublin, to lecture on Jonathan Swift, 18 October 1980.

Below Making socialists: Michael haranguing the faithful, 1981.

Above Michael and Jill with their dogs on Hampstead Heath.

Left Michael and Denis Healey at Heathrow, on their way to meet Soviet leader Leonid Brezhnev in Moscow, 15 September 1981.

Above Comrades and rivals: Garland cartoon, *Daily Telegraph*, 13 November 1981.

Left Welcoming the candidate for Beaconsfield to Westminster: Michael and Tony Blair, 1982.

Below Electioneering bibliophile: Michael on the number 24 bus, 23 May 1983.

With Neil Kinnock at a meeting in Tredegar, 1988.

A faithful follower: Michael and Dizzy on Hampstead Heath.

At the Open University: *left to right*, Lord Callaghan, Tony Blair, Dr John Daniel (Vice-Chancellor) and Michael, c.1990.

Left Cutting the cake: an eightieth birthday party for Michael, with Norman Willis (General Secretary of the TUC) and Jack Jones (also eighty), 23 July 1993.

Below The donkey jacket immortalized: portrait of Michael by Graham Jones, 1998.

A critical test had been a by-election on 24 March in the northern town of Darlington, a seat narrowly won by Labour in the general election of 1979, with a majority of 1,052. Defeat there would make Foot's position unsustainable. In fact, Labour fought a good, old-fashioned 'Old Labour' election, focusing not on nuclear weapons but on the party's traditional domestic agenda. Its candidate, Ossie O'Brien, was a middle-aged local politician of moderate views, not remotely a 'bedsit Trot', and he got home with a solid majority of 2,412. Since many thought the main point of the coming election would be to ensure that Labour remained in second place as the main challenger to the Tories, it was significant that the SDP candidate in Darlington was back in third place. Run by the youthful Francis Beckett, Labour's was a remarkably enthusiastic campaign, resulting in a turnout of 80.1 per cent, a figure of 1950-type proportions. It was a boost for Old Labour, but also its swansong. Not only was Foot destined not to remain leader for long, but poor O'Brien was to be defeated in the general election in June, after only two months at Westminster.[72] His term in Parliament was so short that he did not even appear in the 1984 *Who's Who*.

Labour was ill-prepared for a contest in every way. Its General Secretary, Jim Mortimer, was in no sense an electioneer, and though personally pleasant, was poor at public relations. Much of the electoral organization was shored up by the Assistant National Agent, Joyce Gould, reputed to be on the left. There were only sixty-two Labour agents in post: even in 1979, a bad year, there had been sixty-eight. At the centre there was a lack of preparation in making key appointments: the highly competent Nick Grant was appointed Head of Communications only in February 1983. For the election, younger, rising politicians were brought into the campaign team: Charles Clarke, John Reid, Patricia Hewitt; the staff was eventually built up to over thirty. However, Joyce Gould was to describe this unwieldy team as a 'farce', with trade union leaders with little expertise in running elections playing too large a part, and much suspicion between the different groups.[73] Another serious but inescapable problem was that Labour was likely to suffer from the redistribution of constituency boundaries. The party challenged the implementation of these changes in the courts, but in the end had to settle for defeat, after much expenditure of money. Foot's own constituency would transform from Ebbw Vale to Blaenau Gwent, losing the Rhymney Valley (which went to Ted Rowlands's seat of Merthyr Tydfil) but gaining Brynmawr and Aber-tillery, which made it perhaps even more rock-solid for Labour.[74]

Foot himself was enthusiastic about the campaign, but his team seemed unable to establish any sense of priorities about policy or strategy. He seemed to regard the coming election as part of a long-term campaign of indoctrination, not a contest to win power. He could not understand how the Tories appeared likely to win with unemployment at such a high level. In fact, ever since Callaghan's speech about 'spending your way out of depression' to party conference in 1976, price inflation had been replacing unemployment and growth as the main economic concern. It was a historic shift in priorities which the 1945 generation found hard to fathom. Even more unintelligible to Labour was that more trade unionists seemed likely to vote Con-servative than Labour (which was indeed the case, the figure standing at 33 per cent Tory voters at the start of the campaign). As for unilateral nuclear disarmament, MORI repeatedly told Foot that this was deeply unpopular with the voters, but he ignored their advice. On 6 June, just before polling day, the figures showed that only 22 per cent of the electors thought disarmament was the main issue in any case.[75]

Perhaps the worst handicap from which Labour suffered was entirely self-inflicted, namely its election manifesto. Writing it was still under the control of the National Executive, despite the defeat of the Bennites since 1981, and the Executive's views were shaped by conference decisions. Evidently the manifesto would include all the main demands of the left, including a non-nuclear defence policy, although here Healey was able to modify the previously starkly unilat-eralist statement on Britain's nuclear-armed Polaris submarine by saying that it must form part of a multilateral package of disarmament measures. A pre-election book, *Renewal: Labour Britain in the 1980s*, edited by Gerald Kaufman, contained a piece by Foot denouncing Mrs Thatcher for blindly following American defence policies. These included having a 'dual track' decision on stationing Cruise and Per-shing missiles in Britain without any British control, standing pat on Ronald Reagan's 'zero option' of no further Western arms deployments in return for the Russians abandoning their missile programmes (a very unlikely prospect), and failing to ratify SALT II, the proposed arms limitation policy discussed by Carter and Brezhnev (and Callaghan) in 1979. On Europe, Foot won his battle to have a pledge to pull Britain out of the EC within the lifetime of a single Parliament (the word 'immediately' was dropped). At home, the economy would be expanded with more public ownership. Another hostage to fortune was the pledge that a National Economic Assessment of the state of employment and investment would be made, as a result of which unemployment, currently stable at around three million (after much creative accounting in presenting the figures), would be reduced to one million within five years, a proposal that originated from one of Foot's speeches. The manifesto as unveiled on 29 March was said by the press to be the most left-wing Labour programme since 1945. Entitled *The New Hope for Britain*, it was a potpourri of every Labour policy statement since 1979. At thirty-seven pages, it was not overlong; as Roy Hattersley wrote, 'it only seemed interminable', including a miscellany of proposals from the abolition of the House of Lords to an end to fox-hunting.[76] Gerald Kaufman's description of it as the longest suicide note in history soon went the rounds.

The origins of this manifesto caused much bad blood afterwards, since it was believed, by Kaufman and others, that the published version was in fact only a draft, and that it should have been approved by the Shadow Cabinet. Kaufman had been assured by Foot that it would be. However, this did not happen. A day or two later Foot told his colleagues that it was indeed the final version. Only Peter Shore protested. John Golding, a strong figure, observed bleakly that it didn't matter, since Labour was going to lose badly anyway. A crushing electoral defeat and the far left would be finished, perhaps for ever. At the start of May, Kaufman went on his own initiative to see Foot, after a sleepless night, and told him he should resign as leader in favour of Healey. Foot replied with courtesy that it was too late, which it probably was. He and Kaufman parted company on the most civil of terms, a sense of impending doom having settled on them both. With these inauspicious preliminaries, Labour's electoral bandwagon lurched unsteadily and unconvincingly on its way.[77]

Foot threw himself into the campaign with astonishing energy for a man of nearly seventy who walked with a stick. Jill had done her best to help by buying him several suits from Jermyn Street tailors (possibly including Herbie Frogg of donkey jacket fame) and working on his television style. But the campaign planning was a total shambles. There was talk of the Conservative minister Cecil Parkinson offering to give Labour some organizational help in order to ward off the threat of the Liberal–SDP Alliance. The press commented on Labour's 'wilful amateurishness'.[78] Jim Mortimer was ill at ease in his unfamiliar role. The press office was a mess, with a skilled professional like Tom McCaffrey unable to impose control. Michael Foot made matters worse on this front by regularly departing from prepared press releases and speaking to journalists off the cuff and at length, although London press conferences went rather better. Whereas Mrs Thatcher organized an exclusive interview on ITV, looking commanding, no one at Labour headquarters thought of arranging such a thing for Foot. Instead he appeared looking dishevelled on a windblown Welsh hillside.

The campaign planners, directed by the National Agent and his staff, made matters far worse by dispatching both Foot and Healey all around the country, to locations great and small. Foot visited in total over seventy marginal seats. He spoke at scores of meetings, usually with a very small entourage, perhaps only McCaffrey or Sue Nye, with him, and inevitably his dog Dizzy. It was sometimes difficult to keep in touch with what was happening in other places, and he and Healey occasionally got into difficulties with their respective, and sometimes conflicting, presentations of party policy. Foot looked relatively fresh after it all, but Healey (himself aged sixty-five) seemed exhausted afterwards, and complained bitterly at the speaking schedule imposed on him.[79]

Some of Foot's campaign visits were almost senseless in their indirection. One particularly unfortunate one, well covered in the Conservative press, was of an aged-looking Foot visiting an old people's home in Banbury in Oxfordshire. The congruence of visitor and residents was a point easily made. In any event, Banbury was not a marginal, but had a safe Conservative majority, and there was no point in Foot wasting his time by going there at all.[80] He and Sue Nye had a difficult moment with a hundred angry fox-hunters in Holmfirth in Yorkshire, backed up by foxhounds and terriers. That may have done Foot no harm with core Labour supporters – he hated the cruelty of hunting with dogs anyway – but there was again no value to be gained by being there.[81] Throughout, Foot found his progress around the constituencies hampered by the presence of four Special Branch officers, which he particularly disliked. He did best in 'walkabouts', despite a characteristic tongue-tied shyness in meeting the voters. Sometimes attempted meetings with electors could turn into 'a media scrimmage', although it was certainly not Foot alone to whom that applied. One pleasant touch came when a student in the Manchester suburb of Chorlton-cum-Hardy offered him a copy of *Gulliver's Travels* to sign. He did so with much charm, and gave the audience a short discourse on Swift and how he had prophesied the existence of the bomb. It was one of the rare moments in the campaign when Foot was truly at ease.[82]

Foot was personally very warmly received. The affection widely felt for Labour's Grand Old Man was manifest, and he drew large audiences. But his speeches were invariably invocations to the faithful, to a loyal but diminishing core of old Labour supporters. Nothing much was done to appeal to new voters or to those who had not voted Labour last time. The conversion of Tories was not the point. It was in many respects an old-fashioned campaign, a kind of mixture of Attlee and Nye Bevan. Foot was the last of the party leaders, as Bob Worcester was to observe, who combined the occasional snappy 'soundbite' with travels around the country.[83] At times his progress resembled Attlee being driven erratically down country lanes by his wife in a battered old Humber saloon in the 1951 election. On other occasions there was flamboyant mass oratory that drew large and affectionate audiences to their feet. Towards the close of the campaign Foot addressed sixty thousand people in a People's March for Jobs. It was the kind of event where he felt himself to be in his natural habitat.

But elections were no longer won at mass meetings, demos or protest marches, but in well-managed press conferences, and especially on the television screen, where passages were inserted into speeches to appeal to the unseen audience of millions, without regard for the much smaller audience who happened to be present. As far as Labour's style was concerned, the medium was wrong, and so, often, was the message. Foot's election speeches were too often full of references to historical events with which his audience was quite unfamiliar, or allusions to authors of whom less cultured or educated voters had never heard. An extreme case was his speech at Oxford Town Hall on 19 May, where he suddenly switched back in time and referred to the Oxford by-election just after Munich in 1938, an event that took place long before most of his mainly undergraduate audience were born. He launched an extraordinary attack on Lord Hailsham, now Lord Chancellor and (as Quintin Hogg) the pro-Chamberlain candidate then – 'and he's still in the government'. Foot's assault was close to libellous, but Hailsham preferred to be tolerant and patronizing – 'Poor old Worzel Gummidge.'[84] Throughout, Foot kept campaigning on the issue of the bomb, and came out well in another discussion with Brian Walden on ITV's *Weekend World*. But it did Labour little good. Asked whether they felt Britain would not be properly defended under a Labour government, 53 per cent agreed, and only 32 per cent disagreed. A television newsflash which featured Foot with the American harmonica player Larry Adler and the popular actress Miriam Karlin was not a bonus, since it showed them all happily singing 'The Red Flag'. That did not play well in middle England.

Throughout the campaign Foot was mercilessly pilloried by rightwing journalists like Jean Rook in the *Daily Express* and George Gale. He was depicted as 'a sad old man in the wrong place at the wrong time'. A particularly tasteless episode was a Young Conservative rally attended by Mrs Thatcher which was regaled by a television comedian, Kenny Everett. He urged his audience, 'Let's bomb Russia! Let's kick Michael Foot's stick away!' The Tory throng roared with helpless laughter.[85]

Foot put in a massive effort. He began the campaign with major speeches in Glasgow (with reference to Keir Hardie), St George's Hall, Liverpool (reference to his own time there), Portsmouth (reference to post-1945 reconstruction) and Cardiff (much reference to Nye Bevan). His most effective theme, about which he cared passionately, was unemployment, which 79 per cent of voters thought was a key issue. However, many of them also felt that unemployment was likely to go up faster under a Labour government. Foot seemed to get better as the campaign went on: a MORI private poll on 21 May showed his satisfaction level had gone up six points in four weeks.[86]

But Labour's campaign was constantly disrupted by problems. Most of them arose from nuclear disarmament, on which Foot and Healey had concocted a precarious compromise between their contrasting positions. Healey had insisted that Polaris should not be scrapped unilaterally, but thrown into general disarmament negotiations. On 23 May Foot had to try to clear up confusion that arose when he and Healey had said contrary things on the topic. Healey, and also Peter Shore, had been careful to distance themselves from a commitment to unilateralism; Healey insisted that Labour would not get rid of Polaris if disarmament negotiations failed, whereas Foot had said the reverse. Even to a friendly journalist like Ian Aitken, Foot seemed 'evasive', but he had to say reluctantly that Polaris would only disappear after 'adequate' Soviet concessions. In effect he came to agree with Healey – only for his defence spokesman, John Silkin, to say the opposite. A statement of Foot's to Channel Four on Polaris brought the headline 'Labour Totters on the Brink' in the *Guardian*.[87] A more direct challenge came from the former Prime Minister, Jim Callaghan, who roundly condemned a unilateralist approach in a speech to his Cardiff constituents.[88] This left Foot and party headquarters angry and nonplussed. The truth was that a manifesto which claimed that 'unilateralism and multilateralism went hand in hand' was close to being meaningless. Quite unexpectedly, Foot also had to cover up for Healey, less belligerent than himself over the Falklands, who had accused Mrs Thatcher of 'glorying in slaughter'. One personally difficult episode concerned Jill Craigie, not a politician herself, but under constant media pressure. After badgering from journalists, she appeared to say that Michael, who was almost seventy, was going to retire soon after the election, if he became Prime Minister.[89] This aroused alarm, including the spectre of the demon Benn in number 10, and was negotiated only with much difficulty.

No one expected Labour to win. Bob Worcester's sad judgement was that the party had no hope of winning in 1983 anyway, and that under the leadership of Michael Foot it could never win any election any time.[90] But the results were calamitous, worse than anyone anticipated. Foot romped home in the redrawn Blaenau Gwent constituency with his majority at 23,625, larger than ever, swollen by the redistribution which gave him extra voters in Brynmawr, thereby helping to depress the Labour vote in Brecon and Radnor, which fell to the

Liberals. But in the country as a whole results showed a massive swing against Labour, and a loss of sixty seats. Foot insisted that unilateralism had not damaged the party's cause, though he did grieve for the defeat of Albert Booth in Barrow-in-Furness (where Polaris submarines were made), and wondered whether in fact it had in that case.[91] Another casualty was Tony Benn in the redistributed Bristol South, which brought rather less grief. Foot delivered a courageous speech to his faithful electors in Ebbw Vale and then drove home to Hampstead through the night to see what future he might be able to salvage.

It was a landslide. The new House showed a total of 396 Conservatives against only 209 Labour and twenty-six for the Liberal–SDP Alliance. But the total of seats masked the full extent of Labour's defeat. While the Conservatives polled 43.5 per cent of the votes, Labour managed to win a mere 28.3 per cent, with the Alliance on 26 per cent. Labour had only just clung on to second place. The immediate need was to ensure that it would not slip down to third. It was easily Labour's worst result since it had become an organized nationwide party in 1918. Even in the disaster of 1931, Labour's share of the poll had been 30.8 per cent. Foot kept cheerful. As he prepared to speak to a miners' rally in Northumberland he insisted, 'It's only a setback.' But no one believed him. *Private Eye* depicted him on its front cover, predictably, waving his stick as he took Dizzy for a walk on Hampstead Heath. The balloon from his mouth had him saying, 'Hang on, I haven't finished yet!' But the cruel lead line below read 'Not Waving but Drowning'.[92]

Foot now had to make up his mind about the future. In fact, union leaders, and more particularly Moss Evans and Clive Jenkins, promptly made it up for him. They decided on the evening following the election that Foot should go, and that Neil Kinnock should replace him.[93] It was the last, decisive political throw by union barons. Jenkins saw his ASTMS executive the next day to tell them that Foot had resigned. After dinner with Michael and Jill at Pilgrims Lane that night, Jenkins went further and sent a press release to ITV's *Weekend World*. It was all quite humiliating, with Foot seemingly a pawn in a game to ensure that the unions controlled the nomination, and that centre-right candidates like Hattersley or conceivably Healey would be sidetracked. Tom McCaffrey knew nothing of Jenkins's manoeuvres, and was furious.[94] The leader's office staff were dumbstruck. As he bathed his wounds, Foot went with Jenkins and their wives on a cheerful visit to the cinema to see Richard Eyre's political satire *The Ploughman's Lunch*. Filmed in the aftermath of the Falklands War, it dealt with the rewriting of history to suit political purposes. It would be hard to find a more appropriate theme for Foot's preoccupations in the twilight of his career.

The contest for his successor between Kinnock and Hattersley began immediately, with the unions already having stacked the odds in Kinnock's favour. Foot's political obituaries were set out in the broadsheets. Even in his resignation, the leader had been unable to lead. There was a last spat with Mrs Thatcher over the award of honours, not over a scandalous list like Harold Wilson's notorious lavender-blue-paper nominations in 1976, but Foot's proposal of twenty-seven new Labour peers. Mrs Thatcher promptly turned almost all of them down, even though they included eminent figures like Douglas Jay and despite the huge inbuilt Tory majority in the Lords. The former SDLP leader Gerry Fitt was one of the handful who scraped through. After that, even though he remained leader until party conference, and had the ordeal of addressing it on the election defeat, Michael Foot was effectively gone, off the front bench for ever.

The universal view of the commentators at the time, and of historians later, was that Foot had been totally miscast as leader, and that his years of leadership were disastrous for his party. This view needs qualification, but it is difficult to dissent from it. It is certainly a great exaggeration to say that Foot's period began Labour's recovery. To end up with the worst result in Labour's history, a major defection of important figures to the SDP, and a mood of disaffection and dismay throughout the constituency parties, cannot be anything other than a chronicle of failure. It is true that Foot's time did see the first significant moves to try to curb the hard left. The register which saw the expulsion of five Militants was a symbolic start, but no more than that. It took the brutal head-on confrontation which Neil Kinnock adopted at the 1985 party conference, along with a fundamental rethinking of unpopular policies on public ownership and more socialism, Europe and, most of all, the bomb, for Labour to clamber out of the trough. But Foot was far too tolerant and gentle in style to engage in any of these. However, almost certainly no one else could have succeeded either in 1980–83, so divided was Labour at that time. It is an illusion to imagine that Denis Healey, who took remarkably little interest in Labour's internal squabbles over reselection and the like, and who had a genius for keeping intellectually aloof, would have been any more effective. It required the débâcle of 1983 for anyone to lead the party back. Neil Kinnock was one important participant who felt that in any case Foot had failed to receive the loyalty he might have expected from his own supporters. Many of the Tribune group who had persuaded him to run for the leadership failed to see the obligation to back him once he had been elected, and he suffered grievously for this.[95]

Foot was never elected as leader in order to win an election. To see him as a possible Prime Minister, then or ever, is to use the wrong yardstick. His election campaign in 1983 was always doomed to failure. His leadership rather was moral, educative, in the deepest sense cultural. In the crisis of 1980–83 his role was to keep the party together, and affirm its core values. This he did with patent sincerity and literary flair. In perspective, he clearly won the battle of the socialisms with Tony Benn. It was the constitutional, rational, non-doctrinaire model that triumphed, even if a centralizing Westminster and Whitehall were not necessarily the instruments for it, and Labour embraced devolution. Even in 1983 many felt that Foot had succeeded, since Benn could never be Labour's leader. In later life Benn became a much-admired celebrity on TV chat shows, and travelling around the land reading out extracts from his diary made him the darling of the halls. He bequeathed his personal charisma, his diaries sold well, and the media lapped him up. Foot's legacy was less spectacular – a great party, ailing but still alive, which others could shortly revive. In that sense, without Foot (certainly without Kinnock) there could have been no Blair. Just as Foot's hero Edmund Burke had appealed from the Old Whigs to the New, so Michael Foot presented the face of Old Labour to New. In time, many felt, Gordon Brown might make the connection successfully. Some derided Foot, the 'old bibliophile', for his obsession with history, his intellectual involvement with Hazlitt, Byron or Wells, which often seemed sharper than his grasp of contemporary issues. But Foot had persuaded enough of his contemporaries that his kind of socialism was a faith worth fighting for; in the years after 1990, as the inevitable reaction against Thatcherism set in, his vision seemed increasingly attractive.

In the end it was the Tories, not Labour, who seemed to plummet into almost inexorable decline, and who would lose three elections running. As leaders of their party John Major, William Hague and Michael Howard did far worse than Michael Foot. In 2005 the Tories' tally of seats was eleven below Labour's in 1983. Opinion analysts showed that in 1997 the Tories were so unpopular that Labour would have defeated them even under a Foot leadership. Labour was not much of a machine in 1983. But there survived a ghost in the machine – the democratic socialism whose flame Foot had kept alive in the dark years. His favourite politician was Charles James Fox, who had kept the liberal ideal alive during decades of opposition, for the Whig Lord Grey and the reformers to reclaim after the war with Napoleon. Memory of Fox was the inspiration behind the triumph of Reform in 1832. In a similar way, Foot and his comrades lay behind Labour's renewal in 1997. After retiring as leader, Foot would no longer be a major politician. But he would still have a role as author, journalist, polemicist, man of letters, icon of public life. Nye Bevan had famously said, 'Tell me your truth and I'll tell you mine.' Like Saint-Simon, Michael Foot still had to get up because he had work to do, to make very sure that his truth kept marching on.

12

INTO THE NINETIES

Michael Foot's habitual response to electoral setbacks was to write a book. Not for him the comfortable, sometimes semi-corrupt directorships or consultancies of the defeated ranks of Majorism or 'New Labour', still less a peerage for services rendered. In 1955, after losing his seat at Devonport, he had found solace in writing about Jonathan Swift. In 1979, after the defeat of the government of which he was Deputy Prime Minister, he had turned to publishing *Debts of Honour*. Thus it was after his heavy defeat as party leader in 1983. He immediately began to write up an account of the ideological contest embodied in the general election. The title he chose was *Another Heart and Other Pulses*, taken from a sonnet by Keats. He also contemplated a much more substantial study of one of his admired authors of prose or poetry: either William Hazlitt or Lord Byron appeared to be a likely subject.

However, he was still Member of Parliament for Blaenau Gwent, and there was much to do in protesting against what he saw as the manifold iniquities of the Thatcher government. Foot had stepped down from the National Executive after he ceased to be leader, but there were many who saw him as likely to play a significant, if subterranean, role in advising and encouraging his successor Neil Kinnock, comfortably elected over Roy Hattersley in the 1983 leadership election, with most of the large unions solidly in his favour. The results announced at the party conference showed Kinnock receiving 71 per cent of the votes in the electoral college and Hattersley 19 per cent, with small votes for Eric Heffer and Peter Shore. Kinnock was a formidable politician in many ways, but also a neophyte, aged just forty-one, with no experience at all of office. Even in his modest

projected role as Foot's PPS at Employment back in 1974, his role had
been a shadowy one. Certainly Foot and Kinnock were bound by the
closest ties of personal affection and ideological affinity. Both were
on the left, anti-European as conventionally understood, and staunch
supporters of the Campaign for Nuclear Disarmament. Both were
socialists whose all-time political hero was another Gwent MP, Nye
Bevan. Many saw Kinnock, Member for Bedwellty, next door to
Ebbw Vale, as the eventual heir to the legendary Mantle of Nye, and
he did not altogether disavow this formidable inheritance. He was
indeed reputed to be producing a book on Bevan, perhaps in the form
of a new edition of *In Place of Fear*. Foot, his MP, who had originally
encouraged him to enter Labour politics, had resigned in such a way
as to make Kinnock's succession to the leadership a near certainty.
Kinnock had enormous admiration for Foot's commitment to principle, his socialist sincerity and his strong feel for the social and ideological roots of the labour movement. If Kinnock now sat behind the
wheel of the Old Labour jalopy, Foot was widely surmised to be a
back-seat driver.

In fact, it did not work out like that. Kinnock retained his close
bond of affection with his old mentor, with whom he had so often
discussed socialist principles in their walks in the mountains above
Tredegar. Glenys Kinnock and Jill Craigie were also very close. There
were some issues on which Foot was able to influence Kinnock,
notably persuading him to drop his opposition to Robert Maxwell's
buying up the strongly pro-Labour *Daily Mirror*. But as Foot perhaps
anticipated, Neil Kinnock was going to be his own man, and to deal
with Labour's crisis in his own way. In any case, after the shambles of
the 1983 general election campaign, it would seem prudent not to be
identified with the old leadership or its style. After a period of uncer-
tainty during the 1984–85 miners' strike, which put Kinnock, a miner's
son, at a painful moral disadvantage through conflicting pressures, he
began to assert himself with new force. His eloquent and aggressive
challenge to the Militants of Merseyside at the 1985 party conference
was hugely acclaimed for showing the mainstream of the party fighting
back against the threat of the hard left. Foot warmly applauded Kinnock's stand, but it was never something that a gentle, bookish socialist
like himself could have attempted.

Kinnock then launched a fierce attack on Militant, embarking on a series of expulsions, especially of its leading figures in Liverpool, that went far beyond anything Foot had visualized. Tony Benn called it a witch-hunt, but by the end of the 1980s his authority in the party had vanished, along with that of other left figures like the former head of the Greater London Council and future Mayor of London Ken Livingstone. Benn stood against Kinnock for the leadership in 1988, and was duly crushed by an eight to one majority. It could be said that Kinnock was continuing the process that Foot had begun in 1982–83, but really the Labour Party was now in a quite different mood, and was looking electable in a way that was unthinkable then. Meanwhile many erstwhile Bennites or hard-leftists migrated rapidly to the centre or centre-right of the party, and were in due time to be happily located within the highly revisionist ranks of New Labour. One of them was Chris Mullin, the erstwhile strongly Bennite editor of *Tribune*, later to be a minister under Tony Blair. After Labour managed to ensure in the 1987 election that they would keep well clear of the Liberal–SDP Alliance as the main challengers to the Tories, a series of policy reviews was held in 1987–89. It was orchestrated by Tom Sawyer, the shrewd 'soft left' NUPE official who served as chairman of the NEC Home Policy Committee (and became Party General Secretary under Tony Blair). Labour entered the nineties with its policies on further nationalization, getting out of Europe and unilateral nuclear disarmament totally reversed. Former SDP intellectuals like David Marquand, Andrew Adonis and Roger Liddle came back to the fold. This was once again the Labour Party they had known, and in some cases loved. Symbolically, the veteran Michael Young, a founder member of the SDP in 1981, now rejoined the party whose manifesto he had actually written in the great election of 1945.

Not only were the method of leadership and the thrust of policies quite different from the Foot era, there was relatively little continuity of personnel. Some younger MPs who had once worked for Foot became key figures behind Kinnock, including Patricia Hewitt, John Reid and Charles Clarke. But otherwise, Foot's people rapidly moved on. Dick Clements, who had faithfully run the Political Office under the former leader, briefly worked for Kinnock but then disappeared from party organization. Elizabeth Thomas, a personal appointment, naturally left the political scene with Foot. Tom McCaffrey, who had served Callaghan and Foot with such skill, now retired, although one or two much younger figures remained on the publicity side, including Hilary Coffman. Foot's economics adviser Henry Neuberger worked briefly for Kinnock, producing papers on low pay amongst other issues, but was eventually supplanted by John Eatwell, then worked briefly for Bryan Gould (whose anti-European views he did not share) before returning happily to the Treasury. The most important change of all, however, was not amongst Foot's personal staff but in the party machine. In 1984 Jim Mortimer retired as General Secretary after an unhappy reign, and was succeeded by Larry Whitty, a far more effective manager, both in reorganizing Walworth Road and in giving effect to the restructuring of the party demanded under Kinnock's leadership. Most unusually, after Whitty's ten-year reign the party finances were comfortably in the black.

Foot's links with the top echelons of the party were therefore not strong, other than his and Jill's personal friendship with Neil and Glenys Kinnock. However, there was still plenty for him to do as a prominent backbench MP. Mrs Thatcher's hard-line foreign and defence policy was a wide-open target, especially with the eventual siting of American Cruise missiles at Greenham Common and a continuing strong nuclear policy. At home, the rapid rise of unemployment as monetarist fiscal policies followed their unhappy course, the sharp decline of manufacturing industry, and a rise in interest rates were also obvious themes for Foot to take up. Perhaps the most serious of all the Conservative policies that he attacked was that relating to the trade unions. Already with a moderate Trade Union Bill put through by Jim Prior in 1980, and then a far more swingeing one carried out by Norman Tebbit in 1982, much of the legislative achievement of Foot's time at Employment in 1974–76 had been reversed. In the cautious words of Davies and Freedland, there had been 'a cumulative reformulation of the role of labour law'.[1]

The biggest change came in Tebbit's Bill, under which Section 14 of Foot's 1974 Trade Union and Labour Relations Act was repealed.[2] This meant that trade union funds would now be open to claims for damages after unlawful actions carried out by union officials: the old immunity from tort in civil actions had been significantly eroded. A sliding scale was set for financial penalties that could be imposed. Exposing the unions' funds to attack totally changed the legal context, and indeed placed the unions on much the same basis as all other organizations within the common law. Other measures seriously undermined the closed shop or 'union-only' activities, gave new legal protection to non-union labour, and redefined and greatly restricted the definition of trade disputes. Another Trade Union Act passed by Tebbit in 1984 laid down new conditions for industrial action, including compulsory ballots on possible strike action and continuing the political levy paid to the Labour Party. Not all of Foot's legislation disappeared. ACAS continued, for instance, as a valuable machinery for conciliation. A number of the changes demanded by employers, such as bans on strikes in essential services, were not carried out by the government. Tebbit's legislation in some respects was less forthright than it seemed, and many issues were left uncertain, such as the closed shop. But a series of often violent confrontations, notably in the Wapping dispute in 1986, when the power of the printing unions was broken after Rupert Murdoch's News International moved from Fleet Street to new mechanized premises in London's docklands, confirmed that the government had won. The enhanced status gained for trade unions by Michael Foot and Jack Jones had largely gone for ever. The new legislation, allied to rising unemployment, saw trade union membership falling rapidly throughout the 1980s. But even under Neil Kinnock, Labour showed little inclination to turn the clock back to 1974. Nor did the TUC have anyone remotely of the authority of Jack Jones to defend its interests. Foot's legislation was a world we had lost.

Michael Foot viewed all this with impotent rage. The difficulties of fighting back emerged during an episode close to his heart and central to his Ebbw Vale constituents. The year-long miners' strike of 1984–85 was one for which the government had carefully prepared, both by building up coal stocks at power stations and elsewhere, and by coordinating the police surveillance machinery nationwide. After the experience of 1972 and 1974, they sensed they had public opinion behind them. The strike ended in the total capitulation of the National Union of Mineworkers, or what was left of it, and the coal industry rapidly wound down in the following years.

Foot naturally spoke with warmth on behalf of the miners and their grievances over pay and working conditions. The mining industry was one of the legends of Labour's historic past. But it was also clear to him that the miners themselves were divided. Mineworkers in the Nottinghamshire coalfield worked throughout the dispute, and after the new year in 1985 many others, who had been on strike for almost nine months, drifted back. Foot knew that in south Wales, as in Marine colliery at Cwm in his own constituency, while the strike was rock solid, the miners and their officials were bitterly hostile to Arthur Scargill, the far-left irreconcilable who led the strike nationally, since he was destroying their traditional industry. This was expressed strongly by the Welsh miners' spokesman, a future government minister, Kim Howells. Foot's main demand, therefore, was for a negotiated settlement through ACAS, and he attacked Mrs Thatcher and the National Coal Board's Director, Ian MacGregor, for preventing one. The miners eventually marched back to work defiantly on 3 March 1985, 'heads held high', with brass bands and banners, and the defiant folk music of radical pop groups like the Geordies who formed Lindisfarne, to cheer them on their way. But by the end of the 1980s the Welsh coal industry, including Marine colliery, had effectively disappeared. Just one pit remained, Tower colliery near Maerdy, and that was only to survive at all through Herculean efforts by the local MP, Ann Clwyd, and the miners, headed by Tyrone O'Sullivan, who ran it as a cooperative. Much of the world in which Foot had grown up politically evaporated with its traditional staple industry.

Foot's parliamentary career was further restricted by the result of the 1987 general election. Labour did stage something of a recovery, but the eventual results were very disappointing. There was a net gain of only twenty seats, from 209 to 229, and Labour's share of the poll rose only to 30.8 per cent, against the Conservatives' 42.2 per cent. Labour's vote rose mainly at the expense of the Alliance parties, and Mrs Thatcher presided over a continuing overall majority of 101. In Blaenau Gwent (the redistributed Ebbw Vale constituency) there was the usual landslide: Foot's majority of 27,861 was his largest ever, and the third largest in the country. His parliamentary activities now focused inevitably on more marginal, non-partisan themes – the televising of parliamentary debates, the working of Public Lending Right and, close to home, protecting the environment of Hampstead

Heath. But as he entered his later seventies it was clear that a major parliamentary career was winding down. In 1991 it was formally announced that Michael Foot would retire from Parliament at the next general election.

But there were always books. Throughout the 1980s, and to some degree the 1990s as well, Foot was primarily at work as an author, not a politician. The first of his books was a political retrospective, his account of the 1983 general election, *Another Heart and Other Pulses*, published by Collins in 1984. It provided a selective chronicle of the campaign; emphasized Labour's key themes such as a new Social Contract, the defence of the unions and the ending of the production and deployment of nuclear weapons; and pointed out, very fairly, the way in which heavily biased press coverage had distorted the public's response to Labour's campaign. There were a few revelations, such as the pre-election suggestions from Gerald Kaufman and Jeff Rooker that Foot should resign as leader, and the agreement between him and Healey not to mention the *Belgrano* sinking.[3] The concluding passages were a passionate morality play, contrasting the injustice and inhumanity of Thatcherism with the warm values of the socialist society. The hearts and souls of all Labour voters would respond to such a call, so beautifully expressed, and would continue to do so as the polarization of the country continued in the Thatcher years. But there was nothing in the book to explain why this apparently evil alternative had been so strongly endorsed by the voters, nor why Labour's vote had fallen to its worst ever. The reasons why more trade union voters had voted Conservative than Labour, after the dismantling of much of Foot's own industrial legislation, were not explored. Foot's book, like so much of his writing, was really a text for the converted.

Foot remained a most conscientious parliamentary representative for Ebbw Vale, and could never be accused of neglecting his duties there. He continued to be a pungent commentator and book reviewer in the pages of *Tribune* as it struggled through the eighties. He responded with enormous enthusiasm to the massive changes that occurred internationally in these years, the Gorbachev revolution in the Soviet Union, the unification of Germany and the winding up of the Cold War. In many ways, in his later years his aspirations for the world order were finally coming about. The old anti-apartheid campaigner also welcomed the eventual changes in South Africa and the new status for Nelson Mandela after his release from prison in February 1990. Foot had things to say and write on all of these. Past triumphs for the forces of progress also had contemporary resonance. Thus Foot flew to Paris in 1989 to celebrate the bicentenary of the storming of the Bastille, and won the gratitude of his friend President Mitterrand by rebutting some withering remarks about the French Revolution uttered by the non-historian Margaret Thatcher.

But the main emphasis in his activities now that he was on the backbenches was literary – the purchase, reading and above all writing of books. Thus he intensified his forays into second-hand bookshops on the Charing Cross Road, especially the establishments of Sam Joseph and David Low, to whom his book on Byron was to be partly dedicated. Throughout the 1980s and 1990s, Foot's main prominence came in the world of letters; he worked partly from home, but mostly in a room in the *Tribune* offices in Gray's Inn Road, in a building owned by the TGWU. He preferred to write in manuscript, or failing that by two-finger typing on an ancient typewriter. Like most older men, he never penetrated the world of the word processor. He reviewed regularly in the *Guardian*, the *Observer* and the highly intellectual neighbourhood newspaper, the *Ham and High*, usually on historical topics. As a reviewer he was unfailingly fair and generous: the vitriol he left to soured scholars. He was also a regular and popular speaker at literary festivals, especially the Cheltenham event, where he became close to the organizers, Peter Eaton and Alan Hancox. He often lectured at home and overseas on a variety of authors, spanning the centuries from Milton to the West Indian Marxist writer C. L. R. James. Thomas Paine was a topic that very occasionally persuaded him to visit America, but he would never linger there as he would in India or Croatia. He chaired the judges of the Booker Prize in 1988, and fought in vain to persuade Sebastian Faulks and the other judges to give the award to Salman Rushdie's *The Satanic Verses*, instead of to Peter Carey's *Oscar and Lucinda*. He then took a leading part in promoting Rushdie, and spoke strongly of his qualities in his Chairman's address at the Booker award ceremony in October 1988. He wrote privately to Rushdie comparing *The Satanic Verses* with that famous satire on all religions, Swift's *The Tale of a Tub* – than which, of course, praise could scarcely be higher.[4] Foot was also involved in moves to protect Rushdie from physical harm when a *fatwah* was pronounced against him by Ayatollah Khomeini because of the perceived immorality and blasphemy of his book. Private protests from the Labour parties in Leicester and Blackburn, with their strong Muslim membership, were brushed aside.

Of all his literary heroes, Foot most ardently worshipped Byron, and it was on him rather than on Hazlitt that he decided to focus in his next major book. Byron's poetry had long been a unique inspiration – it was very much a personal one, since Foot's father Isaac, a great lover of Wordsworth like Michael, was not especially sympathetic to Byron's mode of passionate romanticism. Byron was a major link with many of the other honoured members of Foot's cultural genealogy, an enthusiastic devotee of Jonathan Swift, and in his own day a major influence on the lyricism and also the radicalism of Heinrich Heine. Foot was thus a very active member of the Byron Society, which he often addressed, and he served as its President for a time. Through this Society he forged close friendships with at least two eminent Conservatives, Ian (later Lord) Gilmour, who also served as President of the Byron Society and who wrote a fascinating book in 2002 on the early lives of Byron and Shelley, and Robert Blake, the biographer of Disraeli. For Blake, as for Foot, fascination with Disraeli and admiration for Byron went hand in hand. Both enjoyed the Byronesque exoticism of Disraeli's novel *Lothair*, which as Blake wrote 'was deemed by many to be his masterpiece'.[5] Collins gave Foot a contract for his Byron book in 1985, and he spent the next three years working on it, going through the whole of Byron's voluminous corpus of poetry, prose and private letters with an almost scholastic intensity. As in his work on Swift, Foot showed an academic passion for the minutiae of evidence, and the intellectual ability to handle a wide range of sources. He had revealed a similar scholarly enthusiasm in correspondence on the career of Hazlitt with the eminent authority Stanley Jones, who responded warmly to Foot's pursuit of some of the more arcane details of Hazlitt's life.[6] In a different incarnation, Foot would have made a wonderfully imaginative, if discursive, university historian, a kind of politicized Richard Cobb. Equally, he never held back if he felt that professional historians were missing the point or debasing their subject: thus he smote Simon Schama hip and thigh for the disenchanted, anti-Jacobin, even anti-ideological tone of his book on the French Revolution, *Citizens* (1989). This work, declared Foot, consisted of 'assault by innuendo'. Hazlitt, Stendhal and Heine, among other old friends, were called upon to denounce it.[7]

While working on his Byron book, Foot also produced another volume of collected essays, *Loyalists and Loners*, published by Collins in 1986. It is an enjoyable read, even if it lacks the central personalities who dominated *Debts of Honour* in 1980, such as Swift, Beaverbrook and Foot's father Isaac. The book consists of thirty studies, many of them short book reviews published earlier, but a few more extended pieces, including a highly sympathetic study of Jennie Lee. The title of the book is an exegesis of the tension between party and principle. A subtle essay on Enoch Powell brings out the theme of the lifelong 'loner' with rare skill. It compares him effectively with a somewhat similar free-thinking rebel, the Birmingham radical imperialist Joseph Chamberlain, including their respective positions on Northern Ireland.[8] The essays of most contemporary interest were the first ten, covering contemporary Labour personalities. There is a ferocious attack on George Thomas, Lord Tonypandy, for thirty years a Labour MP (and Cabinet minister) and also a recent Speaker of the House. His memoirs, *Mr Speaker* (1985), had included disloyal attacks on former Labour colleagues (his jealousy of Jim Callaghan, elected with him for Cardiff in 1945 and a far more significant politician, is very evident), the sly sycophancy of the Methodist 'unco guid' and, worst of all, the betrayal of confidences over private conversations with ministers behind the Speaker's chair. Foot had strongly attacked this impropriety as 'worse than [Clive] Ponting' (a civil servant unsuccessfully prosecuted for releasing material covered by the Official Secrets Act about the sinking of the *Belgrano*). Reviewers like Robert Blake felt that Foot's attack on Tonypandy was totally justified. Fortunately, no Speaker has written such a book since then.

Of Foot's recent colleagues, there are fascinating, if savage, analyses of David Owen and Tony Benn. 'Ex-Brother David', defector extraordinary as he appears here, is examined via a quotation from Lord Halifax's *Character of a Trimmer* (1688) – 'the impudence of a Bawd is Modesty compared with that of a Convert'; Foot also has sharp things to say about Owen's 'reversionary interest in the future', his eye on the main chance, as Foot saw it.[9] Brother Tony is dealt with even more trenchantly, as his conversion from Anthony Wedgwood-Benn, patrician occupant of the centre ground, to Tony Benn, people's tribune, is dissected. Foot lists as Benn's crimes disloyalty, hypocrisy and unctuous pride. When we read elsewhere in the book of William Lovett deriding Feargus O'Connor in 1840 as 'the great I am' of the Chartist movement, it could be Foot on Benn in 1980.

There are also fascinating insights into Foot's own mental and historical make-up. While due tribute is paid to Churchill as a great war leader, one moving essay shows how Michael, like all the Foots, idolized another premier, another famous Celtic outsider, David Lloyd George, the hero of his West Country youth. There is a memorable *recherche du temps perdu* with an account of the magical experience of a breakfast appointment with the old Prime Minister at the Randolph Hotel in Oxford when Foot was an undergraduate at Wadham.[10] Also, along with tributes to such miscellaneous giants as Stendhal and Herzen, there is a keen appreciation of Heine in all his many-sidedness, his gift of irony, his humanity, his captivating Jewishness, his love of Venice, his importance for Foot's dear departed friend, Vicky. There is a typically generous and well-merited tribute to the great author of *Heine's Jewish Comedy*, Siegbert Prawer, a refugee from Nazism as a boy who became Fellow of Queen's College and Professor of German Literature at Oxford. Prawer and Foot were introduced to each other by the present writer. They were left alone talking animatedly about their literary heroes in an otherwise deserted college dining hall. In *Loyalists and Loners* Foot quotes Heine's self-description, 'an unfrocked romantic'. He could well be writing about himself. Foot had once told the Welsh poet Vernon Watkins, who had published a poem on Heine in the *Spectator*, that 'the company of Heine devotees [was] one of the most fortunate companies in the world'.[11] One reader who much enjoyed the book was Jim Callaghan: 'What I enjoyed particularly about the book was its reminder that when we were young we didn't think of Socialism as only dreary economics and trade balances. If only some of our people would stop snarling at one another for long enough they would realize the uplifting of the spirit that Socialist values can bring.'[12]

Foot's major work on Byron, *The Politics of Paradise: A Vindication of Byron*, was published in 1988. It attracted attention not only because of its eminent author but as an important contribution to a relatively neglected aspect of its much-discussed subject, his political outlook. The dedication page alone tells much of Foot's lives and loves, since the dedicatees variously include Jill, two booksellers, the organizers of the Cheltenham Literary Festival and the electors of Blaenau Gwent, who understood 'the meaning of Byronic resistance to the bomb'. There is also a passage at the end in praise of the Very Reverend Eric Abbott, Dean of Westminster, who in 1968 approved the placing of a plaque of Byron, hitherto excluded on moralistic grounds, in Poet's Corner at Westminster Abbey following entreaties from 'a good Byronist, the late Lord Boothby'.[13]

It is a deeply personal book, in many ways an autobiography, and very moving as the work of a man in his seventies recollecting emotion in tranquillity in his later life. It may not be the most authoritative book on Byron in recent years, but it perhaps gets us closer to its subject's ruling passions than any other. The novelist Brigid Brophy, whom Foot had got to know during the campaign for Public Lending Right, wrote warmly that 'I admire the swiftness (and Swiftness) of your intellectual narrative, your learning, precision and conciseness . . . You have indeed vindicated Byron. Only you could have done so.' She also noted his generosity to other authors. Foot has two tremendous chapters on what Venice meant to Byron and others, and to a degree the Serenissima is as much a hero of the book as Byron himself. 'It is part of the city's secret that she seems to be unveiling her charms individually to each newly arrived suitor,' Foot writes in typically sensuous imagery.[14] Byron, for Foot, rediscovered Venice and made her magic accessible to later generations. The poet was linked not only with Foot's places but with his people. We read of Byron's admiration for the writings of Montaigne, especially when he was returning to the writing of *Don Juan* in 1822. We learn of his praise for Oliver Cromwell. We discover the massive influence on Byron of the writings of Swift. The admiration of Heine for Byron as a spiritual liberator for a revolutionary Europe yearning for freedom is underlined. We are told at some length of Disraeli's fascination with Byron. His *Venetia* was an apology for Byron, while his later novel *Lothair* has a Byronic heroine, 'the divine Theodora'. We read of the particular appeal of

Byron for women, who understood him better than men did. Thus Fanny Brawne had more awareness of Byron's qualities than John Keats had, and he was best understood by women authors and literary critics like Elizabeth Boyd and Doris Langley Moore. (Whether Foot would apply this view to Fiona MacCarthy's 2002 biography, with its suggestions of Byron's bisexuality, seems more doubtful.)

Foot saw in Byron the free-thinking radical, the 'democratical' republican, the champion of freedom across the globe, the man who devoted his maiden speech in the Lords in 1812 to a passionate defence of the poor Nottinghamshire framework-knitters whose lives were being turned upside down by the introduction of new machinery by unfeeling capitalist entrepreneurs. Foot's Byron is a citizen of the world, a man who loves the culture of Greece but whose generous liberalism is stirred above all by his love affair with Italy, 'more tempestuous and languorous by turns, more adult and comprehensive'; he inspires a great hymn of affection from Mazzini, the prophet of Italian national self-determination.[15] Foot denies the charge (once made by Shelley) that *Childe Harold* showed that Byron's revolutionary impulse was waning. Byron is as implacable an opponent as Shelley of Tory ministers like Castlereagh and Sidmouth, he is equally appalled by the massacre of Peterloo and rejoices in the news of Castlereagh's suicide.

Supremely, Byron, a man who witnessed scenes of carnage at first hand in Spain during the Peninsular War, is the opponent of war and the prophet of the horrors of a nuclear holocaust. *Don Juan*, writes Foot, is 'the great anti-war epic in our language, or maybe any other'. Byron felt the cruelty of war to the very marrow of his being. His poem 'Darkness' was cited by Foot in his Cardiff lecture 'Byron and the Bomb' as an evocation of the aftermath of a nuclear catastrophe. Fiona MacCarthy, who sees in it the influence of the child Byron's reading of the Book of Revelation, considers this poem 'grand and terrifying', a study of the last survivors in a ravaged landscape, a Europe made desolate by the bestialities of war.[16] Her book does not over-emphasize Byron's concern with political or social issues. But every author creates a new Byron, a Byron made in his or her own image. Foot sees him as 'the poet of action: more than any other in our language, the poet who cannot watch the fearful human scene without incitement to protest or revenge or perpetual Promethean counter-assault'.[17] His Byron is a thrilling, Manichean poet – and also a thera-peutic one. Foot, in recommending that *Don Juan* be read as a whole (a fairly gargantuan demand), notes: 'I took a copy of *Don Juan* into hospital one week and read it all and recovered.'[18]

The Politics of Paradise – a reference to Byron's comment on his own extremely obscure verse play *Cain* – is a serious, if characteristi-cally partisan, study, one of the best books any politician has ever written about a poet. There are two problems that Foot had to over-come. One was reconciling his two heroes, Hazlitt and Byron. In the first chapter of his book, 'A Cavanagh of a Critic', Foot acknowledges that Hazlitt was a very fierce critic of Byron's poetry, both in style and sense. Hazlitt's essay 'The Spirit of the Age' (which Fiona MacCarthy does not mention at all) was scathing about what he called 'the inordi-nate egotism of the Byronic odyssey'.[19] He was also hugely critical of Byron's use of language and what he saw as his needless obscurity. The poet was upset and angry at Hazlitt's comments. Some of them are demonstrably unfair, or even tasteless, as when Byron's poetic idiosyncrasies are linked to his club foot. Foot can hardly deny the frequently hostile view adopted by Hazlitt during Byron's lifetime, but he also points out how he defended both Byron and Leigh Hunt from 'the practised liars' of the Tory press (compared by Foot with the modern *Daily Mail* and the *Sun*). Byron, Foot states, perhaps not altogether convincingly, was Hazlitt's 'poet-hero'.[20] The other prob-lem is Byron's treatment of women, whom he could both idolize and seriously misuse. As with his other objects of admiration – Swift, Hazlitt and Wells in particular – Foot's view tends to follow the varying lines that Byron's poetic urge dictated a philandering course, and that the women were honoured or dignified by their treatment anyway. For Augusta Leigh and Teresa Guicciolli read Swift's Stella and Vanessa, or perhaps Wells's Amber Reeves and Rebecca West. Jill Craigie was always wary of Michael's perspective in these matters, and she tended to be the more consistent of the two on them. But *The Politics of Paradise* is still a memorable and generous book, highly enjoyable to read, full of astonishingly detailed knowledge of the sources. It explains, as some more scholarly books do not, precisely how Byron could exert a compulsive international appeal for artists like Heine and Pushkin and Berlioz and Delacroix. It shows how Continental intellectual exiles,

Mazzini, Herzen, Ledru-Rollin, even Marx, could not understand why the English placed the more passive poetry of Wordsworth or Coleridge above that of the revolutionary romanticism of Byron.[21] It also shines a powerful beam on Michael Foot's own moral and aesthetic values, his cry of conscience for human redemption.

To Foot, Byron represented the spirit of an 'irrepressible hopefulness'. For all his advancing years, he now turned to another major literary enterprise. Hazlitt remained discarded as a topic for extended work, but there remained the beguiling prospect of one of Foot's first literary and political loves, H. G. Wells. Much of the next seven years would be devoted to studying his life, loves and literature, and in 1995 *The History of Mr Wells*, another important, if equally controversial, biographical study appeared, another labour of love. The Foots' travels at this period were closely linked to Michael's literary enthusiasms – nearly all of which happened to be Jill's also. Venice continued to be a cherished, magical location until the early eighties, when it was challenged and superseded by another sea-girt city with links with Byron and Heine, not to mention Rebecca West – the Dalmatian city of Dubrovnik, known to history as the Venetian Ragusa. Byron had called it 'the pearl of the Adriatic'.

The Foots' travels also encompassed other worlds, especially India, where the attraction was more political than cultural, with Foot's particular contacts with the Gandhi family, partly mediated by the benevolent personality of Swraj Paul, who had brought new work to Ebbw Vale. Foot had never seriously recanted his support for Indira Gandhi during the state of emergency. On the contrary, he praised her for holding an election at all (and then accepting its verdict!) in 1977, and hailed her return to power in 1980 after a period of Janata rule. Throughout he continued to uphold the Indian point of view over Kashmir, and staunchly defended Mrs Gandhi's strong action against the Sikhs, which had involved sending troops into the city of Amritsar and destroying the Golden Temple there. A fellow Labour MP, Oonagh McDonald, was told by Foot that Mrs Gandhi had a prime concern for the unity of India, and could not let Sikh terrorism continue. He strongly criticized the *New Statesman*, in a letter it published on 22 November 1984, for printing attacks on Indira Gandhi by the formerly leftish commentator David Selborne, and accused that old organ of the left of becoming 'the last refuge of neo-colonialism'. He wrote to the cartoonist Abu, a critic of Mrs Gandhi, that 'some appalling filth is being poured out on the subject in some of our newspapers here, led, I am sorry to say, by the *New Statesman*'.[22] He was concerned that because of what the Indians saw as the failure of the Thatcher government to take action against Sikh extremist organizations in Britain, trade between Britain and India was being affected. A £100 million contract for British Aerospace to supply eight Harrier jets to the Indian navy and an £85 million contract for Westland helicopters had been suspended.[23] Foot used his influence to build bridges on these matters with some effect.

In October 1984 he was horrified by news of the assassination of Mrs Gandhi by her Sikh bodyguard; thousands of Sikhs were to be massacred in communal revenge by Hindus. Two long periods of premiership (1966–77, 1980–83) had ended in tragedy. Mrs Gandhi's son Rajiv became the new Prime Minister, and shortly thereafter won a landslide election victory. Foot and Jill visited India at his invitation in January 1985. During his stay Foot gave interviews to the press, including one with the Calcutta *Statesman* in which he praised Indian initiatives on nuclear disarmament, and somewhat hopefully declared that India would not go in for the military use of nuclear technology.[24] When he returned to Britain, he spent much time pressing the British Foreign Office on the need to deal with Sikh activities in the United Kingdom, and pointed out that the Canadian authorities had acted more speedily over extradition[25] – somewhat the same argument that would arise over alleged Muslim 'extremists' after the Iraq war in 2003–05. He had little success. However, India remained profoundly important to him. In 1987 he went again to the country, and took part in a major conference on non-violence and the moral order in Delhi in memory of Mrs Gandhi, along with Bishop Trevor Huddleston, the French politician Simone Veil and others. The assassination of Rajiv Gandhi in May 1991 was a further source of much distress. On 16 June 1991 he gave a passionate address at a Rajiv Gandhi memorial meeting convened by the India League, declaring that both Indira and her son Rajiv had given their lives for a united India. Six years later he went on another visit to India to discuss world disarmament. This reawakened the now octogenarian Foot's passion for a nuclear-free peace, and generated yet another book, *Dr Strangelove, I Presume* (1999). As throughout his life from the 1930s to the 1990s, from Krishna Menon to Foot's friend the Prime Minister Manmohan Singh, Michael Foot always found in India a touchstone for his values, which the 'Nehru-Gandhi dynasty' embodied. He kept aloof from harsh criticisms by Indian commentators of Nehru's legacy, and even more of Indira Gandhi and her sons for cronyism and undermining the institutions and processes of Indian liberal democracy.

But the Foots' most regular and cherished travels were to the walled city of Dubrovnik on the Adriatic. They went originally in 1981 at the invitation of the Yugoslav government, while Foot was leader of the Labour Party. Michael and Jill had heard much of Dubrovnik before from their friend Rebecca West. Her book *Black Lamb and Grey Falcon: A Journey Through Yugoslavia* (1941), however, was far from complimentary about the city, and in conversation she was always inclined to be critical of the artistic priorities of the city fathers, even if she found the old city beautiful. But from the first the Foots were enchanted by Dubrovnik, its fortresses, palaces and cloisters, the cheerful cafés and restaurants around the Rector's Palace and along the quayside, boat trips to the nearby islands, the scenic setting on the Adriatic looking out to the island of Lokrum. Until Jill died in 1999 they would spend a month in Dubrovnik every summer, and would sometimes go there in the spring as well, staying in the Villa Dubrovnik, set beside the sea and a short walk from the battlements of the city. The hotel manageress, Nada Maric, would receive messages from the Foots from other parts of the world saying that attractive as they were, they could not hold a candle to Dubrovnik. Foot resumed his visits to Dubrovnik after Jill's death, seriously disabled though he now was, and they always meant much to him.[26]

When staying in the city, Foot preferred to lead a very private life. He would tend to rise early, soon after 6 a. m., before the staff of the Villa Dubrovnik were really up and about, walk the half-mile to the city, buy some papers, stroll along the main street, the Stradun, sip a coffee in the Kamenica restaurant, famous for its oysters, or perhaps the Festival bar, and generally relax in the leisurely ambience of the old city. He would talk to the locals when he could, but invariably about the arts, seldom about politics. Jill was equally under Dubrovnik's spell, and got to know artists there. The Foots made some good friends amongst the local people, artistic primarily. One particularly close friend was Jan Pulitika, an imaginative landscape painter whom Jill got to know well and some of whose work, with its bright blue colours, was to adorn 66 Pilgrims Lane. Another warm friend, from the early 1990s, was Vesna Gamulin, a multilingual, much-travelled translator of much charm, who along with her seafaring husband Jadran greatly extended the Foots' knowledge of the local community, its culture and Croatia's international difficulties. A more strongly political friend was Dr Hrvoje Kacic, a maritime lawyer who served as Croatia's representative at many international conferences, and a fierce critic of the Serb assault on his native land. As their beloved Venice became increasingly swamped by international tourism, the more private, more gentle charms of Dubrovnik, with its attractive people, became essential to the Foots' way of life.[27]

They visited Dubrovnik at first solely as tourists, enamoured of its setting and culture. But there was soon a very important political dimension. The break-up of the old Yugoslavia in 1991–92 had serious implications for Dubrovnik, as indeed for Croatia as a whole. There were communal tensions throughout the region, especially involving conflict between the Croats (initially in alliance with the Slovenes) and the Serb government of Belgrade, which presided over Serbia and Montenegro, the remnant of the old Yugoslavia. By 1992 there were even worse fratricidal horrors in Bosnia. War broke out between Serbia-Montenegro and Croatia in the summer of 1991, and lasted until 1995. In October 1991 Dubrovnik was under siege, and remained so for the next eight months. Thousands of shells poured down from the mountains into the old city, where 70 per cent of the buildings suffered direct hits, and historic churches, monasteries, palaces and the old city walls were severely damaged, and the nearby airport destroyed. Over a hundred civilians were killed, along with scores of young men defending their city: their memory was to be movingly commemorated in a special gallery in the Sponga Palace in the city centre. Maps around the city walls testify to the extent of the damage for the instruction of tourists. Fifteen years after the war Croatian relations with Serbia, and indeed with Montenegro and Bosnia as well, were no more than tepid.

Michael Foot was utterly horrified at the Serb attacks. His and Jill's sense of outrage at seeing a beautiful and historic city dear to both of them pounded into rubble was obvious. But in addition the siege of Dubrovnik stirred up all the old emotions once let loose in *Guilty Men*, about an almost helpless civilian population being attacked at will by an aggressive dictator. In the past, Foot had been a staunch supporter of Tito's regime (Tito was a Croat, though one generally detested in his own native land) and critical of Croat politicians, especially the Ustasha, who openly sympathized with the Nazis during the war and fought against Tito's Partisans. There were now those on the left (notably his nephew Paul) who felt that Foot was being, as in India and elsewhere, far too one-eyed and partisan, ignoring the attempts at ethnic cleansing of Serbs by President Franjo Tudjman of Croatia, and also his notorious record of anti-Semitism. This was also the view, on the right of the spectrum, of an old opponent, Nora Beloff. She wrote to Foot attacking his 'transparent pro-Croatian bias' and telling him he should be asking for negotiations between Serbia and Bosnia, 'not more violence'. But the balance of aggression clearly came from the Serbs, under the brutal regime of Slobodan Milosevic, hurling weapons of war at a smaller neighbour while the rest of the world did very little. The British Foreign Office seemed to Foot particularly dishonest and spineless, as dishonourable as the appeasers had been in Spain in 1937. His response, therefore, was a final crusade of conscience. It was quite as moving in its way as that of his fellow octogenarian Gladstone's at the massacre of the Armenians in 1896. Foot won new respect from unlikely quarters in Britain. In Dubrovnik, and indeed throughout Croatia, he moved from being a deeply honoured and respected visitor, patron of art and history, to being seen as an international crusader for liberation. There were moves to have him made an honorary citizen of the city, like Dr Kathy Wilkes, a courageous Oxford philosophy don who had made visits to underground groups in Czechoslovakia while it was still under Communist rule and who had stayed in Dubrovnik during the siege.[28]

He had begun his campaign on behalf of Croatia while still an MP in 1991–92. He called for international action to intervene against the Serbs' campaign of intimidation and aggression along the Dalmatian coast, and was scathing about the inertia shown by Douglas Hurd, the British Foreign Secretary. He criticized the uncharacteristically inhumane approach of a friend, the Conservative historian Robert Blake, who had remarked, almost casually, 'No one can stop these tribes slaughtering each other.'[29] Among other things, the historian was guilty of bad history. On 5 March 1992 Foot made what was to be his last speech in the House of Commons, and it was in its way typical of one of the most charismatic and courageous backbenchers ever to sit in the historic chamber. He condemned the failure of the British government and the international community to take more effective action, both military and in terms of sending food supplies, and made acerbic comparison with the failures of the 1930s. He particularly emphasized the assault on Dubrovnik, which he felt was one of the worst acts since the bombing of Guernica during the Spanish Civil War.[30] Little regarded at the time, Foot's speech left its legacy. Another Labour Member, Tony Blair, was to take note when he persuaded the Americans to instigate military action against the Serbs during the similar Kosovo crisis six years later, with heavy bombing raids directed at the heart of the Serbian capital Belgrade.

Foot pointed out in the *Guardian* on 25 August 1992 that the government had no excuse for claiming ignorance of the situation, since journalists had long been writing that the Serb armies were 'destroying Yugoslavia in the name of Yugoslavia'. The Chamberlain government in the late 1930s had received similar press warnings about what was happening to the Jews in Germany, and had also turned several blind eyes. Another Munich was beckoning.[31] Douglas Hurd would not take action to help Croatia. He cited the distinctly mixed record of President Tudjman (as many in the Labour Party did), and resisted pressure from the German government of Helmut Kohl, always traditionally sympathetic to Croatia.[32] In the end, the Serb siege of Dubrovnik came to an end in August 1992, and the shelling of the old city finally ceased. Croatia had by then, like Slovenia, proclaimed itself an independent state, and was recognized officially by the British government. But an uneasy state of cold war continued, and not until 1996 did Croatia and Serbia formally conclude a peace settlement. Meanwhile, with some aid from international agencies, poor, battered Dubrovnik was rapidly rebuilt, until by 2005 its scars were no longer obviously visible and tourism was thriving as never before. In 2004, after a lengthy trial in The Hague, the Serbian General Miodrag Jokic was sentenced to seven years' imprisonment for war crimes connected with the bombing of Dubrovnik. But it was one conviction only, and most of the Serb aggressors in government at the time, including the former President Radovan Karadzic, remained at large. Ex-President Milosevic died in The Hague in March 2006, his trial for war crimes having made only slow progress. Michael Foot's reaction to the Serbs was one of unprecedented ferocity. Opponent of capital punishment though he was, he told Vesna Gamulin that he hoped that Milosevic would be hanged.[33]

Michael Foot witnessed the end of the siege of Dubrovnik as a non-parliamentarian. He had decided not to stand as the Labour candidate for Blaenau Gwent at the next general election, and gave some encouragement to Peter Hain, whom he had met when Hain was leading the 'Stop the Tour' campaign in 1969 to prevent the visit of the South African rugby team, as his possible successor. Hain did not make the shortlist, but was returned for Neath instead. Foot then hoped that he might be succeeded by a woman, but she was voted down by the local party in favour of Llew Smith, an exceptionally traditional Old Labour figure and opponent of Welsh devolution. Smith remained the Member until 2005, when his own retirement provoked a far more serious local dispute about a woman candidate. Foot played less part in the 1992 general election than in any election since that of 1935. He had a quiet start to the campaign, but then, against the wishes of Labour headquarters, went on a week's speaking tour of Wales as far north as Anglesey. Labour made gains in Wales, though not in Monmouth, even though Foot had nostalgically insisted on visiting the constituency he had fought fifty-seven years earlier.[34] Like most observers he thought that the general election would see Neil Kinnock returned to head a new Labour government, but in fact the Conservatives hung on under John Major. Indeed, although the margin in seats between the two main parties was relatively small, at sixty-five, the gap in the vote (42 per cent to the Conservatives, 35 per cent to Labour) was still a very large one. Recovery from the 1983 disaster was still far from complete.

Foot was grievously disappointed, but he departed quietly, saying his emotional goodbyes to the voters of Blaenau Gwent. After the election he began making arrangements with Jill to sell their little home in Morgan Street, Tredegar. A decade later the property was half derelict, the nearby shops boarded up, and almost all the local steelworks was closed down by its owner Corus in 2001. Half a century after the Attlee government's regional policies had brought new hope and employment to the valleys, Tredegar was close to being a ghost town.

For Michael Foot it really was the end at Westminster, after a long and spectacular innings. He refuted with scorn suggestions in the press that he might accept a peerage, and declared that he was quite as strongly in favour of the abolition of the House of Lords as ever he had been.[35] He had always been keenly aware of the history of the Labour and socialist movement. He also had regard for his own history and role in that movement. In 1993 it was announced that his private papers would go to the Labour [later People's] History Museum in Princess Street, Manchester, its most important private collection, to go alongside the archive of the Labour Party, which had been transferred there from Walworth Road.[36] Under the expert custody of Stephen Bird, the archivist, in the scholarly neutrality of the archive store-room, the old rebel's records would be deposited side by side with those of the party apparatchiks he had for so long tormented, lion and lamb reunited.

Then it was back to the Balkans. The main interest had now swung from Croatia to Bosnia, and Dubrovnik returned to something nearer normality as ruined properties were rebuilt. In 1993 the Foots resumed their annual visitations to the Villa Dubrovnik as before. But the legacy of injustice and bitterness remained in the hearts and minds of their friends, and indeed in the Foots themselves. Foot now kept up a strong campaign in the press to get international action to protect Bosnia from ethnic cleansing, to enforce a proper settlement and to restore the authority of the United Nations Charter. He criticized, as did Croatians like Dr Kacic, the Owen/Vance plan for dividing up Bosnia Herzegovina as a victory for the Serbs: David Owen, himself a defector to the SDP, was always destined to be one of Foot's particular *bêtes noires*. Michael and Jill were determined to do more to highlight the atrocities in the Balkans, first in Croatia and then in Bosnia, which the world chose to ignore.

Jill Craigie now revived her career as a film director. After encouragement from friends such as Salman Rushdie and the television presenter Jon Snow, she determined to make a film about Yugoslavia, with Michael as the presenter.[37] They tried in vain to get financial assistance from a former Cabinet colleague, Harold Lever, and also from Sidney Bernstein of Granada Television, but in the end £50,000 was raised, including £12,000 from Michael's superannuation. Michael and Jill went to Dubrovnik in bitterly cold weather in December 1993, and began work. Michael did the main presenting from the city battlements and elsewhere, while there were also appearances from Salman Rushdie, the Conservative MP Sir Patrick Cormack and the Labour MP Malcolm Wicks. Foot's performance, given that he was severely handicapped in his mobility and that he had totally lost the sight of one eye after a severe attack of shingles in the late eighties, was an astonishing achievement of stamina and sheer guts. It was he who supplied a good deal of the substance of the film, after having had conversations with Kathy Wilkes, who had friends at the university in Dubrovnik.

The film was primarily an attack on the ethnic cleansing carried out so brutally by the Serbs in Bosnia, although the Foots were not allowed to go to Bosnia at all, and shot the film entirely in Dubrovnik. The film, entitled *Two Hours from London*, was also a fierce assault on the bland inertia towards Serb aggression shown by successive Tory Foreign Secretaries, Hurd and then Malcolm Rifkind, which, Foot declared on the film, 'was an absolute go-ahead for Milosevic'. Comparisons were made with Munich. An *Observer* interview on 1 January 1995 was headlined 'Foot Names the Guilty Men of Bosnia'.[38] There was much difficulty in getting the film shown. In the end it was cut down by half, to one hour, and shown on BBC television on 1 April 1995. John Naughton in the *Observer* found it very one-sided in its descriptions of the Serbs' 'genocidal nightmare' in Bosnia. Even a friend like Jon Snow noted the absence of any criticism of President Tudjman.[39] But Naughton also found it deeply moving that an elderly couple, one of them in frail health, 'who should be spending their twilight years enjoying the quiet, bookish celebrity to which they are richly entitled', should be so outraged by events in central Europe that they would spend a year and sink their savings in 'a magnificent attempt to counter some of the lies and equivocations which have underpinned the betrayal of the Bosnian people'.

But the cynics (hand-picked for BBC late shows) and British ministers (Naughton referred to the 'Bugger Bosnia' school) derided the
Foots' efforts. John Major assured his backbenchers that no British
troops or other personnel would be sent to Bosnia. There were loud
murmurs in the House of 'Munich'. In Croatia, the film was shown
on a national channel at peak viewing time in uncut two-hour form,
and was regarded as a masterpiece. Vesna Gamulin thought it an extraordinary tribute to Jill Craigie's professional skills as a film director.
An Italian friend of the Foots in Brussels thought it 'an important
achievement in dispelling once and for all the myth of the "tribal civil
war" in the ex-Yugoslavia'.[40] It was generally felt to be easily the most
effective portrayal for the world of the sufferings of the Croatian and
Bosnian peoples.

Michael Foot's health remained generally good for a man of his
age – in his view, testimony to the eternal blessings of the NHS. In
1995, when he was almost eighty-two, he had a serious prostate operation, but soon recovered. Despite other physical problems – serious
arthritis in a leg, the loss of sight in his left eye, the need for a hearing
aid which he found difficult to assemble himself – he lived almost as
active a life as before, much assisted by many affectionate friends. He
was frequently in the news, usually through his own instigation, as
in frequent letters to the *Guardian* and *The Times*, but sometimes
unintentionally. The most extraordinary occasion was in February
1995, when he was suddenly accused of having been a long-term spy
for the KGB. Rumours about Labour politicians were rife at this time.
There had been some prior to the 1992 general election, when the
names not only of Michael Foot but of Neil Kinnock and several
others (including, astonishingly, David Owen) had appeared in the
Sunday Times under the heading 'Kinnock's Kremlin Connection',
only to disappear very quickly. Years later, Dick Clements was to be
another victim. Much of this had to do with the activities of Oleg
Gordievsky, a former KGB spy who had acted as a double agent for
both Britain and the Soviet Union in the later 1970s, and who found
an easy outlet for his suspicions in the British press. On 19 February
the *Sunday Times* ran a front-page headline, 'KGB: Michael Foot was
our Agent'.[41] The story was that Foot had regularly met Soviet agents
in the 1960s, had had lunch with them in the Gay Hussar and had

received occasional payments to help out the finances of *Tribune*. Foot was said by another retired KGB agent, Viktor Kubeykin, to have been an influential agent, while Mikhail Lyubimov, yet another old KGB hand, had had 'several lunches in London restaurants' – than which, clearly, nothing could be more sinister. The KGB men had also targeted Jack Jones, Ray Buckton of ASLEF, the engine drivers' union, Ian Mikardo and the veteran socialist and internationalist Fenner Brockway, but Foot was thought especially important. He was apparently known in KGB code, not very originally it would seem, as 'Agent Boot'.

The following week the *Sunday Times* embellished the original accusations, not with more facts, since there were none, but with more innuendo. Gordievsky's memoirs, for which the Foot allegations were a trailer, began serialization. Andrew Neil, the paper's former editor, declared that Foot was 'a willing proselytizer of Soviet propaganda'.[42] In almost any Cold War crisis, Neil wrote, Foot could be counted on by Moscow to give the Soviet Union the benefit of the doubt – an accusation that was quite extraordinarily untrue, as earlier parts of this book demonstrate. Quoting Lenin, Neil described Foot as 'one of Moscow's useful idiots'. It may be wondered as what kind of idiot Neil himself might be classified.

The *Guardian* promptly dismissed the accusations as nonsense. There were indeed many odd features about the *Sunday Times*'s claims. They depended entirely on allegations from Gordievsky, a known double agent, and it may be asked how such credence could ever be put on evidence from so erratic a source. *Tribune* pointed out that his assertions were based on conversations he had had years before with another agent, and the claim that he had come across a file named 'Boot' which indicated that the Kremlin had once given money to Foot for *Tribune*.[43] Most damagingly for Foot's accusers, Viktor Kubeykin, one of the other KGB men named, denied in a Moscow interview that his meetings with Foot were anything but social. The new editor of the *Sunday Times*, John Witherow, had admitted in the issue of 19 February, and also on Radio Four's *World at One* programme, that claims that Foot was ever a Soviet agent might well be 'utter rubbish', a massive own goal if ever there was one. The paper ended with vague and totally irrelevant meanderings about the huge damage the far left had done to Britain. Foot himself, still not in the most robust of health after his prostate operation, had an edited version of a letter of rebuttal published in the *Sunday Times* after a fierce row with the editors. He totally denied the allegations that he had ever been a traitor or an agent of a foreign power, and made comparisons with McCarthyism and the Zinoviev letter. His complete rebuttal appeared in the *Observer* of 26 February, under the heading 'My Reply to the KGB Smear'. He wrote of his personal pain at being baselessly accused, in McCarthyite terms, of being a traitor to his country. Foot's patriotic sentiments, then and always, could hardly be disputed.

One important figure privately involved was the former Prime Minister Lord Callaghan, whom Foot had contacted. Callaghan wrote to Foot on 23 February 1995, after discussions with the former Cabinet Secretary, Lord Hunt of Tanworth. He told Foot that all ministers had been subjected to additional security procedures, as a matter of routine, when Harold Wilson took office in March 1974. 'In your case there was no evidence that required any action and you were appointed.' It may be of interest, perhaps, that Callaghan's original draft phrased it as 'not (sufficient) evidence to take action'. He added that Gordievsky had reported in the late 1970s that Foot had received some money for *Tribune*, and that the matter had been investigated. 'The Security Service,' wrote Callaghan, 'completely discounted any suggestion of disloyalty or that it represented a security issue, but they did conclude that the Russians had targeted you.'[44]

Foot then sued the *Sunday Times* and its owners, Rupert Murdoch's News Corporation, for libel. He hired a leading civil rights lawyer, the Australian Geoffrey Robertson, who looked forward to tangling with his fellow-countryman Murdoch (who vainly attempted to remove himself from the writ). At this point, in early April, Foot had to go into hospital for an emergency operation, but matters proceeded smoothly nevertheless. Foot won a simple victory without the case coming to court. He received many thousands of pounds of damages in instalments by the end of July, of which *Tribune* received 'about 10,000 quid', with some of the rest going towards a new kitchen in the basement of Pilgrims Lane. There followed a fierce clash with the solicitor for the defendants, Alastair Brett, who made allegations of unprofessional conduct against Foot's own solicitor, David Price, and threw in other attacks on Foot, including a suggestion that he had been put up to the prosecution by *Private Eye*. Foot considered taking the matter further. Perhaps fortunately, this aspect of the affair died away. Michael Foot was strongly defended on all sides throughout, not only by Labour figures like Neil Kinnock and Robin Cook, but by the Liberal Democrat Shirley Williams and also by the maverick Conservative Alan Clark, who compared Foot with Princess Diana and the Queen Mother as 'a national treasure' who could do no wrong. Foot came out of the affair with his reputation and his acknowledged patriotism all the stronger.[45]

A far more palatable event in 1995 came when Doubleday published a three-hundred-page book on which Foot had been working for several years, *H. G.: The History of Mr Wells*. The saga of another literary icon, it was another labour of love, another perfectly serious book, and a further extraordinary achievement from a man of eighty-two. With H. G. Wells, of course, Foot had various important links. He had read Wells's books avidly as a young man. It was works like *Tono-Bungay* and *The New Machiavelli* that made him a socialist in his time at Liverpool. *Ann Veronica* was a powerful text on liberated young womanhood. Foot had also known Wells personally: he had him write book reviews and other columns for the *Evening Standard*, and had joined him in campaigning on behalf of Indian independence and post-war reconstruction. At the time of Wells's death in August 1946, Foot had written a passionate article in the *Herald* describing him as 'the greatest educator of the century'. There was another important link, though perhaps a less straightforward one. The Foots, especially Jill through her work on the women's movement and in promoting feminist literature through Virago Press, were friendly with the now elderly Rebecca West, Wells's mistress and partner over a tumultuous period before, during and just after the First World War.[46] Their son, Anthony West, had written a recent very hostile account of their relationship, of which Foot strongly disapproved. Foot had also been very friendly with Wells's Russian mistress Moura Budberg and her daughter, Tanya Alexander. He went to Moscow with Tanya to make a film about Wells. There he met Mikhail Gorbachev, whose reform of the Soviet system in the *glasnost* period he greatly admired, and presented him with a copy of Wells's book on the First World War, *The World Set Free*.

Foot's book on Wells perhaps shows some sign of waning powers. It is discursive and somewhat padded out by overlong quotations from Wells's books, but it is still a lively and rewarding read. In rehabilitating Wells, Foot had not set himself an easy task. Wells had long lost the cachet he had enjoyed earlier in the century, when he had been seen as one of the world's most influential minds. In the summer of 1934 he had been granted long private interviews successively with Stalin and Franklin Roosevelt, and had argued vigorously with both. After this, poor Wells had to endure jibes by Bernard Shaw and nagging from the *New Statesman*'s editor Kingsley Martin, in his most sententious vein, that he had failed to grasp the wisdom of Stalin's views. At his seventieth birthday dinner at the Savoy there were speeches of tribute by J. M. Barrie, Julian Huxley, Sir Arthur Bliss, André Maurois and his old sparring partner Bernard Shaw. But after his death, his star rapidly waned. His earlier science fiction still excited attention, partly because of the interest of film-makers in books like *The Time Machine*, with its conflict between Eloi and Morlocks, or *The War of the Worlds*, an account of a Martian invasion of Surrey. Wells's most famous novels, the sagas of the comic wage-slave Kipps and Mr Polly, written in his Edwardian high pomp, were seldom read, though in 1949 *Mr Polly* did inspire a fine film starring John Mills. Of Wells's non-fiction, his *Outline of History* (1920), hugely influential in its day and selling two million copies in its first edition, had lost any claim to authority in the face of work by professional scholars, and was at best regarded as a popularizing introduction for the general reader.

Worse still, Wells had latterly not just been ignored but actually condemned. Praised by Norman and Jeanne Mackenzie in their 1973 biography, he was now widely seen as anti-democratic, regarding the masses as 'dull' or 'base'. Other critics noted the anti-democratic elitism of the Samurai in *A Modern Utopia* (1905). John Carey's *The Intellectuals and the Masses* (1992) offers Wells as a prime example of the hostility and contempt with which intellectual authors had frequently viewed the common man. Carey instanced particularly the fears and misanthropy of the early science fiction. This is especially true of *The Time Machine* (1895), where the doltish masses are transmuted into the Morlochs, but Carey even saw novels like *Kipps* (1905) and *Love and Mr Lewisham* (1900) as full of scorn and condescension towards their lower-middle-class subjects. Even the attempts of the amiable Mr Polly ('a failed shop-keeper') at self-education are derided, along with his sense of sexual inadequacy as he sees a pretty young girl swinging her legs astride a wall.[47] A later work like *The Shape of Things to Come* (1933) was a pessimist's dirge. Arnold Bennett, on the other hand, is Carey's hero, and Foot was to deplore Carey's attempt to drive a wedge between him and Wells. Michael Coren's biography of Wells *The Invisible Man* (1993) was more hostile still, laying emphasis on his open anti-Semitism and campaigns against Zionism, along with his attacks on the Roman Catholic Church. Coren claimed that Wells's influence was, 'taken as a whole, pernicious and destructive'.[48]

Foot's response, as ever, is courageous, direct and wholly partisan. He hits back at the great man's critics with much brio and to some effect. For him, Wells was always the literary and ideological inspiration of his younger days, the man who fired his cultural and political enthusiasms and made him a socialist as he took his tram journeys to work in proletarian Liverpool back in 1935. He writes with particular panache on the great Edwardian novels, many of them with autobiographical allusions. *Tono-Bungay* (1909), with its satirical comment on the financial and moral corruption of twentieth-century urban society, and *The New Machiavelli* (1911) with its examination of the value systems of modern politicians as seen through the tortuous career of the Liberal MP Richard Remington, are finely dealt with. *Tono-Bungay* had always been a special book for Foot, read by him and his brother John in turns during their cheerful visit to Paris in 1934. *Ann Veronica* (1909), with its sympathetic evocation of a daring young feminist, also strikes a chord with Foot (as, very much, it did with Jill Craigie). He is also significantly sympathetic to the patriotic tone of *Mr Britling Sees it Through* (1916), a wartime book accused in some quarters of jingoism (Wells, unlike Shaw, unhesitatingly supported the war). Wells's role as a crusader for his own version of socialism is also defended, and his unquestionably destructive role in the Fabian Society (including in connection with numerous Fabian women) applauded, no doubt in part because his opponents were Foot's *bêtes noires*, those disciples of bureaucracy Sidney and Beatrice Webb. He enjoyed the shock caused to their sensibilities by Wells's proclaiming the heady doctrine of free love.

Where Foot was perhaps most open to criticism (of which he received many salvoes over the muesli and marmalade in Pilgrims Lane) was in the way he handled Wells's treatment of women. Almost throughout his life, Wells was a compulsive and demanding womanizer, who disturbed and wrecked numerous lives. In Foot's book this trait became fascinating, almost ennobling, an essential expression of a great mind and a free spirit. Women were part of his quest for experimentation, just as were his early dabblings in science, key specimens in the laboratory of life. Foot concentrates, with much delightful detail drawn from his personal acquaintance with them, on Rebecca West and Moura Budberg, two powerful personalities who gave as good as they got.[49] Their partnerships with Wells enriched both sides. Foot's view was shaped by his intense admiration for Rebecca West, a great friend of Jill's as well as one of Beaverbrook's various mistresses, and for the 'magnificent Moura'. The daughter of the latter, Tanya Alexander, remained a close friend until her death in 2005.[50] Jill was not alone in having doubts about the cruel selfishness of Wells's behaviour, his obliviousness to the lives he ruined, and particularly the shattering effect on some of the younger women he encountered, such as Amber Reeves, far less well equipped to endure the strains involved than were Rebecca or Moura. But for Foot the restless, creative spirit of Wells, like those of Swift, Hazlitt and Byron, required constant female stimulation. His art soared to a new level when he wrote of the feminism of Ann Veronica and Isabel Rivers, the suffragette heroine of The New Machiavelli. His relationships with young women, as much as his writing of brilliant novels in which Foot's book helped to revive interest, were all part of his genius as an artist and as a human being.

The book's critical reception was somewhat mixed. As so often, the reviewers' verdicts reflected their views of the subject rather than of the skills of the biographer. Foot much resented one notice by Peter Conrad in the Observer which bore the headline (drawn from Trotsky's judgement on Wells) 'What a Little Bourgeois'. Professor John Sutherland in the London Review of Books was far more balanced and generous.[51] Michael Foot, at the age of eighty-two, could not be expected to turn the tide of disapproval or apathy towards Wells. But he does provide, without question, an important and extraordinarily well-informed contribution to debate, a necessary corrective, and a deeper personal insight into at least some of Wells's impulses than any other living biographer could have offered.

People imagined that this would be Foot's last book. He was now mainly active in writing brief introductions to new editions of works by Swift, Tom Paine, Orwell and Bertrand Russell; not to universal satisfaction – his brother John wrote of Russell, 'Try as I may, I cannot like the man, any more than I like his son Conrad.'[52] But, to general astonishment, this ceaselessly active man produced yet another book in 1999, *Dr Strangelove, I Presume*, published by Gollancz. This was a reprise of old anti-nuclear themes, a result of his attending the sixth Indira Gandhi Conference in New Delhi in November 1997. The title was a tribute to the American film director Stanley Kubrick, with whom Michael and Jill had become friendly and whom they had entertained in Pilgrims Lane. While in New Delhi Foot met, among others, Robert McNamara, the US Defense Secretary under Lyndon Johnson at the time of Vietnam, now converted into an opponent of the nuclear strategy whose viewpoint was scarcely different from Foot's own long-held unilateralism. It was the stimulus of long, late-night discussions with McNamara which inspired Foot to write the book, along with much enthusiastic prodding from Jill, herself a strong CND partisan. The two-hundred-page book is loosely structured, with some interesting material on the founding of CND in 1958 and the responses of Labour to it thereafter. The case against nuclear weapons is again set out – and Foot rightly underlines how the passage of time, the ending of the Cold War, the change in the nature of conflict, the importance of economic and psychological factors, had made his argument all the more compelling.

But perhaps the book is most interesting about India, where Foot first discussed its themes. He half apologizes for his stand over Mrs Gandhi's state of emergency in 1976, but he also praises her and Rajiv for taking a lead in calling for an end to the production, testing and use of nuclear weapons, advocating world disarmament, and holding back in their confrontation with Pakistan by starting negotiations over defence and other issues with President Bhutto.[53] Nearing the end, as at the beginning, of his political odyssey, Michael Foot always followed events in India avidly. He kept close to Indian friends like Moni Cameron, Swraj Paul and Abu. The dining room table in Pilgrims

Lane was always piled with copies of *Asian Times* or the *Times of India*, and he took a keen interest in the Indian cricket team and its leading batsman Sachin Tendulkar.

Foot was now an old man, but in many ways contentedly so. After all, the landslide election victory of 1997 saw a Labour government returned once again, with a strong grip on power that was to last for over a decade. Tony Blair made much of how New Labour had superseded the Old Labour values of which Michael Foot was the supreme living embodiment. Nationalization, economic planning, re-distributive taxation, universal welfare, legal protection for the unions, non-selective education, withered and fell like the autumn leaves at Vallombrosa. Yet Foot was by no means uncomfortable with New Labour, and in any event was very loath to criticize his successors in any way. He revelled in the fact that Labour under Tony Blair was now a triumphant party of winners, in a way it had not been since 1945. He enjoyed strong relations with key ministers like Robin Cook at the Foreign Office. Cook's successor, Jack Straw, was the former political adviser of Barbara Castle, and her successor as MP for Black-burn. Foot had a particularly good relationship with the Chancellor, Gordon Brown (whose office was run by Sue Nye, as Foot's had once been), and warmly applauded his work at the Treasury. The day after his tenth budget on 22 March 2006, with its stimulus to public investment in the nation's schools, Brown took a private phone call in the Treasury, conveying a cheery message of congratulation from his ninety-two-year-old comrade.

With Tony Blair, apparently distant from his vision of socialism, Foot's relations were perfectly good, and with Cherie Blair better still. He had in fact voted for John Prescott in the leadership contest of 1994. However, Blair wrote warmly to Foot before he became Prime Minister, perhaps in 1996: 'I remember so vividly when we first met and my writing to you afterwards what, when I look at it now, must have seemed a hopelessly naïve and idealistic letter. But I was inspired then, and remain so now, by your passion, commitment and total dedication to our cause. Let us hope it can now be brought to a successful conclusion. Love to Jill.'[54] Blair had found the radical themes of Foot's *Loyalists and Loners* an inspirational force in pushing him into working for the Labour Party. This, after all, was the bright, idealistic

young man by whom Foot had been so impressed during the Beaconsfield by-election back in 1982, and whom he had strongly pushed for
the Sedgefield nomination a year later. He commented with self-
deprecating humour about Tony Blair, 'Anyone who joined the
Labour Party at the time I was leader can't be accused of being an
opportunist.'

Many of the Blair government's policies were highly acceptable to
the sage of Hampstead socialism. He warmly backed the controversial
policy of military intervention over Kosovo in 1999 and endorsed the
bombing of Belgrade by NATO air forces then: it should have happened long ago, when Dubrovnik was being shelled by the Serbs, in
Foot's view. Robin Cook's stance of having 'an ethical foreign policy'
was applauded, and thought far superior to that of his Conservative
predecessors Douglas Hurd and Malcolm Rifkind. Foot also applauded
the Lord Chancellor Lord Irvine's constitutional and legal reforms,
especially the entrenching of human rights in British law and the
ending of hereditary peers' right to sit in the House of Lords, while
the passage of Scottish and Welsh devolution carried through his own
unfinished business from 1979. His former lodger Donald Dewar
became Scotland's First Minister. His good friend Gordon Brown, the
new Chancellor, devoted massive funding to bolster Nye's National
Health Service. Defence policy did not cause great ructions, although
any decision to replace Trident as Britain's nuclear deterrent, at a cost
of perhaps £25 billion, after Polaris lapsed, could provoke a future
great debate. On Europe, Foot, like his party, was a late, surprising
convert. He had never been opposed to European union in the same
way as Peter Shore or Enoch Powell, and had endorsed the idea back
in the later 1940s. Now, influenced by European socialist leaders like
Felipe Gonzales in Spain, Mário Soares in Portugal and George Papan-
dreou in Greece, not to mention his cultural comrade François Mitterrand, Foot warmed at last to the idea of European solidarity, where
the Social Chapter introduced by the EU brought such blessings as the
minimum wage for which Hardie and Lansbury had once crusaded,
improved conditions for working women and greater contractual rights
for trade unionists. Fraternity was surely his natural creed, not isolationist and xenophobic little Englandism. His old Euroscepticism was given
a decent unChristian burial.

Foot otherwise continued his well-tried range of activities in happy mode. He continued to write regularly for *Tribune*, and was very friendly with Mark Seddon, its young editor; he reviewed for the weeklies and gave frequent interviews to Labour historians and others; one honour, greatly appreciated, was honorary membership of his cherished National Union of Journalists. He also continued to enjoy an occasional holiday at the Villa Dubrovnik, despite his growing immobility. Every fortnight during the football season he was driven by his friend Peter Jones on the long journey to see Plymouth Argyle play at Home Park; a television documentary depicted some distinctly cheerful post-match Plymouth youths hailing him as 'a living legend'. He was now a director of Argyle, and claimed that he had introduced them to Paul Sturrock, the manager who set them on the path to promotion out of Division Two into the Championship. Arguments when Sturrock left the club in March 2004, however, led to Peter Jones resigning from the club as director, and Michael Foot, with his habitual loyalty, joined him. Foot also continued to enjoy the comfortable ambience and cuisine of the Gay Hussar, and enjoyed Tuesday lunches there each month with a highly congenial group of friends, Ian (Lord) Gilmour, Ian Aitken, William Keegan, economics editor of the *Observer*, and sometimes Geoffrey Goodman. These lunches had stemmed originally from his friendship with Gilmour through the Byron Society.

His literary interests remained very active, despite his age. Indirectly, he produced yet another book in his ninetieth year. A warmly sympathetic young scholar, Professor Brian Brivati of the University of Kingston, who had already edited an abridged one-volume version of Foot's *Aneurin Bevan*, also edited in 2003 *The Uncollected Michael Foot*, a large and attractive collection of Foot's shorter pieces, notes and reviews. It was well received, and a copy ended up on the shelves of the downstairs restaurant room of the Gay Hussar, with his previous publications as its companions. Elsewhere, Foot continued to be eloquent on many fronts, often addressing the Swift Society, the Hazlitt Society, the Paine Society, the Byron and Irish Byron Societies, and the Wells Society on their respective heroes. He also kept in close touch with the Wordsworth Trust. On 1 April 2004 he opened an exhibition in Dove Cottage, Wordsworth's old home near Grasmere, and announced that most of the thousand volumes in his Hazlitt collection would pass to the Trust when he died. Sixteen years earlier he had 'vindicated' Byron (along with Venice) in a major book. On 10 April 2003 there was yet another vindication, that of Hazlitt, whose writings, both radical and moral (*Liber Amoris* above all), had met with the disapproval of the authorities of St Ann's Church, Soho, at the time of his death, penniless, in nearby Frith Street in 1830. His memorial headstone had badly eroded over the years, and was also damaged during the Blitz. Foot now presided over a ceremony in the little churchyard, attended by notable writers and politicians, including the authors A. C. Grayling and Tom Paulin, and the Conservative peers Ian Gilmour and Kenneth Baker, which made amends to Hazlitt's memory. A new headstone beside the church was unveiled. The indomitable white-haired old man, confined to a wheelchair but his voice firm and clear, spoke for about twenty minutes, first on the glory of Hazlitt, and then on the iniquities of the Tory Party in 2003, in Wells's day in 1903, in Hazlitt's and Byron's in 1803, in Swift's in 1703, and for all eternity. The immortal memory was recalled of 'the hater of the Pride and Power of the Few . . . The unconquered Champion of Truth, Liberty and Humanity'. It was an unforgettable private moment in British political culture.[55]

There was one deep sadness to counter the contentedness of a placid old age. Although Michael looked so frail, and staggered along on his stick ever since the car accident of 1963, it was Jill, two years older than himself, whose health was more problematic. She showed signs of serious heart trouble in 1997–98 but remained stoic, intellectually active and mentally strong. She continued her indefatigable work on the suffragettes even though it was obvious that the book would never be finished. She wrote a delightful personal sketch in *The State of the Nation*, a book edited by Geoffrey Goodman and published in 1997 to celebrate the centenary of the birth of Nye Bevan. The sexual mores of the hero were dealt with delicately, but with some frankness. Bevan is quoted as saying of his marriage to Jennie Lee, 'An element of antagonism kept sex alive.'[56] Jill spoke splendidly at a Bevan centenary dinner in Congress House that autumn. When the story of the Koestler rape broke in mid-1998, after David Cesarani published a new biography of Koestler, she was robust in explaining why she had

had to keep silent, and won immense public sympathy for her ordeal.[57] She and Michael were never closer, the most tender of partnerships. Then catastrophe struck in May 1999. Jill fell in her bathroom and broke a hip. This was serious for a woman of eighty-eight (her age tended to be adjusted), and exacerbated her heart problems. The decline was rapid, and she died on 13 December 1999. Michael, almost uniquely in his life, burst into tears.

It was the end of one of the great partnerships in Labour's pantheon, worthy of being placed alongside that of the Webbs, the Coles or Nye and Jennie Lee. Indeed, unlike the last-named, Michael's and Jill's was emphatically not an open marriage. With the one exception, the partners were faithful in a union based on trust as well as love. Jill was by instinct an artist, not a natural politician. But without her Michael's career, as politician as well as author, would have lost many of its essential qualities. It was Jill who wove the connection for him, as few other women could have done, between culture and political change, and who opened his eyes to environmental and aesthetic issues. Equally, Michael encouraged her to develop her separate professional activities in the film world, and nurtured her deeply-held feminist beliefs. For the remainder of his life, the memory of Jill, her beauty and her radiance were Michael's ever-present inspiration. A meeting of commemoration was held at Conway Hall, Red Lion Square, on 17 January 2000. Tributes were paid by a series of speakers including Michael himself, Paul Foot (now seriously ill himself and able to stand only with difficulty) and, perhaps unexpectedly, Barbara Castle. The ten speakers numbered four men and six women, an arrangement which Jill would no doubt have approved. Afterwards, Foot went with some friends on a quiet visit to Dubrovnik, a very personal way of mourning his dear Jill's memory in their beloved city.

Michael's family and friends were now passing away, the inevitable concomitant of old age. His brothers and sisters had all gone. Dingle died in 1978, Hugh in 1990, John in 1999. Michael, who had suffered from so many health problems earlier on, was the last of the brood. Old political associates were going, too. Harold Wilson had died in 1995, a shadow of his former self. Jim Callaghan, a year older than Foot, lived until March 2005, dying a day before his ninety-third birthday. But he and Foot had had relatively little contact since 1979.

Three personal losses were particularly distressing. In 2001 his long-term personal secretary and warm friend Una Cooze died of cancer after a long and painful illness. Secretarial help thereafter came from the immense personal kindness of Jenny Stringer and Una Cooze's close friend Sheila Noble. A significant blow came with the death of Barbara Castle in May 2002, to the end the closest living confidante of Michael's hopes and dreams. He spoke with strength and humour at a memorial event in Westminster Hall. It was wholly appropriate that those attending should be picketed and leafleted by local public sector workers who were on strike, their own spiky tribute to the author of *In Place of Strife*. Another loss felt with particular acuteness was the death of his favourite nephew, Paul Foot, in July 2004 after a long and distressing illness. With his unique brilliance as a journalist of exposure and his writings on 'Red' Shelley, Paul had seemed to Michael in many ways his natural heir, save for his incomprehensible attachment to the fringe Socialist Workers Party. The death of Stan Orme in April 2005 removed another old Tribunite comrade.

But, as we have seen, Jill's death was by no means the end for Michael. With the devoted and deeply loyal care of Jill's close friend Jenny Stringer, he continued to enjoy a rich and multi-faceted life. He faced up with much resilience to a remarkable series of celebratory parties at the time of his ninetieth birthday in July 2003, with Tony Blair and Jack Straw among the various hosts. Close contact was maintained with *Tribune*, whose offices had now moved to Arkwright Road in Hampstead, near Pilgrims Lane. Foot found the time for another local issue, trying to persuade the local authority to keep the Hampstead ponds free for bathers, and the campaign, supported by many writers and artistic glitterati, was broadly successful.[58] An important family commitment was working on a life of his father Isaac with his niece Alison Highet, the daughter of his sister Jennifer, at her home near Axminster. This work, much enriched by quotations from Isaac's family letters, speeches and sermons, was fulfilling an obligation to write his father's life first discussed when he was in government back in 1977, and in September 2006 the book was published. Its subtitle, *Apostle of England*, evoked Isaac's description of the martyr William Tyndale, who first translated the Bible into English.[59]

Nor was Foot removed from the political controversies of the day.

An interview with him covering the current political scene in the *Independent* in July 2002 led to a pained, but courteous, rejoinder from the Defence Secretary, Geoff Hoon: 'I was disappointed that you should characterize me as talking as if "I might want to use nuclear weapons". I have never spoken that way.' Hoon's letter, however, did not exactly remove Foot's apprehensions.[60] More seriously, when the British government joined the Bush administration in invading Iraq in March 2003 Foot broke with his own precedent and took a vigorous part in denouncing the war. He was one of the speakers who addressed the colossal public anti-war demonstration, probably of well over a million, which marched from Westminster to Hyde Park on 15 February 2003, and condemned any invasion outright. He also sent a message of support to the second anti-war march in March, which took place after the Iraq war had started. Foot would see the Iraq venture as symbolic of the worst features of British foreign policy during his lifetime. He listed the aspects to condemn – the serial untruths about Iraq's alleged weapons of mass destruction and links between Saddam Hussein and al-Qaeda; the ignoring of the United Nations and the weapons inspections methodically being carried out for them by Dr Hans Blix; the illegality of a pre-emptive strike intended to carry through unlawful regime change without any UN mandate; the threats to the independence of reporting by the BBC and others in the media, later the interference of 10 Downing Street in the security services and the Attorney-General's office; the loss of at least fifty thousand Iraqi lives, perhaps many more, through Anglo-American planes bombing homes, mosques, schools and hospitals; the torture of prisoners at Abu Ghraib prison; the chaos and carnage left in Iraq after the formal fighting was over, with many atrocities by US troops recorded. To Foot, it was even worse than the Suez conspiracy in 1956. At least the Americans had been on the right side then. Labour's Iraq venture would be arraigned by history alongside those of Tories like Chamberlain and Eden in the chronicle of history's Guilty Men.

Opinion polls showed, then and afterwards, that it was the anti-war sentiments of men like Michael Foot to which the great majority of people responded, not just in Britain but all over the world. Foot showed signs now of breaking with the loyalty that he had given to the Labour leadership since 1997. At the *Tribune* rally at party conference in

Bournemouth in September 2003, a few months after the invasion, he made an unprecedented attack on the Prime Minister's 'lies', and declared that Britain was now far less safe than before the war. In due time, in July 2005, devastating bomb attacks in London, the work of Muslim extremists stirred to insensate hate partly by the Anglo-American invasion and occupation of Iraq, were to confirm his predictions in terrifying fashion. Foot had made his point, and the press had noticed it. Two days later the accounts of the 2003 Bournemouth conference carried a smiling photograph of him with another nonagenarian comrade-in-arms, Jack Jones.[61]

But, despite Iraq, Foot retained his lifelong loyalty to his old party. This led to an unfortunate episode during the general election of May 2005 in his old constituency of Blaenau Gwent. Here, on the retirement of Llew Smith as MP, party headquarters had proposed an all-woman shortlist, as a result of which Maggie Jones was nominated as official Labour candidate. The local party, however, reacted strongly against having a candidate imposed on them, and many constituency supporters opted for a long-established local figure, Peter Law, Member of the Welsh Assembly. Finally Law stood as an independent candidate against Maggie Jones, who was resident in London though a native of the valleys. Michael Foot, perhaps unfortunately, was persuaded to come down to Ebbw Vale again to endorse a woman candidate, and to urge people not to split the party. He also claimed, most dubiously it has to be said, that Nye Bevan would have supported an all-woman shortlist. This was not well received, and he met with less than his usual cordial reception. In the election, in one of the most astonishing results of the day, there was a 48.2 per cent swing against Labour in Blaenau Gwent, and Peter Law, even though he had had a recent operation for a brain tumour, was elected with a majority of 9,121. Purges of some senior members of an already small local party then took place. The constituency of Nye Bevan and Michael Foot between 1929 and 1992 was the most rock-solid of industrial fortresses. Incredibly, Labour had lost it.[62] Law died in April 2006, and this led to another difficult by-election on 29 June, in which Labour, remarkably, failed to recapture the seat, its candidate losing by 2,484 votes to an independent who had been Law's agent.

Foot took the loss of his old seat with equanimity. In his twentieth election since he first campaigned as a Lloyd George Liberal in 1929, yet another crisis had passed by. His political life had been punctuated by storms and stresses ever since he began his crusading on soapboxes with the Socialist League. His father had taught him that politics was a rough old game, in which landing blows above or below the belt was a matter of tactics, not of ethics. Foot was simply experiencing one more of the extreme vicissitudes that he had known all his life. He was nothing if not a survivor. In the meantime, there was always next week's piece for *Tribune*, and there was still a Labour government in office. Foot enjoyed the celebrations of the party's centenary in February 2006, with a special meeting of the parliamentary Labour Party convened by an old friend, the PLP Chairman Ann Clwyd. Gordon Brown was congratulated on his budget, a misguided critic of Swift was put right in the pages of *The Times Literary Supplement*.[63] The unopposed advent of Gordon Brown as prime minister in late June 2007 was greeted with great enthusiasm, while his former aide, Sue Nye, now became a powerful figure in the office at No. 10. At Foot's monthly lunches upstairs in the Gay Hussar (sadly diminished by the death of Ian Gilmour on 21 September) he rejoiced in Labour's growing lead in the opinion polls, which by October had soared to over 10 per cent before falling again. Inspired by history, Foot could still look forward to new challenges and hope that, one day in some blissful dawn, his England would finally arise. The otherwise unkind cover of *Private Eye* published in June 1983 perhaps unintentionally captured his spirit. The elderly man is shouting defiantly, indefatigably, at the world, 'Hang on, I haven't finished yet!'

ENVOI: *TOUJOURS L'AUDACE*

'No attempt is made at impartiality. Unbiased historians are as insufferable as the people who profess no politics.' These strong sentiments, included in the preface of his first book, *Armistice*, were written in February 1940, at a very early stage of Michael Foot's professional life. But they may well be taken as a parable for his career as a whole. He typecast himself as the utterly committed symbol of permanent opposition, a rebel, a maverick, in eternal conflict with authority, including often within his own Labour Party. One of his favourite words was 'audacity', and his chosen heroes, Swift, Hazlitt, Byron and Wells amongst the authors, Cripps, Beaverbrook, Bevan amongst the politicians, all embodied this life-enhancing quality. Foot was most often seen as a neo-pacifist (though *The Guilty Men*, and his support for the task force in the Falklands war and the bombing of Belgrade suggest a strong opposing tendency). But he warmed to Danton's ardent patriotism during the French Revolution, the era of human history from which he most drew inspiration – '*L'audace, encore l'audace, toujours l'audace.*' In a remarkably long public career, extending from the early 1930s to the dawn of the twenty-first century, he was audacious to the point of recklessness, as backbencher, agitator and journalist, as crusading literary critic, and as a romantic and deeply passionate human being.

Yet he ended up, to the surprise of close friends and probably to his own, as leader of the Labour Party. Certainly his commitment to the party was the mainspring of his career. Ever since he forswore his ancestral Liberalism amidst the dockyard slums of Liverpool in 1935, his selfless dedication to the cause was beyond question. But assessing the precise nature of Foot's contribution both to the party and to the philosophy of democratic socialism is by no means straightforward. It would be difficult to see him as making any special contribution to socialist ideas. His political creed was a passionate response to the social disasters of the thirties, which he characteristically linked with defeatism in foreign policy as well. His views assumed a coherent shape during the collectivism of the 'people's war', and were given practical expression in the Labour manifesto of 1945. Thereafter, Foot's ideas certainly changed on some key policies. In the late 1940s, for instance, he favoured a wages policy and a federal Europe, both of which he vehemently resisted as a minister in the 1970s. But his overall view of corporate state socialism did not greatly change. It focused on public ownership, planning, the redistribution of wealth, full employment, and an enabling welfare state on the centralist model of Nye's immortal National Health Service.

For the rest of his life, his outlook remained much the same; some critics complained that he was trapped in the past, the eternal prophet of a better yesterday. He offered characteristically British recipes, blending Tawney and Keynes with some minor sprinklings from Marx for seasoning. In the late 1960s he was endorsing John Strachey's distinctly revisionist *Contemporary Capitalism* (1956), to the effect that 'Keynesian economics plus democratic pressures' had transformed capitalism and prevented Marx's forebodings about the 'immiseration' of the common people coming about.[1] Foot did not seriously engage with the major debates when the original impetus of the Attlee government's programme had slackened after 1951. Bevanism was doctrinally repetitive. There is no Foot critique of Crosland's *Future of Socialism* – the powerful revisionist view that public ownership was largely irrelevant in a transformed capitalism where management had superseded ownership, and that socialism was now 'about equality'. Education and the argument for comprehensive schools, for instance, on which Crosland's argument placed such emphasis, never seemed to be a topic of great interest to Foot (not that the content of education, as opposed to its organization, ever seemed of much concern to Crosland either), and his speeches on the theme were minimal. Foot countered the ideological challenge of Tony Benn in the 1970s, as he did with the emergence of New Labour's 'Third Way' twenty years later, with a reiteration of the traditional imperatives of Old Labour. His election campaign in 1983 seemed a rendition of the old tunes of forty years earlier. Newer themes, like the environment or globalization, seldom emerged. At the time, his parliamentary approach to socialism clearly carried the day over Benn's more populist approach. It was a supreme irony that the emergence of New Labour in 1997 – heavily managerial, relatively non-ideological, favouring an approach to government that often bypassed not only the party membership but Parliament itself, and even the Cabinet – owed little to either the Foot or the Benn model of parliamentary socialism. After a decade of passionate struggle for the heart and soul of the Labour movement, both combatants appeared to have lost.

The limitations that shaped Foot's ideology were clear enough. His broad lack of interest in economics at any stage of his career was a major factor: perhaps a deep, abiding suspicion of capitalism in any form, and hatred of its instruments within a global economy, made him reluctant to turn his mind to discussing fundamental economic principles. It is doubtful whether he ever really understood them. While in international and Commonwealth affairs he often played an innovative and courageous role, his inability to contribute to economic debates on international development, trade and Third World indebtedness curbed his effectiveness. Such matters did not seem to engage him. Also, his inattention to detail in analysing the machinery of government did not encourage enquiry on his part into how the apparatus of socialist planning might actually work, given the obstacles that it confronted in reality after 1945, 1964 and certainly in 1974, when he was a key minister. He had surprisingly little to say about workers' control or industrial democratization, down to the 1976 Bullock Report. The daily experience of the workers was remote from him until he built up his links with the unions, and with Frank Cousins and Jack Jones in particular, relatively late in his career. His was a socialism of the book, of emotional sensibility rather than empirical analysis. He became a socialist through reading Wells and Arnold Bennett, Jack London and Robert Tressell, on Liverpool's trams, reinforced by imaginative borrowings from radical essayists and poets of earlier generations. Socialism was a mood, a mystique, and it belonged to the ages.

As a result, other than his pamphlet *My Kind of Socialism* in 1980, there is no document that can be seen as Michael Foot's contribution to socialist thought. In this he is unusual amongst Labour's leaders.

Keir Hardie, often accused of simple-minded sentimentalism, produced *From Serfdom to Socialism* (1907), an attempt to pull broad ethical principles together which is full of interest. Ramsay MacDonald's stream of texts promoting Darwinian evolutionary socialism led him to be regarded for a time as an intellectual giant. He recognized that the fledgling Labour Party needed not just instincts but an ideology. The prophet George Lansbury produced a number of statements on the socialist idea, notably *My England* (1934). Even Clement Attlee, derided by the left as an unimaginative, colourless 'calculating machine', set down his credo in methodical fashion in *The Labour Party in Perspective* (1937). While Harold Wilson was essentially a technocrat, enriched by northern nonconformity, Jim Callaghan, no natural intellectual, came to socialism via its philosophy, through reading Harold Laski's complicated texts on democratic pluralism while munching his sandwiches on Tower Hill. It is indeed strange that Michael Foot, so brilliant a communicator, and of immense intellectual stature in the roll-call of labour leaders, produced so little of substance here. But the answer is, no doubt, that this is to look in the wrong place. Foot's socialism was neither ideological nor logical, but inspirational. His great and incomparable contribution to socialist understanding is undoubtedly his massive life of Aneurin Bevan, partisan and often unfair, but a thrilling evocation of what it meant to be a socialist, in philosophy and in the uses of power, seen not through abstract concepts but in what Foot sees as the courage and vision of one towering human being, under whose shadow he always remained. Foot's two volumes on Bevan will survive, long after far more scholarly biographies, as a unique testament to the passion of the ethical socialist faith.

But if Foot the political philosopher is not a rewarding theme, his contribution elsewhere was vivid and consistent. He was the outstanding political publicist and pamphleteer of his day and, through *Tribune*, a crusading editor on the grand scale. His style was naturally pugnacious. As Hazlitt wrote of Cobbett, Michael Foot was the Tom Cribb of the journalistic prize ring, best on the attack. He announced himself in *Guilty Men*, the greatest radical tract since the time of Wilkes, and his unique blend of mordant wit, passionate sensibility and linguistic grace, backed up by a unique fund of historical and literary allusion, made him a celebrated and feared polemicist for the

British left. Much of this was sadly ephemeral, cast in challenging newspaper articles or book reviews; *Tribune*, a genuine competitor to the *New Statesman* in 1945, with marvellous contributors like George Orwell, never sought to cut free from its base in Keep Left and its successors. It became from 1951 inextricably linked with Bevanism, and then CND later on, a persistent voice of criticism of Labour's leadership, and widely seen as essentially destructive. It reinforced a perception of the party as inherently divided and unelectable. The defeat of CND and the absorption of many leading ex-Bevanites into Wilson's government in 1964 seriously diminished *Tribune*'s influence thereafter. By 1974 the paper seemed the voice of the 'soft left', sometimes called the legitimate left, a licensed rebel and essentially safe. Nevertheless, it gave Foot an enduring and influential platform for agitation and protest, which survived the turmoil of the new left disputes of the sixties and seventies, and offered a unique long-term critique. In particular, it was unusual in its attention to international affairs, and here, including in its treatment of India, Palestine and the ideological divisions of Europe (in fact, almost everywhere except the United States), it was important and distinctive. *Tribune* is, among other things, a permanent tribute to Foot's celebration of the profession of journalism. High in his pantheon of heroes were the great editors like Robert Blatchford of the *Clarion*, and of course he revered Beaverbrook as a spearhead of the crusading press. Foot's friendships with journalists he admired were central to his life – Noel Brailsford, Frank Owen, James Cameron, Geoffrey Goodman, the immortal newspaper cartoonists Vicky and Abu. His membership of the National Union of Journalists was deeply important to him, and he fought the good fight on its behalf in the successful campaign for the closed shop in 1975–76. A free society he measured by its free press. It was also the way by which radicals and minority protesters could neutralize the brute force of capitalism. There was, after all, no real answer to the power of literacy.

A question, however, was how far the journalism and pamphleteering of Foot and his colleagues could be seen as basically socialist. With his Liberal background and his ingrained libertarianism, Foot's campaigning almost instinctively took the form of a kind of broad patrician populism, working within a familiar parliamentary mould.

Guilty Men, after all, was in no sense a socialist tract. If anybody, its hero was Winston Churchill. It focused on folly and corruption in high places, much as the 'muckraking' of the American Progressive journalists, Lincoln Steffens or Ida Tarbell or Upton Sinclair, had done earlier in the century. Foot's captivating books of essays, *Debts of Honour* and *Loyalists and Loners*, certainly paid tribute to leftists of the remoter past, but also to colourful Tory outsiders like Disraeli, Churchill and Beaverbrook, well outside the socialist pantheon, not to mention Sarah, Duchess of Marlborough. In ideology as well in style, Foot's books seemed to belong to a much earlier age, perhaps that of his Whig hero Charles James Fox. In some ways they would seem more at home in the late eighteenth century than in the twentieth. Significantly, apart from his highly personal book on Nye, none of his works is a study of the British Labour movement.

Without doubt, one of Foot's unique contributions to socialist and other politics was as a brilliant parliamentarian. Somewhat too rhetorical to be wholly successful in his first spell in Parliament up to 1955, after his return for Ebbw Vale in 1960 he became renowned as the most consistently articulate and powerful speaker in the House, a fusion of the Cornish chapels, the Oxford Union and the soapboxes of the Socialist League. He packed the Commons benches with eloquent and witty speeches, as hardly any other contemporary could do after the death of Bevan. Only Enoch Powell, perhaps, could challenge him, and he and Foot became significantly close friends. Foot was wonderful in Parliament, in large measure because he believed passionately in it – such it was, drawing its historic strength from the victory over Charles I in the seventeenth century, vindicated anew in 1832 and through the triumph of the suffragettes, surviving magnificently and preserving all its historic liberties in two world wars. Churchill and Bevan, in their contrasting styles, were the legitimate heirs of the men on Putney Heath in 1647, embodying the glorious vision of free citizenship. In 1940, whereas Pétain the President saw the French as his 'children', Churchill the parliamentarian regarded his people as freeborn Englishmen. Foot's oratory added its own special nuances. In debate he was often thrilling, leaving much to chance and spontaneous combustion: he told Roy Hattersley that when speaking 'you must always surprise people'. Contemporaries in the 1970s distinguished between the ministerial Foot reading out a civil servant's brief with different glasses, and the uninhibited, spontaneous Foot declaiming his faith and lashing his opponents without mercy. Unfortunately, too many of his great parliamentary performances appeared negative (as with the campaign against Lords reform in 1969), or the products of defeat, as in his memorable performance in March 1979 when the Callaghan government fell, or his attack on Mrs Thatcher over the Argentinian invasion of the Falklands. But they still read finely and move the spirit.

At the same time, he derived strength as an orator from also being, outside the House, amongst the great stump orators of his day. Protest and parliamentarism went side by side. As party leader, Foot always seemed most at home on Marches for Jobs or at demonstrations against nuclear weapons. The Aldermaston marches he took especially seriously. Yet even they always remained a backdrop to the politics of Westminster, which he deeply respected. No one had a greater regard for, or knowledge of, the procedures and conventions of the House. As a backbencher he was zealous in condemning attempts by the whips to curtail the freedoms of honourable Members, and he could be devastating in the hand-to-hand combat of the committee stage. His was a deeply principled attachment to parliamentary sovereignty – yet also a romantic conservative one. It was the sovereignty of Parliament, not the defence of socialism, which provided the basis of his passionate opposition to entry into Europe. It was Parliament which provided the framework for his socialism, in opposition to the left-wing extra-parliamentary (or, as he felt, anti-parliamentary) movements like Militant. Parliament was the foundation of the democratic socialism with which he resisted Tony Benn. Parliament should be inviolable, as for centuries past. Thus he looked with scant enthusiasm at attempts to reform it, for example by voting reform or regional government. Even his taking up the cause of Scottish and Welsh devolution in the 1970s did not really contest the centralizing thrust of his parliamentary socialism. After all, that was Nye Bevan's vision too.

Foot's contribution as a Cabinet minister came late in the day, when he was already into his sixties and in the near-twilight of his career. Previously to that he had been a consistent critic and gadfly, from the Socialist League in the 1930s to the Tribune group in the

1960s. Yet when he became a minister he proved to be an important one, even if inevitably controversial. He moved to the party mainstream in response to what seemed to him the dangers of the historic Labour alliance splitting asunder, especially in relation to the trade unions. He needed little persuasion now to play a controlling role, largely though not entirely as the champion of the unions. As Secretary for Employment his ministerial style was unorthodox but highly effective. In his own fashion he passed no fewer than six major Bills in 1974–76, in a Commons in which Labour had effectively no majority at all. He succeeded for a time in reversing the legal tide in industrial relations. He tilted the balance more equitably in favour of working people in relation to employment rights, trade disputes, membership of unions, health and safety and much else. Many of the criticisms of him as being a creature of the unions, for instance over the protection of the closed shop, were exaggerated, and the import of his legislation was upheld in the courts by judicial notables like Lord Scarman and Lord Denning. It was not Foot's fault that the unions so blighted their image and their popularity in the winter of discontent, after Jack Jones had left the scene. The outcome – the reversal of much of his legislation in the Thatcher years, and the consequent marginalization of the unions in British political life and a 'flexible, deregulated free labour market' – has not helped make Britain a more egalitarian society.

As Leader of the House, Foot's role was different, adaptable, almost atmospheric, in keeping a minority government afloat with a variety of pacts with Liberals, nationalists and Ulstermen. The extraordinary nature of his achievement is often overlooked: certainly without Foot there would have been little enough life in the Labour governments of 1974–79. He acted with scrupulous loyalty, notably in the IMF crisis, and both Callaghan and Healey paid frequent and sincere tribute to him on this score. In his negotiations with the unions in pressing an anti-inflation wages policy he was remarkable in his dedication, and helped massively towards the Labour government's success in the two crucial years 1976–78. As a result, Foot acquired in his later career a stature that went far beyond the narrow ranks of the Labour left. He had been a minister who had contrived to hold the balance between Callaghan and Benn, who had been respected by his civil servants, and who had a clear record of legislative achievement. It was the last, and in some ways, the most effective, phase of the history of the Ministry of Labour and the Department of Employment that succeeded it. It restored a social balance, last enshrined in Bevin's pact with the unions in 1940. In the subsequent eighteen years of Conservative rule there were many former critics (some of whom returned to the fold after their experiment with the SDP) who saw new virtue in the social democracy of the Callaghan years, and felt that, in education, devolution and aspects of social policy, it had anticipated the best of New Labour, well ahead of its time.

As Labour leader, Foot was manifestly out of his element. The television newscaster Jon Snow wrote warmly that he was 'far too honest and interesting ever to be Prime Minister', but this may be over-romantic.[2] Foot had neither the political background nor the temperament to make a success of the job. In the typology of Labour leaders he would be ranked with the minority of protesters – Hardie, Lansbury, the early Kinnock – not with the planners or the 'plodders'. Labour was close to being ungovernable internally in 1980–83, and its election defeat was pre-ordained. It seldom looked like presenting a challenge to Mrs Thatcher, especially with the defections to the SDP, and Foot rarely made a positive impact – ironically, his belligerent speech on the Falklands invasion was one exception, and it eventually worked to Labour's disadvantage, since the left does not normally benefit from jingoism, as the invasion of Iraq in 2003 was to confirm. Foot had no particular vision to offer his party, other than a reiteration of the Old Labour themes of 1945, along with an electorally unwise concentration once again on unilateral nuclear disarmament. Nor did he attempt to look outwards beyond the Labour Party, to try to reclaim those who had defected or who had never been Labour at all. Once a Tory, always a Tory, impenetrable and irredeemable.

But he offered something else, robust and warm, his own image of honesty and integrity. It was a preserving, not a reforming, Labour Party that Michael Foot offered, and after the 1983 general election its standing seemed fragile indeed. But the crisis had nevertheless moved beyond the darkest hour, and renewal was under way. Foot himself, no kind of witch-hunter, had begun the process of weeding out the anti-parliamentary, sectarian far left, Militant and otherwise, from the ranks of the party. His own natural supporters among the soft left turned decisively to uphold the parliamentary, gradualist model; his successor Neil Kinnock encouraged them with courageous leadership and drive that were beyond Michael Foot's temperamental capacity. There was still in being a socialist alternative, however pallid, after Foot's three sad years of leadership. He could never have captured power, but almost alone amongst his contemporaries (including Denis Healey) he supplied a unifying energy and focus, along with a capacity for enlisting trust, that gave his comrades a future still worth fighting for.

But Michael Foot the Labour politician is only part of his story, perhaps the less important part. He commands attention, even fascination, not so much because of what he did – his positive legislative and other achievements, after all, were relatively limited – but because of what he was. In a way unique in his time, he operated as the man of letters in politics. Like the Liberal intellectual grandees John Morley, James Bryce or Augustine Birrell of Edwardian days, he was a genuine voice for public culture, especially historical and literary culture, in British political life. Like them, he saw its origins in the seventeenth century, with Cromwell and Milton as its founding fathers. Journalists who ridiculed him as 'the old bibliophile' or a somewhat manic, dishevelled essayist and book reviewer who had somehow strayed into parliamentary affairs through inadvertence, simply misunderstood him. Foot quite genuinely saw his forays into politics as inextricably bound up with his vision of the culture of the past, its books above all. Inspired always by his father Isaac, he generated for himself a unique cultural genealogy, pivoting on Swift, the *déclassé* outsider who dished Marlborough and the Whigs, but going back to Montaigne, and then moving onwards to Hazlitt, Byron, Heine and H. G. Wells, with Orwell and Silone as more contemporary exhibits.

For Foot, these writers – and their ranks could variously be swollen by Defoe, Wordsworth, Cobbett, Disraeli, Conrad and Shaw, amongst others – were not a mere hobby or 'hinterland', to use the term in Denis Healey's illuminating autobiography. They embodied his values, they shaped his rhetoric. They were custodians of a unique culture, all of them rebels against convention and sometimes driven into isolation or exile, yet all operating broadly within an acceptable context of British-style civility. They all embodied aspects of Foot's political outlook, or at least he claimed that they did. All of them had a sense of history which they had mobilized to subvert present injustices. They also embodied aspects of Foot's personality, especially his romantic vision of personal liberation. Each was a 'sensual puritan', as Foot saw Nye Bevan. Each responded to place and circumstance – not least to the beauties of Venice, almost as central a connecting thread in his literary heroes as were the ideas of Montaigne and Swift. Foot's speeches and writings turned time and again to key statements from his favoured authors, not to strike any forced cultural pose, but because their ideas provided his essential driving force. Defining Jonathan Swift as a 'militant Montaigne' was not just an academic conceit, but a central component of Foot's ideology. He liked to quote Logan Pearsall Smith's aphorism, 'To act and not to read is barbarism.' He put it a different way when quoted in an article which appeared in the *Guardian* in May 2006: 'Men of power have no time to read; yet the men who do not read are unfit for power.'[3] No one in his time in politics has even come close to emulating his unifying vision of the synergy of books and action. With the present-day challenge to the book from electronic forms of information technology, and the relegation of an education that disciplines the intellect in favour of the inculcation of repetitive 'skills', no one is likely to do so again. Our public discourse will be much the poorer.

Apart from his bookishness, Foot's more general public style needs close examination. He seems to offer a relatively simple vision of popular dissent, treasured in the values of the common people over the centuries. In fact, there were many complications in his views, different versions of grit in the oyster. His socialism was at least challenged, perhaps fundamentally modified, by a powerful ancestral background of Cromwellian parliamentarism and old Liberalism. Even when most caught up in protecting the trade unions, Foot always spoke for the free-thinking dissenter, the rebel whatever his or her cause. His endless protests against the Labour leadership from 1935 to 1970 were always framed in the form of a timeless libertarianism that went beyond a mere Liberal defence of civil liberties.

Again, he stood apparently for an internationalism of outlook, powerfully displayed in his enthusiasm for India and Israel, and in idealistic campaigns such as that for rehabilitating a crushed Germany after 1945. Like Wordsworth in 1789, Foot felt himself to be genuinely a citizen of the world. But his was a very British internationalism, indeed 'mere English': even his genuine affection for the Welsh voters of Ebbw Vale was conceived from the outside. Unlike Marx, he found it difficult to grasp an 'unhistoric' nation. In its institutions, its ethos and its culture, England was always his touchstone. Foot in many ways is a key exemplar in the recent annals of English nationalism, no less so than his friend George Orwell in *The Lion and the Unicorn*. Robert Colls's fine book *The Identity of England* (2002) has shrewdly seen Orwell's wartime idea of the English revolution as 'home-grown', an extension of the Englishness that already existed.[4] This would apply equally to Michael Foot. More fully than most socialists, he responded to the clarion call 'England arise.' He felt rooted in his England, whereas a man like Koestler was always displaced and volatile. Foot's opposition to 'Europe' spoke for a deep, abiding insularity. He did not identify politically with England's European neighbours, none of whose languages he spoke, or perhaps wanted to speak, whose history too often was a series of lurches between Bonapartism and anarchy. Foot never drew on the ideas of intellectual socialists like Jean Jaurès or Léon Blum as he might have done, though he did respond strongly to eastern European dissidents like Milan Djilas. The same applied to the USA. American radicalism had had its positive impact on British radicals over the years, on Richard Cobden and Joseph Chamberlain, via Theodore Roosevelt's influence on Lloyd George, down to J. K. Galbraith's impact on the Labour Party of the 1950s. Some of Foot's ideological heroes, Bertrand Russell or Harold Laski, had been genuinely transatlantic in seeing links between America and the British left. His father Isaac, the admirer of Lincoln, had been a strong supporter of the alliance with the United States, which he knew at first hand. But even when the New Deal is taken into account, Michael showed an indifference to the USA that bordered on distaste. Perhaps one of his greatest overseas heroes was Pandit Nehru. Significantly, Nehru was a product of Harrow and Cambridge, a patrician socialist like Foot himself, though more ruthless in the uses of power.

Similarly, Foot's feel for British history, genuine and deeply-felt, was a complex one. History as such was vitally important to him intellectually. He read voraciously Gibbon and Macaulay, Michelet's history of the French Revolution (to which he was drawn by the writings of C. L. R. James) and especially (as an instinctive hero-worshipper) Thomas Carlyle's mighty works on Cromwell and Napoleon. In pamphlets like *Full Speed Ahead* in 1950, or *My Kind of Socialism* in 1981, Foot outlined a kind of popular history of the English people, like E. P. Thompson's vision of the 'liberty tree' down the ages. Those who raised their voices in protest for the common people, from John Ball in the Peasants' Revolt, through the Levellers in the seventeenth century, the Foxite Whigs and radicals like Tom Paine a century and a half later, the Chartists in the early industrial age, the independent Labour Party of Hardie, Lansbury and Bevan more recently, were seen as marching along the long road to political and social liberation. Their eternal enemies were Tories, landlords, generals and industrial capitalists of all descriptions. But this simple-minded populist picture was complicated by other factors, notably a deep patriotic pride in English liberties and institutions (hence his enthusiasm for Fox, far from being any kind of social radical). Newspaper allegations that he indulged in anti-patriotic, even treasonable, activities with Soviet agents are therefore all the more ludicrous.

In his view of history, Foot responded passionately to earlier eras of national glory, the Stuart period above all. Like traditional chroniclers of 'Our Island Story' he believed in British exceptionalism. This Devon man saw not only the freebooting Francis Drake as a symbol of national greatness. Plymouth and the throb of Drake's Drum were as central to his sense of patriotism as were Nelson and the Chimes of Pompey for his colleague Jim Callaghan. Foot extended this to naval heroes over the centuries, from Cromwell's inspired Admiral Blake to Nelson himself, while, despite Swift, he felt there was much to be said for Marlborough and the later Churchills, not to mention Chatham. Like the Elizabethan Welsh mystic John Dee, Foot could even respond to the idea of a 'British Empire', though (like Dee) using neither word in its Victorian colonizing sense. Oliver Cromwell he revered not only as a champion of Parliament but also a powerful agent of maritime greatness, respected across the globe, later recalled by that old cynic Sam Pepys with nostalgic affection. Foot wanted his people to identify with visions of a great cohesive nation, but without its institutional forms being overturned. In practice, provided the rights of back-benchers were respected, he was happy enough with a relatively unreformed House of Commons, and also with leaving as they were institutions like the public schools and the older universities (after all, he had attended them himself, and had deep affection for Oxford in particular). Reforming the unelected Lords was no great priority, even with tales later surfacing of 'cash for peerages': after all, Labour had been content to indulge the corrupt figure of Robert Maxwell when he rescued Mirror Newspapers. There was even something to be said for the monarch, and he respected the patriotic commitment of the Queen, whom in any case he liked on personal grounds, as he did the Queen Mother. On matters like the Commonwealth, he noted, the Queen was far sounder in her instincts than the elected and female Prime Minister of the eighties.

Complexities in his historical outlook also emerged from the human agents of it that he admired. His values were variously embodied by Lloyd George, Stafford Cripps, Lord Beaverbrook, Aneurin Bevan (the strongest force of them all), Jack Jones, the Nehru family, and women in general, as a result of Jill's tutorship. It was inevitably a very mixed vision of culture and social change that these personalities conveyed to him. The most they had in common, perhaps, was a sense that each was a kind of outsider, just as Swift, Hazlitt and Wells had been. Foot's vision was shaped by history in fundamental ways, but a highly usable history, in which he was prepared to impose his principles on the past, and not merely draw from it as 'another country'. He was not, after all, a scholar-historian. None of his books, other than The Pen and the Sword, could be called academic. Most were self-proclaimed 'vindications'. What he did do, however, more powerfully than anyone in political life other than Winston Churchill, was to teach a respect for the past, to see our history as a humane civilizing force with its own validity. Foot was never more himself than when celebrating works of historical literature, especially British. It was in its almost total lack of interest in history that 'New Labour' in his own later years seemed to him most culpably deficient and spiritually dead, Gordon Brown being a distinguished exception. He was not reassured by the spectacle of Tony Blair proclaiming that 'I feel the hand of history on our shoulders,' or telling the American Congress that 'history will forgive' the invasion of Iraq. Dragging in the endorsement of Almighty God was even worse.[5] The historical sense and sensibility of Michael Foot, humanist *littérateur*, reflected a world we had lost.

Michael Foot was a highly intellectual politician. But he was not really an intellectual in politics, certainly not in the same sense as Crosland, Crossman or Denis Healey in using a powerful mental apparatus to define, disentangle and decide on major political issues. Foot operated on a different level, romantic in style but with an ancestral underpinning of rationalism too, as Barbara Castle shrewdly noted of the 'collective Foot type'. He was a fundamentally tolerant man. The frequent air of dogmatism, aggressively conveyed in public (especially towards some fellow socialists, like comrade Gaitskell, whom he seemed to hate more virulently than any Tory, living or dead), was misleading. Norman Tebbit saw Foot as a self-righteous bigot, incapable of being fair to his opponents' position or even of listening to it.[6] In fact, Foot's politics were flexible and eclectic. He was neither moralistic nor Marxist. He preferred by far Disraeli's colourful icono-clasm to Gladstone's evangelical solemnity. The flirtation with Marxist theory undertaken by some of his colleagues in the thirties left him cold, and thereby unencumbered by the dialectic rigidity in his thought-processes which could emerge even in a good social democrat like Healey. After all, Foot's most admired contemporary writers, Orwell, Koestler (with reservations), certainly Ignazio Silone, were all fugitives from the intellectual tyranny of Communism. Their god that had failed was one that Foot had never begun to worship in the first place. He escaped from Cripps's Marxisant mélange in good time. He was in every sense a humanist. For a left-wing socialist devoted to his party, he was not at all tribal, either in his friendships or his instincts. The admirer of the French Jacobins who could revel in Burke's reac-tionary reflections on the Revolution in France was also the liberal anti-racist who could build up a private friendship with Enoch Powell.

Michael Foot's approach to public life was poetic, if partisan. It was also highly personal. People noted that he seemed to be a very private man, distant from children while kind to them, enjoying the solitude of the old books in his library, often curiously shy in conver-sation. He steered well clear of writing his autobiography. In a famous review of Barbara Castle's published diaries he attacked the principle of Cabinet ministers keeping journals, and kept none himself. His books never penetrate or reveal his subconscious. Perhaps his enthusiasm for a rich variety of extrovert heroes and messiahs (nearly all male, save for Indira Gandhi), amongst past authors or present politicians, was a substitute for searching self-analysis. He cleaved to simple human values and loyalties, and very seldom deviated from them. Freud is as much an absentee as Marx in his world view. In so doing, he built up an image of humanity, personal integrity and outgoing generosity that was rare in his lifetime, indeed rare amongst politicians at any time, and he was admired, even loved, for it.

Michael Foot changed relatively few ideas. But he changed a good many lives. In the process he achieved an international respect (notably in the Commonwealth) which few British politicians could match. Like most of his friend A. J. P. Taylor's 'troublemakers', Foot's political legacy was an evanescent one. There was no more eager champion of causes that were irretrievably lost. But, helped always by Jill's inspirational partnership, he taught his comrades how to read, how to feel, perhaps how to live. He brought warmth into his world. Britain's unique contribution to world culture in the later twentieth century, especially powerful in the political class in Africa, Asia and the Caribbean, was its democratic socialist middle way. Much of it flowed through the words and writings of Michael Foot. He touched it with a kind of magic, certainly with his cherished audacity. Like Voltaire (the friend of Dean Swift and the idol of H. N. Brailsford), he devoted a very long life to the pursuit of the highest ideals of free thought, tolerance and civil liberty.[7] He did so with far more social insight, much less cynicism about humankind, than the old French *philosophe* ever managed. But, like Voltaire too, citizen Foot, libertarian and Jacobin, *sans-culotte* of the donkey jacket, was always a great humane reformer, not a revolutionary.

NOTES

Chapter 1: NONCONFORMIST
PATRICIAN (1913–1934)

1. For the older Isaac Foot, see A. M.
   Mobbs, *Horrabridge and District*, Part
   Five: *Isaac Foot of Horrabridge*
   (privately printed, 1982). I am much
   indebted for help on the Foot family
   background to Alison Highet and
   Owain Morgan.
2. For Isaac Foot, see Sarah Foot, *My
   Grandfather, Isaac Foot* (Bossiney
   Books, 1980), and Michael Foot and
   Alison Highet, *Isaac Foot* (Politico's,
   2006)
3. Isaac Foot to Michael Foot, 1945
   (n.d.) (Isaac Foot Papers, courtesy of
   Alison Highet). Also see Churchill to
   Sir Archibald Sinclair, 29 May 1945,
   in Ian Hunter (ed.), *Winston and
   Archie* (Politico's, 2005), p.421
4. Michael Foot's interview with
   Professor Steven Kramer, October
   1981 (Michael Foot Papers, People's
   History Museum, Manchester
   [PHM], C11)
5. Michael Foot, *Debts of Honour*
   (Davis-Poynter, 1980), pp.11ff. See
   also 'The Father of the Foots',
   Sunday Telegraph, 9 August 1970
6. *Observer*, 20 February 1949, later
   reprinted as 'an open letter'
7. John Gross, *The Rise and Fall of the
   Man of Letters* (Weidenfeld &
   Nicolson, 1969), pp.137–8
8. Peter Gaunt to Foot, 26 May 1995,
   Foot to Gaunt, 1 June 1995, and
   other material in Foot private papers;
   Foot to Gaunt, 24 September 1905;

Gaunt to the author, 10 February
2005. I am grateful to the Rev.
Professor John Morrill and Dr Peter
Gaunt for information on the
Cromwell Association.
9. Michael Foot, *Debts of Honour*, p.18
10. Foot and Highet, op. cit.,
    pp.289–95; Christopher Foot to
    Dingle Foot, 23 November 1961
    (Foot Papers [PHM], P1). For an
    account of the materials in Isaac
    Foot's library, see the Online
    Archive of California, http://
    www.oac.cdlib.org.findaid.ark
11. Richard Ollard (ed.), *The Diaries of
    A. L. Rowse* (Allen Lane, 2003),
    p.254
12. Material in Isaac Foot Papers
13. Hugh Foot, *A Start in Freedom*
    (Hodder & Stoughton, 1964),
    p.24
14. Sarah Foot, op. cit., p.28
15. There is an entry on Dingle Foot in
    the *Oxford Dictionary of National
    Biography* (Oxford University Press,
    2004). The Dingle Foot Papers in
    Churchill College, Cambridge,
    Library, are very slight.
16. Interview with Michael Foot,
    17 May 2005
17. *Star*, 25 October 1957
18. Brian Brivati (ed.), *The Uncollected
    Michael Foot* (Politico's, 2003),
    pp.23–7
19. Paul Foot, *The Vote* (Viking, 2004).
    For an affectionate study of Paul
    Foot, see Richard Ingrams, *My Friend
    Footy* (Private Eye Books, 2005)

20. Interview with Michael Foot, 5 July 2005; *Parl. Deb.*, 5th ser., Vol. 840, 1026–8 (6 July 1972)

21. School reports in Isaac Foot and Michael Foot Papers

22. Ibid.; R. M. Chadwick to Isaac Foot, 25 July 1927 (ibid.)

23. A. J. P. Taylor, *Beaverbrook* (Hamish Hamilton, 1972), pp.598–9; *Daily Herald*, 11 April 1947. For Leighton Park, see Kenneth Wright, *Leighton Park: The First 100 Years* (Leighton Park School, 1990), pp.55–9. I am also most grateful for assistance on Leighton Park from Professor Roger Morgan and Mr John Allinson, Senior Master of the school.

24. School reports in Foot private papers

25. *The Leightonian*, March 1931, p.4, and July 1931

26. Michael Foot, 'Travels with a Donkey', ibid., p.59; interview with Michael Foot, 15 November 2004; private information from Professor Roger Morgan and from John Allinson

27. Interview with Michael Foot, 23 January 2005

28. Michael Foot, *Loyalists and Loners* (Hamish Hamilton, 1986), p.304; Philip Williams, *Hugh Gaitskell* (Jonathan Cape, 1979), p.724; interview with Michael Foot, 23 January 2006.

29. See Michael Foot, introduction to Bertrand Russell, *Autobiography* (Routledge & Kegan Paul, 1998 one-volume edition), pp.ix–xv

30. *The Uncollected Michael Foot*, p.101

31. *The Leightonian*, July 1933, p.336; interview with Michael Foot, 23 January 2005

32. *The Leightonian*, December 1932, p.247

33. D. F. Karaka, *The Pulse of Oxford* (Dent, 1933). Also see the same author's *Oh, You English!* (Muller,

1935); Michael Foot to Isaac Foot, 'Friday' 1932 (Isaac Foot Papers)

34. Ibid.

35. D. F. Karaka, *Then Came Hazrat Ali: Autobiography, 1972* (Popular Press, Bombay, 1972), p.48

36. *Oxford Magazine*, 20 October 1932

37. *News Chronicle*, 4 April 1934

38. Barbara Castle, *Fighting All the Way* (Macmillan, 1993), p.77

39. Interview with Baroness Williams of Crosby, 1 November 2004

40. Barbara Castle, *Diaries 1974–76* (Weidenfeld & Nicolson, 1980), p.347 (20 March 1975)

41. *Oxford Magazine*, 1 December 1932, 25 May 1933

42. *Cherwell*, October 1933, p.16

43. See Brian Harrison, 'Politics', in *The History of the University of Oxford*, Vol. VIII: *The Twentieth Century* (Oxford University Press, 1994), pp.406–8; Martin Ceadel, *Pacifism in Britain* (Oxford University Press, 1980), pp.127ff

44. *Oxford Magazine*, 1 June 1933

45. Anthony Greenwood to Foot, 8 June 1933 (Foot Papers [PHM], P1)

46. Eva Foot to Michael Foot, 11 June 1933; Isaac Foot to Michael Foot, 'Saturday', 1933 (Foot Papers [PHM], P1)

47. Foot to Edmund Blunden, 12? January (Harry Ransom Humanities Research Center, University of Texas, Austin); V. K. Krishna Menon (ed.), *Young Oxford and War* (Selwyn & Blount, 1934), pp.19ff

48. Materials on US debating tour in Foot private papers

49. *Atlanta Journal*, 2 November 1934

50. *Yale News*, 20 November 1934

51. *Pitt News*, 14 November 1934

Chapter 2: CRIPPS TO
BEAVERBROOK (1934–1940)

1. W. R. P. George, *The Making of Lloyd George* (Faber & Faber, 1976), p.101 (diary entry of 12 November 1981)

2. Kenneth O. Morgan (ed.), *Lloyd George: Family Letters c.1885–1936* (University of Wales Press/Oxford University Press, 1973), p.14

3. Interview with Michael Foot, 6 March 2003. For a comment on Foot's prowess as a chess player, see Mike Fox and Richard James, *The Even More Complete Chess Addict* (Faber & Faber, 1993), p.84

4. Gwyn A. Williams, 'The Emergence of a Working-Class Movement', in A. J. Roderick (ed.), *Wales Through the Ages*, Vol. II (Christopher Davies, Llandybie, 1960), p.140

5. Michael Foot to Eva Foot, 27 January 1934, quoted in Mervyn Jones, *Michael Foot* (Victor Gollancz, 1994), p.36

6. Dennis Turner to the author, 6 April 2004. I am much indebted to Mr Turner for this most interesting reference.

7. Interview with Michael Foot, 8 April 2003

8. Interview with Michael Foot, 7 June 2004

9. Michael Foot to Margaret Cole, 18 November 1959 (Foot Papers [PHM], T1)

10. Arnold Bennett, *How to Live on Twenty-Four Hours a Day* (Hodder & Stoughton, new edn 1932), p.122; interview with Michael Foot, 8 April 2003

11. Kenneth O. Morgan, *Keir Hardie: Radical and Socialist* (Weidenfeld & Nicolson, 1975), p.191; D. F. Karaka, *Then Came Hazrat Ali*, p.48

12. F. M. Leventhal, *The Last Dissenter: H. N. Brailsford and his World*

(Oxford University Press, 1985), pp.217–22

13. Report on India League meeting, 28 October 1941; India Political Intelligence Papers, File L/PJ/12/453 (British Library, Oriental and India Office Collections, British Library). I am much indebted to Dr Nick Owen for this reference and material.

14. Karaka's *Nehru: The Lotus Eater from Kashmir* (1959) was a scathing attack on Nehru. He also wrote an admiring book about Gandhi, *From Dust He Made us Men*. I am indebted for information on Karaka to Lord Parekh.

15. See the obituary of Mulk Raj Anand, *Independent*, 29 September 2004. I am much indebted to Michael Foot for giving me his precious copy of *The Untouchable*.

16. Interview with Lord Paul, 7 March 2005; correspondence between Michael Foot and Abu (Foot private papers)

17. I am grateful to Professor William Roger Louis of the University of Texas for this information

18. Interview with Michael Foot, 7 June 2005

19. Interview with Michael Foot, 26 October 2004

20. *South Wales Argus*, 2 November 1935

21. *Politics and Letters: Raymond Williams, Interviews with New Left Review* (1979), p.32. I am very grateful to Professor Dai Smith, who is writing a major biography of Raymond Williams, for this reference.

22. *South Wales Argus*, 2 November 1935

23. Ibid., 9 November 1935

24. Ibid.

25. Ibid.

26. Ibid.

27. Ibid.

28. *Western Mail*, 16 November 1935

29. Frank Keating, 'Football and Foot, the Pilgrims' Progressive', *Guardian*, 14 May 2004. Sammy Black scored 180 goals in a career lasting fourteen years.

30. Ben Pimlott, *Labour and the Left in the 1930s* (Cambridge University Press, 1977), pp.54–5

31. Castle, *Fighting All the Way*, p.78

32. Pimlott, op. cit., pp.56–8

33. Castle, *Fighting All the Way*, pp.68–9

34. Ibid., p.80

35. Anne Perkins, *Red Queen: The Authorized Biography of Barbara Castle* (Macmillan, 2003), p.58

36. Stafford Cripps (ed.), *The Struggle for Power* (Left Book Club, 1936)

37. Ibid., p.240; interview of Michael Foot with Francis Beckett (tape given by kind permission of Francis Beckett)

38. Ibid., p.287

39. Michael Foot, *Debts of Honour* (Davis-Poynter, 1980), p.72

40. Kingsley Martin, *Editor* (Hutchinson, 1968), p.296–7

41. *Tribune*, 3 January 1958

42. Ibid.

43. Foot, introduction to Julius Braunthal, *The Tragedy of Austria* (Victor Gollancz, 1942)

44. Interview with Michael Foot, 10 February 2003; see also Peter Clarke, *The Cripps Version* (Allen Lane, 2002), p.75

45. Cripps to Foot, 25 July 1938; Brailsford to Foot, 6 August 1938 (Foot private papers); F. M. Leventhal, *The Last Dissenter* (Oxford, 1985), p.247

46. Brailsford to Foot, ? August 1938 (Foot private papers)

47. Michael Foot, *Aneurin Bevan*, Vol. I (MacGibbon & Kee, 1962), pp.155–7

48. Foot, *Debts of Honour*, pp.72–3

49. Ibid., p.73

50. Ibid., p.95; interview with Michael Foot

51. Foot to Beaverbrook, 15 May 1940 (House of Lords Record Office, Beaverbrook Papers, H/36)

52. Beaverbrook to Foot, 14 May 1940 (ibid.)

53. *Daily Express*, 27 February 1940

54. See Foot's excellent entry on Frank Owen in the *Oxford Dictionary of National Biography* (Oxford, 2004)

55. Michael Foot, *Debts of Honour*, pp.83ff

56. *Evening Standard*, 9 September 1939

57. Ibid.

58. Michael Foot, *Armistice 1918–1939* (Harrap, 1940), pp.110ff

59. Interview with Michael Foot, 10 February 2003

60. For Peter Howard, see Anne Wolrige Gordon, *Peter Howard: Life and Letters* (Hodder & Stoughton, 1969). Howard wrote many books after 1945 for Moral Rearmament, but a particularly relevant work of his here is *Beaverbrook: A Study of Max the Unknown* (Hutchinson, 1964).

61. Interview with Michael Foot, 17 March 2005

Chapter 3: PURSUING GUILTY MEN (1940–1945)

1. Interviews with Michael Foot, 4 November 2003, 7 March 2005

2. 'Cato', *Guilty Men* (Victor Gollancz, 1940), p.19

3. Ibid., pp.103ff

4. Interview with Michael Foot, 7 March 2005; Ruth Dudley Edwards, *Victor Gollancz: A Biography* (Victor Gollancz, 1987), p.317; cf. Sheila Hodges, *Gollancz: The Story of a Publishing House, 1928–1978* (Victor Gollancz, 1978)

5. A. J. P. Taylor, *Beaverbrook* (Hamish Hamilton, 1972), p.586

6. Ibid., p.435

7. E. J. Robertson to Beaverbrook, 4 August 1942 (Beaverbrook Papers, H/36); correspondence between Foot and Owen (Foot private papers); Foot's tribute to Owen appears in the *Evening Standard*, 15 March 1979

8. Foot to Beaverbrook, 3 September 1942 (Beaverbrook Papers, H/248)

9. Ibid.

10. Mervyn Jones, *Michael Foot* (Victor Gollancz, 1994), p.107

11. Beaverbrook to Foot, 20 January 1943 (Beaverbrook Papers, H/248)

12. Taped interview of Michael Foot with Francis Beckett

13. My treatment of Foot's connections with Koestler, Orwell and Silone is based on many conversations with him, especially on 10 October 2005. Also see Foot's introduction to Silone's *Fontemara* (Dent, 1985 edn), and the brilliant essay on Silone, pp.191–242 (and an equally brilliant one on Gaetano Salvemini), in Iris Origo, *A Need to Testify: Four Portraits* (1985). Interesting is Queenie Leavis to Foot, 22 October 1978 (privately owned).

14. David Cesarani, *Arthur Koestler: The Homeless Mind* (Heinemann, 1998), p.188

15. Ibid., p.197; Koestler to Foot, 10 June, 8 July 1942 (Koestler Archive, Edinburgh University Library)

16. Interview with Michael Foot, 26 October 2004

17. Foot to Edmund Blunden, 12? January (Blunden Papers, Austin, Texas). For Foot's health see interview in the *Guardian*, 16 March 2004.

18. Foot to Beaverbrook, 1 November 1943 (Beaverbrook Papers, H/36)

19. Foot to Beaverbrook, ? June 1944 (ibid.)

20. Interviews with Michael Foot, 13 September 2004, 7 March 2005; 'Cassius', *The Trial of Mussolini* (Victor Gollancz, 1943)

21. Interview with Michael Foot, 20 November 2003

22. *The Trial of Mussolini*, pp.80–2

23. Ruth Dudley Edwards, op. cit., p.395; Foot and Highet, *Isaac Foot*, p.230

24. Michael Foot, *Brendan and Beverley: An Extravaganza* (Victor Gollancz, 1944); letter in *The Times*, 23 November 1944

25. *Brendan and Beverley*, pp.66–78

26. Cesarani, op. cit., p.222

27. Paul Addison, *The Road to 1945* (Jonathan Cape, 1945), p.189

28. Patricia Hollis, *Jennie Lee* (Oxford University Press, 1997), pp.100–7

29. Interview with the late Lord Callaghan

30. Michael Foot, *Aneurin Bevan*, Volume 2 (Davis-Poynter, 1973), p.649

31. Bevis Hillier, *John Betjeman: New Fame, New Love* (John Murray, 2002), p.243; interview with Michael Foot, the *Guardian*, 18 March 2002

32. Ibid.

33. Michael Foot, *Debts of Honour*, p.16. For Labour weakness in this region, see Andrew Thorpe, ' "One of the Most Backward Areas of the Country": The Labour Party's Grass Roots in South West England, 1918–45', in Matthew Worley (ed.), *Labour's Grass Roots: Essays on the Activities and Experience of Local Labour Parties and Members, 1918–1945* (Ashgate, Aldershot, 2005).

34. *Western Morning News*, 24, 29 November 1944, 28 June 1945

35. Michael Foot, *Another Heart and*

Other Pulses (William Collins, 1984), p.114

36. *Reynolds News*, 22 October 1944

37. Percy T. Loosemore to Isaac Foot, 29 January 1945 (Isaac Foot Papers)

38. Dingle Foot to Lady Megan Lloyd George, ? 1949 (Megan Lloyd George Papers, National Library of Wales, Aberystwyth, MSS. 20475C, 3174); letter from Dingle Foot to the author, 19 July 1973

39. *Daily Herald*, 1 May 1945

40. For Jill Craigie, see Carl Rollyson, *To be a Woman* (Aurum, 2005)

41. Interview with Michael Foot, 10 February 2003; Foot's article in *Evening Standard*, 19 May 1993

42. Interview with Michael Foot, 15 November 2004

43. Ibid.

44. Castle, *Fighting All the Way*, p.161

45. *Daily Herald*, 29 June 1945

46. *Western Morning News*, 27 June 1945

47. Ibid., 29 June 1945

48. Ibid.

49. See Scott Kelly, ' "The Ghost of Neville Chamberlain": Guilty Men and the 1945 Election', *Conservative History Journal* (autumn 2005), pp.18–24

50. *Western Morning News*, 29 June 1945

51. Ibid., 30 August 1945

52. *News Chronicle*, 27 July 1945

53. A. J. P. Taylor, *English History 1914–1945* (Oxford University Press, 1965), p.60

Chapter 4: LOYAL OPPOSITIONIST (1945–1951)

1. *Daily Herald*, 31 July 1945

2. Ian Mikardo, *Backbencher* (Weidenfeld & Nicolson, 1988), pp.90–1. For Driberg see his autobiography, *Ruling Passions* (Jonathan Cape, 1977), and

Francis Wheen, *Tom Driberg: His Life and Indiscretions* (Chatto & Windus, 1990), and also correspondence between Foot and Alan Watkins (Foot private papers)

3. Interview with Baroness Mallalieu; interview with Michael Foot, 20 October 2003

4. Jonathan Schneer, *Labour's Conscience* (Unwin Hyman, 1988). Despite its title, this is a most informative book.

5. Bertrand de Jouvenel, *Problems of Socialist England* (1949), p.13

6. Interview with Michael Foot, 15 November 2004; Foot's articles in the *Daily Herald*, 23–25 April and 9 August 1946

7. Dalton to Foot, 15 September 1947; Foot to Dalton, 20 September 1947 (Foot Papers [PHM], T1). Niemeyer was Controller of Finance at the Treasury, 1922–27; Catto was Governor of the Bank of England, 1944–49; Eady was Joint Second Secretary at the Treasury 1942–52, in charge of home and overseas finance, also rescuing the British film industry via the 'Eady Levy'.

8. Cripps to Foot, 14 October 1949 (ibid)

9. Hollis, *Jennie Lee*, pp.158–60

10. *Parl. Deb.*, 5th ser., Vol. 413, 336–41 (20 August 1945)

11. Isaac Foot to Michael Foot, July 1945 (Foot private papers)

12. *The Times*, 22 August 1945; *Western Morning News*, 23 August 1945

13. Tom Driberg in *Sunday Express*, 26 August 1945; material in Foot Papers [PHM], M1

14. See Robert Skidelsky, *John Maynard Keynes*, Vol. 3: *Fighting for Britain* (Macmillan, 2000), pp.403ff

15. Cabinet Conclusions, 29 November, 5 December 1945 (National Archive, CAB 128/2)

16. *Tribune*, 14, 21 December 1945

17. Ruth Dudley Edwards, *Victor Gollancz*, p.417. Also see Matthew Frank, 'The New Morality – Victor Gollancz, "Save Europe Now" and the German Refugee Crisis, 1945–46', *Twentieth Century British History*, Vol. 17, No. 2 (2006), pp.230–56.

18. Ibid., p.419

19. *A Palestine Munich?* (Victor Gollancz, 1946)

20. Interview with Michael Foot, 7 June 2005; Cesarani, *Arthur Koestler*, p.264

21. e.g. *Daily Herald*, 14 March 1947

22. Schneer, op. cit., p.58

23. *Parl. Deb.*, 5th ser., Vol. 430, 526ff (18 November 1946); interview with Michael Foot, 15 November 2004

24. *Daily Herald*, 18 December 1947

25. *Keep Left* (New Statesman Publications, 1947). See David Howell's excellent article on 'Keep Left' in *Dictionary of Labour History*, Vol. 12 (2005)

26. *Daily Herald*, 22 August 1947

27. Material in R. W. G. Mackay Papers (British Library of Political and Economic Science, Section 8, File 3)

28. Alan Bullock, *Ernest Bevin: Foreign Secretary* (Heinemann, 1983), pp.396–400; Denis Healey, *The Time of my Life* (Michael Joseph, 1989), pp.105–6; *Tribune*, 6 June 1947

29. *Tribune*, 23, 30 April 1948. Braddock condemned Foot's article as an attempt to curry favour with people who 'will spit in your face, will use you as wage slaves, prostitute your daughters, and make your sons fodder for cannon or worse'. See David Howell's excellent article on 'The Nenni Telegram' in *Dictionary of Labour History*, Vol. 12.

30. *Tribune*, 5 November 1948

31. Ibid., 18, 25 March 1949

32. Philip Williams (ed.), *The Diary of Hugh Gaitskell, 1945–1956* (Jonathan Cape, 1983), p.77

33. Tosco Fyvel in *Tribune*, 17 March 1950

34. Michael Foot, 'A Free Press Means Free Readers', *Daily Herald*, 16 July 1946; *Parl. Deb.*, 5th ser., Vol. 428, 462–71 (29 October 1946)

35. *Minutes of Evidence Taken Before the Royal Commission on the Press* (Cmd. 7330), pp.1–14 (12 November 1947)

36. Ibid., *Thirteenth and Fourteenth Days* (Cmd. 7351), pp.17–26 (18 December 1947)

37. *Royal Commission on the Press: Report*, 1949 (Cmd. 7700), pp.161ff

38. Beaverbrook to Foot, 19 January 1948 (Foot Papers [PHM] P1); interview with Michael Foot, 10 February 2003; Foot, *Debts of Honour*, pp.102–3; *Tribune*, 26 November 1948. In *Debts of Honour*, Foot wrongly gives the year as 1949. The 'Lower than Kemsley' article appeared in *Tribune* on 10 March 1950.

39. Interview with Michael Foot, 10 February 2003

40. Interview with Geoffrey Goodman, 23 March 2004

41. *Daily Herald*, 15 June 1948

42. Ibid., 21 January 1949

43. See Peggy Duff, *Left! Left! Left!* (Allison & Busby, 1971)

44. Morgan, *Keir Hardie*, pp.66–7

45. Peggy Duff, op. cit., p.26

46. Robert Edwards, *Goodbye, Fleet Street* (Jonathan Cape, 1988), pp.32–3

47. Interview with Michael Foot, 17 September 2003; *Tribune*, 10 March 1950

48. Interview with Elizabeth Thomas, 4 October 2003

49. *Tribune*, 30 April 1948

50. Ibid., 30 September 1949

51. Peggy Duff, op. cit., p.26

52. Foot to Phillips, 1 December 1949 (Labour Party Archives, General Secretary's Papers, GS 27/2)

53. Aneurin Bevan to Huw T. Edwards, 20 June 1949 (National Library of Wales, Aberystwyth, Huw T. Edwards Papers)

54. Labour Party NEC minutes, 27 April 1949 (Labour Party Archives, PHM); for Silone, conversation with Michael Foot, 10 October 2005

55. *Evening Standard*, 19 May 1993; interview with Michael Foot, 5 April 2004

56. Jill Craigie to Isaac Foot, ? 1949 (Isaac Foot Papers); *Cornish Guardian*, 27 October 1949

57. David Berry, *Wales and Cinema: The First 100 Years* (University of Wales Press, Cardiff, 1994), p.173

58. Interview with Michael Foot, 13 January 2004; Castle, *Fighting All the Way*, p.161

59. Michael and Jill Foot, telegram to Isaac Foot, 1949 (Isaac Foot Papers); Michael Foot to Isaac Foot, 9 June 1948 (in the author's possession)

60. *Western Morning News*, 28 January 1950

61. Colm Brogan, *Our New Masters* (London, 1948), p.20

62. Foot, *Aneurin Bevan*, Vol. 2, p.276

63. Michael Foot and Donald Bruce, *Who are the Patriots?* (Victor Gollancz, 1949)

64. *Tribune*, 8 October 1948; David Reynolds, *Command of History: Churchill Fighting and Writing the Second World War* (Penguin, 2004), pp.142–3

65. Information from Michael Foot; Foot, *Debts of Honour*, p.149

66. Foot, *Aneurin Bevan*, Vol. 2, p.276

67. *Western Morning News*, 13 February 1950; materials on the 1950 election in Foot Papers [PHM], M1

68. Ibid., 8, 23 February 1950; Foot's column in the *Daily Herald*, 31 January 1947

69. Record of the Dorking conference, May 1950 (PHM, Labour Party Archives, General Secretary's Papers, GS 26/3)

70. Foot, *Aneurin Bevan*, Vol. 2, p.286

71. *Tribune*, 3 March 1950

72. Ibid., 15 September 1950

73. Ibid., 30 June, 28 July 1950

74. Ibid., 28 June 1950

75. Ibid., 21 June 1950

76. Asa Briggs, *History of Broadcasting in the United Kingdom*, Vol. IV: *Sound and Vision* (Oxford University Press, 1979), pp.599–605; Kathleen Burk, *Troublemaker: The Life and History of A. J. P. Taylor* (Yale University Press, 2000), pp.383–4

77. Cabinet Conclusions, 1 August 1950 (National Archive, CAB/18)

78. Cabinet Committee on the National Health Service (ibid., CAB 134/519)

79. Foot, *Aneurin Bevan*, Vol. 2, p.292

80. For a fuller account, see Kenneth O. Morgan, *Labour in Power 1945–1951* (Oxford University Press, 1984), pp.441–61

81. Cabinet Conclusions, 25 January 1951 (National Archive, CAB 128/19)

82. Ibid., 22 March 1951 (ibid., CAB 128/19)

83. *Tribune*, 20 April 1951

84. Morgan, *Labour in Power*, p.454

85. Minutes of Keep Left group, 17 October 1950 (University of Warwick, Modern Records Centre, Crossman Papers, MSS. 154/3/KL/1/1–14)

86. Ibid., 26 April 1951 (Richardson/Mikardo Papers, People's History Museum)

87. Peggy Duff, op. cit., p.38

88. Briggs, op. cit., p.601

89. Foot, *Aneurin Bevan*, Vol. 2, p.342;

Ben Pimlott (ed.), *The Political Diary of Hugh Dalton 1918–40, 1945–60* (Jonathan Cape, 1987), p.547 (1 July 1951)

90. *Tribune*, 13 July 1951

91. Cabinet Conclusions, 2 July 1951 (National Archive, CAB 128/20)

92. *Tribune*, 21 September 1951

93. Williams, *Gaitskell*, p.275

94. *Western Morning News*, 5 October 1951

95. Ibid., 19 October 1951

96. Material on the Foot–Randolph Churchill relationship, including a file of letters, in Foot Papers [PHM], M1; Charles Wintour to Beaverbrook, 12 October 1956 (HLRO, Beaverbrook Papers, H/260)

97. Review of the present author's *Labour in Power 1945–1951* in *Observer*, 4 March 1984

98. Interview with Michael Foot, 20 October 2003

99. Philip Williams, 'Foot-Faults in the Gaitskell–Bevan Match', *Political Studies*, xxvii, 2 (April–June 1949), pp.129ff

Chapter 5: BEVANITE AND TRIBUNITE (1951–1960)

1. *Tribune*, 14 December 1951

2. Janet Morgan (ed.), *The Backbench Diaries of Richard Crossman*, p.143 (27 November 1952)

3. Foot to Gaitskell, 24 October 1952 (University College, London, Gaitskell Papers, F10/2); Foot, *Aneurin Bevan*, Vol. 2, p.376

4. *Backbench Diaries of Richard Crossman*, pp.156–8 (14 October 1952)

5. Ibid., p.186 (3 December 1952)

6. Interview with Michael Foot, 3 June 2003

7. Castle, *Fighting All the Way*, p.235

8. *The Political Diary of Hugh Dalton*, p.583 (7–9 March 1952); Briggs, op. cit., pp.603–5

9. Mark Jenkins, *Bevanism: Labour's High Tide* (Spokesman Press), p.127; interview with Dick Clements, 16 November 2004

10. Keep Left minutes and papers: note by Rose Cohen and Jo Richardson (University of Warwick, MSS. 154/3/KL/3/55)

11. Interview with Michael Foot, 13 January 2004; Castle, *Fighting All the Way*, pp.202–3

12. Castle, *Fighting All the Way*, p.202

13. Richard Crossman, 'Towards a Philosophy of Socialism', in Crossman (ed.), *New Fabian Essays* (Turnstile Press, 1952), p.27

14. Castle, *Fighting All the Way*, p.207

15. *Backbench Diaries of Richard Crossman*, p.971 (8 February 1963)

16. *Daily Herald*, 18 March 1955

17. Robert Edwards, op. cit., p.38

18. Peggy Duff, op. cit., pp.72–3

19. *Tribune*, 10 March 1950, was the original offending article. For Monckton's role see Foot to Lord Birkenhead, 1 February 1968 (Foot Papers [PHM], T1)

20. Ibid., October 1954

21. Ibid., 12 November 1954; *The Times*, 11 November 1954

22. *Backbench Diaries of Richard Crossman*, p.364 (15 November 1954)

23. Interview with Ian Aitken

24. Interview with Elizabeth Thomas

25. Personal knowledge; *Observer* 'Profile', 10 March 1974

26. Files on Cameron and Vicky in Foot private papers, and also Foot's contribution to Russell Davies (ed.), *Vicky* (Secker & Warburg, 1987)

27. *Financial Times*, 8 April 1995; Cesarani, *Arthur Koestler*, pp.399–400

28. Charles Wintour to Beaverbrook, 29 December 1954 (HLRO, Beaverbrook Papers, H/254)

29. Interview with Baroness Mallalieu

30. Information from Michael Foot

31. Pimlott (ed.), *Political Diary of Hugh Dalton*, p.691 (18 June 1958)

32. *Western Morning News*, 16 May 1955; entry on Vickers by Patrick Cosgrave, *Oxford Dictionary of National Biography*

33. Ibid., 24 May 1955

34. Ibid.

35. Isaac Foot to Michael Foot, May 1955 (Foot private papers)

36. *Tribune*, 20 April 1956

37. Michael Foot and Mervyn Jones, *Guilty Men 1957* (Victor Gollancz, 1957)

38. John Campbell, *Nye Bevan and the Mirage of British Socialism* (Weidenfeld & Nicolson, 1987), pp.318–26

39. *Tribune*, 24 May 1957

40. Ibid., 4 October 1957

41. Interview with Michael Foot, 13 January 2004

42. Ibid.; *The Backbench Diaries of Richard Crossman*, p.619 (4 October 1957)

43. John Campbell, op. cit., p.336

44. *Tribune*, 11 October 1957

45. Interview with Geoffrey Goodman; there is some friendly correspondence between Foot and Cousins in the Cousins Papers, University of Warwick, Modern Records Centre, MSS. 282 and 283

46. *Tribune*, 18 October 1957; Hollis, op. cit., pp.192–3

47. Robert Edwards, op. cit.; interview with Dick Clements

48. Information from Michael Foot

49. Jennie Lee to Foot (Foot Papers [PHM], T2)

50. Interview with Dick Clements

51. Pimlott (ed.), *The Political Diary of Hugh Dalton*, p.691 (18 June 1958)

52. Interview with Geoffrey Goodman

53. *Backbench Diaries of Richard Crossman*, p.751 (5 June 1959)

54. *Parliament in Danger* (Pall Mall Press, London), p.18

55. *Tribune*, 28 November 1958

56. *Daily Herald*, 28, 29 May 1958; Foot to Peter Jackson, 16 June 1958 (Foot Papers [PHM] T1); obituary of David Ross by Peter Hitchens in *Guardian*, 17 August 2004

57. *Daily Herald*, 31 May 1958

58. Interview with Michael Foot, 5 July 2005

59. *Western Morning News*, 17 September 1959

60. *Daily Express*, 14 March 1959

61. Foot to Jackson, 16 June 1958; Jackson to Foot, 25 November 1958 (Foot Papers [PHM], T1)

62. Foot to Jackson, 26 November 1958; Jackson to Foot, 27 November 1958 (Foot Papers [PHM] T1)

63. *Western Morning News*, 23 September 1959

64. Ibid., 1 October 1959

65. Ibid., 3 October 1959

66. Foot to Jackson, 8 May 1959 (Foot Papers [PHM], T2)

67. Material on Jackson, ibid.

68. Foot, *Aneurin Bevan*, Vol. 2, p.648

69. Ibid., p.653

70. Ibid., p.655

71. Interview with Michael Foot

72. *Daily Herald*, 9 September 1960

73. Interview with Geoffrey Goodman

74. *Western Mail*, 25 September 1960

75. Ron Evans Papers in the National Library of Wales, Aberystwyth. I am very grateful to John Graham Jones for his assistance.

76. *Daily Herald*, 19 November 1960

77. Ron Evans to Fred Hardwicke, 5 November 1960 (Ron Evans Papers, File 6)

78. Callaghan to Ron Evans, 21 November 1960 (National Library of Wales, Aberystwyth, Ron Evans Papers, File 6); see *Daily Telegraph*, 15 November 1960

79. Gaitskell to Foot, 10 November (ibid., File 7)

80. *Guardian*, 17 November 1960

81. Ibid., 19 November 1960

82. Mervyn Jones, op cit., p.253; Foot to Mackenzie (Mackenzie Papers, Harry Ransom Humanities Center, University of Texas, Austin)

83. *Backbench Diaries of Richard Crossman*, p.862 (4 August 1960)

Chapter 6: CLASSIC AND ROMANTIC

1. Jennie Lee to Isaac Foot, 28 October 1960 (Isaac Foot Papers)

2. Interview with Michael Foot; Michael Foot to Isaac Foot, ? January 1958 (Isaac Foot Papers)

3. Interview with Michael Foot, 13 December 2004

4. George Orwell, 'Politics vs. Literature', *Polemic*, 5, September–October 1946; Foot, *Debts of Honour*, p.207

5. I am much indebted to helpful information and judgements on Swift from Dr James Ward of the University of Leeds. I have also received authoritative advice from Professor Paul Langford, Rector of Lincoln College, Oxford.

6. Foot, *Debts of Honour*, p.206; interview with Lord Kinnock, 30 January 2006

7. Orwell, op. cit.

8. John Foot to Michael Foot, ? November 1957

9. e.g. Swift's *Short View of the State of Ireland* (1728)

10. Roy Carroll, *Modern Ireland, 1600–1972* (Allen Lane, 1988), p.181

11. Foot, *Debts of Honour*, pp.65–9

12. Interview with Michael Foot, 13 December 2004; John Foot to Michael Foot, 7 December 1998 (Foot private papers)

13. Jonathan Swift, *Conduct of the Allies* (Oxford University Press, 1896 edn),

p.48; cf. Foot, *The Pen and the Sword* (MacGibbon & Kee, 1957), pp.323ff

14. Irvin Ehrenpreis, *Swift: The Man, his Works and the Age*, Vol. 2 (Methuen, 1967), pp.484–5; Maximillian E. Novak, *Daniel Defoe: Master of Fictions* (Oxford University Press, 2003 edn), pp.387ff

15. Foot, *The Pen and the Sword*, pp.42ff

16. Foot, *Debts of Honour*, pp.173–5

17. Ibid., pp.185–7

18. Foot, *The Pen and the Sword*, p.9

19. Ehrenpreis, op. cit., p.493

20. Ibid., p.500

21. Interview with Michael Foot, 13 December 2004

22. Foot, *Debts of Honour*, p.208

23. Ibid., pp.206–7

24. Orwell, loc. cit.; interview with Geoffrey Goodman

25. Isaac Foot to Hugh Foot

26. *Sunday Times*, 24 November 1957; *Observer*, 24 November 1957

27. Notably J. A. Downie, *Robert Harley and the Press: Propaganda and Public Opinion in the Age of Swift and Defoe* (Cambridge University Press, 1979) and idem, *Jonathan Swift: Political Writer* (Routledge & Kegan Paul, 1984); David Nokes, *Jonathan Swift. A Hypocrite Reversed: A Critical Biography* (Oxford University Press, 1985); and Ian Higgins, *Swift's Politics: A Study in Disaffection* (Cambridge University Press, 1994). I am most grateful to Lord Rowlands, himself an authority on the career of Robert Harley, and Dr James Ward for their advice on these matters.

28. Robert Walcott, *English Politics in the Early Eighteenth Century* (Clarendon Press, Oxford, 1956)

29. J. A. Downie, *Jonathan Swift: Political Writer*, pp.x–xi, 344–5; Ian Higgins, op. cit., pp.12–13, 171ff

30. CND executive committee minutes, 1958–63 (University of Warwick,

Modern Records Centre, MSS. 181), minutes of 21 January 1958. See generally Frank Parkin, *Middle Class Radicals* (University of Manchester Press, 1968), and John Minnion and Philip Bolsover (eds), *The CND Story* (London, 1983).

31. CND minutes of 28 January 1958

32. Ibid., minutes of 1958–61; Kathleen Burk, op. cit., p.214

33. Mikardo, *Backbencher*, pp.160–1

34. Castle, *Fighting All the Way*, p.257

35. Interviews with the late Lord Orme, 28 October 2004, and Baroness Gould of Potter Newton, 20 July 2005

36. Interview with Dick Clements

37. Ibid.

38. Foot to Peter Jackson, 16 June 1958 (Foot Papers [PHM] T1)

39. Foot, 'Why I Back Cousins on the Bomb', *Daily Herald*, 27 September 1960

40. Foot to Margaret Cole, 1 December 1960 (Foot Papers [PHM] T1)

41. *Backbench Diaries of Richard Crossman*, p.907 (14 December 1960)

42. For a good account of the growth of CDS see Brian Brivati, *Hugh Gaitskell* (Richard Cohen Books, 1996), pp.376ff

43. CND executive committee minutes, 7 March 1963 (loc. cit.)

44. Olive Gibbs to Foot, 16 April 1964 (Foot Papers [PHM] T1)

45. A. J. P. Taylor, *A Personal History* (Hamish Hamilton, 1983), p.227

46. For the diplomatic aspects of the Iraq War, see John Kampfner, *Blair's Wars* (Free Press, new edn 2004), and James Naughtie, *The Accidental American* (Macmillan, 2004). For the context in international law, see Philippe Sands, *Lawless World* (Allen Lane, 2005), especially pp.173ff, 'Kicking Ass in Iraq', a devastating critique.

47. Interview with Michael Foot, 26 October 2004

48. Anthony Powell, quoted in Gordon Bowker, *George Orwell* (Little, Brown, 2003), p.361

49. Interview with Michael Foot, 10 October 2005

50. Ibid.

Chapter 7: TOWARDS THE MAINSTREAM (1960–1968)

1. John Elliott, *The Industrial Development of the Ebbw Valleys, 1780–1914* (University of Wales Press, 2004)

2. Ibid., p.95

3. Interviews with Michael Foot, 26 October 2004, 23 January 2005

4. *Daily Herald*, 1960, quoted in Mervyn Jones, op. cit., p.252

5. See 'Michael Foot on Aneurin Bevan', *Llafur*, 1, No. 3 (May 1974). For the earlier phase of the working-class radicalism of the Gwent valleys see David J. V. Jones, *Before Rebecca* (Allen Lane, 1973) and *The Last Rising* (Clarendon Press, Oxford, 1985)

6. Interviews with Michael Foot, 26 October 2004, 23 January 2006

7. Interview with Alan Fox, 18 March 2004

8. Ibid.

9. Interview with Michael Foot, 26 October 2004; conversation with John Powell's widow, 7 March 2006

10. *Tribune*, 25 November 1960

11. For a full exegesis of Foot's view see his letter to the *Guardian*, 14 December 1961 (draft in Foot Papers [PHM] T1)

12. Correspondence between Foot and Bowden in Foot Papers [PHM], M2

13. Christopher Foot to Dingle Foot, 23 November 1961 (Foot Papers

[PHM] P1); Foot and Highet, *Isaac Foot*, pp.332–42; Mervyn Jones, op. cit.

14. Interview with Michael Foot, 23 June 2004

15. Correspondence between Michael Bessie and Foot (Foot private papers)

16. Anthony Hern to Charles Wintour, 25 June, 27 August 1962 (HLRO, Beaverbrook Papers, H/268)

17. John Campbell, *Nye Bevan and the Mirage of British Socialism*, p.xiv

18. Morgan, *Labour in Power*, pp.455–61. Similar conclusions are reached by Peter Hennessy, *Never Again*, pp.416–19.

19. Dai Smith, *Aneurin Bevan and the World of South Wales* (University of Wales Press, Cardiff); Ben Pimlott, 'The Future of Political Biography', in *Frustrate Their Knavish Tricks* (HarperCollins, 1994), pp.149ff

20. Interview with Michael Foot, 13 January 2004

21. 'Up the Garden', *Spectator*, 22 January 1960

22. *Parl. Deb.*, 5th ser., Vol. 674, 1593–1600 (28 March 1963)

23. Elizabeth Thomas to Ron Evans, 31 October 1964 (National Library of Wales, Aberystwyth, Ron Evans Papers, File 18)

24. Michael Foot to Ron Evans, 7 January 1964 (ibid.)

25. E. P. Thompson, *The Making of the English Working Class* (Victor Gollancz, 1963), pp.746–8

26. Interview with Michael Foot, 5 July 2005

27. Foot, *Debts of Honour*, pp.206–7

28. See Leo Abse, *Private Member* (Macdonald, 1973)

29. Charles Wintour to Beaverbrook, 29 April 1965 (HLRO, Beaverbrook Papers, H/268)

30. Foot, *Debts of Honour*, p.63

31. *Sunday Times*, 29 August 1982 (Vincent's review of T. R. Fyvel, *George Orwell: A Personal Memoir*)

32. Wheen, *Tom Driberg*, p.353

33. Interview with Michael Foot, 13 January 2004; Tony Benn, *Out of the Wilderness: Diaries 1963–67* (Macmillan, 1987), pp.390–1 (11 February 1966)

34. Meeting of Economic Affairs Committee, MISC 1, 17 October 1964 (CAB 129 /119); *Economist*, 28 November 1964; Kenneth Morgan, *Callaghan: A Life* (Oxford University Press, 1997), pp.214–18. The reference to Canossa is to the Holy Roman Emperor, Henry IV, standing in the snow in penance at Canossa in 1077 to try to escape excommunication by Pope Gregory VII.

35. *Parl. Deb.*, 5th ser., Vol. 711, 1646–58 (6 May 1965); interview with Lord Varley.

36. Interview with Lord Orme

37. Morgan, *Callaghan*, pp.224–5

38. See Foot's essay on Vicky, *Debts of Honour*, pp.145–8; and Michael Foot, 'The Anarchist with a Force More Explosive than Bombs', *Evening Standard*, 24 February 1966

39. *Economist*, 23 June 1966

40. Foot to Wilson, 2 August 1966 (Foot Papers [PHM] T2)

41. Interview with Michael Foot, 13 January 2004

42. Interview with Geoffrey Goodman and with Michael Foot, 23 January 2006

43. Foot to Wilson, 26 March 1968; Wilson to Foot, 22 April 1968 (Foot Papers [PHM] T2)

44. 'The Credo of the New Left' (interview with Robin Blackburn and Alexander Cockburn), *New Left Review*, 49 (May–June 1968), pp.19–34

45. *Tribune*, 5 June 1966
46. Edmund Dell, *A Strange Eventful History* (HarperCollins, 2000), p.335
47. Interview with Michael Foot, 1 March 2004; Paul Foot, *The Rise of Enoch Powell* (Cornmarket Press, 1969)
48. Interview with Michael Foot, 1 March 2004
49. Interview with Jack Jones, 15 July 2004

Chapter 8: UNION MAN (1968–1974)

1. Minutes of Advisory Committee on Policy, 6 February 1963 (Conservative Party Archives, Bodleian Library, ACP/63/103)
2. Paul Davies and Mark Freedland, *Labour Legislation and Public Policy* (Clarendon Press, Oxford, 1993), pp.244–5
3. George Thomas to Harold Wilson, 18 June 1969 (Callaghan Papers, private)
4. Barbara Castle, *Diaries 1964–1970* (Weidenfeld & Nicolson, 1984), pp.646–7 (7 May 1969)
5. Roy Jenkins, *Life at the Centre* (Macmillan, 1991), p.288
6. Interview with the late Lord Murray of Epping Forest, 11 December 1996
7. Henry Phelps Brown, *The Origins of Trade Union Power* (Clarendon Press, Oxford, 1983)
8. Morgan, *Callaghan*, pp.360–1
9. *Diaries of a Cabinet Minister*, 1968–70, pp.440–1 (15 April 1969)
10. *Parl. Deb.*, 5th ser., Vol. 777, 84–92 (3 February 1969)
11. Ibid., Vol. 778, 368–79 (19 February 1969)
12. Ibid., Vol. 779, 935–9 (14 April 1969)
13. Alan Watkins in the *Spectator*, 24 December 1965

14. *Parl. Deb.*, 5th ser., Vol. 798, 1491–8 (25 March 1970)
15. *Morning Star*, 11 March 1969
16. *Tribune*, 7, 14 February 1969
17. Rita Hinden, 'Left, Further Left and Protest Left', *Socialist Commentary*, October 1968, pp.8–11
18. Pimlott, *Harold Wilson*, pp.566–7
19. *The Times*, ? 1970: cutting in Foot private papers
20. Correspondence of Michael Bessie and Michael Foot (ibid.)
21. Interview with Michael Foot, 13 January 2004
22. Philip Williams, 'Foot-Faults in the Gaitskell–Bevan Match', loc. cit.
23. Geoffrey Goodman (ed.), *State of the Nation* (1997)
24. Defence statement drawn up by Leon Brittan QC, Desmond Donnelly v. Michael Foot and Davis Poynter, Ltd, 20 November 1973 (National Library of Wales, Aberystwyth, Desmond Donnelly Papers, Box 3); *The Times*, 5 April 1974. The coroner decided that Donnelly took his own life while depressed.
25. Interview with Jack Jones; minutes of the Labour Party/TUC Liaison Committee (Foot private papers)
26. Wheen, *Tom Driberg*, p.401
27. Notes on Shadow Cabinet meetings, 16 July–13 October 1970 (Foot Papers [PHM] C1, entry of 16 July 1970); see Patrick Bell, *Labour in Opposition 1970–1974* (Routledge & Kegan Paul, 2004) for the general context
28. Notes on Shadow Cabinet meetings, 13 October 1970
29. Interview with Eric Varley
30. *Parl. Deb.*, 5th ser., Vol. 845, 933ff; obituary of Lord Donaldson, *Guardian*, 3 September 2005
31. Interview with Jack Jones
32. Interview with Michael Foot, 22 June 2004

33. Eric Heffer to Michael Foot, 23 August 1961 (Foot Papers [PHM] T2)

34. Roy Jenkins, op. cit., p.337

35. e.g. *Parl. Deb.*, 5th ser., Vol. 867, 2009–18 (24 January 1974); and materials in Foot private papers

36. *Parl. Deb.*, 5th ser., Vol. 831, 742 (17 February 1972); materials in Foot private papers

37. Mervyn Jones, op. cit., p.334

38. Raymond Blackburn to Foot, 7 March 1972, and other miscellaneous papers in Foot private papers; *Parl. Deb.*, 5th ser., Vol. 840, 1963–73 (13 July 1972)

39. Interview with Lord Orme

40. Interview with Michael Foot, 5 April 2004

41. Michael Foot, 'My Only Venice', *Art Quarterly*, Vol. 1, No. 1 (1988), pp.35–8; interview with Michael Foot, 20 October 2003

42. Interview with Vesna Gamulin, Dubrovnik, 22 August 2005

43. Interview with Michael Foot, 7 June 2005

44. Indira Gandhi to Foot, 25 October 1972 (Foot Papers [PHM] T1)

45. cf. Douglas Hurd, *An End to Promises* (William Collins, 1975), pp.135–6

46. *Guardian*, 6 March 1974; Ron Evans Papers; interview with Huw Thomas

47. Morgan, *Callaghan*, p.406

48. Interview with Jack Jones

49. Castle, *Diaries 1974–76*, p.35 (5 March 1974)

Chapter 9: SOCIAL CONTRACT (1974–1976)

1. *Parl. Deb.*, 5th ser., Vol. 870, 678 (18 March 1974)

2. *Guardian*, 6 March 1974; Bernard Donoughue, *The Heat of the Kitchen* (Politico's, 2003), p.124

3. Stephen Dorrill and Robin Ramsay, *Smear!: Wilson and the Secret State* (Grafton Books, 1992), p.258

4. Castle, *Fighting All the Way*, p.446

5. Castle, *Diaries 1974–76*, p.159 (30 July 1974); Robert Armstrong to D. H. O. Owen, Lord Chancellor's Office, 16 May 1974; Owen to Armstrong, 17 May 1974 (National Archives, PREM 16/206); obituary of Lord Donaldson, loc. cit.

6. Interview with Roger Dawe, 3 March 2004; Eric Hobsbawm, *Interesting Times* (Allen Lane, 2002), p.170

7. Interview with Albert Booth, 6 July 2004

8. Interviews with Lord Evans of Parkside, 20 July 2004, Lord McNally, 17 January 2006, and Sir Michael Quinlan, 1 September 2004

9. Interview with Albert Booth

10. Interview with Keith McDowall, 29 March 2004; John Fraser to the author, 31 August 2006

11. Ibid.

12. Interview with Caerwyn Roderick, 9 May 2005

13. Interview with Lord Wedderburn, 3 March 2004. I am much indebted to Lord Wedderburn for much valuable help on these matters.

14. Interview with Elizabeth Thomas

15. Interview with Albert Booth

16. Interviews with Elizabeth Thomas and Vivian Williams, 4 October 2003, and with Jacqui Lait, 8 July 2005

17. Interview with Roger Dawe; Castle, *Fighting All the Way*, p.159

18. Sir Kenneth Barnes to the author, 22 June 2004; interview with Lord Hattersley, 15 September 2004

19. Mervyn Jones, op. cit., p.397. I have been unable to contact Sir Donald Derx

20. Interview with Roger Dawe

21. Interview with Keith McDowall; Robert Harris, *Good and Faithful Servant* (Faber & Faber, 1990), p.59

22. Interviews with Keith McDowall, Lord Morris of Aberavon and Caerwyn Roderick, and conversation with Lord Jones of Deeside

23. Dr Andrew Graham to the author, 21 January 2005

24. Edmund Dell, *A Hard Pounding* (Oxford University Press, 1991), pp.105–6

25. Conversation with Baroness Turner of Camden

26. Interview with Roger Dawe

27. *Parl. Deb.*, 5th ser., Vol. 870, 688–703

28. *Guardian*, 19 March 1974

29. Information from Lord Prior

30. cf. Foot's memorandum 'Development of the Social Contract on Pay', 13 June 1975 (CAB 129/183/17)

31. Foot's memorandum, 'Unemployment Measures', 18 September 1975 (CAB 129/184/20) and Cabinet Conclusions, 22 September 1975 (CAB 128/57). For Chrysler UK, see Cabinet Conclusions, 4 December 1975 (ibid.) and Foot's memorandum, 'Chrysler: Redundancy Arrangements', 24 November 1975 (CAB 129/186/15)

32. Interview with Lord Murray of Epping Forest, 7 October 2003

33. Interviews with Lord Varley and Lord Orme

34. *The Times*, 9 May 1974

35. Jack Jones, *Union Man* (William Collins, 1986), p.274

36. Joe Gormley, *Battered Cherub* (Hamish Hamilton, 1982), p.143

37. Cabinet Conclusions, 5 and 7 March 1974 (CAB 128/54); correspondence between Foot and Frank Figgures, 10 March–10 June 1974 (EH 1/129)

38. Cabinet Conclusions, 7 March 1974 (CAB 128/54)

39. Ibid.; interview with Albert Booth; interview with Michael Foot, 1 March 2004

40. *Parl. Deb.*, Vol. 871, 1286–99 (3 April 1974)

41. Memoranda by the Secretary of State for Employment, 'Repeal of the Industrial Relations Act', 20 March 1974 (CAB 129/175/11), 5 April 1974 (CAB 129/175/25) and 25 April 1974 (CAB 129/176/5); interview with Lord Wedderburn

42. Foot's article in *Tribune*, 26 April 1974; 'The Trade Union and Labour Relations Bill' (PPC (74) (2), 3 May 1974 (Conservative Party Archives, Bodleian Library, CRD 4/4/76); John Fraser to the author, 31 August 2006

43. Cabinet Conclusions, 28 March 1974 (CAB 128/54)

44. Ibid., 10 April 1974

45. Ibid., 25 April 1974

46. *The Times*, 1 May 1974

47. Lord Wedderburn, *The Worker and the Law* (Sweet & Maxwell, 3rd edn 1986), pp.586ff

48. *Guardian*, 31 July 1974

49. Wedderburn, *The Worker and the Law*, p.725; idem, *Law and Freedom: Further Essays in Labour Law* (Lawrence & Wishart, 1995), p.361

50. Interview with Michael Foot, 1 March 2004

51. *The Times*, 8 October 1974

52. Ibid., 2 October 1974

53. Ibid., 8 October 1974

54. Jack Jones, op. cit., p.284

55. Cabinet Conclusions, 24 October 1974 (CAB 128/55)

56. Department of Employment: 'Government Proposals for a Conciliation and Arbitration Service,

17 May 1974' (Confederation of Employee Organisations Papers, University of Warwick, Modern Records Centre, MSS. 61/3/4/20); Davies and Freedland, op. cit., p.409

57. Robert Taylor, *The Trade Union Question in British Politics* (Blackwell, 1993), p.239

58. Interview with Albert Booth

59. Davies and Freedland, op. cit., p.395

60. Cabinet Conclusions, 9 October 1975 (CAB 128/57); Foot's memorandum on 'The Law on Picketing', 25 September 1975 (CAB 129/185/15); Jenkins, op. cit., p.417

61. Cabinet Conclusions, 19 June 1975 (CAB 128/56)

62. *The Times*, 17 December 1974

63. Cabinet Conclusions, 11 November 1974 (CAB 128/55); 'Note on the Trade Union and Labour Relations Amendment Bill Debate' (Conservative Party Archives, CRD/4/4/75)

64. Cabinet Conclusions, 11 November 1974 (CAB 128/55)

65. Taylor, op. cit., p.229

66. Brian Brivati, *Lord Goodman* (Cohen Books, 1999), p.232; Nora Beloff, *Freedom Under Foot: The Battle Over the Closed Shop in British Journalism* (Temple Smith, 1976), p.31; Anthony Lester, 'The Home Office Again', in Andrew Adonis and Keith Thomas (eds), *Roy Jenkins: A Retrospective* (Oxford University Press, 2004), p.154

67. Jenkins, op. cit., p.427; interview with Baroness Williams of Crosby; information from Professor David Marquand

68. Interview with Ian Aitken; Paul Nicholson to Foot, 12 March 1976 (COEO Papers, University of Warwick, Modern Records Centre, MSS. 61/3/4/20)

69. *Guardian*, 23 November 1974. cf.

Foot's memorandum 'Freedom of the Press', 3 December 1974 (CAB 129/180/3)

70. Brivati, op. cit., pp.229ff

71. Cabinet Conclusions, 6 November 1975 (CAB 128/57)

72. Beloff, op. cit., p.60

73. Interview with Albert Booth

74. Beloff, op. cit., pp.76–8

75. Brivati, op. cit., pp.231ff

76. Interview with Lord Hattersley

77. *The Times*, 22 January 1976

78. Clause 2, Trade Union and Labour Relations (Amendment) Act, 1976

79. Michael Foot to Ian Gow, 3 February 1976 (Conservative Party Archives, CRD 4/4/76)

80. James Prior, paper on 'Industrial Relations and the Trade Unions' (Conservative Party Archives, ACP/76/1)

81. *Guardian*, 24 January 1975

82. Interview with Lord Healey, 23 October 2003

83. *Guardian*, 16 June 1975

84. Interview with Baroness Williams of Crosby

85. Cabinet Conclusions, 20 June 1974 (CAB 128/54)

86. *Guardian*, 3 March 1975; interview with Lord Morris of Aberavon

87. Cabinet Conclusions, 20 June 1975 (CAB 128/55); Donoughue, op. cit., p.165; Castle, *Diaries 1974–76*, pp.422–3 (19 June 1975)

88. Cabinet Conclusions, 10 July 1975 (CAB 128/57); *Guardian*, 23, 30 July 1975; Edward Pearce, *Denis Healey* (Little, Brown, 2002), pp.443–4; interview with Ian Aitken

89. *Guardian*, 30 September 1975; *The Times*, 30 September 1975

90. Ibid.

91. Interview with Tony Benn, 25 January 2005; Castle, *Diaries 1974–76*, p.45, n.3

92. Castle, *Diaries 1974–76*, p.161 (30 July 1974)
93. Donoughue, op. cit., p.159
94. Interview with Tony Benn
95. Printed in Foot, *Loyalists and Loners*, pp.43ff
96. Crossman, introduction to Walter Bagehot, *The English Constitution* (1963 edn)
97. Crossman's diaries were published jointly by Hamish Hamilton and Jonathan Cape; Anthony Howard, *Crossman: The Pursuit of Power* (Jonathan Cape, 1990), p.7
98. Material in Ron Evans Papers (National Library of Wales, Aberystwyth, File 11); interviews with Lord Morris of Aberavon and with Hugh Thomas
99. Interview with Lord Morris of Aberavon; *Western Mail*, 8 February 1975
100. *Western Mail*, 9 February 1975
101. Ibid., 13 February 1975
102. Interview with Lord Paul; see also his memoirs, *Beyond Boundaries* (Penguin Books India, New Delhi), pp.45–8, 155–7
103. *Western Mail*, 23 November 1978
104. Conversation with Lord Brookman
105. Morgan, *Callaghan*, pp.413ff
106. Foot, Benn and Shore to Wilson, 16 December 1974; Wilson to Foot, 24 December 1974; Benn to Wilson, 2 January 1975; Foot to Wilson, 3 January 1975 (PREM 16/558)
107. Ibid., p.425; Tony Benn, *Against the Tide: Diaries 1973–76* (Hutchinson, 1989), pp.34–9 (17–18 March 1975), gives a full account; Dell, *Strange Eventful History*, p.425
108. Cabinet Conclusions, 18 March 1975 (CAB 128/56)
109. *The Times*, 27 April 1975; Benn, op. cit., p.369 (26 April 1975)
110. Materials in Foot private papers

111. Interview with Lord Callaghan
112. *Guardian*, 19 March 1975
113. Interviews with Albert Booth and Caerwyn Roderick
114. Interview with the late Lord Jay of Battersea
115. Castle, *Diaries 1974–76*, pp.717–18 (5 April 1976)
116. *The Times*, 3 April 1976
117. Diary notes of Lord Callaghan (Callaghan Papers), 3, 5 April 1976
118. Callaghan diary, 5 April 1976; Castle, *Diaries 1974–76*, pp.725–7 (8 April 1976); Foot's comments at Lord Orme memorial celebration, House of Lords, 16 November 2005

Chapter 10: HOUSE AND PARTY LEADER (1976–1980)

1. I am very grateful for information from Mr Clive Saville here
2. Information from Lord Biffen, 29 June 2004
3. Memorandum of duties for the Lord President (Foot private papers)
4. Information from Clive Saville
5. Ibid.; information from Michael and the late Jill Foot
6. Interview by Jim Perrin, 'Figures in their Landscapes', *Guardian*, 16 May 1992
7. Interview with Lord Hattersley; Hattersley's article in *Observer*, 13 July 2003
8. Andy McSmith, *John Smith* (Verso, 1993), pp.76–8
9. Interview with Elizabeth Thomas, 4 October 2003
10. Interview with Sir Michael Quinlan, 1 September 2004
11. Interview with Jacqui Lait, 8 July 2004
12. Information from Clive Saville, along with fine political profiles of Warren in *The Times* (? 1977) by Peter Hennessy, in the *Guardian* (? 1978)

by Simon Hoggart, and an obituary of him in the *Independent* by Lord Glenamara

13. Information from Clive Saville
14. Interview with Vivian Williams, 4 October 2003
15. Information from Clive Saville
16. Private information
17. Interview with the late Baroness Castle; Tony Benn, *Conflicts of Interest: Diaries 1977–80* (Hutchinson, 1990), p.50 (27 February 1977)
18. Interview with Lord Callaghan; interviews with Michael Foot; interview with Lord McNally, 17 February 2006
19. Interview with Sir Thomas McCaffrey, 24 March 2004
20. Callaghan MS notes (in the possession of Baroness Jay)
21. Interviews with Lord Healey, 23 October 2003, and Baroness Williams of Crosby, 1 November 2004
22. Interview with Lord Hattersley, 15 September 2004
23. Foot to Crosland, 15 September 1976 (private possession)
24. Michael Heseltine, *Life in the Jungle: My Autobiography* (Hodder & Stoughton, 2000), pp.170–1
25. Callaghan diary note, 5 March 1976 (Callaghan Papers)
26. Foot to Healey, quoted in Pearce, *Denis Healey*, p.462
27. Pearce, op. cit., p.469 (Healey diary entry of 27 September 1976)
28. Material in Foot Papers [PHM], C11; Judith Brown, *Modern India: The Origins of an Asian Democracy* (Oxford University Press, 2nd edn 1994), pp.375–8
29. E. P. Thompson, *Writing by Candlelight* (Merlin Press, 1980), pp.145–6; Moni Cameron to Foot, 23 February 1976 (Foot private papers)

30. Judith Brown, op. cit., pp.376–7; Ramachandra Guha, 'An Indian Fall', *Prospect*, December 2005, p.34; Michael Foot, *Dr Strangelove, I Presume* (Victor Gollancz, 1999), p.92. Foot admits that Mrs Gandhi's excuses for the state of emergency in 1976 were 'pitifully inadequate'.
31. *Guardian*, 7 January 1977; Rajiv Gandhi to Foot. 15 February 1985 (Foot Papers [PHM], C11)
32. *Times of India* cuttings in Foot Papers, ibid.
33. *Western Mail*, 23 November 1978
34. Morgan, *Callaghan*, pp.544–54
35. Ibid., p.548
36. Interviews with Lord Hattersley, Lord McNally and Baroness Williams of Crosby
37. Benn, *Against the Tide: Diaries 1973–76*, pp.673–4 (2 December 1976)
38. Morgan, *Callaghan*, p.550
39. Ibid., p.552; interview with Lord Barnett, 30 January 2006
40. *Parl. Deb.*, 5th ser., Vol. 921, 834 (30 November 1976); Norman Tebbit, *Upwardly Mobile* (Weidenfeld & Nicolson, 1988), p.192
41. Notes on the Lib–Lab pact, including diary notes (Callaghan Papers)
42. Information from Michael Foot
43. Interview with Lord Steel, 20 July 2004; material in the Callaghan Papers and interviews with Lord Callaghan
44. Interview with Lord Callaghan
45. Material on the Lib–Lab pact in the Callaghan Papers
46. *Guardian*, 29 March 1977
47. Interviews with Michael Foot and Lord Steel, and with Lord Owen, 15 March 2004
48. Benn, *Conflicts of Interest: Diaries 1977–80*, pp.85–91 (23 March 1977)

49. Ibid., p.91 (23 March 1977)

50. Interview with Lord Steel

51. The best scholarly book on this is Vernon Bogdanor, *Devolution in the United Kingdom* (Oxford University Press, new edn 1999)

52. Interview with Sir Michael Quinlan

53. Kenneth O. Morgan, *The Red Dragon and the Red Flag* (National Library of Wales, Aberystwyth, 1989); also see my *Rebirth of a Nation: Wales 1880-1980* (Oxford University Press and University of Wales Press, 1981), p.298

54. *Daily Herald*, 29 December 1950

55. Morgan, *Keir Hardie*, pp.118-19; John Shepherd, *George Lansbury* (Oxford University Press, 2002), p.220

56. Interview with Sir Michael Quinlan

57. Ibid.

58. Interview with Lord Morris of Aberavon, 25 January 2005

59. Information from Clive Saville

60. Interview with Tony Benn, 25 January 2005; Hunt memorandum to Callaghan, ? 1977 (Callaghan Papers, Box 19); interview with the late Lord Hunt of Tanworth, 17 October 1996

61. Interviews with Sir Michael Quinlan and Sir Tom McCaffrey

62. Interview with Sir Michael Quinlan

63. Personal knowledge

64. Interview with Sir Michael Quinlan

65. Information from Alan Watkins

66. See pp.365-7

67. Cledwyn Hughes, diary, 22 February 1978 (National Library of Wales, Aberystwyth, Hughes Papers). There are two communications from Foot on devolution in 1977 (National Library of Wales, Aberystwyth, Labour Party Wales Papers, 51, 112)

68. Derek Gladwin Papers (Bodleian Library, merged with Callaghan Papers)

69. Interviews with Lord Hattersley and Michael Foot

70. Interview with Geoffrey Goodman; notes of 11 September 1978 in Callaghan paper on election decision; Donoughue, op. cit., p.258

71. Interviews with Lord Callaghan and Sir Robert Worcester

72. Morgan, *Callaghan*, p.657

73. Interview with Sir Kenneth Stowe

74. Donoughue, op. cit., p.262; interview with Lord McNally, 17 January 2006

75. Material in possession of Lord Donoughue

76. Benn, *Conflicts of Interest: Diaries 1977-80*, p.438 (15 January 1979)

77. Callaghan diary note (Callaghan Papers); *Parl. Deb.*, 5th ser., Vol. 957, 813-18 (25 January 1979)

78. Donoughue, *Prime Minister* (Jonathan Cape, 1987), pp.176, 183

79. Note on 'How the Government Fell' in Callaghan Papers and Foot Papers [PHM], C1

80. Ibid.

81. Ibid.; Benn, *Conflicts of Interest: Diaries 1977-80*, p.472 (15 March 1979)

82. 'How the Government Fell'

83. Ibid.

84. Ibid.

85. Interview with Lord Hattersley

86. 'How the Government Fell'

87. Ibid.

88. Ibid.

89. *Parl. Deb.*, 5th ser., Vol. 965, 575-84

90. Benn, *Conflicts of Interest: Diaries 1977-80*, p.482 (2 April 1979)

91. *Guardian*, 24 April 1979

92. Donoughue, *Prime Minister*, p.191

93. Foot, foreword to *Debts of Honour*

94. Ibid., pp.71ff

95. David Kogan and Maurice Kogan, *The Battle for the Labour Party* (Fontana Paperbacks, 1982), pp.23ff

96. *Report of the Seventy-Eighth Annual Conference of the Labour Party, 1979*, p.213

97. Conversation with Michael Foot

98. Benn, *Conflicts of Interest: Diaries 1977–80*, pp.150–1 (25 May 1977)

99. Morgan, *Callaghan*, pp.716–17

100. Benn, *The End of an Era: Diaries 1980–90*, p.9 (15 June 1980)

101. *Guardian*, 15 October 1980

102. Stuart Holland to Michael Foot, 17 October 1980 (Foot Papers [PHM] L1)

103. Conversations with Lord Orme, Lord Dubs and others

104. Interview with Michael Foot; interview with Lord Varley, 2 November 2004

105. Interview with Dick Clements, 16 November 2004

106. Interview with Lord Orme, 28 October 2004

107. Information from Alan Watkins; Alan Watkins, *A Short Walk Down Fleet Street* (Duckworth, 2000), pp.180–1

108. Benn, *Conflicts of Interest: Diaries 1977–80*, p.38 (19 October 1977)

109. Mrs Elizabeth Shore to the author, July 2004

110. *Parl. Deb.*, 5th ser., Vol. 991, 601–9 (29 October 1980); conversation with Lord Howe, 19 June 2006

111. Interview with Lord Orme

112. Interview with Lord Kinnock, 30 January 2006; Pearce, *Denis Healey*, pp.540–3; obituary of Philip Whitehead by Roy Hattersley, *Guardian*, 2 January 2006

113. Pearce, *Denis Healey*, p.543; Denis Healey, *The Time of My Life*, p.477; Ivor Crewe and Anthony King, *SDP: The Birth, Life and Death of the Social Democratic Party* (Oxford University Press, 1995), p.75

114. Interview with Lord Kinnock; Giles Radice, *Diaries 1980–2001* (Weidenfeld & Nicolson, 2004), p.20 (20 October 1980)

115. David Owen, *Time to Declare* (Michael Joseph, 1991), p.458; interview with Lord Owen

116. Interview with Ian Aitken. George Lansbury is another, perhaps.

117. Letters to Foot from Tony Benn (11 November 1980), Olive Gibbs (10 November 1980), Bruce Grocott MP (11 November 1980), David Stoddart MP (10 November 1980), Spike Milligan (12 November 1980) in Foot Papers [PHM] L1. Other correspondents sending warm congratulations include Frank Field MP, Nicholas Kaldor, David Ennals MP and Jeremy Bray.

118. Interview with Sir Gerald Kaufman, 10 March 2005

Chapter 11: Two Kinds of Socialism (1980–1983)

1. I have discussed this theme at more length in 'A Comparative Case Study of Labour Prime Ministers: Attlee, Wilson, Callaghan and Blair', in Nicholas D. J. Baldwin (ed.), *Executive Leadership and Legislative Assemblies* (Routledge & Kegan Paul, 2006), pp.38–52; and also in *Labour People: Leaders and Lieutenants, Hardie to Kinnock* (Oxford University Press, 1987)

2. Interviews with Lord Varley, Lord Hattersley, Sir Gerald Kaufman and Geoffrey Goodman; also Geoffrey Goodman, *Fifty Years' Reporting from the Political Front Line* (Pluto Press, 2003), p. 249

3. Interview with Sir Tom McCaffrey, 24 March 2004

4. Interview with Francis Beckett

5. Ibid.

6. Interview with Sue Nye, 17 January 2005

7. Interview with Lord Evans of Parkside, 20 July 2004

8. For Neuberger, see particularly Mark Wickham-Jones, 'Making Economic Policy in the Labour Party 1980–1990', in Neil Fraser and John Hills (eds), *Public Policy for the Twenty-First Century: Social and Economic Essays in Memory of Henry Neuberger* (Policy Press, Bristol, 2000), pp.223ff. I am very grateful for helpful information from Dr Andrew Graham, Master of Balliol College, Oxford, and Dr Christopher Allsop, New College, Oxford. Also interview with Lord Kinnock.

9. Wickham-Jones, op. cit., p.232

10. Information from Lord Hogg

11. *Guardian*, 18 September 1981

12. Ibid., 2 February 1982

13. Information from Lord Lipsey

14. Information from Lord Evans of Parkside

15. *The Times*, 15 November 1980

16. Correspondence in Foot Papers (PHM), C11 and L41/4; *Evening Standard*, 9 November 1981; *Guardian*, 10 November 1981; Watkins, *A Short Walk Down Fleet Street*, p.181; Jim Perrin, 'Figures in their Landscapes', *Guardian*, 16 May 1992

17. William Rodgers and David Owen, 14 November 1982 (University of Essex, Albert Sloman Library, Rodgers Papers, Box 2, File b); conversation with Lord Rodgers; *The Times*, 29 November 1980

18. *Guardian*, 26 January 1981

19. Interview with Ian Aitken

20. Interview with Baroness Williams of Crosby. See Giles Radice, *Friends and Rivals: Crosland, Jenkins and Healey* (Little, Brown, 2002), pp.292–3

21. The authoritative history is Crewe and King, *SDP: The Birth, Life and Death of the Social Democratic Party*, op. cit.

22. Tony Benn, *Office Without Power: Diaries 1968–72* (Hutchinson, 1988), p.161 (16 April 1969)

23. Interview with Tony Benn

24. *Guardian*, 21 May 2005

25. Material in Foot Papers (PHM), L4

26. *Guardian*, 1 June 1981

27. MS of Foot statement, 3 June 1981 (Kinnock Papers, Churchill College, Cambridge, Box 418)

28. Interview with Lord Varley

29. Interview with Baroness Gould of Potter Newton, 20 July 2005

30. Tony Benn, *The End of an Era: Diaries 1980–90* (Hutchinson, 1992), p.135 (3 June 1981)

31. *Guardian*, 30 September 1981; John Golding, *The Hammer of the Left* (Politico's, 2003)

32. *Guardian*, 30 September 1981

33. *Parl. Deb.*, 6th ser., Vol. 12, 494ff (10 November 1981)

34. Foot, *Loyalists and Loners*, pp.107ff

35. Foot, *My Kind of Socialism*, p.3

36. Morgan, *Keir Hardie*, p.168

37. Foot, *My Kind of Socialism*, p.5

38. Tony Benn, *Arguments for Socialism* (Penguin, paperback edn 1985), pp.108–37

39. Tony Benn, *Arguments for Democracy* (Jonathan Cape, 1981), p.183

40. Peter Mandelson and Roger Liddle, *The Blair Revolution* (Faber & Faber, 1996)

41. Benn, *Arguments for Democracy*, p.138

42. Morgan, *Callaghan*, pp.460–2

43. Interview with Michael Foot, 22 June 2004; *Parl. Deb.*, 6th ser., Vol. 24, 484–9 (3 April 1982)

44. Interview with Lord Varley; James Cameron to Foot, 26 May 1982 (Foot private papers)

45. Interviews with Michael Foot, 3 June 2003, 22 June 2004

46. *Guardian*, 15 April 1982

47. Ibid., 28 April 1982

48. Pearce, *Denis Healey*, p.568; interview with Michael Foot, 13 September 2004

49. *Guardian*, 21 May 1982

50. Foot, *Another Heart and Other Pulses*, p.99

51. Neil Kinnock, note on the Falklands, ? May 1981 (Kinnock Papers, Box 112)

52. *Guardian*, 28 December 1982

53. Ibid., 4 September 1982

54. Ibid., 2 September, 28 October 1982

55. Tony Blair to Foot, May 1982 (Foot private papers), quoted in Robert Taylor, 'My Socialist Dream', *New Statesman*, 15 June 2006; the letter is quoted in full on the *New Statesman* website. Tony Blair's nomination for Sedgefield is discussed in Francis Beckett and David Hencke, *The Blairs and their Court* (Aurum, 2004), pp.63–4

56. For Militant Tendency, see John Callaghan, *The Far Left in British Politics* (Blackwell, 1987), pp.196ff; Nick Thomas-Symonds, 'A Reinterpretation of Michael Foot's Handling of Militant Tendency', *Contemporary British History*, 19, 1 (spring 2005), pp.25–49; obituary of Ted Grant, *Guardian*, 27 July 2006

57. Giles Radice, *Diaries 1980–2001* (Weidenfeld & Nicolson, 2004), pp.72–3 (17 June 1981)

58. Labour Party Archives, NEC minutes, 18 December 1981 (PHM); *Guardian*, 18 December 1981

59. *Guardian*, 9 February 1982

60. Material in Foot Papers (PHM), L5, and conversations with Lord Corbett

61. See Peter Tatchell, *The Battle for Bermondsey* (Heretic Books, 1983)

62. Ibid.; Labour Party Archives, NEC minutes, 16 December 1981

63. Material in Foot Papers (PHM), L7, especially Kate Hoey to Michael Foot, 14 December 1981

64. Joan Lestor to Foot, 14 December 1981 (Foot Papers, L7)

65. Bob Mellish to Foot, 1 August 1982, Foot to Mellish. 3 December 1981 (Foot Papers, L6)

66. *Guardian*, 28 September 1982

67. Memorandum by Derry Irvine and Tony Blair (Foot Papers, L6); *Guardian*, 25 February 1983

68. *Guardian*, 26 February 1983

69. Interview with Michael Foot, 22 June 2004

70. Interview with Robert Worcester, 23 February 2005

71. Material in MORI archives, private polling for 1983 general election (with kind permission from Sir Robert Worcester)

72. *Guardian*, 25 March 1983; interview with Francis Beckett

73. Interview with Baroness Gould

74. Interview with Michael Foot, 22 June 2004

75. Material in MORI archives

76. *Guardian*, 30 March 1983; Roy Hattersley, *Who Goes Home?* (Little, Brown, 1995), p.238

77. Interview with Sir Gerald Kaufman

78. *Sunday Times*, 12 June 1983; interviews with Baroness Gould, Sir Tom McCaffrey and Francis Beckett

79. Interview with Francis Beckett

80. *Guardian*, 20 May 1983

81. *Sunday Times*, 29 May 1983; interview with Sue Nye

82. *Guardian*, 28 May 1983

83. Robert Worcester, *British Public Opinion 1970–1990* (Blackwell, 1991), p.129

84. A meeting attended by the present writer

85. David Butler and Denis Kavanagh, *The British General Election of 1983* (Macmillan, 1984), p.114

86. Material in MORI archives
87. *Guardian*, 25 May 1983
88. Ibid., 26 May 1983
89. Interview with Sir Tom McCaffrey
90. Interview with Sir Robert Worcester
91. Interview with Sue Nye
92. *Guardian*, 11 June 1983; *Private Eye*, 20 May 1983
93. Clive Jenkins, *All Against the Collar: Struggles of a White Collar Union Leader* (Methuen, 1990), p.211
94. Interview with Sir Tom McCaffrey
95. Interview with Lord Kinnock

Chapter 12: INTO THE NINETIES
1. Davies and Freedland, op. cit., p.11
2. On these matters, see ibid., pp.425ff; and Robert Taylor, op. cit., pp.265ff
3. Foot, *Another Heart and Other Pulses*, pp.41, 99
4. Foot to Salman Rushdie, 2 November 1988, and other materials on the Booker Prize in Foot private papers
5. Robert Blake, *Disraeli* (Eyre & Spottiswoode, 1966), p.190
6. Stanley Jones to Foot, ? April 1978 and 30 October 1989 (Foot private papers)
7. Review in *Hampstead and Highgate Express*, 16 June 1989
8. Foot, *Loyalists and Loners*, pp.185–92
9. Ibid., p.87
10. Ibid., p.155
11. Ibid., p.269; Foot to Vernon Watkins, n.d. (Watkins Papers, Harry Ransom Humanities Research Center, University of Texas, Austin)
12. Michael Foot, *The Politics of Paradise* (William Collins, 1988), p.364
13. Callaghan to Foot, 7 April 1986 (Foot private papers)
14. Brigid Brophy to Foot, 12 July 1988 ibid.; *The Politics of Paradise*, p.191 and fn
15. Ibid., p.374

16. Ibid., p.397; Fiona MacCarthy, *Byron: Life and Legend* (John Murray, 2002), pp.304–5
17. *The Politics of Paradise*, p.396
18. Ibid., p.244n
19. Ibid., p.79; cf. A. C. Grayling, *The Quarrel of the Age* (Phoenix Press, 2000), pp.205–6
20. *The Politics of Paradise*, p.366
21. MacCarthy, op. cit., pp.544ff; Ian Buruma, *Voltaire's Coconuts* (Weidenfeld & Nicolson, 1999), pp.114–15
22. Foot to Oonagh McDonald, ? 1983 (Foot Papers [PHM] C11/3); Foot to Abu, 22 November 1984 and other material in Foot private papers. Abu had written to Foot on 9 November 1984, 'There is no doubt about it – foreign agencies are attempting to wreck this place. Destabilization has now become universal.'
23. Rajiv Gandhi to Foot, 15 February 1985 (ibid.)
24. Interview for *The Statesman*, Calcutta, 19 January 1985
25. Foot to Baroness Young, 7 August 1986 (Foot Papers [PHM])
26. Interviews with Ms Vesna Gamulin and Ms Nada Maric, Dubrovnik, 23, 25 August 2005; Foot to Ms Maric, 27 February 1998 (privately owned)
27. Interviews with Ms Vesna Gamulin and Dr Hrvoje Kacic, 23, 26 August 2005. Also see Dr Kacic's *Serving My Country* (Bibliotheka Studies, Zagreb, 2002)
28. This account is largely based on conversations with Michael Foot, Vesna and Jadran Gamulin, and Dr Kacic. Also Nora Beloff to Foot, 23 May 1995 (Foot private papers)
29. Michael Foot, 'Dithering While Bosnia Bleeds', *Guardian*, 25 August 1992
30. *Parl. Deb.*, 6th series, Vol. 205, 472–6 (5 March 1992)

31. *Guardian,* 25 August 1992
32. Douglas Hurd, *Memoirs* (Little, Brown, 2003), pp.444ff
33. Interview with Dr Kacic, 26 August 2005
34. Information from Baroness Gale, July 2005, and from Rt Hon. Peter Hain, 24 January 2006
35. *The Times,* 21 March 1992
36. Ibid., 23 July 1993. The reports of the People's History Museum (as it is now called) are a valuable source.
37. Interviews with Michael Foot; Jon Snow, *Shooting History* (HarperCollins, 2004), pp.337–8
38. *Observer,* 1 January 1995
39. Ibid., 2 April 1995; Jon Snow, op. cit., p.338
40. Paola Buonadonna, Brussels, to Michael and Jill Foot, 26 May 1995 (Foot private papers)
41. *Sunday Times,* 19 February 1995, article by David Leppard
42. Ibid., 26 February 1995; *Observer,* 26 February 1995
43. *Tribune,* 24 February 1995, p.2
44. Callaghan to Foot, 23 February 1995 and other MS notes (Callaghan private papers, in author's possession)
45. File on 'Agent Boot' in Foot private papers; Foot's legal affidavit, 17 November 1995 (in the author's possession); interview with Michael Foot, 17 September 2003; interview with Foot in the *Guardian,* 18 March 2002
46. Interview with Michael Foot, 7 June 2004; *Daily Herald,* 16 August 1946
47. John Carey, *The Intellectuals and the Masses* (Faber & Faber, 1992), p.142; cf. Norman and Jeanne Mackenzie, *The Time Traveller: The Life of H. G. Wells* (Weidenfeld & Nicolson, 1973)
48. Michael Coren, *The Invisible Man* (Bloomsbury, 1993), p.11
49. Foot, *The History of Mr Wells* (Doubleday, 1995), pp.113ff and 224ff

50. See the obituary of Tanya Alexander in the *Independent,* 13 December 2004
51. Interview with Michael Foot, 7 June 2004
52. John Foot to Michael Foot, 7 December 1998 (Foot private papers)
53. Michael Foot, *Dr Strangelove, I Presume* (Victor Gollancz, 1999), pp.92ff and 101ff
54. Tony Blair to Foot, ? 1996 (Foot private papers)
55. Attended by the present writer, 10 April 2003
56. Jill Craigie, 'Political Bloodsport' in Geoffrey Goodman (ed.), *The State of the Nation: The Political Legacy of Aneurin Bevan* (Victor Gollancz, 1997), pp.88–105, loc. cit., p.103
57. See pp.168–9. For more detail on the news coverage of Koestler's rape of Jill, see *Observer,* 9, 23 April 1995.
58. *Evening Standard,* 13 December 2004
59. Foot and Highet, *Isaac Foot;* see also Darley Anderson to Dingle Foot, 26 October 1977 (Churchill College, Cambridge, Dingle Foot Papers 8/3)
60. Geoff Hoon to Michael Foot, ? July 2002; interview by Sean O'Grady, *Independent,* 22 July 2002
61. *The Times,* 1, 2 October 2003
62. *Western Mail,* 6 May 2005; 'Labour Kicks out Activists who Backed Welsh Rebel', *Guardian,* 25 May 2005; obituary of Peter Law by Tony Heath, *Guardian,* 26 April 2006
63. *Times Literary Supplement,* 17 March 2006

Envoi: Toujours L'Audace

1. Michael Foot, 'Credo of the Labour Left', *New Left Review,* 49 (May–June 1968), p.24
2. Snow, *Shooting History,* p.148

3. *Guardian*, 26 May 2006, a discussion of Geoff Mulgan's ideas. Foot's passion for reading is well brought out also in in his 'Storied Earth and Unread Heavens', *Times Literary Supplement*, 4 November 1977, with particular reference to Hazlitt, Stendhal, Heine, Swift, Blatchford and his father.

4. Robert Colls, *The Identity of England* (Oxford University Press, 2002), pp.129–30

5. For an interesting discussion of this theme, see Greg Neale, 'Essay', *New Statesman,* 5 January 2006

6. Tebbit, *Upwardly Mobile*, p.192

7. See H. N. Brailsford, *Voltaire* (Home University Library, 1935), described by his biographer, F. M. Leventhal (*The Last Dissenter*, p.239), as 'the most perfect piece he ever wrote'. Also see Roger Pearson, *Voltaire Almighty* (Bloomsbury, 2005), especially pp.395ff

SELECT BIBLIOGRAPHY

A. MANUSCRIPT SOURCES

1. National Archives

CAB 128 (Cabinet conclusions, 1945–51, 1964–70, 1974–75)
CAB 129 (Cabinet papers)
CAB 134 (Cabinet committees)
EH 1 (Pay Board)
PREM 8 (Prime Minister's Office, 1945–51)
PREM 11, 13 (Prime Minister's Office, 1964, 1966)
PREM 16 (Prime Minister's Office, 1974, 1975)

2. Private Collections

Leo Abse papers (National Library of Wales, Aberystwyth)
Lord Beaverbrook papers (House of Lords Record Office)
Edmund Blunden papers (Harry Ransom Humanities Research Center, University of Texas, Austin)
Lord Callaghan papers (Bodleian, Oxford)
Winston Churchill papers (Churchill College, Cambridge)
Lord Cledwyn papers (NLW, Aberystwyth)
Frank Cousins papers (Modern Records Centre, Warwick)
Richard Crossman papers (MRC, Warwick)
Desmond Donnelly papers (NLW, Aberystwyth)
Tom Driberg papers (Christ Church, Oxford)
Huw T. Edwards papers (NLW, Aberystwyth)
Ron Evans papers (NLW, Aberystwyth)
Dingle Foot papers (Churchill College archives)
Isaac Foot papers (courtesy of Alison Highet)
Michael Foot papers (People's History Museum, Manchester)
Michael Foot papers (in the private possession of Mr Foot)
Michael Foot papers (courtesy of Mrs Sheila Noble)
Hugh Gaitskell papers (University College, London)
Judith Hart papers (PHM, Manchester)

Eric Heffer papers (PHM, Manchester)
India Political Intelligence papers (British Library)
Neil Kinnock papers (Churchill College archives)
Arthur Koestler papers (Edinburgh University Library)
Lady Megan Lloyd-George papers (NLW, Aberystwyth)
R. W. G. Mackay papers (British Library of Political and Economic
    Science, London)
Compton Mackenzie papers (Harry Ransom Center, Austin)
Jo Richardson/Ian Mikardo papers (PHM, Manchester)
William Rodgers papers (Albert Sloman library, University of Essex)
Jeffrey Thomas papers (NLW, Aberystwyth)
Lord Tonypandy papers (NLW, Aberstwyth)
Vernon Watkins papers (Harry Ransom Center, Austin)

3. Papers of Other Organizations

Campaign for Nuclear Disarmament (MRC, Warwick)
Conservative Party (Bodleian Library, Oxford):
    Advisory Committee on Policy (ACP) papers
    Conservative Research Department (CRD) papers
Labour Party (PHM, Manchester):
    General Secretary's correspondence
    National Executive Committee minutes and papers
Labour Party Wales archive (NLW, Aberystwyth)
MORI opinion polls (courtesy of Sir Robert Worcester)

B. OFFICIAL PAPERS

Royal Commission on the Press, 1947–8: Minutes of Evidence (Cmd. 7330,
    Cmd. 7351), *Report*, 1949 (Cmd. 7700)
Report of the Royal Commission on Trade Unions' and Employers' Associations,
    1968 (Cmnd. 3623)
Democracy and Devolution, 1974 (Cmnd. 5732)
Our Changing Democracy, 1976 (Cmnd. 6348)
Devolution to Scotland and Wales: Supplementary Statement, 1976 (Cmnd. 6585)
Devolution: Financing the Devolved Services, 1977 (Cmnd. 6890)
Hansard, *Parliamentary Debates*, 5th and 6th series

C. NEWSPAPERS, PERIODICALS AND REPORTS

1. Newspapers

Daily Express
Daily Herald
Daily Mirror
Daily Telegraph
Evening Standard
Financial Times
Guardian
Hampstead and Highgate Express
Independent
India Weekly
Irish Times
Morning Star
News Chronicle
Observer
Reynolds News
South Wales Argus
Star
Statesman (Calcutta)
Sunday Telegraph
Sunday Times
The Times
Western Evening Herald
Western Mail
Western Morning News

2. Periodicals and Journals

Cherwell
Economist
House Magazine
Isis
Labour Weekly
The Leightonian
Nation (New York)
New Statesman
The Oldie
Oxford Magazine
Prospect
Socialist Commentary
Southwark Labour News
Spectator
Times Literary Supplement
Tribune

3. Reports

Advisory, Conciliation and Arbitration Service
Labour Party: annual conference reports
Trades Union Congress

D. MICHAEL FOOT'S PUBLICATIONS
(Place of publication London unless otherwise stated)

1. Books

Armistice 1918–1939 (Harrap, 1940)

Guilty Men (by 'Cato', with Peter Howard and Frank Owen: Gollancz, 1940)

The Trial of Mussolini (by 'Cassius': Gollancz, 1943)

Brendan and Beverley: An Extravaganza (Gollancz, 1944)

Un inglese difende Mussolini (Edizioni Riunite, Milan, 1946)

Who are the Patriots? (with Donald Bruce: Gollancz, 1949)

The Pen and the Sword: Jonathan Swift and the Power of the Press (MacGibbon and Kee, 1957)

Guilty Men, 1957 (with Mervyn Jones: Gollancz, 1957)

Parliament in Danger! (Pall Mall Press, 1959)

Aneurin Bevan, 1897–1945 (MacGibbon and Kee, 1962)

Harold Wilson: A Pictorial Biography (with John Parker and Eugene Prager: Pergamon, 1964)

Aneurin Bevan, 1945–60 (Davis-Poynter, 1973)

Debts of Honour (Davis-Poynter, 1980)

Another Heart and Other Pulses: The Alternative to the Thatcher Society (Collins, 1984)

Loyalists and Loners (Collins, 1986)

The Politics of Paradise: A Vindication of Byron (Collins, 1988)

The History of Mr Wells (Doubleday, New York, 1995; Black Swan, London, 1996)

Dr Strangelove, I Presume (Gollancz, 1999)

The Uncollected Michael Foot (ed. Brian Brivati: Politico's, 2003)

Isaac Foot: A West Country Boy – Apostle of England (with Alison Highet, Politico's, 2006)

2. Contributions to Books

V. Krishna Menon (ed.), *Young Oxford at War* (Selwyn and Blount, 1934)

Stafford Cripps *et al.*, *The Struggle for Peace* (Gollancz: Left Book Club, 1936)

R. H. S. Crossman, *A Palestine Munich* (Gollancz, 1946)

'The Road to Ruin' in ElizabethThomas (ed.), *Tribune 21* (MacGibbon and Kee,1958)

'Labour Britain in the 1980s' in Gerald Kaufman (ed.), *Renewal: Labour Britain in the 1980s* (Harmondsworth, 1983)

Contribution to Russell Davies and Liz Ottway (eds), *Vicky* (Secker and Warburg, 1987)

'Bevan's Message to the World' in Geoffrey Goodman (ed.), *The State of the Nation: The Political Legacy of Nye Bevan* (Gollancz, 1997)

3. Pamphlets

Keep Left (with R. H. S. Crossman and others: *New Statesman*, 1947)

If the Tories had Won (Labour Party, 1947)

Still at Large (*Tribune* pamphlet, 1950)

Full Speed Ahead (*Tribune* pamphlet, 1950)

One Way Only (with others: *Tribune* pamphlet, 1951)

The Case for Freedom: An Answer to Morgan Phillips and the NEC (with others: *Tribune* pamphlet, 1954)

My Kind of Socialism (*Observer* pamphlet, 1982)

4. Lectures, Articles

'Credo of the Labour Left' (interview with Robin Blackburn and Alexander Cockburn, *New Left Review*, 49, May–June 1968)

'Michael Foot on Aneurin Bevan', *Llafur* (*Journal for the Society for the Study of Welsh Labour History*), I, No. 3 (May 1974)

Byron on the Bomb (University College, Cardiff, Evan Davies lecture, 1983)

'My Only Venice', *Art Quarterly*, Vol. I, No. 1 (1988)

'Swift and Europe', *Les Lettres Européennes* (Hachette, Paris, 1992)

Entries on 'James Cameron' and 'Frank Owen' in Brian Harrison (ed.), *Oxford Dictionary of National Biography* (Oxford University Press, 2004)

5. Editions, Introductions

Introduction to Julius Braunthal, *The Tragedy of Austria* (Gollancz, 1948)

Introduction to Jonathan Swift, *Gulliver's Travels* (Penguin edition, 1967)

David Rubinstein (ed.), *People for the People* (Ithaca Press, New York and London, 1973)

Introduction to Ignazio Silone, *Fontemara* (Dent, new edn, 1985)

(ed.), *A Thomas Paine Reader* (with Isaac Kramnick, Harmondsworth, 1987)

Introduction to Jonathan Swift, *A Complete Collection of Genteel and Ingenious Conversation* (Thoemmes Press, Bristol, 1995)

The Writings of Tom Paine (Routledge and Thoemmes Press, 1996)

Introduction to George Orwell, *Down and Out in Paris and London* (Folio Society, 1998)

Introduction to Bertrand Russell, *Autobiography* (one-volume edn, Routledge, 1998)

In addition, Foot wrote thousands and thousands of more ephemeral articles as a staff writer (1937–38), contributor (1945–48), co-editor, editor or editorial director (1948–61) of *Tribune*, sometimes under the name of 'John Marullus'; as contributor or weekly columnist on the *Daily Herald* (1944–63); as staff writer and editor of the *Evening Standard* (1938–43); as weekly book reviewer in the *Evening Standard* (1964 – 73); as book reviewer in the *Observer* and the *Guardian* after 1973; as occasional contributor to the *New Statesman* and the *Hampstead and Highgate Express*; and in a myriad of other publications from 1933 down to 2006.

(E) OTHER WORKS

1. Biographies, Memoirs and Diaries

(Place of publication London unless otherwise stated)

Adonis, Andrew, and Keith Thomas (eds), *Roy Jenkins* (Oxford University Press, 2004)

Beckett, Francis, and D. Hencke, *The Blairs and their Court* (Aurum, 2004)

Benn, Tony, *Office Without Power: Diaries 1968–72* (Hutchinson, 1988)

Benn, Tony, *Against the Tide: Diaries 1973–76* (Hutchinson, 1989)

Benn, Tony, *Conflicts of Interest: Diaries 1977–80* (Hutchinson, 1990)

Benn, Tony, *The End of an Era: Diaries 1980–90* (Hutchinson, 1992)

Bowker, Gordon, *George Orwell* (Little, Brown, 2003)

Brivati, Brian, *Lord Goodman* (Cohen Books, 1999)

Bullock, Alan, *Ernest Bevin: Foreign Secretary* (Heinemann, 1983)

Burk, Kathleen, *Troublemaker: A. J. P. Taylor* (Yale, 2000)

Campbell, John, *Nye Bevan and the Mirage of British Socialism* (Weidenfeld and Nicolson, 1987)

Castle, Barbara, *Fighting All the Way* (Macmillan, 1993)

Castle, Barbara, *Diaries 1964–70* (Weidenfeld and Nicolson, 1984)

Castle, Barbara, *Diaries 1974–76* (Weidenfeld and Nicolson, 1980)

Cesarani, David, *Arthur Koestler: The Homeless Mind* (Heinemann, 1987)

Clarke, Peter, *The Cripps Version* (Penguin Books, 2002)

Coren, Michael, *The Invisible Man: The Life and Liberties of H. G. Wells* (Bloomsbury, 1993)

Crossman, Richard, *The Backbench Diaries of Richard Crossman* (ed. Janet Morgan, Hamish Hamilton and Jonathan Cape, 1981)

Crossman, Richard, *Diaries of a Cabinet Minister. I: 1964–66* (ed. Janet Morgan, Hamish Hamilton and Jonathan Cape, 1975)

Crossman, Richard, *Diaries of a Cabinet Minister. II: 1966–68* (ed. Janet Morgan, Hamish Hamilton and Jonathan Cape, 1976)

Crossman, Richard, *Diaries of a Cabinet Minister. III: 1968–70* (ed. Janet Morgan, Hamish Hamilton and Jonathan Cape, 1977)

Dalyell, Tam, *Richard Crossman* (Weidenfeld and Nicolson, 1990)

Dell, Edmund, *Hard Pounding* (Oxford University Press, 1991)

Donoughue, Bernard, *The Heat of the Kitchen* (Politico's, 2003)

Downie, J. A., *Jonathan Swift: Political Writer* (Routledge and Kegan Paul, 1984)

Duff, Peggy, *Left! Left! Left!* (Allison and Busby, 1971)

Edwards, Robert, *Goodbye, Fleet Street* (Jonathan Cape, 1988)

Edwards, Ruth Dudley, *Victor Gollancz: A Biography* (Gollancz, 1987)

Ehrenpreis, Irving, *Swift: The Man, His Works and His Age* (Methuen, 3 vols, 1962–83)

Foot, Hugh, *A Start in Freedom* (Hodder and Stoughton, 1964)

Foot, Isaac, *Oliver Cromwell and Abraham Lincoln: A Comparison* (Royal Society of Literature, 1941)

Foot, Sara, *My Grandfather Isaac Foot* (Bossiney Books, Bodmin, 1980)

George, W. R. P., *The Making of Lloyd George* (Faber and Faber, 1976)

Golding, John, *Hammer of the Left* (Politico's, 2003)

Goodman, Geoffrey, *Awkward Warrior: Frank Cousins, His Life and Times* (Davis-Poynter, 1979)

Goodman, Geoffrey, *Fifty Years Reporting from the Political Front Line* (Pluto Press, 2003)

Gordon, Anne Wolrige, *Peter Howard* (Hodder and Stoughton, 1969)

Gormley, Joe, *Battered Cherub* (Hamish Hamilton, 1982)

Grayling, A. C., *The Quarrel of the Age: The Life and Times of William Hazlitt* (Weidenfeld and Nicolson, 2000)

Harris, Robert, *Good and Faithful Servant: The Unauthorized Biography of Bernard Ingham* (Faber and Faber, 1991)

Harris, Robert, *The Making of Neil Kinnock* (Faber and Faber, 1984)

Hattersley, Roy, *Who Goes Home?* (Little, Brown, 1995)

Healey, Denis, *The Time of My Life* (Michael Joseph, 1989)

Heseltine, Michael, *Life in the Jungle* (Hodder and Stoughton, 2000)

Higgins, Ian, *Swift's Politics: A Study in Disaffection* (Cambridge University Press, 1994)

Hillier, Bevis, *John Betjeman: New Fame, New Love* (John Murray, 2002)

Hoggart, Simon, and David Leigh, *Michael Foot: A Portrait* (Hodder and Stoughton, 1981)

Hollis, Patricia, *Jennie Lee: A Life* (Oxford University Press, 1987)

Howard, Anthony, *Richard Crossman* (Jonathan Cape, 1990)

Hurd, Douglas, *An End to Promises: Sketch of a Government, 1970–74* (Collins, 1979)

Hurd, Douglas, *Memoirs* (Little, Brown, 2003)

Jefferys, Kevin (ed.), *Leading Labour* (I. B. Tauris, 1999)

Jefferys, Kevin (ed.), *Labour Forces* (I. B. Tauris, 2002)

Jenkins, Clive, *All Against the Collar* (Methuen, 1990)

Jenkins, Roy, *Life at the Centre* (Macmillan, 1991)

Jones, Jack, *Union Man* (Collins, 1986)

Jones, Mervyn, *Michael Foot* (Gollancz, 1994)

Kacic, H., *Serving My Country* (Institute of Social Sciences Ivo Pilo, Zagreb, 1992)

Karaka, D. F., *Then Came Hazrat Ali* (Popular Press, Bombay, 1972)

Leventhal, F. M., *The Last Dissenter* (Oxford University Press, 1985)

MacCarthy, Fiona, *Byron: Life and Legend* (John Murray, 2002)

McKenzie, Norman, and Jeanne Mackenzie, *The Time Traveller: The Life of H. G. Wells* (Simon and Schuster, 1973)

McSmith, Andy, *John Smith: Playing the Long Game* (Verso, 1993)

Martin, Kingsley, *Editor* (Hutchinson, 1968)

Martineau, Lisa, *Politics and Power: Barbara Castle, a Biography* (André Deutsch, 2000)

Morgan, Kenneth O., 'Michael Foot' in *Labour People: Leaders and Lieutenants, Hardie to Kinnock* (Oxford University Press, 1987)

Morgan, Kenneth O., *Callaghan: A Life* (Oxford University Press, 1997)

Morgan, Kenneth O., *Keir Hardie: Radical and Socialist* (Weidenfeld and Nicolson, 1975)

Novak, Maximillian E., *Daniel Defoe: Master of Fictions* (Oxford University Press, 2003 edn)

Ollard, Richard (ed.), *The Diaries of A. L. Rowse* (Allen Lane, 2003)

Origo, Iris, *A Need to Testify: Four Portraits* (John Murray, 1985)

Owen, David, *Time to Declare* (Penguin Books, 1991)

Paul, Swraj, *Beyond Boundaries: A Memoir* (Penguin Books India, New Delhi, 1998)

Pearce, Edward, *Denis Healey* (Little, Brown, 2002)

Perkins, Anne, *Red Queen: The Authorised Biography of Barbara Castle* (Macmillan, 2003)

Pimlott, Ben, *Hugh Dalton* (Jonathan Cape, 1985)

Pimlott, Ben, *Harold Wilson* (HarperCollins, 1992)

Pimlott, Ben (ed.), *The Political Diary of Hugh Dalton, 1918–40, 1945–60* (Jonathan Cape, 1986)

Radice, Giles, *Friends and Rivals: Crosland, Jenkins and Healey* (Little, Brown, 2002)

Radice, Giles, *Diaries 1980–2001* (Weidenfeld and Nicolson, 2004)

Reynolds, David, *In Command of History* (Penguin Books, 2004)

Rollyson, Carl, *To be a Woman: A Life of Jill Craigie* (Aurum, 2005)

Routledge, Paul, *Gordon Brown* (Simon and Schuster, 1998)

Shepherd, John, *George Lansbury* (Oxford University Press, 2002)

Skidelsky, Robert, *John Maynard Keynes: Fighting for Britain 1937–1946* (Macmillan, 2000)

Smith, Dai, *Aneurin Bevan and the World of South Wales* (University of Wales Press, Cardiff, 1993)

Snow, Jon, *Shooting History* (HarperCollins, 2004)

Stanford, Peter, *The Outcasts' Outcast: A Biography of Lord Longford* (Sutton, 2003)

Steel, David, *Against Goliath: David's Steel's Story* (Weidenfeld and Nicolson, 1989)

Stuart, Mark, *John Smith: A Life* (Politico's, 2005)

Taylor, A. J. P., *Beaverbrook* (Hamish Hamilton, 1972)

Tebbit, Norman, *Upwardly Mobile* (Weidenfeld and Nicolson, 1988)

Thomas, George, *Mr Speaker: The Memoirs of Lord Tonypandy* (Century, 1985)

Watkins, Alan, *A Short Walk Down Fleet Street* (Duckworth, 2000)

Westlake, Martin, *Kinnock: The Biography* (Little, Brown, 2001)

Wheen, Francis, *Tom Driberg: His Life and Indiscretions* (Chatto and Windus, 1990)

Williams, Philip, *Hugh Gaitskell* (Jonathan Cape, 1979)

Williams, Philip (ed.), *The Diaries of Hugh Gaitskell 1945–1956* (Jonathan Cape, 1983)

Wilson, Harold, *The Labour Government 1964–70: A Personal Record* (Weidenfeld and Nicolson, 1971)

Wilson, Harold, *The Final Term* (Weidenfeld and Nicolson, 1979)

2. Other Works

Addison, Paul, *The Road to 1945* (Jonathan Cape, 1975)

Beloff, Nora, *Freedom Under Foot* (Temple Smith, 1976)

Bell, Patrick, *The Labour Party in Opposition 1970–1974* (Routledge, 2004)

Benn, Tony, *Arguments for Democracy* (Jonathan Cape, 1981)

Benn, Tony, *Arguments for Socialism* (Jonathan Cape, 1979)

Briggs, Asa, *History of Broadcasting in the United Kingdom. Vol. IV: Sound and Vision* (Oxford University Press, 1979)

Brown, E. H. Phelps, *The Origins of Trade Union Power* (Oxford University Press, 1983)

Brown, Judith, *Modern India: The Origins of an Asian Democracy* (Oxford University Press, 2nd edn, 1994)

Butler, David, and Dennis Kavanagh, *The British General Election of 1970* (Macmillan, 1971)

Butler, David, and Dennis Kavanagh, *The British General Election of March 1974* (Macmillan, 1975)

Butler, David, and Dennis Kavanagh, *The British General Election of October 1974* (Macmillan, 1975)

Butler, David, and Dennis Kavanagh, *The British General Election of 1979* (Macmillan, 1980)

Butler, David, and Dennis Kavanagh, *The British General Election of 1983* (Macmillan, 1984)

Callaghan, John, *The Far Left in British Politics* (Blackwell, 1987)

Ceadel, Martin, *Pacifism in Britain 1914–1945* (Oxford University Press, 1980)

Crewe, Ivor, and Anthony King, *SDP: The Birth, Life and Death of the Social Democratic Party* (Oxford University Press, 1995)

Davies, Paul, and Mark Freedland, *Legislation and Public Policy: A Contemporary History* (Clarendon Press, Oxford, 1993)

Dictionary of Labour Biography, ed. David Howell (Macmillan, 12 vols, 1972–)

Donoughue, Bernard, *Prime Minister* (Jonathan Cape, 1977)

Dorrill, Stephen, and Robin Ramsay, *Smear!* (Grafton, 1992)

Elliott, John, *The Industrial Development of the Ebbw Valleys* (University of Wales Press, Cardiff, 2004)

Fielding, Steven, John W. Young and Jim Tomlinson, *The Labour Governments 1964–70* (Manchester University Press, 3 vols, 2003–05)

Foster, Roy, *History of Ireland 1600–1922* (Allen Lane, 1988)

Fraser, Neil, and John Hills (eds), *Public Policy for the 21st Century* (Policy Press, 2000)

Freedman, L., *Britain and the Falklands War* (Blackwell, Oxford, 1988)

Jenkins, Mark, *Bevanism: Labour's High Tide* (Spokesman, 1979)

Karaka, D.F, *The Pulse of Oxford* (Dent, 1933)

Karaka, D. F., *Oh, You English* (Muller, 1935)

Kogan, David and Maurice Kogan, *The Battle for the Labour Party* (Fontana, 1983)

Minkin, Lewis, *The Labour Party Conference* (Allen Lane, 1978)

Minnion, John, and Philip Bolsover (eds), *The CND Story* (Allison and Busby, 1983)

Morgan, Kenneth O., *Labour in Power, 1945–1951* (Oxford University Press, 1984)

Morgan, Kenneth O., *The People's Peace: British History 1945–2001* (Oxford University Press, new edn, 2001)

Morgan, Kenneth O., *Rebirth of a Nation: Wales 1880–1980* (University of Wales Press, Cardiff, and Oxford University Press, 1981)

Morgan, Kenneth O., *Wales in British Politics, 1868–1922* (University of Wales Press, Cardiff, 1963)

Oxford Dictionary of National Biography, ed. H. C. G. Matthew and Brian Harrison (Oxford University Press, 2004, and subsequently online)

Parkin, Frank, *Middle Class Radicals* (University of Manchester Press, 1968)

Paulin, Tom, *The Day-Star of Liberty: William Hazlitt's Radical Style* (Faber and Faber, 1998)

Pimlott, Ben, *Labour and the Left in the 1930s* (Cambridge University Press, 1977)

Pimlott, Ben, *Frustrate Their Knavish Tricks* (HarperCollins, 1994)

Rosen, Greg (ed.), *Dictionary of Labour History* (Politico's, 2001)

Rosen, Greg, *Old Labour to New* (Politico's, 2005)

Sandbrook, Dominic, *Never Had it so Good* (Little, Brown, 2005)

Schneer, Jonathan, *Labour's Conscience* (Unwin, Hyman, 1988)

Screech, M. A. (ed.), *Michel de Montaigne: The Essays. A Selection* (Penguin Books, 1991)

Shore, Peter, *Leading the Left* (Weidenfeld and Nicolson, 1983)

Tatchell, Peter, *The Battle for Bermondsey* (Heretic Books, 1983)

Taylor, Robert, *The Trade Union Question and British Politics* (Blackwell, Oxford, 1993)

Thompson, E. P., *The Making of the English Working Class* (Gollancz, 1963)

Thompson, E. P., *Writing by Candlelight* (Merlin, 1980)

Toye, Richard, and Julie Gottlieb (eds), *Making Reputations* (I. B. Tauris, 2005)

Wedderburn, Lord, *Law and Freedom: Further Essays in Labour Law* (Lawrence and Wishart, 1995)

Wedderburn, Lord, *The Worker and the Law* (Sweet and Maxwell, 1986 edn)

Wickham-Jones, Mark, *Economic Strategy and the Labour Party: Politics and Policy-Making, 1970–83* (Macmillan, 1996)

Worcester, Robert, *British Public Opinion, 1970–1990* (Blackwell, Oxford, 1991)

Wright, Kenneth, *Leighton Park School: The First 100 Years* (Leighton Park School, Reading, 1990)

3. Articles and Chapters

Ashton, Joe, 'The Last Days of Labour 1979 – A Whip Remembers', *House Magazine*, 2 February 2004

Brivati, Brian, 'Michael Foot – A Life in Books', *Labour History* (Autumn 2003)

Dell, Edmund, 'The Chrysler UK Rescue', *Contemporary Record*, 6/1 (Summer 1992)

Frank, Matthew, 'The New Morality – Victor Gollancz, "Save Europe Now" and the German Refugee Crisis, 1945–46', *Twentieth Century British History*, Vol. 17, No. 2 (2006)

Kelly, Scott, ' "The Ghost of Neville Chamberlain": Guilty Men and the 1945 Election', *Conservative History Journal* (Autumn 2005)

Thomas-Symonds, N., 'A Reinterpretation of Michael Foot's Handling of Militant Tendency', *Contemporary British History*, 19, 1 (Spring 2005)

Thorpe, Andrew, ' "One of the Most Backward Areas of the Country": The Labour Party's Grass Roots in South West England 1918–1945', in Matthew Worley (ed.), *Labour's Grass Roots: Essays on the Activities and Experiences of Local Labour Parties and Members* (Ashgate, Aldershot, 2005)

Williams, Philip, 'Foot-Faults in the Gaitskell–Bevan Match', *Political Studies*, XXVII, 1 (March 1979)

'The Winter of Discontent: A Symposium', *Contemporary Record*, 1/3 (Autumn 1987)

INDEX

Abadan, Iran, 114, 150
Abbey Road, St John's Wood, London, 170, 234
Abbott, Eric, Dean of Westminster, 449
Abdullah, Sheikh, 48
Abercrombie, Sir Patrick, 101–2
Ablett, Noah: *The Miners' Next Step*, 250
abortion, 136
Abraham, Abu (cartoonist 'Abu'), 48, 168, 344, 453, 468
Abse, Leo, 37, 232–3, 261, 356, 377, 414
Abu (cartoonist) *see* Abraham, Abu
Acheson, Dean, 145
Acland, Sir Richard, 95, 148, 201
Adamson, Campbell, 292
Addison, Dr Christopher, Viscount, 108, 147, 396
Addison, Paul, 95
Adenauer, Konrad, 118
Adler, Larry, 432
Adonis, Andrew, Baron, 440
Advisory, Conciliation and Arbitration Service (ACAS), 290–1, 302–5, 328, 442–3
Agee, Philip, 338
Aircraft and Shipbuilding Industries Bill (1976), 340
Aitken, Ian, 129, 166–7, 277, 310, 317–18, 380, 433, 471
Aldermaston marches, 168, 176, 202, 205, 209, 485
Alexander, Tanya, 464, 467
Ali, Tariq, 262, 419
Allaun, Frank, 319, 368, 373–4, 383, 413, 416
Allighan, Garry, 58, 107
Alton, David, Baron, 368
Amery, Leopold, 92
Anand, Mulk Raj, 48
Anderson, Evelyn, 49, 130, 163
Angell, Norman, 34

Anglo-Palestine Committee, 94
Anglo-Persian Oil company, 150
Anne, Queen, 192–6, 199–200
Apsley, Violet Emily Mildred, Lady, 96
Arab–Israeli war (1967), 247
Archer, Peter, Baron, 415
Argentina: invades Falklands (1982), 410–11, 485
Aristotle: *Politics*, 402
Armstrong, Sir William, 281
Ashcroft, Dame Peggy, 202
Asquith, Herbert Henry, 1st Earl, 6
Assheton, Ralph, 129
Astor, David, 94, 310, 311
Astor, Nancy, Viscountess, 6, 100
Astor, Waldorf, 2nd Viscount, 100
Atheneum (US publishers), 225
Atkins, Humphrey, 336
Atkinson, Norman, 240, 374, 400, 413, 426
Atlanta Journal, 35
Attlee, Clement, 1st Earl: 1945–51 premiership, 2, 107, 153; MF meets at Goodfellows, 40; in Independent Labour Party, 42; and Cripps's socialism, 44; MF's view of, 51, 95, 97, 113, 115, 153; on Marxists in Labour Party, 75; Churchill disparages, 105; and victory in Second World War, 108; on Palestine problem, 120; dissident Labour MPs urge middle-way policy between USA and Soviet Union, 121–2; calls 1950 election, 137–9; transfers Bevan to Ministry of Labour, 144; and party split (1950), 145; visits Truman and Acheson over Korean War, 145; supports Gaitskell's defence budget, 146; period in office, 150; and 1951 election, 151, 431; authority diminishes, 156; orders Bevanites to cooperate, 156–7; and nuclear weapons, 158; resigns leadership, 159, 172; enforces party discipline, 178; reviews MF's

533

248; trade union support for, 249–52, 255, 258–9, 272; opposes Barbara Castle's industrial relations policy, 257; supports abolition of House of Lords, 259–61; 'debate of the century', 262–3; loses deputy leadership elections, 264, 276; popular view of, 264; and devolution question, 265–6, 352–9, 365–7; as leader of left, 265, 270; as opposition spokesman on fuel and power, 265; as Shadow Leader of House, 265; and trade unions' resistance to Tory legislation, 268–9; and industrial relations legislation, 271; opposes membership of European Union, 272–6, 323–4, 326–8, 394; extra-marital affair, 279–80; relations with women, 279; visits India, 280–1, 452–4; as Secretary of State for Employment, 283, 286–8, 291–7; staff and aides at Employment Ministry, 286–9; as Lord President of the Council and Leader of the House, 288, 330, 332–6, 340, 486; legislation as Employment Secretary, 297, 299–301, 304–14, 318, 328, 442, 486; settles 1974 miners' strike, 297–8; in October 1974 election campaign, 302; and wage control in inflationary economy, 315–19, 340–1; speech at 1976 party conference, 318–19; and publication of Crossman diaries, 322–3; attempts to prevent closure of Ebbw Vale steelworks, 324–5; emergency operation, 327; challenges for party leadership (1976), 328–9; as deputy leader of party (1976), 332, 337, 339; republicanism, 333; advisers and staff as Lord President, 335–6; working methods, 336–7; supports Lib–Lab pact, 349–51; Callaghan consults over 1978 election, 360–1; and 'winter of discontent' (1978–79), 364–5; and no-confidence motion against Labour (1979), 368; campaigns in 1979 election, 369; and proposed electoral college for party, 374; speech at 1979 conference, 374; wins party leadership (1980), 377–81; leadership principles and qualities, 383–4, 387–90, 415, 435–6, 487; staff and organization as leader, 384–7; breaks ankle, 389; weak eyesight, 389, 460; Cenotaph attendance in 'donkey jacket',

390–1; portrait by Graham Jones, 391; forms Shadow Cabinet, 392; silence at 1981 Wembley conference, 393; and defection of Shirley Williams, 395; hospitalized for operation, 399; speech at 1981 conference, 401; supports Falklands War, 411–14, 479, 487; declares scrapping of independent nuclear deterrent, 415; leadership changes, 415–17; acts against Militant Tendency, 419–25; opposes Tatchell's nomination for Bermondsey, 421–3; in 1983 election campaign, 425–33, 436; attitude to MORI poll, 426; loses confidence of party, 426–7; loses leadership and 1983 election defeat, 434–5; announces retirement (1991), 444; literary activities in later years, 445–8, 470; supports Croatia in conflict with Serbia, 455–7; final Commons speech on Yugoslav troubles, 457; stands down as MP, 458–9; leaves private papers to People's History Museum, 459; presents Jill's film on Yugoslavia, 460; accused of being KGB agent, 461–3; prostate operation, 461; sues *Sunday Times*, 463; converted to Europeanism, 470; as director of Plymouth Argyle, 471; and Jill's death, 473; denounces Iraq War, 475; achievements and principles, 479–86, 493–4; lack of interest in economics, 481; pamphleteering and journalism, 482–3; Englishness, 490;

WORKS: *Above All Things – Liberty* (projected and unpublished), 93; *Another Heart and Other Pulses*, 438, 444; *Armistice 1918–39*, 72, 222, 479; *Brendan and Beverley*, 93–4; *The Case for Freedom – an Answer to Morgan Phillips and the NEC*, 166; *Debts of Honour*, 66, 195, 232, 236, 242, 370, 417–18, 438, 447, 484; *Dr Strangelove, I Presume*, 210, 343, 454, 468; *Full Speed Ahead*, 142, 491; *Guilty Men* (with Owen and Howard), 69, 73–81, 108, 479, 482, 484; *Guilty Men, 1957: Macmillan etc.* (with Mervyn Jones), 172–3; *H.G.: The History of Mr Wells*, 452, 464–8; *Isaac Foot*, 474–5; *Loyalists and Loners*, 24, 86–7, 401, 447–8, 469, 484; *My Kind of Socialism*, 402, 481, 491; 'Ode to Everton' (poem), 41; *One Way*